Engineering the New South

Georgia Tech, 1885–1985

GEORGIA TECH 1885-1985

This work is an official centennial publication done in commemoration of the one-hundredth anniversary of the Georgia Institute of Technology.

Engineering the New South

Georgia Tech, 1885–1985

Robert C. McMath, Jr.
Ronald H. Bayor
James E. Brittain
Lawrence Foster
August W. Giebelhaus
Germaine M. Reed

The University of Georgia Press
Athens

© 1985 by the University of Georgia Press
Athens, Georgia 30602
All rights reserved

Set in Linotron 202 Trump Medieval and Korinna types

The paper in this book meets the guidelines for permanence and durability of the Committee on Production Guidelines for Book Longevity of the Council on Library Resources.

Printed in the United States of America

89 88 87 86 85   5 4 3 2 1

Library of Congress Cataloging in Publication Data

Main entry under title:

Engineering the New South.

  Bibliography: p.
  Includes index.
  1. Georgia Institute of Technology.
I. McMath, Robert C., 1944–
T171.G59E54   1985   620'.007'11758231   85-969
ISBN 0-8203-0784-X (alk. paper)

Contents

Preface ix

ONE   The Shop Culture and the New South Creed   1

TWO   The Administration of Isaac Hopkins and the Commercial Shop Experiment   37

THREE   Dormitories, Diversification, and Discipline: The Administration of Lyman Hall   69

FOUR   Tech in the Progressive Era: The Matheson Years   105

FIVE   The Brittain Era: The Interwar Years   161

SIX   World War II and Expansion   201

SEVEN   The Imprint of Change: The Van Leer Years   235

EIGHT   The Post-Sputnik Era at Georgia Tech   301

NINE   Years of Turmoil and Transition   371

TEN   Toward the Second Century   407

Notes   455

Bibliographical Note   535

Index   541

Preface

For all of its one hundred years, Georgia Tech has been part of two worlds. Firmly rooted in the clay hills of Georgia, Tech has also been at home in a national and international community of engineers and scientists.

Georgians intent on engineering a New South—enlisting the scientist and engineer in the cause of regional industrial development—founded the school in Atlanta, the center of manufacturing in the state. At its centennial, the Georgia Institute of Technology remains an active partner in a coalition of universities, government, and business promoting technology-based economic growth in Georgia.

From the beginning, Georgia Tech has also been national in orientation. Its founders looked to the Northeast for models and found one they liked in the Worcester Free Institute, having passed over Boston Tech (now MIT) as inappropriate for Georgia's needs. Ever since, Georgia Tech has been party to a national dialogue on how best to educate engineers and scientists and on the role of science and technology in the life of the nation.

It is Tech's existence in these two worlds that we wish particularly to explore, for much of its internal history can be explained by the tugging and pulling of different and even conflicting political, economic, and intellectual forces. At the same time, we intend to tell the story of the men and, more recently, women who have shaped the Institute in its first century. In short, we seek to combine an institutional history of Georgia Tech with an analysis of how one particular institution of higher learning has shaped and been shaped by the world around it.

The writing of this history has been a cooperative effort among the six authors. However, primary responsibility for the individual chapters is as follows: 1–3, James E. Brittain; 4, Germaine M. Reed; 5, Ronald H. Bayor; 6–7, August W. Giebelhaus; 8, Lawrence Foster; 9–10, Robert C. McMath, Jr.

All six of us teach history and practice the historian's craft at Georgia Tech. Mindful of the pitfalls of writing one's own history, we have attempted to conform fully to the canons of historical scholarship while, at the same time, telling the story of Georgia Tech in a way that will be of interest to our fellow members of the Tech community and useful to those who will help shape Georgia Tech's second century.

The idea of writing this book was proposed by the co-chairmen of Georgia Tech's centennial celebration, Regents' Professor of Civil Engineering Paul Mayer and Vice President for Institute Relations and Development Warren Heemann. They persuaded us that the time was right to prepare an objective history which would place Georgia Tech's story within the context of higher education in America and would analyze its role in the history of science, technology, and economic development in the southern region and the nation as a whole. Their idea for a new history of Georgia Tech was shared by President Joseph Mayo Pettit. President Pettit encouraged our efforts and has made available to us the official records of his administration, as well as other archival materials under his jurisdiction.

J. Erskine Love, Jr., and Gay M. Love generously provided financial support for the preparation of the book, as did the late William C. Wardlaw and his widow and son, Edna Raine Wardlaw and William C. Wardlaw III. The Georgia Tech Foundation provided additional funding. The Board of Trustees of the Georgia Tech Alumni Association has expressed a continuing interest in the project. Rush S. Smith, Jr., a member of the Alumni Board and former editor of the student newspaper, has helped to see the project through to completion.

The officers, alumni, and friends of Georgia Tech who supported the writing of this book have done so without attempting to influence its conclusions. If the work falls short of the standards of objectivity and analytical rigor set forth at its beginning, the fault is the authors' alone.

Jane Holly Wilson, Anita Wood Bryant, Vickie Estes Polsinelli, and Cindy Jene Dean, all of the School of Social Sciences, typed the manuscript and shepherded our revisions through a cantankerous word processor, all with skill and unfailing good humor. Warren E. Drury III, our research assistant, went far beyond the call of duty in that capacity. His own master's thesis, "The Architectural Development of Georgia Tech," is an indispensable guide to the history of Georgia Tech's campus. Our colleagues in the School of Social Sciences have not only tolerated our preoccupation with the Georgia Tech history project, but have also supported our efforts in many ways.

At the University of Georgia Press, former director Paul Zimmer and his associate Charles East supported the project and provided wise counsel, as has the new director, Malcolm Call. Sandra Hudson and Debra Winter of the Press have done an outstanding job of transforming our mountain of manuscript into a handsome book. Our relationship with the University of Georgia Press demonstrates that no matter how bitter the rivalry between Bulldogs and Yellow Jackets on the playing fields, in matters academic we can work together as a team.

As with other works of history this book could not have been written without the unfailing assistance of librarians and archivists. At our own institution, former Director of Libraries Edward Graham Roberts (now retired) graciously made available to us the resources of the Price Gilbert Memorial Library. Ann Bartlow, head of the Georgia Tech archives department, and Gail Garfinkle, archival assistant, were extremely helpful at every stage of the work. Similarly, Janice Gosdin-Sangster, assistant to the president, facilitated our use of the Institute's central administrative records. Thanks are due also to Charlene Sokal and Carmen Brown, archivists at the Worcester Polytechnic Institute; to Priscilla Sutcliffe, Special Collections, Clemson University; to Virginia Shadron, Georgia Department of Archives and History; to Linda Matthews, Special Collections, Emory University; and to Sally Flocks, who secured materials from the Stanford University Archives.

Family members and associates of former Tech presidents who are now deceased graciously provided us with personal papers and other information. They include Mary Pearson, daughter of K. G. Matheson; Ida Brittain Patterson, daughter of M. L. Brittain; Ella Wall Van Leer and Samuel Wall Van Leer, widow and son of Blake Van Leer; and Doris Dean, secretary to Acting President Paul Weber.

Scores of individuals associated with Georgia Tech have provided us with information and have reviewed portions of the manuscript. Many but by no means all of them are listed as interviewees in the Bibliographical Note. To all those who shared their knowledge with us and to the thousands of others who comprise the Georgia Tech community, we are pleased to express our thanks for their part in the making of Georgia Tech's first century.

Engineering the New South

Georgia Tech, 1885–1985

Chapter One

The Shop Culture and the New South Creed

Overleaf: A view of Atlanta's central business district in 1882 shows Whitehall Street, looking south from Alabama Street. (Courtesy of the *Atlanta Journal-Constitution.*)

The Georgia School of Technology that first opened its doors to students in October 1888 was an institutional response to far-reaching social, cultural, and economic changes. These changes affected the curriculum of the new school and the aspirations of its founders and its students. The emergence in Europe and the United States of new approaches to engineering and industrial education provided alternative patterns for the leaders of the movement in Georgia to establish a technological school. Their selection of the commercial shop approach as exemplified by the Worcester Free Institute in Massachusetts had significant consequences, vestiges of which may still be seen after a century. The founders of Georgia Tech were advocates of an ideology that has become known as the "New South Creed," a doctrine that influenced strongly the expectations of what the school and its graduates might contribute to the economic growth of the state and the region. This creed still continues to affect perceptions of the school and its mission to the present day. Political conflicts and inter-city rivalries were a significant part of the process of founding the school and determining where it should be located.

The Rise of Industrial Education in the Nineteenth Century

The advent of the factory system and the creation of an industrial economy in Great Britain in the late eighteenth and early nineteenth centuries led to the perception of an industrial lag in France as well as in other countries. Although France was a leader in providing formal training in engineering at schools such as the Ecole Polytechnique, by the 1820s the French educational system had failed to produce an adequate supply of engineers with an industrial orientation and appropriate skills. Consequently, a new school, known as the Ecole Centrale des Arts et Manufactures, was established in Paris in 1829. The founders confidently anticipated that the Ecole Centrale would provide the industrial sector of the French economy with a steady supply of graduates equipped to help overtake the British in industrial development.[1] Interestingly, Great Britain had achieved industrial leadership without reliance on formal engineering schools. Instead the British approach emphasized family connections and practical experience in the shop environment. As Anthony Wallace has concluded in a recent study of the British iron industry, the British kinship system produced during several generations a "stable cadre of mechanicians and managers."[2]

The Ecole Centrale developed a curriculum based on the concept of "industrial science" that influenced engineering education elsewhere, including at the Massachusetts Institute of Technology. Industrial science represented an effort to synthesize theory and practice within a "coherent intellectual structure unified by generalizations about natural phenomena."[3] Once the students mastered the principles of industrial science as taught at the Ecole Centrale, they were expected to be "simultaneously scientist, generalist, and expert in finding practical solutions to technological problems."[4] The school served the function of converting "a callow young man vulnerable to political fantasies" into "a sober, industrious citizen who subjected all social commentary to the same critical scrutiny he gave to the blueprints for a steam engine."[5]

While French engineering schools such as the Ecole Centrale provided a pattern for an academic or school culture approach to engineering education, the doctrine that manual training should be integrated with training of the mind also originated in Europe. John H. Pestalozzi, a Swiss educator, founded a manual school at Neuhof in 1774 where he experimented with the use of physical objects and manual labor as a means to teach traditional subjects. He believed that student labor might be used to help pay the cost of their education. Philip von Fellenberg, another Swiss educator, established a manual training academy near Berne in 1799 that served as a stimulus to a manual education movement in the United States that began in the 1820s. He employed skilled technicians to manage shops at the school where the students could learn a trade. He evidently believed that students exposed to this system from the upper as well as lower classes would acquire a work ethic along with a skill.[6]

American interest in manual education as an alternative to the traditional classical education provided by sectarian colleges and state universities dates back to the early nineteenth century. The traditional curriculum included classical languages, mathematics, philosophy, ethics, and science with few if any electives. The state universities were much like the sectarian colleges and were expected to provide religious and moral training. Efforts to reform higher education during the 1820s focused on greater freedom of choice with elective courses and alternative or parallel curricula. A manual labor school movement began around 1825 under the influence of Pestalozzi and von Fellenberg of Switzerland. The expectation that students might pay the costs of their education by manual labor performed in a school setting was thwarted as colleges that experimented with this approach expended more for equipment and instructors than they received from sales.[7]

Interest in the manual labor school declined during the 1830s but pressures for reform persisted in the context of an egalitarian ideology that emerged in the Jacksonian period. The educational implication of this doctrine was that an appropriate education should be available to all, including those who would engage in manufacturing, farming, and commerce rather than a traditional learned profession. Francis Wayland at Brown University and Henry Tappan at the University of Michigan were among the educators who advocated a democratization of higher education with more diversified curricula during the 1840s and 1850s. The transcendentalists such as Emerson and Thoreau also helped set the stage for educational reforms and provided an ideology for the land-grant college movement.[8]

The Morrill Land-Grant College Act and Its Impact

A coalition between educational reformers interested in industrial education and others concerned with agricultural education was forged during the 1850s and became an effective force for securing federal support for a system of colleges of agriculture and engineering. The agricultural community spawned hundreds of local and statewide agricultural societies that provided a forum for the advocates of land-grant colleges and an effective lobby for the enabling legislation. The state of Illinois became a center of the land-grant campaign and was the first state to petition Congress to create a land-grant endowment for state colleges that would teach agriculture and mechanics. Jonathan Turner, a Congregational minister and former professor at Illinois College, began his crusade for the new education with a speech delivered to an Illinois agricultural society in 1851. He contended that the traditional college failed to meet the educational needs of the industrial class that included farmers and mechanics. Turner proposed that Congress authorize the use of public lands to endow a "general system of popular Industrial Education, more glorious in its design and more beneficent in its results than the world has ever seen before." His proposal won the support of the Industrial League and the Illinois State Agricultural Society, both organized in 1853.[9]

Congressman Justin S. Morrill of Vermont introduced the College Land-Grant Act in 1857, proposing that each state be given 20,000 acres of public land or land scrip of equivalent value for each congressional representative. The states were to use the interest on the endowment to establish one or more colleges to teach agriculture and the mechanic arts. The act was passed by the House in April 1858 and by the Senate in February 1859 but subsequently was vetoed by President Buchanan on constitutional grounds. Morrill reintroduced the legislation in 1861 with an increase in the endowment to 30,000 acres for each member of a state's congressional delegation and the stipulation that the schools formed would also offer military training. The act again was passed and was signed into law by President Lincoln in July 1862. The endowment eventually totaled almost 17.5 million acres. Georgia received 270,000 acres that was sold for ninety cents an acre to create an endowment of

$243,000. Seventeen states applied for the land-grant funds by the end of 1863, and thirty-six states were included by 1870. Each state was left to decide how to organize its school or schools and where to locate them with the result being that, as in Illinois, "rival groups gathered like sharks around the carcass of the land grant."[10]

In contrast to most other states, in Georgia the land-grant fund was awarded to the existing state university in 1871. A new college was established at the university in Athens and was called the Georgia State College of Agriculture and the Mechanic Arts. Only one new professor, Henry C. White, was hired for the new college when it was organized in 1872, although several professors nominally were affiliated with the A&M College. White was a graduate of the University of Virginia and a chemist who became an expert in the analysis of fertilizer. He later declined the opportunity to become the first president of Georgia Tech but was elected to head the A&M College at the university in 1890.[11] By the early 1880s it was evident to such advocates of industrial education as Henry Grady that the A&M College of the university was not serving the state's needs adequately in teaching the mechanical arts.

Black students in Georgia did not benefit from land-grant funding until after 1890, when a second Morrill Act provided additional funds with the condition that A&M education be available to blacks as well as whites. An industrial college for black students was established in Savannah and awarded a portion of the land-grant funding.[12] Several privately funded schools in the South, including Hampton Normal and Agricultural Institute in Virginia, Atlanta University, and the Tuskegee Institute in Alabama, provided industrial education and teacher training for black students by the 1880s. The founders of these schools, such as General Samuel C. Armstrong at the Hampton Institute, saw a principal function of these institutions as "the inculcation of Yankee virtues of industriousness and thrift."[13] New South proponents such as Henry Grady expressed similar sentiments with regard to the role of industrial education for white men in the region. The Hampton Institute encouraged the acquisition of a disciplined work ethic by having its students engage in manual labor at the school to help pay the costs of education and by imposing quasi-military discipline. The school's most famous alumnus, Booker T. Washington, introduced the Hampton approach at Tuskegee when it was opened in 1881.[14] Industrial education for women in Georgia became available in 1889 when the Georgia Normal and Industrial School for women was established in Milledgeville with state funding.

The Professionalization of Mechanical Engineering

Mechanical engineering emerged as a profession in response to technological change in prime movers, transportation, manufacturing, and machine tools during the nineteenth century. The skills required to design, test, and improve steam engines, water turbines, milling machines, and powered looms were quite different from those required in the older profession of civil engineering that had been responsible for designing and building roads, bridges, canals, and railroads. Prior to the Civil War, the most important institution devoted to mechanical technology in the United States was the Franklin Institute for the Promotion of the Mechanical Arts, founded in Philadelphia in 1824. It engaged in education, research, and dissemination of information through its *Journal* and periodic industrial exhibitions. The Institute operated a successful drawing school and undertook sponsored research on such problems as steam boiler explosions, the strength of materials, and comparative testing of water engines.[15]

By midcentury, the Franklin Institute's educational role in mechanical technology was challenged and gradually supplanted by new schools of applied science attached to universities and new polytechnic schools. Both Harvard and Yale added schools of applied science in 1847, and the same year William B. Rogers published *A Plan for a Polytechnic School in Boston*, beginning a campaign that resulted in the opening of the Massachusetts Institute of Technology in 1864. The long process of professionalization culminated in the founding of the American Society of Mechanical Engineers in 1880, five years before passage of the enabling legislation for the Georgia School of Technology.[16]

The Shop Culture and the School Culture

In his monograph on the early history of mechanical engineering in the United States, Monte A. Calvert identified two contrasting ap-

9 The Shop Culture and the New South Creed

proaches to the education of mechanical engineers that reflected a conflict between two cultures—the shop culture and the school culture. He found that, in Philadelphia and other eastern industrial centers, the leaders of the shop culture formed a class-conscious elite with a network of family connections.[17] These kinship industrial shop networks were similar to the family networks that Anthony Wallace has shown played a leading role in the British Industrial Revolution. Calvert found that, as college programs designed by school culture advocates began to open the mechanical engineering profession to young men from lower-class and non-shop backgrounds, the leaders of the shop culture became strong critics of the new curricula. The cultural conflict peaked during the 1880s and had significant implication for new schools of mechanical engineering, including the Georgia School of Technology, that were founded during that decade.[18]

The cultural conflict resulted in the creation of two major types of mechanical engineering colleges. One type, designed by leaders of the school culture, included such colleges as the Stevens Institute of Technology, Sibley College at Cornell (after 1885), and the Massachusetts Institute of Technology. Engineering programs in these schools stressed higher mathematics, theoretical science, and original research. An alternative college, preferred by proponents of the shop culture, included the Worcester Free Institute, the Rose Polytechnic Institute, and Sibley College (before 1885). These programs placed greater stress on practical shop work and produced graduates who could work as machinists or as shop foremen, but who were not well prepared for engineering analysis or original research.[19]

Robert H. Thurston was the intellectual leader of the school culture and chief architect of the mechanical engineering curriculum that was adopted at colleges where the school culture was dominant. He graduated from Brown University with a degree in civil engineering in 1859 and served in the Engineering Corps of the United States Navy during the Civil War. He began development of a mechanical engineering curriculum while teaching at the Naval Academy from 1866 to 1871. The new curriculum first was implemented at the Stevens Institute of Technology where Thurston taught from 1871 to 1885, when he was hired to reform the engineering program at Sibley College at Cornell. One of Thurston's most significant innovations, the mechanical laboratory, was introduced at Stevens in 1874 and at

Sibley College soon after he arrived.[20] He contended that such laboratories were needed to produce new knowledge in the form needed in engineering and industry. He anticipated that the school laboratories would help to bridge the cultural gap separating scientists and businessmen.[21] Whether the mechanical laboratory should teach research skills or shop skills became a focal point of the debate between the school and shop cultures.

The Worcester County Free Institute of Industrial Science became the foremost example of the shop culture approach to engineering education and the pattern for the Georgia School of Technology. Worcester Institute was founded as a result of an offer made by John Boynton in 1865 to give $100,000 to a school if the citizens of Worcester would provide land and buildings. The same year Ichabod Washburn, a Worcester manufacturer, offered to provide funds to establish a mechanical shop as a department of the new school. The shop was to be operated as a commercial or construction shop where the students would acquire shop skills while working without pay on the manufacture of products for the market. Worcester opened in 1868 with a 3.5-year program during which the students were required to spend a total of 2,376 hours in the shops. Washburn specified that the superintendent of the school shops should be "a man of good morals and Christian character, having a good English education, a skillful and experienced mechanic, well informed and capable of teaching others in the various parts and processes of practical mechanism usually applied and made use of in the machine shops of the country." The superintendent was expected to "have a care and oversight over the apprentices, such as a faithful master would exercise, to the end that they may cultivate habits of industry, good conduct and attention to their studies." He also was to be given a relatively free hand in making contracts and hiring and firing workmen.[22]

In a paper on mechanical engineering education published in 1884, Thurston stressed the distinction between a technical institute such as Stevens and a "trade school" such as Worcester. He suggested that the graduates of the technical school would be members of a profession that would be served by the trade school graduates. He proposed that the mechanical engineer should be educated as a "designer of construction, not a constructor."[23] In a commencement speech delivered in 1887, Thurston extended his distinction between technical and trade schools to a more general distinction with overtones of intellectual rather than social elitism. He argued that there were two classes of people and that they needed to be educated differently. He described one class as being best suited for intellectual pursuits, while the other was endowed with "constructive faculties." He believed that admission to the mechanical engineering profession should be based on individual ability rather than on social status or family connection.[24]

Unlike some advocates of technological education, Thurston recognized that the polytechnic institute was a necessary but not a sufficient stimulus to the industrial development of a state or a region. As early as 1878 he had formulated a comprehensive plan for the promotion of industrialization in New Jersey. His plan included a four-level system of education beginning with common or elementary schools. At the next level he recommended a system of manual training schools for those destined to work as artisans or laborers. At the third level he proposed a network of trade schools that would prepare students to work in a particular industry such as textile manufacturing. At the final level he advocated the creation of at least one polytechnic school that would produce professional engineers capable of doing industrial research and development. Thurston's overall plan also envisioned direct incentives for industry provided by the state through such means as tax relief or subsidy, improved transportation, and the creation of governmental departments for the promotion of industry. Even then, he concluded that the state might still fail to achieve prosperity through industrialization unless the people of the states were able "to comprehend and to take advantage of the opportunity for self improvement thus offered them."[25]

The New South Creed from a Georgia Perspective

The postbellum educational reform movement that encompassed manual training and mechanical engineering programs, whether school culture or shop culture in orientation, was compatible with a contemporary ideology that became known as the "New South

Creed." During the 1870s the term "New South" was the label for a "movement of social, economic and intellectual regeneration" in the region. In 1870, Edwin De Leon of South Carolina published the essay "The New South: What It Is Doing and What It Wants" in which he advocated cooperation with the North in the promotion of industrialization. His later paper, "The New South," published in *Harper's* in 1874, was read widely and from that time on appeared frequently as the recognized label for the movement.[26]

Benjamin H. Hill became one of the first proponents of the New South doctrine in Georgia. Hill graduated from the University of Georgia in law and represented Troup County in the state legislature before his election to the United States Senate in 1859. He subsequently served in the Confederate Congress as a senator and, following the Reconstruction years, again served in the United States Senate until his death in 1882. In a speech to the Alumni Association of the University of Georgia in 1871, Hill contended that the South's long dependence on slavery and the resultant demeaning of manual labor by whites had hindered the South's ability to compete with the North in industry. He saw a more practical education as being the best way to change southern work values. Hill stated that "education must reach the masses" and "our own sons must be taught to build and operate all machinery." He believed that "we must have schools of agriculture, of commerce, of manufactures, of mining, of technology, and in short, of all polytechnics, and we must have them as sources of power and respectability, and in all, our own sons must be qualified to take the lead and point the way."[27]

During the 1880s, Grady, the editor of the *Atlanta Constitution*, became a powerful force in state politics as a spokesman for the Bourbon Democrats and the New South Creed. He graduated from the University of Georgia and studied law at the University of Virginia before becoming a journalist. He became an editorial writer for the *Constitution* in 1876 and managing editor in 1880. Grady attracted national attention for his speech "The New South," delivered at a banquet of the New England Club in New York City in December 1886.[28] He effectively used the editorial pages of the *Constitution* during the 1880s to promote education, especially manual and practical education.

The International Cotton Exposition of 1881 confirmed the emer-

13 The Shop Culture and the New South Creed

gence of Atlanta as the center of the New South movement and focused attention on the presumed linkage between practical education and industrial development.[29] The initial stimulus for the Cotton Exposition came from Edward Atkinson of Massachusetts, who wrote a letter to the *New York Herald* in August 1880 proposing an exhibition of tools, methods, and products related to the cotton industry. Atkinson, who later was to play a role in the decision to locate Georgia Tech in Atlanta, was involved in the textile business in Boston at the age of fifteen and served as treasurer in several textile firms. He was a founder of the Boston Manufacturers Mutual Insurance Company and served as its president from 1878 to 1905.[30] The *Atlanta Constitution* published an editorial about the Atkinson proposal for a cotton exposition, and he was invited to come to Atlanta in October 1880 to deliver a speech. Atkinson suggested that the exposition be held in Atlanta and a local committee was formed in December, with Joseph E. Brown as president and Samuel Inman as treasurer.[31]

The opening of the International Cotton Exposition on October 5, 1881, led the *Constitution* to herald a "New Era Dawning upon the South."[32] A meeting attended by several representatives of the cotton manufacturers of New England during the exposition led the *Constitution* to predict "much good to come from the mingling of the men of New England and the men of the New South."[33] When Atkinson mentioned during a speech at the exposition that his son at Harvard was an expert blacksmith and carpenter, the *Constitution* speculated on whether the southerners who applauded would have the "nerve and moral courage to do, in the education of their sons, what he has done with his."[34]

Atkinson called the Cotton Exposition a "grand primary school of industry" for the South and predicted that industrial progress of the region would date from the event. He argued that the South probably needed mechanical and industrial education more than his own region and warned that unless education preceded or accompanied capital, the latter would be almost worthless. He stressed that the hand and brain should be trained simultaneously, a theme that would be repeated frequently by Grady and other New South proponents. Atkinson mentioned an exhibit that had been prepared by the School of Mechanic Arts of MIT for the Cotton Exposition and suggested that there was no better lesson than that "taught by that set of bits of iron and steel and wood."[35] The *Constitution*, in the editorial "The Exposition as a Teacher," credited the exposition for having taught the South a significant lesson in industrial progress by showing how other sections had acquired wealth.[36]

The close of the International Cotton Exposition in December 1881 was followed by a period of rapid growth in industrial manufacturing in Atlanta. Early in 1882, the *Constitution* reported that twenty-five men had decided to invest $10,000 each to convert the main exhibition building into a textile mill to be known as the Exposition Cotton Mill. The new factory was described as being the most important manufacturing enterprise yet started in the city.[37] Almost simultaneously it was announced that the Fulton Cotton Spinning Company would begin operation in April with 7,000 spindles. These two Atlanta mills each employed a work force of approximately four hundred before the end of 1882. In September 1882, the *Constitution* reported that Atlanta led the state in the number of mechanics employed and in the value of manufactured products.[38]

Early in 1883, the *Constitution* published an analysis of data based on the 1880 census to show that Atlanta had been the leading manufacturing city in the state as early as 1879, a conclusion that the paper found to be "astonishing." Noting that a large number of new firms had been established since 1879, the *Constitution* served "notice that now we are entering Atlanta for the southern industrial sweepstakes in 1890."[39] Soon afterward the paper followed up this story with a report that, since 1879, the number of industrial firms in the city had increased from 196 to 435, the number of workers employed by these firms had increased from 3,655 to 7,757, and the capital invested had grown from $2.47 million to $5.97 million. The *Constitution* bragged that only two American cities, Lawrence and Lowell in Massachusetts, were ahead of Atlanta in the percentage of the population that was gainfully employed. The numbers cited were: 46 percent for Atlanta, 49 percent for Lawrence, and 50 percent for Lowell.[40]

Atlanta's industries were quite diverse in contrast to cities such as Columbus and Augusta where textile mills were dominant. In 1886 the *Constitution* reported that products manufactured in Atlanta included watches, paper bags, candies, wire fencing, matches, cotton gins, razors, plows, brooms, fertilizers, shirts, furniture, cologne, and carriages.[41] The same year, the Atlanta Manufacturers Association claimed that much of the city's progress was due to its great variety of industries and that it was less vulnerable to economic recession because it was not a "cotton town" nor an "iron town."[42] Atlanta's population increased from 37,840 in 1880 to an estimated 60,000 in 1886 while the average wage paid to industrial workers in the city increased from eighty cents per day to a dollar per day in the same period.[43]

The Campaign for a Technological School in Georgia

Although Atlanta took pride in being the center of the New South movement and the leading manufacturing city in Georgia, it was Macon industrialist John F. Hanson, his newspaper, the *Macon Telegraph and Messenger*, and his candidate for the state legislature, Nathaniel E. Harris, who effectively launched the movement for a technological school in Georgia. Hanson was a self-made industrial entrepreneur who was born in Monroe County in 1840, son of a farmer-preacher. After gaining experience in the manufacture of furniture and brick in Barnesville, Georgia, Hanson moved to Macon, where he founded the Bibb Manufacturing Company in 1876, a textile enterprise that later built or acquired mills in Columbus and elsewhere. In 1881, Hanson became principal owner of the *Macon Telegraph and Messenger*, a paper that became a strong editorial critic of the "Atlanta Ring" and especially of the *Atlanta Constitution* and its Bourbon advocacy. Hanson was a strong protectionist and was a Republican in a state dominated by Bourbon Democrats. He had connections with the railroad industry and became president of the Central of Georgia Railroad in 1903.[44]

Reportedly, it was at Hanson's instigation that Harry S. Edwards composed an editorial that appeared in the *Macon Telegraph and Messenger* of March 2, 1882, and called for the creation in Georgia of a polytechnic college. Edwards pointed to the scarcity of skilled labor for manufacturing in the state and urged that the state do for industry what it already had done for agriculture with the college at the University of Georgia. He recommended that the proposed polytechnic college be tuition-free and open to women as well as men. He noted that Massachusetts and New York had such schools and predicted that once Georgia had established one, "little manufactures of every description will spring up right and left, the idle will be employed, there will arise a demand for everything the farmer can produce, a sale for every article the manufacturer can put forth, and prosperity such as we have never known will rule in the land." In addition to the creation of a school to provide a labor force with diverse skills, Edwards called on the state legislature to provide protection for the state's manufacturing industries.[45]

Nathaniel E. Harris, a young Macon lawyer, became interested in the movement to establish a technological school after discussions with Hanson. With Hanson's support, Harris was elected as a representative of Bibb County in the Georgia legislature in 1882. Harris was born in Tennessee in 1846 and served in the Confederate Army during the Civil War. After the war he came to Georgia and graduated from the University of Georgia. While at the university he became acquainted with Henry Grady and Julius Brown, son of Joseph E. Brown. After teaching school for a short time in Sparta, Harris accepted an offer to become the law partner of Walter B. Hill in Macon. Harris later was elected governor of Georgia in 1915 and served as the chairman of the Board of Trustees of the Georgia School of Technology from its formation until his death in 1929.[46] Harris's contacts in the state legislature and his successful political career became invaluable assets for Georgia Tech as it struggled to survive in its early years.

Grady and the *Atlanta Constitution* strongly supported technological education from the time of Atkinson's speech at the International Cotton Exposition, although the *Constitution* for some time was not convinced that an advanced polytechnic school should be the first step taken. An editorial on practical education published in May 1882 found a deplorable lack of attention to practical concerns in the whole educational system from the primary schools to the college level. The editorial suggested that the schools might even be having a harmful effect by conveying to students the "idea that manual labor is vulgar and that the trades are not respectable." According to the editor, the South had "more lawyers than cases and more physicians than patients" but a shortage of skilled workers for the trades and industry.[47]

In late November 1882, the *Constitution* reported that Representative Harris had introduced a resolution that a committee be appointed to consider the establishing of a school of technology as a branch of the state university. The Harris resolution was referred to the Committee on Education and revised slightly before being brought before the House on December 8.[48] The proposal was passed after the defeat of an amendment that would have had the state school superintendent submit a report on the need for a technical school and another amendment that would have required members of the committee to pay their own expenses. The Speaker of the House appointed a seven-man committee chaired by Harris "to investigate and consider the propriety and expediency of establishing in this state a school of technology under the supervision and direction of the State University, and as a part thereof, to be endowed by the state."[49] Later, three additional members were appointed to the committee that was instructed to prepare a bill for consideration at the session in 1883 if they determined that the school was needed.

Within a few days after appointment of the Harris committee, the *Constitution* published an editorial claiming that the state should first establish trade or industrial schools of a "lower grade," although a high polytechnic school might eventually be added at the University of Georgia. The editor believed that all of the state's industrial cities, including Savannah, Macon, Columbus, Rome, and Athens as well as Atlanta, should have industrial schools. The paper called for schools that would educate artisans, chemists, foremen, contractors, architects, and mechanical engineers instead of "lawyers, doctors and preachers." The editorial concluded that "the only remedy is summed up in technical culture."[50]

The legislative committee on the technological school held its first meeting in Atlanta in May 1883 and decided to travel to the Northeast to inspect several engineering schools. The committee visited Cooper Union in New York City, the Stevens Institute of Technology in New Jersey, Boston Tech (MIT), and the Worcester Free Institute in Massachusetts. The committee was impressed most by Worcester and decided to recommend it as the most suitable model for the school proposed in Georgia. In making this choice they picked the institution most committed to the shop culture tradition and the only one of the four schools visited where products made in the shops by students were sold to produce income for the school. Understandably the committee was less concerned with ongoing debates over educational philosophy between shop and school culture proponents than with economic considerations. This concern was mentioned in Worcester newspapers immediately after the Georgia commission's visit. One article noted with satisfaction that the Worcester system was receiving much praise in Georgia and that they believed that a similar school could be started for $50,000. Another reported that the school had provided much information to the visiting committee, which was very pleased, especially by data on how student work could be used for the benefit of the institution.[51]

The committee's report presented to the Georgia House in July 1883 began by placing technical education in the context of other ways of stimulating industrial and economic development.[52] The report stated that recruitment of immigrants and efforts to attract northern capital had been relatively unsuccessful and that "our Northern brethren have evinced more interest in our politics than in our resources—in our votes, than in the possibilities of development." The committee contended that legislative protection of local manufacture was "practically useless" without skilled labor to start and manage industrial enterprises. The solution, the committee felt, was to be found in technical education that was "necessary to develop our manufactures, utilize our resources, and keep up our state's prestige." The report also argued that technical education would contribute to the solution of the state's social problems by increasing wages, reducing the cost of living and giving "employment to the idle and indigent." The tendency of technical education, according to the committee, was "to stop the drift towards communism, and insure subordination to law and order in all classes of our complex population."[53]

The Harris committee used Worcester as an example of the potential economic impact of a school of technology. The report noted that the city of Worcester had grown from a "comparatively small village" into a "thriving city" of 75,000 since the founding of the

Worcester Free Institute. The school had "made the city a center of manufacturing enterprise" and had "developed the inventive talents of the citizens til the city's ratio of inventions is by far the largest in the state." The committee stressed that the influence of a school such as Worcester was not confined to the city where it was situated but benefited the entire state.[54]

Having given a rationale for creating a technological school in Georgia similar to the Worcester school, the committee turned to details of the curriculum, physical plant, and estimated start-up costs. The academic curriculum was to be almost identical to that of Worcester except for the exclusion of the course of civil engineering that already was taught at the University of Georgia. Included would be professional courses in mechanical engineering, mining engineering, building and architecture, chemistry, and textiles. Three buildings were recommended with one housing a steam engine, a wood shop, and machine tools, while a second would contain a foundry, a blacksmith shop, and facilities for millwrighting exercises. The third building was to be an academic building with lecture rooms, drafting facilities, and a mechanical laboratory. Based on information gathered on its northern tour, the committee estimated that the sum of $65,000 would be sufficient to acquire property, erect the three buildings, equip them with the necessary apparatus, and operate the school for a year. The committee anticipated that a hundred students paying a tuition of $150 per year would provide adequate support. The cost estimates were based on the assumption that the school would not be located at the campus of the university in Athens.[55]

The committee challenged the argument that had been made by the *Atlanta Constitution* that it would be better to establish lower-level technical schools before creating a high-level polytechnic school. According to the committee, the entering student in the school of mechanical arts at Boston Tech "begins his course of instruction by learning to grease machinery, shovel coal into the furnace, and blow the forge bellows." Beyond that, the student only needed to be fifteen years old and take an entrance examination in geography, composition, and arithmetic. The committee felt that such a course was "assuredly graded low enough to satisfy any person however skeptical as to the capacity of the youth of Georgia." In any case, the committee argued that the opening of the technological school in the state would cause other schools with a more practical orientation to be established and would give "a general stimulus to education throughout the entire state."[56]

The *Atlanta Constitution* learned of the Harris committee report well before it was submitted to the Georgia House and was somewhat critical of the committee's findings. In an editorial published in late June 1883, the *Constitution* expressed its regret that the committee had not considered a greater variety of schools during its investigation. The editor acknowledged that the schools in Boston and Worcester were good but added that "excellence is relative." The editorial continued that the kind of excellence needed in a technical school in Georgia was something "far simpler and cheaper" than a richly endowed and developed polytechnic school in Massachusetts. The editor argued that most young men in the South were deficient in mechanical gifts in contrast to Massachusetts, where there was a long tradition of manufacturing and public schools and where there was now a "race of people that begins to whittle and make engines as soon as they get into short clothes." Thus the *Constitution* questioned whether the Massachusetts schools were adapted to the needs of Georgia and compared it to "buying a hat for the baby to furnish our infant industries with a polytechnic school." As an alternative model, the editor preferred the manual school at Washington University in St. Louis as being more suitable for Georgia's "immediate needs." The editor noted that the St. Louis school began at a more elementary level than Worcester and accepted students two years younger. He doubted that many in Georgia were ready to profit from the advanced education of a polytechnic institute.[57]

The *Constitution* soon had second thoughts about its position and decided that the friends of technical education could not afford to fight among themselves. In an editorial published July 13, 1883, the paper took the position that any effort to launch technical education in Georgia was desirable, whether its aim was to produce architects or carpenters or mechanical engineers as opposed to mechanics. The *Constitution* announced that it would lend its support to any effort to start a technical school of some kind and the only difference was over whether it would be better to start at the bottom and build up or to "hold up a lofty idea from the start." The editor stated that he would have preferred the schools in St. Louis and Chicago as patterns, but that other friends of technical education favored a school like those found in Hoboken, Troy, or Boston. Whichever plan was adopted, the editor felt that it should not preclude the establishment of industrial schools in every city as a part of the public school system. The editorial concluded with a call for all of the advocates of technical education to "stand together in support of this new departure in education."[58]

N. E. Harris and W. A. Little of the special House committee on the technological school introduced enabling legislation to implement the recommendations contained in the committee's report.[59] The *Constitution* urged prompt adoption, noting that the school was regarded as experimental only because it was new to Georgia. The editor claimed that only "feeble efforts" had taken place at the University of Georgia in teaching engineering and thought that Georgia ought to take advantage of the years of experience in perfecting technical schools in the North. The bill was presented in the House in September 1883, with several members of the Harris committee recorded as speaking in favor of passage. Harris argued that the proposed school would serve to "practicalize" the education system of the state, while Little explained that no additional tax would be required to start the school. Not enough members were persuaded, however, and the vote was reported as sixty-four in favor of the bill and sixty-three against, which was far short of the vote of eighty-eight needed for enactment.[60] Harris later speculated that some of the opposition probably resulted from the displeasure of some over the actions of a redistricting committee that he chaired at the time the technology bill was being considered.[61] Legislation for a school of technology was not reintroduced until two years later in 1885.

Even as the legislation for a technology school was being defeated in 1883, a modest experiment in industrial education was beginning at Emory, a Methodist college with a traditional classical curriculum located in Oxford, Georgia. Isaac S. Hopkins, who occupied the chair of English and was vice president of Emory, established a school of "Tool-Craft and Design" in 1883 that later became known as the "School of Technology" at Emory. Hopkins was born in Augusta, Georgia, in 1841 and graduated from Emory College in 1859.

He received a degree from the Georgia Medical College in 1861 but did not practice medicine. Instead he became an itinerant Methodist minister serving both white and black congregations. During the years 1869–75 he taught natural science at Emory and then taught physics for two years at the Southern University in Alabama. Hopkins returned to Emory in 1877 and became vice president of the college in 1882. In 1885 he was elected president, a position that included the responsibility for teaching mental and moral science. Hopkins had a strong avocational interest in working with machine tools and in repairing clocks and sewing machines. He discovered that some students at Emory were interested in learning to use shop tools and decided to formalize instruction in the School of Tool-Craft and Design.[62]

Hopkins, who was destined to become the first president of the Georgia School of Technology, was well-informed on the industrial education movement and its manifestations elsewhere in the country. In a speech delivered to Emory alumni in 1883, he called the movement toward industrial education "one of those great revolutions of thought and public sentiment, the results of which are not for a day or a generation, but for all time." Hopkins explained that the purpose of industrial education was to acquaint students with the use of tools under the guidance of a "competent and skilled craftsman" so that they would gain "actual experience and positive knowledge." He dismissed the construction or commercial shop where student-made products were sold as inviting "failure at the outset." He commented that, if the school shop were "operated on such a plan, the department would forego its primary object, namely, instruction, and the articles manufactured could not, in the nature of the case, be such either in design or workmanship as to command a market."[63] Hopkins's critical assessment of the commercial shop as a part of education is quite revealing in light of his later affiliation with Georgia Tech and its commercial shops.

Hopkins believed that industrial education would replace the traditional apprentice system of learning a trade that he characterized as "practically dead." He attributed the decline of the apprentice system to mechanization, the subdivision of labor, and trade union policies. He observed that the need to understand complex machines rather than simple tools was a new factor not provided for in the old system. Thus, Hopkins concluded, the "skilled labor of today requires thinking." His views on the social class implications of introducing industrial education were similar to those expressed by Harris and the editor of the *Atlanta Constitution*. Pointing out that a large majority of criminals came from the unskilled and uneducated segment of the laboring classes, Hopkins argued that it would be much better to teach trades in schools and colleges than "in reformatory institutions and state penitentiaries." But beyond this, he thought that the "undetected and unpunished" crimes that were "committed by the educated classes" might be prevented if they were given some industrial training that would serve "to direct their energies and form their tastes in useful trades." In addition he saw technical education as helping to overcome barriers and lessen conflict between the privileged and working classes by demonstrating the value and dignity of work.[64]

Meanwhile, Nathaniel Harris had not given up in his campaign for a polytechnic school in Georgia. He was reelected to the Georgia House and again introduced enabling legislation for a technological school.[65] His bill came up for debate in July 1885 with the support of the *Atlanta Constitution*, which called it the "most important matter" to be considered during the session. The newspaper characterized the people of Georgia as "ripe for technical education" and stated that if the Harris bill was passed the resulting school would be "recognized ten years from now as the most important factor in the new era that will open gloriously for Georgia."[66]

One of the principal opponents of the bill was Representative Harrell of Webster County, a rural county in southern Georgia. Harrell contended that the state treasury could not stand the expense of such a school and called the proposal a "hydra-headed monster that should be throttled at birth or it will fasten itself upon the state and future legislatures would find it impossible to throw it off." He argued that self-made men rather than the graduates such as the school would produce were looked to for progress and that investment capitalists were more concerned with how the state managed its money than with its educational system.[67]

W. A. Little of Muscogee County, who had been on the technological school committee in 1883 and now was Speaker of the House, stated that the trip north had made him an "enthusiast" for technical education. He believed that Georgia could not afford to spend as much as northern states such as New Jersey and Massachusetts on a technological school but that Georgia could establish a school on a cheaper scale with Worcester as a pattern. He explained that Georgia could get by with less elaborate buildings and fewer professors but that the mechanical department could be made comparable to that of Worcester.[68]

In an editorial published July 29, 1885, the day scheduled for the House vote on the bill, the *Atlanta Constitution* urged those who still had honest doubts "to give the bill the benefit of the doubt." The editor noted that the University of Georgia had educated lawyers, doctors, and salesmen but that the proposed school of technology would produce "great mechanics, great chemists, great scientists and great businessmen who will make Georgia the glorious empire she should be." When the vote was taken, the bill passed with ninety-three votes in favor and sixty-two against.[69] The following day, one representative requested that his vote be added to the majority, making the official vote ninety-four to sixty-two with eighty-eight affirmative votes being needed.[70]

The Georgia Senate passed the school of technology legislation in early October 1885 with a vote of twenty-seven to fourteen but amended the bill so that the House had to vote again on whether to accept the amendments.[71] After some parliamentary maneuvering between Harris and Harrell, the Senate version was accepted by the House on October 12, 1885. The amendments would permit nonsectarian schools to participate in the competition for the location of the technological school and specified that each county would be allowed as many tuition-free students as it had representatives in the General Assembly. The bill became law when it was signed by Governor Henry D. McDaniel on October 13, 1885.[72]

The enabling act established a technological school that nominally was to be a branch of the state university and created a five-person commission to determine the location, establish the school, and serve thereafter as its local board of trustees. The commission initially was to be appointed by the governor but was authorized to create its own rules and to fill any future vacancies as a self-perpetuating governing body. The commission was instructed to locate the school in or near the city or town in Georgia that offered the best inducements with consideration given to accessibility and healthful surroundings. The bill specified that the curriculum was to follow as nearly as practicable the pattern of the Worcester Free Institute. It was to have a president, a shop superintendent, and such other professors and instructors as found necessary. The Tech Board of Trustees was to have responsibility for the "immediate control, supervision and management" although formal governing authority was to be vested in the board of trustees of the University of Georgia. The sum of $65,000 was appropriated to be used in building and equipping the new school and to pay for the first year of operation, but the money was not to be made available until January 1887 and only to be paid out of "any funds in the Treasury not otherwise appropriated." No provision was made for maintenance costs after the first year.[73]

The Selection of a Site for the Georgia School of Technology

In March 1886, the *Atlanta Constitution* reported on the appointment of the commission for the technological school and gave its assessment of the membership. According to the newspaper, it was accepted generally that the cities most likely to be contestants for the location should be represented on the commission. One of the cities was Macon and Governor McDaniel had appointed Nathaniel Harris from Macon, the author of the legislation and the man who was most responsible for its passage. Atlanta's representative on the commission was to be Samuel M. Inman, an appointment that the *Constitution* found so "manifestly fit" that no further discussion was needed. Athens was represented by Edward R. Hodgson, who was described as being one of the most successful and respected young businessmen in the state. Since the small town of Penfield in Greene County, where Mercer University had formerly been located, was expected to be an entrant in the competition, Columbus Heard, a Greene County lawyer who had served as a judge and in the State Senate, was appointed. The fifth member of the commission was Oliver S. Porter, owner of a textile mill in Newton County, and the *Constitution* characterized him as a "man of broad culture and advanced views" who also was a "strong and intelligent advocate" of manual education. The *Constitution* may not have been aware that Porter was born near Penfield, since it believed him to be the one member who had been selected without regard to location. Both Porter and Governor McDaniel were alumni of Mercer University. The *Constitution* concluded that it believed the new commission to be composed of well-qualified and earnest men.[74]

Samuel Inman was one of the most influential members of the commission and of the Atlanta business community. Born in Tennessee in 1843, he graduated from Maryville College and then enrolled at Princeton University, but his studies there were interrupted by the outbreak of the Civil War. After serving in the Confederate Army, he came to Georgia and joined with his father in building a cotton trading business in Atlanta that became one of the largest in the South. He invested in manufacturing industries and was involved in railroad consolidation, banking, and land development. Inman was a close friend of Henry Grady and helped promote the International Cotton Exposition of 1881 and the Cotton States Exposition held in Atlanta in 1895. In addition to his years of service on the board of the Georgia School of Technology, he served on the board of trustees of Agnes Scott College.[75]

Oliver S. Porter was probably the most astute member of the commission in matters pertaining to engineering and manufacturing. He was born near Penfield in 1836 and graduated from Mercer University. He worked as a civil engineer for two years in Madison, Georgia, and then served in the Confederate Army. In 1868 he acquired a cotton mill on the Yellow River in Newton County, an enterprise that later became known as the Porterdale Mill. It was Porter who recruited the first professor of mechanical engineering at Georgia Tech, John S. Coon. Porter frequently used his industrial contacts to benefit the school and became a regular customer of the school's commercial shop. He served on the Tech Board of Trustees until 1911.[76]

Columbus Heard was born near Greensboro, Georgia, and attended Hiawatha College in Tennessee. He also saw service in the Confederate Army before becoming a judge in Greene County in 1866. He was elected to the State Senate in 1870 and remained on the board of the Georgia School of Technology until his death in 1912.[77]

The Shop Culture and the New South Creed

Edward R. Hodgson was born in Athens, Georgia, in 1846 and enrolled at the University of Georgia in 1862 but interrupted his studies in 1863 to enter the Confederate Army. He returned to school after the war and graduated in 1868. His business interests included the Hodgson Oil Company and the Empire Chemical Company of Athens. He was a member of the Georgia Tech Board of Trustees until 1912 and served as its secretary for twenty-six years.[78]

The commissioners held their first meeting April 5, 1886, when they were sworn in by Governor McDaniel and selected Harris as chairman and Hodgson as secretary. The commission decided to notify the mayors of Georgia's principal cities about the competition for the school and that bids would be received until October 1, 1886.[79] In September, the *Atlanta Constitution* reported that the Atlanta City Council had voted a sum of $50,000 to support Atlanta's bid and that there was strong support among the citizens with the city being prepared to do everything that it could do honorably to secure the school. The newspaper mentioned that Athens had entered a cash bid of $35,000 and that it was anticipated that Macon, Milledgeville, Covington, Penfield, and perhaps other cities would join the competition prior to the deadline.[80] Later in the month, the *Constitution* stressed the importance of choosing a suitable location, stating that a mistake would ruin the experiment and set back the cause of practical education for a generation. The editor pointed out the need to attract students and contended that Atlanta could provide more local patronage than any other city because of its population and its leading position in manufacturing.[81]

In late September 1886, it was reported that the chairman of the commission, Harris, was leading a campaign in Macon to arrange a strong bid for the technological school. The report mentioned the possibility that an annuity from railroad companies might be obtained as part of the Macon bid.[82] The competition between Atlanta and Macon for the technological school was carried on in the context of the race for the governorship in 1886 between John B. Gordon and Augustus O. Bacon. Gordon received the strong support of the Atlanta Bourbons and the *Atlanta Constitution*, while Bacon was regarded as Macon's candidate with the strong support of John F. Hanson and the *Macon Telegraph*.[83] Gordon won following a bitter campaign and the *Constitution* gloated in an editorial that "Atlanta's candidate" had defeated "Macon's candidate" by carrying one hundred counties compared to thirty-six for Bacon. The editorial was in response to one that appeared in the *Macon Telegraph* that accused Atlanta of lacking sympathy with the rest of the state. The *Constitution* claimed that Macon had lost several earlier contests and that the *Macon Telegraph* had been "beaten over and over again."[84]

The *Atlanta Constitution* continued its campaign in behalf of locating the technological school in Atlanta by pointing out some potential problems if the school were to be located at the state university in Athens. The editor predicted that the technological students would probably feel a "sense of inferiority," as he implied was the case with agricultural students at the university. He stated that the enrollment in agriculture had declined steadily and that a technological school no doubt would suffer a similar fate if located in Athens. The editorial continued that, in Alabama, the A&M college had been kept separate from the university and was achieving a "remarkable success." The editor concluded that the *Constitution* believed the school should be located in Atlanta and that it would offer more inducements than any other city.[85] Chancellor P. H. Mell of the University of Georgia responded to the editorial with a letter denying that the agricultural students were looked down on by other students or that enrollment had dropped as drastically as the *Constitution* had reported.[86]

A few days before the commission was scheduled to meet to consider the bids, the *Constitution* suggested another reason why it believed that Atlanta would be the best choice. The editor wrote that a major function of the school would be to "elevate the sentiment of labor in Georgia" and popularize industrial education in order that young men would turn from the overcrowded professions toward "humble but more useful avenues." The editorial continued that the school that was to be the "nursery of these ideas" ought to be located in the state capital, which was visited by people from throughout the state. This would, he argued, facilitate the diffusion of the school's doctrine more effectively than if the school were located elsewhere. The editor also called attention to the fact that the legislature had made no provision for the support of the school after the first year of operation. He speculated that if the school were in Atlanta, where it would be highly visible to the legislature, it would be more apt to gain continuing state support in contrast to any other location.⁸⁷

On the day that the commission convened, October 1, 1885, the *Atlanta Constitution* published a letter from Edward Atkinson addressed to Samuel Inman in which Atkinson urged that the technological school be kept separate and distinct from the state university. Atkinson based his recommendation on his experience on a committee that had been asked to consider a merger of MIT with the Lawrence Scientific School at Harvard. Atkinson stated that they investigated numerous other schools and found no example where a technological school flourished when it was annexed to a university. Consequently, the committee decided that MIT should be kept separate and, according to Atkinson, the subsequent results confirmed their wisdom. The *Constitution* noted that the advocates of locating the school in Athens were saying that only one new building and one additional professor would be required. The editor asked "would this not be a rather tame and impotent conclusion to all the agitation for technological education out of which came the present board?" The editorial continued that the board, made up of "practical, level headed, deliberate businessmen," had the opportunity, if they decided to locate the school in Atlanta, to "make themselves the apostles of the new and coming education, by which Georgia must stand or fall." It concluded that forcing the two schools together would sacrifice one without giving any benefit to the other.⁸⁸

The technological school commissioners voted to adopt a policy of accepting no further bids or supplements and then began their evaluation of the bids.⁸⁹ The Atlanta bid included $50,000 from the city, $20,000 from private citizens, one of three sites with a value estimated at $10,000, and an annual annuity from the city of $2,000 per year for twenty years, giving a total bid of $120,000. Athens offered a site on the university campus and a building known as the Rock College. Its delegation pointed out that the technological school would benefit from the existing university laboratory and library facilities and the faculty in civil engineering, chemistry, physics, and agriculture. They argued that it would only be necessary to add and equip a shop facility and add one department instead of the five needed if the school were located at another site. The proponents of Athens estimated the value of their bid at $163,500, with a savings of approximately $266,000 in addition in the long run.[90]

The city of Macon's bid included a sum of $10,000 in cash and an annual annuity of $3,000 for twenty-two years, giving a total of $76,000. Columbus Heard, a member of the commission, presented the bid of Penfield that included three hundred acres of land and the buildings once used by Mercer University.[91] State Representative J. C. Hart of Greene County was quoted earlier as believing that the buildings at Penfield would cost at least $75,000 if built in Athens, Columbus, or Macon. Hart had stated that Penfield was eligible since it was an incorporated town and its geographic location was as good as any other.[92] Chairman Harris presented the bid from Milledgeville that included up to a maximum of $10,000 in cash and a number of old state buildings, which were vacated when the state capital was moved from Milledgeville to Atlanta in 1868.[93]

During the ensuing discussion, Mayor Rucker of Athens was asked whether students would have access to factories if the school were to be located there. He responded that Athens had diverse industrial plants, including cotton mills, a foundry and machine shop, and a door, sash, and blind factory. Professor White from the university faculty responded to the question of whether there would likely be friction between the technological students and other students that he doubted that it would be a serious problem. He declined to speculate on whether placing a commercial shop on the campus would be disadvantageous to the city. Atlanta's Mayor Hillyer argued that it was unfair to include state property as part of a bid and questioned the wisdom of having the school affiliated with a "Literary College." He quoted at length from Atkinson's letter to Inman against putting the school on the campus of the state university and stressed the potential advantage of having the school where the members of the state legislature could easily observe its operation. Hillyer pointed out that Atlanta had numerous manufacturing facilities and that there was scarcely a city block where one did not find a steam engine. He mentioned also that students could find inexpensive housing more easily in Atlanta, with the cost of board in the range of sixteen dollars per month.[94] Henry Grady expressed the view that the commission had not been formed to cheapen public education but as a response to a demand for a new type of education, the lack of which has "made us vassals of New England for a century and without which the South will never achieve full independence." He commented that hiring one new professor in Athens hardly would "signal the new era for which we have all worked and prayed." Grady concluded that if the Athens bid were accepted the likely result would be to "amplify the present educational system and go on in the same old direction."[95]

The commissioners resumed their deliberations October 2, 1886, when Chairman Harris announced that he had received a telegram from Macon shortly before midnight to change its bid. After consultation, the Atlanta delegation, being eager to show "every courtesy to Macon," consented to raise no objection to Macon's amended bid but with the caveat that Atlanta would be permitted to amend its bid if none of the sites were found suitable. Commissioners Porter, Heard, and Inman voted to allow the supplemental bid from Macon, while Hodgson voted against it. A motion by Hodgson that the commission should visit the competing sites before making a final decision passed with the support of Heard and Porter but with Inman voting against.[96]

The commission convened again in Atlanta on October 19, 1886, to make a final decision on which city would get the school. A motion by Porter that the session be closed to the public and press with only written briefs to be considered was adopted. After written arguments on behalf of Athens, Atlanta, and Milledgeville were read, the balloting began with three votes required to give a majority. On the first ballot each of the five competing cities received one vote, with Harris for Macon, Heard for Penfield, Hodgson for Athens, Inman for Atlanta, and Porter for Milledgeville. On the second ballot Porter switched his vote to Penfield, while the others did not change. Porter's vote on the ballot was not too surprising in view of his having spent his early years in the vicinity of Penfield. On the third ballot, again it was Porter alone who switched, this time to join Inman in support of Atlanta. No further change occurred from the third through the twenty-first ballots when the commission decided to adjourn for the night.[97]

The *Atlanta Constitution* quickly learned what had happened behind the closed doors and carried a front-page story the following day entitled "Twenty-One Ballots." The article revealed that Harris reviewed Macon's bid and compared Macon with Athens and Atlanta before the balloting started. Inman gave an assessment of Atlanta's bid in what the *Constitution* stated was an "able and convincing presentation." Hodgson presented a review of the Athens bid and engaged in a discussion with Porter about possible problems if the faculty of the university taught classes containing some technology students together with some who were not. No one was reported to have reviewed the bids of Milledgeville or Penfield. The report concluded that the members maintained their humor and courtesy throughout the protracted balloting and that it was impossible to predict the final outcome.[98]

When the balloting was resumed on October 20 (the twenty-second ballot), Heard joined Harris in voting for Macon, with Inman and Porter voting for Atlanta, and Hodgson for Athens. On the next ballot Heard voted with Hodgson for Athens, while the others did not change. Finally, on the twenty-fourth ballot, Atlanta received the necessary three votes from Inman, Porter, and Heard, with Harris having remained steadfast for Macon and Hodgson for Athens throughout the balloting.[99] Heard explained his decisive vote by stating that he had decided that neither of his first or second choices could win and that he felt the matter should be settled.[100]

Although it had been determined that the Georgia School of Technology would be in Atlanta, the commissioners still had to decide among several available sites for the campus location. Immediately following their selection of Atlanta, the commissioners accompanied Mayor Hillyer, Henry Grady, and others to look at three potential sites: Peters Park, a site on Boulevard and a lot at the end of Capital Avenue.[101] The commission convened in January 1887 to make a final selection with Inman acting as the chairman in the absence of Harris. A citizens' committee attended the session to "press the claims of Peters Park" with a second delegation being present to advocate the Boulevard site. A written brief was received in behalf of locating the school at Grant Park and the commission decided to visit the site in the company of Governor Gordon. At Grant Park they were met by Lemuel P. Grant and others who gave a presentation on the advantages of locating the school in that vicinity. The commissioners were told that the city was growing in that direction and were promised that a street railway and gas and water supply would soon be available in the neighborhood. The proponents also stated that boarding houses that could be used by students would be built nearby.[102]

On the following day, January 26, 1887, the commission voted for the Peters Park site, although only three members, Inman, Porter, and Heard, were present at the time. Hodgson had left a letter stating that he would vote for Peters Park if present, and Harris reportedly had indicated that it also was his first choice.[103] In its account of the selection, the *Atlanta Constitution* stated that a four-acre tract had been donated by Richard Peters with the understanding that he would make additional land available at a cost of $2,000 per acre. The *Constitution* estimated that eight or nine acres would be needed. The property had approximately five hundred feet of frontage on North Avenue and was bounded on the west by Cherry Street. According to the *Constitution*, Peters intended to have a street railway constructed that would run along North Avenue between the Peachtree and Marietta Street lines. This would provide service from the Western and Atlantic Railroad to the school. Among the advantages of the site were the low cost in relation to the number of acres and the close proximity to the business section of the city that would "render the school useful from the start."[104]

Other evidence suggests that Atlanta land developers saw the school as an attraction that might fit in with their plans. As early as June 1883, the *Atlanta Constitution* had predicted that North Avenue would become a fashionable residential street, a "most desirable portion of the city," since it was on a plateau where the "air is pure and invigorating."[105] The following spring, the Peters Park Development Company, organized by Hannibal I. Kimball, purchased a 180-acre tract from Richard Peters at a cost of $1,000 per acre. The tract was between West Peachtree and Marietta streets and was bounded on the south by North Avenue. The transaction was described as the largest real estate sale yet in the city. The Development Company was capitalized at $300,000 with stockholders including Henry W. Grady, Jacob Elsas, and C. W. Hunnicut.[106] Elsas was the founder of the Fulton Cotton Spinning Company that was to become a major customer of the Georgia Tech Shops and was active in the Atlanta Manufacturers Association. Hunnicut was a member of the Atlanta

Manufacturers Association and had joined Grady in taking the commissioners on a tour of the local sites for the school after Atlanta was selected.[107] Kimball had worked for George Pullman and had served as director general of the International Cotton Exposition in 1881.

In an interview about the prospective development of the Peters Park tract into a "magnificent suburb for Atlanta," Kimball mentioned the planned community of Pullman that he had visited and that had been about the size of Peters Park. He anticipated that the investors would realize a gain on the order of 500 percent once the plan was fully implemented. He noted that the city was expanding in the direction of Peters Park and stressed that the company would develop the tract as a whole rather than piecemeal. Kimball stated that a landscape architect would be retained to draw up a complete plan that would include fifty acres in circular parks and thirty acres for streets with half-acre lots for residences. He predicted that the development would be "so delightful that everybody who sees it will want to live there." He expressed confidence that the land would be sold for not less than $5,000 per acre and probably for much more.[108]

Several other land developments were being initiated in Atlanta at about the same time that the Peters Park Development Company was formed. Lemuel P. Grant and his associates were developing land in the vicinity of a park that he donated to the city in 1883 and they hoped to secure the technological school in the same area.[109] Grant's background was similar to that of Peters, with both having come from the North to work as civil engineers during the construction of the Georgia Railroad. Both became wealthy from the sale of lands that they acquired in Atlanta. Still another land development company was active in the Boulevard section of the city by 1884, with the developers also interested in seeing the technological school located in the community.[110] Perhaps it was appropriate that the school ultimately was built on land that had been owned by Richard Peters who had worked as a professional engineer.

The dreams of Kimball and his fellow investors in the Peters Park Development Company that their property would become an elite residential suburb remained unrealized when the decision was made to build the new school on North Avenue early in 1887. The site, however, was in close proximity to what passed for Atlanta's "smoke-stack industries."[111] Nearby were such companies as the Winship Machine Company, the E. Van Winkle Company, and the Atlanta Bridge and Axle Company. George Winship later served on the Board of Trustees of the school as did W. B. Miles, president of the Atlanta Bridge and Axle Company. Other industrial enterprises that were quite near the campus in the 1880s included the Southern Agricultural Works on Marietta Street, the Atlanta Cotton Mill, the Boyd and Baxter Foundry Company, and the Exposition Cotton Mill. Inman, Grant, and Peters were among the investors in the Exposition Mill that became an important customer of the school shop and also provided members of the board such as George W. Parrott and D. N. Speer.[112]

In 1887 the view from the site of the future campus presented a sharp contrast between the vista to the west and south with a growing city, railroads, and the smokestacks of new industrial plants and the vista to the north with wooded hills stretching to the horizon. The promoters of the New South Creed and the new technological school hoped that the young men who would come for the education of their hands as well as their minds would use their acquired skills to make, in effect, the northern vista resemble that seen to the west along Marietta Street and the W&A Railroad. Whether the experiment in transplanting a system of education from Worcester to Atlanta would have the stimulating effects on the industrial economy of the South that were attributed to northern schools or whether the venture might prove as chimerical as the ideal community of the Peters Park Development Company remained in question. But after a protracted political process, the stage for the educational experiment had been selected and the school commissioners confidently prepared to let contracts for the necessary buildings and to select a faculty.

Chapter Two

The Administration of Isaac Hopkins and the Commercial Shop Experiment

Overleaf: Georgia Tech's original physical plant was completed in 1888. The Academic Building is on the right and the Shop Building is on the left. (Courtesy of the Georgia Tech Archives.)

With the selection of the Peters Park site on North Avenue as the future location of the Georgia School of Technology in January 1887, the Tech Commission turned its attention to the design and construction of buildings and to the recruitment of faculty. Except for the shop superintendent and the professor of mechanical engineering, the members of the first faculty were natives of the region and had clerical or military credentials. They welcomed the first students to the new campus in October 1888 with a curriculum similar to that of the Worcester Free Institute. During the early years, the students came mostly from Georgia and a substantial majority of the first graduates remained in the state to work. The commercial shop that was expected to fill the dual function of providing a source of income for the school and giving students actual work experience in an industrial environment had a troubled history that included a disastrous fire in 1892. Tech's existence remained precarious throughout the presidency of Isaac Hopkins. A declining enrollment and other problems, such as a lack of campus housing, set the stage for significant changes beginning in 1895.

Preparations for Opening the School

Since the Worcester Free Institute had been selected as the pattern for the Georgia School of Technology, the commission invited Milton P. Higgins, the superintendent of the Washburn Shops at Worcester, to attend the meeting held in December 1886. The minutes reported that he had discussed the "proper method of organization" of the shop program and that an agreement had been reached to pay Higgins for further assistance and advice.[1] Higgins, born in 1842, had served an apprenticeship at the Amoskeag Manufacturing Company in Manchester, New Hampshire, in the 1860s and graduated from Dartmouth College in 1868. He was recruited by Ichabod Washburn to serve as the first superintendent of the commercial shop at Worcester, a position that he occupied for twenty-eight years. Under Higgins's management the annual income of the Washburn Shops increased steadily from $1,500 in 1870 to $109,000 in 1896. When the Worcester trustees voted in 1896 to dispose of the elevator business that had been the principal source of income for the Washburn Shops, Higgins resigned to become head of a company organized to continue the manufacture of elevators. He was an articulate advocate of the shop culture approach to mechanical engineering education and was active in the American Society of Mechanical Engineers.[2]

Another member of the Worcester faculty, George I. Alden, who taught mechanical engineering, was present at the January 1887 meeting of the Georgia Tech Commission.[3] Newspapers in Worcester soon learned of the visits to Georgia by Higgins and Alden and one account stated that the Georgia school evidently was not content with copying the Worcester school but hoped to recruit members of the Worcester faculty in order "to keep the copy perfect."[4] The *Worcester Evening Gazette* of March 1, 1887, reported that both Higgins and Alden had been offered positions in Atlanta and that they had found in Atlanta a greater "tendency toward industrial training than in any northern city." The same day the *Worcester Telegram* reported that Alden was offered employment as head of scholastic work in mechanical engineering and Higgins was offered a job as head of the shop. During an interview, Higgins described the opportunity as attractive and stated that Georgia's people were "ready for industrial development and will be liberal in their expenditures to secure it."[5]

Higgins and Alden returned to Atlanta early in April 1887 to meet with the school commissioners. The official minutes mentioned that there was much discussion on the organization of the school.[6] Later in the month, a newspaper in Worcester reported that it had learned that the two professors were "not to sing 'Marching through Georgia.'"[7] Commissioners Porter and Inman decided to attend the commencement exercises at Worcester in 1887 in order to investigate further the operation of the school that had been selected as a pattern for Georgia Tech. Ironically, the invited speaker at the commencement was Robert H. Thurston, the principal architect of the school culture approach to mechanical engineering education.[8] In his speech, Thurston stated that education should be provided both for those who were fitted for intellectual pursuits and those who possessed "constructive faculties."[9] The *Atlanta Constitution* reported that it had heard from someone who attended the Worcester commencement and that he found it a revelation that the students did not speak on Homer but on bridges, steam engines, and the paving of roads.[10]

Although Alden and Higgins declined to accept the offer of teaching positions at the Georgia school, the commission developed such a high regard for Higgins that it decided to request that he be granted a one-year leave of absence from Worcester to organize and manage the commercial shop during its first year of operation.[11] The request was opposed by some members of the Worcester board, but it finally voted to grant Higgins a leave at one-half salary with the condition that he be responsible for operation of the Washburn Shops as well.[12] In an editorial entitled "No Man Can Serve Two Masters," the *Worcester Telegram* reported that all was not serene at WPI and that an offer to resign by Higgins would be accepted immediately. The editorial mentioned that Higgins and Alden were known to be involved in starting the Norton Emery Wheel Company and that Worcester students surveyed the site for the new factory. The editor speculated that there might soon be a shake up and that the leave granted to Higgins might be the "entering wedge for a permanent change." The paper mentioned that the last meeting of the Board of Trustees was acrimonious and there was frequent use of the "King's English."[13] Earlier in the year the board received complaints from a local elevator company about the elevators being made at the Washburn Shops using student labor and appointed a committee to look into the matter. The relationship between the Institute and the Washburn Shops continued to be a source of conflict over the next several years until the board decided to dispose of the elevator business in 1896, when both Higgins and Alden resigned to continue the business as a private enterprise.[14]

At the March 1887 meeting of the Georgia Tech Commission, the Executive Committee consisting of Heard, Porter, and Inman reported that an additional tract of land amounting to 4.75 acres had been purchased to add to the four acres donated by the Peters Park Development Company. The Office of Treasurer was created and Inman was elected to serve in that capacity with a paid clerical assistant. During the meeting it was recorded that the architectural firm of Bruce and Morgan had been retained to prepare plans and drawings for the first buildings. Bids on the construction of the academic building were to be advertised in the principal state newspapers and were to be submitted by April 21, 1887.[15] Six bids for the construction contract were received ranging from $53,818 to $67,500 with the low bid submitted by Angus McGilvray. Following negotiations with the Executive Committee, McGilvray agreed to undertake the project for the reduced total of $43,250. The commissioners visited the Peters Park property in early June to decide the exact location of the academic and shop buildings.[16]

At the September 1887 meeting of the commission, a subcommittee consisting of Porter and Inman was authorized to advertise for bids on the shop building.[17] A few days later a reporter from the *Atlanta Constitution* interviewed Inman, who informed him that the shop building was to be a two-story building with outside dimensions of 80 by 250 feet. Inman predicted that the shop would be a "hive of industry" and filled with mechanical apparatus and machines. He explained that the theoretical and practical components of the planned curriculum would be segregated at least physically.[18] The first two buildings of the Georgia School of Technology would reflect the mind-hand dichotomy so often mentioned in New South rhetoric and in the debate between the shop culture and school culture factions of mechanical engineering education. Three bids were received for the construction of the shop building, ranging from $22,866 to $27,000. The commissioners decided to reject the bids and that not more than $20,000 would be spent on the project. A small contract was let in December for the construction of the shop basement and, in April 1888, a contract was awarded to the firm of Petit and DeHaven for $20,600 to complete the shop structure including a foundry.[19]

On the day before Christmas in 1887, the *Atlanta Constitution* reported that the academic building was ready for its roof and that the structure presented an appearance of "symmetry and beauty." The article described the building location as being a "commanding one" that demonstrated that "the light of the school will not be hid." The report observed that the new building was among the finest in the city and that the contractor, McGilvray, seemed "inspired to make the building a monument of his skill." The account mentioned that rapid progress was being made on the shop foundation.[20]

At the November 1887 meeting of the Tech Commission, it was decided that Harris, Hodgson, and Heard would attend the next meeting of the board of the University of Georgia to request authority to organize the new school and hire teachers.[21] When the university board met December 21, 1887, Henry Grady introduced a motion that the Tech Commission be authorized to recruit faculty members and fix salaries with the faculty chairs to be confined to those existing at the Worcester school. When his initial motion failed to pass, Grady introduced a second resolution to establish eight chairs that was approved. The positions were to be in chemistry, mechanical engineering, physics, drawing, architecture, mathematics, English, and geology-mineralogy. The Tech Commission also was authorized to hire a president and a superintendent of the mechanical department or shop.[22] The Tech commissioners had already voted earlier in December to pay Milton P. Higgins a salary of $5,000 to be the shop superintendent during its first year of operation.[23] Shortly after the university board meeting, the *Atlanta Constitution* reported that it had learned that Professor Henry C. White of the University of Georgia would probably be chosen as the first president of Georgia Tech with Higgins to manage the shop. The article stated that other chairs would not be filled before February or March.[24]

The relationship between the University of Georgia and the School of Technology continued to be a source of friction. In July 1887, the *Constitution* responded to the charge that Atlanta was conspiring to take the land-grant fund from the University of Georgia and give it to Tech. The allegation had come up in the context of the selection of a new member of the university Board of Trustees. The editor promised that no such attempt would be made.[25] In January 1888, the *Constitution* responded to an item in the *Athens Banner-Watchman* with a statement that Tech did not aspire to be a rival of the Athens school. The editor asserted that Tech "will be in no sense a classical school." The editorial continued that the question of chairs for the new school was a difficult one and the commission was not prepared to decide exactly which were needed. The governor, however, suggested that all the chairs be named that might possibly be needed, but no more than five were likely to be filled.[26]

Henry C. White, a chemistry professor at the University of Georgia, apparently was on the verge of accepting an offer from the Tech Commission to serve as the school's first president when a new opportunity presented itself. The unexpected death of P. H. Mell, university chancellor, left a vacancy and there soon was speculation that White would be picked for the position. The *Atlanta Constitution* reported that White had decided to accept the presidency of Tech but would decline if he were elected as chancellor. The newspaper account continued that the Tech Commission would begin a search for another candidate but would postpone action until the election in Athens. The article mentioned that there was considerable public sentiment in favor of President Hopkins of Emory to become the Tech president. The *Constitution* did not know whether Hopkins would accept such an offer but observed that there was no doubt as to his "eminent fitness" for the position.[27] At the March meeting of the Tech Commission, a letter from White was read and a resolution was passed thanking him for his interest in the school.[28] Presumably the letter indicated that he was declining to accept the presidency of Tech.

A progressive faction of the university Board of Trustees led by Henry Grady gave its support to White for the chancellorship because it wanted a scientist rather than a minister in the position. White, however, was defeated by one vote, losing to G. B. Strickler, a Presbyterian minister. Strickler declined to accept and William E. Boggs, also a minister, was elected. White later became head of the land-grant college at the University of Georgia in 1890.[29] Ironically,

45 The Administration of Isaac Hopkins

this episode led to the selection of a clergyman rather than a scientist as the first president of the Georgia School of Technology.

Isaac S. Hopkins was nominated for the Tech presidency by Commissioner Inman at the April 1888 meeting of the Tech board. Hopkins was granted a few days to decide, and his letter of acceptance was received and read at the next meeting convened early in May.[30] As discussed in the previous chapter, he had become a strong advocate of manual education and had introduced a shop course at Emory. In addition to his duties as president of Tech, he was to occupy the chair of physics, a discipline in which his credentials were modest at best in an age when physics was undergoing revolutionary change. He had taught physics at the Southern University in Alabama for two years in the 1870s but had held chairs in Latin and in English at Emory.[31] By the late 1880s, it had become the norm for aspirant physicists to take graduate training in a German university or at least to attend Johns Hopkins University, the first American university to offer graduate research degrees comparable to those offered in Germany. Far-reaching changes had occurred, especially in electromagnetic science, since Hopkins had completed his formal education at the Georgia Medical College in 1861.

A few days prior to the June meeting of the Tech board when additional faculty selections were to be announced, the *Atlanta Constitution* reported that there were a few candidates for the chair of chemistry and that the name of Lyman Hall was the one mentioned most frequently for the chair of mathematics. There were around twelve candidates for the chair in English, including Charles Lane, but the reporter pointed out that there had not been a single application for the chair of mechanical engineering from the South, although several had been received from the North.[32]

At the board meeting, Lyman Hall, destined to become the second president of Tech, was elected to the mathematics chair, and Lane was chosen to fill the chair of English.[33] Hall (1859–1905) was born in Americus, Georgia, and attended Mercer University in Penfield before receiving an appointment to the United States Military Academy in 1877. Hall graduated from West Point in 1881, but a physical disability prevented him from pursuing a military career. He taught mathematics and served as cadet commandant at the Georgia Military Academy in Kirkwood for two years and then taught at the

South Carolina Military Academy in Charleston from 1883 to 1886. He became a professor at the Moreland Park Military Academy near Atlanta until he was invited to Tech.[34] Hall was well-qualified to teach mathematics at the undergraduate level and wrote three textbooks on algebra. He also was well grounded in civil engineering as a graduate of West Point, a school that had pioneered in engineering education in the United States with a curriculum patterned after that of the Ecole Polytechnique in France. Although Georgia Tech initially did not offer a degree in civil engineering, Hall included surveying and other engineering applications of mathematics in his courses. He also was a strict disciplinarian, an attribute that became apparent during his presidency. He had an energetic personality and quickly assumed a position of leadership at meetings of the faculty. Charles Lane was an ordained minister from Macon and may have had the support of the commission chairman, Harris, who was also from Macon.

At the July 1888 meeting of the Tech board, R. B. Shepard from Virginia was selected to occupy the chair of mechanical and freehand drawing.[35] His tenure at Tech was brief with a separate chair of drawing being eliminated after the first year. Subsequently, drawing was taught in the mechanical engineering department. The board mounted a strong effort that ultimately was unsuccessful to have a naval officer assigned to teach mechanical engineering at Tech. A motion was passed at the March 1888 meeting that called for Henry Grady and Samuel Inman to travel to Washington, D.C., and request that an officer be detailed to the school.[36] At the board meeting in July, Porter introduced a resolution requesting that the secretary of the navy detail Leo D. Minor to fill the mechanical engineering chair and that Senators Colquitt and Brown be asked to assist in getting Minor's services. An apparent motivation for this effort was to save money, since the resolution included the stipulation that his salary from the navy would be supplemented by only $400 per year.[37] Minor's name appeared on the list of the faculty published in the school prospectus in 1888, but he was not assigned and the chair remained vacant until the following year. It is uncertain why the effort failed since the navy did have a program during the period from 1879 to 1896 of assigning officers to teach in college programs of mechanical engineering. The curriculum at Annapolis stressed mechanical engineering just as West Point stressed civil engineering.[38]

In August 1888, William H. Emerson (1860–1924) was added to the faculty as professor of chemistry.[39] Thus only five of the designated eight chairs were filled when the school opened in October 1888. Emerson's academic credentials clearly were the most outstanding among the members of the first faculty. He was born in Tunnel Hill, Georgia, and graduated from the Naval Academy in 1880. After three years of service in the navy he enrolled in the graduate school at Johns Hopkins University, where he received a doctorate in 1885. He then taught at the South Carolina Military Academy until 1888.[40] Lyman Hall may have encouraged him to apply for the vacancy at Tech since they shared a military background and their periods of teaching at the Citadel overlapped. Emerson was only one of many students from the southern states who were attracted to the graduate school at Johns Hopkins after it opened in 1876. An outstanding program in chemistry was established at Johns Hopkins by Ira Remsen, who directed the dissertation work of more than one hundred students who received their doctorates between 1879 and 1902. Reportedly, Remsen's students were "strongly directed to teaching" and many founded new departments. Despite his German education, Remsen took little interest in industrial research, an attitude that presumably influenced his graduate students.[41] Emerson was professionally active, at least by the standards of Tech in its early years, as a member of the American Chemical Society and the Society for the Promotion of Engineering Education. He published at least one paper in the *Journal of the American Chemical Society.*[42]

Thus the first faculty who prepared to welcome students in the fall of 1888 was dominated by southerners, mostly Georgians, with the notable exception of the shop superintendent, Milton P. Higgins. There was a balance between professors with clerical and military backgrounds with Hopkins and Lane being ordained ministers and Hall and Emerson being graduates of service acadamies. These callings were quite compatible with the Old South culture but were not necessarily the most appropriate for educating young southerners in the industrial culture that the adherents of the New South Creed were trying to promote.

48   Engineering the New South

In early September 1888, the *Atlanta Constitution* reported that the academic and shop buildings were completed, the machinery was being installed in the shop, and all was in readiness for the students who would begin their work October 3. President Hopkins informed the reporter on details of the curriculum and stated that the students' time would be divided "about half and half between brain and body." He explained that the student would be expected to devote "a full working day of ten hours" to each of the major departments, shop and academic, and thus would "accomplish a great deal more than he would if his time were broken into bits to be distributed out among studies and work hours."[43]

In order to qualify for admission to the apprentice (first-year) class at Tech, applicants were required to be at least sixteen years old and to pass an entrance examination that included arithmetic, algebra, Amerian history, geography, and English. The first entrance examination was administered to eighty-four candidates in the chapel of the Academic Building on October 3, 1888. Free tuition was available for students from each county in Georgia up to a number equal to the number of representatives in the state legislature from the county, while out-of-state students were required to pay $150 per year for tuition. In the beginning, there were no dormitories on the campus, but prospective students were provided with a list of off-campus lodging that ranged in cost from $12.50 to $20 per month.[44]

The Opening of the Georgia School of Technology

The formal opening of the Georgia School of Technology occurred October 5, 1888, with the official transfer by the Tech Commission to the trustees of the state university. Following a brief inspection of the academic building, the attending dignitaries entered the shop building where a polished forty-horse-power steam engine that had been constructed by students at the Worcester Polytechnic Institute waited with its throttle wheel "ornamented with three blue, red, and gold rosettes." A steam whistle was sounded at noon and Miss Nellie Inman, escorted by former Governor McDaniel, opened the throttle to start the engine that powered the shop machinery as the crowd applauded. Ironically, it was to be many decades before women would be permitted to study the design and testing of engines at Georgia Tech.⁴⁵

Following the starting of the engine, Milton P. Higgins, the first superintendent of the Tech Shops, gave a short talk in which he outlined the role that the shops were expected to play in the education of those who enrolled at the new school. He stated that the educational method would be "simple and direct" with the student being placed in "an environment not unlike what he may expect to find when he enters the active duties of life." He continued that the shop experience would give the student valuable skills but that "the greatest value of shop training . . . is the marked effective influence upon the mind and character of the pupil." Higgins argued that, to be effective in molding character, it was necessary to "have a real shop, where real difficulties are overcome and where real successes are achieved" and that "a play shop cannot do it."⁴⁶

A highlight of the opening day ceremonies was a speech by N. E. Harris, who had led the legislative campaign to establish the school. A principal theme of his speech was that the new school represented a response to the needs of the working class. He claimed that the gap between the classes was narrowing and that the "lower classes have risen upward and higher classes have moved downward." He continued that the lower classes "do not boast the blue blood of the cavaliers—they use their hands in making a living. It is no disgrace now." Harris mentioned the friction between the city of Atlanta and the middle and southern portions of the state. He stated that Atlanta's "people were not like our people, the push and energy of her citizens, the rapid strides which they made in wealth and prosperity gave her more the appearance of one of our western or northern cities than of a southern metropolis." Harris concluded that the students who came to Tech would be taught nothing but the "gospel of labor."⁴⁷

Governance in the Early Years

In the early years the school president and the other professors met weekly as a committee of the whole to decide curriculum changes, disciplinary action, suspensions or dismissals due to poor grades, and other issues. President Hopkins's managerial style might be characterized as clerical rather than authoritarian. William H. Emerson later recalled that Hopkins had impressed him as a "dignified, kindly man of broad sympathy and understanding." Emerson observed that the first faculty had divergent views on what was the proper curriculum and on the relative importance of the various departments. He noted that the faculty meetings were not "love feasts" but that Hopkins remained calm and impartial and worked diligently to harmonize discords. According to Emerson, Hopkins's chapel talks were "always thoughtful, clothed in elegant language, and delivered in a most charming manner."[48]

The faculty held its first meeting October 5, 1888, and elected Lyman Hall as secretary. They discussed the results of the entrance examination and voted to admit all but seven who had taken it. The following day the faculty decided that those few who had been unable to qualify by examination would be permitted to remain on probationary status and receive remedial instruction to qualify them for the apprentice class. At a meeting held October 19, 1888, the faculty decided that they would meet each Friday with a regular agenda that included reports on student conduct and scholastic standing.[49]

The Tech Board of Trustees met less frequently after the school opened with the official minutes indicating no quorum in November, February, March, and April of the first academic year. At the December 1888 meeting, the board voted to reimburse Professor Aldrich from Philadelphia for his expenses to come to an interview for the still vacant chair of mechanical engineering. Most of the business transacted involved approval of payment of bills. At the May 1889 meeting, the board authorized Professor Emerson to spend four hundred dollars on the chemistry laboratory but declined to act on a request from Hall for extra compensation for his duties as faculty secretary. During the same meeting the board passed a motion by Oliver Porter to place the department of mechanical drawing under mechanical engineering and to inform Professor Shepherd that his chair of drawing would be declared vacant effective October 1, 1889.[50]

Another significant action taken by the Tech board at the May 1889 meeting was the hiring of John Saylor Coon to occupy the chair of mechanical engineering.[51] Coon was a much needed addition to the Tech faculty since mechanical engineering was the only degree offered at the time, and he would serve as both mentor and role model for the students. During a career of nearly forty years at Tech, he determined the style and substance of the mechanical engineering curriculum. When he joined the faculty in 1889, Coon was the only professor with both an engineering degree and years of experience in industry. With the departure of Higgins and the consolidation of the drawing and mechanical engineering departments, Coon arrived with an opportunity to be a powerful force on the faculty and in engineering education in the region. Born in Burdett, New York, he graduated in mechanical engineering from Cornell University in 1877, when it was still dominated by the shop culture approach. Coon taught at Cornell for a year and then worked as an engineer with the Calumet and Hecla Mining Company for eight years with responsibility for inspecting and testing heavy mining and pumping machinery. He was a charter member of the American Society of Mechanical Engineers, formed in 1880, and published several contributions to its *Transactions* in the 1880s. He later was a founding member and first chairman of the Atlanta section of the ASME. Coon worked approximately two years as an engineer at the Anaconda Copper Company in Montana and became a professor at the University of Tennessee in 1888 before accepting the position at Georgia Tech the following year.[52]

Oliver Porter took an active role in the recruitment of Coon. M. L. Brittain, who had access to some of Porter's correspondence with Coon, wrote that Coon had expressed some doubt about accepting the position at Tech because his teaching methods were "rather unorthodox." Porter reportedly responded by assuring Coon that "he was not trying to secure a Sunday-School teacher."[53] Porter was also a member of the ASME and may have learned of Coon's credentials for the position through reading his papers in the *Transactions* or from other ASME connections.[54] Coon became commonly known as "Uncle Si" by the Tech engineering students, and a booklet of his pithy "sayings" in class later was printed by a former student.

J. B. McCrary, one of Coon's first students at Tech, characterized him as "very rigid and exacting as a professor, but his practical experience and forcefulness of character made a strong impression on the young men who later went out into the engineering world." Another former student, J. H. Lucas, stated that Coon's greatest attribute was his "ability to inject more than textbook knowledge into students."[55] Coon, who had helped a Cornell professor to build one of the first electric dynamos built in the United States, wound the first electrical machines built in the Tech Shops and eventually became superintendent of the shops in addition to his duties as head of mechanical engineering. He engaged in some outside consulting work and used data and drawings from his years in industry as teaching materials in his courses. He was known for tossing a steam gauge or "other flying missiles" at students who dozed in class or otherwise irritated him.[56]

A significant change in the makeup and operation of the Tech board followed a request to the state legislature in October 1890 for authorization to increase the board membership from five to seven.[57] The requested change was approved, and two Atlanta manufacturers, D. N. Speer and W. B. Miles, were elected to the board in January 1891. At the same time Porter resigned as auditor of the shops, and Inman, Speer, and Miles were appointed as a committee to audit expenditures of the school, including those for the shops. In addition, Inman and Miles were appointed as an executive committee to represent the board in the administration of school affairs with full authority to act.[58] Miles was president of the Atlanta Bridge and Axle Company located near the campus. The company employed around 350 men and manufactured steel bridges and did other large-scale structural work. Speer was president of the Exposition Cotton Mill, also located near the Tech campus, and was active in the Atlanta Manufacturers Association, as were Miles and Inman. These changes in the Tech board greatly increased the influence of the manufacturing community in Atlanta on the management of the school. Speer's tenure on the Tech board proved rather brief due to his death in 1893, but his replacement elected in June 1893 was another manufacturer, George Winship, who was president of the Winship Machine Company located near the Tech campus.[59]

The Commercial Shop, 1888–1896

When the school opened in the fall of 1888, the shops occupied a two-story building with a tower that resembled that of the academic building. The first floor was devoted to metalworking and housed a drawing room, office, machine shop, engine room, blacksmith shop, iron foundry, and brass foundry. The equipment in the metal shops included fifteen lathes, two upright drills, a milling machine, a core cutter, a shaper, and a variety of small tools. The iron foundry contained a large cupola and an oven for baking the mold cores. The wood shop on the second floor was described as having "the very best machinery of the latest pattern." Equipment included thirty-two work benches, six lathes, six jig saws, a band saw, three planers, a tenon machine, and a mortising machine. It was reported that the woodworking department had ample space for sixty-eight students to work at one time.[60]

The superintendent managed the shop with the assistance of four foremen who supervised work in the machine shop, the blacksmith shop, the foundry, and the wood shop. The shops also employed some skilled paid workmen, but much of the work was by Tech students who were unpaid unless they were employed in the shops during summer vacations. Although the ostensible function of the shops was educational, they were run for the first several years as contract job shops that were largely autonomous from the academic departments. The shop system closely paralleled that of the Washburn Shops at Worcester with the first two superintendents of the Tech Shops and at least two of the first four foremen having worked at the Worcester Shops.

The description of the shop course printed in the first catalog of Georgia Tech followed closely the description in the Worcester catalog and at least some passages were identical in wording. The description, presumably authored by Milton P. Higgins, stated that, after the first lesson, "the practice is on commercial goods and follows the best methods of commercial production." It continued that the shops were "organized and managed as a manufacturing establishment and the great variety of work always in process of construction will enable the students to have constantly before them the wholesome atmosphere of real business." The account stated that the apprentice class would concentrate on woodworking while the upper class would work mostly with iron. Students also were expected to learn to operate and maintain the boiler and steam engine, and members of the senior class were required to build one or more complete machines using their own drawings.[61]

Much of the business for the Tech Shops came from Atlanta, although some orders were filled from customers elsewhere in Georgia and, less frequently, from out of the state. Among the more frequent customers were the Fulton Cotton Spinning Company, the Exposition Cotton Mill, and Oliver Porter's cotton mill in Porterdale.[62] The Fulton Company was located in east Atlanta and was owned and managed by the Elsas family. Oscar Elsas, a son of the founder of the company, was a member of the junior class during the first year, one of several students admitted with advanced standing. Elsas later became an executive in the Fulton Company and provided assistance to Lyman Hall in starting a textile school at Georgia Tech. During the first year, the Tech Shops received orders for pattern work, 400 loom castings, and 2,000 pickers from the Fulton Company. Other orders included gears for the Atlanta Paper Company, castings for the Exposition Cotton Mill, patterns for Oliver Porter, and castings for the Atlanta Cotton Factory.[63]

The balance sheet for the Tech Shops during the first year with Higgins as the superintendent showed that the net cost of operating the shop was $1,866, excluding the superintendent's salary. The shops took in $1,688 for the sale of manufactured products and $1,324 from castings from October 1888 to July 1889. Only two months, February and April, showed a positive cash flow. The number of paid employees during the first year ranged from nineteen to thirty-seven and their average pay ranged from twenty to twenty-eight cents per hour. Although Higgins left to return to Worcester on July 1, 1889, the shops continued to operate during the summer and some students were provided with paid summer employment.[64] In May 1889, Inman, the treasurer of the Tech board, notified W. F. Cole of the Washburn Shops that he had been elected to the position of superintendent at the Tech Shops. G. E. Cassidy, the foreman of the wood shop, was authorized to handle shop correspondence pending the arrival of Cole to assume his duties in September.[65]

W. F. Cole (1859–1942) had good credentials for the position at Tech, which he assumed would be a permanent appointment. He was a native of Massachusetts and had a bachelor's degree in civil engineering. He taught mechanical engineering for a year at Iowa State University before accepting a position at the Washburn Shops in 1885. Following a year as superintendent of the shops at Georgia Tech, he returned to Worcester as assistant to Higgins at the Washburn Shops. In 1896 he joined Higgins in organizing the Plunger Elevator Company and served as its general manager.⁶⁶

The Tech Shops experienced a chronic lack of working capital. In October 1889, Cole informed a local customer that the shops could not accept a ninety-day note but that transactions were on a cash basis with payment due by the fifteenth of each month. In April 1890 Cole contacted the Thomson-Houston Electric Company asking prompt payment of their bill since "we have almost no working capital and need to make collection every month." Cole explained that the shop was "entirely independent of other departments" and that if an electrical plant were to be installed it would be paid for by funds other than those from the shop. He wrote to the Davis Water Wheel Company of Macon that further pattern work would not be undertaken for them until they paid for work outstanding.⁶⁷

Cole sought to diversify to take advantage of Tech's location and opportunities in newly developing industry. He wrote to Oliver Porter that the Tech Shops needed a large gear-cutting machine and that, if it had one, it could be kept busy every day of the year. He pointed out that the new and expanding electric streetcar industry used many large gears and that Tech should be able to get the business in much of the South if it were equipped to make them. Cole stated that such gears would provide a "very desirable class of work" for the Tech Shops and it would be most unfortunate if the chance to secure this business were missed. He asked Porter whether "some way can be found for us to seize it and make the most of it."⁶⁸

Superintendent Cole's tenure at Tech ended in August 1890 when his contract was not renewed due to what the Tech board felt to be the financial "uncertainty of the future." G. E. Cassidy, the wood shop foreman, was made acting shop superintendent effective September 1, 1890.⁶⁹ The lack of managerial continuity in the position of superintendent undoubtedly contributed to the disappointing economic performance of the Tech Shops. Certainly Higgins and Cole were more experienced in the management of educational commercial shops than were their successors. The evidence suggests that the educational function of the shops received less emphasis during the period between the departure of Cole and the consolidation of the shops under mechanical engineering in 1896.

Cassidy was faced with the cash flow problem that had plagued his predecessor from the start. In December 1890 he wrote to Pratt Furnace, from which the Tech Shops purchased pig iron, that he could not pay the due account but that an appropriation bill was pending in the state legislature. Cassidy asked that Pratt wait for a few days rather than initiate litigation to collect. He wrote to another creditor, a coal mining firm in Virginia, to explain why Tech had not paid its bill for foundry coal. He stated that there was no money to pay the bill but that it would receive prompt attention when the state appropriation was received.[70]

Tech's commercial shop was dealt a severe setback when a fire destroyed the shop building in April 1892. The *Atlanta Journal* reported the disaster, stating that the chief of the fire department believed that the night watchman at Tech had been asleep, since the alarm had been turned in by a policeman who had seen the flames burst through the roof. The fire department was delayed in getting to the scene because of the muddy condition of North Avenue and had to detour to Simpson Street. A further delay resulted when a fire hose had to be stretched 2,100 feet to reach the nearest hydrant at the corner of Marietta Street and North Avenue. The report continued that the only things saved had been three chests of tools that been rescued by students and that a large quantity of contract work had been destroyed. The *Journal* stated that the "most important branch of the school" probably would have to suspend operation for a considerable time.[71] The loss was estimated at over $30,000 with the insurance covering only $18,000.[72]

The Tech Board of Trustees met on April 29, 1892, to consider what actions were needed in the aftermath of the fire. It was mentioned that there had been some public criticism over not having enough insurance but that this was unfair since it was customary in Georgia to insure such property at about half of its value. Board members Miles, Speer, and Porter were appointed as a building committee to be responsible for replacement of the structure and equipping it as quickly as possible. Miles, both a board member and president of the Atlanta Bridge and Axle Company, stated that work contracted prior to the fire would be completed at the shops and foundry of the old works of the Atlanta Bridge and Axle Company. Four bids ranging from $11,886 to $20,000 were received in June 1892 for the rebuilding of the shops. The contract was awarded to the low bidder, F. P. Heifner.[73] The shop records after the fire reveal a steady increase in the monthly deficits associated with running the Tech Shops, reaching $2,155 in December 1892. The Executive Committee of the Tech board met December 21, 1892, and selected Alfred Jessop to replace Cassidy as shop superintendent.[74] Jessop's background is obscure, although he is known to have worked for the Southern Agricultural Works before becoming superintendent of the Tech Shops. This firm had been organized in Atlanta in 1882 and manufactured plows and other agricultural implements. Its plant was located near the Tech campus between Marietta Street and the W&A Railroad and employed about two hundred.[75] It seems likely that he was recruited through the network of the Atlanta manufacturers who dominated the Tech board at the time.

Jessop provided the Tech board with a financial report on shop operations during the year ending June 30, 1893. The report showed a deficit of $6,620 for the year, not including the shop superintendent's salary of $200 per month. Jessop attributed $1,685 of the deficit to "worthless accounts" that antedated the fire and the cost of replacing patterns for valued customers whose business otherwise would have been lost. Thus he argued that the actual deficit was $5,159 and that total expenses were only slightly greater than for the "prosperous year just before the fire." He also noted that the shops had not resumed full operation until around December 1 and that there had been some loss of customers following the fire. Jessop noted that $1,766 was charged to the woodworking shop but that no revenue business had been done by students in that department. He stated that he was confident that the deficit could be reduced in the future. The shop payroll during the year had varied from a low of $364 in September 1892 to a high of $2,035 in January 1893. The cash flow had varied from a maximum monthly deficit of $2,155 in December 1892 to a maximum monthly surplus of $1,146 in March 1893.[76] Despite Jessop's optimistic forecast the shop still showed little promise of becoming a source of net income for the school with the operating deficit in the fifth year being more than 3.5 times that of the first year under Higgins.

The commercial shop experiment at Tech ended in January 1896 with a decision by the Tech board "to change it from a commercial to a purely education institution as soon as possible." Mechanical

Engineering Professor John S. Coon was put in charge of the shops, eliminating their semi-autonomous status and the separate position of shop superintendent.[77] The 1896 Tech catalog asserted that the contract system was abandoned not because of "any lack of efficiency in the management of the shops under the former method" but because the "exigencies of local trade filled the shop with a class of work not always adapted to the most efficient instruction." The statement continued that the student could learn to do a "poor, cheap job, after graduation" when the "scramble for the mighty dollar may force it upon him."[78] This passage presumably reflected the thinking of Professor Coon and may have been composed by him.

Athough the contract system was ended in 1896, the Tech students continued to spend much of their time on shop work. The catalog for 1896–97 indicated that members of the apprentice class would continue to work in the shop for two eight-hour days per week while, in the remaining three years, one day per week would be spent in the shop. The same catalog mentioned that planers made entirely by the students were for sale and were "guaranteed to be a strictly first-class job and to give entire satisfaction." Another product that still was offered for sale was a wooden case for large drawings. The entry claimed that no other school in the country placed as much emphasis on "the practical skill and experience to be gained in machine shop work of the very highest order."[79]

The Academic Curriculum in the Early Years

The prospectus printed in 1888 listed six academic subjects in addition to the shop course: mathematics, physics, chemistry, mechanics, drawing, and English. The curriculum included no electives but had daily recitations that were graded. The students were to devote five hours per week to mathematics during the first three years and during the first semester of the senior year. Algebra and plane geometry were included in the apprentice year, while the junior class was to study geometry, trigonometry, surveying, and orthographic projection, including some topographic work. The middle class was to study analytic geometry and beginning calculus, while the senior class would continue in calculus. The classes were divided into sections with fifteen to twenty-six students in each. As was the case with almost everything taught at Tech, mathematics was taught with a practical emphasis that included field work in farm surveying and leveling and was, in effect, an introduction to civil engineering even though a degree was not offered in that discipline.[80]

In the original curriculum, the students were to devote two hours per week to physics in the first year, three hours in the junior year, and five hours in each of the final two years. Students in the advanced classes were informed that they would study hydrostatics, dynamics, pneumatics, acoustics, electricity and magnetism, optics, the transmission of power, and telegraphy and telephony. The work in applied electromagnetics amounted to an introduction to the field of electrical engineering, a degree also not offered prior to 1896. The first Tech students were to study chemistry for two hours per week in the first year, five hours in the junior year, and three hours in the final year. The chemistry courses included inorganic, analytic, and industrial chemistry, along with some consideration of geology and mineralogy as they related to the mining industry and the mineral resources of Georgia. In the last semester of the senior year, the students learned about industrial applications of chemistry and reported on articles from chemical journals. Again, they were introduced to chemical and mining engineering, although degrees were not offered in either.[81]

The 1888 prospectus was somewhat vague in its description of what would be studied in mechanical engineering outside the shop, probably because a professor of mechanical engineering had not yet been found. The entry indicated that the students would study theoretical and applied mechanics, the strength of materials, gears, transformation of energy, and steam.[82] A revised description, probably written by Coon, was included in the catalog for 1889–90 which stated that all instruction in the mechanical engineering department "is based on strictly utilitarian lines." The entry continued that "the graduate's commercial value on leaving the technical school is invariably based on his helpfulness—on what he can do and not on what he knows. He must know things and how to do them, and not simply know about them." According to this catalog, the students would learn kinematics, analytic and applied mechanics, machine design, the materials used in engineering structures, steam engineering and prime movers, and engage in laboratory experiments.[83]

The first Tech faculty soon learned that a substantial number of the young Georgians who sought admission to Tech were unprepared to begin college level courses. Consequently, Tech found it expedient to introduce a subapprentice class beginning in 1891, and 56 out of the total of 167 students were placed in the subapprentice class during the year 1890–91.[84] By 1899 around 125 students were enrolled in the subapprentice class and Lyman Hall wrote to Nathaniel Harris that Tech was gaining a "splendid reputation" for its preparatory teaching methods and that many "students prefer coming here to remaining home and attending high school."[85]

Extracurricular Activities in the Early Years

All students were expected to attend services at a place of worship according to their denominational preference on the Sabbath and were required to attend the daily chapel service at Tech unless excused for good reason. By 1890 Tech students had organized a branch of the YMCA and were holding regular meetings in the school chapel. The Phi Eta Sigma Literary Society was organized in 1892 and was said to have copies of the latest magazines and scientific periodicals that were available to its members. A student publication known as the *Technologian* was started in 1891 but soon was discontinued. A second student publication, *Georgia Tech*, was started in 1894 and survived until 1908.[86]

Georgia Tech's first football team was organized in the fall of 1892 and participated in a series of games played in Atlanta in which teams from the University of North Carolina, the University of Virginia, Vanderbilt, Alabama A&M (Auburn), and Mercer University participated. The *Atlanta Constitution* carried a story in October 1892 about an upcoming game between Tech and Mercer and reported that the Tech team was practicing each afternoon under the direction of F. O. Spain or E. E. West. Spain was a graduate of the South Carolina Military Academy (Citadel), where Lyman Hall and W. H. Emerson had formerly taught, and was an adjunct professor of mathematics at Tech. West was a graduate of the United States

Naval Academy at Annapolis and was an adjunct professor of physics at Tech. The *Constitution* stated that West was serving as the team's captain and played the position of left halfback. The article noted that he was an experienced player who had played at Annapolis and was "the most scientific player" on the Tech team.[87]

In 1893 the *Constitution* published an article entitled "A Great Sport—How the Modern Game of Football Is Played." The writer called football the "most exciting and scientific athletic sport now engaged in" and noted that northern newspapers were giving the sport extensive coverage. The story continued that the South was just "waking up to the importance of the game" and that college football essentially had arrived in the region in 1891, when a game was played in Atlanta between the University of Georgia and Auburn that was attended by three thousand people. The article included a description of the game and its rules and stated that a good season was anticipated in 1893 since the players of the principal teams had spent the summer practicing "passing, kicking and falling on the ball."[88]

The results of Tech's first football contest with the University of Georgia were reported by the *Constitution* of November 5, 1893. According to the story, Tech had won by a score of 28–6 but the fans of the university had complained that Tech's team had players who were not legitimate students and that the umpire was a brother of Tech's trainer and had made unfair decisions. Tech supporters in turn objected that a professionally paid trainer had played for the university. Tech's leading player in the game had been Leonard Wood, an army surgeon stationed at Fort McPherson who had enrolled at Tech. The story claimed that Wood had been able to handle the opposing guard "almost as if he were a child." The Athens fans also objected to Tech's use of Park Howell who had played fullback but was a medical student and was believed to have enrolled at Tech only to play football. The University of Georgia team had fared better in the second half, when they had used a trick "turtleback play" that Tech's team had not seen before. The article mentioned that a number of young ladies from the Lucy Cobb Institute for Girls had attended the game and supported Tech by wearing the "white and gold" colors of the school. It also was reported that Tech's players had been "rocked and threatened" and that the train that was bringing the team back to Atlanta had collided with a freight train near Lawrenceville but that no lives had been lost.[89]

The First Tech Students and the Employment of Early Graduates

The enrollment at Tech during the first academic year was 129, a total that included 116 in the apprentice class, 11 juniors, and 2 in the middle class. Almost all the students at Tech for the first several years came from the state of Georgia. The only out-of-state student in the first year was from Chattanooga, Tennessee, and in 1890–91 only one member of the apprentice class came from a state other than Georgia. A list of students in the 1893–94 catalog indicated that one member of the middle class was from West Virginia and that two members of the subapprentice class were from South Carolina, while all the rest were from Georgia.[90] The rate of attrition was quite high. A quantitative comparison of the number of graduating seniors with the number who had enrolled four years earlier reveals that the percentage who graduated varied from a low of 17.2 in 1892 to a high of 25.7 in 1894 during the period from 1892 to 1896. The highest percentage prior to 1900 was 30.8 in the class of 1897.[91]

Of the sixty students who graduated from Tech from 1890 to 1895, all were from Georgia and came from twenty-nine counties. Seventeen of these graduates (28.4 percent) were from Fulton County, where the school was located, followed by Richmond County (Augusta) with four, and DeKalb, Chatham, and Floyd counties with three each. Six counties were represented by two graduates with the remaining graduates coming from eighteen other counties. Thirty-eight of these early graduates came from urban counties (63.3 percent), including twenty-six (43.5 percent) from counties near Atlanta. An analysis of where these graduates were employed in 1896 reveals that forty-six (76.6 percent) were working in Georgia and that twenty-six (43.3 percent) worked in Atlanta. Only eight (13.3 percent) of the graduates had found employment in the North at that time. Forty-three of the first sixty graduates were employed in manufacturing, transportation, or in various business enterprises in Georgia, while two had become, at least temporarily, farmers in Georgia. Interestingly, twelve (20 percent) of these graduates were employed in various segments of the electrical industry (including street railways). Five worked in the textile manufacturing industry in Georgia.[92]

George G. Crawford (1869–1936), who was one of the first two graduates of Tech in the class of 1890, became one of the school's most eminent alumni. Born in Madison, Georgia, he was the son of a surgeon who later taught at the Southern Medical College in Atlanta. Crawford attended the Georgia Military and Agricultural College in Milledgeville, Georgia, before enrolling at Georgia Tech as a third-year student in 1888. While in Atlanta, he served as a lieutenant on the Gate City Guard, a drill team that had Lyman Hall as captain. M. L. Brittain, who was to become the fourth president of Tech, also became a member of the drill unit in 1888.[93] Crawford was an expert draftsman, and his drawings of the floor plans of the academic and shop building were included in early catalogs of the school. Following his graduation from Tech in 1890, he studied chemistry at the University of Tubingen in Germany and then worked as a draftsman at the Sloss Iron and Steel Company in Birmingham, Alabama. He joined the Carnegie Steel Company in Pittsburgh in 1893 and became superintendent of furnaces at the giant Edgar Thomson steel mill in 1895. In 1901, Crawford became president of the Tennessee Coal, Iron and Railroad Company in Birmingham, a subsidiary of the United States Steel Company. In 1930 he became president of the Jones and Laughlin Steel Company in Pittsburgh. He was a member of the Tech Board of Trustees and received an honorary doctorate from Tech in 1931.[94]

Henry L. Smith was from Rockdale County and was the other member of the first graduating class in 1890. His first job was as superintendent of the bleachery at the Fulton Bag and Cotton Mill in Atlanta. He later founded the Smith Manufacturing Company in Dalton, Georgia, and was a civic leader in that city.[95] Two members of the graduating class of 1891, W. H. Glenn and J. B. McCrary, began their careers with the Consolidated Street Railway Company in Atlanta. Both men participated in the organization of the Georgia Tech Alumni Association in 1906, and Glenn was a leader in founding the Georgia Tech Alumni Foundation in 1932. McCrary became a partner with another early alumnus, J. S. Moore (class of 1891), in a mechanical engineering firm in Atlanta in the late 1890s.[96]

64   Engineering the New South

The End of the Hopkins Administration

Hopkins's final months as Tech's president were marked by a sense of malaise with a growing concern over the school's perilous financial situation. At a meeting of the faculty in May 1895, Lyman Hall introduced a motion asking that Hopkins contact the Tech board to ascertain whether the faculty would be paid for the remainder of the year. At the next meeting Hopkins reported that the treasurer had assured him that "there was no immediate cause for apprehension" with regard to salaries.[97] The same month, Hopkins submitted his resignation with the request that it become effective either on July 1, 1895, or January 1, 1896. His request was tabled until the June meeting of the Tech board. At the same time, the trustees were seeking ways to reduce the operating costs of the Tech Shops and were concerned over low enrollment and disciplinary problems at the school.

Professor Lyman Hall was invited to attend a meeting of the Tech board on June 25, 1895, at which he gave a presentation on the needs of the school. His remarks were not recorded in the official minutes, but subsequent developments suggest that he probably stressed the need to build dormitories so that the students could live on campus. It later became evident that he saw a link between disciplinary problems and the lack of housing on the campus. Hall probably recommended a more aggressive recruitment of students, a policy that he implemented when he became president. He may also have discussed personnel changes such as those made at a board meeting the following day.[98]

At its meeting on June 26, 1895, the Tech board instructed its Executive Committee to look into the possibility of constructing temporary dormitories. The official minutes revealed that Hopkins had withdrawn his letter of resignation and that he now would occupy the chair of English instead of physics. Charles Lane, who had held the English chair since the school opened, was placed in charge of the subapprentice class. In another action, the Executive Committee was told to arrange for the faculty to travel over the state during the vacation period for the purpose of "awakening further interest in the school and securing a larger enrollment."[99]

Six months later, the Hopkins presidency ended at the same time that the contract shop system was abolished. Rumors of Hopkins's impending resignation already were public knowledge before the meeting of the Tech board on January 3, 1896, and were discussed by the *Atlanta Constitution* in an article entitled "Are All to Resign?" The story, published on the day of the board meeting, reported that Hopkins had been interviewed upon his return from Macon the previous day and had denied that his resignation was "due to any pique on his part" over the recent actions in the Georgia House. He had expressed regret that his motives had been "misunderstood and misconstrued." Hopkins had stated that his decision to resign had been motivated by his recent election as pastor of the First Methodist Church of Atlanta and his feeling that he could not do "justice both to the school and the church."

The *Constitution* article went on to say that there had been reports that Chairman Harris and the rest of the Tech board would resign because of the recent action in the state legislature. The reporter explained that the legislature had been appropriating the sum of $22,500 annually for the support of Tech and had refused to increase this amount at the recent session. Senator Harris (the Tech board chairman) from Macon had introduced a bill to appropriate an additional $15,000 to build dormitories at Tech, and another bill had included $5,000 to start a department of electrical engineering. However, both bills had been voted down in the House. According to the *Constitution*, the fact that Hopkins had submitted his resignation had led to reports that his action had resulted from failure to get the requested increase in the state appropriation.[100]

At the board meeting, Chairman Harris read Hopkins's letter of resignation, which was accepted as effective immediately. Several possible candidates to succeed Hopkins were proposed during the meeting, including the state school superintendent, the school superintendent of Rome, Georgia, and Professors Hall and Lane of the Tech faculty. A motion by S. M. Inman, however, was adopted to postpone a decision and make Lyman Hall the chairman of the faculty with the full authority of the president for a period of six months. Lane was returned to the chair of English being vacated by Hopkins. At the same meeting the Executive Committee was authorized to proceed with the construction of dormitory and dining facilities, and the positions of shop superintendent and foundry foreman (and their salaries) were eliminated. Finally, the board elected Robert M. Quick to fill a position that now was called the chair of electrical engineering and physics.[101]

Further background on the historic board meeting was provided the following day by the *Atlanta Constitution*. The article stated that, contrary to expectation, "nothing sensational" had happened at the meeting and that "ruffled feelings" had been "assuaged" by the governor and "all was now well." The account continued that a report prepared by the Executive Committee had been read which showed that the school's system had been altered and improved so that the academic and mechanical (shop) departments would work more "hand in hand" with "the progress of the one measured by the progress of the other." The report explained that the board's decision not to elect a new president had been made for two reasons, to save money and use it to expand the physical facilities and to avoid the difficulty of electing a new president in the middle of a term. According to the *Constitution*, the board had authorized construction of dormitories and a mess hall to fill an urgent need because students of limited means could not afford the costs of boarding off campus. Noting the selection of Hall as the faculty chairman who would carry out the duties of a president, the *Constitution* stated that he was well known in Georgia and "possesses liberal ideas, is abreast of the times and fully qualified to conduct the school successfully." The reporter asserted that "from now on the policy and object of the college will be instructive as well as constructive."[102]

In June 1896, the Executive Committee of the Tech board reported the completion of two dormitories at a cost of $4,000. A motion by Oliver Porter was approved that called for the rules and regulations of the school to be rewritten and submitted for approval. The board encouraged the faculty to impose "rigid discipline" in the shops in the future. At the same meeting, the Board of Trustees elected Lyman Hall as Tech's second president.[103]

Isaac Hopkins's clerical style of management was perhaps not well suited to the needs of a newly established technological school that was trying to survive in an adverse financial climate of legislative skepticism and frugality. He was less proficient than his successor in lobbying the legislature and in the use of funds from outside sources as leverage to gain increased appropriations. Hopkins's managerial approach was probably better suited to the needs of an established sectarian college such as Emory than to a school with the avowed mission of preparing boys from the working classes for employment in shops and manufacturing industries. Edgar H. Johnson later wrote in a biographical essay on Hopkins that he "had little relish for administrative duties, but found pleasure in his study and worship."[104]

Lyman Hall's approach to the management of Tech was to be quite different from that of Hopkins, and Hall adopted tactics in his campaigns to expand the school and add to its physical plant that he might have learned at West Point. Judging from the results, his dynamic and aggressive policies were probably more appropriate to the needs of a school that still had to convince skeptics of the value of technological education than the Hopkins laissez-faire policies had been.

After leaving Tech, Hopkins continued his career as a clergyman for many years with his last church being in Athens. According to one biographer, he "delighted in metaphysics rather than physics," and his "metaphysical tendency manifests itself to some extent in his sermons." However, the same writer commented that Hopkins probably would cast aside both physics and metaphysics in order "to study the details of some new piece of machinery."[105] Hopkins returned to Atlanta during the last years of his life and was appointed to the position of warrant clerk in the state government by the governor.[106] Hopkins participated in the twenty-fifth anniversary ceremonies at Tech in 1913, which took place a few months before his death in February 1914.[107]

Chapter Three

Dormitories, Diversification, and Discipline: The Administration of Lyman Hall

Overleaf: Students operate power looms in classes at the Textile School, circa 1902–1903. (Courtesy of the Georgia Tech Archives.)

The themes of the Hall administration were discernible in the first few months of his presidency. They included the building of dormitories, a greater emphasis on disciplinary rules, the establishment of new degree programs, a more aggressive recruitment of students, and an almost constant effort by Hall to increase the funding of Tech by the state and by private benefactors. Tech acquired its first dormitories in the form of two temporary frame buildings in June 1896, just as Hall became the school's second president. This began a process that inevitably led to greater separation between the school and the city, a common tendency among urban colleges in the late nineteenth century. As Thomas Bender has pointed out, "some sort of physical isolation" was thought necessary in order that colleges be able to "assert their distinctive and superior values." He noted that such schools as Johns Hopkins and Harvard that "once opened onto the life of their community, turned inward" and erected walls and gates.[1] Such a policy only became realistic if a majority of the students could be housed on the campus. Lyman Hall's conviction that stricter rules of conduct were needed than had existed under his predecessor was compatible with making Tech into a more isolated enclave than it had been at the start.

The decade of Hall's presidency was notable not only for a substantial increase in the school's physical facilities but also for the addition of new degree programs in electrical engineering, civil engineering, textile engineering, and engineering chemistry. This diversification served to attract more students and promote a steady growth in enrollment. The school also began to attract a substantial number of students from outside Georgia, which Hall encouraged by such means as offering cash bounties to recruiters in neighboring states for each student they could persuade to enroll at Tech.[2] In his effort to obtain funding for new dormitories and new academic departments, Hall devoted much time and energy to seeking the financial support of wealthy philanthropists, such as Aaron French and Andrew Carnegie, as an alternative to state funding that never seemed adequate.

In contrast to the clerical managerial style of Hopkins, Hall, a graduate of West Point and captain of the Gate City Guard, adopted a more authoritarian style with an emphasis on disciplinary rules and regulations. The introduction of quasi-military discipline at Tech served the function of creating social bonding and a sense of esprit de corps among students from diverse economic and class backgrounds. The Hall system played an important role in the production of a disciplined industrial and engineering culture as the students learned respect for authority and became accustomed to cooperative behavior in a well-regulated environment.[3]

The Fencing of the Campus, the Knowles Dormitory, and New Rules of Conduct

In November 1896, Hall requested permission from the Tech Board of Trustees to enclose the school with a fence in order "to protect the property against tramps" and was instructed to obtain an estimate of the cost. The following month, the trustees appropriated $500 to build the fence and make other campus improvements.[4] When Hall informed the faculty about the fence, he mentioned that they could save $250 by using a barbed-wire fence on the back side of the campus. A whitewashed picket fence was erected on the North Avenue side.[5]

Probably the most significant development during Hall's first year as Tech's president was the passage of a bill by the state legislature that included supplemental funds to build and equip a permanent dormitory. At its meeting held in November 1896, the Tech board gave formal approval to Chairman Harris's action of having had legislation introduced that included money for a dormitory in addition to the usual appropriation for maintenance of the school.[6] The *Atlanta Constitution* reported that Hall had appeared before the finance committee of the Georgia House to speak in favor of the increased appropriation that also included funds to equip a program in electrical engineering. He had testified that a dormitory resident could save approximately fifty dollars per year as compared to the cost of living in a local boarding house. He estimated that students from outside Atlanta would save enough in two years to pay for the cost of the proposed new dormitory.[7] The newspaper reported that Nathaniel Harris also had been present to urge approval of Tech's request. He was quoted as stating that "we teach seven trades and one profession there" and that any school that could do that certainly was worthy of support. The *Constitution* commented that the lack of dormitory facilities was preventing many poor boys from attending the school.[8]

Clarence Knowles, who represented Fulton County in the Georgia House and was an Atlanta businessman, became the leading advocate in the legislature for increasing the appropriation for Tech The *Atlanta Constitution* gave him credit for the favorable action of the finance committee. According to the paper, Knowles found that there were "doubting Thomases" on the committee, and escorted members of the committee to the school to "let them see with their own eyes the splendid service being done the boys of the state there and pointed out the school's needs." The *Constitution* characterized Knowles as being among the "ablest businessmen" in the city and suggested that the same qualities were making him an effective legislator. The reporter commented that no member of the Georgia House was more popular than Knowles.[9]

During the debate on the Tech appropriation by the full House in December 1896, Knowles disputed the notion that most of Tech's students were natives of Atlanta and noted that only 25 of 157 enrolled were from the city. He presented data on the occupations of the fathers of Tech students with the largest single category being farmers with 49, while only 3 were "capitalists." He informed the legislators that Tech currently received only $22,500 from the state and $2,500 from Atlanta for an aggregate annual income of $25,000. Of this total, he explained that $16,000 went to pay the salaries of the thirteen professors, instructors, and foremen, with $8,000 allocated for shop expenses and the remaining $1,000 for contingent expenses. Knowles pointed out that the value of the school was not limited to its graduates since those who attended for a year or more without graduating were able to earn a living as skilled laborers. He opposed the suggestion that smaller and less expensive dormitories should be built that might be expanded later. He called this proposal "short-sighted and unwise," asserting that "the business-like policy would rather be to build for future needs and avoid frequent additions, which are always more expensive than if included in the original contract." He concluded that the number of students at Tech would double within two years and that the school's efficiency would be much improved if it received the additional funding. Representative Johnson from Hall County also spoke in favor of the increase and stated that the school benefited all classes. He asserted that "the poor man's son works beside the rich man's son in the school." A representative from Bibb County favored passage of the bill and commented that "technical education is the basis of wealth, the basis of power."[10]

The *Constitution* published an editorial shortly before the bill finally was passed that made the point that boarding houses might be acceptable in smaller towns and rural areas where the "temptations are not so great." But the editor contended that the situation was different at Tech, where the students were the "state's wards" and "they are literally turned loose upon the city" with no restraint. The *Constitution* argued that it was the "moral duty" of the state to provide dormitories in order that this "splendid institution" might achieve "its highest efficiency."[11]

The bill that passed in December 1896 increased the annual appropriation for Tech by $10,000 for both 1897 and 1898. It imposed the requirement that the Tech board furnish an annual report that would provide details on faculty salaries, where the students came from, the amount of tuition received, and the disposition of the products produced in the school shops.[12] At its meeting in late December 1896, the board voted to spend $7,000 from the supplemental appropriation on a new dormitory during 1897 and $2,000 for apparatus for the newly authorized program in electrical engineering. The trustees also authorized $700 for the installation of electric lighting on the campus. They expressed their appreciation to Knowles for his effective effort that had gained the increased appropriation and agreed that the new dormitory should be called the "Knowles Dormitory."[13] The building was designed by the local architectural firm of Bruce and Morgan, which had designed Tech's original academic and shop buildings. At a meeting of the Tech board in June 1897, it was reported that a contract for the new dormitory had been awarded to Black and Hilliard for $13,000.[14] The structure was completed by September 1897 when George Winship, chairman of the building subcommittee, informed the other trustees that the work had been completed satisfactorily "within the amount of the contract except for about $14 extra." The treasurer was authorized to borrow the balance due the contractor using the supplemental appropriation for 1898 as collateral.[15]

The Knowles Dormitory included thirty-six rooms, a gymnasium, shower facilities, and a dining room. A professor was assigned to live in the dormitory and enforce the dormitory regulations. On the basis of two students per room, the new dormitory, together with the two temporary dormitories that had eight rooms each, provided on-campus housing for approximately one hundred students. Sixteen students were given permission to operate a separate mess in a temporary dormitory that used "country produce" received from home, which enabled them to reduce the cost of board to $5.50 per month compared to the normal fee of $10 per month.[16] President Hall alluded to the question of possible bias felt toward residents of the more economical dormitory in a letter written to the mother of a prospective student in August 1898. He wrote that some of Tech's best students from the best families were residents of the cheaper dormitory and "there is no feeling among the students that students in the cheap dormitory are inferior in any way." Later the same year, Hall referred to complaints about the food served in the dormitory mess hall. He explained that an effort was being made to keep the prices very low for the benefit of students of limited means and that this prevented much variety in the fare.[17]

Within a year after completion of the Knowles Dormitory, Hall informed Harris that the dormitory facilities were "entirely inadequate," with three students housed in rooms designed for two. Hall asked for $15,000 to build another dormitory, which he said was necessary if the school was to stay up-to-date and to remain the equal of other schools of engineering.[18] In October 1898, Hall provided the governor of Georgia with information about Tech for possible inclusion in his annual message. Hall stated that the dormitory space at Tech was inadequate to accommodate the hundreds who desired to attend the school with its low cost and "wholesome regulation." He suggested that parents liked to have their sons in dormitories where they would be under the "continual guardianship and protection of the authorities."[19]

President Hall read proposed regulations for dormitory students at a faculty meeting in March 1897, several months before the completion of the Knowles Dormitory, and they also appeared in the Tech catalog for 1897–98.[20] The regulations specified that the students must have written permission from the professor in charge to leave the school property, "except to visit the ball-ground or walk on North Avenue, between Plum and West Peachtree streets during the day hours." Any student who left the campus before the time requested or who returned late was to be "considered absent without leave, and will be punished by expulsion from the Dormitory." The dormitory students were forbidden to have playing cards and if "found with intoxicating liquors" were subject to expulsion from the dormitory. The students were required to keep their rooms in good order with "frequent inspections" being made. Life in the dormitory was closely regulated, with the typical day beginning with the ringing of the "rising-bell at 6:30 A.M." The breakfast bell sounded at 7:00, by which time the rooms were expected to be in order and the beds made. The "call to quarters" bell was rung a half hour after supper when the students were expected to go to their rooms for study until 10:15 P.M. when the "bell for retiring" sounded and lights were to be extinguished by 10:30, "except in rooms of division inspectors." The division inspectors were appointed by the school president and were responsible for inspecting rooms in the morning and evening and reporting the results to the professor in charge. Each inspector was to report any "breaches of regulations" observed or "any irregularities, such as damage to property, unusual noise, etc., occurring in his division."[21]

Hall expressed his philosophy on student discipline in a letter to a parent in 1898. He stated that "as long as I am here, all students must be treated alike and under no circumstances will I ever allow a student to defy the laws of the institution without a penalty."[22] In January 1899, Hall wrote to Harris that the enforcement of regulations was having a "splendid effect on our student body." Hall commented that a recently hired professor from New York had stated that he had never seen a body of college students "under such thorough discipline" as those at Tech in his entire professional career. Hall concluded that "this discipline is making the school."[23] Later the same year Hall wrote to Chairman Harris that the dormitory students were subject to regulations that differed only slightly from those in an army barracks. Hall suggested that the state legislature be requested to authorize the Tech Board of Trustees to put the apprentice and subapprentice classes "under Military Discipline which will be brought to a high standard." He stated that "the enforcement of military regulations benefits young students in many ways and assists in the management of large bodies of young men." He explained that military discipline served to "cultivate systematic and orderly habits, improve personal appearance and give a polish and bearing to our graduates which will increase their opportunity for success in life."[24]

New Degree Programs in Electrical and Civil Engineering

An important element in Lyman Hall's strategy to attract more students to Tech and to broaden the school's role of providing graduates who could lead Georgia and the South in industrial diversification was to add new degree programs. The first two to be added were in electrical and in civil engineering and were authorized by the Tech board in December 1896. Professor of Physics Robert M. Quick designed the electrical engineering curriculum.[25]

A program in electrical engineering seemed quite attractive at Tech in 1897 since it could be introduced at a modest cost by taking advantage of existing strengths in physics and mechanical engineering and offered a number of potential benefits. As noted in the previous chapter, a substantial number of Tech's early graduates in mechanical engineering had found employment in the electrical power or transportation industries. The field was becoming even more exciting and more relevant to the goals of the New South proponents as a result of technological innovations in alternating-current power generation, transmission, and utilization introduced during the 1890s. The world's largest hydroelectric generating plant began operation at Niagara Falls in 1895 with power being transmitted by high-voltage transmission lines to Buffalo by November 1896.[26] The technology demonstrated at Niagara Falls was to be used to develop the extensive water power resources of north Georgia and other southeastern states in the early twentieth century. Another significant development that coincided with the inauguration of Tech's program in electrical engineering was the successful introduction of alternating-current motors in the southern textile industry. The combination of cheap hydroelectric power and industrial electrification stimulated a rapid expansion of textile manufacturing in the region and insured that electrical engineering graduates would be in demand.

The degree requirements of typical electrical engineering programs, including that at Tech, served to increase enrollment in mechanical engineering courses and also affected the mechanical engineering course content. For example, a greater emphasis on non-steam engineering was a common result of the interaction. More significantly for schools such as Tech with its shop-culture heritage, "electrical engineering gave impetus to the argument that engineering education was a function of the schools more than the shops and required a thorough training in science and mathematics." As pointed out by Robert Rosenberg, "electrical engineering was the focus of powerful social forces at a most opportune time for higher education, a time when schools of all types were feeling pressure for change and expansion." Electrical engineering served as "the prototype of the new scientific engineering" that "combined the academic world of physics, the shop world of mechanical engineering, and the business world of the new electrical industries in a pattern that became the accepted way of education in the twentieth century."[27] An electrical engineering program also happened to conform admirably with the expansionary goals of Lyman Hall and his New South supporters.

Professor Robert Quick, who designed the electrical engineering program and taught its first students at Tech, was a New York native who graduated from Cornell in 1894. He taught for a year at Cornell before coming to Tech as the successor to Hopkins as professor of physics. He may have been recruited by John S. Coon, who usually spent his summers in New York State. In 1898, Hall referred to Quick as "one of the most prominent instructors in electrical engineering in the country."[28] The program designed by Quick was listed in the Tech catalog for the year 1897–98, which stated that there was no deviation from the mechanical engineering curriculum until the senior year when the theory of electrical machinery took the place of steam engines and materials used in construction. Among the subjects that were included in the electrical engineering course were the theory, design, and construction of direct-current dynamos and motors. Also covered were alternators, rotary transformers, alternating-current motors, electric lighting, and power transmission.[29]

Tech's newly established electrical engineering program suffered a serious blow in September 1899 with the death from typhoid fever of Professor Quick. President Hall informed George Winship of the Tech board of Quick's death and mentioned that he already had written to Coon, who was near Cornell, asking him to secure a possible replacement. Ezra F. Scattergood was hired as the new professor of physics and electrical engineering. It was during Scattergood's brief tenure of two years at Tech that a successful effort was mounted to get funding for a new electrical engineering building. Albert H. Ford was hired to replace Scattergood in 1901.[30]

Albert Ford possessed impressive credentials for the position and his achievements later led to his being selected for inclusion in a series of articles on distinguished electrical engineers published by the *Electrical World and Engineer* in 1905. He graduated in electrical engineering from the University of Wisconsin in 1895 and was awarded an advanced professional degree in electrical engineering from Wisconsin in 1896. He held a fellowship at Columbia in 1897 and took the famous Test Course at General Electric in Schenectady before taking a job with the Western Electric Company in his native Chicago in 1898. Ford taught electrical engineering at the University of Colorado during the 1900–1901 academic year and engaged in research on the magnetic properties of iron and the efficiency of electrical transformers. He was a member of the American Institute of Electrical Engineers and gave an AIEE paper in April 1900 concerning the effect of the composition of iron and steel on the magnetic hysteresis of transformers. He also was a member of the Society for the Promotion of Engineering Education. A year after Ford's arrival at Tech, the trustees voted to separate the physics and electrical engineering departments with Ford occupying the chair of electrical engineering and J. B. Edwards being appointed to the chair of physics.[31]

Tech introduced a degree program in the field of civil engineering at the same time as electrical engineering, but it proved less successful in attracting students during the Hall years. Although civil engineering was an older profession than both mechanical and electrical engineering, the rationale for adding a degree program at Tech in the 1890s was not compelling, especially since this was a degree offered by the land-grant college of the University of Georgia. It appears probable that the degree was authorized more as a consequence of the personal interest of Lyman Hall in civil engineering than because of an evident need for more trained civil engineers. With Hall's approach to teaching mathematics, the civil engineering curriculum could be viewed as being linked to mathematics in a manner analogous to the connection between physics and electrical engineering. Hall not only included field work in surveying and mapping in his mathematics classes but also supplemented his teaching salary by conducting surveys and other engineering assignments in the Atlanta area before he was elected president of Tech. However, by the time the civil engineering degree was approved, Hall's duties as president prevented him from taking direct charge of the program. At a meeting of the trustees in June 1898, T. P. Branch was appointed to the position of junior professor of mathematics and also was placed in charge of civil engineering.[32]

Tech did not produce its first graduate in civil engineering until 1902, and there was a cumulative total of only seven graduates up to 1905 as compared to forty-six in electrical engineering. In 1910 five of the first seven civil engineering graduates were still employed in Georgia, although one owned a grocery firm in Atlanta and another worked as a chemist with a company in Athens. W. F. Montgomery (class of 1905) was employed as a mining engineer in Tennessee and W. F. Pringle, Jr., was with the Army Corps of Engineers in the Canal Zone in Panama.³³ Headed by a junior member of the faculty and without much promotion, the civil engineering program did not develop the status and momentum of the new degree programs in electrical engineering and textile engineering in the early years.

Origins of a Textile Program at Tech

Lyman Hall discovered a magical formula for multiplying the resources for expansion of Georgia Tech during his campaign to establish a degree program in textile engineering. The formula that he employed effectively for the remainder of his tenure involved the use of New South rhetoric, conditional gifts from philanthropists, and conditional appropriations by the state legislature. The conditional funding provided leverage to obtain still more donations from friends of the school. Hall's selection of textile education as the focus of his first use of the formula in 1898 was well timed, since the economy was beginning to recover from the long recession that had begun in 1893 and the textile industry in Georgia and in the Carolinas was just entering a period of rapid expansion. The number of textile mills in Georgia increased from sixty-two in 1886 to seventy-five by January 1, 1900; twelve more were in operation by September 1, 1900, and twenty-four more were under construction.³⁴ The creation of a network of high-voltage power lines throughout the piedmont of Georgia and the Carolinas prior to the First World War enabled a continued growth of the textile industry, since it was no longer necessary to locate mills primarily in cities such as Columbus and Augusta at the falls of large rivers. The rapid expansion of the textile industry in the South meant that there would be employment opportunities in the region for the graduates of textile schools. The phenomenon seemed to confirm the expectations of Hall and the many friends of Tech who contributed money or equipment to launch the textile engineering program that the long-awaited New South was arriving with the turn of the century.

In early November 1897, Nathaniel Harris informed the Tech trustees that a bill had been introduced in the state legislature requesting an appropriation of $10,000 to establish a textile department. Soon afterward, it was recorded in the faculty minutes that the meeting had been scheduled earlier than normal so that Hall might go to the capital and "aid our friends in the work for the Textile Department." In December 1897, the legislature approved an appropriation of $10,000 for the proposed new department but made it conditional on the school raising an equal sum from other sources.[35]

As the founders of Tech had done in the 1880s, Hall selected a Massachusetts school as the pattern for the new textile department. Only a few days after the Georgia legislature passed the bill with the conditional appropriation, Hall traveled to Lowell, Massachusetts, to collect information about the textile school located there. When he returned and informed the Tech board of the results of his trip, the trustees agreed to appropriate $350 as a consulting fee for the services of C. P. Brooks, who headed the Lowell school. Brooks was to fill the same role, at least in the planning stage, that M. P. Higgins had filled in the planning of Tech's commercial shop.[36]

In February 1898, Hall turned his attention to the urgent task of raising the $10,000 needed to match the state appropriation. He decided to contact Aaron French, a Pittsburgh manufacturer whom he had met at a resort in North Carolina the previous summer. In a letter to the Pittsburgh industrialist, Hall explained the recent action by the Georgia legislature and asked whether French might make a donation. Hall assured him that, if he would donate $10,000, the proposed new structure at Tech would be "named the French Textile Mill" and that he would "be regarded as a benefactor by the state." Hall continued that "if you do not feel like becoming immortal at one stroke, as indicated, can you not give us a donation of some kind?" Hall predicted that the new textile department would "work a revolution in our industries" and that the state would support it. He commented that it was "depressing to those of us trying to lift the standard of industrial excellence in the South that we have no Rockefeller to help us in the work."[37]

Hall wrote to John D. Rockefeller in February 1898 telling him of Georgia's desire to "lift her young men to positions where by their skill and expert knowledge in industrial pursuits they may take rank with their brothers in the north and west." Hall stated that, if Rockefeller would donate the $10,000, he believed that the building would be "called the Rockefeller Textile Mill."[38]

Hall prepared a circular for distribution to cotton mills in Georgia and to friends of the trustees or other potential donors to the textile fund. He explained in the circular why he believed that a school could provide better quality instruction than could be obtained in the mills. He argued that the mill superintendents lacked time and were not specially qualified to provide instruction. He pointed out that the machinery in any one mill was apt to be limited in variety and that "no systematic or scientific training can be had in a short time." Hall commented that there was little opportunity in southern textile mills for instruction in the manufacture of the higher grades of cotton fabric. The circular concluded by soliciting the help of those who were interested in advancing the textile manufacturing industry and "the scientific manipulation of that great staple in whose fibers are to be found the future greatness, wealth, and prosperity of our people." In a cover letter to Harris, Hall stated that a thousand copies would be made with twenty-five copies sent to each trustee and a copy sent to each cotton mill. A month later Hall wrote to Knowles that he had written to every cotton manufacturer in Georgia but had received no response. He thanked Knowles for his donation and predicted that the enrollment would increase from its current level of around 270 to 500 if the textile department were established successfully.[39]

In a letter written in early March 1898 to Clark Howell, editor of the *Constitution*, Hall employed New South rhetoric and military metaphor in an eloquent appeal for local support for the proposed textile department. He complained that he had as yet received no reply or offer of assistance from the cotton manufacturers of Georgia who had been sent circulars. He contrasted this lack of response to that of "the cotton men in New England" who had established "without state aid, the Lowell Textile School which is the equal in equipment and efficiency of the best schools in Europe." Hall reported that he had collected approximately $2,000, including a donation of $1,000 from a Tech trustee, and asked if Howell could suggest a plan to raise the remaining $8,000 by June. Hall stated that he already had the plans of the building and a list of machinery needed so that "the money is the only thing lacking in the South to make the first step towards a great future for her manufacturing industries." He predicted that "when the first brick is laid in the textile department of the Georgia School of Technology, the South declares war against New England; a war not of secession but of aggression, a war against slavery and we are the slaves who shall be free." He anticipated that "industrial warfare is to be the conflict in the future between the sections of this country, as well as between nations."[40]

In late February 1898, Hall wrote to Aaron French to thank him for a donation and for his encouragement. Hall mentioned that a trustee had given $1,000 but that the trustees were "despondent" about raising the amount needed. He stated that they planned to lower the minimum age limit for admission to the textile program to 15.5 years and that the requirements would be "lower than for the engineering work." Hall believed that the cotton industry offered "the greatest future for the young men in this section" and that "there are large fortunes awaiting every progressive manufacturer of cotton goods here, as he has the staple at his command and water power in abundance."[41] Although he was probably disappointed at the rather small donation initially received from French, Hall remained optimistic about the prospects. He wrote to Harris that his "millionaire friend" would be in Atlanta soon and asked for authority to name the building for French if he would supply the balance needed of $8,000. Hall commented that French had made substantial contributions to Methodist education in North Carolina and that his confidence in Hall was such that he "would risk my administration in any matter of education with which he happened to be interested." Hall concluded that he was confident that he could make Tech "the greatest institution in the southern states if I am given the support of the state." A few days later Hall wrote to French to ask that he consider "fathering this movement" and to assure him that a gift of $8,000 would be sufficient to name the building for him. Hall expressed the hope that French soon would be in Atlanta and promised to show him the school and convince him "that we have the nucleus of the greatest technical school in this section."[42]

Since obtaining the needed donations in cash by the June deadline seemed increasingly problematic, Hall decided to solicit donations of textile machinery from northern manufacturers. He wrote to C. P.

Brooks at Lowell to request a list of the makers of each machine that would be needed in the textile department with a ranking in order of quality, since he wanted initially to seek donations from the makers of the best machines.[43] Hall welcomed an offer of assistance in contacting the machinery manufacturers from Oscar Elsas, a former Tech student who had become vice president of the Fulton Bag and Cotton Mill in Atlanta. Hall informed Harris that Elsas was making a trip to the North to visit most of the textile equipment firms mentioned by Brooks and had promised to do what he could on behalf of Tech. Elsas's efforts met with considerable success and he was given credit in the 1899 Tech catalog for obtaining through donations "most of the magnificent equipment of cotton manufacturing machinery." The estimated value of the machinery had reached approximately $20,000 by the time the tribute to Elsas was written.[44]

A few days after the deadline that had been set by the legislature to match the $10,000 appropriation, Hall informed the Georgia governor that Tech had complied with the condition and asked that the state appropriation be made available in order that the building could be erected. Hall listed the donors of machinery that included eleven Massachusetts firms, seven in Rhode Island, two in Maine, and two in Pennsylvania. He estimated the total value of the machinery offered at $10,786 and pointed out that these all had come from northern companies except for a saw gin valued at $180 from the Winship Company in Atlanta. He reported that cash contributions amounted to $1,577 so that the total donations were equivalent to $12,363.[45] The machinery donations obtained with the aid of Oscar Elsas had proved decisive, since the large contribution anticipated from French had not yet materialized.

Early in July 1898, Hall received the good news that French had decided to donate $2,500 to the textile fund and that he would give another $3,000 with the condition that friends of the school contribute an equal amount. Hall wrote to French that his generosity had created great enthusiasm at Tech and that his name would henceforth be a "beloved name in the history of Georgia." Hall promised that the new department would be called the "A. French Textile School" and that his name would be "placed on the front of the building for all time." Hall decided to ask the city of Atlanta to match French's conditional gift and wrote to the editor of the

Atlanta Constitution to seek his support in persuading the City Council. Hall listed all the contributions that had been received and calculated that the total, including the conditional state appropriation, would be approximately $32,000 if the city would match French's offer. Hall asked whether Atlanta would allow a stranger to donate $5,600 and fail to meet his requirements that $3,000 be raised locally. He called again on New South rhetoric stating that "unless Georgia awakes at once to the solution of this problem, our people will remain hewers of wood and drawers of water, while more skilled and better posted men from other sections will come among us to reap the greatest profits from the manufacture of our unlimited product in cotton."[46]

In August 1898, the *Atlanta Constitution* published an editorial defending Lyman Hall against criticism by a textile trade journal. The *Southern and Western Textile Excelsior* had questioned Hall's qualifications to manage the proposed textile department saying that textile education was being put into the hands of men who only were "versed in Greek and Latin." The *Constitution* called Hall "one of the ablest young educators in the country, north, south, east or west." It credited him with having infused Tech with "his own vigorous energies" and with having made the school into one of "the most progressive and wideawake schools of its kind in the United States." The editor stated that Hall had been so intent on enlarging the scope of Tech that he had "scarcely allowed himself sleep or rest for months." The editorial concluded that Hall was more responsible than any other person for the establishment of the new textile department.[47]

The new textile program at Tech attracted attention outside the South. Hall wrote in November 1898 that there was great interest in every section of the country and that Tech was receiving inquiries from Europe and Australia. He commented that this response served to demonstrate that "the sun never sets" on the development that had been started by the Georgia legislature in 1897.[48] The textile school was discussed in an article published in the *Scientific American* in June 1900. The article described the French Building in detail and stated that it embodied "the very latest ideas of mill construction" and that its equipment was "very complete."[49] Another article on Georgia Tech was published in the *Scientific American Supplement* in August 1901. It reviewed the history of the school and noted that it had not exhibited "any special signs of progress" until 1896. The article stated that the French textile school had an advantage over other textile schools in that the textile engineering course included shop work, mechanical drawing, and some mechanical and electrical engineering. The writer commented that those who had already completed the textile program at Tech were having little difficulty in finding employment as foremen and superintendents in textile mills in the South. According to the article, it was the intention of the trustees and the president of Tech to continue to expand until technical training could be "obtained in all the arts, industries, and manufactures which may flourish or are peculiarly fitted for the southern states." The article pointed out that the cost of attending Tech was far lower than for northern schools and that the school probably would attract students from the North if it chose to advertise. In addition to the modest cost, the writer cited the "splendid climate" of Atlanta that would attract students whose health "might break down under our rigorous winters at the North."[50]

Hall's phenomenal success in attracting outside support for Tech along with a rapid increase in enrollment led to an attempt to make him the chancellor of the University of Georgia in the spring of 1899. In a letter to Nathaniel Harris in March 1899, Hall alluded to a conversation that they had had during a train ride back from Washington concerning the University of Georgia and "some steps to be taken by my friends." Hall stated that he would make no personal effort in the matter. A few days later he elaborated on the situation and informed Harris that he would not go to the university without a prior understanding. Hall mentioned that certain members of the university Board of Trustees were working to have him appointed and that some alumni of the university were supporting the movement. He pointed out that his influence with French would be affected adversely if he left Tech and that he would accept only if he could retain his position at Tech "in name and partly in fact." Hall stated that he was unwilling simply to exchange places with Chancellor Boggs, since he anticipated that the position at Tech soon would offer more inducements than the one at the university. He wrote to French that there had been talk of making him chancellor at the university but that he would not accept unless he could continue as head of Tech. Hall speculated that he probably was "too much of a worker and too little of a politician to suit the University."[51]

In May 1899, Hall wrote to Harris that he was not seeking the chancellorship but that he was "at the mercy of some very enthusiastic friends" who thought it would benefit the university. Hall mentioned that petitions were being circulated asking that the university board consider him in its election in June. He mentioned that Governor McDaniel had consented to a request that Hall appear before the board to express his opinion on how the university should be managed. He reiterated that he was not willing to release his control of the school of technology. Hall stated that, if he could have the men he wanted as principal assistants both at Tech and at the university, he would be willing to give time to both schools if he were paid $2,500 per year by each. He concluded that such an arrangement would enable him to "build up both the working school and the University."[52] Early in June 1899, Hall informed Harris that gifts of $3,000 each from French and another donor would "place us at the crest of a wave." Hall predicted that, if Harris "should get me placed where your last letter intimated," they could "do a lot of good and you would have to be governor per force if I succeeded." The university board apparently was unwilling to meet Hall's conditions, since Walter B. Hill, a law partner of Nathaniel Harris in Macon, was elected as the university chancellor in June 1899 and served until his death in 1906.[53]

The textile program enjoyed immediate success, and Hall wrote to French in October 1899 that more than 125 students already had enrolled in the textile course. Hall mentioned that the executives of several cotton mills in the South had visited the new department and were pleased with its equipment. The first five students to graduate in textile engineering from Tech were members of the class of 1901. Fifty students graduated in textile engineering in the period 1901 to 1905, a total that compared favorably to mechanical engineering with forty-five, electrical engineering with thirty-three, and civil engineering with seven for the same years.[54]

The Electrical Building and the Swann Dormitory

Hall applied the lessons that he had learned during his textile campaign in seeking both state and outside support in adding another academic building and another dormitory at Tech. In September 1899, the *Atlanta Constitution* reported that applications had already been received from 230 who wished to live in the dormitories and that Hall was advising future applicants to make arrangements to live in the city. The report mentioned that only 109 students could be seated at one time in the dormitory mess so that it would be necessary to have two seatings at each meal. The following month, the *Constitution* reported that 400 students were "crowded into the institution" and that another 400 waited who "must be doomed to the slavery of the hoe" unless the legislature acted to expand Tech's facilities. The editorial stated that the subapprentice class would have to be abolished unless the state was willing to provide more space. The editor viewed this prospect as alarming since this class admitted students from locations that failed to prepare students for college. The editor asserted that "the trained hand is worth one hundred hands not trained" and continued that the Tech trustees had "felt as if they were but beggars." The writer pointed out that even the appropriations that had been made had come with strings attached that meant that private individuals such as Aaron French were having to do the "work that belongs to the state." The editorial concluded that "the young men of Georgia plead for a chance" and asked whether the legislature would give them this chance.[55]

Hall wrote to Aaron French about the dormitory situation and mentioned that two buildings adjacent to the campus had been rented and would be used as temporary dormitories. Hall observed that it seemed a pity that no Georgian could see fit to help Tech to carry out its "great work." He asked if French would be interested in investing $20,000 in a dormitory that would pay a rental of $1,000 per year. In October 1899, Hall informed N. E. Harris that negotiations were underway with J. W. Rucker for a dormitory to be built between the Academic Building and the Knowles Dormitory at a cost of about $10,000. Early the following month, Hall suggested to

Harris that the trustees meet and take action to eliminate the subapprentice class unless new buildings were provided. He thought that such an action would "confront the legislature with the school's condition." Soon afterward, Hall wrote to Trustee W. B. Miles that Tech planned to admit no more students unless they could be accommodated two to a room and that no students would be accepted for the subapprentice class after November 15, 1899. Hall stated that the new policy on admissions would be changed if the legislature approved the appropriation requested and that bills had been introduced seeking $20,000 for a dormitory and $10,000 for a new academic building. Hall wrote to several friends of Tech asking that they help lobby for the passage of the legislation. Despite the efforts of Hall, the *Atlanta Constitution,* and other friends of Tech, the Georgia legislature declined to approve state funds for the new buildings during the 1899 session. However, Hall informed the Tech trustees in January 1900 that Aaron French had made a contribution of $3,500 to enable Tech to continue to accept applications for the subapprentice class.[56]

In contrast to the disappointments of 1899, Hall enjoyed considerable success with the legislature and with outside donors in 1900. At the October 1900 meeting of the Tech board, the treasurer reported that Tech's finances were in relatively good shape. Chairman Harris was instructed to ask the state legislature for an appropriation of $40,000 for annual maintenance of the school and for a supplemental appropriation of $10,000 for the construction of an electrical building and $6,000 for the purchase of textile machinery. The *Atlanta Constitution* strongly supported Tech's request for additional funds for the electrical engineering and textile departments. The article stated that Tech was of "inestimable value" to the state and had proved to be among the best investments ever made by the legislature. The writer commented that the development of the electrical and textile industries were very important to Georgia. The report characterized electricity as "the science which promises to revolutionize conditions in the industrial world."[57]

Samuel M. Inman, a former trustee and one of the founders of Tech, apparently introduced Hall to James Swann, who became a major benefactor of the school. After Swann had visited the Tech campus in October 1900, Hall wrote to Inman that Swann had expressed an interest in helping the school. Hall suggested that Inman try to persuade Swann to make a gift that could be used for the construction of a much-needed dormitory. Swann agreed to give $20,000 with the condition that an additional $15,000 be collected from other sources. Hall subsequently was able to use the gift as leverage with the state legislature as it considered Tech's request for an increased appropriation.[58]

In early December 1900, the *Atlanta Constitution* reported on the effort to win legislative support for Tech. The newspaper stated that the friends of the school had done their best during the past week to make the legislature aware of the needs of the school. The article mentioned that a special exhibition had been given at Tech for the legislators with the students dressed in their working clothes and at work in the shops. The report continued that Tech's trustees were seeking an increase in state funding from $30,000 to $40,000 and that if this was not done the school would have to reduce its student body and faculty by about 50 percent. The *Constitution* mentioned that J. W. English had brought up Hall's offer to match the requested supplemental appropriation "dollar for dollar" with contributions from Tech's friends. Asking rhetorically whether any other school made such proposals, English had answered "no, not one." English had asked, "How can Hall do this?" and had explained that Hall had "convinced men of means of the great work the school is doing for the manufacturing interests and business interests of the South." The *Constitution* stated that Hall was scheduled to speak at an industrial convention and that it hoped he would not find it necessary to report that his own state, which had pioneered in industrial education in the South, had "crippled our school of technology." The paper concluded that Tech's friends viewed the situation as a crisis and asked whether the legislature would place itself on the "side of progress."[59]

In its account of the debate on the Tech bill in the Senate, the *Atlanta Constitution* reported that Senator Baker had argued that he could see no good that the school's graduates were doing for the state. He had claimed that common schools were all the state needed and that he thought an institution for the education of legislators would be more beneficial to Georgia than a school of technology. An amendment that would have reduced the annual maintenance appropriation from $40,000 to $30,000 was defeated by a vote of twenty-eight to eight, and the $16,000 supplemental appropriation for the electrical building and textile equipment was approved on the condition that $25,000 be raised from outside sources. President Hall had announced that the money needed to meet the condition already had been subscribed with $20,000 having been promised by Swann. The following day the *Constitution* reported in a front-page story that Tech would have the unprecedented sum of $87,000 to spend for improvements. The article stated that $25,000 already had been raised to match the $31,000 condition imposed by Swann and the legislature and that little difficulty was expected in getting the rest from the friends of Tech. A *Constitution* editorial gave credit to the legislature for making possible a "great educational revival" that would be dated from the session of 1900.[60]

Hall requested and was granted the services of Fulton County convicts to grade the sites for the new Electrical Building and for the Janie Austell Swann Dormitory, named for the wife of James Swann. Walter T. Downing, an Atlanta architect who had designed a house for Inman, served as the architect for the two new buildings. Bids for construction of the Swann Dormitory were opened in early April 1901 and ranged from $28,987 to $33,700. The contract was awarded to the low bidder, Harry H. Miles, who had graduated from Tech in 1893. The new dormitory was designed to house a hundred students. Both of the new buildings were completed in time for the fall session in 1901.[61]

Engineering Chemistry

The fourth and final new degree program introduced at Tech during Hall's administration was in engineering chemistry. As had been the case with electrical engineering with its close link to physics and civil engineering and its link to mathematics, a degree program in engineering chemistry seemed a logical extension of the existing but non-degree courses offered in chemistry. Another stimulus to launch the new degree program was provided by the textile program with its dyeing department that taught applications of chemistry in the field of textiles. The courses taught by W. H. Emerson had included industrial applications of chemistry from the start of the school in 1888. Other faculty members in chemistry who had come to Tech by the early twentieth century had impressive credentials and could be expected to offer a strong degree program. Similar programs were being introduced at about the same time at schools such as Boston Tech (MIT), where the faculty in chemistry was attempting to create a chemical engineering curriculum and to resolve differences of educational philosophy that were similar to the school culture versus shop culture conflict in mechanical engineering education.[62]

Professor Emerson appeared before the trustees in January 1901 to provide them with an outline of a proposed program in "commercial chemistry." Emerson mentioned that Professor Homer V. Black had proposed to go to Johns Hopkins University to qualify in this area, if he could receive a portion of his salary while away. In April 1901 the Tech board voted to establish a chair in engineering chemistry and estimated that this would entail an additional expenditure for equipment of $500. At the same meeting Black was employed as an assistant in chemistry at a salary of $1,000 per year. The 1901 Tech catalog stated that the new degree program in engineering chemistry provided specialized training in those branches of chemistry that were applied in industry and a broad foundation in both general and theoretical chemistry.[63]

By 1904 the Tech faculty included three chemistry professors with doctorates, W. H. Emerson, Homer V. Black, and Gilbert H. Boggs. When the Georgia section of the American Chemical Society was organized in 1904, Emerson served as the presiding officer and Black as the secretary. The first meeting held in Atlanta in May 1904 attracted an audience of thirty-five chemists and Emerson delivered a paper, "The Heat of Combustion of Coal Calculated from DuLong's Formula." Boggs became the secretary of the Georgia section in 1907. He later became head of both the chemistry and chemical engineering department at Tech.[64]

Extracurricular Activities

The Phi Eta Sigma literary society that was originally organized by members of the middle class in October 1892 was revived in 1901 after a brief period of inactivity. At the time it was reported by the *Georgia Tech* that more than half of Tech's graduates since 1892 had been members of the society. Members of the literary society participated in competitive debates with students from other local colleges. After one such debate where the Tech debating team "did not come out last," Lyman Hall commented that other schools tended to view oratory as a business and that to them "defeat means inferiority." He explained that Tech students regarded oratory as a pastime and that "defeat does not reflect on what we profess to teach." Among the debate topics was "resolved that technical schools do more for the advancement of the country than literary colleges." An early Tech catalog commented that oratory originally had been thought to have no place in a school of technology but that the faculty had recognized the benefit and had encouraged the activity. An essay entitled "Why Tech Men Should Become Orators" appeared in the *Georgia Tech* in May 1902. The writer asserted that in the future the politician was destined to be humiliated and that "the man of industrial pursuits . . . shall hold the reins of power." The article continued that there should be "more men of mechanical training and industrial ability in our legislative halls" and that there was a great need for men with a technological education "who can express themselves in public." By October of 1901 a second literary society, known as Phi Omega, was organized, and the faculty agreed to excuse the members of both literary societies from duty by 4:00 P.M. on Fridays.[65]

An engineering society was organized by Tech students in October 1901 and it held regular meetings on the first and third Fridays of each month in the physics lecture room. The first meeting featured a lecture on the subject of power transmission by Floyd C. Furlow, who had graduated from Tech in mechanical engineering in 1897 and had been hired as an assistant professor at Tech. His lecture reportedly gave the students the benefit of his experience gained the previous summer when he had worked in Boston. By 1910 Furlow had left Tech to work for the Plunger Elevator Company that had been founded by Milton P. Higgins, who had served as the first shop superintendent at Tech. The Plunger Company was acquired by the Otis Elevator Company of which Furlow eventually became the president. He also became a member of Tech's Board of Trustees. In

November 1901 the Tech faculty was informed that its members had been elected to the engineering society and that they would be welcome to attend all meetings. They voted to accept the invitation.[66]

The *Georgia Tech*, a monthly magazine produced by Tech students, contained contributions that are quite revealing on student attitudes and values during the time when Hall was Tech's president. Charles H. Kicklighter, a mechanical engineering student who was among Tech's best orators in competitive debates, contributed the essay "The Future of the Technological School" to the issue published in December 1900. He wrote that "this school sends forth men who are men, not afraid of oil and dust, but men who will produce something." He predicted that in the twentieth century the South would become "the foremost industrial and commercial country of the earth" and that technological education would become "more and more necessary to the use of delicate and complicated machinery." He noted Tech's location on a hill that overlooked Atlanta and the surrounding countryside and saw this as symbolic of "the story of her future." In a later issue of the magazine, Kicklighter reported on a field trip to Birmingham by the senior class. He stated that they had learned more during the three-day trip than they could have "in as many months by the study of texts on the subject." He commented that there were graduates of Tech who were holding good positions in Birmingham and that there were "Tech boys all over the South." After graduating in 1902, Kicklighter became a professor of mechanical engineering and drawing at the University of Florida.[67]

An Athletic Association was organized at Tech in January 1901 when the *Georgia Tech* reported that the association met to discuss the debt and decided to hold a benefit function to raise money. They also decided to field a football team again, despite the disappointing winless season of 1900. Professors Coon and Randall were elected to the Athletic Association's Advisory Board that included students from the various classes. The association had a membership of eighty-three in the spring of 1901. There was considerable discussion at the time over whether control of intercollegiate athletics should be in the hands of students or the faculty. Early in 1902, the *Georgia Tech* reported that the Athletic Association had been incorporated and planned to sell stock to raise money. The plan was to

96   *Engineering the New South*

sell four hundred shares at five dollars per share, and the magazine forecast that this development would begin a new era in the athletic history of Tech.[68]

Tech's record in intercollegiate football improved to four wins and one tie of five games played in 1901 but dropped to a record of 0–6–2 in 1902 and 2–5–0 in 1903. The overall record from 1892, when the first games were played through the season of 1903, was 8–32–5. Tech hired its first full-time football coach, John W. Heisman, from Clemson in November 1903, with the Tech Athletic Association agreeing to pay him an annual salary of $2,000 to be supplemented by 30 percent of the gate receipts for both football and baseball games. Heisman's first Tech football team enjoyed a record of 8–1–1 in 1904, and he compiled a winning record of 100–29–6 during his tenure at Tech that ended with the 1919 season. Space for a playing field was leased from the Peters Land Company by the Athletic Association and graded by convict labor. The field was fenced and a wooden grandstand was built by Tech students in time for the baseball season in 1905.[69]

Student Origins and Tech's Impact on Regional Development

During Hall's tenure, total student enrollment at Tech increased dramatically from 180 in the year 1896–97 to 511 in the 1904–5 academic year. The rate of attrition also was high. Hall reported to the trustees in June 1900 on the causes of reduction in the senior class that had started with eighty and declined to fourteen. He stated that thirteen had left for financial reasons and thirteen due to failure to study. He continued that five had been lost due to bad conduct and five for lack of aptitude for the work. Of the remaining losses, he attributed eight to students who had gone to work, five to poor health, two to "mental deficiency," one to death, and the rest due to unknown causes.[70]

In 1898 Hall prepared data for the state legislature that revealed that there were students at Tech from sixty-nine Georgia counties and eight students from South Carolina, four from Florida, one from Pennsylvania, and one from Alabama. There were fifty-nine from Fulton County, twelve from Floyd, and eight each from Cobb, Richmond, and DeKalb counties. Approximately 56 percent of the students from the state were from towns with a population of over 2,500. Hall also collected data on the occupations of parents of Tech students as of November 1898 with the results indicated by table 1. This may be compared to data that was gathered on the occupations of parents or guardians for 499 Tech students in 1905, as shown in table 2.[71]

Hall frequently compared Tech to other engineering schools both in the region and outside. He wrote to Harris in June 1898 that the standard of scholarship was high at Tech and was at least equal to that of the better northern engineering schools. He noted that Tech graduates who had gone on to study at northern universities had done quite well. Hall wrote to a correspondent in Tennessee that Tech offered advantages equal to larger northern schools except that "we are not rich enough to offer the extended laboratory work in engineering given in Boston and at Cornell. He mentioned that a few

Table 1
Occupations of Parents of Tech Students in November 1898

Occupation	Number of Students
Farmer	38
Merchant/businessman	37
Laborer/clerk	21
Lawyer	15
Railroad employee	9
Minister	9
Manufacturer	8
Contractor	7
Local official/government employee	7
Traveling salesman	7
Craftsman/artisan	6
Banker	6
Physician	6
Bookkeeper	5
Engineer	4
Army	1
Editor	1
Congressman	1
Total	188

Table 2
Occupations of Parents of Tech Students in 1905

Occupation	Number of Students
Merchant	89
Farmer	80
Manufacturer	51
Lawyer	32
Clerk	29
Workman	26
Traveling salesman	23
Physician	19
Insurance agent	18
Engineer	17
Railway agent	17
Teacher	16
Cotton merchant	12
Contractor	10
State official	6
Other	54
Total	499

Tech graduates had finished a degree at Cornell within a year after leaving Tech. He expressed the belief that Tech was "better equipped than other southern scientific schools." Data collected in 1904 comparing Tech with twelve other schools indicated that Tech required more hours per year in most subjects than the average of the twelve other schools. Tech was above the average in hours devoted to chemistry, English, mathematics, drawing, and shop, but slightly below the average for physics.[72]

Of the eighty-seven graduates of Tech during the years 1890–98, sixty-one (70 percent) were employed in Georgia in 1899 with thirty-three (38 percent) being in Atlanta. Twelve (13.8 percent) of these early graduates were employed in other states in the South while only thirteen (15 percent) had taken work outside the region.[73] By way of comparison there were seventy-seven graduates of the Clemson A&M College during the years 1896–1900, and fifty-one (66.2 percent) were employed in South Carolina in 1901. Seven (9.1 percent) of these Clemson graduates were employed elsewhere in the South while nineteen (24.7 percent) worked outside the region.[74] As late as 1909, 98.8 percent of Tech's graduates were from the South, and 92.5 percent were from Georgia. The available evidence indicates that a majority of the early Tech graduates and of the neighboring A&M colleges in North Carolina, South Carolina, and Alabama found employment in the region. However, an increase in the out-migration of Tech graduates did occur after 1900. By 1909 only 53 percent of Tech's graduates were still employed in the state of Georgia, although another 24 percent were still in the region. Atlanta gained in the number of Tech graduates employed in the city at the expense of the rest of the state, but the state suffered a substantial loss during the first decade of the twentieth century.[75]

Data on the employment of the 251 living Tech graduates in 1906 are shown in table 3.[76] The data indicate that 221 (88 percent) were working in technical fields for which their education at Tech had prepared them and that Tech was in fact adding significantly to the regional pool of industrial managers and engineers, as the New South proponents had anticipated when the school was founded. The actual impact of Tech on the industrial work force in the region was considerably greater than the number of graduates would indicate, since the high attrition rate meant that a far larger number

Table 3
Occupations of Tech Graduates in 1906

Occupation	Number of Graduates
Mechanical engineer	86
Electrical engineer	43
Textile engineer	39
General engineer	22
Chemical engineer	20
Merchant/real estate agent	13
Civil engineer	11
Teacher	3
Army officer	3
Physician	2
Minister	2
Farmer	2
Lawyer	1
Other	4
Total	251

received some technical training without completing the requirements for an engineering degree.[77]

A Tech Alumni Association had been organized and was holding an annual meeting by June 1899 when H. L. Smith, a member of the two-man graduating class of 1890, spoke to the alumni. He observed that Tech might turn out hundreds of graduates but that it would "amount to nought unless the individual alumnus commands the respect and confidence of his employer." Smith stated that an important purpose of the Alumni Association was to find positions for all Tech alumni and help those already employed to gain promotion to higher positions. He pointed out that new opportunities were opening in the southern textile mills and a variety of other industries but that many top positions still were being filled by northern men "because we have not heretofore proven our ability to cope with the requirements of the positions." Smith noted, however, that Tech now was sending alumni "into the same territory from which we have been drawing our supply and they are filling the most responsible positions."[78]

The Final Years

During the last few years of his administration, President Hall worked diligently at fund raising, following the pattern established earlier of conditional contributions and appropriations matched by collective contributions by friends of Tech. Since the campus still consisted of less than ten acres and was becoming crowded with buildings, he began to explore the possibility of acquiring more land for expansion. In October 1901 he wrote to Aaron French to inquire whether he might be willing to invest around $25,000 to purchase land adjacent to the campus that would put the French Textile Building near the center of the Tech property rather than near the boundary. Hall suggested that the added land could be called "French Field."[79]

During the 1901–2 academic year, the General Education Board, a philanthropic organization endowed by John D. Rockefeller, offered to give Tech $10,000 with the condition that Hall raise an equal sum by the time of the commencement exercises in June 1902. As the deadline approached, the *Atlanta Constitution* reported that Tech was within $1,000 of the total needed to get the conditional gift and that the school planned to use the $20,000 to purchase equipment for the electrical and experimental laboratories. The article was accompanied by a photograph showing Professors Homer Black and Floyd Furlow during an analysis of gases released from the smoke stack behind the shop building. During the commencement, Hall announced that Tech's friends had given the $10,000 required to secure the conditional gift of the Educational Board. The *Constitution* reported that a portion of the technological fund would be used to establish a Department of Experimental Engineering that would be directed by Professor Furlow. Hall informed the Tech trustees that the money would be divided with $4,000 for the shop, $4,000 for electrical engineering, $5,000 for the experimental department, and $500 to the textile department.[80]

In January 1903 the Tech board approved a plan to enable Hall to live near the campus by building a house on North Avenue. The trustees agreed to pay Hall $500 per year with the option to buy the house at cost within three years as a permanent residence for Tech presidents. At the same meeting the trustees appropriated $500 for construction of a building to permit isolation of students with contagious diseases. This action was taken after the state legislature had refused to grant Tech's request for $5,000 to build a hospital and $15,000 for construction of a chemistry building. In January 1904 the Tech trustees voted to purchase Hall's home that was appraised at $11,000, and he was given $2,000 as partial payment. Funds for this acquisition came from the estate of James Swann, who died in May 1903 and whose will provided an additional bequest of $10,000 to Tech. Tech used $2,800 from the Swann bequest to purchase a tract adjacent to the president's house on North Avenue.[81]

Hall's announcement of a large gift for Tech became almost a normal event of commencement exercises, and the pattern continued in June 1903 when he reported a $5,000 gift from William R. Hearst. Hall stated that he hoped that the friends of Tech would augment the Swann bequest and the Hearst gift so that accommodations might be built for another two hundred students. The *Atlanta Constitution* reported on the Hearst gift and wrote a laudatory editorial on Hall, stating that he had worked with "indefatigable devotion" to make Tech the peer of other schools of its class. The editor stated that Hall's "success has been phenomenal and the far reaching values, introduced in trained intellectuals and skilled hands, that he is creating for the South are amazing even to those familiar with the institution and its work." The *Constitution* also mentioned that Hall had issued his "annual order" that all Tech students dressed in work clothes should be at work in the shops that were open to the public during the morning of graduation day. The paper estimated that there were 1,000 visitors to the shops that day.[82]

Samuel Spencer, president of the Southern Railroad Company, spoke at Tech's commencement in 1904 and characterized Tech's students as "cadets in the West Point of industry," an analogy that must have pleased Lyman Hall. Spencer's talk was entitled "Industrial Education" and stated that it was becoming an "intensely industrial and commercial age" and "the industrial war . . . is upon us." Hall also spoke to the graduates and commented that the record indicated that Tech was fulfilling the objectives for which it had been founded. He noted that engineering education was in the "forefront of progress" and that the laborer would always be "in the rear guard of the progressive industrial army." Hall did not anticipate that any of the graduating class would become professional politicians since "your training has been deductive rather than seductive, mechanical rather than tyrannical, for draughting rather than grafting." He noted that Tech already had graduated two hundred men who had "become bread winners, developers, manufacturers, managers, superintendents and presidents." He asserted that an adverse report had never been received on a single Tech graduate as to "character, ability, energy or competency."[83]

In 1904 the Georgia legislature appropriated $10,000 for the construction of a chemistry building at Tech with the usual condition that it be matched by an equal amount from outside donations. In April 1905 Hall informed the Tech trustees that he had raised $7,500 thus far and expected to obtain the remaining $2,500 by the time of the June commencement. The success of what was to be Hall's final fund drive was announced in June 1905. A few weeks later, on August 16, 1905, Hall died at a health resort in Danville, New York. The Tech trustees voted that the new chemistry building be called the Lyman Hall Laboratory of Chemistry in his honor. At the same meeting the trustees voted to elect Hall's protégé K. G. Matheson as the faculty chairman with the duties of an acting president. The faculty drafted a memorial statement that credited Hall with exhibiting the "best qualities of the new industrial South," while at the same time retaining the best of "the traditions and ideals of the old South."[84]

An inventory of Tech's physical assets was prepared for Matheson in October 1905 and indicated that Hall's continuous fund raising efforts had left Tech with an impressive legacy. The total assets were valued at $251,900, of which $194,700 consisted of buildings and land, and the machinery and equipment was valued at $57,200. There were nine buildings, including the president's house, as compared to the two buildings when Hall became Tech's president in 1896. The 1905 inventory valued the two original buildings, their equipment, and the land at $111,000, so that Tech's physical plant had been increased by approximately $140,900 during Hall's tenure.[85] This was equivalent to an average annual increase of almost $16,000. Hall's legacy also included five degree programs compared to one and an enrollment that was 3.3 times higher than when he had succeeded Hopkins.

Lyman Hall had inherited the presidency of a school that was perceived as little more than an Atlanta trade school, struggling to survive in a climate of legislative indifference if not hostility. During the next nine years, he managed to gain the support of local newspapers, key members of the state legislature, and several philanthropists, and he orchestrated an almost continual series of fund raising campaigns that served the latent function of creating a growing number of friends for Tech. He left the school with the reputation of a dynamic center of excellence in technological education in the region with aspirations for national prominence. The selection of K. G. Matheson, who had been taught and recruited by Hall, as Tech's third president made it seem probable that Hall's agenda for Tech and his disciplined style of management would continue.

Chapter Four

Tech in the Progressive Era: The Matheson Years

Overleaf: The school culture side of engineering education is evident in an early class in descriptive geometry. (Courtesy of the Georgia Tech Archives.)

The man who succeeded Lyman Hall as president of Georgia Tech was Kenneth Gordon Matheson, professor and head of the English department. Elected chairman of the faculty in August 1905, he was appointed to the presidency the following June, serving there until April 1922, when the combined effects of overwork, inadequate legislative support, and concern for his family led him to leave Tech for the presidency of Drexel Institute in Philadelphia. Matheson was born in Cheraw, South Carolina, in July 1864. After graduating in 1885 from the South Carolina Military Academy, now the Citadel, he served as commandant of cadets at Georgia Military College in Milledgeville, Georgia (1885–88), and the University of Tennessee (1888–90), where he also taught English. In 1890 Matheson went to the Missouri Military Academy in the same capacity, remaining there until 1896 when he resigned to enter Stanford University. Awarded a master's degree in English the following year, he joined the Tech faculty as a junior professor of English. However, the unexpected and somewhat mysterious resignation of his department head, Charles Lane, resulted in his rapid promotion to a full professorship early in 1898.[1]

Matheson and Lyman Hall, who were both at the Citadel between 1883 and 1885, knew each other well before Matheson came to Tech. They were working together closely by 1900, when Hall, not given to delegation of authority, left the selection of a new English instructor to his subordinate's discretion. A week after Hall's death on August 16, 1905, Matheson was elected chairman of the faculty and acting president because, as one professor put it, he was "the person best able to take up Dr. Hall's work."[2]

Praised as a man who represented the best qualities of "the New Industrial South—Progressivism tempered with Conservatism," Hall was a worthy model for Matheson. The West Point–trained disciplinarian taught Georgians "the essential difference between technical training and technical education . . . [drawing the line] between the artisan and the engineer." Matheson's task was to build upon the solid foundation laid by his predecessor, to expand the school physically, but more important, to broaden its educational activity so that it might better serve the city, state, and region.[3]

Physical Expansion

The first and most compelling problem faced by the new president was an old one: where to get enough money to keep the institution running. In 1905–6 Georgia Tech's total income from all sources amounted to $64,522, of which wages consumed about $48,000. Given that the recently completed chemistry laboratory lacked equipment, that the chapel had been cut up into classrooms to accommodate growing enrollment, and that Knowles Dormitory had neither electricity nor steam heat, it is no wonder that Matheson's *Annual Report* dismissed the state's regular appropriation as "totally inadequate."[4]

Like Hall before him, Matheson had to lobby the legislature and the Atlanta city council, solicit gifts and donations from businessmen and philanthropic foundations, and conduct organized fund-raising campaigns to match or supplement whatever the lawmakers saw fit to appropriate. Like Hall, Matheson enjoyed some measurable successes. Between 1906 and 1923, the campus expanded from roughly eleven acres to twenty-five, the number of principal buildings doubled, and regular state and local government support grew threefold. Even more impressive were the amounts the president raised through campaigns among "friends" of Georgia Tech.[5]

Matheson's expansion efforts began in the summer of 1906. The Peters Land Company, which owned most of the property surrounding Tech, had given the school nonrenewable options to purchase some land by January 1, 1907. An additional parcel on North Avenue, just east of the campus, had been leased to Tech's Athletic Association in 1904. Matheson hoped to acquire all of it. With a special legislative appropriation and funds raised from "friends" of the institution, he was able to purchase the four acres that make up the southern two-thirds of the present Grant Field and a number of lots on Cherry, Kimball, and Fowler streets. The "friends," incidentally, responded to form letters that invoked for the first time Matheson's vision of a "Greater Georgia Tech."[6]

In succeeding years Matheson continued to press Tech's Board of Trustees to expand the campus. Otherwise, he argued, rising land prices would prevent growth and the school would be unable to fulfill its mission, which, by 1915, he defined as "teaching first, then research, and finally extension work among the people of the State." The Peters Land Company agreed in 1912 to sell Tech three acres of land on the north side of the campus for half its appraised value, and a year later it granted the school a five-year option and free use of four more acres located to the north of the existing athletic field.[7]

In the last two years of his presidency, Matheson urged the Board of Trustees to acquire more land on the northern edge of the campus before the Peters Land Company built residences on it. By that time, relations between the school and Peters were strained because Tech had been slow to retire its long-standing obligation to purchase the northern half of Grant Field.[8] One acquisition was not solicited by the enterprising president or anyone else. In September 1906, Julius Brown, son of a former Georgia governor, left two-thirds of his estate to Georgia Tech because he thought it was worth more than any other school in the state. The bequest consisted of a valuable collection of books, furniture, real estate in Atlanta and Fulton County, and over four thousand acres of land in Texas.[9]

Matheson's building program for Georgia Tech began with a library to house the small collection he began to accumulate while still head of the English department. By 1905 the library had over 2,500 volumes and periodicals, largely donated, and a competent librarian to oversee it, but it was crammed into quarters on the second floor of the Academic Building. Matheson sought the aid of Andrew Carnegie, and in March 1906, he was informed that the philanthropist would pay for a library building, provided its cost did not exceed $20,000 and Tech would agree to spend at least $2,000 a year on the library's upkeep.[10]

When Tech celebrated its twenty-fifth anniversary in June 1913, three new buildings greeted visitors to the campus: the Joseph Brown Whitehead Memorial Hospital, the first three units of a planned five-part shop building, and an imposing YMCA building, which became the center of student activity at Tech. Matheson enlisted the Federation of Women's Clubs of Georgia, primarily the Atlanta component, in a fund-raising project for a campus hospital in 1909. Mrs. Joseph Brown Whitehead, a member of the local group and widow of a Coca-Cola Bottling Company executive, contributed $5,000 to the drive, and within a year construction of the two-story facility was begun. Located on Cherry Street, and now used to house the offices of the dean of students, the building was formally dedicated in November 1911.[11]

Meanwhile, Matheson was working tirelessly to secure funds for a new shop building. With help from certain alumni prominent in Atlanta business circles, he persuaded the legislature to appropriate $35,000 for the facility, provided the school managed to raise $15,000 for the first unit of the planned $100,000 five-part structure. In fact, largely through the efforts of the Atlanta Chamber of Commerce, more than $22,000 was raised and three units of the building were ready for occupancy by January 1912. A fourth section constructed in 1920 relieved the extreme overcrowding of facilities that followed World War I, but not until 1938 was the fifth unit of the Mechanical Building finally completed.[12]

Certainly one of the most important additions to the Georgia Tech campus from the students' point of view was the YMCA Building, which was located directly across North Avenue from the main campus and the athletic field. Matheson called it the center of "social and moral life" on campus.[13] Dedicated formally on June 7, 1912, the building was constructed with funds from philanthropist John D. Rockefeller and an additional sum raised among "friends" of the college. Besides a bowling alley, poolroom, restaurant, and barbershop, the facility housed offices, student publications, reading rooms, meeting places for the band and literary societies, an auditorium, guest quarters, and a third-floor dormitory. A school bulletin assured parents that students would find "a wholesome atmosphere and adequate amusement [there], making it unnecessary for a boy to go to the city to spend his idle hours."[14]

If the YMCA was the center of "moral and social" life on the Tech campus, the athletic field was its corporeal center, at least on weekends in the spring and fall. As noted, the first part of the field, four acres fronting on North Avenue, was leased from the Peters Land Company in 1904, purchased in 1906, and added to in 1913, when E. C. Peters agreed to lease four more acres just north of the first parcel to the school with an option to purchase them within five years. The lease allowed Tech to improve the site, and with convict labor donated by Fulton County, the entire acreage was graded and leveled. Meanwhile, in 1913, a prominent businessman, John W. Grant, offered to donate $15,000 for the construction of the first concrete stands on the site. Tech responded by naming its athletic complex for the donor's deceased son, Hugh Inman Grant. Two years later, Grant, the Athletic Association, and the Board of Trustees contributed additional funds to complete the stands, and in 1920 another sizable donation from Grant helped to retire Tech's obligation to the Peters Land Company, two years late.[15]

The most ambitious and the most expensive building project undertaken during Matheson's presidency was the construction of a new power plant. Tech's rapid expansion made the existing system obsolete. By the early months of 1912, gifts of equipment from various industrial firms, including General Electric, Westinghouse Electric, and the National Tube Company, had been promised to Tech, and a site was selected at the rear of the school between Cherry Street and the athletic field. Meanwhile, Professors J. S. Coon and H. P. Wood, heads of the mechanical and electrical engineering departments, respectively, began designing a modern heating and lighting plant capable of supplying all existing and planned structures on campus. Matheson asked the state for $20,000 to build the new plant, noting in his *Annual Report* that of the $150,000 spent for recent construction on the campus, only $35,000 had come from the state, while "another State college" was recently given a $40,000 building and a $10,000 increase in its annual maintenance appropriation.[16]

The state refused to appropriate for the power plant in 1912 and again in 1913, despite Tech's pledge to raise an additional $10,000 and its often expressed fear that unless a building for the plant were erected soon, the manufacturers' donations of equipment would be canceled. Even the promise that Tech hoped to become the state's engineering experiment station, "ready and willing at all times to extend industrial and engineering information" to the citizens of Georgia, did no good. By 1914, frustrated by legislative inaction, Matheson and the Board of Trustees moved ahead on their own. Besides securing more pledges from northern manufacturers, the school obtained free site preparation from the Fulton County Commission and enough free crushed stone from the city of Atlanta to build necessary retaining walls. Finally, early in the summer of 1914, the school launched the Greater Tech Campaign, a fund drive, which despite the declaration of war in Europe and the consequent economic dislocation in the United States, managed to produce over $80,000, enough to begin construction of the power plant building. Most of the money came from Atlanta businessmen; a planned statewide effort to raise $500,000 had to be postponed as the nation's attention was increasingly diverted by events abroad. An effort to revive the campaign early in 1918 was quickly aborted because of squabbles among the fund raisers and word from Washington that campaigns to raise money for college buildings "at that time were out of order."[17]

President Matheson's conception of what the new power plant ought to do for Tech underwent considerable change between 1912 and 1918. Initially, Tech sought to modernize an old facility at modest cost. Later the project was seen as part of a larger plan to provide power laboratory experience and research facilities for faculty and students. And finally, it was viewed as the capstone of an elaborate industrial research scheme that could develop Georgia's natural resources and supply scientific and technical solutions to knotty industrial problems. If it did all this, the "laboratory," as it came to be called, would certainly go a long way to satisfy Matheson's expressed criteria of what a modern college ought to provide: "teaching first; then research, and finally, extension work among the people of the State."[18]

Academic and Administrative Reform

Tech's increased revenues and physical expansion paled by comparison with the educational, administrative, and professional changes introduced during the Matheson presidency. Dubbed the Progressive Era by contemporaries as well as historians, the first twenty years of this century were marked by a spirit of optimism, a desire to improve existing conditions, and a drive to increase material wealth through the application of scientific and technological expertise. Reform was the watchword from the White House to the court house. The school house, too, attracted the reformers' attention. Matheson, alive to the changes occurring in higher education, particularly in engineering education, could not help but be affected.

One of his first acts as president was to change the names of Tech's undergraduate classes. Formerly labeled subapprentice, apprentice, junior, middle and senior, they became apprentice (that is, preparatory), freshman, sophomore, junior, and senior in 1906. More cosmetic than substantive, the revised nomenclature did modify somewhat Tech's trade school image.[19]

Of far greater significance was Matheson's determined effort to raise entrance requirements and to do away with the preparatory class altogether. This took time, primarily because most Georgia secondary schools failed to prepare their graduates well enough, particularly in mathematics and science, to meet Tech's minimum freshman requirements. The apprentice class allowed deficient students to catch up. It also competed with public and private high schools, which they hardly appreciated. To smooth relations, Tech's *Annual Announcements* in 1906 advised high schools on the University of Georgia's "accredited" list just what mathematics and English courses their graduates must have mastered to be admitted to Tech's freshman class by certificate rather than by entrance examination.

But three years later the Tech admissions officer told a friend that admitting "certified" students had its drawbacks. Some high school principals, he noted, "certify what is clearly not there."[20]

Although some of the pressure to upgrade entrance requirements came from within the faculty, Tech was also responding to a nationwide movement to raise standards. President Matheson returned from a meeting of the Association of Southern Colleges and Preparatory Schools in November 1908 to advise his colleagues that the association would require a minimum of ten high school units for freshman standing by 1909 and fourteen two years later. A faculty committee was already working on the problem and reported early in 1910 what thirty leading colleges and universities, north and south, expected of entering freshmen. Tech could not be so demanding because of "local conditions," but it could move gradually toward the same goals, and did. The fourteen high school units mandated by the Southern Association in 1911 were required at Tech by 1914.[21]

The inadequacy of Georgia high schools was only one obstacle in the way of raising standards and abolishing the subfreshman class. The Board of Trustees, especially Chairman N. E. Harris, was reluctant to authorize either, fearing that a precipitous decline in enrollment would invite legislative retaliation. Neither occurred. When the board finally allowed Tech to drop the subfreshman class in the fall of 1915, more students enrolled than ever before and the legislature increased its annual appropriation by $10,000. By 1921 Tech required a minimum of fifteen units for admission to the freshman class, which was standard among public and private engineering and liberal arts schools all over the country.[22]

Enrollment figures climbed steadily from the beginning of Matheson's presidency. From approximately 500 students in 1906, the number enrolled in all programs for 1916–17 totaled 1,129. The next year, with America at war, it was 1,291, and the increase continued following the Armistice. By early October 1920, the *Technique* recorded more than 2,400 students on campus, over 1,450 of whom were enrolled in full-time collegiate programs. A year later, the Board of Trustees reported an expected enrollment in all programs of 2,671. Of these, 1,612 were in regular degree-granting curricula. In other words, Tech's daytime collegiate student body more than tripled between 1906 and 1921.²³

As he had in the case of undergraduate class names, President Matheson moved to change the terms used to describe faculty rank. He also wanted to rename the school and raise faculty salaries. First proposed in 1909, the adoption of traditional terms for faculty rank did not occur until January 1911, when Chairman N. E. Harris withdrew his objections. Changing the name of the school took longer. The faculty first suggested a shift from "Georgia School of Technology" to the "Georgia Institute of Technology" on June 12, 1906. Five years later they were still talking about it. All agreed it was a good idea, if only to make clear that Georgia Tech was a college, not a high school. Meanwhile, the board authorized Matheson to poll the alumni on the subject. In his letter to the alumni, Matheson argued for the name change first, because practically all of America's leading engineering schools used the term "institute," unless engineering formed only a department of a university, and secondly, because Atlanta had a Tech High School. The confusion with Georgia Tech "would be funny if not so humiliating and embarrassing." The president advised the former students that while the term "polytechnic" in the name might give the administration a great boost in building the institution, its use would also stir up opposition from those who did not want to see Tech broaden its focus. Not a single response favored retention of the name "Georgia Tech" or "Georgia School of Technology." But to no avail. Tech did not become the Georgia Institute of Technology until 1948.²⁴

Beyond their small salaries, Tech faculty received no pensions or fringe benefits and enjoyed very few amenities in 1906. The younger bachelors organized a kind of banquet study club to pass some of their time. Others, single or married, thought the school ought to provide space for a faculty club. J. B. Crenshaw, professor of modern languages, campaigned through the columns of the *Technique,* noting that at Sewanee the administration had fitted up a common room for the use of trustees and visitors as well as faculty. Matheson named a committee to study the proposal but nothing seems to have come of it. Not until 1949 was a faculty club formally organized.²⁵

Faculty salaries did little to attract ambitious young instructors to

Georgia Tech. In 1906, for a faculty and staff of forty-five, the total payroll amounted to only $46,520. Chairman Harris thought Tech professors probably earned less than the faculty of comparable schools anywhere in the world. Noting that "this class of educators" was in great demand, he predicted difficulty in future recruitment. Matheson echoed Harris's remarks, adding that unless salaries were increased, the school would lose the faculty it had.[26]

The prediction came true. By 1910 increasing enrollment required more work from an already overburdened staff. Some faculty members left, and inexperienced recent Tech graduates replaced them in the classroom. Yet even they were leaving for better positions elsewhere. Matheson noted in 1912 that his annual recruiting tour of northern universities was less productive in all fields: "In the past we had no difficulty in securing a large number of candidates for . . . English but [this time] . . . I had only a few men to offer for the two vacant instructorships. . . . If this be true of the Literary Department how much more so it is in the Scientific field, where the demand is great and thoroughly prepared men are few."[27]

World War I exacerbated Tech's staffing problems. With more students and programs than ever before and faculty lost to industry, the military, or government service, a heavy burden fell on those who remained. After the war the meager support provided by the legislature made Tech unable to compete in the recruitment sweepstakes at a time when diminished supply and inflation allowed qualified instructors to command premium salaries. Matheson's tour of Harvard, Yale, Princeton, Columbia, and MIT in the spring of 1919 did not secure a single man because seniors and graduate students refused to enter a profession that paid so poorly.[28]

A major administrative reform introduced at Tech when Matheson became president was the restructuring of its internal government. Under Lyman Hall everything was centered in the president's office. Routine matters were submitted to the faculty at weekly meetings, but as J. B. Crenshaw, professor of modern languages, recalled, final decisions were made "almost exclusively by Captain Hall, who managed even the smallest detail." When Matheson took over, rapid expansion in every aspect of the school made Hall's system "cumbrous and timewasting." The new president, who had a reverence for "efficiency," soon scrapped the full meetings for a kind of councilor system. Composed of department heads who served on various standing and ad hoc committees, the "inner council" met weekly with the president. The full faculty assembled only when called. Besides relieving Matheson of considerable drudgery, the system freed him to engage in activities like fund raising, public relations, and meetings with other educational leaders.[29]

Additional administrative changes occurred in 1909 with the appointment of Tech's first dean, William Emerson, and the substitution of an executive committee for the existing "inner council." Chaired by Emerson and comprised of representatives from all of the school's major divisions, the executive committee lasted until 1921, when yet another reorganization designed to cope with Tech's increasing size and complexity took place. A faculty council composed of all full professors and associates met every Friday to act upon an agenda framed beforehand by a steering or advisory committee. By that time Tech boasted a bursar and deans of the night school, the commerce school, the cooperative program, and student affairs, as well as a dean of faculties. Throughout his tenure, President Matheson did not relinquish final decision making on important matters. But he clearly shared the policy-making process with his senior colleagues.[30]

Matheson's administrative reforms broke no new ground, but they did move Tech into the mainstream of higher educational practice. So did his constant efforts to encourage the growth of professionalism among the faculty through participation in educational meetings, membership in learned societies, research, and publication. The president set the tone himself by traveling frequently to represent Tech at conferences of educational administrators and meetings on engineering education. He also read widely in popular and profesional journals, making it a point to call pertinent articles to the attention of his faculty.[31]

Georgia Tech did not belong to any educational association when Matheson became president. In 1895 the Southern Association of Colleges and Secondary Schools was organized in the school's chapel, but Tech could not qualify for membership because it had a preparatory or subfreshman department. Even the Georgia Educational Association attracted no representatives from Tech in 1910, although Matheson urged Tech faculty to attend their meetings.[32]

Faculty membership and attendance at the meetings of scientific and professional organizations were just as spotty. A few individuals belonged to associations in their respective disciplines; J. S. Coon, for example, was a charter member of the American Society of Mechanical Engineers, and William Emerson and Gilbert Boggs belonged to the American Chemical Society. But in 1914 the American Association for the Advancement of Science had to urge Tech professors to attend a session held in Atlanta, and both Matheson and Dean Emerson regularly had to remind the faculty that the library subscribed to professional journals like the *Bulletins* and *Proceedings* of the Society for the Promotion of Engineering Education.[33]

Before the First World War, Tech professors concentrated almost exclusively on teaching. There is practically no evidence in the official records of administrative pressure to encourage research and publication among the faculty. Nevertheless, a few individuals did produce scholarly work. President Lyman Hall authored two mathematics textbooks, and W. G. Perry of the English department published articles in the *North American Review* and the *Sewanee Review*. Professors J. S. Coon and William Emerson also contributed articles to professional journals early in their tenure at Tech. In 1914 planning for the new power plant stimulated interest in industrial research. George Baldwin, an executive of the Savannah Power and Electric Company and a member of the Board of Trustees, proposed that Tech raise money for the new facility among Georgia industrialists and businessmen by promising to solve their industrial problems. Baldwin's concept had mushroomed by 1916. The new power "laboratory," declared the *Annual Announcements*, would make it possible to establish a State Research Bureau and a Bureau of Standards at Georgia Tech. Not only the new equipment in the power "laboratory" but all of the school's facilities could be made available for "industrial research and testing." Thus, state and local governments, as well as the private sector, could look forward to a prosperous future through the development of natural resources, new products, processes and machinery, materials testing, and standardization, all made possible by a "Greater Georgia Tech."[34]

Unfortunately, the war disrupted Tech's ambitious research and service plans. They were not revived until 1921 when President Matheson, then in the midst of another fund-raising effort, reported numerous requests from Georgia manufacturers for help in solving industrial problems. At his suggestion, the faculty agreed to the appointment of a research committee. On May 5, 1921, it recommended that the faculty council ask the Board of Trustees to: (1) provide for the beginning of research work at Georgia Tech; (2) establish a postgraduate course leading to the degree of master of science; (3) appoint research fellows and teachers in order to allow department heads enough time to direct research and graduate work; and (4) require department heads to submit lists of postgraduate level courses that could be offered with Tech's existing equipment. The faculty council approved the proposal, and also accepted a research committee suggestion that a medal, the gift of associate and full professors, be awarded to the instructor or assistant professor who presented the best paper based on original research conducted at Georgia Tech. By November 1921, eight junior faculty indicated their intentions to enter the competition.[35]

Curricular Innovation

In addition to raising educational standards, restructuring governance, and promoting professionalism among the faculty, President Matheson introduced extensive curricular reform at Georgia Tech. New courses and degree programs were added in response to advances in scientific and technological developments, the expressed needs of local leaders in business and government, and a growing consensus among American engineering educators that the cultural horizons of their students ought to be broadened. J. B. Crenshaw, head of Tech's modern languages department from its inception in 1904, wrote in 1938 that Matheson's entire presidency "was marked by a strong and definite cultural tendency" and a determined effort to "liberalize" the curricula. Crenshaw recalled that his first appearance on campus was not hailed with "an oversupply of cordiality." But Professors K. G. Matheson and J. S. Coon both staunchly supported at least two years of modern language study for Tech students. "Others were not so sure," despite the fact that time for the new course was deducted from Matheson's and Coon's departments, English and mechanical drawing.

In time students in every degree program except textile engineering had to complete two years of French or German to graduate. Spanish was added in 1908, and thereafter most students chose it because it was said to be easiest. The administrators offered more compelling reasons to teach all three: Spanish had value for those going into business or government; French was essential for architecture students; and every budding chemist had to know German. The "cultural and literary" dimensions were also important: "English and the modern languages are the only cultural forces [that are] mingled in the future engineers' education with science, math, physics, chemistry, mechanics, etc. They are necessary to produce men able to communicate with doctors, lawyers, statesmen and financiers on an equal footing. Without [them] . . . the technical man never reaches full potential."[36]

Some of President Matheson's early efforts to reform Tech's curricula were successful; others were not. For example, while still chairman of the faculty, Matheson proposed and the Board of Trustees approved the creation of a department of mining engineering to begin operations in the fall of 1906. But a year and a half later he announced that the effort would be abandoned because the legislature had failed to provide a building for equipment donated by "New York friends." Meanwhile, schools in Alabama and Tennessee organized similar programs. Matheson thought there was not enough demand in the Southeast for Tech to persevere.[37]

Instead, the president proposed a course in architecture, for which there did seem to be a demand. The board agreed and the program began in the fall of 1908. Recognizing that architecture was "essentially a Fine Art," the degee requirements included the study of the history of architecture as well as the "work of construction in practical form." Courses in building materials and construction were supplemented by field trips to quarries and brickyards. Provision was also made for those who wanted to stress architectural engineering rather than design in the last part of their programs. Tech students would have their work monitored and judged by members of the profession practicing in Atlanta.[38]

Some of the curricular and degree changes in Matheson's early years as president were designed to tailor programs more precisely to the needs of industry. Chemistry was required in every degree program but did not itself lead to any degree until 1901, when the bachelor of science in engineering chemistry was introduced. An amalgam of certain mechanical engineering and general chemistry courses, especially those "most usually applied industrially," it was the forerunner of what became the chemical engineering degree at Tech in 1931. As for chemistry, per se, the board authorized a bachelor of science degree in chemistry in 1906. This program omitted math and engineering subjects after the first year, substituting courses in minerology, geology, and crystallography, as well as more language study. Billed as preparation for those planning to enter "general" chemical work, metallurgy or assaying, it also required work in the history of chemistry. The number of degrees granted in both branches, particularly in "pure" chemistry, was small compared to those in mechanical or electrical engineering. Consequently, the bachelor of science in chemistry was dropped in 1919, not to be reintroduced until the 1930s.[39]

One of the most successful programs begun at Tech during Matheson's presidency was the night school. Designed to meet the needs of Atlanta manufacturers for skilled labor, the night school opened on March 2, 1908. Over the course of an academic year some twenty-four "trades" or short courses were offered in addition to elementary English and mathematics. The city council supported the program with $2,500 a year to supplement the small registration fees paid by students. Initially, support for the program was lukewarm, both on and off the campus. Some feared night school classes would lessen the dignity of the college. But for those who had to work during the day, the program was a means of self-improvement and a ticket to a better job. Over a hundred students signed up for the first session directed by Professor J. N. G. Nesbit, head of the department of experimental engineering. They took courses in foundry practice, machine and wood shop, mechanical drawing, and textile work. Nesbit, who was dean of the night school by the time he resigned to go to war in 1917, was succeeded by A. B. "Froggy" Morton, director of Tech's summer school. In 1923 Professor R. S. Howell replaced Morton as director of the night school, which by that time had been renamed the Evening School of Applied Science. Its offerings had been considerably upgraded in 1919 and the course of study reorganized into a three-year program.[40]

At the collegiate level, two of the most important curricular reforms introduced in the Matheson years were the cooperative program and the commerce course. Tech's cooperative program was modeled on the pioneering co-op plan of the University of Cincinnati. Begun in 1906 by Dean Herman Schneider, the Cincinnati cooperative program in engineering education was largely the outgrowth of that school's inadequate shop equipment. Rotating weekly, paired students spent half of a six-year undergraduate program on campus doing regular class work and half in the shops, mills, or laboratories of Cincinnati businessmen. Because they spent all but four weeks a year working on campus or with the cooperating business, no time was lost from the regular undergraduate course. The Cincinnati plan, concluded a Tech committee that studied the matter in 1909, offered several advantages for the school and the student: (1) it identified and eliminated weak students early; (2) it developed seriousness and maturity among those who remained; (3) it brought students into contact with up-to-date equipment and modern industrial practice which no school could hope to match; (4) it enabled graduates to go directly into productive work without a training period; and, perhaps most important, (5) it enabled students from poor families to work their way through school. The report, however, advised against adopting the system immediately unless the board agreed to hire more faculty.[41]

Three years passed before the cooperative program came to Georgia Tech. President Matheson cultivated support among local business leaders and arranged for them to meet with Dean Schneider of the University of Cincinnati. Twelve students enrolled as co-ops in 1912 and twenty-six signed up two years later. The war interrupted the program briefly, but by the fall of 1919 it was reintroduced. Despite a rapid turnover of key faculty and the serious economic downturn of the postwar years, Tech co-ops were employed in twenty-six different establishments in and around Atlanta by the end of 1920. Professor Cecil A. Kapp urged them to "stay on the job and put forth the very best effort possible." Noting that wages and prices had fallen and that manufacturers were responding by "tighten[ing] down on their money," Kapp reminded the co-ops that *"thousands of men are being laid off all over the country, . . . good jobs are already scarce and will be doubly so in the near future."*[42]

Tech in the Progressive Era

The introduction of a commerce program at Tech represented another major curricular reform during the presidency of Matheson. Engineering educators began to appreciate the need to include economics in the undergraduate curriculum by the late nineteenth century. In no sense did they consider it of comparable importance to mathematics or the physical sciences, but the growing role of the engineer in industry and public life developed a new attitude among the curriculum makers toward economics and related subjects.[43]

At Tech the English department made room for such courses as "political economy" or "economic theory," but clearly the brief exposure was not enough to prepare students for the world of business and industry. According to an article in the January 31, 1912, issue of the *Technique*, J. B. McCrary (class of 1891) first approached Professor J. S. Coon about a business course for Tech students in 1908. Later, he and his business manager, W. M. Fambrough (class of 1903), mailed a circular to alumni in which McCrary asserted that a course in "business science" would increase every Tech man's chance for success by 100 percent. Ignorant of Georgia's industrial and business possibilities, too many Tech graduates were going north to work for large corporations rather than staying at home to develop the state and enrich themselves.[44]

William Fambrough's public efforts to interest alumni and the Tech administration in business courses began early in 1911. A few months later he promoted the idea at commencement exercises. The response was positive, and by early fall juniors and seniors were campaigning for a department of commerce. President Matheson presented the plan to his faculty in October, noting that alumni strongly favored it and that other colleges had long since introduced similar programs. Meanwhile, a drive to raise $25,000 for the proposed course was meeting with considerable success, and in February 1912 an evening lecture series featuring J. B. McCrary, W. M. Fambrough, Joel Hunt, a well-known certified public accountant, and Samuel Inman, a member of Tech's first Board of Trustees, was announced by the school paper. Juniors and seniors were urged to attend; they would be excused from other duties if they did not "abuse the privilege."[45]

Encouraged by the experiment, Tech authorities scheduled a full series of monthly lectures on business economics to be delivered by leading Atlanta businessmen, lawyers, and accountants during the academic year 1912–13. Later, a part-time faculty for a new School of Commerce was also appointed from Tech's regular staff. Wayne S. Kell, formerly an assistant professor of metallurgy and geology, became dean of the school and professor of accounting and finance; E. C. Gruen, an instructor of mechanical engineering, taught banking; and S. S. Wallace, head of the English department, offered economics and business English. Outside lecturers from local business firms filled in with classes in accounting, commercial law, and marketing.[46]

By September 1913, the School of Commerce was offering two programs. The first, designed to meet the need of businessmen and taught by the "commercial division," met evenings between six and eight; the second, intended to provide regular engineering students with essential business training, was conducted during regular daytime hours under the direction of the "engineering division." In 1916 the trustees authorized the day school to grant the degree of bachelor of science in commerce. Besides business subjects, the four-year program required Spanish, mathematics, engineering, and machine shop. Graduates of the night school earned a bachelor of commercial studies degree after two years of study plus two years of practical business experience.[47]

From the beginning, both divisions of the School of Commerce attracted significant numbers of students. Twenty-one enrolled in the day school in 1913–14; an additional twenty-three attended "irregular" or night school classes. By the following year, the numbers rose to fifty-four and twenty-seven, respectively. A new dean, J. M. Watters, replaced W. S. Kell, who resigned unexpectedly in the middle of an academic year, but progress was not interrupted. By 1917, night school classes had been moved from the campus to the Walton Building in downtown Atlanta. In the fall of 1917 women students were admitted to the evening school. One of them, Anna Teitelbaum Wise, became Tech's first woman graduate in 1919, a full year before the legislature passed a law allowing females to attend the evening school. Mrs. Wise scored another first in 1919 when she joined the faculty of the evening school as instructor of commerce. That feat would not be repeated on the main campus until 1960.[48]

Federal legislation and the First World War also caused curricular innovation at Georgia Tech. In 1917 Congress passed the Smith-Hughes Act to promote vocational training in secondary schools. Administered through state departments of education and funded jointly by the federal government and participating states, the act provided money for the training of secondary school teachers of vocational subjects. Tech moved quickly to develop a teacher training course. Begun in the fall of 1918, Tech's Department of Industrial Education admitted three classes of students: elementary and high school graduates with two years of work experience, Tech graduates, and Tech students planning to earn a bachelor of science in industrial education. Elementary and high school graduates would receive "certificates of proficiency." Tech graduates and those who took the full four-year course, it was assumed, would become principals and superintendents in the state's vocational education program.[49]

Enrollment in the industrial education department was small, which allowed for what Matheson claimed were "unusually efficient results." He expected more rapid growth as extension centers were set up around the state. But the program remained small, and in 1932 it was discontinued by the newly established Board of Regents.[50]

World War I also brought curricular change to Tech. During and immediately following the conflict, Tech conducted a ground school for cadet aviators and supply officers, trained several hundred enlisted men as army technicians, and began a reserve officers training program that was later expanded and made a permanent feature of the institution. The federal government also asked Tech to run a motor transport school for army officers and enlisted men and a rehabilitation program for disabled soldiers. A geology department was also established at federal request and expense in 1919.

Finally, many curricular changes introduced during Matheson's presidency were designed to promote efficiency, specialization within an existing degree program, and good relations with the community. In 1919 a new department of mechanics put all work of that class under the authority of a single unit, and two years later seniors in mechanical engineering could elect an automotive specialty. Tech also cooperated with Fulton County by introducing a highway engineering course in the civil engineering degree program. The school tested road materials and the county gave it an annual appropriation besides letting students use its road grading equipment. Similarly, Tech provided the city of Atlanta with a special course on "municipal and sanitary engineering," and Atlanta increased its annual appropriation to the school.[51]

Most of the programs just discussed did not cost the state any money. In fact, the income from the local and federal government programs, added to money raised from private sources, kept the school solvent in 1919–20 despite the fact that enrollment had doubled since 1917 and inflation had cut the purchasing power of state appropriations in half.[52]

Community Relations

From the beginning, Georgia Tech administrators did all they could to cultivate good relations with the local community. A large part of the student body came from the immediate vicinity and so did a sizable part of the school's regular income. Atlanta businessmen provided the means for much of Tech's early expansion, and they came to its aid when the legislature would not. Throughout his presidency, Matheson made every effort to build bridges by publicizing what Tech had to offer, by promoting student and faculty participation in community affairs, and by instilling a sense of pride in the institution among the local citizenry. Specifically, he advertised in local newspapers, encouraged the faculty to deliver public lectures, and urged the students to enter their work in Chamber of Commerce exhibits and the State Fair. A movie made on the campus for distribution in commercial theaters also helped to popularize the school, as did visits of prominent persons such as William Howard Taft, General Leonard Wood, and Josephus Daniels. William Jennings Bryan was scheduled to speak at commencement in 1913, but developments in Washington forced him to cancel at the last moment.[53]

Commencement services proved to be the most effective means of enhancing Tech's reputation within the community. Before 1911 commencements were relatively brief and simple affairs, but that year Matheson charged a special committee to develop "a new policy for a more dignified commencement season." "Season" was the right word. What the committee devised took two-and-a-half days and involved dances, a class day, dinners, speeches, baccalaureate services, and a procession besides the distribution of diplomas. The president thought the expanded program would build recognition for the school as "a high grade institution" and promote his plans for its future growth.[54]

Tech authorities welcomed recognition from the home folk but prized it even more when it came from America's leading industries and engineering institutions. On a 1912 trip through the Northeast to recruit faculty and solicit donations of equipment, Matheson was cordially received everywhere. Massachusetts Institute of Technology, recently given two and a half million dollars and forty acres for a new campus, "hands it to us when it comes to the class of men we turn out," he reported. The same welcome greeted the Tech president at General Electric and Westinghouse. At the latter's Pittsburgh works Matheson heard many favorable comments about Tech graduates such as Cherry L. Emerson, employed at the company's district headquarters in Charlotte, North Carolina. The department of architecture at the University of Pennsylvania also praised Tech students enrolled in its program. So did engineering departments at Cornell and Columbia. In 1915 Charles Schwab, president of United States Steel, told Matheson that any school which turned out men like George Crawford, class of 1890, head of its subsidiary, the Tennessee Coal and Iron Company, was well worth all that had been put into it.[55]

What disturbed Matheson was that Georgia might not appreciate just how valuable an asset it possessed in Georgia Tech. He knew of no school with a brighter future if enough support were extended, he wrote in 1919. The United States Department of Education, after an exhaustive study, reported its conviction that the only proper location for an engineering school was an industrial city where large manufacturing facilities could serve as "industrial clinics" for engineering students. Qualified experts concurred that the South was on the eve of great industrial expansion which could make it the leading industrial section of the country. Therefore, Tech had most of the ingredients for success: the right municipal and regional location, high standards, and a well-established reputation. The only thing missing was enough money to ensure the future. "In a spirit of patriotism," Matheson entreated, "we call upon the legislators and the people of Georgia . . . to support properly their State technical school, which has already done much for the prosperity of the State and which has all the possibilities of far greater and more fruitful service."[56]

Student Activities

Student life at Georgia Tech underwent dramatic change during the first twenty years of this century. In 1916 Dean William Emerson recalled that campus athletics and student activities were practically nonexistent in his early years at Tech. But two decades later the growth of organized sports, clubs, publications, and fraternities was so rapid that it alarmed the faculty. Too many extracurricular attractions might undermine the school's main purpose: the production of well-trained engineers dedicated to the development of a progressive and prosperous New South. President Matheson raised the issue early in 1913, and a faculty committee responded by surveying twenty-one engineering schools on the subject. The result was a recommendation that extracurricular activities be limited to three per student. Members of athletic teams were already subject to suspension if their grades fell below a certain level.[57]

As mentioned already, the YMCA was the hub of student activity on campus. Begun before the turn of the century, the Tech Y met in various campus locations before moving in 1912 to its new home on North Avenue. J. L. Neill, hired in 1906, became the Tech Y's first full-time general secretary. He left after a few months and E. A. Turner, who remained at Tech for six years, replaced him. Student activities conducted, sponsored, or housed by the Y multiplied so swiftly that an associate secretary, H. F. Comer, was appointed. He became general secretary when Turner resigned in 1913 for service as a missionary in China.[58]

J. L. Neill began the principal work of the Tech YMCA by organizing Bible study classes among the students. By 1915 over 350 students were participating regularly as well as attending weekly devotional and Sunday evening services. Other Y-sponsored activities involved lectures and workshops on issues of current concern.[59]

Each fall the Tech YMCA provided an orientation program for incoming students. Called College Night, it usually featured welcoming speeches by President Matheson, Coach John Heisman, star athletes, and the general secretary. Talks about campus activities, songs, and college cheers, as well as information about the annual Y encampment in western North Carolina, also formed parts of the program. The YMCA played a major role in other campus organizations as well, if only because they were headquartered in its building. It published the annual *Students' Handbook*, conducted fund drives for YMCA work in Europe during World War I, and sponsored a series of revivals in the postwar era, when a kind of demoralization and apathy seemed to afflict the Tech student body.[60]

Tech's first lasting student publication, *Georgia Tech*, appeared in the 1890s. The few issues in the school's archives, dating from the early 1900s, contain fiction, short essays, articles on science and athletics, editorials, and "humor." Alumni and faculty, as well as students, contributed regularly. In 1908 *Georgia Tech* was superseded by a similar publication, the *Yellow Jacket*. New features, such as alumni news and theater reviews were added, along with "news" of the various departments of the school. Meanwhile a college annual made its debut. Called the *Blue Print*, the initial volume was dedicated by the class of 1908 to Nathaniel E. Harris, chairman of Tech's Board of Trustees.[61]

In the fall of 1911, the first issue of the *Technique* appeared on campus. Published weekly, the initial issues concentrated heavily on football. Later the editors found space and time for other campus news and even launched a mini-crusade during the spring of 1912. In a column headed "Lest We Forget," the paper reminded students every week what Tech men should be working for: literary clubs, a business lecture course, better commencement exercises, a swimming pool, a faculty lounge, and student support for campus publications. "Subscribe to the *Technique*," urged the editor, "don't sponge on your roommate."[62]

Initially, two faculty members oversaw the *Technique*'s staff, "serving merely to establish the tone, policy and support of the paper before giving it into the hands of the student managers altogether." By March of 1913 they must have relinquished control. Professor J. S. Coon did not want to hurt anyone's feelings, he told his colleagues, but he felt obliged to protest the "sloppy manner" in which the paper was being printed. It was discouraging to contribute something only to discover later that misspellings and punctuation errors practically destroyed all meaning.[63]

During the last year of Matheson's tenure, a few students made a short-lived effort to produce a humor magazine. "Tech needs a comic magazine like the [Cornell] *Widow* and the *Harvard Lampoon*," declared the *Technique*. One issue, named the *Tornado*, appeared in April 1921. But the *Tornado*'s promoter, it was revealed, was not a Tech student at all. He was out only to exploit the school's vaunted athletic reputation for personal gain. President Matheson consulted with the trustees, who asked one of their number, L. W. "Chip" Robert (class of 1908), to investigate the situation. If the would-be entrepreneur did not desist, the board authorized Matheson to take legal action.[64]

Other student activities that blossomed in the dozen years between 1910 and 1922 included intercollegiate competitions by students in Tech's departments of architecture and electrical engineering, a proliferation of honor societies, music, drama and dance clubs, and a growth of social fraternities. Tech architecture students consistently took top honors in regional competitions, and the electrical engineers placed first in a contest to design a high-voltage transmission line and substation in 1914.[65]

Honorary societies began at Georgia Tech with the establishment of Anak in 1908 and Koseme some four years later. Open to seniors and juniors respectively, both Anak and Koseme were local organizations dedicated to the promotion of leadership, the development of worthy campus activities, and the cultivation of school spirit. The first national honorary society represented at Tech was Phi Kappa Phi. In 1914 Chemistry Professor Gilbert Boggs and H. P. Wood, head of electrical engineering, petitioned for a chapter. Established the following year, the Tech chapter admitted faculty of "ripe scholarship," high character, and leadership, as well as outstanding seniors.[66]

Even those who were not "leaders" or outstanding students could find some group to join. In 1910 Matheson suggested that every department follow the lead of the civil engineers in forming a student society. By the following year, Tech boasted organizations for chemists, architects, and mechanical, electrical and textile engineers. The groups met monthly to hear student papers or lectures by practicing professionals in the various disciplines.[67]

Clubs at Tech were not all service-oriented or meant to promote some educational interest. Many existed simply for fun and entertainment. The Bull Dogs, the Glee Club, and the Drama Club are cases in point. Organized in 1909, Bull Dogs were selected "strictly on a basis of personality and compatibility" rather than athletic or intellectual prowess and devoted themselves to having a good time. Why the club chose the symbol of Tech's arch rival for a name is a mystery. According to one account, Tech's first Glee Club consisted of eight or ten young men who met informally every afternoon in the basement of the Academic Building in 1906. Recognized by the faculty two years later, they made road trips to Savannah, Augusta, and Macon in the 1910–11 academic year. A dispute with their manager in 1912 caused the club to disband temporarily, but by 1914, having reorganized, it gave several concerts around the state and a major performance in Atlanta. The Drama Club made its appearance on campus in 1912. Under the direction of Carolyn Cobb, the students presented "Brown of Harvard" at the Atlanta Theater late in the year. The play was a sellout, but plans for a second production in the spring were quickly squelched. Seniors, decreed the faculty, could lose no more class time if they expected to graduate.[68]

Dancing was extremely popular at Tech, especially after the Athletic Association arranged to convert the old foundry into a combination basketball court and dance hall. Dubbed the "Crystal Palace" by Professor Coon, the facility opened with a formal dance sponsored by the Athletic Association early in 1912. "Get You a 'Skirt' for the Big Occasion," urged the chauvinist *Technique*. A few weeks later a dance club, the Cotillion, organized formally. Members and invited guests met monthly at Segadlo's, a popular Atlanta dance hall. Fraternities also gave dances, as did the junior and senior classes during commencement week. Finally, the faculty had to impose limits. In December 1912, new rules required house dances at fraternities to end by midnight, restricted each fraternity to one formal dance a year, limited the Cotillion Club to five dances annually and the Bull Dogs, Koseme, and the Panhellenic Organization to one each.[69]

Not all the dancing among Tech students took place on campus or at school-sponsored affairs. Segadlo's featured tea dances at which well-known artists like W. C. Handy performed to the delight of Tech students and their dates. One enterprising student organized his own dance club. In 1921 Arthur Murray formed the "Club de Vingt." Composed of the most popular members of Atlanta's younger set, Murray's club included about twenty Tech men and met weekly every Thursday afternoon at the Georgian Terrace Hotel.[70]

Most of Tech's existing musical, dancing, and dramatic clubs suspended operations in late 1917 because of World War I, but the band was an exception. Organized informally in 1908, it acquired its most colorful director in 1914 when Frank "Wop" Roman officially assumed that post. Because no one could imagine military training without martial music, the authorities allowed the band to continue, effecting an arrangement whereby the baseball team was allowed to practice on the athletic field if the band agreed to play for drill. Cooperation continued after the war. Always in demand for civic functions in other Georgia cities, the band traveled to its concerts in trucks belonging to Tech's Reserve Officers' Training Corps units.[71]

Other student groups organized at Tech during Matheson's presidency included a rifle club in 1915 and one called the Kluck Kluck Klan in 1910. This Klan was apparently a recognized student activity, at least it appeared along with all other campus organizations in the *Blue Print* for several years. The 1917 *Blue Print*, however, pictured only a Ku Klux Klan, whose members wore ordinary clothing, but no names were listed under the photograph. By 1921 the Ku Klux Klan appeared in full regalia, complete with cross (unlit) and American flag. Again, no names were given under the photograph. In the same year, President Matheson ordered the *Technique* not to accept a Ku Klux Klan advertisement soliciting new members on campus. Later he asked the Executive Committee of the Board of Trustees to approve his action, stating that "the faculty will not countenance the entrance here of any organization which we believe to be [dedicated to] the usurpation of established law and order." Whether the 1921 *Blue Print* photograph represented a student prank or outright defiance of the authorities is not clear.

But there is no question about where the administration stood on the subject.⁷²

Organizations that the administration *did* authorize in the postwar period included a Tech chapter of the American Legion, a chapter of a national military fraternity, Scabbard and Blade, and chapters of national commerce and journalism fraternities. Student interest in service to the community, begun before the war but suspended in 1917, also revived following the Armistice. Tech's Christmas tree for poor children started in 1916 when 475 children came to the Crystal Palace for carols and gifts contributed by students and friends of Tech. By 1920 Tech had begun to participate in the Empty Stocking Fund drive. Sponsored by the *Atlanta Georgian*, the fund provided gifts for orphaned children. Tech students collected money for the presents, and the Tech Band and Glee Club provided entertainment when they were distributed.⁷³

Social fraternities began at Tech in 1888, the year the school opened. The existence of secret organizations at state-supported colleges offended some people, who thought they had no place at "democratic" institutions. Mississippi barred them in 1913, and Texas was expected to follow suit. At Georgia Tech the faculty thought fraternities could be directed toward "worthy purposes," but the president urged careful supervision of their activities. By 1922 the *Blue Print* listed chapters of sixteen national fraternities and two locals on the Tech campus. However, the attempt of a few Jewish students to secure official recognition for a chapter of Alpha Epsilon Pi encountered opposition. The Student Activities Committee rejected their application in January 1921, and again four months later. The national requested faculty reconsideration the following year, but again recommendation from the Student Activities Committee was negative.⁷⁴

Two additional categories of student activity during the first twenty years of the century deserve consideration: efforts to develop student government and Tech's early involvement in radio. President Matheson's official report for 1914–15 announced the faculty's intention to "increase gradually the principle of self-government in the student body, and thus better prepare [it] for the duties of citizenship." A tentative first step was taken in 1912 when the Georgia

Tech Student Association, an organization designed to control all student activities other than athletics, was created. Promoted by Anak, the association was overseen by a governing board composed of three student members elected by the student body and three faculty appointed by the president. The board nominated candidates for office in all student organizations under its control and assumed financial responsibility for their operations.[75]

For some, the "principle of self-government" was still missing from the campus in 1920 when the *Technique* published a letter of W. P. Stubbs, a brash freshman. Stubbs pointed out that most American colleges and universities had long ago given full governing power to the students. "Our college has not," he complained, because "a few senile members of the Faculty (obviously not so progressive, but with a controlling influence) . . . desire to adhere to old methods rather than keep pace with the advancement of today."[76] The criticism must have hit home. A few months later Dean William Emerson informed the faculty of an Anak-sponsored plan to establish a student council, and by November 1922, its constitution was approved.[77]

Radio came to Tech well before student self-government. While the stack for the new power plant was under construction in 1914, Professors H. P. Wood (electrical engineering), J. B. Edwards (physics), and P. V. Stephens, consultant for the power plant, met with several radio "bugs" on the campus and in the city to plan a new radio station to replace older facilities in the Electrical Building. They arranged to have a large iron ring sealed into the brickwork near the top of the stack and an aerial suspended from it to the steeple of the Academic Building. A room built in the upper end of the boiler room was also planned to serve as a radio room, but the war interrupted developments. Everything was dismantled and the radio room in the power plant was turned over to the aviation cadets, then in training on the Tech campus. Nothing more was done until after the war, when R. B. Flowers and A. D. Whitaker, Jr., decided to push for reactivation of the old station. In the fall of 1919, the Atlanta Radio Club arranged with Professor C. P. Eldred, the new head of electrical engineering, to use the station as its official home, in exchange for which it supplied some equipment and operators. Most of the apparatus in the station was the same as that used in 1916. However, the

135 Tech in the Progressive Era

Signal Corps unit of the Reserve Officers' Training Corps came to the rescue, supplying the station with Atlanta's first radio phone set. More improvements followed and more "bugs" joined the staff. In March 1920, Tech staged a "wireless dance," the first ever held in the South. Tech's band, playing on campus, transmitted music to the Capitol City Club Roof a mile away, where two hundred dancers waited eagerly to participate in the great event. During the summer and fall more funds for radio equipment were secured, and by April 1921, the radio station was operating almost every night. Its supporters hoped the Greater Georgia Tech Fund Drive, then in full swing, would help make it the best equipped station in the country.[78]

Sports and the Tech-Georgia Rivalry

Sports at Georgia Tech, especially football, have been treated extensively by several authors. Only the broad outlines of Tech's athletic history during the Matheson years can be dealt with here. By 1906 athletic affairs were run by the Athletic Association under the control of a faculty-dominated board. W. N. Randle, director of textile engineering, was also director of athletics. It was his job to arrange varsity schedules and to oversee financial affairs of the association, subject to the approval of the faculty. The school physician, Dr. William Jackson, was in charge of a required physical training program for all first-year students, then barred by conference rules from participating in varsity athletics. Matheson and some members of the faculty thought everybody should be required to take Jackson's course, but "mass athletics," a concept developed during World War I, did not come to Tech until 1919.[79]

Tech belonged to the Southern Intercollegiate Athletic Association, a group organized in 1894 soon after football came to the Deep South. The relationship was not always smooth, and in 1914, unwilling to accept certain procedural changes, Tech left the conference. The question of eligibility and who should determine it was one sore point; the large and varied membership and the extensive geographical territory represented in the association also constituted problems from Tech's point of view. Vanderbilt and Alabama had already dropped out. Tech authorities thought Georgia,

Tulane, Louisiana, and Texas would, too, if Tech left. Unable to prevail at an Atlanta meeting on July 1, 1914, Tech resigned from the association a week later, making it clear that it intended to "maintain athletics at the Georgia Tech on the same high plane as in the past." In time, however, Director Randle came to believe that Tech's independent status placed it at a disadvantage. There was a move afoot to organize another conference of the stronger southeastern colleges, something the SIAA planned to discuss when it met in New Orleans in mid-December 1915. Tech sent three representatives to the meeting with authorization to enter the new conference or, if they thought it advisable, to reenter the SIAA. They rejoined after Sewanee proposed a resolution ordering the association to apologize for the incident that caused Tech to withdraw in 1914.[80]

Tech's athletic program suffered a minor setback when W. N. Randle's resignation, signed by his wife, was presented to the Board of Trustees in September 1917. After purchasing a Gainesville, Georgia, cotton mill that proved unprofitable, Randle, "in a moment of panic . . . left the city for parts unknown." He left, owing Georgia Tech for used textile equipment about to be replaced by newly donated machinery, but not before borrowing $1,500 in the name of the Tech Athletic Association and converting it to his own use.[81]

Professor J. B. Crenshaw, head of the modern languages department, replaced Randle as director of athletics. He had to face what President Matheson feared was a disturbing trend toward "professionalism" then developing in college athletics. In November 1917, the president charged that the "sporting element" was exerting great pressure on authorities to schedule post-season games. Matheson was totally opposed. A "pernicious and undermining element" acting in the name of patriotism, he told the trustees, was using "subterfuge" which, if successful, would only result in lowering the school's standards. Following the war, Matheson's fears deepened. Newspaper stories reported enormous expansion and specialization in college athletics. A very few men received great attention from the coaches and the public while the vast majority of the student body did not participate in any athletic activity. The president was particularly irked by gambling and the press accounts that seemed to contribute to it. He pledged to do all he could to combat the trend, and the faculty vowed their support. They named a committee to investigate ways and means to fight the evil.[82]

Immediately following the Armistice, a move developed in American colleges to adopt the physical training system employed so effectively during the war. Called "mass athletics," it required regular daily exercise by all students rather than highly specialized training for a few. Professor Crenshaw attended a meeting of the National Athletic Association in January 1919 at which the program was discussed. He hoped it would result in a department of physical training at every college under the leadership of someone who enjoyed professorial rank. Due largely to the establishment of several ROTC units on the Tech campus, much of Crenshaw's vision became reality. President Matheson reported in 1920 that, thanks to the "sanitary living" required by the ROTC and the Department of Athletics, more students than ever were taking part in exercises or various forms of athletics. And it was paying off. Even a recurrence of the dreaded flu did minor damage; only two deaths were recorded that year, and one of those resulted from "unavoidable" surgery.[83]

When K. G. Matheson became president of Georgia Tech, the school fielded only two varsity teams: baseball and football. Baseball, played in Brisbine Park before Tech had its own field, was the moneymaking sport before John W. Heisman became Tech's first professional full-time coach in 1904. As a member of the Atlanta Basketball League, Tech played basketball in 1906 against the city's Athletic Club, the YMCA and Fort MacPherson. Games with Georgia and Auburn were also scheduled. But in 1910 more ambitious plans to play other schools had to be canceled because Tech had no suitable place to practice. The conversion of the old foundry into the Crystal Palace made intercollegiate basketball possible in 1913 for the first time since 1908. Varsity play was finally regularized in 1919, and in 1921 Tech met the University of Georgia in a Southern Intercollegiate Athletic Association Tournament. Ironically, athletic relations with Athens had been severed two years earlier. No scheduled meetings between the two had occurred since the break, but as the *Technique* commented, "Both schools had entered the meet, the forces of destiny had ordained that they should meet—who can . . . resist Destiny?"[84]

138   *Engineering the New South*

Track, swimming, boxing, tennis, and golf were all part of Tech's sports program by the time Matheson left Atlanta in 1922. Only track had a full-time coach; students ran the other teams. Tech's participation in the Intercollegiate Golf Association, urged by Atlanta alumni of Princeton, Yale, and Harvard, was delayed briefly because Athletic Director Crenshaw forgot to reply to a notice that the school had been elected to membership. Meanwhile, R. T. "Bobby" Jones, described then as a "golf specialist," began studying mechanical engineering at Tech. He graduated in 1922 and by 1930 had made golfing history by winning the United States and British Open and Amateur titles.[85]

As described in chapter 2, football began at Georgia Tech in 1892, but the game played the following year in Athens is the one most fans remember because Tech's thirty-three-year-old playing trainer-coach, Leonard Wood, led Tech to its first victory over the University of Georgia. During the next ten years, Tech played what one unidentified commentator described as " 'in and out' football, mostly out." The team lost to Georgia, Auburn, Sewanee, and others so often that a dedicated few started a drive to hire Tech's first professional full-time coach. From the beginning, the officers and "friends" of Tech's Athletic Association knew they wanted John W. Heisman, Clemson's coach, and by the 1904 football season, they had him. In his first year, Heisman led the team to victories over Tennessee, Florida, and Cumberland, a tie with Clemson, and most satisfying of all, a 23–6 win over Georgia.[86]

Heisman's first contract called for him to coach football and baseball, for which he would receive $2,250 plus 30 percent of the net gate receipts from all varsity games. Later contracts raised his salary but dropped the gate percentage feature. He also began coaching basketball and track and secured permission from Tech authorities to serve as president of the Atlanta Baseball Association and athletic director of the Atlanta Athletic Club. In 1918 Heisman cut back his duties, contracting to coach only football between September 1 and December 15. A second contract that year obligated him to coach the Student Army Training Corps teams as well. By that time Heisman was spending part of his time in private business.[87]

By all accounts Heisman was a colorful, even eccentric, character whose principle contribution to football, besides the winning record

Tech in the Progressive Era

amassed at Tech, was the forward pass, which he claimed was suggested to him while scouting a game between Georgia and the University of North Carolina.[88] Tech was unbeaten and tied only twice during the 1915, 1916, and 1917 seasons. Named southern champion three times (1916, 1917, and 1918), the Golden Tornado won national recognition when it beat Heisman's alma mater, the University of Pennsylvania, 41–0 in 1917. A 98–0 victory over the Carlisle Indians and a 68–7 triumph over Auburn on Thanksgiving Day was frosting on the cake.[89]

The *Technique* thought the 1917 football schedule was tougher than any ever played by a southern college. Besides Pennsylvania, Carlisle, and Auburn, Tech met Wake Forest, Furman, Davidson, Washington and Lee, Vanderbilt, and Tulane. Vanderbilt partisans did not wait for the game to start before attacking Tech. On October 21 a sportswriter for the *Nashville Banner* sneered that while the Commodores might make no headlines on the gridiron that year, their record would not be equaled by any school in the "larger game" being waged in Europe. Listing the names of Vanderbilt football greats who were in service, the columnist demanded: "Is there any other Southern college that can exhibit such a record? What have the Yellow Jackets to show that they are behind the government in the struggle with Germany? Instead, the Georgians are content to sit steady and boast of their chances of winning . . . the southern football championship (again). . . . What right has any team to brag . . . when the U.S. is in need of just such men as these?"[90] Morgan Blake, sports editor for the *Atlanta Journal* and a Vanderbilt alumnus, denounced the "slander" of Tech's patriotism. Noting that the entire senior class volunteered when America went to war, he proceeded to list the current status of the 1916 squad. Fifteen were on active duty, two had applied for aviation school, one was in "industrial service," four were exempt, three were under age, and one had a very high draft number. Despite the loss, Tech still had a great 1917 team of which it was very proud. Tech beat Vanderbilt 83–0 a couple of weeks later.[91]

Whatever Nashville thought, New York and Philadelphia were impressed. So were Grantland Rice and Walter Camp. Quoted in a Chicago paper copied by the *Technique*, Camp declared: "If someone does not soon do something to our old friend J. W. Heisman and his

Georgia Tech team, the football prestige of the North will be dimmed past brushing up."[92]

Perhaps the most glowing praise for Tech came from the *New York Sun*, whose sports expert thought that anyone questioning Tech's supremacy following the beating it gave to Auburn on Thanksgiving Day must be suffering from a "Turkey hangover." It was too bad that Heisman's best team materialized in a "lack-lustre" football season, he thought. If Tech had all the veteran players who went to war, she would have been even more formidable. On the other hand, the war made it possible for Tech to attract national attention. Without it, Penn would have played Army and Carlisle some other northern team, not the Golden Tornado.[93]

Tech played the undefeated University of Pittsburgh in 1918, losing 32–0, but shutting out every other opponent on its schedule. In 1919 Pittsburgh beat Tech again by a narrower margin. That was Heisman's last year at Tech, and authorities began a frantic search to find his successor. They finally located him in the assistant coach's office where he had served as Heisman's second in command for several years. W. A. Alexander, or "Coach Alex," graduated from Tech in 1912 as valedictorian of his class. In addition to his duties in the athletic department he taught mathematics until elected head coach in April 1920. Some doubted Alexander's ability to keep Tech's winning streak alive, but the team and the *Technique* did not. "The fellows seem to work even better under him than under Coach Heisman," reported the newspaper in late September. By October the editor detected a "real change" in football under the new management. No longer were students and visitors barred from practice; "broader," more "reasonable" training rules were introduced and a friendlier, more cooperative spirit seemed to prevail, especially among alumni. Adored by his players who found him a good listener and adviser as well as a respected leader, Coach Alex was also popular with the student body. They gave him a gold watch before the Davidson game in 1920. As the *Technique* put it: "Since Coach Alex has taken charge there is a change in the team. The youngest coach [30] in major football, he is probably the most popular, and bids fair to prove himself the peer of them all. Not only is Coach the idol of the members of the team, but of the student body as well."[94]

Alexander's first three seasons as head coach were very successful.

Only Pittsburgh beat Tech in 1920, and only one other team, Georgetown, managed to score a single point. The next year Tech lost only to Rutgers, and in 1922 it defeated every team on the schedule but Navy and Notre Dame. The southern championship went to Tech for all three years, but there was criticism as well as praise for Tech's performance under Alexander. In 1920 fans of Centre College in Kentucky charged the Georgians with unnecessary roughness and the visiting crowd with unsportsmanlike conduct. Pitt claimed that Tech used ineligible players, and Vanderbilt called the Golden Tornado a "bunch of hoodlums who regard football as a prize fight." All three refused to play Tech the following year. The *Technique* issued a sarcastic rebuttal, noting that a Tech player suffered a broken jaw in the Vanderbilt game, and even the northern papers considered Pittsburgh's complaint "feeble."[95]

Obviously the well-circulated attacks, some of which came from other schools in the SIAA, stung Tech authorities. An article in a national magazine, the *Outlook*, stimulated a letter to the editor from President Matheson early in 1921. The magazine ought to check out the facts before printing "rumors," he complained. If it had, it would have learned that Tech had been absolved of the unnecessary roughness charges by the game officials and of the ineligibility charge by the SIAA. Tech ought to have a press club, commented the *Technique*, so it could counteract the biased coverage of a hostile press. Efforts to found a Tech news bureau began at once and by the following spring a press club, headed by English Professor J. E. McDaniel, made its appearance on campus. At first it planned to concentrate on athletic events, but later it promised to feed news of student achievements, the co-op program and other campus activities to over one hundred dailies throughout the country.[96]

No history of Georgia Tech can avoid at least a cursory glance at the series of events that have contributed to the long-standing athletic rivalry between Georgia Tech and the University of Georgia. The trouble began in 1893 when Tech, led by a superannuated sub-apprentice with a Harvard medical degree and a commission in the army, visited Athens to play football. As Captain Leonard Wood ran touchdowns and Tech's score mounted, the crowd grew rowdy. Missiles rained on the field, fist fights developed among the spectators, and finally, the game over, the hosts chased the visitors to the train.

142   *Engineering the New South*

In the next ten years, the captain having returned to active duty, Georgia beat Tech five times. They tied once and did not play at all for four seasons. But then Heisman came to Tech and Georgia lost four years straight, which may have contributed to the next imbroglio.[97]

In November 1907, Tech was accused of violating SIAA recruitment rules and paying players through a shady "scholarship" scheme devised by President Matheson, Coach Heisman, and a prominent alumnus. Specifically, Tech authorities were charged with persuading, by improper means, a promising football player to enroll at Tech rather than Georgia, which also wanted his services. In exchange for steering Tech students to a certain haberdashery shop, the athlete could expect to earn as much as six hundred dollars a year. The charges were brought by alumni of the University of Georgia and "outsiders"; officers of the Athens school were not officially involved. Finally, after a lengthy investigation by the executive committee of the Southern Intercollegiate Athletic Association, Tech and all of its personnel were exonerated. In Matheson's view, the whole incident was the work of "Tech's avowed enemies in Atlanta."[98]

Relations between Tech and Georgia were so strained in the spring of 1911 that officials of both schools considered cutting all athletic ties. Instead they agreed to enforce diligently a ruling of the University of Georgia Board of Trustees that barred all signs and pictures from their respective athletic fields which might "excite feeling of resentment" among visiting teams and spectators. This tactic worked for the 1911 football season. A December issue of the *Technique* printed an official letter of thanks from the Athens student body, commending Tech for the cordial reception and "fair treatment" accorded at a recent game in Atlanta.[99]

The era of good feelings did not last long. At a baseball game in Athens in May 1916, Tech was grossly insulted when a senior parade ended its march around the field by dumping a load of manure in front of the stands occupied by Tech sponsors. Other tasteless "stunts" suggested that the gold in Tech's colors, or "yellow" as Georgia called it, was an accurate reflection of Tech's spirit. President Matheson and his faculty demanded an immediate apology if relations between the two schools were to continue. It came, but in

Matheson's view, with so many qualifications that it seemed insincere. In a subsequent letter addressed to the chancellor of the university, Matheson noted that several years earlier, when a far less serious "discourtesy" was shown to Georgia, Tech's faculty and student body found the guilty party and expelled him. Tech thought Georgia ought to do as much.[100]

The final confrontation came in 1919. Again the occasion was a baseball game, or rather a three-game series. On May 9 the university visited Tech. After the game, which Georgia won, students from both schools began snatching freshman hats or "rat caps" and a fight was narrowly avoided. A few minutes later, a former university student deliberately zigzagged his car through crowds crossing North Avenue and injured a Tech student. Later, more cap-snatching took place as well as a number of street fights. At another game the next day, trouble was avoided at the field, but more disturbances occurred before the Georgia crowd boarded the train for Athens.

Tech and Georgia had a return match scheduled for Athens the next weekend. Fearing trouble, J. B. Crenshaw, Tech's athletic director, proposed to his counterpart at Georgia that some kind of pledge by the students of both schools be taken before the teams met. It was agreed that all students would behave as gentlemen and that trophy caps would be left at home. On Saturday, May 17, Georgia's seniors, having marched through town, wound onto the field for their annual parade. Leading it was a float bearing a tank marked "Argonne" and carrying a sign on one side reading "Georgia in France 1917." Behind it was an automobile occupied by three persons dressed in Tech old gold sweaters and wearing Tech caps. Its sign said "Tech in Atlanta." A printed program distributed throughout the stands made the same point: while a patriotic Georgia was fighting in France, a cowardly Tech was playing football in Atlanta. Other affronts of a similar nature inflamed the visitors. Alert Tech faculty moved quickly through the stands to control student resentment, but it was not easy. Finally, its patience exhausted when no apology was forthcoming, Tech broke all athletic ties with the university.[101]

Relations between the two schools did not resume for years. But almost from the beginning, journalists, Atlanta businessmen, and alumni of both schools made strenuous efforts to effect a rapprochement. As long as Matheson was president, he made it clear that unless Georgia offered "due apologies" he would never change his mind. If overruled, he would resign. It did not come to that because Matheson found another job in 1922. But it is also clear that enormous and not always subtle pressure was being exerted on Tech students and faculty to resume relations. Finally, a series of conferences between J. B. Crenshaw and S. V. Sanford, chancellor of the University of Georgia, ended the controversy in 1924.[102]

Tech and World War I

The First World War had a tremendous impact on American colleges and universities. Some liberal arts institutions practically ceased operations. Other schools, because of their specialized nature, expanded dramatically, adding new departments to their regular offerings and retaining much of the new work after the fighting stopped. Tech fell into the latter category.

In 1916, even those government officials who pledged to "keep us out of war" felt compelled to prepare for any eventuality. One phase of the national preparedness campaign called for the training of 50,000 military officers. The nation's colleges and universities seemed ideally suited to the purpose, and in June 1916, Congress passed the National Defense Act, which led to the establishment of the Reserve Officers' Training Corps on the campuses of institutions that could qualify.[103] Tech's first ROTC unit was not formally approved until March 1918, but that did not prevent the school from placing itself at the nation's disposal. Even before Congress declared war in April 1917, President Matheson was in Washington conferring with the War Department about how Tech might contribute. The school also joined the Intercollegiate Intelligence Agency, a Washington-based private organization engaged in compiling a census of all college students and alumni with special training who were willing and able to serve their country. But most important, through Phinehas V. Stephens, a 1905 alumnus, lobbyist, and consultant to Georgia Tech, Matheson was in touch with the Aero Club of America, an organization planning to establish, endow, and equip departments of aeronautics at colleges that could qualify. The club was interested in Georgia Tech, and the Board of Trustees instructed Matheson to cultivate that interest.[104]

Phinehas Stephens also tried to secure federal support for a department of aviation at Tech, but nothing came of it until after war was declared. In late May 1917, Matheson announced that Tech had been selected as one of eight aviation cadet training centers to be established immediately. Tech had to provide quarters and instruction for twenty-five cadets by mid-June and a total of two hundred shortly thereafter. The program called for eight weeks of intensive training in physics, mechanical and electrical engineering, and laboratory work. Three men from Tech's staff were dispatched immediately to study an operating program in Toronto with instructions to be back in Atlanta by June 11 in order to meet their first classes. In exchange, the government contracted to pay Tech $5,000 per month, provide all necessary equipment, and assign to the campus a drill sergeant and commissioned officer to oversee the whole program.[105]

To accommodate the incoming cadets, Tech moved commencement ahead by two days, canceled most of the usual festivities, and allowed all students not graduating to go home early. Many of the seniors were gone already, having been graduated ahead of schedule in order to enter service. But a number of changes had to be made before the regular student body returned in the fall. These involved converting the old gym in the basement of Knowles Dormitory into a mess hall, building a new kitchen, and finding other quarters for the freshmen who usually occupied Knowles.[106]

The School of Military Aeronautics at Tech was strictly a ground school designed to provide basic instruction for flight training elsewhere. The object was threefold: to teach fundamental "military duties," to provide the technical courses prescribed by the Signal Corps, and to eliminate those candidates who were found to be mentally or morally unfit for a commission. From July 5, 1917, to January 12, 1918, the Tech Military Aeronautics program trained some four hundred future pilots. Then its mission was changed abruptly to the production of aviation supply officers. Much larger than its predecessor, the Supply Officers' Training School was the only school of its type in the United States, which the *Technique* took to be a great honor for Georgia Tech. In fact, the pilot cadets were transferred to the University of Texas and Princeton because the entire program was being consolidated and those schools possessed mechanical equipment superior to that at Georgia Tech. In May 1918, the Supply Officers' Training School closed down, too. By that time Tech authorities were planning the operation of other war-related programs.[107]

Some of Tech's prewar facilities were already "mobilized." Wireless telegraphy began seriously at Tech in 1912, and by 1916 student operators were in contact with amateur radio "bugs" all over Georgia, gaining valuable experience that they could employ in war or peace. When the Military Aeronautics School arrived, it used Tech's station, as did seniors enrolled in a special radio course designed to train them for service in the Signal Corps. The corps supplied the most modern equipment, and the students, on completion of the course, were eligible to enroll in an army radio school which trained radio officers.

Other wartime programs established at Georgia Tech included a motor transport course for personnel stationed at Camp Gordon in the northeastern outskirts of Atlanta and a training operation for 550 army draftees. Designed to produce carpenters, machinists, blacksmiths, mechanics, and technicians of all types, the program went a long way to replace the military personnel and income Tech lost with the shutdown of the Supply Officers' Training School.[108]

The aviation cadets were not the only ones in uniform on Tech's campus in 1917. Soon after war was declared the authorities decreed that all students had to drill one hour a week unless they were physically disabled. Not much was accomplished before the term ended, but during the summer the faculty adopted rules that significantly altered the look if not the behavior of Tech undergraduates. All were required to wear uniforms and report for drill every day. A regular army man, "Sergeant Blake," tried to whip the boys into soldiers, but with relatively little success. Late in November 1917, the *Technique* railed at students who appeared all over town in odd mixtures of "half civil, half soldier" garments, and the commandant of the School of Military Aeronautics declared that men who took no pride in the uniform should not be allowed to wear it. Things improved considerably when Lieutenant Colonel E. W. Hubbard, a retired Coast Artillery officer, was ordered by the War Department to take charge of Georgia Tech's newly created Department of Military Sci-

Tech in the Progressive Era

ence. As commandant and professor of military science and tactics, Hubbard soon effected improvements, leading the *Technique* to hope that Tech might soon win recognition as an officers' training school.[109]

Early in 1918 President Matheson, Chairman of the Board Harris, and Colonel Hubbard went to Washington to secure arms, equipment, and formal approval for ROTC units on campus. Promised one hundred rifles by the adjutant general's office, they were assured recognition as an ROTC institution as soon as the weapons reached the campus. The guns arrived on March 26, and so did official authorization for signal corps and coast artillery units. But circumstances prevented the complete organization of either. Instead, Tech had a de facto infantry unit, not formally authorized until later in 1918.[110]

Faculty members also went to war. At least two professors of electrical engineering left with the seniors to join the officers' training program at Fort MacPherson in the spring of 1917. One of them, H. P. Wood, resigned in order to come back to Tech as vice president of the academic board in the School of Military Aeronautics, but he left that post also to go on active duty as a captain in the army engineers. Two English instructors were in service by June 1917, as well as two men from Heisman's coaching staff, R. A. Clay and W. A. Alexander. By the middle of 1918, besides Wood, Clay, Alexander, and the two English instructors (Robert M. Burrowes and Richard Kirk), Tech contributed Major James N. G. Nesbitt, experimental engineering, to the ordnance department, and G. A. McKee, modern languages, and T. R. Weems, instructor of physical culture, to active service.[111] Even President Matheson donned a uniform. In March 1918, the Board of Trustees granted him six months leave of absence to go to France as a member of the National War Work Council of the YMCA. The council studied conditions at the front and planned welfare services for members of the American Expeditionary Forces. The students staged an impressive parade and military review in Matheson's honor. Planned by Colonel Hubbard, the ceremonies included stirring renditions of "Dixie" and "Ramblin' Wreck" by "Wop" Roman's band and the entire student body marching past the reviewing stand in their new khaki uniforms.[112]

President Matheson returned to the United States and Georgia Tech in September 1918, just in time to preside over the school's participation in the Student Army Training Corps. Organized by the War Department for the purpose of keeping men in school for military and scholastic instruction until they were required in active service, the program was under the direction of the War Department's Committee on Education and Special Training. Its aim was to disrupt the students' regular education as little as possible while at the same time preparing them for immediate service when called. Plans called for the traditional four-year program, with necessary military modifications, to be completed in two by conducting schools twelve months a year. Army officers assigned to each campus supplied military instruction and discipline, and the government paid each school a regular daily fee per man.

Tech's ROTC program was discontinued when the SATC appeared on campus and Colonel Hubbard was ordered to a new assignment. Major Radcliffe Hermance took charge of the new operation. Students who qualified physically were inducted into army, navy, or marine SATC units at Tech, one of only a few schools in the country to boast a marine unit. The SATC was also divided into an A (collegiate officer training) section and a B (vocational) section. The B section incorporated the enlisted men in Tech's existing technician training program, begun in June 1918.[113]

No one regretted the demise of the SATC, which came about a month after the Armistice. During its brief existence, elements of military life overshadowed everything on campus. Schedules were disrupted, coursework suffered, classrooms and sleeping quarters were makeshift and crowded, and student morale deteriorated by an alarming degree. Consequently, college administrators welcomed the program's end, even though it meant another series of wrenching adjustments in scheduling and curricula. Replies to a War Department survey early in December 1918 indicated that 75 percent of all participating schools wanted to drop the program at once. So did the students. According to the 1919 *Blue Print*, the end of SATC was "a godsend." Tech "readjusted herself admirably," claimed the yearbook, "and in less than a month had successfully eliminated many of the disagreeable features that had crept in during . . . the war."[114]

The end of the war and the SATC did not mean the end of everything military at Georgia Tech. The faculty voted to reactivate an ROTC program in December 1918. The board heartily approved and so did Washington; only the students objected. On February 14, 1919, President Matheson reported a "Bolshevik movement" that developed when drill was reinstituted. He met with representatives of each class (some of whom were more "Bolshevik" than others) to explain why they must conform. First of all, drill contributed to student health; second, the school would receive no material benefits from the ROTC program unless the students accepted it; and third, the War Department was making sure that America would never again be caught unprepared. Colleges had to do their part by furnishing the officers for any future war. Disarmed, the "Bolsheviks" went back to their dormitories, and by the time Matheson resigned, almost 90 percent of some 1,500 eligible students participated in ROTC. By that time also, Tech boasted six military units (infantry, coast artillery, signal corps, air service, motor transport, and ordnance).[115]

With the war over, the SATC dismantled, and something like normality restored to the campus, President Matheson spent the last three years of his tenure in an effort to realize what he began earlier: a "Greater Georgia Tech." To do it, he had to appeal for support in Washington and New York as well as in the state legislature and the Georgia business community, and he had to compete with partisans of the University of Georgia, who hoped to secure for that institution some of the same facilities and funding he wanted to win for Georgia Tech. Given the long-standing rivalry between the two schools, the traditional disinterest (not to say hostility) of rural legislators for projects based in Atlanta, and the severe economic dislocation that followed World War I, it is surprising that he achieved as much as he did.

Matheson never had any misgivings about seeking federal support for Georgia Tech. In 1907 he endorsed a lobbying effort in Congress, organized by the National Association of State Mining Schools, saying, "I am thoroughly in accord with the movement to secure federal aid. The Department of Mining is in its infancy here and needs all the help it can get."[116] Tech's Industrial Education Department was funded in part by the federal government through the Smith-Hughes Act of 1917, and war-related programs like the School of Aeronautics, the motor transport course, and the technicians' training course were totally supported by Washington. So was a program for the rehabilitation of disabled veterans begun in 1919. But the federally assisted program that Tech authorities hoped to attract above all others after the war was still in the talking stages.[117]

Postwar Frustration: The Engineering Experiment Station and Inadequate Funding

As part of the preparedness campaign in 1916, Congress considered the Newlands Bill, a measure to fund state engineering experiment stations. Patterned after earlier legislation to promote agricultural science, the Newlands Bill as originally drawn planned to award $15,000 a year to existing land-grant colleges. In Georgia that meant the money would go to the State Agricultural College in Athens. Amended to death, the Newlands Bill died in committee, and a substitute, written by Phinehas V. Stephens, allowed state legislatures to locate the proposed engineering experiment stations at the state school possessing the best engineering program. Stephens was a Tech graduate of 1905 and on the school's payroll as a lobbyist and consultant. He found two Georgians, Senator Hoke Smith and Representative William S. Howard, to introduce his bill, but, like the Newlands measure, it met stiff opposition. Besides offending land-grant colleges, the Smith-Howard Bill challenged the recommendations of the National Research Council, which wanted to award federal money on the basis of "meritorious projects" in each state rather than to allocate it on an "institutional level." R. C. MacLaurin, president of Massachusetts Institute of Technology and a friend of Matheson's, formed a national committee in December 1918 to salvage the Smith-Howard Bill, but to no avail. Like its predecessor, the measure died in committee.[118]

While opposition to the Smith-Howard Bill was building in Washington, Matheson learned it was also organizing in Athens. In October 1918, he told Tech's Board of Trustees that Professor A. M. Soule, head of the State Agricultural College in Athens, planned to set up a "technical department" in that school. Soule also intended to secure the engineering research station should the Smith-Howard Bill pass. The board directed Matheson to arrange a meeting with Soule, but six weeks passed and no reply came from Athens. Finally,

Soule declined to see Matheson because he did not think "an interview on the subject was necessary." Soule continued his efforts, even after the legislature voted in August 1919 to locate the prospective experiment station at Tech. Later that year, Matheson and Phinehas Stephens visited Chicago for a meeting of the American Land-Grant College Association. On the agenda was the Smith-Howard Bill, which the engineering section of the association supported unanimously. But when the presidents' section convened, Soule strongly dissented. His school wanted the original association-sponsored (Newlands) bill, which gave proposed engineering experiment stations to land-grant colleges only. By a narrow margin, Soule's faction prevailed, despite the fact that the rank and file in the convention supported Smith-Howard. Back in Atlanta, Matheson told the board:

> Now that [Soule] has openly declared his intention of developing [engineering] at the State Agricultural College, it is clearly the duty of the Georgia School of Technology to bring the matter squarely before the people of the State and have the State decide the functions of the Colleges composing the University System; otherwise the opportunities, harmony and efficiency of the University System will be jeopardized and disruption will follow.[119]

The conflict intensified. Matheson pressed the board to protect Tech's interests, and the board responded by naming a committee, including Matheson and Chairman Harris, to meet with a committee of the State Agricultural College Board to work toward some kind of reconciliation. The committee was unsuccessful. By June 8, 1920, Tech's board adopted a resolution that as "a matter of justice and equity," Tech should be the land-grant college of engineering in Georgia and therefore entitled to what it had never had: income from the Morrill Acts of 1862 and 1890. Meanwhile, efforts to pass a successor to the Smith-Howard Bill continued in Washington, and President Soule continued to declare that he would do everything in his power to secure for his school whatever it might provide. By 1922 Tech's board was still talking about "equity and justice" but still hoping also to narrow the "unbridgeable chasm" that was developing between the schools. A meeting with the Prudential Committee of the University of Georgia took place on March 1, 1922. Phinehas Stephens was there and Tech made a strong case for its right to the proposed experiment station, citing its charter, enrollment, and national reputation as an engineering school. It also noted that the state legislature had made Tech the state engineering experiment station, eligible to receive whatever funds might accrue from a federal bill. The Tech group proposed three resolutions: that at the next legislative session Tech be designated the engineering division of the land-grant College of Georgia and authorized to receive one-half of the funds from the first and second Morrill Acts; that officials from the University of Georgia stop opposing Tech's efforts to secure passage of the engineering experiment station bill then before Congress; and that all friends and alumni of both schools urge passage of the federal bill so that Tech could proceed to organize the engineering and industrial research authorized by the state of Georgia and proposed in the Greater Georgia Tech Campaign launched in 1921. Tech also proposed that the Carnegie or Rockefeller foundations conduct a study in order to define the exact mission of the university and the technological school. With luck, it would improve relations and overcome the "almost chaotic" situation in Georgia's system of higher education, a situation that was the result of long-standing "political and economic expedience."[120]

The University of Georgia Prudential Committee made no response to Tech's resolutions, so on March 24, 1922, N. P. Pratt, chairman of the Executive Committee of the Tech Board of Trustees, jogged its collective memory. In fact, the Prudential Committee had met but did not deign to advise Tech of its deliberations until Pratt prodded the committee's secretary. The Prudential Committee had essentially referred everything to the full University System Board of Trustees, expressing its opinion, meanwhile, that what Tech proposed would cause serious damage to the educational interest of the state. By that time Matheson had resigned and his successor had to cope with the problem.[121]

As if jurisdictional disputes and struggles with the University of Georgia over federal largesse were not enough, Tech authorities also had to deal with a severe shortage of funds. In 1919, the school was serving 1,365 full-time collegiate students in a plant designed to accommodate 700. Its regular income from the state was the same as that provided in 1915 ($100,000), yet inflation had essentially halved the value of the dollar. The federally supported educational programs already discussed helped a great deal, but increased state appropriations were essential if Tech were to fulfill its mission.[122]

In 1919, Tech department heads were urged to make personal appeals to private industry in order to upgrade their worn-out and obsolete equipment. President Matheson found that young instructors earned as much as $2,750 elsewhere; Tech's maximum offer was $1,400. There was no gymnasium because Tech's had been converted into a dining hall during the war. Students were sitting in hallways and every classroom was occupied every hour of the day. Consequently, when the legislature met in the summer of 1919 Tech asked, among other things, for a $25,000 increase in its maintenance fund (to $125,000) and a special appropriation of $125,000 to complete the Mechanical Engineering Building begun in 1911. It secured the first and most of the second ($100,000). Nevertheless, Matheson directed a professor of commerce to begin a lobbying campaign for an additional increase in Tech's maintenance appropriation.[123]

Extracting funds from the legislature in 1920 was more difficult. Rumors reached Tech that students of the University of Georgia were using Tech's severance of athletic relations as a talking point "against Atlanta" in the capitol. Matheson feared that Tech's appropriation bill, which called for an increase to $250,000, might be in trouble because the increase requested by the entire University System totaled almost a million dollars that year. The president's concern was well founded. At a called meeting of the Board of Trustees, Matheson reported that despite Tech's "almost desperate" financial situation, and House approval of the $125,000 increase, the Senate cut Tech's amount to $100,000. Then, due to differences between the two Houses having nothing to do with Tech, the increased appropriations bill was tabled and therefore lost. Without it, Matheson told the board, Tech could not operate.[124]

The legislative oversight touched off a frantic scramble for ways to raise enough money to run the school. Convinced that the lawmakers at their next session would vote funds to cover whatever Tech might borrow, the board devised a scheme to issue notes in various denominations up to $100,000. Then, to show its faith, the board personally subscribed for $10,000 worth. Meanwhile, Georgia Rotarians mounted a campaign to raise a loan fund for the school. By mid-October 1920, Atlanta members had pledged $54,000. But the notes issued by the Board of Trustees were not moving well, leading the trustees to ask the governor for a special session. President Matheson did manage to pull one financial rabbit out of a philanthropic hat: in November 1920 he secured a gift of $40,000 from the General Education Board. Together with the amount realized from the Rotary loan, about $30,000, and a generous grant from the Atlanta city council, Tech had enough to operate for the academic year.[125]

Matheson's heroic efforts to scrape together enough money for bare essentials in 1920–21 led the Tech faculty to adopt a resolution praising his "unwearying efforts" and "unfailing tact." They were especially pleased that their salaries had not been cut or withheld, something which had occurred at the University of Georgia when the state, due to depressed economic conditions, failed to meet its obligations on time. But the situation did not improve. After the 1921 legislative session, Matheson told a called meeting of the board that because only $112,500 of a requested $225,000 had been appropriated, Tech could expect a deficit of $100,000 in 1921–22. As a last resort, the faculty voted to charge tuition, something recently approved by the General Assembly. The board set the figures at $100 per year for state residents and $175 for all others. Matheson estimated that 1,300 students would produce $60,000, leaving about $40,000 to be "found" elsewhere. Meanwhile, department heads were enjoined to cut every cost to the bone in order to avoid salary cuts and reductions in force. In the end, Tech had to float a loan to get through the 1921–22 academic year. N. P. Pratt, acting as "interim executive" after Matheson left for Drexel on April 1, 1922, secured a $125,000 line of credit from the Fourth National Bank of Atlanta. For collateral, the school used pledges to the Greater Georgia Tech Campaign, due to be collected in October.[126]

The Greater Georgia Tech Campaign

The phrase "Greater Georgia Tech" first appeared in Matheson's fund-raising correspondence in 1906, when he was soliciting funds to purchase a few land lots adjacent to the original campus. By 1914 the term was tied to Tech's first professional fund-raising campaign initiated to provide Georgia Tech with a new power plant, better laboratory facilities, and a research bureau. Phinehas V. Stephens, on the payroll as consultant for the construction of the new building, agreed to head a drive for $500,000. Business conditions were poor early in 1914 and many Atlantans thought Stephens would do well to raise $25,000 in the city. But he thought a little "education" about what the new plant could do for Georgia business and industry might change some minds. About $80,000 was subscribed in the city before the outbreak of war in Europe caused a postponement of the campaign. Three years later, interest revived but an ineffective fundraiser and dissatisfaction in the Board of Trustees resulted in another postponement.[127]

When the war ended, increased enrollment and antiquated facilities made new construction imperative. President Matheson pressed the trustees to implement Stephen's overall plans for campus expansion, but they were unresponsive until March 1920, when they authorized the consultant to direct a full-scale Greater Georgia Tech Campaign. More ambitious than anything undertaken before, Stephens's grand design called for the organization of a national alumni association, the generation of "ample funds" for campaign expenses, and the employment of enough trained assistants to carry out his elaborate scheme. All, he argued, were essential to success.[128]

Stephens began by interesting the New York club of Tech alumni in the Greater Georgia Tech Campaign. Under his leadership, they spearheaded a drive to locate all former Tech students and to consolidate some twenty existing Tech alumni clubs scattered throughout the country. Attempts to organize Tech alumni began years earlier, but lasting success was not achieved until 1920. By October the organizing alumni agreed to raise $100,000 among their own members to put the Greater Tech Campaign before the public, nationwide as well as in Georgia. Tech's board responded appropriately by supporting a move to make the president of the National Alumni Association an ex officio member of their body.[129]

With alumni organization underway and "ample funds" promised, Stephens moved quickly to secure the necessary trained assistants. He found them through Wickes Wamboldt, a professional fund raiser whom he recommended to Tech authorities as associate director of the Greater Tech Campaign effort, and by the fall of 1920, the campaign train was ready to roll, literally. Exhibits at state and county fairs, canvassing by field men assigned to confer with business and industrial leaders all over Georgia, statewide committees, contacts with trade associations—all were preliminary to a spectacular staged in November 1920. A large party of "prominent Georgians," led by Governor Hugh Dorsey and several important alumni and joined later by President Matheson, embarked on a steam-driven odyssey to Cincinnati, Pittsburgh, Buffalo, Niagara Falls, Boston, New York, and Washington. They inspected universities, plants, and laboratories, listened to lectures by industrialists, educators, and government bureaucrats, and dined well and often. Back in Atlanta in time for the Tech-Auburn Thanksgiving Day game, the industrial tour was pronounced a huge success as an educational experience. More than 125 influential Georgians had been treated to a closeup view of what Tech was trying to bring about: "A Greater Georgia Tech for a Greater Industrial Georgia."[130]

The successful outcome of the northern tour seems to have encouraged Tech authorities to broaden the scope of the Greater Tech Campaign. Despite the bleak economic situation and internal feuding between the campaign directors, Phinehas Stephens in New York and Wickes Wamboldt in Georgia, they approved an expanded proposal to raise five million dollars over the next five years in order to develop a physical plant that could accommodate five thousand students. They also endorsed a plan designed to attract wide support from industry. Under this scheme Tech would provide an Industrial Development Service that would survey the state's resources, find and interest capital to develop them, and disseminate all the data generated. With the "right" director in charge, Campaign Director Wickes Wamboldt thought the service would pay tremendous dividends.[131]

The big push to secure pledges for the Greater Georgia Tech Campaign came between April 20 and 30, 1921. To show people what they would get for their money, the *Technique* printed architectural drawings of what the campus would look like in five years. An industrial conference in Macon featuring prominent visitors like Drs. A. D. Little of Boston, W. S. Stratton of the Bureau of Standards, and Raymond Bacon, director of the Mellon Institute, also "prepared" Georgians for the fund drive. In Atlanta there were mass meetings, exhibits, concerts by the Tech band, Glee Club, and Yellow Jacket Quartette, vaudeville acts, and speeches. A pep rally, fireworks, parade, and sham battle topped off Tech's efforts in the capital city. Meanwhile a state industrial tour visited thirty-one Georgia towns and cities, all of which turned out for banquets, dances, barbecues, and the stirring music of "Wop" Roman's traveling Tech band.[132]

The Greater Georgia Tech Campaign raised about $1.2 million in subscriptions by June 1921, but none of it was available immediately because the first installment on pledges to be paid over the next five years was not due until October. Meanwhile, the school was barely staying alive thanks to the loan from the Rotarians and the gift from the General Education Board. To complicate matters, continued infighting among the campaign directors led to personnel changes in both the New York and Georgia campaigns. The depressed economy also made continuation of the campaign impractical, and on the advice of the new campaign director in New York, Ivy Lee, it was shut down until the fall of 1922. By that time Matheson had left Georgia Tech for his new position at Drexel Institute in Philadelphia. Well before his departure, however, the outgoing president secured a major donation from the Carnegie Corporation to the Greater Georgia Tech Campaign Fund. In June 1921, the corporation agreed to give $150,000 to Tech for the construction of a physics building. If the proposed structure could not be completed with that amount, Tech authorities pledged to supply whatever was needed to finish and equip the facility.[133]

When Matheson left, the Board of Trustees named the chairman of its executive committee, N. P. Pratt, to act as "administrative executive" until a new president of Georgia Tech could be elected. Pratt moved at once to make the Greater Georgia Tech Campaign operation more "efficient." He cut its budget, moved its headquarters to the campus, reduced the staff, and called for weekly status reports detailing precisely how much it cost to solicit and collect each dollar subscribed. Meanwhile he also negotiated with Stephens and Wamboldt in an effort to settle their claims for services in Tech's behalf. Within five months "after the new order had begun on April 1, 1922" only two people, W. J. Milner and a stenographer, remained on the Greater Georgia Tech Campaign payroll, mainly for the purpose of collecting subscriptions when due. All told, about $1,720,000 was subscribed to the campaign. Most of it was collected in currency but some paid off their pledges in liberty bonds, building materials, office furniture, and services. One donor contributed a purebred Guernsey cow. Reporting in March 1923, Milner noted that in ten days, April 20–30, 1921, Atlanta alone subscribed $750,000 to the campaign. Considering the $150,000 Carnegie gift and the funds subscribed by Tech alumni, he thought the campaign so far had been a success: "The work it was intended for is progressing rapidly . . . and if the payment of pledges continues as it has . . . Georgia Tech will soon be equipped in the thorough and complete manner which it rightfully deserves."[134]

As English professor and president, K. G. Matheson served Georgia Tech selflessly for almost twenty-five years. He could not leave the school that he described as "my first love" without regret. Yet when Drexel Institute of Philadelphia offered him its presidency in September 1921, he hesitated only briefly. Tech's Board of Trustees made a substantial counteroffer to keep him in Atlanta, but his own income was not the issue. He could not stay for reasons made clear in an extraordinarily candid statement issued on Saturday, October 8, 1921. The *Atlanta Constitution* printed it the next day, noting that it would doubtless "arrest the serious attention of thinking people throughout the state, for it touches on a subject of state educational policy that is vital, not only to Georgia Tech, but all other state institutions of learning."[135] In substance, Matheson told the public that he had resigned because it had become a "humiliating burden" to secure enough money from the legislature to run the school and enlarge its facilities to the degree required by modern technical education. More than that, he had been informed bluntly that nothing would change until the state's "archaic system of taxation" was overhauled, something no informed observer expected in the foreseeable future. After watching Georgia politics for twenty-five years, he doubted that the state's higher educational institutions could afford to wait. Matheson decried a system that required presidents of state colleges to spend their summer vacations "begging" for alms in the corridors and committee rooms of the state capitol. He saw no reason to continue so futile a pursuit. Besides, it was unnecessary. "Georgia, with her matchless resources," he declared, "is not so poverty-stricken as to justify the possible sacrifice of family and self in order to secure the support for her technical school which she is so abundantly able to supply."¹³⁶

Matheson was aware of the state's precarious financial situation in 1921; it was not his duty to "locate responsibility" for it. But he certainly deplored the lawmakers' decision to retrench by cutting appropriations for higher education before any other activity felt the knife. That in itself, he thought, revealed how much Georgia needed what she obviously valued so little. Matheson's own words express best the frustration he must have felt:

> It was our hope and belief that by developing an efficient technological school, the legislators would amply support it. In spite of many handicaps and discouragements, we gave to the state what competent critics declare to be the second engineering college of the nation—the first [MIT], by the way, having recently spent $28,000,000 in its development. Notwithstanding . . . [soaring] enrollment, donated equipment totaling many thousands of dollars in value, $1,500,000 in subscriptions from friends and other evidences of growth, the legislatures of the past two summers have appropriated only half the amount actually needed for the operation of the school. In 1920, upon the failure to appropriate the additional $100,000 necessary to keep Tech's doors open, I again became a modern Lazarus and successfully begged from Atlanta to New York the crumbs from the rich men's tables which a rich mother had denied. . . . Again [in 1921] we have met the emergency at a disruptive and destructive cost which cannot be continued.¹³⁷

Matheson profoundly regretted having to leave the presidency before his vision of a Greater Georgia Tech was fully achieved But no man was indispensable and he was sure the school would one day attain its goals and contribute thereby to the development of a truly Greater Georgia. "The foundations of the school have been laid strong and deep," he concluded, "and when Georgians realize its value as they certainly will they will demand and provide the generous and adequate support necessary for its maximum efficiency. This is my prayer and belief."¹³⁸

Chapter Five

The Brittain Era: The Interwar Years

Overleaf: The Daniel Guggenheim School of Aeronautics was made possible by a gift from the Guggenheim Foundation in 1930. (Courtesy of the Georgia Tech Archives.)

On August 1, 1922, as Marion Luther Brittain assumed the presidency of Georgia Tech, the school was poised on the brink of a long period of expansion, curriculum changes, political reforms and disputes, and sports victories. The 1920s and 1930s represent an era of both great expectations and achievements, and missed opportunities and disappointments. It was a period that required the guiding hand of an educator sophisticated in the ways of local, state, and national politics.

Brittain's value to Georgia Tech was recognized early and surely played a role in his selection. For example, Nathaniel E. Harris, president of Tech's Board of Trustees, noted in 1923 that Brittain "has a vast number of friends and acquaintances growing out of previous associations, and this carries a promise of incalculable value to be realized in the administration and discharge of his intricate duties as head of this institution." M. L. Brittain had a long history of service to education in Georgia and, although he had not been involved in college or engineering education in his previous positions, could serve Tech well as an influential and politically knowledgeable spokesman. Before coming to Georgia Tech, Brittain had served as superintendent of Fulton County Schools (1900–10), and state superintendent of education (1910–22). He had also been president of the Georgia Education Association (1906), of the Southern Education Association (1913), and of the Council of State School Superintendents of the United States (1917). Brittain had earlier incurred the wrath of Senator Tom Watson, who tried to oust Brittain from his position as superintendent of education. Despite Watson's constant attacks, Brittain stayed in the position, aided by his many supporters in politics and education in Georgia. Brittain's ability to withstand Watson's abuse indicated that he was well-respected in the state and also prepared him for future battles with other demagogues.[1]

Brittain's actions during the 1920s indicate a strong concern with securing adequate state funding and national recognition for the Georgia School of Technology. His efforts resulted in an outburst of building activity, curriculum additions, faculty improvements, and finally a reorganization of the University System of Georgia.

Building and Funding

As part of the Greater Georgia Tech campaign, begun in 1921 under Matheson, the Carnegie Educational Fund agreed to contribute $150,000 to Tech if over $1,500,000 was pledged during the fund drive. Brittain held the Carnegie Foundation to its promise and with these funds was able to fulfill the decision made under the Matheson administration to use this money to construct the Physics Building that opened in 1923, the first of many new buildings for Tech during the Brittain era. During the rest of the decade, construction was completed on a Ceramics Building, the Julius Brown Memorial Hall (a dormitory), the Emerson addition to the Lyman Hall Chemistry Laboratory, the Senator N. E. Harris Dormitory, the Army ROTC Building, and the Brittain Dining Hall. In addition, renovations were made on the Knowles Dormitory, the Swann Dormitory (remodeled for use by the commerce department as a classroom building), the Mechanical, Textile, and Academic buildings, and Grant Field. The changes to the stadium included a new concrete grandstand on the east side with an indoor track beneath it, a rounded connecting grandstand to join the ends of the east and west grandstands, and a basketball court built at the north end of Grant Field. The seating expansion at the stadium resulted in its being the largest south of Baltimore "and one of the ten largest in the entire country."[2]

Brittain was an admirer of the English collegiate style of architecture, and many of the buildings of this era reflect that style. In an effort to provide some uniformity to the Tech campus and a plan,

Harold Bush-Brown of Tech's architecture department was often called upon to design these additions to the campus. Also, other departments at times provided their services. The Brittain Dining Hall was truly a joint project of Tech's departments—the architecture department designed the building, the ceramics department manufactured the tile for the floor of the tower, the mechanical engineering department supplied the wrought iron for the light fixtures in the main hall, and the textile department made tapestries for the walls.[3]

Although further building was desired (for example, Brittain constantly appealed for a new gymnasium and auditorium), the amount of construction during the 1920s was prodigious. The new buildings of this decade and after, however, illustrate a common problem of the Brittain era—lack of funds. Whatever was built at Tech was done with private contributions, indicating a state government little concerned with improvements of its higher education facilities. The Julius Brown Memorial Hall was built with money received from the Brown estate and Greater Georgia Tech Campaign, the Emerson addition was paid for with money contributed to the Greater Georgia Tech Campaign, and the Harris Dormitory, at a cost of $106,000, saw completion due to this same funding campaign. Even when state appropriations were involved, as in the Brittain Dining Hall, the bulk of the money came from other sources—in this case from a large contribution from the Athletic Association and the Georgia Tech Expansion Fund.[4]

The lack of funding on all levels was a recognized problem on campus. Brittain noted in his annual report in 1923 that "there are more students in Georgia Tech than in any other two colleges in Georgia, and we have the smallest appropriation of them all," a theme he would reiterate many times in numerous appeals for more money. Brittain and Harris also made the point that Georgia could never become a great manufacturing state unless its technological school was properly funded. And a 1926 editorial in the *Technique* commented that "it is a lamentable situation that exists in Georgia insofar as the granting of money to educational institutions is concerned.... It seems that the citizens of the great State of Georgia do not realize that the Georgia School of Technology needs money to operate, to grow and to expand." The editorial went on to note that Tech gets less state appropriations than any other state college in the South and concluded that Tech could not live on its reputation. Either the school had to receive more money or it would be surpassed by other southern colleges.[5] President Brittain was not going to let this happen and used his skills to find the funding to allow Tech to grow and develop.

Enabling Tech to expand and to enhance its reputation required more than campus construction. What was also needed was the development of new departments, new fields of study, and the attraction of faculty members. Brittain was active in this regard, too, as indicated by the establishment of new ceramics and aeronautical engineering departments. For many years there had been discussion of starting a ceramics engineering department at Tech. As always, however, lack of funding had prevented its appearance. Finally Brittain was approached by some of Georgia's business leaders, particularly those connected with the Central of Georgia Railroad, who were aware of the state's large deposits of kaolin and other clays and unhappy that these materials were shipped elsewhere for analysis and manufacturing and then sent back to Georgia as finished products. The business leaders wanted the development of a ceramics industry in Georgia, and, of course, trained engineers were needed. In 1922, Brittain established a committee of those interested in creating a ceramics department at Tech. An invitation to join this committee was sent to Georgia-based companies and individuals interested in the manufacturing of clay products. The response was enthusiastic. As Brittain commented, "So intense was the feeling and enthusiasm developed that these industrial leaders offered to make subscriptions to begin this important work and show its value to the State in creating payrolls and giving Georgia the benefit of this new wealth." Three committee meetings were held in 1922–23 with mineowners, manufacturers, and others. Brittain also visited the ceramics engineering department at Ohio State University, which was considered the center of ceramic work in the country, in order to calculate the cost of developing and operating such a unit. On the basis of the committee meetings and Brittain's projected budget for this department, subscriptions were received from a number of companies, including, for example, the B. Mifflin Hood Brick Company, the Central of Georgia Railroad, and the Atlanta Terra Cotta Company. Financial aid was also contributed by the Atlanta Chamber of Commerce and the Fulton County Commission. Sufficient money ($46,300) and materials were pledged in this manner so that there was enough to construct the building, buy the machinery, and run the school for at least a year. Harris, of Tech's Board of Trustees, hoped that this strong showing would convince the legislature "of the advantages to be derived from the education of experts in this very important manufacture." The Georgia General Assembly in 1924 agreed to commit $10,000 annually to the project.[6]

Brittain, along with the business leaders, had been successful in pointing out to the state legislature the importance of this department and industry to Georgia. As Brittain noted later of the new ceramics department, "Its distinct purpose is to serve Georgia in every way possible in the effort to develop our clay industries."[7] The Ceramics Building was dedicated on November 15, 1924, with A. V. Henry, formerly of Ohio State University, as the department's first chairman.[8] The organization of this department and the development of the industry in the state, as well as the recruitment of qualified faculty, was largely the work of President Brittain. Georgia Tech thus became the first school in the south to have both a ceramics department and building. As an article in the *Technique* stated, "The installation of a ceramics department, with an up-to-date building, is an innovation in southern institutions, and marks the movement among southern industries to establish a more efficient ceramics development throughout the South." With the introduction of ceramics engineering, Tech not only achieved a new level of leadership among southern schools but also secured national recognition. As a result of this new department and the efforts of the Central of Georgia Railroad, the American Ceramics Society held its annual convention in Atlanta in 1926 with about one thousand ceramics specialists attending. Brittain was fully aware of the implications of this meeting and made sure to include in his annual report that "from the visit of this important group of ceramic experts, we are expecting nationwide notice of the possibilities of our resources in this field." And the *Technique* reported at the time of the meeting

168 Engineering the New South

that "the industry in the South has been given marked impetus by the interest fostered by the convention, which is the first that the Ceramics Society has ever held in the South." Many delegates also visited the department at Tech and were impressed by what they saw.⁹

Guggenheim Award

Tech's development and increasing national prominence was further enhanced by Brittain's ability to secure the prestigious Guggenheim award in 1930. For a number of years Tech had been slowly developing an aeronautical engineering curriculum and showing interest in the field. In 1926 a new course in aeronautics was offered in the machine design department for those students who might later concentrate their studies in aeronautical engineering, and in 1928 an aeronautics course was added to the Night School course of study. In 1927 the War Department gave Tech a complete aeronautical library (250 books), which provided the school with the best library of this type in the South. Also in 1927, in a visit paid for by the Guggenheim Fund, Charles A. Lindbergh came to Tech and spoke at Grant Field. Later he flew his "Spirit of St. Louis" over the stadium. The purpose of the visit was to "further public interest in aviation and aeronautics," which at Tech was already evident.¹⁰

Brittain was clearly interested in developing this curriculum at Tech and in securing the Guggenheim award to construct a building for an aeronautical engineering department. As early as 1926, he met with representatives of the Guggenheim Fund and stressed to them the idea of establishing a chair in this field at Tech. The Daniel Guggenheim Fund for the Promotion of Aeronautics had already awarded grants to a number of other schools, but none in the South. Twenty-seven southern colleges were being considered for this honor. The Guggenheim board surveyed the various institutions, taking into consideration their "location, aviation equipment, cosmopolitan character of the student body, and standards of scholarship." The final choice was among Rice, Vanderbilt, Alabama, and Georgia Tech. Brittain worked hard to make Tech suitable to receive the award. He toured the other schools that had won the award and tried to improve his knowledge of aeronautical studies. Also, to upgrade the faculty in this area, he secured Montgomery Knight as the chairman of an aeronautical engineering department. Knight already was a recognized scholar in this field, having been involved in the design of helicopters. He had also taught at MIT and served as director of the atmospheric wind tunnel unit of the National Advisory Committee for Aeronautics. Finally, plans were being developed for the building to house this new department.[11]

Apparently the Guggenheim board was impressed with Brittain's efforts and Tech's reputation. There was, however, hesitation in offering the grant to Tech due to the well-known and constant lack of financial support that the school received from the state. The board wanted to be assured that Georgia would continue to provide funds for the aeronautical engineering department in the years ahead. As Brittain noted later, "The members of the Board hesitated some weeks before sending us the money after they reached the decision as to the final award. . . . I called in for conference the then Governor, Treasurer, Secretary of State, and other officials, and all assured him [Guggenheim Representative Captain Emory S. Land] that his fear was without foundation, and if the money was forwarded, they would see that the department would be amply supported for its research work." The state promised to provide a minimum of 6 percent of the $300,000 award ($18,000 a year) as support. On the basis of that meeting and promise, Tech, largely through Brittain's efforts, received the important Guggenheim award on March 3, 1930. The $300,000 grant was the largest single award that the Guggenheim Fund presented and the largest amount of money that Tech or any other southern technological college ever received in a single gift. It was also the last grant that the Guggenheim Fund gave.[12]

Brittain viewed the Guggenheim award as one of his most important achievements. In one stroke he had enhanced the curriculum at Tech and the reputation of the school. That the fund and the other universities that had previously won the award (and had to vote approval of Tech) had agreed to give this grant to Tech was a clear indication of the national recognition that Brittain sought for Georgia Tech. Brittain was a little disappointed and angry with the response to the news on the Tech campus, for he commented that "the Tech students took in their stride, as a matter of course, the receiving of the greatest honor ever bestowed upon the school, or, for that matter, upon almost any Southern college, for it was quietly received and without fanfare." Other schools, however, recognized the importance of the award. Among the congratulatory messages that Brittain received was one from Chancellor Kirkland of Vanderbilt University, who commented, "I would have secured that award for Vanderbilt if you and D. M. Smith, your fine head of mathematics, had not filled that department at Georgia Tech with those excellent Ph.D. instructors from Harvard."[13]

Improvement of the faculty had long been one of Brittain's goals, and therefore it is not surprising that Kirkland would refer to this. From the very beginning of his tenure, Brittain insisted on interviewing all new faculty candidates before they were approved by the Board of Trustees. He personally was involved in upgrading the faculty, as was Matheson before him. Periodically he would visit northern schools looking for qualified professors to bring back to Tech. Even when traveling on other business, he always included in his itinerary a visit to top universities to secure instructors. For example, after attending a meeting of the National Education Association in 1926 (held in Washington, D.C.), he went to Johns Hopkins, Princeton, and Harvard in search of faculty for Georgia Tech. Attracting professors from other schools could only be successful, of course, if Tech had something to offer them. Brittain fought long and hard to raise faculty salaries at Tech and made a point of noting who the school was losing due to low salaries. In his first year as president, he made clever use of a pamphlet published by a small area school that commented derisively about Tech's low salaries. Brittain was able to utilize this pamphlet as political leverage on the legislature in an effort to secure more money for the school. And he was successful in his efforts, thereby immediately raising salaries at Tech during the early period of his long tenure.[14]

National Recognition

The attraction of quality instructors always remained an important goal of Brittain. It was part of his desire to improve the school and secure national recognition for Tech. In many ways this recognition

The Brittain Era

came to Tech during the 1920s, not only with the ceramics department and Guggenheim award already noted, but with other events as well. In 1926, for example, a Navy ROTC unit was established at Tech under Commander John L. London. The school was one of only six colleges in the nation selected by the Navy Department for a training course. Brittain saw the establishment of this ROTC unit, the first in the South, as a particularly important achievement. "The marked characteristic," as Brittain noted of the choice of Tech for the naval unit, "of faculty and students to insist on the best academic standards at Georgia Tech was the direct cause, therefore, of the first great national distinction the school received."[15] The architecture department also showed significant accomplishments during this period. In 1926, the architecture school was admitted to membership in the Association of Collegiate Schools of Architecture—the only southern school to be admitted. The association consisted of the best architectural schools in the country. "To meet the requirements of the association a school must include in its curriculum a well balanced and thorough professional course and must show a very high order of student attainment." Certainly this department had achieved much. Brittain noted in 1927 that the school had won first and second place in the Southern Intercollegiate Competition in Architecture for five years in a row, and the seniors in design had "won First Mention in the Beaux Arts Competition in New York." Also Brittain's efforts to improve the curriculum during the 1920s led to Tech's election to membership in the Southern Association of Colleges and Secondary Schools in 1925, an important achievement and an indication of Tech's growing status. "The School was formerly barred," noted the *Technique*, "because of its strictly technical nature, but with the institution of the General Science course that objection ceased to be."[16]

Sports also provided regional and national recognition for Georgia Tech during the 1920s. The great sports rivalry between Tech and the University of Georgia was resumed in 1924 after a five-year hiatus. The last athletic event, a baseball game, was played in 1919. The last football game between the two schools took place in 1916 (and was won by Tech 21–0). Optimistically, as the teams once again met each other in athletic competition, Brittain's annual report noted that "the representatives of both institutions have agreed to be friends in the future, and to put an end to the long-standing antagonism." Football games between the two colleges began again in November 1925 (with Tech winning the first game 3–0). The restarting of this athletic competition was welcome news to fans across the South. Tech teams did well in all sports during the 1920s, although football provided the main attraction. In 1926, for example, Tech's baseball, swimming, rifle, tennis, and lacrosse teams won championship titles. In 1929, the basketball team won the Southern Conference Tournament. Later in the 1930s, Tech still continued to distinguish itself in sports when the track and tennis teams won the Southeastern AAU championship and the Southeastern Conference championship respectively. The highlight, however, for Tech sports during the entire Brittain era came in 1929 with the Rose Bowl game.[17]

The football teams under Coach William A. Alexander were as impressive as the coach. Alexander had started at Tech in 1912 as an assistant to Coach Heisman. He became head coach in 1920, and during this decade had winning seasons for 1920–25 and 1927–28. He led the "Golden Tornado" to five conference championships—in 1920, 1921, 1922, 1927, and 1928. The 1928 team, which went to the Rose Bowl, was undefeated (having amassed 213 points in 9 games against 40 for the opposition), and the bowl game against California on January 1, 1929, provided special excitement. Not only did Tech win by only one point (8–7), but the game included an unusual play still remembered by many fans. The play, as told by end Frank Waddey of the 1928 Tech team, occurred as follows:

> The score was 0–0 and we had the ball on our 23 near the sideline. We had a play which faked toward the sideline and came back. Stumpy [halfback J. C. "Stumpy" Thomason] was carrying the ball and fumbled, California's Riegels [center Roy Riegels] grabbed it while it was still in the air. It was my business to block halfback Benny Lom but when Riegels got the ball it became Lom's job to block me.
>
> Riegels took two steps in the right direction, but as I was bearing down on him he headed for his own goal. Lom was caught short and we both set out after the ball-carrier.
>
> We ran like a team, with me one stride behind Lom, who finally caught Riegels at the one. Lom grabbed Riegels by the right shoulder with his left hand and spun him around. Then I hit him high and spilled

him into the end zone, where he lost the ball and we recovered. I've never been able to understand why we didn't get a touchdown, but they gave the ball to California on the one.

The ball was so close to the sideline that [Vance] Maree, our left tackle, moved over outside right tackle. No one stopped him as he went in with arms crossed to knock the punt clear out of the end zone for two points.[18]

Riegels ran sixty-two yards in the wrong direction and thereby created the situation for the two-point safety. The play decided the game—each team went on to score a touchdown, but the wrong way run was the deciding factor in the Tech win. The Tech Rose Bowl team included many stars, such as Captain Peter Pund (All-American center), Warner Mizell (All-American halfback), and Frank Speer (tackle who "won the Associated Press composite selection for All-American tackle"), and was the best Tech was to have for many years. Tech did not produce another winning team until 1937 nor another bowl appearance and win (Orange Bowl against Missouri) until 1939.[19]

The Rose Bowl victory not only brought national prominence to Tech but also financial rewards. The school received $76,000 as a result of the game. Tech was able to use this money to purchase what became Rose Bowl Field, a ten-acre tract of land from Fifth to Eighth streets between Fowler and Cherry streets. The first interest in this land occurred a few months earlier, when Tech put a down payment of $15,000 on it. Then, to pay off the rest of the money owed ($65,000) to the Peters Land Company, a loan was secured. The Rose Bowl revenues allowed the loan to be repaid, with some money left over, and Tech had full ownership of this valuable property.[20] Another athletic acquisition for the school, and a unique one, came in 1928 when Brittain took a long trip to Europe and the Middle East. He sent back a large block of marble from the site of the Battle of Marathon in Greece to be used as a marker at Grant Field to show the start and finish of races and to inspire Tech athletes.[21]

While Georgia Tech's scholastic and sports activities were giving the school a national name, awareness of Tech came from another, more unusual source. In July 1923, Clark Howell, Sr., editor of the *Atlanta Constitution* and a member of Tech's Board of Trustees, gave Georgia Tech the newspaper's radio equipment as a gift. A few months later, after receiving a license to broadcast, Tech operated a station first under the call letters WGM, then WBBF, and finally in 1925 WGST. Broadcasting from the Electrical Engineering Building and run by that department until 1930 and then by the Southern Broadcasting Company from the Ansley Hotel and elsewhere, the station offered a variety of Tech programs, including lectures by faculty and music programs by the glee club and by the band under the direction of Frank Roman. Also, there was an interesting contest to pick an announcer for the year. Each student who tried out for the job made a short announcement; listeners were then asked to send in letters stating their preferences. Surprisingly, letters were received from twenty-six states and one Canadian province.[22] Surely Georgia Tech was achieving national recognition in a variety of ways during the 1920s as the school grew and changed.

Campus Activities

Some other changes on campus took place during this period that are worth noting. The organization of the Student Council was proposed and approved in 1922 in an effort to allow "for more direct government of the various activities of the school by the students themselves." A fee of twenty-five cents was collected from each student to support the work of the council. The honor system was discontinued in 1925 because students and faculty believed that it was not working. Perhaps this was a result of a perceived impersonality of campus life. The *Technique* in 1926 complained of a loss of bond among the students at Tech and an increasing lack of friendly contact. In contrast, however, fraternities flourished, and a number of new chapters were organized, as was the Inter-Fraternity Council, which replaced the old Pan-Hellenic Council. But whether or not there was, as the *Technique* feared, a growing unfriendliness at Tech, certainly there was continued improvement and recognition. In 1922, before Brittain assumed the presidency, a chapter of Pi Delta Epsilon, the national honorary journalism fraternity, was established at Tech, and in 1925 chapters of Phi Psi, the national textile society, and Tau Beta Pi, the national honorary engineering society, were started. In 1930, Omicron Delta Kappa (ODK), a national honorary society, was organized at Tech.²³

Funding, the Depression, and Reorganization

By the end of the decade, after eight years of the Brittain presidency, Tech had accomplished much, but often in spite of, rather than due to, state assistance. Lack of funding remained an issue. Throughout the decade, Brittain kept up a steady plea for more money for salaries, dormitories, academic buildings, and expansion. These statements were echoed in editorials in the *Tech Alumnus* (the publication of the Georgia Tech Alumni Association that first appeared in 1923) and the *Technique*. Faculty, administrators, alumni, and students were all aware of the problem.²⁴ Brittain's concern with the funding issue led to some innovative suggestions for the state's college system. As early as 1926, he was speaking out in opposition to the creation of more colleges in Georgia. He suggested that the state should fund the University of Georgia at Athens, the State College of Agriculture, Tech, and two or three colleges for women. The establishment of more branches of the University System would simply divide the resources of the state into too small portions.²⁵ The concept of providing a better management system for the state's colleges so that expansion could be beneficially controlled and funding allocated more evenly began to take shape as a proposal when the country was plunged into the Great Depression in 1929.

The Depression made the funding and expansion issues crucial to Tech's survival and led Brittain to make a suggestion that had a major impact on higher education in Georgia. Brittain proposed on April 27, 1930, to a group of Tech and Georgia alumni meeting in Savannah that the University System be reorganized. As Brittain said:

> The time has come for this State to stop drifting, and plan a clear, definite policy as to our higher educational institutions. . . . To continue a spineless course not only spells calamity to the University System but is unfair to the State and means ruin for every hope for Georgia to hold up her head with her sister commonwealths in the field of higher educa-

tion. . . . No other State even dreams of maintaining more than one University for Liberal Arts, one College of Agriculture, and one College for Advanced Technical Training. To attempt the support of two dozen or one in every county, as seems the present tendency, means that none will be worthy of the name.

In this hard-hitting, timely, and candid speech, Brittain also asked for some organization and plan for the state's colleges—particularly a state system of junior and senior colleges under central management. Although he was not the first to suggest reorganization of the University System, Brittain attracted much attention with his speech.[26]

In an effort to bring about a close working relationship between the educational institutions of the state and to ensure efficient management, the General Assembly and Governor Richard B. Russell, Jr., secured the passage of an act in 1931 establishing the University System of Georgia and creating an eleven-member Board of Regents to replace the individual boards of trustees. On January 1, 1932, the new system went into operation. Although the concept was good, Tech unfortunately initially suffered from the change, for when the Board of Regents was created, no Tech alumnus was appointed. The University of Georgia, however, had a majority on the board. The underrepresentation of Tech on the Board of Regents, and its implications, continued to plague Brittain throughout the 1930s.[27]

In a parting message, the Tech Board of Trustees outlined its ideas for the future of Tech and sent the letter to the chairman of the regents, W. D. Anderson, on January 7, 1932. The eight suggestions included: that Tech remain a men's school; that the present location of the school be maintained; "that the Institution be kept entirely a technical school, with proper and sufficient allied commercial courses"; that out-of-state students remain a large percent (as much as 50 percent) of the Tech student body; that more dormitories be built to provide sufficient housing; that money be available for a yearly expansion program; that the Athletic Association continue to handle athletic and student activities; and finally, in a plea to the regents, the trustees concluded by noting, "We beg to call your attention to the fact that although the State of Georgia has appropriated but a very few hundred thousand dollars to the plant and equipment at Georgia Tech, the Institution through its policies and its position of national prominence, and through its friends and alumni has accumulated a property value for the State in excess of several million dollars. This Board and members, who have gone before us, have given close business study to the operation of this Institution and in many instances lent their personal endorsement to see that its progress was never retarded." Acknowledging the lack of support from the state, and the generous support from private sources, Tech's Board of Trustees urged that the progress of the school be continued.[28]

The nation's deepening financial crisis during the 1930s initially impeded the progress and development of Tech, but later as the federal government became active in alleviating the effects of the Depression, Tech benefited. At first, Tech suffered from decreasing enrollments, a cutback in state funds, and an attempt to make the University System more cost efficient.

Enrollment fell continuously in the early stages of the Depression (from 3,271 in 1931–32 to 2,944 in 1932–33), finally bottoming out in 1933–34 with a 2,482 total and then rising slowly over the next few years as economic conditions in the country improved. Along with a decreasing student body and a reduction in state revenue collections came a reduction in state funding. This decrease affected all aspects of campus life. Salaries, for example, were reduced. Brittain was forced to inform the faculty in the early part of the Depression that "we are unable to meet the payroll in full this month." He was only able to pay 60 percent of the salaries with the hope of offering another 30 percent in a few months. Ten percent "represents almost certainly a permanent cut." In Chemistry and Chemical Engineering, lack of money necessitated the firing of graduate student assistants. Also the renovation of buildings was delayed, and there was concern that the buildings on campus would deteriorate.[29]

In an attempt to cut expenses further, an effort was made to eliminate duplication in the University System. Basing their action on the report of experts called in to advise the regents on an improvement of operations in the University System, the board decided in April 1933 to transfer all engineering courses at the University of Georgia to Tech and also to transfer all commerce courses at Tech to the university, effective July 1, 1934. While the engineering work transferred from Athens was minimal (consisting of a small civil engineering program), Tech's commerce school was substantial, and a number of the athletes on campus were commerce majors. The regents noted in their 1933 annual report that "the University System could not afford to continue two competing Schools of Commerce within sixty-eight miles of each other. It became necessary to determine which school should be discontinued." The regents went on to say that the "Georgia School of Technology is primarily an engineering school and a splendid one. It does not have, and is not likely to develop, a Department of Economics. Taking these matters into consideration and the further fact that Emory University provides business training for students in Atlanta who cannot leave the city, it was decided to discontinue the School of Commerce at Georgia School of Technology". The regents were sensitive to the criticism that a major business center like Atlanta should have a commerce school and thus mentioned the Emory courses and also decided to set up Tech's Evening School of Commerce as an independent unit of Adult Education of the University of Georgia and no longer a part of Tech. All evening work was moved to Atlanta. The Evening School of Commerce "will meet the demands and needs of that considerable body of students who must be employed during the working day."[30]

There was widespread dissatisfaction on the Tech campus with the regents' decision. The transfer of the school came as a surprise to the students, but they quickly realized its implications and rallied and demonstrated against the move. A number of commerce students formed a protest group called the "Students' Justice Committee," and a student mass meeting organized by Willard Turnbull, editor of the *Technique,* was held on the Tech campus and threatened to march on the state capitol.[31]

Brittain also spoke out forcefully against the transfer. Noting that the Tech faculty was concerned about other, future losses, Brittain decided to go public with his protests. Speaking at the annual Homecoming Day luncheon on November 25, 1933, Brittain commented that "my own view is that this should be a distinct technical college rather than an Engineering Department of the University. Engineers certainly need training in business administration." Brittain noted his fear of the loss of other departments such as architecture "with the purpose of making Georgia Tech a mere Department of the University at Athens instead of a complete technical college as I desire. Georgia cannot afford to dim the lustre of the school which has won fame in this country as well as abroad through the excellence of its work. We have too few colleges whose reputation extends beyond the Mason and Dixon line." Continuing by pointing to many of Tech's achievements, Brittain concluded by raising the issue that apparently was troubling many Tech supporters. "Not intentionally would the fine personnel of the Board of Regents diminish this hard won position, but I am frank to say that this loss of our Commerce Department would never have occurred—in spite of our Survey Commission—if Tech had been given its just share of members on the Board of Regents with the instinctive and natural leanings toward their Alma Mater." Brittain did not accept financial concerns as a reason for the removal of the school and insisted that Atlanta was a logical place for it. "Not only is this the greatest commercial center of the State, and consequently is there more demand by the sons of these business leaders, but there is the further fact that engineers above all men need this training." He noted that 43.9 percent of the 460 commerce students came from Atlanta. A year later, Brittain was still complaining about the effects of this loss. In a letter to Chancellor Philip Weltner, Brittain stated that "this department of Commerce was one whose income showed a profit of eight or ten thousand dollars annually over expenditures. In consequence, we were crippled to this extent financially"—not a small matter during an economic depression.[32]

The *Technique* and student body were very supportive of Brittain's speech and shared his concerns. An editorial in the *Technique* worried that the architecture school might be removed from Tech, since "it is not strictly in the engineering field." And, the editorial continued, "if the N.R.A. [National Recovery Administration] succeeds in 'booming' the textile industry sufficiently, there will no doubt be ample proof presented by Georgia alumni that the textile field has changed and it is no longer an engineering department."[33]

The regents held their ground despite the discontent. Faced with the demonstrations and protests, all Regents Chairman Hughes Spalding could say to Brittain was, "That is all right for you fellows to act that way. If I were a Tech man, I would do likewise, but we are going to stand firm anyhow for we are compelled to economize and cut out duplication."[34]

The fight over the commerce school actually ended better for Tech than one would have imagined in 1934. Within a short time plans were made to establish an industrial management department. The *Technique* noted that this program was being developed in fall 1934 not only to replace the commerce school but also to allow the engineering students to have some business training. And according to one observer, the department was initiated in order to provide a place for football players to take courses—"a program that was less mathematical and that the Regents would approve." With the return of a business program and an upturn in the economy by 1935, Tech's student body began to increase in size. The registration for the freshman class was 50 percent higher in 1935 than in 1933. As the student paper noted, the Depression and the loss of the commerce school "dealt Tech's registration a blow from which the school is now rapidly recovering."[35]

However, problems caused by the Depression continued in many areas. In his presidential reports in the early years of the economic collapse, Brittain spoke often of the continued contributions of the school to the state in the face of decreased funding and unfulfilled requests. In 1934, for example, he expressed Tech's need of a gymnasium, a building for the Experiment Station, and for Civil Engineering, as well as space and equipment improvements for Chemistry and Chemical Engineering. One of Brittain's most often expressed concerns was for the funding of the aeronautical engineering department, which he believed needed to improve its course of study. "It is sad to recall," he stated, "that the deficiency is caused by the failure to meet the pledges made by the State and local authorities in accepting the Guggenheim award." As late as 1939, he was still concerned about the state's unwillingness to comply with their original promises of proper funding for this department and hoped that the reduction of state money in this area would be corrected quickly, "because the State's pledge and honor . . . are involved."[36]

Even sports were not exempt from financial difficulties. The loss of the commerce school hurt the athletic program, as did the elimination of athletic scholarships and a switch instead to a loan program for the athletes. Also, football revenues decreased by over 50 percent from 1930–32, resulting in sparse times for the entire sports program. Not until 1937 did the football team have a winning record (6–3–1). In 1932 and 1933, cutbacks in major sports and the elimination of minor sports seriously undermined Tech's athletic standing. A notice posted by Coach Alexander in spring 1932 revealed that in football, equipment would be limited to fifty men, and in baseball and track to forty, with no money available for trophies, banquets, tutors, or any other sports. Swimming, golf, boxing, lacrosse, and tennis were eliminated.[37]

The team members and other students rallied to save their sports. The swimming team began raising its own funds, and in 1933 and 1934 benefit shows were held to secure money for the golf, swimming, and tennis teams. Anak, Tech's honorary society, sponsored dances every Saturday night to raise money for minor sports. As the *Technique* commented, "The discontinuance of minor sports was a challenge to the students of Georgia Tech." And they rose to that challenge. School spirit was always strong at Tech, and the students often joined together to aid the school. In financial help to the teams or in events like the Ramblin' Wreck Parade (which began in 1932), Tech students showed their support for school activities. As a further indication of this support, the Student Council voted to lend the Athletic Association $1,250 in 1933 and $500 in 1934, when a bank loan was refused. Even with a loan, the minor sports would be dropped unless, as the council noted, they could finance themselves. Difficulties continued throughout the decade. The baseball and swimming teams were funded in 1937 after having been cancelled the previous year.[38]

Georgia Tech Foundation

Help for Tech came not only from the students but, as the financial problems mounted and all aspects of campus life suffered, from the alumni, and later, as part of a national program, from the federal government. Based on Tech's usual funding problems and the coming of the Depression, two alumni began to develop the plan that eventually became the Georgia Tech Foundation. G. M. ("Pup") Phillips and Everett Strupper, both former football stars whose occupations were now insurance agents, suggested a plan to set up a separate nonprofit corporation that would receive and administer dividends for Georgia Tech from insurance policies issued to individual alumni. By buying an insurance policy and signing over any dividends to this corporation for Tech's use, the school could benefit financially. Phillips and Strupper developed the new corporation and began issuing policies in 1931. To provide leadership for the corporation, six prominent alumni were asked to petition the state for a charter and to serve as the corporation's first Board of Trustees. (The six included Y. Frank Freeman, William H. Glenn, Robert Gregg, George Marchmont, Floyd McRae, and Frank Neely.) The corporation approved by the state in December 1931 was the Georgia Tech Alumni Foundation, Inc. Although the Tech Foundation was poorly funded in its early years due to the inadequacies of the insurance plan, it served later on as an important source of needed money for the school and even during the 1930s indicates the commitment of Tech's alumni to solve finally the funding problem.[39]

The New Deal and Tech

Tech survived the Depression intact mainly due to large amounts of money channeled into building programs by the federal government. The amount of construction, renovation, and repair work that took place on or around the campus was significant. In Brittain's annual report of 1933–34 alone, he listed more work done through government help than Tech had seen in years. For example, he noted that the Civil Works Administration (CWA) was responsible for repairs to the athletic fields, the painting of the Chemistry, Library, and Physics buildings, and construction of a chemistry lab for research and a Naval Armory building. "Since December," as Brittain continued, "we have received considerable assistance from C.W.A. and F.E.R.A. [Federal Emergency Relief Administration] in repair, painting, etc. We secured about 30,000 hours of labor; about $3,997.48 worth of material."[40] And that was just the beginning.

In subsequent years, various New Deal agencies were either wholly or partly responsible for construction of an annex to the

The Brittain Era

Chemistry Building for the Chemical Engineering Laboratory (built in 1936 with the aid of the WPA [Works Progress Administration]); a long-sought auditorium-gymnasium in 1938 (PWA and WPA) and the addition of a swimming pool in 1939 (WPA); the Mechanical Engineering Building (John Saylor Coon Building) in 1938 (PWA); the Civil Engineering Building in 1938 (PWA); a renovation of the Physics Building in 1938 (WPA) and an addition to the Ceramics Engineering Building in 1939 (WPA); the Clark Howell, Sr., Dormitory and the George W. Harrison, Jr., Dormitory in 1939 (PWA); and the Research Building for the Engineering Experiment Station (WPA) in 1939 and the Athletic Association Building in 1941 (WPA). Also FERA in 1935 rebuilt many of the machines for Mechanical Engineering and constructed new benches for the shops with materials supplied by the CWA. Other construction completed during this period, with money from private sources, included the Cloudman Dormitory (1931), the Naval Armory (1935), and the ODK Banquet Hall (1941). The Naval Armory was built with a gift from alumnus Ferd M. Kaufman and also with help from the CWA.

The New Deal also provided needed jobs for Tech students during those troubled times. As the *Technique* reported in 1934, "Georgia Tech students felt the first direct benefits of the 'New Deal' student employment program and professors found a new luxury in their positions Monday, as over 100 needy students reported to jobs provided by the C.W.A. Most of the jobs were in the offices or laboratories of professors and heads of departments." Students worked during their spare time, earning forty cents an hour up to a maximum of fifty hours a week. Aid continued in 1935 with the work of the National Youth Administration (NYA). Students worked in various departments or government agencies and earned an average of $11.06 per month. In 1935, 281 Tech students were so employed, and by 1939, 510 Tech students were under this program. Various government employment programs were essential since the Depression made it difficult for Tech's students to find jobs. Co-ops and graduating seniors looking for full-time work also had great difficulty, and therefore full-time government jobs were in high demand as late as 1938 because of continuing problems in the private sector. Without New Deal agencies, many Tech men would have faced unemployment, although the problem with finding jobs varied from year to year. In an effort to aid students in finding employment, George Griffin, assistant dean of men, established a central placement office in the early 1930s, and thereby initiated Tech's Placement Center.[41]

One of the major New Deal programs for the Tech area gave the school only one dormitory but changed the neighborhood considerably. Secretary of the Interior Harold Ickes (also PWA administrator) came to Tech in September 1934 to preside over the official beginning of Techwood Homes, the first federally subsidized public housing project in the United States. Prior to the construction of this project, the area bordering Georgia Tech was a large slum of shanty houses with a creek, in which raw sewage was dumped, running through the area. "Students at Georgia Tech could look out the college windows and be close enough to count more than 197 miserable shacks huddled in the valley below them." The slum area not only prevented Tech from expanding south, but it hindered any development between the school area and downtown and also adversely affected surrounding neighborhoods.[42]

Because of these deplorable conditions, Brittain was interested in clearing out this area. He served on the Board of Trustees of Techwood, Inc., and then as chairman of the Techwood Advisory Committee, thereby having an important voice in the development of the project. Two Tech alumni, Flippen Burge and P. D. Stevens, were chosen to design the project. The first unit, a dormitory for Georgia Tech, was completed in September 1935. To celebrate this historic event, President Franklin D. Roosevelt presided over the dedication of the project on November 29, 1935, and spoke to a large crowd at Grant Field.[43]

The opening of this new dormitory was an important addition to Tech. A year earlier a report had been issued noting the need for more on-campus housing. The unsuitable housing conditions for students living off campus, mainly in rooming houses, was noted and a Housing Bureau was created under the dean of men to supervise off-campus housing. The opening of a new 189-room dormitory partially alleviated the housing problem. The new dorm (which Tech leased from the government) housed 350 students, and as Chancellor S. V. Sanford commented, it "takes many of the students away from undesirable boarding houses and places them more directly under the influence of the school." Brittain was able to work closely with the government officials on this dorm and noted that "he found the Federal officials willing at all times to consider favorably any point affecting our institution, and in particular I have been pleased with their willingness to change the location of several of the houses as first proposed and give us the benefit of air and sunshine through tennis courts and park arrangements between the buildings and North Avenue."[44]

When Techwood was completed, it included 604 apartment units in twenty-three buildings on twenty-five acres of land. The buildings were of brick-and-concrete construction, and the units consisted of mainly three-, four-, and five-room apartments. The development also contained social rooms and central laundries. In 1940, with the building of the adjacent Clark Howell Homes, the entire project increased to a 56-acre, 1,234-unit development. Given the location and well-built construction of the projects, Brittain had hopes that all of it would eventually be given to Georgia Tech. In commenting on the building of the project, Brittain noted that "for several reasons, therefore, Georgia Tech will always be grateful for the success of the delicate and difficult task brought to completion by the building of Techwood Project: First, the acquisition of a handsome new dormitory costing at the time a quarter of a million dollars . . . ; second, the removal of a group of slattern, ill-appearing slum houses near her campus; third, the creation of the first and at this date the best and most attractive of the government's building projects; fourth, a possibility which has been mentioned discreetly more than once that possibly and particularly if the Republicans regained political power—and how much that would sweeten the pill—the Government might turn over not only the dormitory but all of the apartments as well to Georgia School of Technology. Possibly a dream but one which I think may come true with the bitter partisan feeling against the New Deal."[45] Of course, Brittain's hopes remained just that.

Engineering Experiment Station

Nonetheless, the improvements made at Tech under the New Deal were substantial, and the school continued to show major progress during this time. One new area that eventually was to have a significant impact on Tech was the development of the Engineering Experiment Station. This research station was officially established in 1919 but was not put into operation until July 1, 1934, when the regents voted a $5,000 budget for the station in order "to study engineering problems of commerical, economic, and social interest to Georgia and the South." As Chancellor S. V. Sanford noted in 1935, "This step resulted from a growing realization of the great effectiveness of other such stations located in most of the states. . . . Moreover, the obvious need to discover new uses for the natural products in the State of Georgia was a final compelling reason for establishing a scientific and engineering research agency at the engineering institution."[46]

The genesis for the station, other than the state legislative action in 1919, came in 1929 when a group of faculty belonging to Sigma Xi started a Research Club at Tech that met once a month. Those who met together (about twenty faculty, including W. Harry Vaughan, associate professor of ceramic engineering), read technical papers and offered comments. Vaughan later suggested that a group of subjects relating to Tech, such as library development, or the development of a state experiment station, be selected for discussion. As part of the study of the experiment station topic, the other stations around the country were reviewed, and the report was completed by Harold Bunger (head of chemical engineering), Montgomery Knight, and Vaughan in December 1929. The report gathered dust until S. V. Sanford, then president of the University of Georgia, suggested in 1933 that a technical research activity be established at Tech. Brittain and Dean William Vernon Skiles subsequently asked to see the report. Skiles then called together the various department heads and secured approval of the station. Brittain had already voiced his approval of the idea. Vaughan was appointed as acting director in spring 1934.[47]

The station was funded directly through the regents; Chancellor Philip Weltner wanted it to be the State Engineering Experiment Station of the University System with funding to be independent of Georgia Tech. For this reason, Weltner dealt directly with Vaughan. The acting director was asked to hand in a list of his projects to the chancellor and then was initially given $5,000 to pursue them.

There was at first some opposition to naming Vaughan, an associate professor, as director and thereby giving him so much authority, but with the creation of a Faculty Advisory Council (to serve as a board of directors to the director), opposition was stilled.[48]

The early work of the station was carried out in the basement of the Shop Building with Vaughan's office in the Aeronautical Engineering Building. There were no full-time researchers for the station at this time, but instead faculty members worked there part-time in addition to their teaching. Even Vaughan doubled up as head of the station and also of ceramic engineering as of 1938. Initial work at the station involved, for example, the development of rayon from pine pulp. The funding of the station improved considerably over the next few years reaching a state appropriation of $40,000 in 1940 plus considerable outside money as well.[49]

As an adjunct to the station, the Industrial Development Council was established in 1938 by Weltner and Preston Arkwright, Sr., president of Georgia Power Company. The IDC was set up as a contractual agency for the station to administer patents and to help develop its research projects. Vaughan, as director, served as secretary to the council with Arkwright as president. Vaughan resigned as director in 1940 to take a position with the TVA and was replaced by Bunger and then by Gerald A. Rosselot in 1941.[50]

Tech's Fiftieth Anniversary

The considerable progress at Tech by the late 1930s, although lack of funding and the lagging economy remained problems, resulted in a joyous fiftieth anniversary celebration in 1938. The event lasted two days (October 7–8, 1938) beginning on Friday afternoon with a golf foursome including the legendary Bobby Jones (who had graduated from Tech in 1922 with a mechanical engineering degree), a tennis match on Tech's courts, a show of scientific magic by the physics department, and for visitors to the city, a guided tour of Atlanta. The day finished with a reception for official delegates and members of the Tech faculty at the governor's mansion (Governor E. D. Rivers), a tea dance in the new auditorium gymnasium, a president's dinner for alumni, and finally an evening dance in the auditorium.[51]

On Saturday morning, an academic procession into the auditorium was held and included over 150 delegates from other colleges, members of the Board of Regents, Governor Rivers, Tech faculty, and the Student Council members. In the auditorium the main speech was given by Frank P. Graves, New York State's commissioner of education and president of the State University of New York and of the Phi Beta Kappa Society. In an address that surely must have made Brittain proud of his work, Graves commented that "people in the North have generally failed to realize the magnitude and efficiency of the training afforded at 'Georgia Tech.'" Graves went on to note the accomplishments of the school: "Probably the best evidence of the scholastic standing of Georgia Tech . . . is found in the recognition of her in recent years received from agencies outside the State. In 1925 the Naval Department of the United States Government selected this institution in the South, together with Yale, Harvard, Northwestern, Washington and California Universities in the North and West, for R.O.T.C. naval training, and stated that the choice was made by reason of the high standards here." Graves also mentioned the Guggenheim award that was made to Tech "because of their high standard of scholarship," but concluded by noting that "the effectiveness of the training at Tech is better evidenced by the record of its graduates than by any description of its courses and activities. Distinguished alumni of the school are found in many fields of industry and in the North, South, East and West of the United States and in many foreign countries." Graves's speech, which was preceded by Governor Rivers's short address "What Georgia Tech Means to the State of Georgia," was followed by other activities.[52]

Right after the auditorium ceremonies, a variety of activities took place: a president's luncheon for official delegates, then a football game between Tech and Notre Dame, an open house at all the fraternities, a late afternoon tea dance, a Phi Beta Kappa dinner, and last, a final dance in the auditorium. During the two days exhibits were displayed in the Naval Armory and in various departmental buildings, including exhibits on fifty years of engineering development, a scale model of the first campus, and a Georgia textiles exhibit. It was a well-attended and noteworthy commemoration of Tech's national importance. The celebration was also a way to bring together the old and new at the school. Representatives from every graduating class were present.⁵³

Education at Tech and Funding

Tech's high standard of scholarship that Graves mentioned in his speech was evidence of the many years spent by Brittain and others to improve and expand the curriculum. Although it was true that Brittain knew little about engineering, and, according to one observer, there were some faculty and alumni complaints about him because of his lack of technical training and thereby his inability to fit in with the state's industrialists, still the course of studies was considerably improved during his years as president.⁵⁴ In the 1920s, for example, not only were the ceramics engineering and aeronautical engineering programs developed, as already noted, but also the co-op program added new courses (for example, chemical engineering) in 1928; earlier, a general science course was added to Tech's offerings, and additional courses were added to various departments to keep up with the ever-changing fields. In addition, biology became a department in 1925.⁵⁵

Brittain also tried throughout his presidency to improve the library, noting that "my purpose was to secure as soon as possible membership for the school in the Southern Association of Colleges, and designation by the Association of American Universities on its preferred list of American institutions of learning. Both required certain standards of excellence for the libraries of applicants." Both goals were achieved in 1930. His concern for the library also reflects his emphasis on fundamentals—to in-depth training in mathematics and English. As late as 1939, Brittain was complaining that the high schools were easing their requirements, and therefore students were arriving at Tech not as well-prepared as earlier.⁵⁶ If Brittain was not an engineer, he certainly was an educator.

During the 1930s other programs of study were added or changed. Survey courses in social sciences became part of the curriculum in 1934, and a Department of Economics and Social Science was formed. Courses in general engineering and industrial management were also added in that year. The architecture department switched in 1937 from offering a four-year bachelor of science degree in architecture to a five-year bachelor of architecture degree. In 1938 the bachelor's degree in public health engineering became one of many degrees offered by Tech. And the school continued to be honored for its excellence. In 1939, for example, Tech was one of only seven schools in the nation selected by the Civil Aeronautics Authority to initiate a program for the training of civilian pilots. Tech was chosen "because of the pioneer work it has done in aeronautical engineering." Also in 1939 the architecture department won international recognition with the awarding of the University Medal by the Societes des Architectes Diplomas par le Gouvernement Francais, Groupe Americain.[57]

Yet even with these changes, additions, and honors, Tech held true to what Trustee Harris said in 1922 when describing the education at the school: "It is an education in which the machine is made the textbook and the workman's labor dignified by a collegiate training." A number of Tech departments (Mechanical, Civil, Ceramic, and Textile Engineering) required practical work before a degree would be awarded. This approach to engineering education came under some criticism in the 1930s, when a report was issued by the Society for the Promotion of Engineering Education in 1930 (vol. 1) and 1934 (vol. 2) based on an investigation of education in this field conducted between 1923 and 1929. The report noted that "the present trend is placing greater emphasis on general rather than technical educational values. Specialized training follows graduation." The society commented that since World War I there had been a movement away from overspecialization during the undergraduate years. The intention of the college curriculum is not to provide a "complete professional training" but rather "to supply a grounding in scientific principles and the methods of engineering together with the elements of liberal culture." The emphasis on a detailed technical training at Tech put its curriculum at odds with the trend in the field.[58]

Education at Tech was still sound, as noted in reports by Harry P. Hammond on engineering education in Georgia issued in 1932 and 1942. Hammond, president of the Society for the Promotion of En-

The Brittain Era

gineering Education as of 1936, was a well-respected authority in the field of engineering education. Noting the heavy technical load, however, the 1932 report suggested a reduction of requirements in drawing, shop work, and minor engineering subjects, as well as a general reduction of curriculum requirements to match that of other engineering schools. Those facets of the curriculum that were part of the beneficial national trend to broaden engineering studies could be retained, as in humanities (English, languages, economics) and mathematics. "Special approval is given to the time devoted to English and Mathematics and no change should be made in the requirements in these subjects."[59]

The 1942 report continued to note the heavy load at the school and the lack of ability to engage in elective work. However, the requirements for graduation had been reduced by 1942 and "the stem of humanistic studies has been strengthened." To Tech's credit, even the 1932 report concluded that the school's curriculum included all the necessary engineering fields except metallurgical engineering, which the report stated should be started soon as part of an expansion of the chemical engineering courses. However, as the report also commented, "The school has undoubtedly gone as far as it should, certainly for the present."[60]

The reasoning for this conclusion lies in the area of funding, an issue raised repeatedly in the report. "Revenues of the Georgia School of Technology are approximately half of those of other separately organized colleges of engineering and schools of mines. It is evident from these figures that the Georgia School of Technology is doing its work, and has been doing it for some years, on a scale of revenues considerably below its legitimate needs." Tech was receiving less per day school student per year than endowed universities, endowed polytechnic universities, state universities, schools of mines, and land-grant colleges. As a result, the report continued, "there is some question as to whether the school has not already spread its slender resources over too broad a field." The lack of funding affected all areas of the school's functioning. "An observer is struck with many evidences of unsatisfactory conditions, almost every one of which may be traced to lack of funds as the cause," including an overburdened faculty, the limitation of research and graduate study, the low salaries, the inadequate laboratory equipment, and the poor physical plant.[61]

In 1942 the second report reaffirmed the continuing problems mentioned in the first in the area of funding. Noting how little the state had given over the years, while acknowledging the generous contributions of private individuals, this study concluded that "in effect, the Georgia School of Technology is a publicly controlled but privately supported institution." Once again the school was said to suffer from inadequate faculty salaries, a limited graduate curriculum, excessive teaching loads, and a lack of upkeep of its physical plant. Both reports, however, while acknowledging the financial limitations imposed on Tech, also concluded that the school was doing well. The 1932 study commented that Tech "has never secured the financial support which an institution of its size and importance requires, but it has, nevertheless, acquired a position of both regional and national significance in the country's general system of engineering education." And the 1942 report stated that "the wonder is that this institution should have done as good work as it has on the basis of such inadequate financing."[62]

Brittain continued to hammer away at the funding issue during the 1930s, commenting "that no other technological college of our rank in the country receives so little from its state." He was especially worried about the loss of good faculty to other universities, a concern of his since the early days of his presidency. Salaries cut during the early 1930s still had not been increased to their previous level by 1937, although the nation's economy had improved considerably. There was even some discussion in 1938 among alumni and faculty about trying to make Tech a private school since the state was not providing adequate funding support. Even with Brittain's friends in the legislature, in the higher levels of the University System, and in the federal government, he was not able to rectify the situation at Tech. One of those who helped Tech immeasurably during this period was Alumnus L. W. "Chip" Robert, Jr. Robert was a member of Tech's Board of Trustees and, as of 1937, the Board of Regents. He was also the assistant secretary of the treasury for the United States from 1933–36 and secretary of the Democratic National Committee in 1936. Robert was an influential voice on Tech's

The Brittain Era

behalf on the national and state levels, but even with his substantial help, Tech continued to face financial difficulties.[63]

Governor Talmadge, Georgia Tech, and the University System

Important as lack of funding was to Tech, it paled as a problem when compared to political interference in the University System, which had immediate and dire consequences for the school. Although the most serious repercussions of this political meddling came in 1941–42, the issue could be observed as early as 1935. Governor Eugene Talmadge made repeated attempts to exert more control over the University System and the Board of Regents. For example, Talmadge supported a bill in 1935 that would give the governor more control over funds appropriated to the regents. The bill would also transfer to the state the title to all property of the University System and threatened to allow the state to absorb all trust funds and investments of the University System. Title was at the time vested in the Board of Regents and before that in the Board of Trustees of each institution. To secure support for his bill, the governor threatened to oppose any appropriations to the regents until the bill passed. Talmadge clearly aimed to gain control over the Board of Regents' money as well as all its property. Yet the bill had even more serious implications. If the state held title to the property, PWA loans could not be secured, since the state could not make a loan or incur any liabilities. The PWA had already allocated money to build a gymnasium at Tech in 1935, but this construction was now threatened by the Talmadge bill. The governor's plan was seen by others as simple political interference. As Marion Smith, chairman of the Board of Regents, commented, "The whole plan embodied in the bill, to make the university system a football of politics, is in my opinion disastrous to the efforts being made to build up a great university system." Lamar Rucker, a state senator from Athens, stated that "if you pass this bill you will make it possible for some future dictator to ruin the university. . . . Don't make the university system subject to the whim and fancy of any governor." The outcome was that a compromise was reached. If the bill passed with regents' support, Talmadge agreed to endorse a final appropriation to the University

System to construct the buildings that were to be funded by the PWA loan and also agreed to exempt athletic fees, dormitory receipts, and board revenue from being turned over to the state treasury. However, Talmadge's desire to control the regents and interfere in the University System was clear, and became more so later.[64]

The second attempt by Talmadge to exert his power involved an effort to support the career of his friend David I. ("Red") Barron, who was a 1920s Tech football star. In May 1941, with Barron head of the Georgia Vocational and Trades School in Monroe, Talmadge proposed him as a vice president at Tech in what appeared to be an obvious effort to replace Brittain. Brittain, having reached the age of seventy-five, was already thinking about retirement in 1941. In January of that year, Brittain had offered his resignation to the chancellor and the Board of Regents. Chancellor Sanford refused to accept it due to concern that Talmadge "will dictate the appointment of a personal or political friend as your successor." There was also concern among the Tech faculty that the school would be hurt by Brittain's resignation at the very point when Talmadge appeared interested in meddling in university affairs. For these reasons, Brittain withdrew his letter of resignation.[65]

The subsequent attempt to appoint Barron as vice president then seemed an evident case of Talmadge's desire to get a friend in as president of Tech. As the *Journal* reported it, Talmadge had been interested in putting Barron in as president for a number of months. Barron had been active in the governor's reelection campaign and had been promised the Tech position. Talmadge also wished to have Brittain retire. Among other points of controversy, Brittain had recently opposed the sale of WGST "to a group of private citizens represented by attorneys close to the present administration." When word of the proposed appointment became known at Tech, the students staged a protest. As Frank Hudson, president of the Student Council, said, "Our one purpose in the demonstration was to voice our opposition to any plan that would make a political football of the presidency of Georgia Tech." A plan to march on the state capitol was called off, but the students did hold a mass meeting on campus. Instead of vice president, however, Barron was offered the position of dean of men, replacing Floyd Field, who had held that position since 1921 when the Office of Dean of Men was established. Field was to be given another job. Although neither Brittain nor the chancellor recommended Barron for this post, he was approved by the regents at Talmadge's insistence. Barron, however, decided to remain as president of the school in Monroe, and the incident, another example of Talmadge's interference, was closed.[66]

The last and most serious incident of the governor's meddling occurred just after the Barron case and initially involved Walter Cocking, the dean of the School of Education at the University of Georgia. Dean Cocking had presented a report, "The Study of Higher Education of Negroes in Georgia," to the Board of Regents in 1938. The report recommended more education for Negro teachers, industrial training and education for all males, and the creation of new schools for Negroes. It did not suggest that the two races go to the same schools. Nonetheless, Talmadge claimed that Cocking, as well as others in the University System, supported integration of the schools and the "coeducation of the whites and blacks." Although these accusations were denied by Cocking and by his superior, President Harmon W. Caldwell of the University of Georgia, Talmadge insisted on making an issue of it. Cocking and others suggested that Talmadge raised the charge as part of his effort to get reelected. Certainly it was a good campaign issue, and racism had helped Talmadge before in his election bids.[67]

Therefore, when the Board of Regents met on May 30, 1941, Talmadge asked it to fire Cocking, although the dean was already supported for reappointment by President Caldwell and Chancellor Sanford. Talmadge brought Cocking to trial before the regents on June 16, pressuring them to do his bidding, but the regents refused by a vote of 8–7 to find Cocking guilty and instead reappointed him for the next year. This action angered Talmadge, and in an effort to impose his will on the regents, he forced three of the board members opposed to his desires to resign and appointed three others favorable to his plan. With the regents stacked in his favor, Talmadge called for a new trial on July 14 for Cocking and one for Marvin Pittman, president of the Georgia Teachers College. This time the board voted 10–5 against Cocking and also Pittman. Moreover, eight other University System employees were fired without a hearing. (None were from Tech.)[68]

The regents' actions invoked a response from the Southern Association of Colleges and Secondary Schools. A committee of the association, after investigating the situation in Georgia, concluded that Cocking and Pittman had been innocent of the charges, "that the Board of Regents . . . has violated sound education policy" in the dismissals as well as in the appointment of Barron, that the governor has interfered with the University System and violated proper procedure, and that "the Board of Regents does not appear to be an independent and effective educational board of control." Talmadge's right to revise the regents' budget without the board's approval was an example of his interference. On the basis of the committee's report and recommendation, the association voted on December 3, 1941, to suspend the ten colleges of the University System of Georgia from membership in the association, with the suspension to become effective on September 1, 1942. The loss of accreditation and also the removal of the University System schools from the list of approved colleges of the Southern University Conference and the Association of American Universities turned into an issue that Talmadge could not control.[69]

Talmadge's political advisors, as well as his family, had tried to talk him out of pursuing this fight, warning him that the accreditation issue could cost him the next election. Talmadge, however, was stubborn, and according to Ellis Arnall, his opponent in the next gubernatorial election, Talmadge felt he could win on this issue and therefore decided not to back off. Under the county unit system, Talmadge could lose Atlanta and the total popular vote and still win the election by capturing the rural counties. He may have believed that once again a segregationist racist position would propel him into office. On this basis, there was little room for compromise. Although the governor indicated verbally that he might be interested in correcting the situation and ending the controversy, nothing was done, one reason being that Arnall constantly baited Talmadge, saying he would change his mind and could not stick to one position. This political tactic may have encouraged the governor's stubbornness.[70]

The accreditation issue provoked a tidal wave of protest. Students at Tech and other colleges of the University System rose in protest against the governor. A resolution passed by the Tech Student Council urged that the legislature correct the situation and ensure that it would not happen again. A conference of campus leaders from around the state met in Macon in October 1941 in an effort to pressure the legislature to hold a special session to save the University System. The Macon meeting, which was attended by Tech Representatives Bill Cromartie (president of the Student Council), Harry Arthur (vice president of the Student Council), Bill Garrison (nonfraternity president of the YMCA), Tom Hill (editor of the *Technique*), Chase Read (nonfraternity leader and co-op student), and Ed Thompson (student representative), urged statewide student action against the governor's interference in the University System. The Tech Student Council also sent a letter of protest to Talmadge, which read in part that "if the University System is discredited, you alone will bear the blame." The letter continued by proclaiming, "We, the students of Tech, are demanding action!" The council insisted that Talmadge do something to correct the expected loss of accreditation that was soon to be voted on.[71]

Administrators also protested against the governor. In an effort to present a united front of all units of the University System, the heads of all the colleges met to plan a joint strategy and a joint statement. Brittain, who attended this meeting, also spoke out forcefully on his own, for he saw the loss of accreditation as destroying all that he had worked so hard for over the years. As Brittain noted in relation to one repercussion of the loss, "In all of our history at Georgia Tech, we have never had such difficulty in keeping our teachers. Several have left us, and we are endeavoring to supply these vacancies, but we have found unusual difficulty from those who were, before this accrediting trouble, eager to join our ranks." Brittain also wrote to Fernandus Payne, chairman of the Committee on the Classification of Universities and Colleges for the Association of American Universities, asking for more information on Tech's removal from the approved list of colleges. Brittain, in an effort to defend his school, noted that Tech had maintained high academic standards as shown by the Guggenheim award and the Naval ROTC being established and indicated his feeling of the unfairness of the ruling. Payne responded that the action was not meant to criticize Tech's academic quality. "In a sense it may be a very unkind and unjust act to your institution individually. . . . It is our only method, however, of telling the Governor and the people of Georgia that we do not approve his action." And to Chancellor O. C. Carmichael of Vanderbilt University (chairman of the Committee of the Southern Association of Colleges and Secondary Schools, which had investigated the situation in the Georgia University System), Brittain again defended Tech by claiming that there had been no political interference at his school. "Every man, recommended by me as presented, was approved as shown in my annual budget." On that basis, Brittain urged that no penalty be placed on Tech and ended his letter with a P.S., which stated that "there was a report or rumor that a friend of the Governor would be here as a Vice-President or Dean, but it did not materialize—perhaps due to opposition by the students." To W. Elliott Dunwoody, Jr., a member of the Board of Regents, Brittain claimed that "if we are dropt from our places on the accredited lists, . . . a million dollars will not compensate for this hurt."[72]

The accreditation battle had the potential of seriously damaging the school. The suspension in 1942, for example, could result in the inability of University System students to qualify as army or navy pilots, since admissions for pilot training required at least two years at an accredited college. Also, students wishing to go elsewhere for their graduate studies would be hindered. Brittain, realizing the danger to Tech, became active politically against Talmadge. He urged that Tech students and faculty join with their counterparts in the other colleges and organize to defeat Talmadge. He also called on them to convince their parents and friends to vote against the governor. A Student Political League, made up of representatives from most colleges in Georgia, including Tech, was set up to work against Talmadge's reelection. The Tech chapter of the league, in explaining its participation, stated that "it has become increasingly hard to get good students and good teachers to come to the Georgia institutions or to stay in them."[73]

The wave of protest and the political organizing against Talmadge was responsible for his defeat in 1942. Talmadge even admitted that "it was the university issue that defeated me." Arnall, who had made the accreditation loss the major issue of the campaign, was elected amid promises of rectifying the situation. Arnall, who was attorney general in Talmadge's administration, believed that the removal of regents' members was illegal and that the issue was not segregation but academic freedom. The university community rallied around Arnall on the basis that he would end political interference in the education system.⁷⁴

Arnall kept his word. Working with Brittain, Chancellor Sanford, Caldwell, and others, Arnall drafted legislation to improve the University System. He also appeared before the Southern Association on December 1, 1942, and explained what he intended to do. He attended the association's meeting in Memphis, along with Chancellor Sanford and Marion Smith (Arnall's Board of Regents chairman designate). To set up this meeting, Sanford had written in November to M. C. Huntley, executive secretary of the association, asking for reinstatement of the University System on the basis that Governor-elect Arnall had promised to seek legislation which would reorganize the Board of Regents and ensure its independence. As Sanford concluded, "The people have elected the governor and the members of the General Assembly, in large measure, on the University System issue—to remove it forever from political domination, by a constitutional *amendment* and do all things necessary to restore it at once its accredited standing."⁷⁵

Arnall and the others told the association about the planned House Bill No. 1, which would create a largely independent Board of Regents (and which Arnall was told would definitely pass), and also of an amendment to the state constitution guaranteeing an independent Board of Regents. Arnall also favored the elimination of the governor's ability to remove from the budget any individual or expenditure after the budget was approved by the regents. Only the Board of Regents would have the power to revise the budget of the University System. On the basis of this testimony, the Executive Council of the Commission on Institutions of Higher Education recommended to the Executive Committee of the Southern Association that accreditation be restored as soon as there was indication that the governor's promises had been fulfilled. The suspension was lifted after Arnall took office, House Bill No. 1 was passed, and the new Board of Regents was created. The University System was returned to its good standing as of September 1, 1942, the original date of the suspension action.⁷⁶

The changes enacted by the new governor were significant and were to prevent interference from future political leaders. Arnall's House Bill No. 1 terminated the Board of Regents and established a new one that was independent from outside control. The amendment to article 8, section 6 of the state constitution was submitted and approved by the voters in 1943. It provided for permanent protection against political interference. The regents were given full control of the University System, the governor was no longer a member of the board, and the regents were given staggered seven-year terms so that the governor could never control all of the members. The University System therefore emerged from its fight with Talmadge in a stronger position than before.[77]

During the period when the accreditation battle raged, the United States was thrown into turmoil by the Japanese bombing of Pearl Harbor and America's entry into World War II. Georgia Tech responded to the new events and responsibilities, as did the rest of the nation. Brittain, nearing retirement, once again provided the firm leadership he had given Tech since 1922 and led the school through yet another crisis.

Although the war brought great changes to Georgia Tech, much remained the same. Brittain's 1942 report listed the usual complaints about inadequate funding, including "the failure of State and local authorities to give us the promised aid when we received the GUGGENHEIM AWARD," which now limited the development of the important aeronautical engineering school during the wartime emergency. He also noted that due to the war, plans for a new chemistry building had to be eliminated. Yet the war also provided new opportunities. The federal government, for example, provided $50,000 worth of equipment to the mechanical engineering laboratories and machine shop because of the importance of this area of study to the war effort.[78] The war, providing the capstone to Brittain's career, was to change Tech considerably, yet leave the school with many of its familiar problems.[79]

Chapter Six

World War II and Expansion

Overleaf: Navy V-12 officer candidates march past the gymnasium on the Tech campus in 1943. (Courtesy of the Georgia Tech Archives.)

For Georgia Tech, as for American higher education in general, World War II represented a major watershed. During the war itself the campus became "militarized" to a large extent, as scores of students enrolled in designated programs, such as the Navy V-12 and Army Specialized Training Program (ASTP), soon outnumbered the regular school population. The physical appearance of the school and its military atmosphere paralleled developments apparent in 1917–18 under the presidency of K. G. Matheson. Yet, the Second World War would come to represent far more than a temporary break with the traditional, low-key atmosphere that dominated on "the flats." Lasting changes resulting from the impact of the war would extend well into the postwar era and up to the present day.

The mass influx of veterans into the school under the auspices of the postwar GI Bill served to democratize the campus at Georgia Tech, as it did other colleges across the nation. Although the level of research activity at Tech during the war itself remained small when compared with that at other universities, there was a significant increase that provided a major impetus for postwar expansion. The collective success of the Manhattan Project and other government-subsidized research projects had placed the role of science and technology on a higher plane in both the strategic thinking of our national government and in the minds of its citizens.[1] University research would no longer be thought of only in terms of the isolated work of individual scholars or inventors, but as the effort of large teams of academics, assisted by graduate students and increasingly larger numbers of support personnel. At Georgia Tech the research thrust would transform the Engineering Experiment Station, which began to hit its stride in the years after World War II, and trigger a systematic attempt to expand graduate education.

To accommodate the changes effected by these new dynamic forces, the school underwent a number of significant adjustments. Just to meet the pressures of an anticipated doubled enrollment by the late 1940s, the administration undertook a massive campus expansion program in the ten years following the war. In order to manage the larger physical plant, the increased size of the student body, and expanded curricular programs, the traditionally centralized administrative structure, which President M. L. Brittain had directed for over twenty years, would give way to a more decentralized mode of operation under Colonel Blake Ragsdale Van Leer, Georgia Tech's president from 1944 to 1956. To meet the demands of growing undergraduate enrollment and an expanded graduate program, Van Leer encouraged the hiring of large numbers of young faculty members, a greater percentage of whom held the doctoral degree or its equivalent and who became agents for change in the creation of a new Georgia Tech. As the first engineer to head the school since its founding in 1885, Van Leer also strove to bring Tech programs into conformity with his own notions of engineering education. Under Van Leer's leadership, Georgia Tech was ready to capitalize on the changes that the war had caused.

The Coming of War

The international events that unfolded in the late 1930s and President Franklin Roosevelt's program of war preparedness inevitably penetrated the Tech campus. As part of these efforts in May of 1939, the Army Air Corps announced that it was going to double the number of pilots in training and enroll some twenty thousand college students beginning that September. Tech was one of thirteen selected schools that had begun the program earlier under the auspices of the New Deal National Youth Administration (NYA). Supervised by Professor Montgomery Knight and the Guggenheim School of Aeronautics, forty Tech students began the program that spring, with an additional forty-five enrollees planned for in the summer term.[2]

There were dissenting views on the Tech campus as to the merits of Roosevelt's preparedness program and what appeared to be a drift toward war. A *Technique* editorial in October 1939, following the outbreak of war in Europe, argued that "we firmly believe that the power politics of the decadent nations of Europe is beyond the understanding of most honest straight-forward Americans." It concluded, however, that if the United States were attacked, "Tech men will fight."[3] As events proceeded throughout 1940 and into 1941, Tech men as well as students across the nation were faced with uncertainty. With the enactment of the first peacetime draft in history in April 1941, President Roosevelt specifically requested that college students remain in school until they were drafted so that they would be prepared "for greatest usefulness to their country."[4] The *Technique* explored this theme in a March 1941 editorial entitled "Engineers Fight Modern Wars." In trying to dissuade the Tech student from leaving school to enlist, the writer admonished that "the best possible way for us to demonstrate our patriotism and to do our duty *is to stay!* Have you ever thought of it that way?"[5]

Tech students had other distractions in the spring of 1941 in addition to their studies and the routines of campus life. The uproar over Governor Eugene Talmadge's aborted nomination of "Red" Barron as Tech vice president in May, discussed in chapter 5, had become the dominant topic of discussion among the student body. Subsequent political interference by Talmadge with the University System continued to hold a high level of campus interest into the 1941–42 academic year. The removal of accreditation from the University System by the Southern Association of Colleges and Secondary Schools on December 3, 1941, aroused the students as never before.[6]

The war had temporarily taken a back seat to this political turmoil at home, but the specter of the draft and the conflict in Europe still lurked in the background. Dean Vernon Skiles, while acknowledging that most engineering students were receiving deferments from their draft boards, stressed that these young men were not "draft dodgers," but patriotic citizens preparing for the armed forces' desperate need for technical personnel.[7] After Pearl Harbor, however, pressures on college students to enlist increased. The *Technique* urged students not to "desert" or be intimidated by the charge of "slacker." The war would be one of production, and "the first duty of every Tech man is to remain in school and get a good technical education as soon as possible."[8]

A compromise became possible whereby students would be able to enter specialized army and navy programs, while guaranteeing, at least for a time, continued schooling. A telegram from Frank Knox, secretary of the navy, to President Brittain in April 1942 announced the first of these options, the Navy V-1 program, which extended naval training beyond the regular ROTC option. Men between the ages of seventeen and twenty could enlist immediately as apprentice seamen, while staying in college to continue their regular course until at least the end of their second year. Classification examinations, to be given in March 1942, would offer these men the opportunity to qualify for specific training leading to commissions as aviation or engineering officers. Only days later, Brittain received a similar telegram from H. H. Arnold, commanding general of the United States Army Air Forces, announcing a revised aviation cadet program for enlistment on a deferred service basis that gave the student the option of continuing his college course while serving his country.[9]

Because of its competitive examinations and threat to take men from school after only two years, the Navy V-1 program received generally unfavorable acceptance. There was more interest in both the Army Air Corps and Marine Corps programs, which allowed students to complete their college work before induction. Both President Brittain and Dean Skiles believed that all engineering students should be allowed to obtain their degrees before being assigned to either military service or war industry and thus discouraged the Navy V-1 and a similar Army Reserve plan, which threatened to curtail degree completion. Fred W. Ajax, assistant dean of men and placement director, presented Tech's views in June 1942 at a Washington meeting on manpower needs affecting higher education. Ajax, formerly of the English department, had been working in the Office of the Dean of Men since March 1941 when Assistant Dean George Griffin had been called to active duty with the Naval Reserve. In September 1941 Ajax assumed the duties of assistant dean of men and assistant placement director. These administrative changes were but part of a facelift that war was beginning to give to the campus.[10]

Wartime Changes

In February 1942, upon request of government authorities in Washington, Tech changed its school calendar from the previous regular semester system of nine months to an accelerated twelve-month trimester system. Under this plan, the year became divided into three trimesters of sixteen weeks each, which enabled the student to complete a regular four-year course of study in three years. Tech maintained its traditional summer session of eight weeks for high school students in need of further preparatory work prior to beginning their college studies.[11]

With the exception of students of architecture, who were experiencing some difficulties with their draft boards, by the summer of 1942 Dean Skiles could report success in having engineering students deferred into Selective Service Classification II-A. All freshmen and sophomores with grades in the upper third of their class and juniors and seniors showing normal progress toward a degree were so designated. Because of the anticipated drop in enrollment due to the draft, however, the administration suspended the degree program in architecture for the duration of the war. The department instead concentrated on a degree in architectural engineering after the completion of nine semesters of work, and architecture faculty taught courses in other units as needed. Harold Bush-Brown, professor of architecture, attended a two-week camouflage program at Fort Belvoir, Virginia, in order to learn techniques that could then be imparted to Tech students.[12]

Total full-time enrollment actually remained relatively stable during the war. The figures for 1940–41 were 2,866; 1941–42, 2,910; 1942–43, 2,875; and 1943–44, 2,854. Increasingly, however, students enrolled in the military options began to outnumber the civilian body. During the fall term of 1943, for example, out of a total number of 2,732 students, 990 were classified as army, 1,036 as navy, and only 706 as "other." These army and navy students were mostly part of the two largest specialized war programs that had begun in early 1942, the Navy V-12 and the Army Specialized Training Program (ASTP).[13]

Both the V-12 program and the ASTP grew out of negotiations in the fall of 1942 among the Joint Army-Navy Personnel Board, the War Manpower Commission, and the American Council on Education's Committee on the Relationships of Higher Education to the Federal Government. President Edmund D. Day of Cornell, chairman of the American Council on Education, also chaired its special committee. The War Department had planned in September 1942 to revise its reserve programs, both the Army Enlisted Reserve Corps and the Navy V-1, V-5, and V-7 specialized programs, at the time that the draft age would be lowered to eighteen. The government conceived the Navy V-12 and ASTP college training programs, whereby selected candidates were inducted into the service and assigned on active duty to designated colleges and universities to follow special courses of study specified by the Departments of the Navy and Army. Georgia Tech became one of the 280 schools selected to participate in these programs, which were to begin officially on July 1, 1943.[14]

In announcing Tech's selection in February, M. L. Brittain explained that the government was not planning to "take over" the school, but to send 2,000 men to Atlanta for their studies. Since the school had a capacity of only 2,900, there would only be room for 900 nonmilitary students. "There must be no mistake," Brittain added, "Georgia Tech is still Georgia Tech. Our regular staff of teachers is simply shouldering the added job of training soldiers and sailors for Army and Navy jobs. The school is still being operated by the same staff."[15]

Brittain leased part of the school's facilities to the War Department on March 6, 1943, making Tech the first school in the Southeast to enter the ASTP. The army students faced a curriculum, prescribed by Washington authorities, that focused on civil, chemical, mechanical, and electrical engineering, with supplemental work in physics, mathematics, and mechanics. Tech entered into a similar agreement with the navy in March. Coach W. A. Alexander assumed responsibility for coordinating physical arrangements. An anticipated seven hundred ASTP men would be housed in Techwood Dormitory and additional units in Techwood Homes obtained from the Atlanta Housing Authority. Another three to four hundred men would receive lodging in temporary wooden barracks moved from a Civilian Conservation Corps (CCC) camp in Bartow County, Georgia, and erected at the corner of Third Street and Techwood Drive. All Navy V-12 personnel would reside in dorms and fraternity houses. The administration arranged eating accommodations for both groups in Brittain Dining Hall and a temporary CCC mess hall located on the Techwood and Third property.[16]

The ASTP began earlier than anticipated, as 500 trainees arrived on campus in mid-March 1943. By the beginning of the summer trimester in July, there were 1,050 navy trainees, 1,000 ASTP trainees, and 850 regular students. Because of the prescribed curriculum, President Brittain planned to cut back the teaching staffs in architecture, biology, ceramic engineering, geology, and textile engineering, while maintaining or expanding the faculties of electrical, civil, mechanical, aeronautical, and chemical engineering, mathematics, physics, English, and economics and social sciences. The ASTP trainees took twenty-four hours of class work, four hours of military study, and one hour of drill a week, with physical training every day. The Navy V-12 trainees enrolled in a regular civilian program of study in engineering curricula and one hour daily of physical fitness.[17]

Prior to the war there had been no regular physical training courses offered at Georgia Tech, and it was assumed that the three hours of military drill required for all freshmen and sophomores enrolled in the basic ROTC programs was sufficient. Beginning in September 1941, however, Coach Alexander had instituted classes for those students who for any reason were not taking either the basic military or naval courses. Alexander hired a new instructor, Fred Lanoue from Springfield College, and reassigned Coach Norris Dean to handle these classes. The Athletic Association provided a large share of these two men's salaries, with President Brittain picking up the rest from general funds. Coach Lanoue developed his famous "drownproofing" swimming techniques while working with Georgia Tech students during the war. Navy personnel assigned to the campus coordinated physical training for the V-12 students, while

Coach Alexander and his staff put the army trainees through their paces on the playing field and obstacle courses. The Army Specialized Training Division (ASTD) did not allow army personnel to participate in intercollegiate athletics, while the Navy V-12 program encouraged its people to join in. The presence of several V-12 football players was largely responsible for a resurgence of Tech's football fortunes during the war years.[18]

By July of 1943 there were five separate classifications of students on the campus: civilian, cooperative civilian, Army ASTP, Army ASTP-ROTC, and Navy and Marine Corps. The influx of military trainees in the financially difficult year of 1943 was a great boon to the school. University System Chancellor S. V. Sanford had been concerned about declining enrollments as a result of the draft and the accreditation battle. Speaking for the entire system, he had wondered "whether our institutions could operate unless selected by the army, navy, and air forces to train men in the armed forces." In fact, enrollments in the University System increased by some 30 percent over the previous year.[19]

Georgia Tech's military trainees performed well on the standardized tests administered by the military. Results of the ASTP test of November 25, 1943, for example, showed Tech students coming in second out of forty-seven schools in mathematics and fifth out of forty-six in chemistry. Similar creditable scores were registered in English, physics, and geography. Promised a guarantee of completing their college training as long as they performed adequately on their examinations, the ASTP trainees could not have envisioned the events of early 1944 that brought their world crashing down.[20]

In January 1944, with the ill-fated Anzio invasion and the subsequent realization that the Italian campaign would be difficult, the Pentagon became quite concerned with manpower shortages. In February the War Department announced that due to the immediate need for 200,000 troops it was discontinuing all ASTP training before April 1. The entire Tech contingent received orders and abruptly left campus on March 28, 1944, most of them to be shipped overseas shortly thereafter. The army's boast that the infusion of the intelligent ASTP forces would strengthen the fighting power of its troops was of little solace to these men.[21]

The loss of the ASTP unit presented an immediate financial crisis to the school's administration, since in 1943 Tech had received $132,543 to cover the cost of ASTP training. Upon learning of the ASTP termination, Captain J. V. Babcock, commanding officer of the Navy V-12 program on campus, contacted the Navy Department in Washington on behalf of President Brittain. He made known the availability of the Techwood dormitories and the possibility of increasing the V-12 complement, while reporting "the very serious problem confronting the school as regards the faculty, particularly following July 1." Although uncertainty remained for some time, the V-12 program did increase substantially and remained fully operational on campus through 1945.[22]

Despite M. L. Brittain's earlier admonition that Georgia Tech had not been taken over by the military, the imprint of the armed forces was very evident indeed. From April 1, 1943, until the close of the war, for example, the College Inn became classified as a Post Exchange (PX) and carried special products for the military. Civilian pilot training begun in 1939 was taken over completely by the army in 1942. By July 1944 over 742 army, navy, and civilian students had enrolled in the program, with 91 percent having completed flight training. The net proceeds of $24,826 from this program were placed in a reserve fund for aeronautical research conducted at the Engineering Experiment Station.[23]

The war also greatly affected the evening school, as large numbers of its students enrolled in one of three special federal training agencies: the Vocational Education for National Defense (VEND), Engineering Science and Management War Training (ESMWT), and Division of Emergency Training (DET). The ESMWT and VEND programs begun at Tech in 1942 were designed to provide practical technical training to civilian personnel working in the industrial war effort. Professor R. L. Sweigert of civil engineering directed the large ESMWT program, whose classes met on the Atlanta campus and at other locations throughout the state, including Savannah, Brunswick, Toccoa, Augusta, Warner Robins, Rome, and Marietta. Curriculum ranged from theoretical courses to practical industrial subjects such as ordinance inspection and production engineering. The VEND program, headed by Professor R. S. King of mechanical engineering, provided training to high school vocational education teachers who would in turn prepare their students for jobs in wartime production plants. The government phased out the VEND program in 1944, replacing it with DET classes. Of a total of 1,469 evening students during the 1944–45 school year, there were 338 tuition, 995 ESMWT, and 26 DET enrollees. Income from these federal programs helped to keep the evening division operational for the war's duration.[24]

Nationally, the war was a major force for social change affecting women, as "Rosie the Riveter" became a symbol of a new women's role. Even at Georgia Tech, a bastion of masculinity, some small gains were achieved. In November 1939 the M. L. Brittain debating society had addressed the proposition of "Should There Be Women at Tech?" The women's side lost the debate, and it would not be until 1952 that the first women would be admitted as full-time day students. For the sake of the war effort, however, the school tolerated small compromises. In spring 1942, thirty-two women enrolled in a special training program sponsored by the United States Chemical Warfare Service conducted in the Mechanical Engineering Building. The following spring, fifty Navy Waves preparing to be link trainer operators resided at the Biltmore Hotel and took their meals at Brittain Dining Hall. These were small programs to be sure, but they represented chinks in Georgia Tech's all-male armor, which would be further probed in the immediate postwar years.[25]

Wartime Research: EES, 1940–45

Prior to World War II, research on the Georgia Tech campus was limited in scope. Although some faculty members conducted research programs from within their academic departments, the Engineering Experiment Station represented the main focal point of activity. Heavy teaching loads, a norm of fifteen hours, tended to preclude much time for research, especially when such a heavy premium was placed on undergraduate instruction. Of a total faculty of 165 in the academic year 1939–40, only thirty-one members held doctorates, with seventy-three having earned a master's degree. Doctorates, particularly in engineering, were not so common prior to World War II as they are today, but the evidence suggests that there had been relatively little encouragement for faculty to pursue a research degree.

Men such as Paul Weber in chemical engineering and Homer S. Weber and Phil C. Narmore in engineering drawing and mechanics had earned their doctorates in the 1930s out of their own intellectual curiosity and interest. In some cases faculty members were actually discouraged from pursuing further study. Time off campus to fulfill residency requirements, for example, was perceived as an infringement upon teaching responsibilities.[26]

High hopes for station research in 1938–39 and 1939–40 dwindled when the state cut the EES budget by 40 percent those two years. EES Director Harry Vaughan informed the faculty of these funding difficulties in the spring of 1940 and indicated that the same situation would most likely prevail during the 1940–41 years. The Faculty Advisory Council of the station recommended that the EES concentrate its efforts on the developmental phases of three to five projects and undertake no new efforts. Vaughan invited faculty members to submit applications for new projects with the understanding that they could not begin until 1940–41.[27]

The station's cooperative projects (meaning outside-sponsored funding was involved) included the processing of domestic flax, helicopter research, the Georgia Economic Survey, paint primers for southern yellow pine, study of the properties of abietic acid, application of the attic fan in southern homes, x-ray study of synthetic fibers as affected by changes in processing, and birefringence due to a strong electric field. Station research still concentrated on Georgia and southeastern regional economic development and had not gravitated toward any significant war-related activity. Founding EES Director Harry Vaughan left Georgia Tech in 1940 to accept a higher paying position as chief of the Regional Products Research Division of the Tennessee Valley Authority (TVA), and Professor Harold Bunger, who held the concurrent post as director of chemical engineering, succeeded him. Professor Gerald A. Rosselot of the physics department became assistant director. Bunger, in poor health for some time, died during the summer of 1941 while on vacation in Minnesota. That same summer, Professor Gilbert H. Boggs, longtime director of chemistry and chemical engineering, also passed away. The unit was formally split into a separate Department of Chemistry headed by Professor J. L. Daniel, who remained dean of the Graduate Division at Tech, and a full Department of Chemical Engineering headed by Professor Jesse W. Mason. Rosselot moved up to the directorship of the Experiment Station, and Paul Weber of chemical engineering became assistant director.[28]

The Industrial Development Council, the nonprofit corporation created in 1938 to serve as contracting agency with industry and administrator of patents emanating from station research, did not function aggressively after Vaughan's departure and during Bunger's brief tenure as director. The level of research in 1941–42 remained essentially the same as in the previous year. Despite the fact that the always small number of graduate students had been further reduced by the war, some nineteen projects were undertaken. M. L. Brittain singled out wind tunnel testing of airfoil designs for industry and Montgomery Knight's helicopter work as the only important war-related research.[29]

State and regional rather than national priorities still dominated the station's research efforts, even after Pearl Harbor. One of the most significant new developments cited in 1942–43 was the establishment of a State Industrial Economics Research Agency, administered by Professor H. F. Dennison of industrial management, which compiled basic economic data for regional agencies and industries. This work, an extension of the state economic surveys formerly conducted by J. B. Hosmer, was in the mainstream of the promotion of industrial activity within Georgia. In addition, there remained a small but steady stream of contracts with regional industry, including textiles, pulp and paper making, and lumber.[30]

By 1943 the accelerated pace of the war had begun to have an impact on research at Georgia Tech. The station budget for 1943–44 for the first time reflected more than half (58 percent) of its budget coming from federal government and industrial contracts. Thirty different projects involving seventeen full-time and nearly one hundred part-time workers were active. War-related contracts existed with the Army Ordnance Department and the Office of Scientific Research and Development (OSRD).[31]

Members of the Guggenheim School were particularly fortunate in being able to supplement their income through contract work. Research continued on the Georgia Tech "autogyro" designed by Montgomery Knight, and the large wind tunnel operated an average of ten to twelve hours a day conducting tests for firms, including

United Aircraft, Glenn L. Martin Aircraft, Nemeth Helicopter Corporation, and McDonnell Aircraft. Income earned from these contracts augmented the special fund for aeronautical research maintained by the Experiment Station.[32]

The accumulation of such funds began to raise concerns that they might become "lost in the general shuffle," and the EES sought ways to segregate monies brought in from externally supported operations. Station Director Gerald Rosselot, an increasingly aggressive spokesman, addressed the issue in his 1943–44 annual report. The school could accomplish this separation of funds within the structure of the treasurer's books, by utilizing the Industrial Development Council as a third party, or with the creation of a Georgia Tech Research Foundation analagous to similar bodies at other large state institutions. After the war, the solution was realized through the creation of the Georgia Tech Research Institute (GTRI). It is significant to note, however, that the increase in contract research *during* the war provided the initial impetus for its creation. In his comments on the operation, function, and needs of the station, Rosselot also urged that there be *official* and not simply informal coordination of Graduate Division and Experiment Station activities. It was essential to coordinate all research through the station, he added, because "this institution is not yet wealthy enough to efficiently support and develop several separate and unrelated research programs." At the same time, Rosselot urged that activities such as the special regents' grant for Dennison's industrial economic research be continued with the goal of generating increased cooperative research funds from industry.[33]

The funding successes experienced in 1943–44 extended into the following year. The 1944–45 EES operating budget totaled approximately $236,792, a whopping 61 percent of which came from cooperating agencies, industry, and the federal government. The acceleration of work placed serious strains on space in the research building, and Rosselot noted a need for additional floor space. A much larger number of specific projects were now related to the war effort, such as contracts with the Army Air Force, the National Advisory Committee on Aeronautics (NACA), the Army Signal Corps, and the navy. Classified research for the Office of Scientific Research and Development (OSRD) represented the most significant of all of these war-related projects. This research focused on three related aspects of electronic communication—the development of a high selectivity, high-gain audio amplifier, a rugged portable "mini-band" amplifier, and the investigation of the use of lock-in amplifier circuits in the separation of one microsecond pulse signals from thermal noise.[34]

Tech's connection with OSRD, although relatively limited, was nevertheless significant. President Roosevelt had established OSRD's predecessor agency, the National Defense Research Committee (NDRC), on June 27, 1940, largely as a result of the efforts of Vannevar Bush of the Carnegie Institute. Tremendously successful in organizing scientific and technical research for the war effort during its first year of operation, the committee became subordinated to the newly created OSRD in June 1941. This major agency of World War II was important not only because it spent research dollars (the army and navy both spent more on research development), but because, in the words of historian of technology Carroll Pursell, "It became the training ground for that generation of science administrators who shaped the postwar scientific establishment."[35]

The OSRD (and NDRC before it) had spent some $453,656,657 on a broad program of research by the end of fiscal year 1945–46. Money had originated from a special fund established by President Roosevelt, supplemented by transfers from the military budget. By 1942–43 increased military transfers and special congressional appropriations increased dramatically. For the most part, funds flowed to a relatively small group of well-established research centers. In dollar volume, the top five university contractors were MIT, Caltech, Harvard, Columbia, and the University of California, while Western Electric led a list of top corporate contractors including, among others, Du Pont, RCA, Eastman Kodak, and General Electric. There was some political criticism during the war that OSRD contracts were regionally biased, a fact which no doubt aided in obtaining Georgia Tech's relatively small award in 1944–45. By comparison, California received 106 OSRD contracts totaling $14,384,506, while MIT led all universities in total dollar value with $116,941,352. In order of magnitude, the EES contract with OSRD was relatively insignificant; as a harbinger of things to come, however, it was of great importance. Postwar expansion of the EES would become increasingly tied to defense contracts, a large share of which centered in the field of electronics.[36]

Early Postwar Planning

President M. L. Brittain was already an elderly man of seventy-five and looking toward a well-earned retirement when war erupted. He submitted a letter of resignation to Chancellor S. V. Sanford in January 1941, only to be persuaded to withdraw it by the chancellor and members of the Board of Regents, who feared the actions that Governor Talmadge might take. These concerns were well-founded as evidenced by the subsequent events of 1941 and 1942. Flushed with the political victory of Ellis Arnall in 1942 and the resulting reforms in the University System, and at the same time weary with the increasing pace of wartime activity on campus, Brittain again submitted his resignation in January 1943. Chancellor Sanford delayed presenting the resignation to the Board of Regents, and Brittain agreed to remain until the end of his current term on August 31, 1943.[37]

It became clear to many that a new president for Tech was inevitable, given the increased pressures of the job and Brittain's advancing age. In a letter of August 4, 1943, to Marion Smith, chairman of the Board of Regents, the Georgia Tech Alumni Association stated that it had "no dissatisfaction with or criticisms of Dr. Brittain," but that "the unsettled conditions now existing because of the war, and the presence of both Army and Navy students at Georgia Tech, combined with Dr. Brittain's advanced age, make it, in our judgement, necessary that some assistance be given him and that some plans be made looking to the future of the institution."[38]

In 1941 an alumni committee had been formed to make recommendations for a new president at the time of Brittain's initial letter of resignation. This committee now endorsed Robert P. Russell, former MIT professor of chemical engineering and vice president of the Standard Oil Development Company, the research and development subsidiary of Standard Oil (New Jersey). Not only did Russell have strong academic and corporate research credentials, but his wife was a Georgia native, which some alumni felt might be a lever in attracting him to Tech. In 1943, however, Russell was tied to his responsibilities as a member of the Technical Advisory Committee of the Petroleum Industry War Council in Washington. Because of Russell's unavailability, the Alumni Association recommended that Cherry Emerson, then president of the association, a well-respected engineer with Robert and Company, a Georgia Tech engineering graduate, and son of former Dean William S. Emerson, be hired as either a part-time or full-time assistant to President Brittain. With his own career at Robert and Company apparently at an impasse when passed over for the presidency of that firm, Emerson was available to lend assistance to his alma mater.[39]

The regents formally appointed Emerson to the post of part-time vice president of Georgia Tech on September 8, 1943, "relieving Dr. Brittain *only* of such duties and activities as Dr. Brittain directs." The regents specifically charged Emerson to build up the Alumni Association, interest "well-to-do" individuals to contribute to the school, and develop industry interest in Tech's research program. Moreover, Emerson was to further cooperation with the army, navy, and air force, become acquainted with federal policy trends in postwar education, and aid the chancellor in obtaining greater federal financial support for the University System. President Brittain, now seventy-eight years of age, again submitted his resignation, to become effective on July 1, 1944.[40]

In the midst of the turmoil of the war, the political fights surrounding the accreditation dispute, and the growing concern over Brittain's successor, the school had devoted little attention to specific issues of postwar planning such as campus expansion and curriculum improvement. The administration for the most part functioned, as did most colleges during wartime, on a level of crisis management rather than long-term planning. Yet, as early as June 1942, Harold Bush-Brown, head of architecture, had raised several planning issues in a report forwarded to the regents under Brittain's signature. Bush-Brown wrote that "the government, it appears, is looking forward to conditions of the post-war situation. . . . This means establishment and adoption of a *master plan* for future development as an initial and major step."[41]

The Bush-Brown report designated as immediate needs a new boiler for the central power plant and the acquisition of more land. Ranked in descending order of importance, urgent needs included dormitories, a new administration-library building, a physics and architecture building, a chemistry and chemical engineering building, a textile building, a military armory, and new equipment. Less urgent needs encompassed more land, a mechanical engineering building, a new hospital, a faculty club, a student union, a new chemistry plant, a new auditorium and chapel, a new president's home, faculty housing, still more equipment, and additional dormitories. The future needs category listed still more land, an academic building, an electrical engineering building, an engineering drawing and mechanics building, an additional EES building, a service building, and a large exhibition hall. The report recommended that a minimum commitment from the regents would require the expenditure of $1.8 million or $300,000 a year for a six-year program.[42]

On October 13, 1943, the regents authorized President Brittain to engage the architecture department at Georgia Tech, under Bush-Brown's direction, to draw up a long-range development plan, with the cost of preparing the plan coming from profits earned by radio station WGST. In May of that year the regents had taken over active operation of the station through its radio committee, chaired by Regent Frank M. Spratlin. This action had followed an FCC ruling that directed the school to terminate its contractual agreement with the Southern Broadcasting Company to operate the station. This represented a windfall for Tech in that higher profits would now accrue to the school, much of them ultimately going toward the postwar land acquisition program.[43]

With the WGST funds, Bush-Brown established an Office of Long-Range Development within the Department of Architecture as of November 15, 1943. The first drawing or "master plan" prepared and labeled "M-1" depicted the campus as it existed on January 1, 1944. The roots of the master plan concept lay in what Brittain termed the "master key plan," which existed in 1922 when he took over the presidency from K. G. Matheson. This plan had evolved during the 1920s and 1930s and was more or less in place when the war broke out. A series of subsequent drawings, executed between January 1 and February 11, 1944, and numbered M-2, M-3, M-4, and M-5, detailed various stages of a comprehensive future plan for both land acquisition and building construction. Under the plan, the teaching and working area would stay to the west, the living area to the east, with recreation and athletic areas in between as the campus grew in a northerly direction.[44]

Aside from planning for physical expansion, there were also concerns for the status of Georgia Tech's educational programs in the immediate postwar era. President Brittain appointed three separate faculty postwar planning committees between late fall of 1943 and spring of 1944 to address these issues. They recommended that Georgia Tech's instructional program be kept at the college level and offered more specific suggestions, including a careful and critical review of the engineering curricula, encouragement of graduate study and research, and an improved salary schedule and promotion system aimed at bolstering faculty morale. Perhaps reflecting the fact that the regents had accepted Brittain's resignation in February and announced the selection of Blake R. Van Leer as the new president, the third committee seized the opportunity to address specific areas of concern affecting faculty status. Here was a chance to signal major faculty concerns to the new man before he officially assumed his duties on July 1, 1944. The committee advocated that staff hired for additional work (evening and summer school teaching) should be paid an amount equal to their rate of basic pay and strongly urged that the school provide generous aid and encouragement to faculty research, a better salary scale, and paid leave for study, travel, and other appropriate activities. The committee also recommended that the school calendar be adjusted so that cooperative and regular students be synchronized, since co-ops had remained on the quarter system, while the regular civilian and military students had moved to the accelerated trimester system developed during the war.[45]

In a memorandum to Brittain and the presidents of all of the units in the University System on January 13, 1944, Chancellor S. V. Sanford put forth a program of ten objectives for 1944. Three of these goals affected Georgia Tech to the extent that they were relevant to the entire system. They included a plan to provide for the education of returning veterans (the GI Bill had been introduced in Congress and would be passed on June 22, 1944), to secure larger appropriations from the legislature, and to create an expanded graduate school. Aims specific to Tech included Sanford's stated goal to make the school the outstanding engineering institution in the Southeast and expansion of the Engineering Experiment Station over a five-year program. Sanford also directed Brittain to appoint five faculty members to a new committee to study Georgia Tech's postwar curriculum.[46] In a variety of ways, then, there had been significant efforts at planning for postwar Georgia Tech months before Brittain's successor would set foot on campus. There is a tendency to associate the rapid change that occurred in the immediate postwar era with Van Leer, and much of this is clearly justified. There was also, however, evident continuity with earlier planning concepts, particularly with regard to physical expansion.

The Colonel Arrives

It is unclear from the record precisely when Colonel Blake Ragsdale Van Leer became a candidate for the Georgia Tech presidency. More than likely, however, the first connection was made in September 1943 when two events coincided. President Brittain again submitted his resignation to Chancellor Sanford at the beginning of the 1943–44 school year, and on September 14, 1943, Colonel Van Leer addressed a meeting of the ASTP Advisory Committee at the Municipal Auditorium in Atlanta. At the time, Van Leer was on leave from his post as dean of engineering at North Carolina State and was on active military duty as chief of the facilities branch (ASTD) in Washington. He had held this military position since June 1943 and had certainly been in contact with Georgia Tech authorities in conjunction with his duties. Van Leer was anxious to return to academic life. It is reasonable to assume that he learned of the Georgia Tech vacancy at the time of his Atlanta trip and decided to apply. His former personal secretary at the Pentagon has confirmed that it was Van Leer who took the initiative in contacting Georgia Tech about the job.[47]

The regents were apparently impressed with Van Leer's credentials, for on February 15, 1944, they elected the colonel to become the fifth president of Georgia Tech, with his appointment officially beginning on July 1, 1944. At the same time, the regents honored M. L. Brittain with the post of president emeritus. Brittain was allowed to remain in the president's home on North Avenue and would have general supervisory duties looking after bequests that had been made to the school, including the Texas property that had come from the Julius Brown estate, radio station WGST, the Florence Hinman bequest, and the Florence H. Brownell estate. Brittain was also directed to write a history of Georgia Tech, a labor of love that he had contemplated doing for some time.[48]

Colonel Van Leer became the first true engineer to head the Atlanta school. He brought to the job an impressive list of qualifications from the academic community, private industry, professional engineering societies, and the military. In many ways, he was the ideal person to lead Georgia Tech during the most explosive growth period in its history up to that time. In May, at the time of his first visit to Atlanta following his election in February, Van Leer outlined his vision for the school: "It has always been my ambition to see a great technological school built up in the South comparable to the Massachusetts Institute of Technology in Boston. Georgia Tech has a fine chance to become this great Southern technical school." He added, however, that "I hope you will be patient, as it will require a lot of hard work to place Georgia Tech where the institution properly belongs." In a seemingly romanticized story often told by Van Leer, and independently confirmed by his wife, the Colonel had, as a young man, stated the goal of one day becoming the president of Georgia Tech. If the story is true, his life-long dream had now become a reality.[49]

Fifty years old at the time of his appointment, Van Leer was born in Mangum, Texas (now Oklahoma), on August 16, 1893. He graduated from Purdue with a bachelor's degree in electrical engineering in 1915 and went to the University of California at Berkeley as an instructor and head of the hydraulics laboratory there. An ROTC student at Purdue, Van Leer entered the army as a second lieutenant in 1917, remaining on active duty until 1919 and rising to the rank of captain. Overseas for thirteen months in World War I, he received the French Croix de Guerre for service in the 316th Army Engineers. While in France, he also took a certificate in engineering from the University of Caen in 1919. Returning from active military duty to Berkeley in 1919, Van Leer earned a master's degree in mechanical engineering in 1920, and in 1922 received the degree of master in engineering from Purdue. He remained at the hydraulics laboratory in Berkeley, marrying Ella Wall, an art student at the Berkeley school of architecture, in 1924. In 1927–28, Van Leer was the recipient of the Freeman Traveling Scholarship awarded by the American Society of Mechanical Engineers to study in Europe and attended courses in hydraulics at the University of Munich.[50]

Upon returning to the United States, Van Leer worked briefly as an engineer with the Southern Pacific Railroad and the Bryan-Jackson Pump Company before taking a position in Washington, D.C., as assistant secretary of the American Engineering Council. From there he went to the University of Florida at Gainesville as dean of engineering, a post he held from 1932 to 1937 before taking the same position at North Carolina State. Van Leer, a major in the Army Reserve Corps of Engineers at the time of Pearl Harbor, was recalled to active duty in May of 1942 and promoted to lieutenant colonel on October 17, 1942. He became chief of the facilities branch (ASTD) in June 1943 and was promoted to full colonel in October 1943. In 1943, Washington and Jefferson College of Washington, Pennsylvania, awarded Van Leer the honorary degree of doctor of science in recognition of his many contributions to engineering education in the United States.[51]

Van Leer possessed broad knowledge and experience of engineering education. He had a respected reputation within professional engineering societies and had increased his visibility during the war through his work with the ASTP. During his spring visit prior to his assumption of duties, Van Leer informed the regents that his first priority was to extend graduate education and research work so that Georgia Tech would be in a position to better serve southern industry. Striking a theme that he would echo repeatedly over the next several years, the often brash colonel told his new bosses that the development of Georgia Tech would take money. In the past, he noted, the regents had spent approximately $247 to $287 per student, whereas other engineering schools typically expended $1,000 per student.[52]

Van Leer's emphasis on the theme of southern regional industrial growth triggered a warm response from Ralph McGill, editor of the *Atlanta Constitution*. Citing the words of his predecessor, Henry Grady, McGill wrote a column extolling the role of Georgia Tech in the process of industrialization. The New South Creed sounded again as McGill wrote that "there is a new stirring and a new hope for the future. Blake Ragsdale Van Leer is a part of it. He is one of the weapons that the South must use in the competition of the postwar future."⁵³ Intuitively an activist, Van Leer did not hesitate before launching himself at McGill's target.

The Colonel Takes Command

Blake R. Van Leer preferred always to be addressed as colonel rather than as president or doctor. In part, this may have been just the symptomatic use of military titles during World War II and the immediate postwar period; it may have been, as suggested by some, that the lack of an earned doctorate touched a raw nerve. The latter concern had never bothered M. L. Brittain, whose doctorates from Emory, Mercer, and Georgia were honorary. Certainly the title of colonel fit Van Leer's bearing and approach to administration, which were both by all accounts decidedly military. On the positive side, Van Leer seemed able to make tough decisions while at the same time demonstrating a willingness to listen to other points of view. He also decentralized administrative authority in a model similar to that of a military staff structure. More negatively, Van Leer's somewhat gruff exterior often rankled the conciliatory academic mindset, and his bluntness, particularly with the regents, sometimes came across as overly combative when diplomacy may have been more productive. To reassure those apprehensive of what the Van Leer era might bring, in July 1944, soon after his arrival on campus, he implored the Georgia Tech community to "please don't get the idea that I'm one of those fellows who jump in to revolutionize things and shift everything around. It'll be months before changes are made, if any."⁵⁴

It may have been months before changes came, but just barely. Since their adoption in 1891, Georgia Tech had operated with only a very general set of formal statutes, a situation that struck Van Leer as odd when compared with his past experiences at other schools. The regents had decreed that each unit should develop a detailed outline of organization and responsibility, and the University of

Georgia had compiled new by-laws in 1943. It would be necessary for Tech to follow Georgia's general guidelines in amending its statutes, but Van Leer insisted that the Atlanta school's regulations must reflect the differences of a technological institution. On July 8, 1944, exactly one week after his inauguration, Van Leer wrote to Professor Ralph Hefner of the mathematics department, appointing him chairman of a Committee on Regulations, Constitution, and By-laws and empowering the committee to draft a new set of statutes for Georgia Tech. In his selection of Hefner, Van Leer indicated an administrative style of singling out younger faculty with initiative and appointing them to positions of authority. Van Leer then proceeded to give Hefner an idea of what he, the president, wanted to see in the statutes.[55]

Van Leer desired an organizational chart that gave the faculty final authority on all academic matters, with administrative and executive functions left exclusively to the president and other administrative officers. All teachers were to be members of the General Faculty, but he thought it unwise to give votes to instructors. He preferred that there be four deans: one each for graduate studies, engineering, general studies, and student affairs, and recommended that Dean Skiles's office be converted into that of vice president in charge of academic matters to supervise and coordinate the four deans and the registrar's office. The president suggested that Hefner might seek models in the statutes of the University of Florida, North Carolina State, Purdue, and the University of California (where Van Leer had experience), as well as those at the University of Chicago and other leading academic institutions.[56]

William Gilmer Perry, dean of general subjects, wrote to Chairman Hefner of the faculty regulations committee listing his concerns about the proposed statutes based on his long tenure and experience at Tech. Perry had served under Presidents Lyman Hall, K. G. Matheson, and M. L. Brittain and represented an important voice of continuity. He attached a useful historical sketch of government at Georgia Tech, highlighting the growing power of the post of dean at the school after the resignation of Matheson in 1922. Perry stressed that governance at the school had been, despite its flaws, both flexible and successful and said that "Georgia Tech was a *pleasant* place to work." In conclusion, the dean iterated that "the most valuable asset of any organization is morale; and whatever destroys, or even lowers the morale does the organization a grievous injury."[57]

Hefner's faculty regulations committee worked over a period of some ten months to hammer out the first detailed by-laws in the history of the school. Under the plan the number of administrative officers directly reporting to the president were reduced to fourteen, a move toward decentralization fully supported by Van Leer. The document, finally adopted by the faculty in the spring of 1945 and later approved by the regents, also decentralized the duties and responsibilities of Dean W. Vernon Skiles.[58]

Skiles was appointed to the new position of executive dean, a far less demanding post. Although he had assumed enormous responsibility during Brittain's declining years, Skiles had not been in good health, and the added strains of wartime had greatly taken their toll. Cherry L. Emerson, temporary vice president since 1943, succeeded D. P. Savant as dean of engineering with Savant remaining as vice dean. Phil C. Narmore moved in as acting dean of basic studies with the ailing Professor Perry remaining as vice dean. Robert Irving Sarbacher was brought in to head up Van Leer's expanded Graduate Division. Holding a bachelor's in electrical engineering from Florida, a master's from Princeton, and a doctorate of science from Harvard, Sarbacher, whom Van Leer had known at Florida, had been director of research and development in aircraft radios and radar for the navy from 1942 to 1944.[59]

In his first annual report of 1944–45, President Van Leer indicated that his initial priority had been to hire and retain a distinguished faculty, while the expansion of the school's physical plant had remained a second major goal. He moved to address the first with the appointment of an Advanced Planning Committee in the fall of 1944. The committee report highlighted the excessively high teaching loads and low salaries at Georgia Tech, citing the 1942 study of engineering education in Georgia by H. P. Hammond, dean of engineering at Penn State, that had termed teaching loads "abnormally high." The report included extensive comparative salary data with selected colleges and universities in the Southeast, and leading engineering schools across the country, which clearly found Tech's pay scale wanting. It concluded that "if the Georgia School of Technology is to attract and hold men who are outstanding in their work, there must be a marked increase in the present salary scale, particularly in the upper brackets."[60] Van Leer picked up the cry, and constantly fought for higher salary appropriations from the regents.

Van Leer had also acted quickly on his stated goal of improving the Georgia Tech physical plant. In July 1944 he asked the members of his Advisory Council to submit a list of campus needs and priorities. Their recommendations, combined with a progress report submitted by Harold Bush-Brown on July 15, 1944, all entered into the president's thinking as he assembled a master development plan for the campus. Bush-Brown's report was based on the M-5 plan submitted to M. L. Brittain on February 11, 1944. Van Leer implemented minor changes into a new M-6 plan submitted to the Board of Regents in the fall of 1944.[61]

On October 21, 1944, the regents formally adopted Van Leer's comprehensive master plan. In most respects it was consistent with the previous documents that had originated in the campus architect's office under Bush-Brown's direction. The M-6 plan contained a master building plan for the next ten years and envisioned a comprehensive expansion to 135 acres of land. The Atlanta campus would remain relatively compact, built on three sides of a major arterial highway. Under this plan Tech would approximately double its size over the next ten years. The Board of Regents gave Van Leer approval to accomplish the first phase of expansion, and Regents Frank Spratlin, Rutherford Ellis, and Marion Smith of Atlanta were to work with Tech's president on his long-range plan.[62]

In order to explain his vision for the new Georgia Tech and in the hope of generating support for his plans, Van Leer created the first Office of Public Relations on the campus. Everyone knew about Tech's football team and rich athletic heritage, but few outside of Georgia and the Southeast were aware of its programs in engineering education and research. Eugene O'Brien, former ASME president and an experienced publications administrator, suggested that Van Leer seek out a person with both engineering credentials and public affairs experience to head up such an information program. He recommended Lieutenant Colonel Leslie R. Zsuffa, then on active duty with the army in Washington. Zsuffa, a thirty-four-year-old engineering graduate of New York University, had been assistant editor and public relations officer for ASME before the war. On active military duty for five years, he had served as a staff officer under General Dwight Eisenhower at SHAEF and was then attached to Army Service and Supply, which was assigned to do work on auxiliary plants connected with the Manhattan Project. Zsuffa was interviewed for the job in the summer of 1945 and hired on July 11. Van Leer pulled strings to obtain Zsuffa's military release, and Zsuffa assumed his duties on campus in September 1945. In his role as director of public relations and assistant to the president, Zsuffa played an influential and often controversial role in the president's office. In the minds of many faculty, the new public relations director too often beat the drum for Van Leer personally rather than for Georgia Tech.[63]

Within months of his arrival, Van Leer had demonstrated that he was a mover and a shaker. His swift action to adopt governing statutes and his support for faculty salary increases did much for bolstering morale. His forceful advocacy of the campus expansion plans which had been around for years indicated that great change lay ahead. With the end of the war in sight and the prospect of increased enrollments of returning veterans, the administration had to address the school's academic programs.

Curricular Developments

Blake Van Leer had been intimately associated with the development of engineering education nationally for many years. He understood the importance of integrating Tech's programs into the main currents of engineering education, while at the same time seeking to take advantage of innovative curriculum development. In October 1944, for example, Georgia Tech became the first school in the South to establish a Veterans Guidance Center under the auspices and funding of the Veterans Administration. Intended to be the center of a personnel program for discharged veterans, its establishment led to other significant developments.

Not only did the Veterans Guidance Center provide for the scientific testing and guidance of entering students and a clinic for counseling mentally and emotionally disturbed veterans, it led to the creation of Georgia Tech's Department of Psychology. Captain Joseph E.

Moore, assistant chief of the Military Processing Board, Fourth Service Command, came to campus as professor of psychology, director of the Veterans Center, and head of the new Department of Psychology. Under contract with the Veterans Administration (VA), the center received twenty dollars per advisement and soon became self-sustaining. Run on a cooperative basis between Tech and the VA, the center accepted for advisement all veterans with a Georgia address. Following a battery of tests and interviews with each veteran, the center endeavored to locate the right college, vocational school, or job for him.[64]

In the spring of 1945, Van Leer brought in two men from the outside to administer major departments at the school. Lieutenant Colonel Frank F. Groseclose, a former colleague of the president at North Carolina State, became head of the new Department of Industrial Engineering. Holding both a bachelor's and a master's in mechanical engineering, Groseclose had been professor of engineering mechanics at West Point since 1942. The death of Franklyn C. Snow, head of civil engineering, created a vacancy that was filled by Lieutenant Colonel Thomas H. Evans, who held bachelor's and master's degrees from Caltech and who had previous teaching experience at Yale and Virginia. Their appointments took effect on July 1, 1945, at the same time that Cherry Emerson became dean of engineering and Robert Sarbacher dean of graduate studies. The onslaught of so many colonels on the campus gave pause to more than one faculty member, but with the war still on, the military aura was to be expected.[65]

Another innovation begun by Van Leer soon after his arrival was the creation of a new Department of Safety Engineering. During the war several engineering schools, including Georgia Tech, had established extension classes in safety engineering in conjunction with the United States Departments of Labor and Education. Van Leer was interested in extending this safety work into the postwar years by integrating programs into the overall engineering curriculum. Secretary of Labor Frances Perkins wrote to the colonel in December 1944 that "your plan to incorporate safety into your regular engineering courses is a real contribution toward better control of industrial accidents." In the spring of 1945 Georgia Tech was one of four schools, the others being New York University, California, and the Illinois Institute of Technology, to receive a renewable grant of

$8,000 from the National Safety Council to institute a safety engineering program. Tech planned to integrate safety into all regular engineering courses, to reorganize, and re-equip all laboratories and shops to incorporate safety practices, and to develop a graduate program in safety engineering in cooperation with private industry. Professor W. N. Cox, Jr., arrived on campus as head of the new Department of Safety Engineering.[66]

Van Leer viewed the accelerated trimester school calendar adopted during the war as further barrier to curricular reform. While all other units of the university system had now moved to a quarter system, Tech's student body in 1944–45 still included 70 percent Navy V-12 trainees, and the school had to stick with three sixteen-week trimesters. In order to bring Tech's program into conformity with the rest of the University System, to accommodate the cooperative program more effectively, and to create greater flexibility in vacation time, Van Leer recommended the adoption of a quarter system at Georgia Tech. Approved by the regents in September 1945, the new calendar was slated to go into effect in the fall of 1946.[67]

Other new programs adopted in 1945 included a hotel management undergraduate major in the industrial management department and the first graduate program in that school, a master of science in industrial management. The hotel management program, partially sponsored by the Georgia Hotel Association, became operative in 1947 but was not very successful. The original condition imposed by the regents was that the program would become self-sustaining after five years, but it did not generate sufficient enrollment and was terminated. The more successful master's degree in industrial management became the first professional management degree awarded in the state, preceding the University of Georgia's master of business administration degree by five years. The 1945–46 school year saw the completion of the first required physical training courses for all students. All civilian freshmen (veterans were excluded) had to take three hours a week of physical training for one hour's credit. A direct outgrowth of the small program begun by Coach Alexander in 1941 and the extensive classes conducted for ASTP students, the physical training department was located within the College of Basic Studies but was largely financed by the Athletic Association.[68]

At Colonel Van Leers's urging in 1944–45, Tech made title changes in the engineering degrees that it awarded. Following the recommendation of the American Society for Engineering Education and the Engineers' Council for Professional Development, the word "science" was dropped from all professional degrees. Thus the degree would now be a bachelor of civil engineering rather than a bachelor of science in civil engineering.[69]

Van Leer continued to make graduate education one of his top priorities. He stated in 1945 that "if our graduate school is strong, students will naturally be attracted to the undergraduate courses, just as they are to the Massachusetts Institute of Technology."[70] In addition to $20,500 in matching funds for the support of graduate fellowships obtained from the General Education Board (Rockefeller Foundation) in 1945, the regents appropriated another $15,000 for graduate studies at Georgia Tech for 1945–46. Fellowship awards up to $1,800 a year for graduate study were given in the expanded graduate division headed by Sarbacher. Van Leer supported the adoption of a new doctoral program in engineering to add to the existing master of science programs at the school. So as not to conflict with degrees offered at the University of Georgia, the president stressed the "applied" nature of such a doctoral degree. On April 10, 1946, the regents approved the recommendation that Georgia Tech for the first time offer courses leading to the degree of doctor in engineering.[71]

Student Life

As the war began to wind down in 1944–45, the heavy military imprint on the campus waned. As of July 1, 1944, for example, there were 717 Navy V-12 students on campus; one year later the number had declined to 330. The Departments of the Army and Navy in 1945 assured Georgia Tech that its military training programs would continue in the form of Army and Navy ROTC units. The school was slowly returning to civilian status, but the rich history of military training dating back to World War I would continue on the prewar ROTC basis.[72]

Football, by far the major sport at Georgia Tech, had survived the war through the creative use of civilian 4-F and Navy V-12 students, who were allowed to participate in intercollegiate athletics. In the spring of 1942, after Pearl Harbor, the Board of Regents had briefly considered dropping intercollegiate football for the duration, but opted instead to follow a national movement supporting the playing of the game to bolster morale. Led by freshman halfback Clint Castleberry, the first wartime season of 1942 began well with victories over Auburn, Notre Dame, Chattanooga, Davidson, Navy, and Duke, the best start since the championship team of 1939. When Coach W. A. Alexander suffered a heart attack after the Duke game, however, the season appeared threatened. Chief Assistant R. L. "Bobby" Dodd led the squad to successive wins over Kentucky, Alabama, and Florida but lost the season finale to a powerful University of Georgia team and the Cotton Bowl to Texas.[73]

Coach Alex recovered and stayed on to complete his last two seasons in 1943 and 1944. The 1943 season (7–3–0) culminated with a victory over Tulsa in the Sugar Bowl, making Tech the first team in history to have played in each of the four major bowls: Rose, 1929; Orange, 1939; Cotton, 1942; and Sugar, 1943. Alex's last team in 1944 finished with a record of 8–2–0, losing only to Duke and Notre Dame during the regular season. In the postseason Orange Bowl, Tulsa avenged the previous year's loss with a conquest over Tech. Bobby Dodd succeeded legendary Coach Alexander in 1945, with the old master staying on as athletic director. The season ended with a disappointing 4–6–0 record, but the wartime crowds continued to flock to Grant Field.[74]

Dodd soon returned Georgia Tech to winning ways in 1946 with an 8–2–0 season capped by an Oil Bowl victory over St. Mary's in Houston, but the school came close to losing its dynamic young coach. Offered the job of succeeding Frank Kimbrough as head football coach at Baylor, Dodd finally decided to stay on with the Yellow Jackets. In a comment at the time, the *Atlanta Journal* suggested a theme that ironically would later haunt Dodd. In predicting that Tech would be unable to win many more bowl games, the sportswriter argued that "its a matter of curricula. Tech doesn't have courses competitive with big league participation." Dodd overcame this problem effectively in the late 1940s, however, posting winning campaigns in 1947, 1948, and 1949 before recording a disappointing

5–6–0 record in 1950. Dodd's continuing success on the field engendered continuing rumors that he was leaving. In January 1948 stories circulated that Dodd had agreed to coach Dan Topping's New York Yankee team in the professional All-America Conference. The completion of the new west stands at Grant Field that added 9,700 additional seats and new press boxes may have been one major reason why Dodd remained in Atlanta.[75]

Dodd differed from Coach Alexander in many ways. He substituted the "T" formation offense for the single wing and replaced the old, drab yellow uniforms that hearkened back to the "Golden Tornado" of the 1920s. More important, Alex's fair but harsh training rules gave way to a more relaxed regimen. The success of the football program represented an important link with the past as well as a key factor in integrating the campus—students, alumni, and faculty—as the school made the transition from wartime to peacetime.[76]

An End and a Beginning

The war witnessed the end of one epoch in Georgia Tech's history and ushered in a new era. M. L. Brittain's well-earned retirement and the inauguration of Blake R. Van Leer in 1944 serve as convenient benchmarks to this transition, but it went far deeper. The relatively small prewar institution had established a deserved reputation as the South's leading engineering school, but in terms of research, graduate education, and national and international recognition, it had not yet achieved its often-stated goal of becoming another MIT. Arguably, Tech has still not approached this level of achievement and reputation, but it has come much closer in the new scientific and technological world that has emerged in post–World War II America.

Forces set in motion with the growth of sponsored research during the war and the influx of students under the GI Bill would build momentum during the crucial decade from 1946 to 1956, the year that Blake Van Leer died in office. During this ten-year period the administration and faculty of the Atlanta school moved ever closer to the status of a major technological university. A doubling of the undergraduate student body, a comprehensive campus building program, the dramatic expansion of graduate education, and a concomitant growth of research activity all contributed to bring about this change.

Chapter Seven

The Imprint of Change: The Van Leer Years

Overleaf: Engineering Experiment Station personnel operate the AC network calculator in the late 1940s. (Courtesy of the Georgia Tech Archives.)

By any measure the era of tremendous growth at Georgia Tech after World War II will be forever associated with the administration headed by Blake R. Van Leer. The achievements, and there were many, as well as the shortcomings were not Van Leer's alone, however. In seeking to understand historical change it is imperative to discriminate between the men and women who shape events and the dynamics of the environment in which they are operating. In the case of Colonel Van Leer, it is not meant to denigrate his personal role by pointing out that he assumed the mantle of leadership at a unique time in Georgia Tech's as well as the nation's history. In many ways, he was at the right place at the right time. It is equally important to acknowledge the respective roles played by a large number of other individuals among the administration, faculty, and staff who contributed mightily to these events.

While focusing on change, one must also not underestimate the forces of continuity that prevail at any institution. New opportunities to expand Tech's service in the promotion of state industrial development were consistent with the culture of the New South Creed prevalent at the time of the school's founding in the late nineteenth century. Despite efforts to further graduate education and research, Georgia Tech remained predominantly an undergraduate engineering school, conscious of its role in Georgia and the Southeast, and proud of its mission. Although moving toward the goal of becoming a major technological university, a status symbolically if not literally demonstrated by its name change in 1948 to the Georgia "Institute" of Technology, the school continued to exhibit characteristics identified with its past. Unlike the Massachusetts and California institutes of technology, whose athletic activities centered on the intramural rather than the intercollegiate level of competition, at Georgia Tech varsity football remained a centerpiece of student life and alumni involvement. It is somewhat paradoxical that while the school was seeking to reach a new level of recognition as a center of scientific and technological excellence, it enjoyed its "golden era" of football success with the great Bobby Dodd teams of the late 1940s and mid-1950s, reaching a zenith with a record-setting six consecutive major bowl victories from 1952 to 1957.

In yet another and somewhat ironic instance of continuity with the past, Tech found itself struggling to obtain a greater share of funding from the University System to implement its expanded programs. Van Leer's annual reports continuously focused on the relatively small amount of per capita student appropriations the engineering school received when compared with other units within the University System.

The decade 1946–56 marked a period of both great achievements and major disappointments, such as the dip in enrollment in the early 1950s associated with the end of the flow of World War II veterans under the GI Bill. The fifties was a conservative era politically and educationally across the nation, and the Yellow Jacket version of the "silent generation" participated in its share of fraternity parties and pep rallies. But it was also a time of social change that saw the admission of women on a full-time basis and the initial rumblings of racial integration within the University System and at Georgia Tech. On balance, the forces of change ultimately outweighed the countervailing pressures of tradition as Georgia Tech made enormous strides toward Blake Van Leer's vision of a great technological university.

Southern Technical Institute

From the beginning of his presidency, Van Leer had pressed to expand graduate education at Georgia Tech, but he was also aware of developments in engineering education that addressed postwar needs in another area—a critical scarcity of trained technicians.

This idea was embodied in a growing "technical institutes" movement, in which the Engineers' Council for Professional Development (ECPD) played a leading part. Although figures showed a national enrollment of 21,079 students in two-year technical institutes in 1945–46, a study reported that some 400,000 technicians attended similar programs in the Soviet Union. Aware that the federal government was contemplating the support of such two-year institutions, Van Leer had recommended the establishment of a technical institute at Georgia Tech. Seen as an educational experience somewhere between a trade school and an engineering college, such programs appeared to be ideal for returning veterans of World War II. At Georgia Tech the technical institute concept represented a symbolic link with the shop culture past. On April 19, 1945, the Board of Regents approved Van Leer's recommendation.[1]

The president appointed a five-member faculty Committee on Technical Institutes, which in August 1945 recommended that Tech begin a terminal two-year curriculum program for technicians, possibly to be located on the campus of a junior college in Americus, Georgia, in the southern part of the state. Van Leer was wary of the Americus location for several reasons, among them the concern that there might arise a movement to establish a rival four-year engineering college in the area. A separate three-man faculty committee investigated locating the technical institute on property formerly belonging to the United States Navy in Gainesville, north of Atlanta. This committee recommended the creation of a center for radar research, a flight training school, a branch of Georgia Tech's extension division, and a technical institute providing terminal courses of from six months to two years for high school graduates.[2]

The regents rejected the Gainesville site on the grounds that the new institute should be located close to Atlanta. Moreover, they believed that radar research, then just getting underway at the Experiment Station, should be conducted at the main campus. The regents' own technical institute committee recommended that Tech investigate either the Naval Air Station in Chamblee or Rickenbacker Field in Marietta. A feasibility study of the Chamblee site reported that the twenty-three buildings at the Naval Air Station were available for housing, feeding, and instructing 650 students. In

July 1946, Georgia Tech leased nine of the navy buildings at the Chamblee Air Station, valued at $1.5 million, for one dollar a year.[3]

The situation remained static for the next several months, as the regents withheld a final decision. Meanwhile, the technical institutes program was booming nationally as returning vets began to flood the educational market. Professor C. W. Beese of Purdue presented a paper at the December 1946 meeting of the Association of Land-Grant Colleges and Universities summarizing the interests and experiences of a large number of schools in the program. Finally, in May 1947 the regents authorized their chairman to appoint a committee to study the creation of a technical institute on the Chamblee property, on which Georgia Tech now had a lease. Still, however, the regents vacillated.[4]

Colonel Van Leer, through his public relations director, Leslie Zsuffa, had mobilized support for the technical institute in many quarters. The Associated Industries of Georgia (AIG), a trade association, lobbied the regents for the technical institute, making particularly good use of a slogan which Zsuffa had given to them. Whereas Georgia Tech would continue to train the captains of industry, the technical institute would prepare the "sergeants of industry." Influential Tech alumnus and Rich's Department Store executive Frank Neely, apparently at Van Leer's urging, wrote to new University System Chancellor Raymond A. Paty that the Georgia Tech Alumni Association might consider taking over all extension work as well as the contemplated new technical school, independent of the University System. This proposal never gained momentum, but it did serve to hasten the regents' action to fund the school. On September 10, 1947, the regents allocated an additional $60,000 to Georgia Tech's budget for the fiscal year ending June 30, 1948, with the money to be used for the establishment of the technical institute at the Atlanta Naval Air Station in Chamblee.[5]

Van Leer, anxious to get the new "polytechnic" under way by January, had previously recommended that R. W. Mayer be appointed as director. Mayer, an army colonel, had been director of training for the Quartermaster Corps and had been interested in opening a trade school in the Atlanta area. When the Mayer connection failed to work out, Van Leer recommended Professor Lawrence V. Johnson to head the new school. Johnson, a graduate of Ohio State, had come to Tech in 1931 as an instructor in physics. He became coordinator of the pilot training program administered by the Guggenheim School during the war and acting director of the School of Aeronautics in 1946. The choice of Johnson, which became effective on October 15, 1947, was fortuitous. More than any other individual, he became the guiding hand of what would later become the Southern Technical Institute.[6]

With basic funding assured, Van Leer looked to the pressing need for equipment at the Chamblee campus. Tech itself was woefully lacking and had little to spare. Graduate Dean Robert I. Sarbacher had left Georgia Tech in the summer of 1947, concluding a stormy three-year tenure. As a member of the Advisory Council of the War Assets Administration in Washington, he offered his services in successfully obtaining surplus government equipment for the new technical institute.[7]

On March 24, 1948, the Technical Institute, officially a unit of the Engineering Extension Division of Georgia Tech, opened its doors in Chamblee to 166 students. From the beginning, L. V. Johnson and Van Leer supported a distinct identity for the two-year school under the supervision of Georgia Tech. This manifested itself, for example, in a separate athletic program—the institute's mascot name was the Green Hornets as contrasted with Georgia Tech's Yellow Jackets—and the distinctive school colors of green and white. Larry Johnson also fought to assure that the Technical Institute got its fair share of veterans wanting to pursue a two-year rather than a four-year program of study.[8]

The business community warmly welcomed the creation of the new institute. Those who were in the forefront of Georgia's continuing march to industrialize understood the desperate need for trained technicians, the "sergeants of industry." Leaders such as R. S. Lynch of Atlantic Steel publicly praised the new school. Professor H. P. Hammond of Penn State, chairman of the ECPD Committee on Technical Institutes, was hired as a consultant by Van Leer. Impressed by what he saw on an initial visit to the Chamblee campus in April 1949, Hammond made recommendations that helped to clear the way for an ECPD inspection leading toward full accreditation of the institute's programs. In order to give the two-year school a clearer identity prior to accreditation proceedings, on May 11,

1949, the Board of Regents approved a name change from the Technical Institute to the Southern Technical Institute.[9]

On September 6, 1949, the first commencement of the Southern Technical Institute took place. Much of the credit for the inception of the school must go directly to Van Leer. Vice President Cherry Emerson acknowledged as much when he referred to Southern Tech in 1948 as Van Leer's "baby." As an expedient step to meet the needs of the veteran, and as a way to mesh with a new trend in engineering education in the immediate postwar period, Southern Tech was a great success.[10]

Veterans' Affairs

Within a month of his inauguration as president, Van Leer had appointed a committee to study veterans' affairs. He viewed this as but one more important step in Georgia Tech's overall plan for expansion in the postwar era. The establishment of the Veterans' Guidance Center and Southern Tech represented specific responses to the growing impact of World War II veterans on our nation's campuses. In the fall of 1946, for example, the enrollment at American colleges was 57 percent higher than the comparable figures for 1939. At large universities veterans comprised 78 percent of the male student population. The GI Bill, passed in 1944, would change higher education in America to the extent that our colleges and universities would never again be the same. The influx of former soldiers caused serious shortages in classroom space, faculty, books, and at Georgia Tech, slide rules, but the greatest immediate need was for dormitory space.[11]

Georgia Tech responded to the housing crisis by becoming the first college in the country to make available low-cost FPHA facilities to married veterans entering school under the GI Bill. Fifty vacated apartments at the Bell Bomber plant in Marietta became available on November 1, 1945, at a rental of fifteen dollars a month, less than half the going rate for equivalent housing in Atlanta. This and other programs were placed under the administration of Phil C. Narmore, coordinator of veterans' affairs. To further alleviate the crunch for veterans' housing, Georgia Tech obtained 228 apartments for married student-veterans located in the Lawson General Hospital complex adjacent to the Chamblee Naval Air Station.[12]

Although Tech was hard-pressed to provide facilities for the expanding postwar enrollments, it nevertheless vigorously recruited veterans. In 1945, Leslie Zsuffa prepared a slick brochure designed to attract veterans to the school. In an introductory message, Van Leer appealed to the veteran to take advantage of the GI Bill "while preparing in one of the specific fields of engineering." He also stressed the special programs of counseling and guidance available through the Veterans Guidance Center.[13]

The veterans collectively represented a new breed of student on campus. Men who had been in a foxhole in the Pacific or on the beach at Normandy were not interested in many traditional aspects of college life. Freshman hazing had virtually disappeared with the war, but student leaders attempted to return the "rat cap," pep rallies, and freshman cake races previously enjoyed. Veterans became conspicuously outspoken on issues affecting their lives at Tech. Led by veterans, for example, students planned a sit-down strike of four to five thousand students at the 1946 navy football game unless the Athletic Association accepted their demand for better seating at games. James M. Crawford of the American Veterans Committee stated that "Georgia Tech has been run for a long time by a tyranny of certain business, faculty, and student groups, and we must co-operate to smash this ring." He then threatened a sit-down strike on the playing field. Van Leer responded that he would not stand for threats, but quietly supported a compromise to arrange some better seating.[14]

Jim Williford, a talented cartoonist for the *Technique* and himself a veteran, frequently aimed barbs at the difficulties which veterans, particularly married veterans, experienced while trying to survive on the financial allotment of the GI Bill. Other comments in the student newspaper give a clear impression that the veteran was a different kind of person altogether. Serious in his studies and frequently strapped financially, he approached his college life soberly. There was, of course, another side of the coin—the "civilian" student's perception of the veteran. The campus humor magazine, the *Yellow Jacket*, had ceased publication during the war in 1943, but reappeared at Christmas 1946. In its second issue, a typical piece entitled "Talk of the Campus" took a good-natured jibe at the "malarkey" one constantly heard from the veteran recounting his wartime experiences.[15]

Administrative Adjustments

Many faculty members had long believed that the institution's official name, the Georgia School of Technology, did not adequately reflect the focus of the college. President Van Leer concurred and supported a name change to the Georgia Institute of Technology. In 1946 a study commissioned by the Alumni Foundation recommended that the name be changed to the Georgia Institute of Technology so that "Tech would benefit in general public regard, and the character and scope of its work would be more adequately described."[16]

First formally proposed in the spring of 1947, 5,000 returned alumni questionnaires out of 17,500 mailed showed a 3–1 majority in favor of the new name. The minority, however, was caustic in its opposition. One offered the following poem:

> Rooty-toot-toot
> Rooty-toot-toot
> We are the Boys from the Institute
> We don't smoke and we don't chew,
> And we don't go wid the boys what do.[17]

Others less humorously criticized the penological connotation of the term "Institute," and urged that the name be left alone. Faculty balloting conducted in January 1948 indicated a slim lead in favor of the change. Van Leer proceeded, submitting a formal request to the regents, who approved the change to go into effect on July 1, 1948. The president indicated that he planned to recommend an internal administrative reorganization to coincide with the name change.[18]

In a letter to Chancellor Raymond Paty on July 12, 1948, Van Leer outlined the reasons for his proposed changes. Since his arrival in 1944, the enrollment of full-time day students had increased from approximately 2,000 to 5,000, and faculty members from 125 to over 400. Concomitant expansion had occurred in research, engineering extension, and building programs. The 1944–45 statutes had made strides toward decentralization, but twenty individuals still reported directly to the president, and Van Leer believed that some divisions, such as the Engineering Experiment Station, were not receiving adequate supervision. "The time has come," he argued, "when it is necessary to re-shift the responsibilities and put the most capable men in the most responsible positions."[19]

A number of sweeping changes took effect on September 1, 1948. Dean Vernon Skiles, who had long run the academic activities at the school, had retired as executive dean in January 1946 to be succeeded by Phil C. Narmore. In the 1948 reorganization, however, Narmore was passed over and the post of executive dean weakened. The new position of dean of faculties would have general supervision of all academic work. Van Leer appointed Registrar Lloyd Chapin, "an able speaker and writer who has the admiration and respect of the faculty," to this important post. The coordination of religious affairs, the YMCA, the infirmary, and the campus director of health was to reside in Dean of Students George C. Griffin, who had replaced Dean Floyd Field upon his retirement on July 1, 1946. In a third major move, the colonel created the new position of vice president (in charge of research, engineering extension, planning, and construction) for Cherry L. Emerson, who had been dean of engineering since 1945. Jesse W. Mason, head of chemical engineering, moved up to replace Emerson as dean, and Paul Weber took over as head of chemical engineering.[20]

Emerson's presence had posed an administrative problem for Van Leer from the beginning. A competent engineer and an efficient administrator, Emerson lacked the academic qualifications for the position of dean of engineering, possessing only a bachelor's degree in engineering from Georgia Tech. He had served his alma mater well as temporary vice president during M. L. Brittain's last years and as dean of engineering since 1945. He had been an effective force in implementing many of the changes on campus, particularly with regard to campus expansion. Moreover, Emerson had excellent contacts with the alumni and Atlanta civic leaders. In appointing Emerson to the vice presidency, Van Leer charged him specifically to reorganize the Engineering Experiment Station, organize the campus planning and construction division, implement the extension division and its new Technical Institute (Southern Tech), and work on the building program.[21]

Captain Robert Strite, who had come to Tech in April 1945 as Navy V-12 commanding officer, had been made controller in July 1946 upon the retirement of longtime financial officer Frank I. Houston. The following year Van Leer elevated Strite to assistant to the president and Jamie R. Anthony became controller, thus capping a meteoric rise from office boy to purchasing agent to chief financial officer. On July 1, 1948, Strite was called to active naval duty and was then out of the picture.[22]

In 1948 Georgia Tech ranked fourth in size in a group of 143 engineering colleges in the United States. Its enrollment had doubled since 1945, extension work had increased tenfold, EES research had increased fivefold, and buildings and grounds had been expanded sevenfold. The new administrative structure provided for two colleges within the Institute (engineering and general), twelve schools (all degree-granting units), and five departments (nondegree-granting service units). Under the new plan only eleven individuals now reported directly to the president rather than the previous twenty-two.[23]

Other changes in administrative personnel had occurred in July 1948, just prior to implementation of the new reorganization. Chemistry Director J. L. Daniel retired to be replaced by Paul K. Calaway, and A. J. Walker took the reins of the English department from William G. Perry. The newly created Department of Social Sciences was spun off from the larger unit of economics and social sciences, with Glenn L. Sisk becoming its first head. This left the new Department of Economics and Industrial Management headed by H. L. Dennison. The new administrative organization was now complete.[24]

The Campus Expansion Program

With the approval of the master development plan in October 1944, Van Leer and Cherry Emerson had moved quickly to implement the badly needed building program. The colonel met with the Atlanta City Planning Commission in early 1945 to discuss the ten-year program planned at Georgia Tech. Among other things, the school would need city cooperation in closing off streets that cut through the campus. A visitation committee from the Georgia General Assembly complimented Van Leer and his staff on their long-range planning efforts and supported the appeal for new construction funds. The legislators noted that several structures on campus were "firetraps," and added that Tech "must receive fair treatment from the state or else it will be relegated to secondary standing."[25]

The most pressing need remained dormitory space to accommodate the increased enrollment of veterans. In a bold and innovative move, Cherry Emerson arranged in 1946 for Georgia Tech to issue $4 million in self-liquidating revenue bonds to build housing for 1,150 student veterans. Three regular dormitories for 928 unmarried students and apartment units for 222 married couples comprised the package. The earnings from all dormitory and apartment fees were pledged to repay the bonds. The Burge married student high-rise apartments at the corner of North Avenue and McAffee Street were named in honor of architect Flippen David Burge, a Georgia Tech graduate and designer of the 1930s Techwood Homes project. The Callaway Apartments on Tenth Street were completed and occupied December 1, 1947, and Smith, Glenn, and Towers dormitories between September 15 and December 15, 1947.[26]

Van Leer continuously modified the 1944 master plan in order to incorporate changes in campus priorities. The president wrote to architect Harold Bush-Brown in early 1945 that "the 1944 Development Plan is 'a' plan. I have never looked upon it as 'the' plan . . . you will recall that I had very little, if anything, to do with the preparation of the 1944 Development Plan." The regents approved a modified 1945 plan (M-8) in November of that year and a new M-9 plan in November 1946. Enrollment during the 1947–48 academic year reached 5,402 full-time day students; the physical plant was equipped to serve approximately 2,600. As a result, classes met from 7:00 A.M, to 10:00 P.M. in order to accommodate such large numbers.[27]

In his annual report of 1945–46, Van Leer had listed his top building priorities as an academic classroom building, a new textile building, a new architecture building, a new library, and a research building annex. In the fall of 1947 the regents added to a special governor's grant to construct a new textile building, and the Textile Institute, the leading trade association in the state, pledged additional funds for staffing and other operating expenses. Textile executive William Harrison Hightower had led the drive to promote textile education at Georgia Tech, and so the building was named after him. The school itself had to lobby diligently for the state appropriations that made the building possible.[28]

With postwar expansion underway at the EES, there was a desperate shortage of space. In 1945 the regents had set aside funds for a new research building, but bids showed the amount to be inadequate. Tech opted to use the money for construction of a small annex to the existing building to house an alternating current network calculator presented to the school by the Georgia Power Company. Tech now campaigned for an additional allocation to be supplemented by private funds to construct a much larger research annex. Van Leer reminded Governor Melvin E. Thompson that the EES had performed $600,000 of research the previous year, practically none of it paid for by the state. Formal plans for the new addition proceeded in 1949 with funds from the Hinman Trust, a bequest obtained in 1944, and state money from Georgia Tech surplus funds. The Research Building and its annex would formerly be named the "Thomas Phillip Hinman Memorial," in honor of the prominent Atlanta dentist.[29]

Another major goal of several alumni was the construction of an official presidential home on the campus. M. L. Brittain had been allowed to stay in the modest wooden-framed structure on North Avenue, and the Van Leers had been living in rented quarters. A permanent residence would not only be a home fitting for Tech presidents but would serve as a focal point for social activity. A gift from Fuller E. Callaway, Jr., a prominent LaGrange textile magnate and Georgia Tech alumnus, set plans in motion in January 1948. The money came with the provision that the donor remain anonymous and that no publicity be given to the contribution. A site on Tenth Street was acquired, and groundbreaking ceremonies took place in May 1948. The regents approved an expenditure for furnishings, which alumnus Frank Neely arranged to supply at a discount from Rich's Department Store.[30]

After a struggle, the extensive building program envisioned in the various master development plans had begun, but still a list of important priorities remained. A new library, architecture building, heating plant, and classroom building headed the list. The old Carnegie library had long been outdated, but the increased enrollments after the war made the situation critical. Beginning in 1939, the librarian, Mrs. Dorothy Crosland, had been successful in obtaining valuable grants for purchasing books from the General Education Board of the Rockefeller Foundation. Additionally, in the fall of 1945 Crosland obtained a grant from the Carnegie Foundation, which she used to purchase back issues of technical journals and rare scientific books in Europe. The Georgia Tech Alumni Association paid for her immensely successful trip, the value of seventeen boxes of duplicate journals obtained from Leeds University alone covering the cost of travel. The problem increasingly became one of where to store all of these new materials.[31]

The 1945 Georgia legislature inspection committee had found in the library "thousands of priceless volumes and technical papers which have seriously overcrowded the quarters, causing much loss of time on the part of students engaging in research work." Following a visit to the campus in September 1948, A. Hollis Edens, associate director of the General Education Board, wrote to Crosland that "it appears to me that you cannot expect the support you deserve until provision had been made for an adequate building." Dorothy Crosland used these comments as further ammunition in her continuing struggle to get a new library. "If humanly possible," she wrote to Edens, "I am going to get Georgia Tech a library building."[32]

Among the many people whom Crosland enlisted in her campaign was Judge S. Price Gilbert, a former justice of the Georgia Supreme Court, who served as a member of the Board of Regents from 1943 to 1950. His eldest son, S. Price Gilbert, Jr., was a Georgia Tech graduate, and Judge Gilbert gave the commencement address in June 1944. Long interested in higher education in Georgia, Gilbert had worked for the establishment of the Georgia State College for Women in Milledgeville and had donated money for the construction of the Gilbert men's infirmary at the University of Georgia. Indicating to Crosland that he wanted to do something for Georgia Tech, Gilbert told her in 1946 that "I should like nothing better than to start the ball rolling for a new library building."[33]

Because of Judge Gilbert's strong support and his promise of financial aid for the planning phase of the library project, Van Leer concurred with Crosland in 1947 that the new facility, when completed, would be named the S. Price Gilbert Library. Gilbert provided funds for the preliminary studies, including architectural drawings that were prepared by Tech architect and faculty member Paul Heffernan. In February 1951 the University System Building Authority funded the construction of the new library as designed by Heffernan. The library, completed and dedicated on November 21, 1953, received much favorable publicity locally and in national architecture journals. The facility quickly became a very popular visitor's attraction and a major boost to faculty and administration efforts to upgrade graduate education and research at Georgia Tech.[34]

In 1949–50 the regents had allocated $12 million for an overall two-year building program in the University System. Georgia Tech's two priorities then were an architectural building and a new library, while the University of Georgia requested a new library and a girls' dormitory. Regents Chairman Hughes Spalding asked Van Leer if he wished to alter his priorities to obtain funding first for the library. To the chagrin of Mrs. Crosland at the time, Van Leer stuck with his plans because the architectural school was in some danger of losing accreditation due to its inadequate facilities. Construction thus began first on the architecture building, which was dedicated on September 20, 1952. The project was unique in that the state of Georgia provided all of the funds for the building, which the architecture faculty designed and supervised. The building conformed to the master plan by providing sufficient space around it to avoid crowding and ensure the possibility of future expansion.[35]

Colonel Van Leer continued to take a personal interest in the building program. Although Vice President Cherry Emerson had direct responsibility for campus construction, Van Leer became irritated when Emerson approved architectural details without consulting him. Citing his personal embarrassment at not always knowing of these plans when in public discussions, the president instructed the often-independent Emerson that he "would like to be consulted before any structures are built, even though they are of a semi-permanent nature."[36]

Georgia Tech still had a priority list of planned buildings that Van Leer believed were desperately needed. These included a classroom building, an athletic arena, a third floor annex to the Chemistry Building, an electrical engineering building, a research building wing, and a chemical engineering building, among others. The research building addition (Hinman Building) was dedicated on April 27, 1951. In 1953 there was a departure from the practice of employing the firm of Bush-Brown, Gailey, and Heffernan as campus architects. The firm, composed of faculty from the School of Architecture, had maintained a monopoly on campus projects for many years on the grounds that it was cost effective, but other architects in the state had voiced displeasure over the practice. Both the University System Building Authority and the Board of Regents bowed to pressure in 1953, directing that all future projects be placed out on bid.[37]

During his final years, Coach W. A. Alexander had nurtured a dream of constructing a huge athletic coliseum with a seating capacity of thirteen thousand spectators. At an estimated cost of $2.5 million, this facility would become the largest such arena in the Southeast and second only to New York's Madison Square Garden at the time. Alexander believed that the Athletic Association could raise $1.5 million, but that the rest would have to come from donations. On April 21, 1950, Alexander, who had been in declining health, went to his physician complaining of a cold; he died in his sleep the next morning. The Athletic Board, meeting on April 25, two hours after Coach Alex's funeral, named Bobby Dodd as athletic director and authorized the construction of the Alexander Memorial Coliseum at a cost of $2.5 million. Cherry Emerson chaired the fundraising committee charged to raise the additional money. To be located on the corner of Fifth and Fowler streets, the coliseum would seat sixteen thousand—and ten thousand for basketball games.[38]

The Athletic Association's fund-raising campaign attracted $1,436,000 in pledges, but many of these later turned out to be "soft," with some $560,000 remaining unpaid. Moreover, the inflationary spiral that accompanied the Korean War ballooned costs out of sight; the original estimate of $2.5 million climbed to $4 million.

In September 1953, Tech officials and alumni announced plans to build a scaled-down structure at a cost of $1.5 million, which could be met from honored pledges and Athletic Association funds. Van Leer announced the construction contract for the new Alexander Memorial Physical Training Center (later changed to the Alexander Memorial Coliseum) on April 23, 1955, and groundbreaking began on May 9. The domed structure, located on the land bordered by Eighth, Tenth, and Fowler streets and the interstate expressway, was dedicated on October 27, 1956, after Van Leer's death.[39]

One of Colonel Van Leer's last acts was to preside at the dedication of the Rich Electronic Computer Center in December 1955. The first facility of its kind in the South, it was made possible by two grants from the Rich Foundation and the Georgia Tech Research Institute (GTRI), plus a matching appropriation from the University System Building Authority. The Rich Foundation grant partially paid for an NCR-102-D digital computer. The National Cash Register Corporation contributed the balance for its 102-D machine, and the Remington-Rand Corporation contributed an ERA-1101 large-scale, high-speed computer. This facility enabled Georgia Tech to enter the rapidly expanding field of digital computation at a crucial time. Of all the things accomplished in his more than eleven years as president, Van Leer was most proud of the campus expansion program.[40]

Financial and Budgetary Issues

The struggles to obtain funding for the library and Alexander Memorial Coliseum highlight what had been a constant impediment to Van Leer's expansion plans—the fact that Georgia Tech received inadequate state support. While other University System units obtained from 54 to 80 percent of their instructional costs from the state, Tech received only 38 percent, forcing it to secure necessary income from endowments, gifts, and rents. In a letter to Chancellor S. V. Sanford in July 1945, Van Leer stated: "I respectfully urge that the Regents treat the Georgia School of Technology exactly the same as it treats the other units of the system and give us all the same amount *per student per year* or the same percentage of our *educa-*

tional cost." This disparity, particularly in terms of a comparison with the University of Georgia, continued throughout the entire period of Van Leer's presidency, despite his frequent and often strident protests. He believed that the University of Georgia dominated the Board of Regents and that it was impossible for Tech to get a fair shake.[41]

Furthermore, soon after his arrival, the new president was chagrined to learn that Georgia Tech received none of the federal funds available under the Morrill (1862), Smith-Lever (1914), and Bankhead-Jones (1918) acts, a situation which had so greatly irked President K. G. Matheson back in the early 1920s. All land-grant appropriations went to the University of Georgia, the designated land-grant institution. Van Leer wrote in 1945 to W. Wilson Noyes, treasurer of the Board of Regents, that "as far as I know the Georgia School of Technology, which is a land-grant college as far as the engineer is concerned, does not receive a penny of this money." Unfortunately, this continued to be the case.[42]

The administration sought various ways to support basic educational programs with external funds. In addition to the General Education Board grants obtained for the library, in 1945 Van Leer negotiated money to purchase scientific instruments. The regents authorized matching funds in 1945–46 and 1946–47. In 1947 the Georgia Tech Alumni Association initiated the annual Alumni Roll Call, asking graduates to contribute to their alma mater an amount based on their ability to pay. This approach, suggested by alumni leaders and organized by Leslie Zsuffa for Van Leer, superseded the dues-membership concept that had been in force during the first twenty-three years of the association's existence. Although contributions in the first year of 1947–48 were modest, the Roll Call soon became a major tool for bringing sorely needed funds to the Georgia Tech Foundation for the school. Increased enrollments after the war had fortunately also brought greater tuition income. The regular day student enrollment of 4,200 in 1945–46, for example, was twice the figure for 1944–45. This number increased to 5,681 for 1946–47 and 6,424 in 1947–48. A 1948 survey reported by the American Society for Engineering Education (ASEE) showed Tech's enrollment as first in the South and fourth nationally among 143 accredited engineering schools in the United States, while its graduate division ranked twelfth. Out-of-state enrollment represented about 50 percent of the full-time student body, a figure Van Leer defended because of the income brought in ($472.50 a year versus $172.50 a year for in-state students). The president also viewed this high out-of-state enrollment as an educational advantage.[43]

When enrollment began to drop after 1948, however, it brought a concomitant decrease in tuition revenue. Nationally, engineering enrollment peaked in 1948. Tech's full-time enrollment dropped from a peak figure of 6,424 in 1947–48 to 5,174 in 1950–51, and 3,308 in 1951–52. Ironically, because of this decline state per capita contributions in 1951–52 reached an all-time high, twenty dollars greater than that for 1950–51. Van Leer planned to use surplus funds to increase faculty salaries, which remained in the lower third when compared with other engineering institutions. But despite his hopes, the state was not forthcoming with additional appropriations. State funds for 1952–53 represented only 25 percent of total educational costs, compared with what Van Leer claimed was the 50 to 80 percent provided at other similar institutions throughout the country. Enrollment picked up for the 1953–54 year, but Georgia Tech received 22 percent less from the state that year than it did in 1951–52. Protesting this inadequate support, Van Leer stated that "many of our laboratories are woefully short of equipment and our accrediting is threatened."[44]

Similar drops in enrollment at the Southern Technical Institute created a serious budgetary shortfall for Tech's sister institution. Southern Tech had never become self-supporting, but when it appeared in the spring of 1951 that income would not nearly be adequate to cover operating expenses, and the regents indicated that no supplemental funds were forthcoming, Van Leer announced plans to move the small program to the main Georgia Tech campus as a cost-saving measure. He appointed a committee chaired by Cherry Emerson to investigate this possibility. When the regents indicated their disapproval of this possible action, Van Leer threatened to close Southern Tech as of June 30, 1951.[45]

Causes for the precipitous decline in STI enrollment were many. The Korean War emergency, the change in Georgia public school education from eleven to twelve years, the decrease in the birth rate during the worst years of the Depression in 1931–33, and the termination of the college training program under the GI Bill all played a role. Southern Tech had submitted a budget of $301,000 for the 1951–52 year, but income from student fees was estimated at only $140,000, less than had been anticipated. The regents had allocated $80,000 to the school and claimed that the shortfall resulted from the fact that Van Leer had used all but $19,000 of the Southern Tech money to cover other costs at Georgia Tech. It was the colonel's problem, not theirs, and the regents opposed his decision to close the school. Meanwhile, as a contingency plan in the event that he would have to go ahead with his threat, Van Leer opened negotiations with Jim Cherry, superintendent of schools in DeKalb County, Georgia, on a plan for the county taking over Southern Tech. Under a tentative agreement, Georgia Tech would turn over most of the technical equipment at STI (worth about $200,000). In return, the county agreed to offer technical institute training, at least until the students presently enrolled had completed their work, absorb and continue all STI instructors for a year, and assume all of Georgia Tech's obligations to the navy, which still owned the Chamblee site.[46]

Director L. V. Johnson of Southern Tech enlisted all of the support he could to keep the school from closing. In letters to individual regents he cited the 1949 Strayer report, commissioned by the University System, which had praised the work of Southern Tech, and again mobilized the private support of the Associated Industries of Georgia. H. P. Hammond, dean of engineering at Penn State, stated in a letter to Van Leer that "discontinuance of the Southern Technical Institute would be a severe loss to technical and engineering education in the country."[47]

There is reason to believe that Van Leer's announced closing of STI was a bluff designed to shake loose additional revenue from the Board of Regents. If so, it failed completely. On March 21, 1951, the regents directed Van Leer "to restore the sum of $80,000 or some part of that sum as is necessary to operate the Technical Institute at its present location at Chamblee, and adjust the budget of Georgia Tech accordingly, or to close the Technical Institute." Citing "intense pressure from industry," on April 9, 1951, Van Leer rescinded his recommendation that Southern Tech be closed. By reducing salary increases and eliminating capital outlay and supply items from the Georgia Tech budget, he was able to reallocate most of the $80,000 originally earmarked by the regents for Southern Tech.[48]

In Van Leer's view he had merely deprived Georgia Tech of badly needed funds. In the next several months he sought ways to attract external money to Southern Tech in order to keep the school functioning. Negotiations with the Air Force resulted in the awarding of a contract to train 140 airmen in the fundamentals of armament electronics, an important beginning of contract work at STI. The school later arranged cooperative work with Lockheed Aircraft, the Air Force Material Command, and AT&T. Southern Tech enrollment began to rebound by 1953–54, thus insuring a healthier base of income from student fees. The average enrollment had reached almost 474 students per quarter. Southern Tech had survived its greatest financial crisis and could look forward to anticipated enrollment increases projected for the rest of the decade. The school estimated that the student population would reach 1,500 by 1960 and 2,500 by 1965. The total level of state support for all Georgia Tech programs, however, still remained inadequate in the early 1950s.[49]

Van Leer referred to the 1954–55 year as the most difficult one he had experienced during the eleven years he had been at Georgia Tech and cited lack of adequate financial support from the state of Georgia as the reason. State support had remained the same even as enrollments had risen. The "slow, insidious inflation" that had come in the wake of the Korean War further exacerbated the situation. The inability to get the Georgia legislature to appropriate the funds necessary to create the MIT of the South that he envisioned remained the greatest failure of Van Leer's presidency.[50]

The Expansion of Research

Van Leer had made clear that if Georgia Tech were to become an engineering school of national reputation, the school needed to expand research and graduate education. One step in this direction occurred in 1947 with the establishment of a new hydraulics laboratory located within the School of Civil Engineering. Directed by associate professor C. E. Kindsvater, this facility would address problems related to the production of hydroelectric power, the conservation and regulation of water supplies, and flood control. Including a miniature dam used to simulate hydraulic flow conditions, the entire lab was about the size of a large garage. Van Leer's own research specialty earlier in his career had been in hydraulics, and he took a particular interest in this work. Two anonymous donations made the erection of the laboratory possible.[51]

In order to promote research more generally on campus, Van Leer enlisted faculty support through the informal Research Club, established in the 1920s and largely responsible for the activation of the Engineering Experiment Station in 1934. Several of these men, along with Van Leer himself, were members of Sigma Xi, the national honorary and professional scientific research society. Van Leer saw the establishment of a local Sigma Xi chapter at Georgia Tech as an important step in accelerating a research consciousness at the school. Accordingly, in January 1946 he directed Acting Dean of General Studies Ralph Hefner, a member of both Sigma Xi and the Research Club, to contact all society members on campus with the aim of obtaining a charter from the national organization. The informal group elected Professor W. M. Spicer of chemistry as its chairman and proceeded to work with Van Leer in achieving the first goal, a Sigma Xi club. Sigma Xi brought together those older faculty members who had supported research in the past with younger, recently hired staff such as William Eberhardt in chemistry and Waldemar Ziegler in chemical engineering, a former Tech undergraduate who was inducted into the society while earning his doctorate at Johns Hopkins. Both Eberbardt and Ziegler would become active Sigma Xi supporters for several years.[52]

In 1947 the Sigma Xi club instituted a research prize to be awarded on a competitive basis to a scholarly paper written by a Tech faculty member. Alumnus Monie Ferst donated funds for the annual faculty award, and Professor Paul K. Calaway of chemistry won the first award of three hundred dollars in 1947. The club also applied to the national society for the full chapter status that would give the group the authority to induct new members. After a campus visitation in March 1950, on May 22 Sigma Xi's Executive Committee informed the Tech club that its petition had been deferred because it viewed the present policies at Georgia Tech as restrictive on faculty time for independent research. At the December 1950 society convention in Cleveland, Waldemar Ziegler, president of Tech's club, and EES Director Gerald Rosselot were able to confer with Sigma Xi officials on the problems at Georgia Tech. They acknowledged the school's deficiencies but stressed the changes under President Van Leer and how important the Sigma Xi club had been in improving the "climate" for research. They supplied additional information detailing the research programs underway at Georgia Tech, and Van Leer pledged his support for improving the situation at the school. These efforts were rewarded with the granting of full Sigma Xi Chapter status in 1953. The initial rejection of a charter became important ammunition used by the research-conscious faculty in their attempts to obtain a greater administrative commitment for research.[53]

The expansion of graduate education at Georgia Tech was a positive development that had impressed the Sigma Xi Executive Board. By 1952 Tech offered the doctoral degree in chemical engineering, chemistry, and electrical engineering. In 1950 William L. Carter became the first student to complete the requirements for a doctorate in chemical engineering, and eight others were awarded by 1952. Forty-six students were pursuing work leading to the doctorate in that year. R. L. Sweigert, who had succeeded R. I. Sarbacher as dean of graduate studies in 1949, noted in 1951 that Tech's graduate enrollment had increased by 865 percent since 1940 as compared with a national average increase of 103 percent. Many of these graduate students conducted thesis and dissertation research in conjunction with the EES, where several faculty members had joint appointments. This was a policy generally supported by the Engineering College, but one in which friction would increasingly develop with the Department of Chemistry and other "pure science" units within the General College. The question was whether basic research could be conducted within the context of contract work.[54]

The EES: Postwar Growth and the Creation of GTRI

As discussed in chapter 6, the volume of work at the Experiment Station had dramatically increased during the last two years of the war as a result of military-related research. Georgia Tech had negotiated contracts directly with various federal agencies, but some complications resulted when accrued funds overlapped from one fiscal year to the next. The situation came to a head with the announcement of a new regents' procedure adopted on July 11, 1945, which stated that "no official of the Board of Regents nor any official of the branches of the university system is authorized to expend any funds which he accrued from balances from previous periods or from income from any subsequent period unless the expenditures are approved by the Board of Regents." Van Leer strenuously opposed this policy, believing that it discriminated against Georgia Tech.[55]

These overall financial concerns, plus a recognition of the great potential of the EES in bringing in external research dollars, prompted Cherry Emerson (then engineering dean) and Van Leer to begin working with key alumni from industry in the revival of the old prewar Industrial Development Council in the form of the Georgia Tech Research Institute (GTRI). Emerson drew up the initial plans for the organization in September 1945. An independently chartered, nonprofit corporation, this institution would serve as a contracting agency for the Experiment Station and handle all "profits" that came from such research in the form of overhead (indirect costs). As administrator of all external contracts, the GTRI would be able to accrue and redistribute funds as well as carry over projects from one fiscal year to another. An independent Board of Directors, one member of which would be the president of Georgia Tech, would run the organization. Fuller E. Callaway, Jr., a Tech alumnus, agreed to serve as chairman of such a board, provided that it hire a full-time, paid business manager as president. The GTRI, under contract with the Board of Regents, would use all of the facilities of the EES. Callaway recommended Harry Baker, Jr., a 1934 chemical engineering graduate of Georgia Tech, for the job as GTRI president. The board interviewed Baker in January 1946 and hired him for the post. The board then met in February to formally amend the Industrial Development Council charter, changing its name to the Georgia Tech Research Institute. As of February 9, 1946, the GTRI had become a reality. As Emerson wrote to board member Raymond Jones, "We very definitely expect to operate the GTRI at a profit for the benefit of the Georgia School of Technology only, and not for the profit of any individual."[56]

In the spring of 1946 Harry Baker visited a number of research foundations around the country to obtain information useful to the operation of GTRI. Among those he looked at were the Callaway Institute, Inc., the Institute of Textile Technology, Armour Research Foundation (Illinois Institute of Technology), Ohio State University Research Foundation, Battelle Memorial Institute, the Purdue University Foundation, and the Institute of Paper Chemistry. Of this group, Baker concluded that the Ohio State Research Foundation offered the most useful model in that it was a private corporation very closely integrated with the university and it used its facilities and personnel whenever possible.[57]

The EES budget for 1945–46 represented 67 percent funding from contracts with cooperating agencies, industries, and the federal government. There were forty-four separate research projects employing thirty-one full-time and sixty part-time personnel. The *Research Engineer*, the station's new bimonthly bulletin edited by EES public relations officer Ben H. Weil, made its initial appearance during the year. The regents authorized the construction of the Research Building annex to house the new AC network calculator, a $100,000 gift from the Georgia Power Company. To be operational by early 1947, this state-of-the-art equipment would enable engineers to electronically reproduce power station and circuit conditions so as to simulate load division, short-circuit, and stability problems. Use of the calculator would be contracted out to private industry in the Southeast, thus providing important service to industry as well as attracting external funds. The network calculator was the sixth to be installed by an educational institution, following those at MIT, Purdue, IIT, Texas A&M, and the University of Kansas.[58]

During the first full year of operation under the GTRI, the EES had its busiest year in history with an operating budget of $451,000, 87 percent of which came from contracts. The budget supported a full-time staff of fifty-six and a part-time group of ninety-five researchers—the equivalent of eighty-seven full-time employees. Within the mix of contract research there was an increasing amount of classified work. One of the most important studies in 1946–47 was Project 109, "Propagation Studies of Electromagnetic Waves," conducted by Professors F. E. Lowndes and James E. Boyd. This was followed by a large contract obtained by Boyd with the Navy Bureau of Ordnance on radar research and development, the first of what would become a steady stream of classified radar research. Boyd, a member of the physics faculty from 1935 to 1942, had spent time in the navy, where he worked with the Research and Development Division of the Bureau of Ordnance on radar-directed fire control. He had returned to Tech as a full professor of physics in 1946 with a joint appointment at the station. Other classified projects were undertaken for the NACA, the Army Chemical Warfare Service, and the United States Navy Bureau of Ships.[59]

A 1948 study of the dollar value of research at twenty-four state-supported experiment stations conducted by the Association of Land-Grant Colleges and Universities listed the EES second in the nation and first in the South, ranking it behind Purdue only. With the growth in external funds, the station's growing autonomy on campus inevitably caused friction with faculty members not intimately involved in its projects. Professor Thomas H. Evans of civil engineering, a member of the EES faculty advisory council, complained to both President Van Leer and Vice President Emerson that the group had not met for several months. Unless EES Director Rosselot gave the council a useful function and responsibility, he indicated that he was prepared to resign. Still frustrated by Rosselot's refusal to call a meeting, Evans did so in January 1949. Under pressure from Van Leer, the EES director called the council together on February 4, 1949, and announced that there would be regular quarterly meetings. Underneath these isolated incidents was a common feeling in some quarters that the station was becoming the tail that wagged the dog.[60]

The station itself was undergoing growth pains in a number of areas. Just as deans and department heads were having difficulties recruiting and retaining qualified faculty members, so was the EES in hiring full-time research staff in competition with industry. Georgia Tech was simply not yet in a position to offer competitive salaries. Moreover, there was a significant drop in operational funds from the state of Georgia in 1949–50, the first time that the EES budget had fallen below that of a previous year. Cherry Emerson, now vice president in charge of research, applied to the General Education Board in 1949 for a grant of $16,000 a year for three years to supplement EES salaries.[61]

Van Leer went along with these supplementary salary increases but in principle opposed raises after the submission of the annual budget. General Sandy Beaver, one of the most outspoken of the regents, also raised objections when Van Leer made a request for a supplemental appropriation to match the General Education Board grant. Beaver argued that Van Leer "should employ the highest type of *combination teachers and researchers* that are obtainable within your budget so that our boys can receive *both instruction and research training* from the most outstanding men we can employ." This fundamental difference concerning the nature of research at Georgia Tech would be clearly evident in the next few years. Van Leer realized that faculty should be assigned a teaching load realistic enough to support a research program, but he also believed that the only way to foster research at all at Georgia Tech was to make use of contract dollars funneled to the EES through the GTRI.[62]

In 1950–51 a decided increase in defense contracting as a result of the Korean War resulted in a dramatic increase in the station's budget, 95 percent of which represented sponsored funds. James E. Boyd moved up to become full-time director of the Physics Division at the station, and the new Hinman Building (the old Research Building plus the new annex) added 20,000 additional feet of floor space. The future course of development at the EES—an overwhelming reliance on sponsored contract research, the majority of which was Department of Defense related—had now been established.[63]

The EES: Growing Pains and Administrative Adjustments

Under the 1948 administrative reorganization the director of the station reported directly to Vice President Emerson rather than to President Van Leer. Points of contention between EES Director Gerald Rosselot and Vice President Cherry Emerson, two strong individuals, emerged in the early 1950s to place severe strain on station operations. The first apparent signs of tension occurred in the wake of the 1949–50 cut in state operational funds, which required a transfusion of GTRI money to keep the station solvent. Rosselot agreed to implement specific administrative changes aimed at effecting tighter managerial control and improved financial operations, including the hiring of Captain Dewitt C. Redgrave, director of the Materials Laboratory at the Brooklyn Navy Yard, as the vice president of GTRI. Redgrave would have specific responsibility in assisting GTRI President Harry Baker in obtaining sponsored contracts from industry and government.[64]

Rosselot followed through with these initial steps to Emerson's satisfaction, but the vice president expressed irritation at the EES director's foot-dragging in implementing other administrative changes. In a testy letter of June 17, 1950, Emerson chided Rosselot for his delay, stating that "your failure to fulfill the statement made in your letter of April 7 leaves me to wonder whether or not any of the other things which you stated as your definite plans have been carried out." The tone of this and additional memos between the two men suggests that their personal relationship had deteriorated, a fact confirmed in discussion with individuals peripherally involved at the time.[65]

Further friction occurred when Rosselot agreed to accept the presidency of Scientific Associates, a direct spin-off from the station incorporated on October 31, 1951. This private firm later evolved into Scientific Atlanta, a multimillion dollar Atlanta-based electronics corporation. Georgia Tech administrators today look with great pride to Scientific Atlanta as an example of how the school has helped to create a "high tech" infrastructure in the state of Georgia. Although there is no explicit reference in the files indicating the case, several principals have suggested that Vice President Cherry Emerson viewed the participation of EES personnel in this private research concern as a potential if not direct conflict of interest. Policies did later develop under Emerson that required a written request to the president in order to undertake outside work with Scientific Associates. Emerson also suspected that Scientific Associates competitively sought contracts that otherwise would have gone to the station.[66]

The falling out between Emerson and his subordinate erupted in a serious confrontation over budgetary issues in the fall of 1952 that led directly to Rosselot's resignation. The 1951–52 EES budget operated at a record high of $1,324,000, 80 percent of which represented military research. These contracts brought in a great deal of overhead that went directly to GTRI. In September 1951 the Board of

Regents directed the chancellor's staff to undertake a detailed study of the financial operation of the station. According to a letter from its treasurer, the Board of Regents' main concern was a suspicion that the station's reporting of overhead income was inadequate. Regents Treasurer James Blissit stated that he had little doubt that every dollar received by the station had gone for the good of Georgia Tech, but that it was necessary for the station's budget and reports to conform with University System procedures.[67]

Van Leer, Cherry Emerson, GTRI President Harry Baker, Controller Jamie Anthony, and EES Director Rosselot met to have a "dry run" on Blissit's letter. The upshot of this meeting was to recommend that an independent firm of certified public accountants audit the previous year's EES accounts and that Georgia Tech develop a new set of financial operating procedures. In the interim, however, Blissit had prepared his own report on EES operations for the fiscal year 1951–52 and discovered a discrepancy in excess of $100,000 between his figures and those previously submitted by Tech Controller Anthony. After a consultation with Anthony's assistant, accountant Ewell Barnes, Blissit discovered that the difference lay in the accounts receivable as of June 30, 1952, which the station had reported to Anthony's office. Blissit confronted the EES with this discrepancy and learned that because the regents had failed to provide adequate funding for the station, it had become common practice for the unit to withhold information on receivables for one month in order that it might have additional working capital.[68]

Although EES Director Rosselot strongly denied that there was any intent to render a false report and that it was simply a matter of not considering any item as a receivable until it had actually been billed, this represented the final straw for Cherry Emerson. He insisted that action be taken, and Van Leer forwarded Rosselot's letter of resignation to the chancellor, to be effective on March 1, 1953. As of Monday, November 24, Herschel H. Cudd, an EES staff member and head of its Chemical Sciences Division since 1950, became acting director of the station while Rosselot went on leave.[69]

In many ways Rosselot's leaving represented a severe loss to Georgia Tech. As director of the EES for over ten years, he had been largely responsible for the expansion of its research activity during and after the war. A physicist himself, he was also the principal investigator of several prime electronics projects, including the original OSRD study funded in 1944. As a former member of the faculty, Rosselot also had relatively good relations with the teaching staff. As evidence of his reputation, Rosselot landed on his feet, accepting a post with the Aviation Division of Bendix Corporation at a significantly higher salary than he had been earning at Georgia Tech. One also sympathizes with the difficulties Rosselot faced in attempting to expand the station while receiving inadequate basic operating funds from the state of Georgia. The line between "creative financing" with external funds and impropriety is often a fine one indeed, and honest men may disagree about the methods Rosselot used that led to his dispute with Cherry Emerson. It has been suggested that Emerson had been looking for a weapon against Rosselot, and he found it in the charges of financial impropriety leveled by the regents. For his part, Rosselot retained fond memories of the EES and Georgia Tech, if not for Cherry Emerson, and maintained a corresponding relationship with several old friends at the school. He could justifiably be proud of the "Rosselot Era" at the Engineering Experiment Station.[70]

The main task facing the new station administration in the post-Rosselot period was the establishment of a set of financial policies that would satisfy all parties involved—the various contracting agencies, Georgia Tech, GTRI, and the Board of Regents. Negotiations on these issues consumed much time during the first three months of 1953. In addition to the previous question of station overhead reporting and the regents' feeling that more indirect cost income should go into Georgia Tech general operating funds, a report filed by the United States Army Audit Agency in January added a further complication. As a result of this study, the army dropped Georgia Tech's overhead rate from 60.4 percent to only 46.05 percent. The main reason given for this action was the relatively small increase in indirect personal services. Although overhead should not have increased at as great a rate as direct costs, it should have moved further upward than it did. The end result was that the new overhead rate was inadequate to support auxiliary services during the remainder of the fiscal year. In a strongly worded memorandum to President Van Leer, Emerson stated that "I merely wish to emphasize that the Engineering Experiment Station and the Georgia Tech

Research Institute will suffer severely in regard to their income during the calendar year, 1953, because of the poor management of the preceding administration of the Engineering Experiment Station, which almost amounts to negligence. It appears that the administration of the Station should have been changed at an earlier date than was actually the case."[71]

A key agreement worked out among Georgia Tech, GTRI, and the regents in 1953 spelled out the duties and responsibilities of all three bodies and specified a precise method of reporting all EES budgetary transactions. For its services, GTRI would receive 10/46 of any overhead allowed by the army and other branches of the armed forces. Any balance of funds over and above operating costs could be left in trust in GTRI accounts to promote research at Georgia Tech and the station. Georgia Institute of Technology would receive 13/46 of overhead to defray physical plant, administrative, and bookkeeping costs tied to running the station. The remaining 23/46 of all overhead would go directly to the station to cover internal administrative expenses and support services. With this agreement all parties expressed hope that past differences between Georgia Tech and the regents over EES management would now be put to rest.[72]

Soon after taking charge of the station, Herschel Cudd recommended that the station officially revert to use of the name designated in the original 1919 enabling act, the "Engineering Experiment Station," rather than the title of "State Engineering Experiment Station." The former name had become common usage anyway. Van Leer and Emerson had charged Cudd to integrate station activities more into the general educational programs and academic life of Georgia Tech, and by now referring to the unit as the "Georgia Tech Engineering Experiment Station," they hoped to encourage this attitude. Both Chancellor Harmon Caldwell and Van Leer expressed the view that it was more desirable to promote a research program in which a substantial number of faculty participated, rather than just a few full-time EES researchers. The latter model had begun to characterize Rosselot's operation, and several faculty members had expressed dissatisfaction. It had irked many, for example, that the large sign over the EES main building which labeled it as "Research" implied that this was the only place where research was being conducted. It is noteworthy that the first annual station report under Cudd's management highlighted the fact that sixty-six faculty members from fifteen schools at Georgia Tech had conducted cooperative research at the station.[73]

In a further spirit of faculty-EES cooperation, Cudd addressed the contentious issue of faculty rank assigned to full-time EES staff not engaged in teaching. There were grievances on both sides of this issue. Several members of the faculty objected to station personnel holding professorial academic rank while, at the same time, station employees were getting turned down for advancement by the regents because they did not hold a doctorate or otherwise did not meet promotion and tenure qualifications. Cudd recommended a policy of assigning station research personnel new equivalent titles, including senior research scientist or engineer, research scientist or engineer, junior research scientist or engineer, or research assistant. These titles would be analogous to professor, associate professor, assistant professor, and instructor. Those currently on staff who accepted the new ranks would not be subjected to the usual regents' requirements for advancement in faculty rank or limitations on their salaries. They would, in exchange, forego the possibility of tenure. Those full-time EES employees who valued professorial rank and the tenure which accompanied it could retain their status but would be subject to regular regents policy on advancement in rank and salary. The regents approved this policy in the spring of 1953.[74]

The presence of increasing numbers of full-time research personnel at the station also raised questions about their membership in the General Faculty as defined by the 1945 statutes. Negotiations over revised statutes addressed this issue as well as refinement of the committee structure. Under the new statutes approved on May 13, 1953, station research engineers were defined as "adjunct members" of the General Faculty but excluded from membership in the Faculty Senate, that body dealing with all academic matters. Herschel Cudd also made known to the faculty members of the EES advisory council that he planned to meet with them on a regular basis and follow their advice, a previous point of friction during the Rosselot era.[75]

There remained growing faculty concern with the station. In 1954, the committee appointed to conduct the Institutewide self-study "The Aims and Objectives of the Georgia Institute of Technology" addressed the subject in its final report. This committee, funded in part by the Alumni Association, was chaired by Professor W. M. Spicer of the chemistry school. The committee noted with concern that the station budget of $2 million for 1953–54 represented 83 percent research support from government agencies, about two-thirds of which was classified. Committee members viewed this situation as undesirable except as a temporary expedient and quoted from the 1953 American Council on Education report on institutional research policy which stated: "It is recognized that classified research contributes very little of value to the academic objectives of an institution." The committee urged that this situation change at Georgia Tech and also noted the "lack of liaison" between the EES and the academic departments.[76]

The School of Chemistry led in promoting department-based faculty research as opposed to work exclusively managed through the Engineering Experiment Station. The passage of the National Science Foundation (NSF) Act in 1950 had opened new possibilities for federal funding of basic scientific research, and chemistry was the first unit on campus to obtain NSF grants. Vice President Emerson noted that "certain of the faculty of the Institute have indicated a desire to be free of the dominance of the Engineering Experiment Station." He was concerned, however, with NSF's low rate of overhead—15 percent of all budget cost (equivalent to 20–30 percent of payroll costs)—compared to the higher rates received from armed forces contracts. Emerson believed that Tech should "play ball" with the NSF as it would gain in importance over the years. He also supported individual grant requests to administer projects through the departments instead of the "rather ponderous mechanism" of the EES. While Emerson viewed NSF versus DOD sponsorship primarily in terms of dollars and cents, many academic faculty perceived the difference in another light. Could truly basic research be carried out through performance contracts negotiated through the station? This issue was not so clear-cut, and several individuals involved at the time argue today that it was unfair to make a blanket criticism of EES research on these grounds. The stage had been set, however, for a continuing controversy over the proper conduct of research programs at Georgia Tech.[77]

To his credit, Herschel Cudd, who advanced from acting director to director of the station on July 1, 1953, attempted to effect better relations between the teaching faculty and the station. In addition to increasing EES service functions above the level maintained during the Rosselot administration, he had also expanded existing laboratories and created new facilities. These laboratory improvements were in part an attempt to enhance relations with the academic side of the school. Cudd encouraged faculty members to seek connections with EES and undertake research projects there. Unfortunately, this spending created another serious financial drain during the year that Cudd was in charge. It became necessary for GTRI to cover a deficit of slightly over $20,000 in order to balance the operating budget for 1953–54. Although this deficit was not severe, it retarded the expansion of EES research.[78]

Cudd was an activist and, like Rosselot, remained impatient with the conservative administration of Vice President Cherry Emerson. When, for example, Cudd recommended that the station seek external funding to participate in the Point Four Program of foreign aid for the less-developed world in 1953, Emerson rejected the idea, citing the station's small staff and the difficulty of sending scientists to "small remote countries." Emerson's practical considerations were valid, but, given the expansion of the station's involvement in the third world in recent years, one must also give credit to Herschel Cudd's prescience. On November 30, 1953, Cudd resigned his post to accept a position as manager of research and development at the American Viscose Corporation at a salary over four times what he received from the Institute. Cudd stressed this point at the time of his leaving in order to emphasize the difficulty of maintaining a first-rate research operation on the woeful salary scale authorized by the regents.[79]

Professor Paul K. Calaway, director of the School of Chemistry, succeeded Cudd, and the competent and popular Jim Boyd moved up to the post of assistant director in charge of scientific affairs. Van Leer and Emerson hoped that the selection of Calaway, who had come from the very vocal chemistry school, and Boyd, who although now identified with EES was very well respected, might serve to ease tensions between the station and the academic units.[80] In 1953–54, for the first time in ten years, the total volume of EES research failed to increase, and Van Leer cited a lack of floor space, a shortage of qualified scientific personnel, and inadequate state funds to investigate Georgia industrial problems as the reasons. The following year saw an increase in total budget of which the state provided only 7.1 percent. The lion's share of sponsored work centered in fifty-two government and eighty industrial contracts. Radar and microwave propagation projects again headed the government work, but other significant research included, among others, microwave optics, missile tracking frequency control, ultra-high frequency interference, antenna design, and underwater acoustics. Van Leer also noted a positive trend in sponsored projects toward more basic and unclassified research. Additionally, a large number of industrial projects meshed well with the school's historic role of aid to Georgia industry.[81]

During 1955–56, the last year of Van Leer's presidency, the Experiment Station achieved a peak in research income and patent activity but established a negative record with a new high in personnel turnover. Van Leer had effectively used the station to expand research programs during the nearly twelve years of his presidency. He wrote in 1954: "It is now generally understood that Georgia Tech is a technological university. It now engages in all of the activities of a great technological university and that is shown by its three major activities: 1) instruction, 2) research, and 3) extension services."[82] Yet, in promoting the station to achieve research growth, Van Leer had raised other issues. Among these were the questions of classified versus unclassified research, and station-based versus department-based research. EES achievements were impressive, but, increasingly, some members of the faculty questioned whether the station had become too powerful a force within the overall framework of the Institute.

The Integration of Women

One of the most significant changes on the Georgia Tech campus occurred on April 9, 1952, when the Board of Regents, by a split vote, admitted women to the school on a full-time basis. Much of the credit for this achievement must go to Blake Van Leer, who long had been committed to removing barriers to admission at the school based on sex. In a letter of June 1945 to L. R. Siebert, regents secretary, the colonel indicated that he would not immediately challenge the exclusion of women but stated, "My position, however, is that I believe this law and this regulation are unconstitutional, and that if any girl ever takes them to the Supreme Court, they shall be so declared." Van Leer's views were no secret among a student body which, for the most part, opposed the admission of women. The April Fool's edition of the *Technique* in 1946 reported that "President Snake Van Sleer" has been replaced as president because of the "prolonged agony Van Sleer administered to Tech students for their refusal to wholeheartedly accept Van Sleer's proposal to convert Georgia Tech into a co-ed school." The entire Van Leer family was committed to engineering education for women. Mrs. Van Leer was a graduate in art of the School of Architecture at the University of California, Berkeley, and the Van Leers' daughter, Maryly, had to pursue her engineering degree at Vanderbilt because no school in the state of Georgia offered an engineering curriculum for women.[83]

When in the spring of 1947 Van Leer proposed to the regents that they consider changing the policy at Georgia Tech, they directed him to appoint a study committee. Although the Tech faculty narrowly supported the change, General Sandy Beaver, head of the regents' Education Committee, strongly opposed the idea, and student opinion as indicated by letters in the *Technique* was also negative. A student editorial cited a list of reasons for opposing the move that included the rearrangement of dormitories and classes, the need to maintain strict rules of attitude, speech, conduct, and appearance, the fact that girls were an "academic distraction," and that it would probably mean even worse football seats![84]

Textile Professor Herman A. Dickert, chairman of the campus Committee on Co-education, obtained a legal opinion from the Georgia Attorney General's office indicating that the ban was not statutory, but rather reflected long-stated policy of the Board of Regents. The original enabling act of 1885 had made no mention of sex, and a subsequent law of 1920 had made it specifically lawful to admit women into the old Georgia Tech School of Commerce. Georgia Code Section 32-123, codified in 1933, stated that all of the branch colleges of the University of Georgia, except Georgia Tech and the Negro colleges, shall be open to white female students. Though not of legislative origin, this exception had taken on the full force of law. In the opinion of the Attorney General's office, however, the Board of Regents had the authority to change the policy. This was the thrust of Van Leer's appeal to the regents that voted against change on June 11, 1947.[85]

When the Technical Institute (Southern Tech) opened its doors in the spring of 1948, it did so as a coeducational institution. The Georgia Federation of Business and Professional Women's Clubs congratulated Van Leer on this policy, but the first woman student, Miss Barbara Hudson, did not enroll until the fall. The regents remained firm toward Georgia Tech, refusing even to reimburse resident female students who were forced to go out-of-state for an engineering degree, a benefit that they already provided to black students. In 1938 the United States Supreme Court, in the Gaines decision, had ruled that it was the duty of the states to provide equal educational opportunity for all their citizens. Since Georgia had no black engineering college, the legislature authorized tuition payments for out-of-state schools. Anne Bonds, daughter of an engineer with Robert and Company, had tried unsuccessfully to gain admission into Georgia Tech beginning in 1943. Forced to go outside Georgia to Auburn, Miss Bonds applied to the regents for tuition reimbursement, only to have her request denied.[86]

Following the regents' rejection of his coeducational proposal in 1947, the colonel had called in Tech's librarian, Mrs. Dorothy Crosland, asking to see what she could do to get women into Georgia Tech. Crosland's personal influence with certain regents, particularly Rutherford Ellis, apparently contributed to a slow change of attitude on the board. At the same time, Van Leer directed Cherry Emerson to study the lavatory facilities on the campus so as to have information available for the regents when this delicate subject came up. The study indicated that it would take a sum of $50,000 ($5,000 per toilet) to retrofit the campus with ladies' rest rooms, but that all new buildings were being designed with women's facilities included. Van Leer sent this "toilet report" to Chancellor Harmon Caldwell along with the intelligence that women's organizations were raising funds to challenge the policy in court.[87]

Outside women's groups mobilized their forces over the next three years, and in early 1952, the Women's Chamber of Commerce in Atlanta formally petitioned the regents to change its policy at Georgia Tech. Both Van Leer and Dorothy Crosland had worked behind the scenes with this group. The petition cited a gross discrimination to the females of Georgia and noted that declining enrollments in 1951–52 made space no problem. This was an important debating point, since the flood of returning veterans in 1947 had been a factor weighing heavily against the admission of women at that time. The Women's Chamber also stressed that there was a national shortage of engineers, that "moral" arguments opposing technical careers for women had wavered in the state, and that student attitudes were now generally favorable. The Student Council had adopted a resolution favoring admission of women, practically all Georgia Tech administrative officers favored the change, and the faculty had overwhelmingly voted to recommend their admission. Many Tech students, however, still remained opposed. One undergraduate criticized the Student Council in the *Technique* for its failure to adequately sample student opinion and complained of the lowered standards and restrictions on classroom activities that, in his view, would inevitably develop.[88]

The regents had forwarded the petition from the Women's Chamber to Van Leer, requesting a formal recommendation. In a strongly written letter of March 6, 1952, the colonel recommended that qualified female students be admitted to Georgia Tech on the same basis as male students. On March 12, Regent Rutherford L. Ellis, now chairman of the Education Committee, sponsored a resolution to change the policy. Over the next month the Women's Chamber orchestrated a letter-writing campaign from various women's organizations in support of Ellis's resolution.[89]

On April 9, the regents passed the resolution by a vote of 7–5, after a frank and sometimes bitter exchange of views. Regent Edgar Dunlop of Gainesville opposed the change, noting that "here is where the women get their noses under the tent. . . . We'll have home economics and dressmaking at Tech yet." The policy was initially a limited one; women were eligible to apply only to those programs not offered at other units within the University System, which included engineering, architecture, and the master's degree in applied mathematics. Aware of the negative feelings that some of the regents still held, Van Leer instructed Registrar W. L. Carmichael: "We must be very strict about this matter. If any questions arise about the admission of a young woman, the case should be decided against her . . . no women are to be admitted with any entrance deficiencies whatsoever."[90]

When it learned that the regents' policy was not an all-inclusive one, the Women's Chamber of Commerce protested, urging the policy be expanded. In fact, it would be several more years before Tech opened all of its degree programs to women. Van Leer personally advocated open admissions but in the meantime sought to make school policies free from sex discrimination. He encouraged the ROTC to move toward accepting women so that "we can truthfully say we are making no exceptions as far as women students are concerned." The first four women accepted to Georgia Tech for the fall of 1952 included: Coleman Douglass, Nashville (architecture); Regina Marie Didden, Washington, D.C. (chemical engineering); Barbara Diane Michel, Houston (aeronautical engineering); and Elizabeth Herndon, Atlanta (electrical engineering). Mrs. Van Leer volunteered to serve as an unofficial dean of women, and since there was no girls' dormitory, out-of-state women were provided accommodations in efficiency apartments near the campus. Only Mrs. Herndon, a World War II widow, and Miss Michel actually enrolled in the fall. Partially because there were only two females, the transition went smoothly, In a letter to the *Technique* replying to charges of a privileged double standard for parking on campus, Mrs. Herndon made the case well for all who followed her path-breaking efforts: "I do not seek any special privilege, or ask any special favors because of sex. I hope to obey all rules just as all freshmen are required to do."[91]

Two additional women enrolled in the winter quarter, but in the spring only Herndon and Michel remained in school. Although a small minority, women soon integrated themselves into campus life. With Mrs. Van Leer's assistance in 1953, eleven students established the first local sorority, Tau Sigma, which became a colony of the national organization, Alpha Xi Delta. Ann Brown of Decatur became the first female cheerleader in the fall of 1953, and the following fall saw the first two women as ROTC cadets attached to the air force unit. In the fall of 1955, President and Mrs. Van Leer were able to enjoy a personal reward as a fruit of their efforts. Their daughter, Maryly Van Leer Peck, an honors graduate of Vanderbilt in

Isaac Stiles Hopkins, President, 1888–1896. (Courtesy of the Special Collections, Robert W. Woodruff Library, Emory University.)

Lyman Hall, President, 1896–1905. (Courtesy of Mr. Lyman Hall Robertson.)

Kenneth George Matheson, President, 1906–1922. (Courtesy of Mrs. J. O. Pearson.)

Marion Luther Brittain, President, 1922–1944. (Courtesy of the Georgia Tech Archives.)

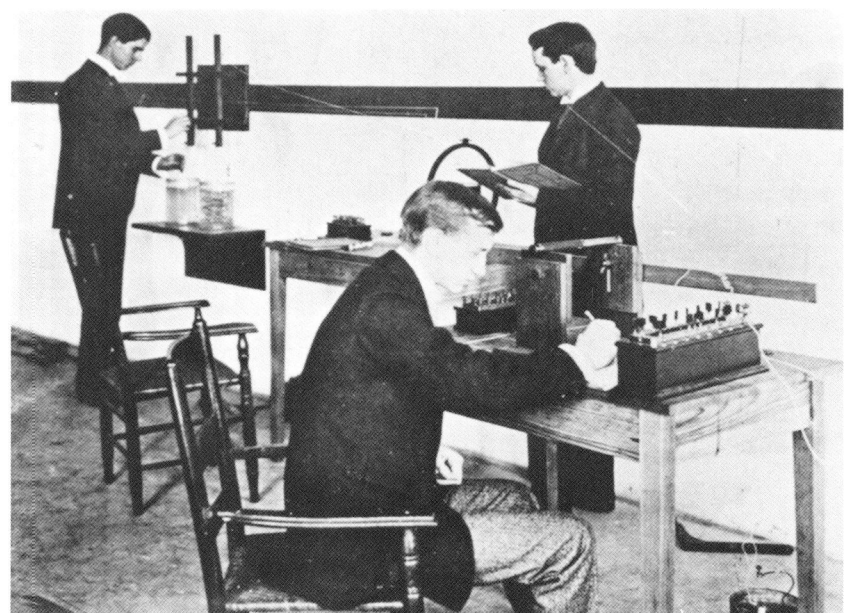

Students in an early electrical laboratory, circa 1896–1897, determine current and test the resistance of a battery. (Courtesy of the Georgia Tech Archives.)

Aviation supply officers in training are bivouacked in front of the Academic (Administration) Building, as the campus becomes partially militarized in 1917–1918. (Courtesy of the Georgia Tech Archives.)

John W. Heisman, legendary Georgia Tech football coach, 1904–1919, for whom the Heisman Trophy is named. (Courtesy of Mr. H. Wayne Patterson.)

William A. Alexander (Coach "Alex"), head football coach, 1920–1944, and director of athletics, 1934–1950. (Courtesy of the Georgia Tech Archives.)

University of California center Roy Riegels executes his famous sixty-two-yard run toward the wrong goal line during the 1929 Rose Bowl game won by Georgia Tech, 8–6. (Courtesy of Mr. Joe Westbrook.)

The Techwood Homes Project, completed in 1935 with Public Works Administration funds, was the first federally subsidized public housing project in the United States. (Courtesy of the Georgia Tech Archives.)

A student examines the wind tunnel located in the Guggenheim School of Aeronautics, which M. L. Brittain considered to be his finest achievement. (Courtesy of the Georgia Tech Archives.)

Blake Ragsdale Van Leer, President, 1944–1956. (Courtesy of the Georgia Tech Archives.)

Edwin Davies Harrison, President, 1957–1969. (Courtesy of the Georgia Tech Archives.)

Arthur Gene Hanson, President, 1969–1971. (Courtesy of the Georgia Tech Archives.)

Joseph Mayo Pettit, President, 1971 to the present. (Courtesy of the Georgia Tech Office of the President.)

In June 1956, Acting President Paul Weber confers the baccalaureate degree on Ms. Barbara Diane Michel, the first female graduate under Tech's new admissions policy. (Courtesy of the Georgia Tech Archives.)

Students obtaining "hands-on" training at the Southern Technical Institute reflect a linkage with Georgia Tech's shop culture past. (Courtesy of the Georgia Tech Archives.)

Robert L. "Bobby" Dodd, head football coach, 1945–1966, and director of athletics, 1950–1977. (Courtesy of the Georgia Tech Archives.)

John "Whack" Hyder, head basketball coach, 1951–1973. (Courtesy of the Georgia Tech Archives.)

Student protest of Governor Griffin's proposed cancellation of participation in the 1956 Sugar Bowl led to a confrontation in front of the governor's mansion during the early morning hours of December 3, 1955. (Courtesy of the Georgia Tech Archives.)

Since the admission of the first black students in 1961, minority enrollment at Georgia Tech has gradually increased, as shown by this 1982 group photograph of the Society of Black Engineers. (Courtesy of the Georgia Tech Archives.)

Former governor George Busbee, with Dr. Joseph Pettit looking on, formally greets Chinese ambassador to the United States Zhang Wenjing at the opening of the exhibit "China: 7,000 Years of Discovery," a part of Georgia Tech's centennial celebration. (Courtesy of the Georgia Tech News Bureau.)

chemical engineering, with a master's degree from the University of Florida, became the first female doctoral candidate at Georgia Tech. Unfortunately, President Van Leer did not live to see the first woman graduate. In June 1956, Barbara Diane Michel received her bachelor's degree in industrial engineering from Acting President Paul Weber. The presence of the many outstanding young women at Georgia Tech today represents a most fitting monument to Blake R. Van Leer's leadership.[92]

Student Life

Georgia Tech had always taken pride in its demanding curriculum and somewhat austere campus life. Colonel Van Leer alluded to this in his annual message to the incoming student body in 1946: "Georgia Tech is a man's institution. It is not intended for crybabies or weaklings. Here we expect you to play a man's part, to look after yourselves in so far as that can be done without trespassing on the rights of others."[93] Despite this typical Spartan message and the colonel's overall military bearing, he became a president willing to listen and communicate with the student body.

In 1946, Van Leer attended a stormy mass meeting with the student body in the gymnasium to discuss their grievances with football seating arrangements. He began to attend student council meetings to discuss campus problems with the elected leadership of the student body. When in 1950 students, many of them veterans, reacted bitterly to an announced plan of compulsory contract feeding for dormitory residents, Van Leer was not afraid to meet them in a tumultuous mass meeting at the YMCA. Underneath his sometimes gruff and always military exterior, the "Colonel" also possessed a softer side. How many college presidents, for example, would have agreed to have his services as a chauffeur for a student and his date for the 1952 Military Ball auctioned off to raise funds for the World Student Fund? Van Leer consciously tried to overcome the image of aloofness that had characterized his first few years as president. In the fall of 1952 the president inaugurated a program of entertaining the Student Council and other campus leaders at his home for Sunday evening discussions on common campus problems. The *Technique* reported favorably on the practice, noting "the affair was the first of its kind, but we trust it will not be the last." Van Leer was never a beloved president, but by the end of his career at Tech, he had earned the respect of a majority of the student body.[94]

Many of the prewar student activities disbanded for the duration began to revive in the late 1940s. The campus dramatic group known as the "Marionette" reemerged in February 1947 as the Georgia Tech Dramatic Club, later to become today's "DramaTech." The players presented a set of one-act plays in the spring of that year, two shows in 1947–48, and in the fall of 1948 decided to do a production every quarter. The group was first directed by Glenn Jones and local radio personality Zenas Sears, but in 1950–51 local actress Mary Nell Ivey took over. The Georgia Tech band gave its first postwar concert on February 1, 1948, and the Glee Club, also revived after the war, toured the South on a regular basis and conducted lengthy northern swings in 1948 and 1949. During Christmas break in 1949, the club, directed by Walter C. Herbert, made a foreign tour of principal German cities. On Sunday, October 11, 1953, the Glee Club reached a high point in its history with an appearance on the Ed Sullivan "Toast of the Town" program on the CBS network, where it performed "Ramblin' Reck," "Nothing Like a Dame," and "Alma Mater."[95]

With the return of Robert C. "Charlie" Commander, the popular and dynamic YMCA secretary, to the campus in 1946, following forty-six months of army service, the Y began to return to its former role of importance as a center of student activity. The Student Council, which had controlled publications and campus organizations since 1921, had ceased functioning during the war because, as one student writer put it, "Georgia Tech was militarized." In 1945, however, the council was reorganized. The newly constituted body became involved in mild controversy as student opinion split over charter affiliation with the new National Student Association (NSA). In addition to supporting international student contact, the organization was committed to the removal of "economic, religious, and racial barriers to educational opportunity," a position seen as too liberal by many Tech students. After a campus debate during the fall of 1947, the council voted 17–3 in February 1948 to ratify the

USNSA constitution and formerly affiliate with the national organization. The situation remained unsettled, however, and dissent over this relationship continued into the 1950s.[96]

Student life in the 1950s generally paralleled national trends. Scholars and pundits alike have dubbed the students of this decade as the "silent generation." If indeed this is an accurate description, students were simply reflecting the views of an entire American society that was tired of war, afraid of inflation, and frightened by an alleged internal communist conspiracy. He or she dressed blandly, disdained political involvement, seemed more interested in football than in social change, and for the most part worked hard at academic studies. Issues that motivated students to action were those which focused on their personal lives. When Van Leer announced the new compulsory eating plan mentioned above, for example, opposition mobilized through the Student Council and campus mass meetings. In this case, protest was successful as the contract feeding option remained, but only on a voluntary basis.[97]

The unsteady life of the *Yellow Jacket*, the campus humor magazine, demonstrates the kind of cause that captured campus attention. Revived after the war in 1946–47, the often off-color publication had generated frequent student and faculty criticism. Several faculty members, led by English Professor A. J. Walker, had wanted to ban the *Yellow Jacket* in 1950, but it barely survived with the support of George Griffin, the dean of men. In November 1952, however, controversy arose when the Baptist Student Association strongly opposed an issue and W. R. Metcalfe of the English department resigned as faculty advisor because he had not been consulted prior to publication. The Baptists had taken particular exception to some irreverent pokes at the Christian religion. This material, plus a few risqué jokes, appear quite tame when viewed against later levels of campus humor. The *Yellow Jacket* endured a brief suspension and resurfaced in December 1953. Dean Griffin had warned in 1950, at the time of the *Yellow Jacket*'s previous difficulty, that he would recommend abolishment if trouble again emerged. When, in the spring of 1955, an issue of the magazine included Griffin's secretary in an unkind parody of Georgia Tech staff, it lost its most loyal friend and went out of existence. In a black-bordered "obituary" of June 3, 1955, the *Technique* reported that the "orphan child of the publications family passed away quietly Tuesday morning 11:00, May 31, 1955, after 46 years of ill-health, laid to rest by the faculty senate."[98]

Despite the continuing role of the YMCA Building as a focal point for campus activities, momentum was underway in the 1950s for the construction of a new multipurpose student center, a project which had long been discussed. Professor Fred B. Wenn of industrial management and Dean George Griffin were the biggest boosters of the idea, and they successfully enlisted Van Leer to their cause. On September 22, 1951, the Bradley Building addition to the Administration Building opened to replace the crowded and outdated facilities of the College Inn, whose dining room in the basement of the Administration Building was converted to a senior lounge. Made possible by a grant from the W. C. and Sarah H. Bradley Foundation, this new snack area, soon rechristened "the Robbery," represented a major improvement in student services, but Georgia Tech still lacked amenities when compared to other state-supported schools of its size. With the new library under construction in the spring of 1952, Griffin suggested to Van Leer that the old Carnegie Building be converted into a student union. The president rejected the idea on the grounds that the building should be near the dormitory rather than the academic area of the campus. In the spring of 1953 the Tech Athletic Association agreed to turn over the proceeds from the "T-Day" intrasquad football game to the student union fund that Omicron Delta Kappa (ODK) had been collecting. The following year students voted to raise activities fees two dollars a quarter for the building fund, and in the fall of 1954 the regents authorized plans for a $300,000 student activities building. Money raised from student fees eventually provided the financial base for construction of the building, but there would be many frustrating delays before the groundbreaking ceremony in 1967.[99]

The Georgia Tech administration supported the fraternity system in the postwar years for very pragmatic reasons. By encouraging fraternities to build new dwellings, the campus housing crunch partially could be ameliorated. Construction of the interstate highway adjacent to the campus in 1948–49 had exacerbated the situation by adversely affecting a row of fraternity houses near Williams Street. Organizations were forced to sell or move their houses to other locations. In 1951–52, Kappa Alpha, Kappa Sigma, Sigma Chi, and Sigma Nu constructed new houses in the designated area on the master plan, and Theta Chi began construction on a new building. But housing on campus still remained tight.[100]

Although Tech's full-time enrollment had reached over 4,000, dormitory capacity was limited to 1,900, a situation requiring the continued encouragement of fraternities to build. In addition, many of the older wooden-framed fraternity houses were fire traps desperately needing correction. An inspection by the Atlanta Fire Department in 1955 found only one fraternity house on campus, Phi Delta Theta, adequate to receive a state certificate of occupancy. It was up to Associate Dean of Men John Pershing to issue ultimata to the deficient fraternities that their houses would be closed unless they took corrective measures. On the bottom of the copy sent to Van Leer, Pershing asked for the president's backing "when the wolves come!" Pershing, who had come to Tech as George Griffin's assistant in 1945, usually drew the tough task of enforcing regulations, while the beloved Griffin remained the students' friend. As one former faculty member recently recalled, "Pershing got them into trouble, and George got them out."[101]

By the early 1950s student life had begun to return to its more traditional prewar patterns as the influx of veterans subsided. Freshmen were reminded periodically, for example, that those who refused to wear their "rat caps" were subject to the infamous "T-cut" haircut, a Georgia Tech variant of the shaved scalp which left only a T visible. Plans began in late 1951 to create Tech's first private radio station, WTJY, later to evolve into the present WREK. At first the student-operated station broadcast only into the dormitories via a small transmitter.[102]

If the attitude on the nation's campuses in the 1950s was related to a search for economic security, as has often been suggested, developments at Georgia Tech fit into this pattern. Engineers were in great demand during the booming years of the Eisenhower administration, and the Tech Placement Center became a beehive of Yellow Jacket activity. Associate Dean of Men Fred W. Ajax directed the Placement Center into a model of its kind, maintaining communication with over seven thousand firms in the United States. The average salary offered to Tech engineering graduates in 1953 was a healthy $345 a month, with oil companies paying the highest starting figure. Citing 1953 as the "biggest boom ever" in the job market for engineers, Ajax reported that his office had arranged over twenty-five thousand individual interviews between Tech students and prospective employers. Perhaps more than the average college student of the 1950s, Georgia Tech graduates were truly "men on the make."[103]

But new cosmopolitan ideas consistent with the emerging international role of the United States also could be found on campus. The World Student Fund (WSF), sponsored by the YMCA and begun in 1949–50, sought to aid world peace, friendship, and professional competence through a foreign exchange program. The organization supported foreign students who studied at Georgia Tech, while selected Tech men spent a year abroad. In 1951–52 five foreign students were enrolled on campus as part of the program. Much of WSF's success must be attributed to YMCA Secretary Charlie Commander. As the first WSF committee chairman Roy Barnes has recalled, "Commander was the father, mother, and midwife to the World Student Fund. It was his project; his work made it a success."[104]

Georgia Tech students were also in tune with more controversial issues. In an editorial entitled "McCarthyism versus Americanism" in 1954, the student writer supported the United States Senate's censure of the Wisconsin crusader, citing his "little respect for personal and civil liberties of persons that have happened to fall in the path of the McCarthy Smear Campaign." The student body also demonstrated a growing concern for that most volatile of all social issues in the South of the 1950s—race. A *Technique* editorial in December 1953 advocated a position most probably consistent with the general campus attitude. It criticized an antisegregation editorial that had appeared in its sister publication at the University of Georgia, the *Red and Black*, but defended the right of the Georgia students to express their views from the state politicians who had threatened to cut off funds from the Athens student publication. When the Warren Court announced its landmark antisegregation ruling in the 1954 *Brown v. Board of Education, Topeka, Kansas*, case, the entire educational structure of the South appeared threatened. Student editorials and comments generally opposed the Brown decision. In subsequent letters to the newspaper, however, a healthy

281   *The Van Leer Years*

dialogue began to emerge which demonstrated that dissenting views existed among the student body.[105]

For its part, the school administration had also become concerned with growing agitation for racial integration. The regents feared that one of the recent number of applications received from black students might represent a legal test case. Georgia Tech referred all such applicants to the chancellor's office, which sent the candidate a form letter informing him of regents' policy. A "scholarship" available to black students forced to go out of state for an engineering education consisted of a tuition reimbursement equal to the difference between the out-of-state tuition and what was charged in the University System, plus a two-way rail coach fare, one each calendar year. The form letter pointed out that Georgia blacks could attend one of several accredited engineering schools in the East, including the Negro colleges, Tuskegee Institute, North Carolina A&I, Tennessee A&I, as well as northern integrated engineering schools such as MIT, Cornell, NYU, Purdue, Illinois, and Wisconsin. After receipt of one particular application in early 1953, regents staff wrote to Van Leer suggesting that Georgia Tech implement an entrance exam as a way to screen out black students. The assumption seems to have been that blacks would automatically fail such an exam. Van Leer demurred, pointing out the general problems with standardized entrance exams and the fact that such a test implemented at this time would be "ex post facto." The colonel made clear his general views on such an exam: "If it is fair, *any* qualified student can pass it, and if it is not fair, I have no desire to be a party to it." Racial integration would not come to Georgia Tech until 1961; in the interim, the prospect of increasing pressure for the admission of blacks caused increasing consternation within the administration.[106]

The question of race was the backdrop to one of the most painful episodes of the Van Leer presidency—the Sugar Bowl football game of 1956. Following a highly successful 1955 season of 8–1–1, Tech's football squad accepted a bid to play the University of Pittsburgh in the Sugar Bowl in New Orleans. This would make five straight major bowl appearances for the school, which was at the peak of its football prowess in the Bobby Dodd era. Pittsburgh had a starting black player, fullback Bob Grier, but the Tech Athletic Association and President Van Leer had not balked at signing the game contract since the University of Georgia had recently played out-of-state games against racially mixed teams. Tension was high in the South in the wake of the Brown decision, however, and Coach Dodd received a telegram from a White Citizens' Council in Augusta asking the Tech team not to play in the game. Governor Marvin Griffin had given Dodd private assurances of his support, but he stunned the Tech campus when, on Friday, December 2, the governor sent a wire to the Board of Regents chairman, Robert A. Arnold, requesting that Tech not participate in the game. Griffin asserted: "The South stands at Armageddon. The battle is joined. We can't make the slightest concession to the enemy in this dark and lamentable hour of struggle." Under pressure from militant segregationists in the state, Griffin had caved in.[107]

Chairman Arnold called a special meeting for Monday, December 5, to decide the matter, but in the meantime the Tech campus erupted in protest. Students organized an impromptu protest rally on campus, and on Friday at midnight a large group hung the governor in effigy and ignited a bonfire. The crowd then marched on to Five Points, the state capitol, and the governor's mansion, hanging Marvin Griffin in effigy at each stop. The crowd did some minor damage to the governor's mansion before state representative "Muggsy" Smith, a Tech alumnus, succeeded in dispelling the demonstration at three-thirty in the morning. Colonel Van Leer had been ill in bed with the flu, emerging only briefly on December 2 for the dedication of the Rich Electronic Computer Center. His only statement to the media on Saturday, December 3, was: "I am 60 years old and have never broken a contract. I do not intend to start now."[108]

At the end of a stormy meeting of the Board of Regents on Monday, Chairman Arnold announced that Georgia Tech would be allowed to play in the Sugar Bowl on January 2. But the regents also condemned the "riotous" behavior of Tech students, and directed Van Leer to investigate the demonstration and punish those responsible. The new policy on athletic contests stated that all laws, customs, and traditions of host states would be respected but that all games played in Georgia would be segregated, a policy not reversed until 1963. Only Georgia Tech alumnus David Rice among the regents directed his criticism against Governor Griffin instead of the behavior of the students. The *Technique* praised Rice as the "only man with the moral conviction to stand up against Griffin, Roy Harris [a staunch segregationist] and co." Further evidence of campus attitudes came on Thursday, December 6, when President Van Leer received a five-minute standing ovation at the regular monthly meeting of the Faculty Senate.[109]

Van Leer filed his formal report to the chancellor and the regents on January 5, 1956. In the meantime, Georgia Tech had defeated Pittsburgh 7–0 in the most ironic twist of the entire episode. Pittsburgh's black star, Bob Grier, was penalized for pass interference in the end zone, giving Tech a first down on the one yard line, and an early touchdown. The score proved to be the margin of victory. Van Leer's report to the regents concluded that the student body had not been protesting segregation, but the governor's attempt to take away "our game." Since the demonstration had occurred just before final exams, Van Leer also noted that a percentage of students who expected to fail anyway had joined in the "shirt-tail parade" looking for a good time. To further deflect the wrath of the governor and the regents from the Tech student body, Van Leer also introduced the theory that outside agitators had inflamed the demonstration. In this case he mentioned a mysterious thirty-five-year-old man with glasses and unidentified "media people" who eyewitnesses suggested had incited the crowd.[110]

The strain of this incident had taken a tremendous toll on Blake Van Leer, and he died only six weeks later. There are many who share the opinion that the episode shortened his life. Although the colonel had publicly stated only his refusal to break the Sugar Bowl contract, in private he had become very bitter toward those politicians who had made the game into such a "cause célèbre."[111]

Aside from its racial overtones, the Sugar Bowl victory over Pittsburgh represented a record of five straight major bowl victories for Bobby Dodd's Georgia Tech team. In 1950 the squad had salvaged a mediocre season with a 7–0 win over Georgia, the second worst record since Dodd became head coach in 1945. But the following year the Yellow Jackets won the Orange Bowl, the next two years they won the Sugar Bowl, and following the 1954 season they triumphed in the Cotton Bowl before defeating Pittsburgh in the 1956 Sugar

Bowl. The 1951 team, which went on to the Orange Bowl, was the school's first undefeated squad since the 1928 "Golden Tornado" of Rose Bowl fame. Ironically, it was in the midst of this outstanding season that a serious movement began within the Board of Regents to deemphasize football at both Georgia Tech and the University of Georgia.[112]

Much of the regents' concern had emanated from the cost of maintaining a major intercollegiate football program under the two-platoon system that had developed after the war. The free substitution rule had been introduced in 1941, and during the war Coach Earl "Red" Blaik of West Point and Fritz Crisler at Michigan used the separate offensive and defensive unit system to develop powerful teams. The system had hit the South, forcing all major teams wishing to remain competitive to field squads of at least fifty men. This meant increased numbers of scholarship grants-in-aid and larger coaching staffs to teach the now-specialized college game. A cheating scandal that rocked Red Blaik's West Point football team in 1951 had exacerbated the situation by heightening the national concern for abuse in big-time college football. It appeared to many as if the football programs at major universities were in need of restraint.[113]

In 1951 the NCAA Council unanimously adopted a resolution urging that institutions and conferences "must take aggressive action" to save the dignity of intercollegiate athletics. At the September 1951 regents meeting, Sandy Beaver introduced a resolution to reexamine the athletic objectives and practices at Georgia Tech and the University of Georgia. Several regents cited various "irregularities" that they personally had observed and expressed similar concerns. Chancellor Harmon Caldwell requested Presidents Aderhold of Georgia and Van Leer to forward their recommendations to the regents. Aderhold proposed to abolish spring football practice, limit the number of athletic grants-in-aid, and abolish the two-platoon system. Van Leer summoned a meeting of the Athletic Board to discuss the regents' request and forwarded a letter to Caldwell on October 1, 1951, with his suggestions. After first defending the record of the Georgia Tech Athletic Association (GTAA) and practices at Georgia Tech, the colonel also supported the elimination of spring football practice and the two-platoon system, as well as the curtailment of athletic scholarships. The regents appointed a special committee, chaired by Robert Arnold, to determine a proper course of action.[114]

The situation came to a head in October, with a number of powerful voices in the state coming to the support of the football programs at the two major schools. Regent Roy Harris of Augusta spoke for a large majority of the state: "So far as I'm concerned, I'm ready to stand behind what the coaches recommend. Football teams of Georgia and Georgia Tech have given the finest advertising the State of Georgia ever had. I am not in favor of doing anything to cripple or embarrass our athletic program." The special regents committee, meeting on October 20, 1951, recommended that the management of intercollegiate athletic affairs should continue to rest with the proper authorities at Tech and the university. The full board passed the resolution at its November 14 meeting, thus bringing an end to the deemphasis movement for the time being.[115]

Nationally, the issue did not die, however, and in 1953 the NCAA Rules Committee voted to end the free substitution rule, thus eliminating two-platoon football. Bobby Dodd, who favored the two-platoon game, voted against the rules change. Never comfortable with the "iron man" football advocated by his mentor, Tennessee's General Bob Neyland, Dodd realized that his smaller, lighter players would have difficulties playing both ways. The coach adjusted quickly; his 1953 team, the first under the new rules, posted a 8–2–1 record and a victory over West Virginia in the Sugar Bowl. After the West Virginia win, however, there were numerous rumors that Dodd would step down as coach, remaining only as athletic director. Two seasons later, on the eve of the controversial Sugar Bowl game with Pittsburgh, Dodd turned down an offer to coach the professional Philadelphia Eagles team. Having adjusted to the new rules, although still not liking them, Dodd remained committed to Georgia Tech and stayed on as coach through the 1966 season.[116]

Football remained in central focus at Georgia Tech in the early 1950s, with most other sports taking a back seat under Athletic Director and Head Football Coach Bobby Dodd. The basketball team, led by Coach John "Whack" Hyder, did have its moments of glory, however. Hyder succeeded Roy McArthur as head basketball coach in the spring of 1951. McArthur, who had been at Tech for twenty-two years, had resigned following a series of losing seasons. Hyder had only marginally more success in his first years, but in 1955 earned the reputation of "giant killer." In January Tech defeated the number one ranked team in the country, Kentucky, by a score of 59–58 in Lexington, the first time that Adolf Rupp's Wildcats had been defeated at home in 129 games. In early February Tech did it again, this time on its home court. This was the first time that any Rupp team had lost twice to the same opponent in one season.[117]

Georgia Tech students differed little from their counterparts at other schools in the 1950s. Athletics, fraternity and sorority life, parties, and extracurricular activities all served as important distractions from the rigorous undergraduate academic program. A rather perverse pride also remained in overcoming the many obstacles which "Ma Tech" threw in the way of that ultimate diploma. Colonel Van Leer again touched upon this theme in the last of his annual welcoming messages, given to the incoming class of 1959: "At Georgia Tech we judge your manliness not by the number of bad habits you acquire but by your ability to 'take it' without complaining. Senseless grumbling, kicking, and complaining do no good. They are harmful to you because no one likes a malcontent, and employers will never employ one if they can get someone else."[118]

Curricular Developments

Two reports compiled in the mid-1950s, one internal and the other external, provide insights into the development of engineering education at Georgia Tech in the crucial postwar decade. An internal self-study report previously mentioned, *The Aims and Objectives of the Georgia Institute of Technology*, was first assembled in May 1954 and published the following September. A broad external study, the American Society for Engineering Education (ASEE) *Report on the Evolution of Engineering Education*, commissioned in 1952, appeared in January 1955. This "Grinter report" (named for chairman L. E. Grinter), was a successor to the influential Wickenden report of 1923–29 and the Hammond reports of 1940 and 1944. Both reports, the Georgia Tech *Aims and Objectives* and the ASEE Grinter study, dealt with the changes in engineering education wrought by the war, particularly the new role of science in advanced technological development and the expansion of research.[119]

The *Aims and Objectives* made twenty-two specific recommendations in its final report. It focused on the need to emphasize quality within the present Georgia Tech curricular framework rather than developing new programs and recommended that resources be devoted to a "hard central core" of studies. The report encouraged "creative scholarship" and stressed the need to strengthen and expand graduate education, but not at the expense of undergraduate programs. Reflecting the influence of the 1940 and 1944 Hammond reports, which had recommended the division of each engineering curriculum into a "scientific-technological stem" and a "humanistic-social stem," the Tech committee urged the liberalization of instruction with the expanded use of the "historical and philosophical approach." The committee also recommended a raising of entrance requirements, a move toward a "true quarter system" of five-hour courses, and a return to the practice of required final examinations in the last part of the quarter rather than during a designated exam period. Finally, it urged that Georgia Tech take full advantage of its opportunities and abilities for supporting regional industrial growth.[120]

Despite the attention the self-study gave to liberal, nonengineering studies, Professor Samuel J. Mantel, Jr., of the social sciences department compiled a formal critique of the *Aims and Objectives* that focused on the recommendations in its chapter on liberal studies. On a list of twelve engineering schools Mantel compiled, Georgia Tech ranked last in the average number of hours in social sciences taken by its students. Cal Tech led the list with thirty-eight hours, while Georgia Tech ranked a distant last with an average of only eight hours. Mantel recommended a minimum of twenty-two hours, quoting from the 1944 Hammond report, which had suggested a minimum of approximately 20 percent of engineering course work in the humanities–social sciences stem.[121]

The two major recommendations of the ASEE Grinter report, made public in 1955, were to strengthen work in the basic sciences, including mathematics, chemistry, and physics, and to continue to concentrate efforts to expand and integrate work in the humanities and social sciences. The Georgia Tech Faculty Senate reviewed these recommendations during the 1955–56 school year. The Educational Aims Committee of the senate supported the goal to make the engineering curriculum more rigorous and scientific, thus "bringing it in line with present-day demand." It also seconded the recommendation to strengthen the humanities and social sciences in the curriculum so as to be more consistent with the new standards emanating from the ASEE and Engineers' Council for Professional Development (ECPD). Actual implementation of curricular changes would not be effected until after Van Leer's death.[122]

Significant curriculum developments did occur under Van Leer in the 1950s. In October 1951, the President announced a contractual agreement between the Norfolk Naval Shipyard and Tech's Cooperative Education Division, a working relationship which has functioned successfully up to the present day. In 1953 Tech entered into its first "three-two" joint program with a liberal arts college. Under an agreement with the University of the South at Sewanee, students would take three years of work at the liberal arts school and two years at Tech, a liberalized five-year program leading to two degrees, a bachelor of arts or a bachelor of science. This educational plan had proved successful elsewhere, and Georgia Tech opened negotiations with several other liberal arts schools to establish similar relationships. With the approval of the new bachelor of science degree in applied mathematics in 1953, the former Department of Mathematics became the degree-granting "School" of Mathematics. In conjunction with the opening of the Rich Computer Center on campus, the School of Mathematics developed its first sequence of courses in digital computation.[123]

The Grinter report had also recommended that engineering schools take steps to hire faculty members with the capacity to teach the new science-based curriculum. Georgia Tech had improved its staff since World War II and now possessed a much more research-oriented faculty. In 1955 there were eighty-two full-time faculty members holding the doctorate whereas ten years before there were less than twenty. Graduate school enrollment was holding at between 250 and 300 students and doctorates were now awarded in chemistry, chemical engineering, physics, and electrical engineering. The Board of Regents approved a doctorate in civil engineering in the spring of 1955. Georgia Tech had made significant progress toward Van Leer's stated goal to make the school into a true technological university.[124]

Faculty Relations

From the beginning of his presidency Van Leer had fought to improve faculty salaries. Although successful to a degree, the relatively low payscale at the school remained a chronic problem. A study conducted in 1953–54 showed that Tech faculty still received less than their counterparts at a sample of large state universities, private southern schools, leading institutes of technology, and southern engineering schools. Van Leer noted, "If this situation continues, it will become increasingly difficult for us to maintain our position as one of the leading engineering schools of the country and the leading engineering school of the South." Even though average salaries increased by 13 percent over the next two years, Georgia Tech was still not competitive in recruiting against the leading engineering institutions in the country.[125]

In response to constant requests for increased appropriations for salary, the regents had countered with appeals for greater faculty accountability. Van Leer had resisted strongly a regents attempt in 1946 to impose a standardized twelve-month salary schedule for the entire system. Arguing that different conditions existed at different schools, the Tech president was aware that he had to compete with industry to obtain engineering faculty and needed greater flexibility in contract negotiation. He and Cherry Emerson also objected to the wording of the proposed standard contract, which spelled out terms and conditions of employment in great detail. Emerson pointed to the great improvement in faculty morale since Van Leer had become president and feared that the new contract, with its lack of professionalism, would threaten relations with the faculty. He assured the regents that "our president, while regarded as a sincere friend of every faculty member, is also a hard task-master." Van Leer argued that the proposed contract "will make us the laughing-stock of the educational world. It will drive good men away from us and encourage faculty labor-unionism. I urge that our contract be simple and similar to those used in all first-class institutions of higher learning." He further noted that the contract violated established principles of the American Association of University Professors (AAUP) and the American Council on Education.[126]

Although this contract proposal died in 1948, there remained a Board of Regents faction that viewed the academic faculties of the University System with cynicism. Regent Sandy Beaver again trumpeted the charge in 1951 that the board needed to get "more for their money." President Van Leer was fully aware that heavier teaching loads, similar to those at General Beaver's military school for boys, would seriously undermine his efforts to further research at Georgia Tech. He had previously written to Chancellor Harmon Caldwell of his strong objection to the effort to keep faculty on an inflexible forty-hour week, arguing that professionals should be free to stagger their work load as they desired. Van Leer also supported other policies aimed at encouraging faculty advancement and creativity. He announced a new policy in 1948 whereby Georgia Tech would pay a faculty member's expenses to go to professional meetings when presenting an academic paper. Van Leer had also introduced a sabbatical policy in 1946–47 entitling a faculty member to one quarter's leave with pay for each eight quarters of service. Citing cost, the Board of Regents rescinded this benefit in June of 1951. Thereafter, all requests for leave were to be decided on an individual basis.[127]

Because of the relatively low salaries he was able to pay, Van Leer tried to recruit and keep good people with other inducements. Promotion and tenure tended to be rapid at Georgia Tech, a policy that engendered regents' criticism. In 1947–48 Tech had only 39.9 percent of its faculty at the higher ranks of associate and full professor; by 1953–54 this figure had grown to 58 percent. The regents' Committee on Education, concerned that Tech was becoming top-heavy, urged caution in recommending additional promotions in the future. The regents had also objected to a growing practice of faculty taking graduate work in the departments in which they themselves taught. Van Leer defended the policy as a benefit available to junior faculty, citing his own experience of earning a master's degree at California in the early 1920s. Van Leer and Lloyd Chapin, dean of faculties, did agree to curtail the practice sharply. In 1953 Professors J. M. DallaValle of chemical engineering, Mario J. Goglia of mechanical engineering, and C. E. Kindsvater of civil engineering became the first three Regents' Professors at Georgia Tech. Van Leer saw this move as only partial relief from the growing threat of top faculty leaving. Primarily because of low salaries, the school had lost fifty-two faculty members during the 1952–53 school year. Among that group, Van Leer reported, were ten men of international reputation.[128]

A serious issue of faculty morale arose in 1954 over a security questionnaire that Governor Herman Talmadge required all state employees sign. The questionnaire was above and beyond the loyalty oath that every faculty and staff member had completed at the time of initial employment. The regents had established the loyalty oath in 1949 during the first stages of the "Red Scare" that accompanied the cold war. Now employees were directed to complete an additional form attesting to their loyalty to the United States and the Constitution and listing their affiliations, including religion. In a special general meeting on March 16, 1954, the Georgia Tech faculty passed a resolution calling on university officials, the Board of Regents, the Georgia Attorney General, and Governor Talmadge for "relief from the burdens and dangers of the present questionnaire."[129]

Ralph E. Himstead, general secretary of the AAUP in Washington, had cabled Van Leer on March 15 protesting the proposed questionnaire and offering the services of the AAUP in fighting it. Van Leer declined the AAUP offer of intervention. Meanwhile, Herman Talmadge remained firm, stating that "I cannot conceive of any good citizen refusing to respond to the questionnaire. However, the law requires the questionnaire to be executed." As a compromise, Talmadge granted faculty a thirty-day time extension for filing. The task of obtaining 1,685 completed questionnaires from Georgia Tech employees and then turning them over to the state security officer created enormous headaches for the Tech administration. The majority of the faculty construed the entire exercise as harassment; not all objected to the questionnaire on civil libertarian lines, but saw it as a useless, time-consuming task. In his annual report of 1954, Colonel Van Leer expressed his hope that a reexamination of the law would allow some of the loyalty oaths to be eliminated so that employees would not have to execute something like this every year.[130]

Administrative Change and the 1955 Reorganization

A changing of the guard at several units on campus in the 1950s served to strengthen academic programs. In 1950–51 Robert E. Stiemke from Penn State succeeded Thomas Evans as director of the School of Civil Engineering. That same year D. P. Savant retired as head of electrical engineering after thirty years of service to Georgia Tech. His successor, William A. Edson, had earned a doctor of science degree at Harvard, worked at Bell Laboratories, and was on the faculty at Illinois Institute of Technology before coming to Atlanta. Professor James E. McDaniel, director of the cooperative program since 1927, resigned in 1950 to accept a permanent position with the military government in occupied Germany. J. G. Wohlford succeeded McDaniel as director of the Cooperative Division.[131]

The fall of 1953 saw the return of two influential campus figures who had been on leave. Jesse Mason, dean of engineering, returned in September after a year at the engineering department of E. I. du Pont de Nemours in Newark, Delaware. His leave was part of the "year-in-industry" program sponsored by Du Pont. While Mason was away, Paul Weber had served as acting dean of engineering. Colonel Leslie Zsuffa, director of public relations and presidential assistant, returned on October 1, 1953, after two years of active military service. In 1951 the Army Quartermaster Corps had called Zsuffa to become project leader for the construction of a new $11 million Quartermaster Research and Development Laboratory in Natick, Massachusetts.[132]

D. M. Smith, former head of the mathematics department and considered to be one of the best teachers and most influential faculty members on campus, retired at the end of the 1953–54 year. In addition to his forty-one years of teaching mathematics to Georgia Tech students, Smith had also been long associated with the Athletic Association as head of its tutorial program for varsity athletes. He had developed this program with his close friend, Coach W. A. Alexander, and had continued his affiliation under Bobby Dodd. At halftime of the annual "T-Day" game in April, the GTAA presented Smith with a 1954 two-toned sedan, which he drove slowly around the field, and a check for $1,500.[133]

An era of Georgia Tech history ended with the deaths of two legendary campus figures. On February 19, 1951, the longtime foreman of the woodshop, John Henika, affectionately known by everyone as "Uncle Heinie," passed away. Retired but still visible on the campus, Henika had become ill following a fall at his home, and the ninety-five-year-old Uncle Heinie never regained his strength. Famous to students, faculty, and alumni for his philosophy and sayings as well as his dedicated service, Henika was much mourned. In his honor, Van Leer proposed to rename one block on campus, formerly part of Ponce de Leon Avenue, N.W., and where Henika once lived, as "Uncle Heinie Way." With regents' approval the change became effective in 1954. Then on July 1, 1953, President Emeritus M. L. Brittain died after a brief illness. He had completed his history of Georgia Tech, published in 1948, and was living out his retirement in the old presidential home on North Avenue. In honor of President Brittain, the administration suspended all classes on Thursday and Friday of that week.[134]

In 1954–55 a number of factors, including Blake Van Leer's health, the pending mandatory retirement of Vice President Cherry L. Emerson, concern about the presidential succession, regents' criticism of the relationship between teaching and research at Georgia Tech, continuing budgetary problems, and friction between Van Leer and some of his top administrators, coalesced to bring about the second sweeping organizational change to occur during the colonel's presidency. Van Leer first proposed the changes in a letter to Chancellor Harmon Caldwell on September 15, 1954. Citing Emerson's retirement on July 1, 1955, and the need to effect economies by reducing the number of officers reporting directly to the president, Van Leer proposed three major changes. He recommended the abolishing of the position of executive dean, then occupied by Phil C. Narmore, and the creation of a dual vice presidency. The first vice president would be in charge of education (abolishing the Office of Dean of Faculties) and the second in charge of research and extension, a post analogous to Emerson's job. This was a model that would much later emerge at Georgia Tech. Van Leer's last recommendation was to transfer the buildings and grounds department from the existing vice president's authority to that of the controller, a practice "followed in 90 percent of our institutions of higher learning." Caldwell commented with favor on these recommendations with one major exception. He was not convinced that the dual vice presidency was the best way "to provide the needed coordination of teaching and research."[135]

Van Leer's concerns about his own health and his possible successor were clearly on his mind. The colonel had a history of minor strokes going back to his days as dean of engineering at Florida, a condition exacerbated by an accidental head injury he received in 1950. These problems ultimately led to surgery to remove a blood clot on his brain, a very serious operation in those years. Van Leer recovered from the surgery well, but his health had begun to deteriorate as a result of high blood pressure, coronary disorders, and emphysema.[136]

Contained in Van Leer's correspondence with Chancellor Caldwell in September is an illuminating passage suggesting a connection between his health and his proposed organizational changes:

> We already have a vice president in charge of research, extension, planning and construction, and buildings and grounds. The trouble is that he, being the only one, is usually listed as vice president, inferring that he succeeds the president in authority, when, of course, that is not the case. . . . I do not want to give the public, the Regents, or anyone else the impression that the officer who is in charge of research and extension actually is of greater importance than the man who has charge of our truly educational activities, and that is the reason I propose two vice presidents and that their titles be: 1) vice president in charge of research and extension, and 2) vice president in charge of education.[137]

Van Leer had inherited Cherry Emerson as temporary vice president when he arrived in 1944. He made Emerson the dean of engineering in 1945, a post for which he was academically unqualified, and in 1948 promoted him to vice president in the new organizational structure. The two men had enjoyed a sound relationship for the first several years, but by 1954 the relationship had become strained. Emerson had seized every opportunity to exercise authority, and in the minds of several faculty members, was really running the Institute. This was particularly the case at times when Van Leer was at the Atlanta Veterans Hospital for treatment or otherwise out of the office. The colonel wanted to ensure that the chief academic officer, dean of faculties or vice president for education, was the designated successor. But who would hold such an all-important post at this critical juncture in the school's history?

Van Leer had appointed Registrar Lloyd W. Chapin to dean of faculties in 1948. They had worked well together for many years, but two factors, one external and academic, the other internal and personal, had worked to undermine Chapin's status. The ASEE Grinter study, begun in 1952, first appeared as an interim report in the September 1954 *Journal of Engineering Education*. Its principal recommendation was to strengthen science-based work in engineering education. Yet, Georgia Tech's dean of faculties, its chief academic officer, was a former professor of English without a doctorate. There was growing pressure to place a technical person with a doctorate in this post. In the official news release of March 1955, at the time of the reorganization, Van Leer stated that "it is no reflection either on [Chapin's] ability or character that the professional aims of the institution now require that the academic work be under a person trained in engineering."[138]

The other issue that worked against Chapin had grown from the dean's role in a controversial nonrenewal case earlier in 1954. Physics Professor George F. Wheeler had received notice that his contract was not being renewed for the 1954–55 school year. Wheeler had originally come to Georgia Tech in 1940 as an instructor in physics but resigned in December 1943 to take a position conducting war-related research at the radiology laboratory at MIT. He returned to Tech as an assistant professor in 1946 but resigned again in 1948. Wheeler later obtained a job at the Experiment Station and in the spring of 1953 was hired back on the teaching faculty.[139]

Wheeler received an appointment for the 1953–54 school year but was not offered a contract in the next year. He had alienated many powerful people in the state by writing a critical letter to segregationist Congressman James C. Davis of Stone Mountain, Georgia. Davis had made an inflammatory speech on the floor of the United States House of Representatives opposing desegregation of public facilities in Washington, D.C. Wheeler had written the letter on his private stationery, and had not indicated a Georgia Tech affiliation. Nevertheless, Davis had apparently sent the letter to Governor Herman Talmadge, who in turn had forwarded it to Van Leer. Wheeler's letter most certainly played a role in the decision not to renew his contract.[140]

Wheeler appealed his case through the local chapter of the AAUP and enlisted the support of the organization's national general secretary, Ralph E. Himstead. Lloyd Chapin supported the professor's right to free speech and petitioned both Van Leer and the regents to reconsider the case. The petition, signed by Chapin, Dean Ralph Hefner of the General College, and Director J. H. Howey of the physics school, listed Wheeler's excellent teaching, the scarcity of physicists, the AAUP's interest in the case, and Wheeler's personal misfortune—his wife was terminally ill—as points in the appeal. Van Leer, stating that he had "no objection" to the petition, but not endorsing it, forwarded it to the regents. On June 18, 1954, Chapin, Hefner, and Howey personally appealed to the regents' Committee on Education, but to no avail. Citing the fact that the untenured Wheeler had not pursued training beyond his master's degree and was therefore not eligible for promotion to associate professor, the regents refused to reverse its decision, which was based on Van Leer's recommendation. The record also shows, however, that "consideration was also given to Mr. Wheeler's actions in writing intemperate and critical letters." Wheeler obtained a teaching position at nearby Oglethorpe University and remained active in state AAUP affairs for many years. By pushing the Wheeler case all the way to the regents, Chapin had shown courage and integrity; he also undermined his own position with president Van Leer.[141]

Personalities also apparently played some role in Van Leer's decision to demote Executive Dean Phil Narmore. Since 1948, when Narmore assumed the title, the post had gradually eroded in importance. The executive dean's chief responsibilities were campus space allocation and chairing the committees on scholarship aid, student standing, and commencement. Beyond this, however, the relationship between Narmore and Van Leer had grown far apart. Narmore had criticized several of Van Leer's actions, and it has been suggested that Narmore was interested in the colonel's job. The president's relations with the regents were strained, Van Leer confiding to a friend in early 1955 that "he had just barely gotten reappointed for one more year." There appears to be general agreement that there was no love lost between Van Leer and Narmore.[142]

In the fall of 1954 negotiations among Van Leer, Chancellor Caldwell, and the regents resulted in an impasse over the colonel's two vice-presidency proposals. Van Leer concluded: "It now appears that the question has become involved with one of personalities as to who is to occupy the various positions and execute certain responsibilities." Conceding that his proposal would now be opposed, Van Leer withdrew his recommendation and indicated that Georgia Tech would continue to operate under the statutes approved on May 13, 1953. On February 3, 1955, however, a high-level policy meeting was held at the Capital City Club in Atlanta to attempt a compromise acceptable to both Van Leer and the regents. The regents assured Van Leer that they would follow his recommendations if limited to only four main points: abolish the office of vice president and appoint no one to succeed Cherry Emerson; abolish the executive dean's office and offer Narmore a regents' professorship; relieve Chapin as dean of faculties and give him a regents' professorship also, his successor to be an engineer with a doctoral degree; and change the present dean of engineering, Jesse Mason. The first three recommendations carried through and were presented to the regents for approval at their March meeting. Van Leer withdrew his recommendation to replace Mason because "in view of the above drastic changes, it is recommended that no other changes be made in the academic administration of Georgia Tech at this time." A highly competent and strong engineering dean, Mason had alienated several faculty members by his sometimes autocratic methods. Mason was a logical candidate to get Chapin's job, but Van Leer had already decided on Paul Weber instead.[143]

The regents approved the changes on March 9, 1955, and Van Leer made them public at a special meeting of the General Faculty the next day. The colonel gave his reasons for the reorganization as economy, the need to strengthen the instructional staff of the institution, and the retirement of Vice President Cherry Emerson on June 30, 1955, because of statutory age limitation. The president assumed the functions of Emerson's office with the exception of buildings and grounds and planning and construction, which were reassigned to Controller Jamie Anthony. Under this new arrangement, both the EES and Extension Division reported directly to President Van Leer. The position of executive dean was abolished and Narmore was appointed as a Regents' Professor of Mechanics. Van Leer assigned the former duties of executive dean to the registrar, the dean of students, and the student grant-in-aid and scholarship committees, of which Phil Narmore remained chairman. Dean of Faculties Lloyd Chapin received a leave of absence from July 1 to October 1, 1955, at which time he became a Regents' Professor of English. Effective July 1, Paul Weber became the new dean of faculties. Rising to speak at the General Faculty meeting, J. E. Moore, head of the psychology department, captured what was in the minds of many that day. Expressing "no joy" at seeing "the lifelong dreams and hopes of colleagues shattered and wrecked," Moore raised his deep concern over the use of the honored title of regents' professor to "cushion" the reassignment of any administrator, no matter how able. Moore concluded with an appeal to support the new Dean of Faculties and to show "a deep concern for Tech in her hour of need."[144]

Lloyd Chapin and Phil Narmore both had their supporters on campus, but Chapin in particular was very well liked. Had Paul Weber himself not commanded such great respect, the situation would have been untenable. As the former EES director, Gerald Rosselot, stated to Weber in a letter of March 13, 1955: "I frankly don't know how the Colonel is going to handle all the business next year, the way it is set up. He is in no shape to do so, as far as I can see. It looks like it will have to be done with the help of Weber, Mason, and Anthony and others. 'Tis quite a job you've got cut out for yourself next year—you are the only guy around there who can pull the faculty back together." With Weber's help Van Leer implemented the many specific administrative changes necessary to comply with the new structure. Several faculty committees, for example, had to be adjusted. Weary from his long fight over this issue and recovering from a gall bladder operation, Van Leer departed on June 19 with his wife for a five-week European tour. Confident of Paul Weber's abilities and personal integrity, the colonel could leave the campus with a clear mind.[145]

Van Leer returned from his vacation in August, ready to begin his twelfth year as head of Georgia Tech. Although not critically ill, he still suffered from high blood pressure, heart disease, and emphysema. The colonel had to check into the Veteran's hospital that fall for periodic treatments of these ailments. Certainly the pressures brought on by the 1956 Sugar Bowl controversy did not help matters. Van Leer entered the hospital on Sunday evening, January 22, complaining of chest pains. He suffered a coronary thrombosis, but rallied during the night. On Monday, his secretary visited him with some papers to sign, but she said that he appeared very weak and let him rest. At 4:15 that afternoon he suffered a massive heart attack and died with his wife at his bedside. The school, the evening school, the Experiment Station, and Southern Technical Institute all closed Tuesday and Wednesday and opened after the interment. Dean of Faculties Paul Weber assumed the duties of the president, and in February the regents appointed him acting president, a post he would fill with distinction for eighteen months.[146]

The Van Leer Years: An Assessment

The colonel took greatest pride in the massive expansion of Tech undertaken during his tenure. The campus had enlarged from 51 to 128 acres, and the value of the physical plant increased from $4.5 million in 1944 to more than $25 million in 1955. State appropriations had grown from $143,386 in 1945–46 to $1,704,000 in 1954–55. Undergraduate enrollment had risen from 2,911 students in 1944 to over 5,762 in 1956, and graduate students from only 6 in 1944 to over 300 in 1956. The EES budget had grown from $50,000 to $2 million, and research opportunities for both faculty and EES personnel had risen proportionately. The GTRI was an established institution, and the AC Network calculator, hydraulic laboratory, and Rich Electronic Computer Center were all constructed. The new library, textile building, and architecture building, as well as new dormitories and apartment houses also marked the physical expansion of the campus. But Van Leer had left additional legacies.[147]

The Southern Technical Institute, which boasted almost seven hundred students in 1955–56, had been a personal project. By effecting the procedural name change from the Georgia School of Technology to the Georgia Institute of Technology in 1948, Van Leer had also encouraged substantive change. All engineering curricula had attained accreditation by the appropriate societies, and the colonel had attempted to keep Georgia Tech programs abreast of the latest developments in engineering education. By fighting for increased salaries, faculty housing, and expanded research opportunities, Van Leer had accomplished much to boost faculty morale. His strong personal convictions had given backbone to the long struggle for the admission of women to Georgia Tech, a goal achieved in 1952. Governor Marvin Griffin, who had recently been locked in controversy with Van Leer over the Sugar Bowl incident, served as a pall bearer at his funeral and publicly praised the colonel's major achievement of bringing Georgia Tech into high regard nationally. Another pall bearer, former Governor Herman Talmadge, cited how Van Leer had worked night and day for Georgia Tech.[148]

Perhaps the most fitting tribute to Blake R. Van Leer is the consensus of everyone interviewed who worked with him. Whether they admired his methods, military style, and personality or not, all agree that, as the first engineer to head the school, Van Leer led Georgia Tech into the future. No longer a small regional school mired in the shop culture and known primarily for its football team, the post–Van Leer Georgia Tech had started on the road to becoming a nationally recognized center of excellence in engineering education. Under the stewardship of Acting President Paul Weber and his successor, Edwin D. Harrison, the Institute consolidated its gains and initiated new departures.

Chapter Eight
The Post-Sputnik Era at Georgia Tech

Overleaf: Construction of the new Montgomery Knight Aerospace Building with the older campus viewed in the background is symbolic of the massive physical expansion that took place during the Harrison presidency in the 1960s. (Courtesy of the Georgia Tech Archives.)

The death of Colonel Blake Van Leer on January 23, 1956, saddened the Georgia Tech campus. Much had been accomplished under his presidency to improve campus facilities and academic quality. Yet the currents of change that the postwar era and Van Leer's presidency had unleashed did not cease with his death. Instead, they continued and accelerated during the able interim presidency of Paul Weber for more than seventeen months and under the popular presidency of Edwin D. Harrison for nearly twelve years until 1969. Despite ongoing strains and challenges, the period was one of unprecedented growth and achievement, both for the nation and for Georgia Tech.

Nationally, the period roughly encompassed the years between the Soviet orbiting in 1957 of the first manmade satellite, Sputnik I, which stimulated the United States to self-examination and a drive to catch up, and the United States landing of a man on the moon in 1969. The postwar surge of enrollment in higher education, which began with the return of the veterans under the GI Bill, continued and accelerated during the 1960s as the "baby boom" generation reached college age. Rapid increases in the numbers of students interested in higher education posed new challenges and encouraged greater academic selectivity, especially at the best schools. Growth in the United States economy, combined with fear of the Soviet threat, encouraged both public and private commitment to improving education. Standards of student performance rose, numbers of faculty members and their salaries increased, and great new building and expansion programs were undertaken. Concerns were expressed for revising and strengthening the curriculum, both in technical fields and in the liberal arts. Professionalism of faculty increased and a drive toward graduate education developed. It was an age when, for a time, all things seemed possible.

Georgia Tech was both the beneficiary of these national currents of change and a contributor to them. Under Weber's leadership, plans were set in motion that would dramatically raise student entrance requirements at the Institute during the five-year period from 1959 through 1963, and steps were initiated to increase faculty salaries so that they would be more competitive nationally. These efforts were continued and accelerated under Harrison's presidency. Curricular offerings were strengthened; the percentage of faculty members holding advanced degrees and engaging in scholarly publication rose; and graduate programs began to be offered in most areas of engineering, the physical sciences, and mathematics. Under the stimulus of a major urban renewal program, the size of the campus more than doubled, and new buildings appeared to be rising everywhere.

Contributing to these changes was the greater availability of federal, state, and private funds. Georgia Tech's outstanding alumni contributions, in particular, led the school repeatedly to be recognized as first in the nation in sustained alumni giving to a public institution of higher education. Support for research doubled every five years, and eventually such funds were channeled both through Georgia Tech's Engineering Experiment Station and through the academic departments. Undergirding and directing many of the changes at Tech were a series of institutional studies, undertaken with the assistance of the Georgia Tech Foundation, which would culminate in a major administrative reorganization in 1965 that sought to enable the Institute to coordinate its rapidly expanding programs more effectively.

These institutional changes were closely associated with the development of student life at Georgia Tech. Tech students had always worked and played hard, but rising academic standards and the increasing size of the institution tended to accentuate extremes. On the one hand, students increasingly exercised responsible roles through a strengthened student government, through candid discussion of issues in student organizations and in the *Technique*, and through involvement with community service activities. On the other hand, students expressed restiveness about the perceived pressures and impersonality of the institution. In the absence of a student union building until 1970, extracurricular life continued to revolve around the fraternities and around the YMCA, which served many of the functions of a student union.

Many student traditions at Georgia Tech gradually were modified during these years. Freshman customs such as the wearing of "rat caps" became increasingly difficult to enforce. In loco parentis restrictions eventually were relaxed, though not without considerable sparring between students and administrators. The first black students peacefully entered Georgia Tech in 1961, and women at Tech increased slightly in numbers and in general community acceptance. Compulsory ROTC fell by the wayside in 1965, primarily the victim of higher academic standards and student desires for greater freedom of choice. Georgia Tech continued to field many fine teams in football, as well as in other sports, yet even the leadership of Coach Bobby Dodd was unable entirely to avoid slippage in Tech's sports record. National student unrest over the Vietnam War and over social issues during the late 1960s stimulated a ripple of concern among a small minority of students, but surplus idealism of Georgia Tech students generally was quietly devoted to community uplift projects in the poorer communities that surrounded the campus. Despite the many subtle changes that took place in student life, continuity was at least as noticeable as change throughout the period.

The Weber Interim

The profound changes that Georgia Tech underwent during the 1950s and 1960s were guided by several key administrators. One of the most important individuals who managed the day-to-day operations of the Institute during the decade between his selection as dean of faculties in 1955 and his change of position following the reorganization of 1965 was Paul Weber. Weber had originally come to Georgia Tech in 1927 as an instructor in chemistry. After leaving temporarily to get his doctorate in chemistry at Purdue in 1934, he returned to teach in the Department of Chemistry and Chemical Engineering. In 1941, when Gerald Rosselot was named director of the Engineering Experiment Station, Weber became his assistant. When Jesse Mason stepped into the position of dean of engineering in 1948, Weber replaced him as director of the School of Chemical Engineering. In July 1955 when Van Leer undertook his controversial administrative reorganization, centralizing power in the hands of the president, dean of faculties, and controller, Weber was named to the number two spot as dean of faculties. Upon Van Leer's death eight months later, Weber was appointed acting president of Georgia Tech, serving in that position for more than seventeen months. During that time, he continued to handle many of the duties of the dean of faculties, a position he formally retained.[1]

Weber brought considerable strengths to his various administrative roles within the Institute. Quiet, soft-spoken, and methodical, he slowly but thoroughly investigated issues before developing new programs. He loved detail work and was very good at it. He seemed always to be knowledgeable, with the relevant facts on diverse issues at his fingertips. Yet Weber's reserve and meticulousness did not contribute to his success in public relations. Although he could make good speeches, he intensely disliked such assignments. One close friend commented that his presentations tended to be a bit dry. Another spoke of his rather "Teutonic" demeanor that made it difficult for him to engage easily in the more casual exchanges necessary for effective public relations. Within the Institute, however, Weber increasingly gained the confidence and respect of faculty members of widely varying persuasions because of his thoroughness, fairness, and ability to probe to the heart of an issue.

Weber's appointment as acting president in February 1956 made him potentially a prime contender for the presidency of Georgia Tech. Popular wisdom holds that "he had no desire whatsoever to become president," largely because of the "political and social responsibilities which that entailed."[2] Initially this appears to have been true. As Weber increasingly became adjusted to the role of president, however, he found strong faculty support for his continuing in the position, and a faculty petition on his behalf was sent to the regents. Gradually, he reassessed his stand, keeping in close contact with a friend who was vigorously supporting his candidacy to the Board of Regents.[3] Yet after Edwin D. Harrison was selected president, Weber served unstintingly as a trusted supporter and friend. Weber was the only individual to be singled out in every president's report during the Harrison years for his outstanding service to Georgia Tech. Only many years later, following Weber's own death, would Harrison learn through a close mutual friend that Weber had once desired the presidency of Georgia Tech.[4]

Whatever Weber's own attitudes may have been, finding a new president for Georgia Tech proved an unusually lengthy process. The formal search lasted more than seventeen months, whereas previous presidential searches had never taken more than four. The hope was to have a new president by the fall of 1956, yet the search continued. Atlanta newspapers and the *Technique* commented on the delay and speculated on its reasons. Two primary factors appear to have hindered the attraction of an external candidate. First, the president's salary at Georgia Tech, like that of its faculty members, was not competitive with comparable schools nationally. Second, few candidates for the position were prepared to deal with the looming issue of racial integration at the Institute, given a state government that seemed adamantly opposed to any change in the status quo on that matter.[5]

While the search went on, Weber continued to move the school along on an even keel. His basic premise was to make little or no significant changes in administrative organization but to handle immediate needs and prepare for future growth. One key problem was faculty salaries, which were not competitive with those in engineering schools elsewhere. Teaching loads were heavy, reducing the quality of instruction and the time available for research. The limited support for research came mainly from the Engineering Experiment Station. The result of the inauspicious teaching and research conditions was that during Weber's first interim year, more good faculty members were lost than acquired. By the following year, however, the vigorous efforts of Weber and other friends of Tech were helping to turn the situation around. First, an extra $300,000 for the operation of Georgia Tech was made available by the Board of Regents. Second, the Georgia Tech Foundation initiated a faculty salary supplementation program with a total of $150,000 for supplementing faculty salaries and aiding with additional expenses for the 1957–58 year. This support, only one example of the active role of the foundation in improving conditions at the Institute, would continue to grow and would play a vital part in upgrading the quality of education at Georgia Tech.[6]

In addition to financial efforts, Weber continued the campus development program started by Van Leer. The most substantial building complex constructed during Weber's tenure was the Alexander Memorial Coliseum, completed and dedicated on October 27, 1956. Also completed were new laboratories, buildings, or annexes for Civil Engineering, Mechanical Engineering, and Aeronautical Engineering. Several older buildings on campus were renovated, and Tech purchased and began renovation of the Techwood Dormitory. Preliminary planning began for the Radioisotopes and Bioengineering Laboratory, the first of Georgia Tech's extensive nuclear research facilities. Planning for a new classroom building, which had been in the works since the 1940s, finally was underway in 1956. The building, eventually named after Dean William Vernon Skiles, was completed in 1959.[7]

The Early Harrison Years

Edwin D. Harrison became Georgia Tech's sixth president in August 1957 at the age of forty-one. Born in Evadale, Arkansas, he had lived in many parts of the country and in Puerto Rico as the son of a career army officer. After graduating from the Naval Academy at Annapolis in 1939, he served in the navy through 1945, rising to the rank of lieutenant commander. He then earned his master of science degree in mechanical engineering from Virginia Polytechnic Institute in 1948, and received his doctorate, also in mechanical engineering, from Purdue University in 1952. He began his administrative career as an assistant dean at Virginia Polytechnic Institute and then moved on to become dean of engineering at the University of Toledo in Ohio.[8]

The selection of Harrison as president of Georgia Tech came about almost coincidentally. In May of 1957 two executive members of the Georgia Board of Regents, Chancellor Harmon Caldwell and Executive Secretary L. R. Siebert, visited a number of schools with engineering programs to see if they could locate possible presidential candidates. The president of the University of Toledo was unavailable for consultation, so instead they chatted with Harrison. After leaving, they realized that Harrison himself might be an excellent candidate. He was invited twice to campus and was offered the job—all in the space of two weeks.[9]

Harrison's rapid rise and continuing success in administration owed much to his outgoing personality. He was an excellent off-the-cuff speaker, with a natural ability to form warm personal friendships. It was no accident that during his presidency, and with the assistance of Joe Guthridge and many other able administrators, faculty members, and alumni, the Institute's fund-raising efforts through the Georgia Tech Foundation and the Joint Tech-Georgia Development Fund appeal rose to a new high. Harrison maintained warm and effective contact with the Atlanta business community and alumni. He recalls speaking at almost every alumni club in the United States, and at one time he knew personally approximately one-half the members of the state senate and one-third of the members of the state House of Representatives.[10]

On the other hand, Harrison was bored by bureaucratic detail. His philosophy of administration was to appoint able subordinates and give them authority to act, subject to correction only if they failed to accomplish their tasks effectively.[11] Harrison was fortunate in being able to delegate much of the day-to-day paperwork of the Institute to a number of capable administrators. Foremost among them was Paul Weber. Harrison and Weber worked well together, with Harrison focusing primarily on external relations and fund raising and Weber being chiefly responsible for overseeing a wide range of internal matters. Also important during the years before 1965 were the dean of engineering, Jesse Mason; the dean of the Graduate Program, Mario Goglia; the president's assistant and director of development, Joe Guthridge; and the controller, Jamie Anthony. Further down the chain of command of the Institute were numerous influential department heads and faculty leaders who set their mark on various aspects of the Tech program. Although the Institute's leadership structure had much in common with that of the military (four of Georgia Tech's first six presidents had come from military backgrounds), within the hierarchical structure of command there was much flexibility for individuals to see a need and respond to it effectively.

Harrison's first year at Georgia Tech, 1957–58, saw the culmination of many projects that had been in the planning stages for as long as a decade. The sense of excitement of that first year, which coincided with the launching of Sputnik I and the beginning of the "space age," was conveyed in Harrison's first president's report, "Technological Education and the Future." The report presented a platform for curricular revision in technological education that was heavily influenced by the Grinter report and similar studies. Harrison noted with approval the new emphasis on "reducing the amount of purely descriptive material and the amount of training in the skills and eliminating some of the outmoded, traditional courses." He felt that material to be added should stress "a more thorough and more advanced emphasis on the fundamentals of science and mathematics applicable to the further field of study." The goal of the new engineering education was to be "a new type of engineer or scientist, one able to adapt himself readily to new concepts and new fields as they are developed," yet "possessed of enough so-called 'practical' knowledge that, with a reasonable period of orientation, he is able to serve capably at the operating level."[12]

In order to improve engineering education at the Institute, a number of changes were made in entrance requirements. Georgia Tech's curriculum was already too difficult for students who lacked a sound academic background, as the high attrition rate illustrated. "To discourage those students without promise of success as well as to raise the level of performance of the better qualified students by lightening the teacher's load" Harrison announced that higher admission standards would be instituted over a five-year period beginning in 1959. This would enable Georgia Tech "to provide essentially the same number of graduates without the exorbitant expenses of a greatly expanded physical plant. During the period when some colleges speak of doubling their enrollment, we feel that a modest expansion of approximately 50 per cent of our present enrollment will achieve, for us, the same results."[13]

Georgia Tech went substantially beyond the state of Georgia, which had already instituted statewide requirements, beginning in 1957–58, that Scholastic Aptitude Test scores be submitted by all applicants to state colleges and universities. In addition, the Institute gradually strengthened its required course preparation for entrance, so that by 1963 it required four units of English, two of algebra, one of plane geometry, one-half unit of both trigonometry and advanced algebra, and one unit of both chemistry and physics.[14] The raising of entrance standards, as well as the addition of fellowships and scholarships to try to attract more of Georgia's outstanding students, would not only improve the freshman class at Georgia Tech but would also stimulate higher standards within the Institute.

A second major goal enunciated in the 1958 report was to improve salaries and so attract better-qualified faculty members. Harrison noted that salaries for college teachers had not been competitive with those for other professions, but that now teachers' salaries were beginning to move upward at a "steady though moderate rate." Georgia Tech itself had been able to increase faculty salaries in 1957–58 with the aid of additional state and alumni support. That increase had made salaries at Tech competitive with those of similar schools in the region but still left them below the level of schools with which they were competing nationally. Teaching loads had not increased in 1957–58, but actually had declined slightly, for the first time since 1952. As a result of these factors, Georgia Tech for the first time in several years had retained or gained more good teachers than it had lost. Faculty morale appeared to be at the highest level in Tech's recent history.[15]

The most dramatic accomplishment of 1957–58 was the impetus given to Georgia Tech's ambitious building program, "the biggest building program in its history," as the 1958 report noted.[16] This program marked the culmination of earlier efforts and continued throughout Harrison's presidency, providing his most tangible legacy to the Institute. The momentum behind the construction efforts could be seen by the fact that just five days after Harrison assumed the presidency, Governor Marvin Griffin pledged $2.5 million in state support for Tech's new nuclear reactor, the most expensive construction outlay in the Institute's history. Within a year, Georgia Tech would also secure an additional grant of $750,000 toward the building from the National Science Foundation. Other major building projects begun that year included the Radioisotopes and Bioengineering Laboratory; the New Classroom Building (Skiles); the Electrical Engineering Building; the campus physical plant near Marietta, Georgia, for the Southern Technical Institute, then under Georgia Tech administration; five dormitories; and an infirmary.[17] These buildings, which began to reach completion by 1959, significantly helped reduce overcrowding in both teaching and research. The full force of Georgia Tech's building expansion was not felt until the mid to late 1960s, however, when with the aid of urban renewal, including federal and state funds, the Institute would more than double the size of its campus and initiate an even more ambitious program of construction.

The Integration Crisis

The first major crisis and one of the greatest achievements of the Harrison presidency was the peaceful integration of Georgia Tech in 1961. This action was the first occasion on which any public institution of higher education in the Deep South had achieved racial integration peacefully and without court order. The seeming ease of the process was deceptive. Underlying the move was conscious effort, careful planning, and skillful leadership. The inside story of this process, which could have led to a damaging crisis had it been mishandled, can only be understood fully in the context of national, regional, and local considerations.

The roots of racial integration in the nation as a whole and in the South in particular go back at least as far as the 1930s and 1940s. During this period, the South slowly began to move into the mainstream of American life. The turning point for the integration of education came with the 1954 United States Supreme Court decision in the case of *Brown* v. *Board of Education*. That decision overturned the earlier *Plessy* v. *Ferguson* doctrine of "separate but equal," stating that "separate educational facilities are inherently unequal" and that the Fourteenth Amendment to the Constitution outlawed racial discrimination in public education. A year later the Court called on school authorities to submit plans for desegregation and gave local federal courts the responsibility of deciding whether the plans constituted "good faith compliance." The Court concluded by ordering action "with all deliberate speed."[18]

White responses to the Court decisions often were quite negative, especially in the Deep South. There, resistance to school integration hardened during the mid and late 1950s into what has been called a policy of "massive resistance."[19] Numerous ingenious expedients were utilized to try to block integration. Among the most drastic of these was the threat to close public schools that were subject to integration by court order. Georgia was one of the hardline states. In 1959, for example, Governor Ernest Vandiver declared: "We will fight [integration] wherever it rears its ugly head. . . . We have only just begun to fight."[20] Also firmly behind such sentiments, at least in public, were the state legislature and the Board of Regents of the University System. The legislature even passed a bill mandating the closing of any public educational institution to become integrated. Hoping, nevertheless, to prevent such an undesirable happening, the legislature and the regents tinkered in the meantime with regulations that sought to make black admittance impossible. As each of these regulations was, in turn, struck down by court order as discriminatory, yet another effort was launched.[21]

In the face of this increasingly fruitless effort, a moderate counterreaction began to develop. In Georgia, the city of Atlanta and the Georgia Institute of Technology became prime movers in the more moderate approach. Although Atlanta businessmen generally were opposed to integration, they were even more concerned about the consequences that racial disturbances could have in retarding Atlanta's rapid economic growth. Increasingly an accommodation was sought. As early as 1955, Atlanta Mayor William Hartsfield made his famous characterization of Atlanta as "a city too busy to hate" and quietly helped during the mid and late 1950s to ease the way for the peaceful integration of municipal golf courses and bus and trolley lines. During the early 1960s, the chief racial crisis in Atlanta developed over the issue of desegregating public lunch counters and public primary and secondary schools. After some delays, federal courts ordered that Atlanta's public schools be integrated by September 1961.[22]

Georgia Tech, in the meantime, had also been struggling with the issue of integration. As we have seen, one of the reasons that the search for a successor to Van Leer took nearly eighteen months was the reluctance of many potential presidential candidates to come to Georgia Tech, given the state's hardline policies against integration. By 1957, following the school integration crisis in Little Rock, Arkansas, the *Technique* began to discuss with students their options regarding integration. Almost no attention was devoted to the merits of integration per se; the assumption was that students opposed integration and that the school should resist it as long as possible. Rather, the question that was repeatedly asked was: What should Georgia Tech's response be in the event that it were forced to integrate? Tech student Howard Arnold identified three options, none of them palatable. First, Tech might be temporarily closed. This would be catastrophic, both for students and for the institution. Second, the school could be integrated in opposition to state law, which held that it was a felony to operate an integrated public school. Third, the school could be made private, in which case many students would find it financially impossible to attend.[23] When given a choice between closing Georgia Tech or accepting integration, students polled by the *Technique* in January 1959 voted by a 71 percent margin to keep the school open.[24]

Student desires for moderation notwithstanding, the situation could easily have gotten out of hand had not effective planning and appropriate action been taken by the administration. The type of situation that Georgia Tech hoped to avoid was highlighted by events at the University of Georgia in Athens. Violence broke out there on the night of January 11, 1961, two days after the university had been integrated as the result of a ruling by a federal judge in Macon. A particularly heated basketball game between Georgia and Tech, which Tech won in overtime, was followed by a riotous student demonstration. It began in front of the dormitory in which Charlayne Hunter, one of the two black students, was living. Looking back, Robert B. Wallace, Jr., succinctly summarized the consequences of the affair:

> Out of the demonstration came the expulsion of several Georgia students for leading the riots, the indictment of two students and a member of the Ku Klux Klan by members of the Grand Jury in Athens, a faculty petition from the University of Georgia, a resolution by the Georgia House censuring the faculty for its petition, a series of four bills by the General Assembly which effectively declared a local option basis

for future integration attempts on Georgia's public schools as well as set up a tuition-grant system for private schools, and news and editorials in almost every newspaper in the country and many abroad.25

Such problems and negative publicity were exactly what Georgia Tech administrators hoped to avoid. In a letter to President Harrison on January 16, 1961, the associate dean of students, James E. Dull, recommended some possible approaches. He had just attended the annual meeting of the Southern Deans of Students and Deans of Men held at the University of Alabama. With the University of Georgia disturbances on their minds, individuals discussed how to prevent potential campus disorder. Based on these discussions, Dean Dull suggested the general outlines of an "Emergency Plan" for possible implementation at Georgia Tech. As a starting point, the Institute should immediately make clear that it does not condone "student involvement in riots, demonstrations, and disturbances" and that "students who do involve themselves in such situations will be instantly dismissed (suspended, expelled) from school." Dull described suggested procedures for implementing crowd control, and suggested that the resources of city, county, and state law enforcement be utilized if necessary.26

Georgia Tech's public response, following many of Dull's recommendations, was given by President Harrison in a crowded all-student meeting of over two thousand in the Old Gym on January 17, 1961.27 In a brief opening statement, Harrison stressed the distinctiveness of Georgia Tech as "the only technological school in the southeastern United States with a national reputation," and he emphasized that "any actions and activities which you could undertake if and when a crisis should arise on our campus will affect greatly the future of our institution." At a student's request, he then asked how many would "openly resist forced integration," and only a few hands—variously estimated at between ten and thirty—went up.

Harrison then read a policy statement, which for the following decade would be repeated, in slightly modified form, to all incoming classes:

> The Georgia Institute of Technology does not condone student involvement in riots, demonstrations, and disturbances likely to become

riotous. Students who do involve themselves in such situations will be instantly dismissed, which means expelled from the institution. Moreover, students should understand that any action anywhere tending to instigate or add emphasis to a riot, demonstration or disturbance, using pyrotechnics, making inflammatory statements, inciting to riot, obstructing law and order, or perpetrating actions of this general nature will be sufficient grounds for immediate dismissal. All students should also know that should a riot, demonstration or disturbance occur, they are to go immediately to their place of residence and remain inside. Students in classes, the Library, and other areas on campus, should remain where they are until instructed otherwise.[28]

Asked by students to clarify the specifics of possible integration at Georgia Tech, Harrison responded that the situation was still hypothetical as no blacks had yet applied, that student self-interest would in any case support peaceful and responsible behavior, and that no definite decisions had yet been reached regarding how the specifics of integration might be handled.

Behind the scenes, the Georgia Tech administration continued working on plans to ease a transition they saw as inevitable. By the end of March 1961, the administration was beginning to contact various campus groups about the issue, including the YMCA, the Student Council, the Advisory Council to the President, the Dormitory Staff, and the Interfraternity Council.[29] Of special significance was a series of invitational dinners sponsored by the YMCA, along with leaders of campus religious organizations, to bring together selected faculty and students in the spring of 1961 to discuss constructively all aspects of the impending situation. Cooperation was also sought and obtained from the Atlanta police and other public agencies. The goal was to keep the school operating normally, while privately encouraging groups that were seeking to defuse potential conflict.

On May 11, 1961, Harrison formally announced to his top advisors and to the public his decision to admit three out of thirteen black applicants for admission to Georgia Tech. To his advisers, he observed that the step was essential to keep the federal courts from dictating admission policies or placing a blanket injunction against Tech. To the public, he also stressed that the decision to accept or reject the black applicants had been made after a fair and full review of their records.³⁰ He concluded his public statement: "During the past few months I have sought the advice of hundreds of interested parties on the problem. They include alumni, members of the Board of Regents, my own administrative staff, and top legal authorities in this area. Considering all of the circumstances involved, I believe that I have made the only possible decision concerning these applicants."³¹ The response to this decision was overwhelmingly positive from those who counted most. Of course, numerous negative phone calls and letters were received as expected. But other private letters came in from leading Atlanta business and political figures backing Harrison, the Alumni Board of Trustees issued a statement supporting the move, and most newspapers in the state, even those defending segregation at any cost, endorsed the Tech approach.³² At the Georgia Tech faculty dinner following his announcement, Harrison received a standing ovation from grateful faculty members. The *Technique* and other student groups also backed the move. A pointed editorial in the *Technique* advised students who were not prepared to behave responsibly in the face of integration not to return in the fall.³³ In addition, a variety of special meetings and discussions were held to ease the forthcoming transition.

When integration finally came to Georgia Tech in September 1961, it seemed almost anticlimactic. Two weeks before Tech was scheduled to open, Atlanta public schools had peacefully commenced integrated operation. Possibly the biggest press excitement at Georgia Tech came on Friday, September 15, three days before the scheduled arrival of the students, when Public Relations Director Fred Ajax announced the decision to bar the press from the campus during the integration process. News media representatives were assigned to a press headquarters in the YMCA just off campus, but were not allowed inside any campus buildings, were not allowed to provide television or radio coverage on campus, and were restricted to interviews arranged by the public relations department, most of which were held at press headquarters.³⁴ The administration was determined to keep the campus operating normally and not to allow any activities that might encourage disruptive displays. Press reaction to the decision to restrict outside access was intensely negative, and the restrictions were accepted only with the greatest of reluctance.

On Monday, September 18, President Harrison in his talk to incoming students at the Alexander Memorial Coliseum reiterated the need for maturity. At 11:02 in the morning that same day, three black students—Ford Greene, Ralph Long, Jr., and Lawrence Williams—arrived at the Tech infirmary for their required physicals. Watched from a distance by plainclothes police and by reporters, the three entered the infirmary and went through their physicals without incident.[35] Their itinerary for the first week, planned almost to the minute, also passed without incident, as did their attendance at their first classes on September 27. The only reported incident of any kind was the brief playing of the song "Old Black Joe" from a fraternity house.[36] By the end of the first week of classes, the campus had settled back to its normal routine.

During the remaining years of Harrison's presidency, additional changes in school policy toward blacks gradually were implemented. Under student pressure, the unwritten policy of not allowing black entertainers on campus at all school functions was removed, effective in the winter of 1963 when a concert by Ray Charles was scheduled for Alexander Memorial Coliseum by the Interfraternity Council.[37] In the winter of 1964, the internationally acclaimed Dave Brubeck jazz quartet, which included one black member, gave a popular concert.[38] During the 1965–66 school year, a brilliant and likable black physics major, John Gill, became editor of the *Technique* and oversaw some of Tech's finest student journalism. His work received special commendation in the Institute's 1966–67 annual report.[39] Athletics was slower to become integrated. Georgia Board of Regents restrictions were changed in April 1963 and Georgia Tech announced the school's new policy in April 1965, but not until the fall of 1969 did the first black athlete, Eddie McAshen, come to Georgia Tech on a football scholarship.[40]

Throughout the period, the influence of blacks at Georgia Tech remained minimal, largely because of their limited numbers. As late as the 1967–68 school year, only twenty-eight blacks were in attendance at Georgia Tech out of a total undergraduate enrollment of 7,526.[41] In the spring of 1968, just two weeks before the assassination of Martin Luther King, Jr., seventeen black and white students formed the Georgia Tech Afro-American Association to try to raise student consciousness about black-related issues.[42] In the fall of

1968, the first black instructor, William Peace, began teaching in the Department of Social Sciences.[43] That year also saw the first dormitory sponsor a black woman for homecoming queen.[44] Overall, however, blacks did not make a significant impact on life at Georgia Tech until the early 1970s, when they began to arrive on campus in larger numbers, eventually comprising more than 6 percent of the undergraduate student population.

Charting the Future

Prior to the late 1950s, Georgia Tech had struggled to compensate for recurrent shortages of funds, while also developing a first-rate program. During the late 1950s and increasingly in the 1960s, however, money became more readily available at Georgia Tech, as well as throughout the nation, to upgrade scientific and technological education and to enlarge the campus physical plant and equipment. While it is easy to see how severe shortages of funds could create difficulties, rapid growth in funding and in numbers of faculty members and students also posed new challenges at Tech that demanded creative management. Could administrators and administrative techniques adapted to working under conditions of scarcity successfully deal with the problems of rapid expansion and relative affluence? How ought the increasingly available new resources best be utilized for the benefit of the Institute?

In an effort to chart its future course both for expansion in the size and improvement in the quality of its programs, Georgia Tech during the early 1960s undertook a major institutional self-study, completed by May 1963 and in time for the Institute's seventy-fifth anniversary celebration. During the early to mid-1960s, a series of studies by external management consultants also was conducted on campus expansion, the reorganization of campus administration, and Tech's relationship with economic growth in the state. Much of the immediate impetus for the internal self-assessment and the external studies came from Joe Guthridge, who had come to Tech in 1958 and had served since 1960 as director of development and assistant to President Harrison. Guthridge had a broader view of the Development Office than simply a money-raising operation. His vision also encompassed planning and coordination for a substantially enlarged Georgia Tech of the future. As he stated in the 1961–62 annual report: "The true function of a Development Office is the total development of the Institute," including "(1) greater overall institutional planning, (2) a clearer image of education to the publics on whom support of education depends, and (3) a more systematic method of long-range financing of programs."[45]

Toward those larger ends, an institutional self-study was initiated in 1961 and Guthridge helped secure funding from the Georgia Tech Foundation and the Georgia Tech National Alumni Association for four external studies to help chart the future of the Institute. The Tech Foundation funded the Keck report, *Formula for Growth* (1962), which set the stage for Georgia Tech's future urban renewal plans, and the Perkins and Will *Comprehensive Campus Development Plan* (1965), which provided a master plan for campus growth during the next twenty years. The Tech Foundation and the National Alumni Association each provided half of the funds for the Booz, Allen and Hamilton study (1965), which presented plans for a major reorganization of campus administration. The Arthur D. Little report, *Georgia Tech: Impetus for Economic Growth* (1963), conducted at the request of the National Alumni Association with financial support from a leading Georgia concern that preferred to remain anonymous, sought to determine ways in which Georgia Tech might give additional impetus to development of the economy of Georgia and the Southeast.[46]

Internal and external examination of the future direction of Georgia Tech also was stimulated by planning for the seventy-fifth anniversary celebration of the opening of the institution, held primarily during 1963. Planning for the celebration was envisioned as yet another means of helping to develop "a new set of goals and ambitions to which faculty and students can strive with enthusiasm and vigor."[47] Although the external observer might well have seen Georgia Tech as remarkably stable during the early sixties, nevertheless issues were being quietly addressed that would significantly shape the future development of the Institute. This section and the one that follows will look at the internal side of the growing self-consciousness at Georgia Tech, as expressed through the institutional self-study and the seventy-fifth anniversary celebration. External management studies will be discussed subsequently in the sections to which they are applicable.

The 1963 self-study was first formally proposed in a letter of December 8, 1960, from President Harrison to Elford Morgan of the Southern Association of Colleges and Secondary Schools. The letter indicated that as part of an effort to begin "active and vigorous planning for the growth of our physical plant . . . it is essential that both the current mission of the Institution be understood and that a planned program of academic research and growth be developed." A self-study was necessary to determine the "long-range plans for physical growth."[48] Following approval of the study, a committee of five men was chosen to coordinate the study, headed by Mario Goglia, the associate dean of faculties and dean of the Graduate Division. Beneath that committee were ten others, chosen to include individuals who reflected the divergent viewpoints and concerns that were present at Georgia Tech.[49]

Perhaps the most revealing section of the 1963 self-study dealt with "The Purpose of the Institution." The section began by exploring earlier statements of purpose going back to the enabling act by the state legislature in 1885 that had made possible the establishment of the school. That statement, previously discussed in chapter 2, saw Georgia Tech as essentially a trade school, following the model of the Worcester Institute in Massachusetts. That practical "hands on" emphasis had continued strong throughout the years. Gradually, however, the scope of education at Georgia Tech had broadened with the addition of new programs. Especially after World War II, increasing concern for research and for graduate education developed. Theoretical as well as practical knowledge became more and more a part of the program. Tensions began to be felt between the practical and the theoretical emphases in engineering education, as well as between the Engineering College and the General College. Some even began to raise the possibility that Georgia Tech might eventually become a technological university, with a full range of programs in the sciences and liberal arts.[50]

The administration's concern to assess the underlying goals of the Institute was highlighted during the October 3, 1961, meeting of the general faculty at which President Harrison presented a major policy address, "Quality is Our Constant Goal,"[51] and announced plans for the institutional self-study. At that time, he also invited all members of the faculty to submit written statements indicating what they thought the purposes of the institution and their own school or department should be. These statements were submitted up the chain of command to the president, and to the steering committee of the self-study for use in creating a new, comprehensive statement of the purpose of the Institute. Of the more than five hundred persons in administration, teaching, and research eligible to contribute a statement, only 185, less than one-third, responded, including less than one-quarter of the Engineering College and less than one-half of the General College.[52]

The results of the survey, unrepresentative though they might be, highlighted a polarization among faculty members over the purpose of the Institute. Leaving aside the thirteen individuals who were noncommittal, seventy-five felt that the present purpose of the institution should be preserved and ninety-seven felt that its purpose should be enlarged. Faculty members favoring the status quo stated that the present goals of the Institute were, variously: "undergraduate engineering education," "more and better engineering graduates," "engineering and applied scientists," "management, science and engineering," and "technical education." Faculty members favoring broadening the scope of the Institute believed that its goals should be, variously: to "become a university of Engineering and Applied Science (including Management Science)," "engineers and scientists, broadly trained," "broaden, even to include humanities degrees," and "become a first-rate university."[53]

These divergent concerns were reflected in the vigorous discussions on Institute goals held as part of a series of ten faculty forums during 1961–62 to secure faculty input into the self-study. Those who favored the status quo sometimes expressed discomfort at the freewheeling discussions. One faculty member, for example, criticized the facultywide forums as leading to faultfinding criticism and gratuitous attacks on engineers. The discomfitted faculty member also expressed broader criticisms of the direction in which engineering education nationally was moving, seeing it as increasingly disappearing from the curriculum to make way for more humanities, science, and mathematics courses: "If the current trend continues, engineering will completely disappear from our former engineering schools and will have been replaced by a hybrid course most closely resembling a traditional physics course of study."[54] The lukewarm attitude toward the self-study that administrators such as Jesse Mason expressed may well have reflected similar conservatism.[55] Such tensions would reappear in the divided faculty reactions toward the firing of Mason as dean of engineering, an action that would be associated with the major administrative reorganization of 1965.

The Seventy-fifth Anniversary

The 1963 self-study was only one component of the larger seventy-fifth anniversary celebration planned for the 1963 calendar year. The committees for both the self-study and for the seventy-fifth anniversary celebration were appointed at the same time in the summer of 1961 and they were tied together through common involvement in meetings such as the faculty forums of 1961–62. The titular chairman of the anniversary committee was President Harrison, while Guthridge acted as coordinator. Numerous other committees also were developed to help handle the complex tasks of planning for the celebration. Georgia Tech's anniversary was envisioned as an occasion for stimulating self-examination and improving the institution's external image. The anniversary committee attempted to encourage and publicize activities that were going on at Tech, serving a liaison role by giving support when needed and asked, but not trying to act as a censorship board. A prime external goal of the committee was to attract national attention to Georgia Tech's "75 years as a growing institution [in] the south, the so-called backward or frontier section of the United States. To shake off this regional stamp is no small task."[56]

Toward these ends the committee coordinated an impressive series of programs. During the first six months of the celebration in 1963, the liveliest and most productive period, over one hundred well-known scientists, engineers, educators, and business leaders visited the campus. A monthly lecture series brought prominent and occasionally controversial figures to campus, including Earl Warren, chief justice of the United States Supreme Court. A Symposium on Engineering for Major Scientific Programs brought to campus many of America's top scientific and technological leaders in February 1963, and in November 1963 a Symposium on Utilization of Research Reactors brought other distinguished scientists to Tech. The Fiftieth Anniversary Celebration of Cooperative Education at Tech in April 1963 had as its keynote speaker President Walter Langsam of the University of Cincinnati, the institution that originated cooperative education in the United States. Among the many other activities were an alumni institute, a student employment forum, completion of the institutional self-study, and publication of Wallace's history of Tech, *Dress Her in White and Gold*.

One of the most highly visible activities of the anniversary celebration was the monthly lecture series, organized by a faculty committee headed by Paul G. Mayer, a professor of civil engineering. The lecture committee sought to bring outstanding speakers to Tech in fields ranging from politics to science and from literature to technology. The first four speakers suggest the broad backgrounds of those brought to campus. The first speaker was General Lucius D. Clay, a native Georgian whose distinguished military career had culminated between 1947 and 1949 when he acted as commander in chief of the United States forces and United States military governor of Germany. Having recently served as President Kennedy's personal representative during the Berlin blockade crises of 1961, General Clay spoke on the topic "America and the World Today." Another speaker, of special interest to Georgia Tech, was William G. Pollard, executive director of the Oak Ridge Institute of Nuclear Studies, who discussed "Prospects and Problems in Scientific and Technological Education." More controversial by Tech standards were two other speakers. Ralph W. McGill, Pulitzer prize-winning editor of the *Atlanta Constitution*, was described locally as both the most highly respected and the least highly respected newspaper writer in Atlanta, largely because of his advocacy of racial moderation during the turbulent integration struggles of the 1950s and 1960s. His presentation was provocatively entitled "Look Away Dixieland."[57]

Greatest attention, however, was generated by the appearance on campus of Chief Justice Warren, who had presided over the unanimous Supreme Court desegregation ruling of 1954. His decision to appear at Tech marked the first time since his appointment to the

Supreme Court that he had spoken in the South. Not surprisingly, numerous letters and calls criticized his alleged "profanation and rape" of the United States Constitution and described him as "the worst hated man in Georgia."[58] His speech also created controversy because it was inadvertently scheduled for February 12, Abraham Lincoln's birthday. A small weekly newspaper, the *North Side News*, issued a vitriolic attack on the visit and, more generally, on Georgia Tech. Such actions created great interest and called forth a strong counterresponse. The *Technique* described the *News*'s attack as "libel, implication and lies," and called upon Tech men to support their school vigorously.[59] Privately, President Harrison reassured irate correspondents that Warren had been invited as one of a number of distinguished Americans of differing persuasions, not because Tech approved of his specific views.[60] The excitement of the episode eventually drew to Warren's speech at the Alexander Memorial Coliseum an audience of more than 3,700, more people than attended any other seventy-fifth anniversary academic function except the October 7 convocation. Audience response was respectful and no untoward incidents occurred. Warren spoke of what he called "the lag of the law behind technology and resulting social change," complimenting Tech on its role in technological development during the preceding seventy-five years. He said: "I wish we had made comparable advances in my profession of law."[61]

More characteristic than such occasional controversial speakers was a host of scientists, engineers, educators, and business leaders who participated in special symposia, institutes, forums, or visitor programs. Of the gatherings, perhaps the most scientifically distinguished was the Symposium on Engineering for Major Scientific Programs, held in February 1963. Planned by a faculty committee headed by Maurice Long, then chief of the Electronics Division of the Engineering Experiment Station, the symposium attracted more than 250 participants and attenders to the two-day session, including leaders in scientific research, business, and government. The November 1963 Symposium on Utilization of Research Reactors, and a variety of other special speaker programs throughout the year, also helped bring many prominent figures to Tech.[62]

By far the greatest amount of activity during the seventy-fifth year was devoted to public relations and alumni affairs. Although all of the anniversary activities could be viewed as part of an effort to enhance Georgia Tech's stature and public support, a variety of special programs had as their primary goal the strengthening of alumni and business backing. Among the most successful of these programs was the Student Employment Forum, first held in December 1962. It brought to campus David S. Lewis, a Tech graduate who had become head of McDonnell Aircraft Company; Robert H. Roy, dean of engineering at the Johns Hopkins University; and Governor-elect Carl E. Sanders, who delivered a major policy speech, "Georgia's Industrial Future." Also highly successful was the special Alumni Institute on Management in the Sixties, held October 25–27, 1962. An innovation in alumni offerings for that fall was a one-day program of special lectures by outstanding Georgia Tech teachers from diverse fields, which attracted so much attention that it was continued in the fall of 1963 as well.[63]

Other publicity activities peaked in the fall of 1963. A special seventy-two-page Georgia Tech anniversary issue of the *Atlanta Journal and Constitution Magazine* appeared on September 15, 1963, celebrating the school's past and looking toward a glowing future.[64] Also published in the fall was the colorful Georgia Tech history *Dress Her in White and Gold*, written by Robert B. Wallace, Jr., a 1949 industrial management graduate, editor of the *Georgia Tech Alumnus*, and publications director. The history, which would be revised and enlarged in 1969, provided a lively and informative in-house view of the development of Georgia Tech.[65] The 1963 homecoming celebration, the biggest ever, was also a rousing success, highlighted by a satisfying victory over the Duke University Blue Devils.

Climaxing the formal aspects of the anniversary celebration was a major convocation planned for October 7, 1963. The intent of the anniversary committee had been to secure as the speaker for that occasion a "world-renowned" figure. Talk had initially centered on inviting former Presidents Eisenhower, Truman, or both, to participate in events on that day. On January 3, 1963, however, President Edwin Harrison of Georgia Tech wrote a letter instead to President John F. Kennedy, asking him to present the convocation address.[66] In May 1963 that invitation was formally accepted.[67]

Much excitement, both positive and negative, ensued. The *Technique* announced the engagement with pride, noting that it would constitute Kennedy's first Atlanta visit since becoming president of the United States.⁶⁸ At the other extreme, however, was vicious and frightening criticism, expressed in both anonymous and acknowledged phone calls and letters. In the time since Harrison's invitation to Kennedy had originally been tendered in January, the president had announced support for a major civil rights bill, eventually passed in 1964 following his assassination. That bill was scheduled for preliminary debate in Congress early in the fall of 1963, precisely when he was to appear at Georgia Tech. Reconstruction of the events that followed must remain speculative, but the general outlines may be suggested. A year following Kennedy's assassination in Dallas, Texas, on November 22, 1963, J. B. Fuqua, the former chairman of the Georgia Democratic party, indicated in comments reported on television and in the *Atlanta Constitution* that he had personally arranged for a private meeting with Kennedy in the summer of 1963. Fuqua stated that at that meeting he had expressed his concerns about possible insults to the president, bad publicity, and even personal danger.⁶⁹ Whatever the reasons, on August 13, 1963, a letter was sent by Kenneth F. O'Donnell, special assistant to the president, regretfully indicating that "recent circumstances" had made it necessary to change the president's plans for the fall.⁷⁰ Arrangements subsequently were made for Secretary of Defense Robert S. McNamara, who had already been invited to present a speech that day, to give the convocation address.

The seventy-fifth anniversary convocation on October 7, 1963, in the Alexander Memorial Coliseum went smoothly, once the preliminary planning was completed. The impressive ceremony began with a full academic procession that included representatives of 275 of America's colleges, universities, and learned societies. Brief statements were made by Governor Carl Sanders, Mayor Ivan Allen, President Edwin Harrison, and other figures, including David Harris, Tech alumnus of 1912 and son of Tech founder Nat Harris. The address by Robert S. McNamara to a crowd of as many as 4,500 predictably praised Tech's accomplishments, suggesting that the fact "that nearly half of your students are drawn from outside Georgia, [and] that you draw to this campus faculty and students from all over the world" indicates "that you have a place, and a contribution to make, in this nation and in the world." He went on to urge that institutions such as Tech "produce men who are more than narrow specialists," and he stressed that the great need of the United States was "for more leaders who are trained to think in terms of the overall interests of the country rather than the narrower interests of a particular service or agency or specialized policy area."[71]

How successful was Georgia Tech's seventy-fifth anniversay celebration and what, in retrospect, had it accomplished? These were questions that the anniversary committee raised with participants. Responses generally were positive, while also often suggesting that if much had been accomplished at Tech, much more still remained to be done. One outside research director wrote: "For years Georgia Tech was better known as the home of a good football team than a scientific organization. With this anniversary and the opening of the reactor, Georgia Tech took a long step forward to become identified as the leading institution in the Southeast." Another respondent observed: "The 75th Anniversary program, while not a corrective in itself, was instrumental in calling attention to this transmutation of the role of Tech as a truly technological university and not exclusively an engineering school."[72]

Criticism as well as praise was also voiced, of course. Most common was the disappointment at lack of sufficient participation in programs by Tech faculty members, and especially by students. Student apathy was "overwhelming" despite efforts to include them in the planning phases and the implementation of the program. As one memo noted: "The committee is at a loss to explain why there was no more student interest than there was unless Tech's workload is such that students just don't have enough time for anything except weekend programs."[73]

Perhaps the greatest significance of the anniversary celebration was in highlighting the tremendous advances that Tech had made in alumni and public relations during the sixties. Beginning in 1955 with the establishment of the Joint Tech-Georgia Development Program, a variety of new methods had been utilized to secure substantially more private financial support for the Institute. The growing success of Georgia Tech's fund raising, which showed a sharp upturn during the anniversary celebration and which by 1968 was bringing more than one million dollars a year into the Georgia Tech Foundation,[74] helped make possible great improvements in Tech's buildings and programs during the 1960s. During those years, Georgia Tech was repeatedly recognized as foremost in the nation among public institutions in the extent of its alumni support and the excellence of its alumni publications. The coordinated development program in which Joe Guthridge, Robert Wallace, Roane Beard of the Georgia Tech National Alumni Association, and thousands of other alumni and friends of Tech participated bore the most eloquent possible testimony to the past achievements of Tech and the future possibilities looking beyond the seventy-fifth anniversary.

Administrative Reorganization

Much growth and change had occurred at Georgia Tech since the beginning of Edwin D. Harrison's presidency, yet the structure of Georgia Tech's administration and the personnel that comprised it had remained largely static between 1957 and 1965. The same few administrators were responsible for handling rapidly increasing amounts of paperwork, often using antiquated methods. The annual budget of the Institute, for example, was compiled manually by Paul Weber, utilizing full budget statements from each school, every part of which was required to be fully compatible with the others, even with regard to the exact margins of the typescript pages. Even more demanding, in order to compile annual reports of academic data needed for several national reports, Weber utilized three-by-five cards on every faculty member, each of which was color-coded for different sets of information. The entire project required his attention almost every night from August through November. Even for an individual such as Weber whose hobby was work and who was devoted to Tech, such a task was mammoth.[75] Similar personal control over even the most minute aspects of administrative detail was maintained by Jesse Mason, the dean of engineering, and by other key administrators. The organization clearly was cumbersome; as President Harrison observed, "Tech had outgrown its administrative structure."[76]

Perhaps the greatest single crisis in President Harrison's career at Tech came in 1965 when he attempted to reorganize both the top administrative structure and the personnel of the Institute in order

330 Engineering the New South

to deal with the growing administrative weaknesses that he and others perceived. As in all such reorganizations, personality factors played a part in the change of Tech's administration. Yet the structural and philosophical issues of the reorganization of 1965 were in the long run even more important, causing it to stand as a watershed in Tech's history. What had been an essentially personal institution, run largely through informal individual contact and still focusing largely on undergraduate engineering education with emphasis on practical training was gradually giving way to a more formally structured bureaucracy that placed greater emphasis on the theoretical aspects of undergraduate education, while also stressing research and graduate education. The crisis provoked by the 1965 reorganization highlights fundamental issues in engineering education and management that have not to this day been resolved either at Georgia Tech or elsewhere.

One of the principal figures affected by the 1965 reorganization was Jesse W. Mason, who had served as dean of engineering since 1948. Formally, Mason ranked third in the administrative chain of command in 1965, behind Harrison as president and Weber as dean of faculties.[77] Like Weber, Mason was responsible for much of the day-to-day operations of Georgia Tech. He had a mind like a steel trap, with an extraordinary memory for detail, and knew how to get things done. He played an active role in selecting the heads of many of the engineering schools, and he vigorously advocated the engineering program when questions of allocation of funds within the Institute were raised. Weber and Mason shared common background and loyalties from having both been head of Chemical Engineering before moving into higher administrative positions at Tech. Although Weber was formally Mason's administrative superior in 1965, some felt that he deferred to Mason's judgment on important questions.[78]

The factors that led to the disagreement between Mason and Harrison are difficult to reconstruct in detail. Initially, Harrison, Mason, Weber, and other top administrators appear to have been close, both professionally and socially. By the early sixties, however, more distance was apparent between Harrison and Mason. Differences in personalities may well have played a part. Mason could be autocratic and dour at times, and he lacked Weber's willingness to defer to higher authority. Rather, Mason preferred to do what he thought best, no matter what the consequences might be. He had already almost lost his position as dean of engineering in 1954, as noted in chapter 7, but he had succeeded in creating a considerable personal empire by the early sixties. Mason also, throughout his career at Tech, remained a staunch advocate of engineering vis-à-vis other programs, and he particularly supported undergraduate engineering education with a "shop culture" flavor. As early as 1959, at the same time that Harrison was calling for broadening engineering education and stressing more theoretical training, Mason was vigorously warning of the dangers of too much movement away from the traditional "hands on" approach and toward science and the liberal arts.[79] According to Harrison, the chief factor which convinced him that Mason must be removed from an administrative position with financial authority occurred early in 1965. At that point, Harrison discovered that Mason had been "squirreling away" funds, which he then could make available to support engineering projects of his own choosing. When Mason refused to cease engaging in the practice, Harrison felt that Mason could no longer be trusted in an administrative position with responsibility for financial matters.[80]

The Booz, Allen and Hamilton study of Georgia Tech's internal management, which had been under consideration since 1963, began in March 1965 under grants from the Georgia Tech Foundation and the Georgia Tech National Alumni Association. This confidential study, paid for "without a penny of taxpayer's money" and "intended solely for the information of the client to whom it is addressed,"[81] was undertaken in close cooperation with the Office of Development. The report's tentative findings and recommendations were discussed at progress meetings in May and June and a summary of the final report was presented on September 3, 1965. The study put forward numerous proposals for revamping and strengthening Georgia Tech's administrative structure. The chief goal of the study, as summarized in the 1966 president's report, was ultimately to permit "much greater decentralization of administrative functions while retaining unified direction of the Institute's academic and research efforts."[82]

The immediate importance of the study, however, was twofold: it provided a specific plan for a new top administrative structure for the Institute, with six (soon revised to five) vice-presidential positions reporting directly to the president, and it provided an apparently "objective" external justification for removing Mason as dean of engineering and creating a more unified administrative team. The report noted, using typical bureaucratic jargon:

> It became evident during the survey that there are decided feelings of uncertainty and divergent opinions among officers of the administration regarding the specific interpretations to be made of basic purpose and objectives and their translation into short-range goals for programs and services. More importantly, there is a lack of uniform understanding and support of the broader implications of the "goal of excellence" that is asserted for the Institute. Goals of many programs are uncertain and long-range program planning is incomplete and uncoordinated.[83]

The overall message of the report, stripped of details, was that "early strengthening of top organization and administration of Georgia Tech is a necessary first step to the realization of potential opportunities for growth and development."[84]

Armed with an external justification and plan for his administrative reorganization, Harrison moved rapidly in late September and early October to put the specific plan for that reorganization into effect. In the new top administrative structure, there would be vice presidents for academic affairs, financial operations, development, planning, and special projects, all of whom would report directly to the president. Individuals already at Tech were slated to fill each position. As vice president for academic affairs—the most powerful role, which had hitherto been held under the title dean of faculties by Paul Weber, now nearing retirement age—Harrison intended to select Mario J. Goglia.[85] Goglia's academic and administrative career had been a distinguished one since he had come to Georgia Tech from Purdue in 1948. He had progressed to Regents' Professor of Mechanical Engineering, had served under Weber as associate dean of faculties, as well as acting as dean of the Graduate School, and had chaired the 1963 self-study. For vice president and controller, the current controller, Jamie Anthony, was selected. As vice president for development, Joe Guthridge was the obvious choice to coordinate a greatly expanded program. The role of vice president for planning, to undertake long-range planning for the aca-

333 The Post-Sputnik Era

demic, research, and service functions of the Institute, was assigned to Paul Weber. A final, ill-defined position, presented essentially as an afterthought in the Booz, Allen and Hamilton report, was that of vice president for special projects. Jesse Mason was proposed for that position, and his acceptance of it would necessitate his relinquishing his powerful role as dean of engineering.

The new positions and the individuals who would fill them were slated to be presented to the faculty on October 5, with action by the Board of Regents on October 13. Events did not progress smoothly according to plan, however. When Harrison told Mason that he was being asked to move to a new position as vice president for special projects, Mason was furious. He demanded to be retained as dean of engineering, and when he was told that he could not remain in that position, he mobilized eleven of the twelve directors of the engineering schools to protest the decision sharply in an action that verged on academic mutiny. Hostility also came from some of the engineering directors toward the placement of Goglia in the most important vice-presidential position in the reorganized administration. The feelings, coupled with anger about Mason's removal, were so strong that Harrison came to believe that Goglia could not under the circumstances function effectively in the position. Reluctantly Goglia's name was withdrawn from the new administrative slate.[86]

The faculty meeting of October 5 proved to be one of the most heated in Tech's history. President Harrison began by discussing the changes at Tech since the late 1940s that necessitated changes in the administrative structure: "The two major shortcomings of the present structure—designed in 1948 for an institution of some 5,000 students, mostly undergraduates, and for a blue-sky research budget of $1,000,000—are the inability to develop current short-term and long-term institutional plans to carry out our goals and responsibilities and the lack of specific policy and procedure guidelines to permit simplification of routine administration in an institution that has grown to roughly 7,300 students with a research budget approaching $7,000,000." Harrison then proceeded to discuss the Booz, Allen and Hamilton management study and its plan, refined in cooperation with his office: "Dr. Paul Weber, an outstanding Dean of Faculties will become Vice President for Planning and will serve as Vice President for Academic Affairs until that position is permanently filled. Mr. Joe Guthridge, currently Director of Development for the institution, will become Vice President for Development in an expanded program that will better coordinate all of the areas of development which have become so important to present-day universities. Mr. Jamie Anthony will become Vice President-Controller and will direct the financial operations of the institution."[87]

Controversy was aroused by Harrison's concluding announcement about Jesse Mason. Harrison stated: "Dean Mason has declined to serve in the position of Vice President [for Special Projects] which I had requested him and, in effect, has informed me that he will not serve the institution as *I* wish—but only as *he sees fit*. For *that* reason I am recommending to the B[oard] of Regents that he be relieved of his responsibilities as Dean of Engineering and revert to his tenured position as Prof[essor] of Ch[emical] E[ngineering]. This action I perform with greatest regret."[88] In response to this announcement, Professor Ben Dasher of electrical engineering read a prepared statement that he said represented the views of all but one of the Engineering College directors. It read in part: "We are convinced that some of your decisions are based on incomplete and inaccurate information and that they are not in the best interests of this institution. We have presented to you our reasons for opposing this action, and we have asked you to reconsider these decisions. . . . We regret that we cannot agree with the position you have taken."[89] Mason then eloquently defended himself and his position. A barrage of intense questioning of Harrison followed, which he handled with a calm and composed demeanor. At one point, Professor Earl M. Daniels of Physics spoke in defense of Harrison and received an extended round of applause.[90] Though lasting little more than an hour in all, the intensity of the debate was all but unprecedented for a faculty meeting of the institution.

Correspondence received by Harrison before and after the October 5 meeting highlights many of the broader issues raised by the administrative action, as well as the larger transition Tech was undergoing. Only a few individuals, usually full professors in engineering, committed themselves prior to October 5 to a written defense of Mason, but they were eloquent. One professor wrote how disturbed he was at Mason's removal from a position that had in fact been "the equivalent of vice president for academic affairs. . . . We consider this man [Mason] to be the bulwark of Georgia Tech's academic program." Another professor wrote that he considered the most serious shortcoming of the reorganization plan to be "the removal of the present Dean of Engineering from the direct line of administrative authority. Almost singlehandedly he has promoted a positive philosophy of engineering education. At the undergraduate level, Georgia Tech has moved ahead of such 'name' schools as MIT, where engineering has been prostituted to the early twentieth century German concept of the research institute or the present, USSR approach of specializing more and more on less and less."[91]

A much larger group of letters before and after October 5 supported Harrison's actions, often with an eloquence equal to those who had opposed him. Such letters came largely from the General College, as well as from the Engineering Experiment Station, from some junior professors in engineering, and from Kenneth G. Picha in Mechanical Engineering, the one engineering school director to support Harrison. A research analyst at the Experiment Station compared the action to the necessary reorganization he had experienced in the army when individuals were replaced if they "could not or would not accept changes for the good of the army as a whole." A faculty member wrote: "Even though expressions from opponents dominated the recent faculty meeting, I am confident that the vast majority of the faculty either now agree with your position or will soon recognize the value of the changes when the inevitable benefits to the Institution become apparent." Another wrote: "This begins my tenth year at Tech; within my first year it was obvious that such a reorganization that you now instituted was necessary for Tech to become the school it really has the potential to become. I was beginning to despair, frankly; now I can see the light of great promise, provided a firm attitude toward progress is maintained."

Perhaps the best overall assessment of the faculty meeting, representing even the views of some faculty members who opposed Mason's removal, was: "You took a considered position, stated it decisively, handled a difficult crisis (a large group, some 'loaded for bear') charged with emotion; and you did this in a dignified and magnificent manner. Only a very strong and 'big' person dares to do this."[92]

The 1965 reorganization constituted a major step away from the older Georgia Tech, which had focused almost exclusively on undergraduate engineering education with overtones of the shop culture, and toward the Georgia Tech of the 1980s, with more emphasis on theory in undergraduate education, on graduate education, and on research. Yet the move was and remains incomplete. Mason was removed from his position as dean of engineering and returned to teaching, but the old guard remained powerful at Tech. Harrison was unable to put his entire team into place in 1965, and prior to his departure as president of Georgia Tech in 1969 he would be unable to secure and retain a fully effective administrative team, as we shall see in the concluding section of this chapter.

Campus Expansion

The most enduring legacy of the Harrison era may well have been the tremendous increase in the size of the campus and in the number and value of campus buildings. During Harrison's eleven-year presidency, both the size of the campus and the value of campus buildings more than doubled.[93] By the close of the Harrison presidency, the space available for teaching and research activities was beginning to approximate the needs of the institution for the first time in its history. This achievement was possible due to a combination of carefully conceived campus planning and an auspicious external environment in which support for urban renewal and expansion of the campus was possible from federal, state, and local sources.

Much of the story of Georgia Tech, like that of many other institutions of higher education in America, could well be written as a never-ending struggle for space and for facilities sufficient to house its programs and make possible their expansion. When Van Leer arrived on campus, Georgia Tech comprised only sixty-three acres, with severely inadequate buildings and facilities. The end of Brittain's presidency had seen the first steps in 1944 toward development of a comprehensive campus plan for expansion, and this preliminary planning was followed up under Van Leer's presidency in a series of master plans, M-6 through M-11, until 1952. By the time Van Leer died in January 1956, Tech had acquired or was in the process of acquiring fifty-one additional acres, and new dormitories, a library, an architecture building, and an athletic facility were completed or under construction. Yet despite efforts to create a comprehensive plan and secure necessary buildings, shortages of funds resulted only in piecemeal additions to campus. Severe space strains remained when President Harrison arrived in August 1957, and he soon became very much aware of the need for additional space and for new buildings. Eventually Harrison's presidency would see the campus expand by an additional 128 acres.[94]

Harrison, like Van Leer before him, became president of Tech at an auspicious time for campus expansion. Federal, state, and local support for urban renewal was increasingly available during the 1950s and 1960s. Although federal requirements were enacted in 1954 to set comprehensive standards of eligibility for federal urban renewal aid, widely differing local objectives were allowed to coexist under the redevelopment umbrella. Concurrently with the expansion of urban renewal programs, the rapid economic growth of the fifties and sixties, the desire to surpass the Russians following their launching of Sputnik I in 1957, and the increasing arrival on college campuses of the "baby boom" generation by the early 1960s, led both public and private sources to see support for education, including building programs, as a high priority. Locally, Tech benefited from having many prominent alumni in Atlanta—such as Mayor Ivan Allen, Jr.—who enthusiastically supported the expansion and strengthening of their alma mater. The most important remaining task was for Tech itself to determine its needs and to make application for assistance in meeting them.[95]

In his letter of December 8, 1960, proposing an institutional self-study, President Harrison had indicated that an important motive for the study was the desire to lay the groundwork for "active and vigorous planning for the growth of our physical plant."[96] The first major step toward exploring options for expansion was a study by the Atlanta firm of Keck Engineering Associates entitled *Formula for Growth*, completed in 1962. The primary purpose of the study was to establish Georgia Tech's eligibility for a federally assisted urban renewal project and to suggest some of the initial steps that Tech could take to acquire land in surrounding areas of predominantly substandard structures. The study argued that a unified urban renewal approach was preferable to Tech's earlier expansion by piecemeal and uncoordinated acquisition of land. Although the Keck report did not provide a comprehensive analysis of what should be done, it did suggest setting fifty-eight acres as the first goal for acquisition and noted that part of Hemphill Avenue to the west of campus would have to be closed if Tech were to be able to expand effectively in that, the most promising, direction.[97]

Building on the groundwork laid by the Keck report, but presenting a far more detailed analysis with specific proposals, was the Perkins and Will *Comprehensive Campus Development Plan*, completed in March 1965, with a shortened version, entitled *A Bold Future*, highlighting its key findings.[98] The comprehensive report noted: "Over the past several years, the campus has crept outward, parcel by parcel; a slow and very costly process." Now is the time for "a major breakout. Land and buildings must be added at an unprecedented rate. Such rapid expansion, however, must not be allowed to be explosive; it must be controlled, scheduled, given direction by as comprehensive, wise, and farsighted a planning process as can possibly be conceived."[99] The report presented a twenty-year plan, at the end of which it envisioned a student population of 12,500 and a campus of nearly four hundred acres, including all land north and westward to Tenth Street, Northside Drive, and almost to Marietta Street. Different Institute functions would be located in different zones. Almost all instructional buildings would be contained within a roughly circular district one-half mile in diameter. The Engineering Experiment Station would be moved further out from main campus and consolidated in an area where it could expand. A new student housing zone would be located in the northwest sector of the ultimate campus. Large open spaces would allow for recreational activities and possible future expansion. Hemphill Avenue, a busy traffic artery that divided this proposed campus expansion in two, would be closed off and traffic rerouted along a new "Tech Parkway."[100]

The basic provisions of the 1965 campus plan have in large measure been achieved twenty years later. Inevitably, of course, certain features of the plan eventually were modified or eliminated altogether due to changing circumstances. New political and economic conditions by the early 1970s, for example, delayed the school from expanding to the full four hundred acres or constructing all the desired buildings on the land that was acquired. The proposed relocation of Grant Field and the administration building failed to be carried out due to considerations of tradition and finance. Inertia also prevented removal of some older buildings that had been slated for demolition. And some of the more idealistic proposals to unify the campus and make it more appealing still remain only partially realized.[101] Yet the degree to which the basic 1965 plan has been followed is impressive. Much of this achievement must be credited to the campus planner, Clyde D. Robbins, and to the campus architect, David O. Savini, both of whom worked closely with Perkins and Will representatives in developing the original plan and have continued since then to cooperate with each other in carrying it out to the fullest extent possible.

Robbins's role as the first and only official Tech campus planner to date has been particularly noteworthy. Robbins came to Tech in 1964, working half-time as an assistant professor in architecture and half-time as campus planner to aid the Perkins and Will team in developing their master plan for the campus. Robbins brought to Tech a diverse background that included undergraduate degrees in forestry and landscape architecture; graduate degrees in city planning, real estate, and economics; employment as a planner with the United States Forest Service and National Parks Service; and work with private firms on downtown renovation, mall studies, and campus hospitals in Pennsylvania, Ohio, and West Virginia.[102]

The major efforts through which Tech, under Robbins's direction, sought to aquire land through the federal urban renewal program were the R-85 and R-111 plans. The objective of the R-85 plan was total clearance for two goals: to acquire land for the expansion of Tech and to create a corridor of redevelopment in the private sector between the campus and Marietta Street. The Atlanta Housing Authority was the agency that formally acquired the land, cleared the neighborhood, assembled the parcels of land, and sold them to Tech or retained them in the private sector. Tech administrators, including Controller Jamie Anthony, Campus Planner Clyde Robbins, and others, personally dealt with hundreds of individuals who owned and often lived on the approximately 1,100 parcels of land, soothing feelings and helping with individual relocation. In part because of skillful handling of such grass roots relations with individuals, no organized opposition to the project developed either in the Tech area or in Atlanta during the 1960s. By the late 1960s when the R-111 plan, essentially an extension of the highly successful R-85, was proposed, however, federal and municipal priorities were changing from total clearance to renovation. The result was that the only part of the proposed R-111 plan which was approved and funded was the completion of the Tech Parkway to replace part of Hemphill Avenue that was closed in 1972. As in the case of other urban renewal projects associated with universities, the net impact of urban renewal for Tech was to allow the Institute to expand rapidly and efficiently at far lower cost than if the parcels had been acquired piecemeal.[103]

On the land that Tech acquired for expansion during the sixties, an impressive array of buildings began to rise that significantly reshaped the appearance of the campus. During the years between 1960 and 1969, architectural plans for all or part of nineteen buildings or complexes were developed.[104] The major buildings started or completed during this period may be briefly indicated. In the fall of 1961, five new dormitories housing approximately 750 students were opened. Also that fall, Southern Technical Institute relocated from the Naval Air Station at Chamblee and began operations at its entirely new campus in Marietta, capable of accommodating approximately 1,600 new students in its laboratories and classrooms. Winter 1962 saw occupation on the Georgia Tech campus of a new Electrical Engineering Building, capable of serving the program for many years.

The 1963–64 school year saw a surge in building activity, funding, and planning. The $4.5 million Frank H. Neeley Nuclear Research Center was completed, and plans were approved for new buildings for physics and for chemistry, as well as for two additional buildings for the Engineering Experiment Station. A one million dollar grant from the National Aeronautics and Space Administration was received to help with the construction of the first of what would eventually become three Space Science and Technology Center buildings. In the fall of 1964, the new Chemical Engineering–Ceramic Engineering Building was occupied. During the 1964–65 school year, plans began to be developed and funded for a six-story Graduate Library addition to the Price Gilbert Memorial Library, which was completed in 1968. During the 1966–67 school year, plans for double-decking the west stands of Grant Field, adding 7,509 seats, were also set in motion. In the course of the 1966–67 academic year, building projects under construction totaled almost $15 million. If projects in the design stage were included, the total rose to almost $33 million.[105]

The long-awaited Student Center, which was first approved in 1967 and was completed in 1970, was in many ways a fitting climax to the building programs of the Harrison era. Although the idea of a student center had originally been proposed by the academic honorary society Omicron Delta Kappa in 1939, the construction of the Student Center Building had languished both for lack of funds and because of the opposition of powerful groups such as the YMCA, which felt that such a center would undercut their influence on campus. Financing for the $2,744,122 Student Center Building ultimately came from the widest source of funds in Tech history.[106] The spacious facilities, including an auditorium, a large hall, large and small meeting rooms, lounges, bowling lanes, an art gallery and music listening area, and a cafeteria, among other things, seemed to many to have been well worth the wait. In conjunction with the new men's, women's, and graduate dormitories, completed during the early seventies, the Student Center greatly helped improve student life at Georgia Tech. The many buildings completed or conceived during the Harrison era represented a most impressive legacy for the future of the Institute.

Student Life

Student life at Georgia Tech showed much continuity during the late 1950s and early 1960s, but profound forces leading to change also were at work, both at Tech and nationally. The immediate aftermath of World War II had seen the influx of veterans returning to school under the GI Bill. Their presence not only had enlarged the student body but had contributed a group of highly motivated, nononsense individuals who wanted to complete their schooling and get on with their lives. By the mid-1950s as the relative numbers of veterans declined, students became more insular in their interests and backgrounds, described by some as a "silent generation," narrowly focused on student life and concerns, often without much awareness of the outer world. This was the heyday of fraternities as the focus of social life. Togetherness, parties, and the round of social events often was the primary concern of students rather than the academic program.

By the early 1960s, a shift was underway as students born during the era of the Great Depression increasingly gave way to students born during the postwar baby boom. Postwar affluence and growing numbers of college age students combined to contribute to overcrowding and the tightening of academic standards. Nationally, student awareness of the outside world was stimulated first by involvement with the civil rights movement and then by the Vietnam War and its corollary, the draft. In the meantime, beginning as early as the Berkeley demonstrations of 1964, students across the country began to protest against what they perceived as the inadequacy and impersonality of academic programs. Protests of all kinds became more frequent and attracted media attention. Paralleling the academic and political frustrations, but not necessarily directly connected with them, was the rise of cynicism, the drug culture, and the "turn on, tune in, drop out" mentality. College faculty members, deans, and presidents faced many difficulties in dealing with the new unrest.[107]

At Georgia Tech, student life reflected some of the national currents of change, yet like other schools in the South and like technical schools nationally, Tech would be less influenced by the rise of protest movements and by the counter culture that developed by the late 1960s. During the midfifties, Tech, like most schools, was dominated by fraternities. The typical student was pragmatic, hardworking, and hardplaying. The rising academic standards of the late fifties had a profound impact, contributing initially to student restiveness and frustration at what was perceived as the increasing impersonality of the school. Moves toward greater freedom and responsibility were reflected in the growing role of Student Government, the expanding influence of the YMCA, reduction of in loco parentis restrictions, and the ending of compulsory ROTC. The absence of significant public protest at Georgia Tech in the late 1960s can be attributed to the more conservative southern tradition, the inertia of a student body primarily committed to career goals, and the relatively responsive administration. Student concerns about the outside world were reflected primarily in one-to-one efforts at community service. Tech students tried always to "live within the system," with allowance for occasional rowdy behavior to let off steam.

Two institutions dominated student life at Georgia Tech during the 1950s and early 1960s. The first was the fraternities. They remained the most important single force throughout the period, despite some lessening of their influence during the late sixties as more dormitories were constructed and as the Student Center neared completion. In the absence of a Student Center Building or regular campuswide program of activities for all students during the period, fraternities served as the focal point for extracurricular life. For example, at Tech there were only a few women and they were typically dismissed as dating possibilities, so fraternities organized parties and brought in women from Agnes Scott, Emory, and local nursing schools. Fraternities held unquestioned control over Student Government, the *Technique,* the Ramblin' Reck Club and nearly all aspects of Tech "traditions" and extracurricular life. Given the relatively tight restrictions in the dorms, fraternities also offered greater freedom in male-female relations, use of alcohol, and avoidance of in loco parentis restrictions. There were fraternities that catered to amost every type of student, from the most sociable to the most studious. Coordination of fraternity activities and joint action on common problems was achieved through an Interfraternity Council.[108]

The second important institution for students at Georgia Tech throughout the 1950s and much of the 1960s was the YMCA under its dynamic director Robert Charlton ("Charlie") Commander. The Y was described by some as "a fraternity for non-fraternity members," but it actually served a broad range of functions for fraternity and nonfraternity members alike. In the absence of a student union building until 1970, the three-story Y building on North Avenue at the edge of campus served as an unofficial student center, housing offices for the *Technique,* Student Government, game and meeting rooms, and even dormitories on the third floor. The Y had started the off-campus "freshman camp" to orient new students, beginning in the early 1950s, and by the late 1950s and early 1960s a substantial minority of all incoming freshmen participated. Upper-class advisers, including fraternity men, invited faculty members, and administrators participated in freshman camp and other Y-sponsored activities, gaining status and power thereby. Equally if not more influential was the World Student Fund, started in the late 1940s by the Y to encourage international student exchange. It served as one of the most prestigious organizations on campus, with membership by invitation only—not unlike a super fraternity.[109]

Commander continued actively expanding the Y operations throughout the late 1950s and early 1960s until cancer and his death in 1967 intervened. One of the most highly praised new Y activities was the student-faculty-industry conferences held at Callaway Gardens beginning in 1963. The conferences brought together specially selected faculty members, student leaders, and prominent businessmen, helping to groom certain elite students for positions of leadership at Tech and following graduation.[110] Meanwhile, major campus religious faiths—Baptist, Methodist, Presbyterian, Episcopal, Catholic, and Jewish, among others—formed or strengthened their student organizations and gradually began to acquire attractive facilities of their own.[111] Nevertheless, the YMCA remained the dominant campuswide organization outside the fraternities. It even received a mandatory donation of student fees, an increasing anachronism in a public institution.[112]

Despite the basic stability of Georgia Tech student culture and institutions during this period, strong forces for change were also at work. The rising academic standards and pressures at Tech, as at other American colleges and universities, were associated with social tensions, as well as with increased student involvement in both the school and in the world. During the late 1950s and 1960s, pressures on students were reflected in considerable rebelliousness and rowdy behavior. In response to unfortunate incidents, the administration briefly prohibited off-campus fraternity house parties in 1958, and in 1960 it issued an absolute and unenforceable rule against the drinking of intoxicating beverages at any student functions.[113] Disorder appears to have peaked in 1960, perhaps in part because of the tighter restrictions. In late February 1960, some five hundred students, unhappy that President Harrison had refused to cancel classes due to the icy weather, gathered in front of his house, threw snowballs and assorted projectiles at it and upon returning to campus broke a few windows on the ground floor of the women's house.[114] In October 1960, approximately three hundred Tech students, most of them freshmen, engaged in a traditional shirttail parade, snaking their way into downtown Atlanta after a football game, and eventually were dispersed by police.[115] That same fall, the Varsity drive-in ended the practice of cashing student checks after annual losses of nearly $3,000.[116]

The rebelliousness and "mutual barriers" between students and the administration were of concern to both sides. As early as October 1958, President Harrison held the first all-student meeting, in which 1,200 students participated, to try to bring students, faculty members, and administrators together. Those meetings continued throughout the early 1960s until declining student interest led to their quiet elimination.[117] In the fall of 1960, the dean of students office was reorganized, following the departure of Associate Dean of Students John J. Pershing, and a Student Advisory Board was also approved by the Student Council to meet with President Harrison to discuss problems concerning student affairs.[118] That advisory board continued to meet periodically throughout the sixties. In the fall of 1962, the first Annual Leadership Conference, sponsored by the YMCA, was held at Callaway Gardens and was described in an editorial in the *Technique* as "the first great breakthrough in student-faculty relations."[119]

The early 1960s also saw changes in various Tech traditions. In the summer of 1960, the administration announced that it would no longer tolerate enforcement of freshman customs such as the wearing of "rat caps" by means of the "T-cut."[120] Without effective means of enforcing freshman practices, they gradually became increasingly honored in the breach, and by 1965 the Ramblin' Reck Club acknowledged the change by shortening the period during which rat caps were to be worn and admitting the practice was "traditional" but no longer "compulsory."[121] While many bemoaned the changes, others celebrated the greater freedom. A satirical article in the *Technique*, for example, bore the title, "Ramblin' Reck Spirit Will Die If We Can't Castrate Frosh."[122] A column by student Ed Patterson in the *Technique* saw the decline of such traditions as reflecting a more mature and less insular student environment and called for the development of new and more appropriate traditions for the present, including a more effective orientation program for incoming students.[123]

The drive toward greater student independence and self-expression involved much more than the breaking down of old traditions. Most important, it also contributed to a greater student sense of responsibility and involvement. Student Government, which had previously been little more than a debating society for elite fraternity men, acquired new powers, developed several new and enlarged constitutions, and broadened its electoral and leadership base, stimulating a voting turnout of as much as three-quarters of the eligible students in some races. The 1956–57 school year saw the first Student Activities Night, the first Burdell Ball, and the first Tech Greek Week in the postwar years.[124] The *Technique*, though far from typifying student opinion on many issues, nevertheless broadened its coverage beyond purely campus topics. Simultaneously it also became more aggressive in pursuing student concerns. Whereas in 1956 a relatively bland student letter critical of the quality of dining room food had led the unfortunate student to be given a choice of retracting the statement or facing possible legal action,[125] by the mid-1960s constructive criticism and comment was frequent in the paper. Occasionally the paper did push beyond the bounds of good taste, as in the 1964 April Fool's issue of the *Technique*, whose editor was summarily fired when the paper lampooned both religion and sex, but in general student involvement was positive and well accommodated by the administration.[126]

The retirement of the popular dean of students, George C. Griffin, in 1964 marked the end of an era for students at Tech. Almost all of Griffin's adult life had been associated with Tech. He had originally entered the school as a member of the last of the subfreshman classes in 1914 and, following service as a naval officer during World War I, earned his degree in civil engineering in 1922. During his student years he was a scrub football player, a cross country and track man, and a member of most of the major campus organizations for which he was eligible. He returned to campus in 1930 as an instructor in mathematics, and he simultaneously acted as assistant dean of students, a position he held for a decade until he went into active duty again with the navy. At various times at Tech, Griffin served as personnel officer of the school, alumni club organizer, alumni placement director, student placement director, and in various other positions. One of his more notable achievements was starting Tech's central placement office, the second of its type in the country. His most important role at Tech, however, was as dean of students, a position he held for eighteen years. During that time, he became beloved of generations of students, helping to get them out of trouble, making speeches, and starting innumerable campus organizations and plans to aid students. As absentminded as any professor (sometimes by design), Griffin started the "sackbrain club" for those who were so forgetful that they ought to "carry their brains around in a sack lest they forget them," and he regaled students with tales of days gone by. Although Griffin remained a fixture on campus for years following his retirement, the Office of the Dean of Students would never be quite the same thereafter.[127]

The political concerns of Georgia Tech students were primarily conservative and pragmatic. Unlike many other schools that experienced disruptive political demonstrations during the late 1960s, Georgia Tech remained almost without interest in external politics. A poorly attended debate sponsored by the Young Americans for Freedom in 1965 and modest on-campus attendance at "Affirmation Vietnam" meetings in 1966 favoring United States Vietnamese policy reflected the predominant student sentiment, if political interests were voiced at all.[128] Counterfeelings were expressed about the war in the more liberal *Technique*, especially after United States draft policy changed so that students became increasingly aware of the possibility of serving in Vietnam. Most Tech students, nevertheless, remained strongly supportive of United States policy. The ending of compulsory ROTC in March 1965, for example, did not reflect any lack of support for the armed forces but rather pragmatic internal considerations and a change in federal policy. The *Technique* commented that the program did not appear to measure up to the rigorous standards of other programs and argued that the credit hours needed to be devoted to other more academic subjects.[129]

The social idealism of Georgia Tech students focused primarily on student efforts to help better the local community and on attempts to get the Institute to become more involved in dealing with immediate community problems. During the 1968–69 school year, for example, students worked in the Techwood Tutorial Project, participated in the Urban Corps and in the Model Cities Program, and designed and built a creative playground in the Vine City area of Atlanta.[130] Efforts to encourage greater Institute involvement with local social problems were reflected in a seven-point "Open Letter" of April 25, 1968, to the administration, which was signed by 570 students and faculty members, including approximately 7 percent of the student body. Among other things, the letter requested that the school encourage more active faculty and student involvement with improving conditions in slum areas, that an urban studies program be instituted in conjunction with other Atlanta schools, that employee wage scales at Tech be made more equitable, and that course credit be given for certain projects in ghetto areas which related academic studies to actual problems in the outside world. The Georgia Tech administration responded graciously to the letter, proceeded to make some of the proposed changes, and began to consider the others, thus defusing the likelihood of conflict.[131]

Women at Tech

As with student life generally at Georgia Tech, the experiences of women students showed basic patterns of continuity, along with subtle but nevertheless far-reaching changes, especially during the sixties. The number of female students, like the number of black students, remained minuscule during the period, with little direct effect on patterns of student life and behavior. Gradual progress was made in expanding the programs in which women could major, the organizations in which they could participate, and the attitudes that male students and faculty members held toward them. As late as 1968, however, there were just over one hundred undergraduate women at Tech—approximately one out of every one hundred students. Throughout the sixties, Georgia Tech had a higher number of women studying engineering than in any other school in the country, yet the Institute remained basically a male preserve. Integrating women into Georgia Tech was in many ways even more difficult than racial integration, even though women had come to Tech nine years before blacks. Just as a few outstanding black students such as John Gill broke through the racial barriers, so, too, a few outstanding women such as Paula Stevenson began to break down the stereotypes of female students at Georgia Tech. Only during the early 1970s, however, did substantial numbers of both women and blacks begin to come to the Institute and to play a more active role in the life of the school.[132]

The first two women entered Georgia Tech in 1952, but many factors mitigated against others coming to the school in large numbers during the 1950s and 1960s. One major obstacle was limited housing. Throughout the period, the only on-campus housing for women was a converted house on Fifth Street that had a maximum capacity of eleven girls. In 1958 alone, the *Technique* announced that seven women had been rejected because of the lack of housing facilities.[133] Not until 1969 would additional facilities be completed to house sixty women in a new dorm complex. On campus there were similar problems of inadequate facilities for women. Initially, all women's restrooms on campus had to be opened with a secretary's key, so whenever there was a need to use a washroom a secretary first had to be found. Only gradually were such inconveniences overcome.

Attitudes of male Tech students and instructors were trying at times. As one male graduate of the midsixties reflected: "A lot of people came to Tech simply to be in an all-male domain and they felt terribly threatened by the presence of women."[134] Reported campus humor during the early fifties included mention of "ruffled T-Squares," "Nell of an Engineer," and "I'm a Ramblin' Wreck from Georgia Tech and I keep my lipstick near."[135] Repeatedly males asserted that women came to Tech to find husbands rather than to become engineers, but as one of the first female graduates noted, there certainly were much easier ways to find a husband![136] In January 1959 it was reported that women's scholastic averages at Tech had risen steadily and now surpassed those of the men, but a year later when women's averages dropped back below those of the men there was gloating comment in the *Technique*.[137]

Despite such tensions, changes gradually took place during the fifties and sixties, both in the participation of women in campus organizations and in academic life. In the spring of 1956 a student chapter of the Society of Women Engineers, a national engineering society, was begun on the Tech campus. A year later Tech's first women's freshman camp, sponsored by the Georgia Tech YMCA, was held, and the YMCA women's organization, Gamma Psi, was organized. Also in that year, Paula Stevenson became the first woman to be elected to the Ramblin' Reck Club. Other campus organizations gradually were opened to women throughout the fifties and sixties. Academic life similarly saw changes. Women initially had only been allowed to major in engineering or in architecture, but by 1965 all programs except industrial management had been opened to women, and that school followed suit in 1968 as well.[138]

By 1968 much had been acomplished and the groundwork had been laid for the later expansion in the numbers of women at Tech, but more still remained to be done. In that year it was reported that women who applied to Tech and were accepted without having an interview routinely were sent a letter from the admissions office that warned them of the difficulties they would face. The letter served to discourage all but the most hardy. It read in part: "Your application for admission has been received, but before taking action on your application I wanted to let you know some special factors about life as a coed at Tech which may or may not affect your desire for attendance here. We have a student body of about 7,300, only 100 of whom are girls. This may at first seem attractive to you, but many of the girls who have attended Tech have found it to be quite disconcerting. Very few concessions are made for coed students here at Tech."[139]

Athletics

Georgia Tech's excellence in sports, especially intercollegiate football, was a key factor in making the school known throughout the country during the first half of the twentieth century. Perhaps the highest point in Georgia Tech's sports reputation had come during the 1950s when, under Coach Bobby Dodd's football leadership, Tech won six bowl games in a row with his 1951 through 1956 teams. Dodd would remain head football coach until 1967 and would continue to field many outstanding teams. Yet even his leadership was unable to compensate entirely for national changes in intercollegiate football and the tightening of academic requirements at Tech, which increasingly hindered recruiting. Outwardly, Tech's reputation and student life continued to revolve to a remarkable degree around sports, both intercollegiate and intramural. The full force of the changes in the athletic program at Tech, however, only became visible in the 1970s and 1980s.

By the late 1950s, both national and local trends were leading toward greater professionalism in college football. The emphasis was less on simply playing a game and having fun, and more on winning and making money. The growing pressure to win at any cost led many schools to cut corners and engage in unethical practices of various sorts. At Tech, Dodd resisted such tendencies. During the early fifties he had the best of both worlds: he played primarily for fun, treated his players well, *and* won an exceptional series of victories. Dodd's style had a certain noblesse oblige to it, stressing sportsmanship even if one lost.[140] Dodd got the very best out of his players, not by driving them till they dropped or by demeaning them, but by inspiring their loyalty and dedication. He attracted outstanding athletes who wanted to play on a fine team and be treated fairly as well.[141]

In addition to the challenges posed by national changes in collegiate football, Georgia Tech's internal changes created increasing problems for the athletic program. The Institute's rising academic standards were felt by all students, but especially by athletes. It became more and more difficult to attract and retain the best players. Dodd recalls how coaches from other schools sometimes tried to discourage students from going to Tech by showing them a calculus textbook and asking them if they would be capable of handling such work.[142] Georgia Tech also stood in a unique position in the country in combining a purely engineering and technical curriculum with big-time athletics. All programs had a heavy mathematical component, and there were no general humanities or social science degrees to broaden possible opportunities for study. Only Industrial Management gained a reputation for offering a somewhat easier degree, and even that could prove quite challenging. In an interview in 1958, Dodd frankly admitted the problems that higher standards posed, saying: "Yes, it will hurt us very much if the high schools do not give the right preparation for entrance. We will probably have to go more out of state to get players who meet requirements for school here."[143]

Aggressive efforts were made to deal with these challenges. Only students deemed capable of handling the Tech program were accepted. Players were able to preregister for courses before the majority of students. A regular tutoring program was instituted every week night for students with a 2.0 average or lower, players were not allowed to cut classes, and their academic progress was closely monitored. If an athlete was unable to graduate in the normal four years because of the additional pressure of playing football, he was brought back for a fifth year and every effort was made to see that he graduated.[144] Difficulties in recruitment and retention remained, however. Discrete inquiries were made to see if other forms of "academic relief" might be possible by instituting a program in industrial management that would not be so heavily dependent on mathematics as the existing ones, but this possibility was not formally pursued at the time because it was clear that the faculty would not support any curricular changes for such purposes.[145]

The problems of playing teams or individuals that were determined to win at any cost were most painfully illustrated during a game in November 1961 when Darwin Holt, a senior Alabama linebacker, struck Georgia Tech player Chick Graning in the face with his left elbow. The injury was worse than that suffered by any Southeastern Conference player in many years. The full diagnosis, as indicated by the Tech team physician, was: "fracture of facial bones, five missing upper teeth and remaining front teeth broken, fracture of nasal bone, fracture of right maxilary sinus and sinus filled with blood, fracture of bone beneath right eye, cerebral concussion, possible fracture of base of skull."[146] Despite the violation of sportsmanship, clearly recorded on film, Coach Bear Bryant of Alabama refused to remove Holt from the squad or even issue a public apology. Great anger was generated by the incident. In January 1962, Coach Dodd announced that as of the expiration of the contract in 1964, Tech would no longer play Alabama.[147] Officially, any connection with the Holt case was disclaimed, but Tech did not play Alabama again until shortly before Bear Bryant's death, by which time memories of the incident had abated somewhat.

The impact of national changes in college football and of the internal tightening of standards at Georgia Tech can be seen in Tech's decision to withdraw from the Southeastern Conference in 1964.

The primary stated reason for the withdrawal was the conference's rule that no school could have more than 140 athletes on football and basketball scholarships at one time. If 20 scholarships were allotted to basketball, this left 120 for football, or approximately 30 per class. If a school accepted substantially more than 30 each year, then the excess players who did not live up to initial expectations would, under the 140 rule, have to be "run off" by various devious means. Tech's policy, however, was to continue scholarship support for all its football players throughout their time at Tech and to encourage them to graduate, even if the individuals were unable to continue playing on the team or contributing to its success. Adhering to such a policy under the 140 rule placed Tech at a substantial competitive disadvantage with less ethical programs. When Tech was unable to secure a change in the 140 rule in 1964, it withdrew from the Southeastern Conference. This action, though not popular with many alumni, appeared almost inevitable under the circumstances if Tech were to be able to continue to live up to its principles in football.[148] The action also would have proved advantageous financially if Tech had been able to continue to maintain a winning tradition and, as an independent, retain exclusive control over television and bowl revenues.

The 1966 football season was a highly successful one for Dodd, with a 9–1–0 record that took Tech to the Orange Bowl. Nevertheless, the handwriting clearly was on the wall for Tech's football program. Dodd had brought the team back to a respectable showing after a series of less successful years in the late fifties and early sixties, yet by 1965 he observed: "Over the past few years we simply have not been able to recruit good linemen who are also good students. We all know how difficult it is to be admitted to Tech, much less stay in school."[149] Following the 1966 football year, which had surpassed all expectations, an editorial in the *Technique* entitled "Goodbye, Grey Fox?" commented on the importance of a great sportsman stepping down gracefully while he still had the respect and poise of a champion.[150] On February 6, 1967, Dodd issued an announcement that he was resigning as head football coach due to personal health problems.[151] He did, however, remain as athletic director at Tech, a post he continued to hold until 1977. Dodd's retirement after twenty-two years as head football coach at Tech, with an enviable 165–64–8 record, marked the end of a great era in Tech football. Dodd's successor, Leon H. "Bud" Carson, faced the combined challenges of succeeding a legend and trying to revive Tech's winning ways.

Although football dominated the athletic program at Tech during the fifties and sixties, financially and in almost every other way, Tech also achieved considerable success in many other areas of sports activity. Following the opening of the Alexander Memorial Coliseum in 1956, basketball coach Whack Hyder was able to revitalize Tech's basketball program by the early 1960s. Swimming coach Freddie Lanoue became nationally known during the mid-1950s for his innovative "drown-proofing" methods, which were adopted as a required course for all students attending Tech. Throughout the period before 1964, Tech fielded teams in all Southeastern Conference sports: football, basketball, baseball, tennis, track, golf, cross country, and swimming.[152] In addition to intercollegiate competition, Tech also sustained a strong program of intramural athletics. Despite the lack of space or funding, more than 50 percent of all Tech students usually participated each year in the intramural program.[153] Overall, the late fifties and early sixties saw a strong athletic program at Tech, yet one which, because of higher academic standards, was unable in some sports to achieve the full competitive success of earlier years.

Undergraduate Curriculum Revision

Revision of the undergraduate curriculum at Georgia Tech during the 1950s and most of the 1960s proceeded at a slow pace. Efforts to reform and revitalize engineering education had been apparent well before Harrison assumed the presidency of Georgia Tech in 1957, of course. The aftermath of World War II had seen increased emphasis on broadening engineering education and the Grinter report in 1955 had provided a national rationale for such change. Georgia Tech's September 1954 report on its aims and objectives had put forward as its goals improvement in the quality of students admitted; upgrading of course quality; a more unified academic program, including a core curriculum for the first year; a more well-rounded education, including additional attention to the humanities and social sciences; improved teaching standards and more attention to superior students; greater flexibility in programs, including introduction of an undesignated bachelor's in engineering; reduction of excessive faculty teaching loads to allow more time for faculty self-development and research; and improvement of research and graduate education.[154] By the end of Harrison's first year at Tech, his presidential report echoed similar concerns, calling for a reorganized and better-coordinated program that would place more emphasis on understanding basic principles and would reduce purely descriptive material. Enunciating such goals was one thing; putting them into practice was another. Tremendous inertia would prevail at Georgia Tech, especially within the dominant engineering schools, until the 1965 administrative reorganization and beyond.

Initial steps to improve the quality of the student body and the undergraduate curriculum at Tech came primarily through Institute-wide decisions. As noted earlier in this chapter, in 1957 Tech went beyond the new Georgia requirement that SAT scores be submitted by all applicants to state colleges and universities, announcing that in addition Georgia Tech from 1959 through 1963 would gradually raise the standards of high school course preparation that the Institute required for admission. Internally, standards were strengthened by the decision, passed by the Faculty Senate in November 1957, to replace the existing final exams during regular class periods with a week of three-hour finals that allowed learning to be tested more fully. In December 1959, in an effort to allow more time for strictly academic courses, the Faculty Senate approved a policy that students entering in the summer of 1960 and after could only count nine hours of advanced ROTC credit toward graduation.[155] Despite numerous minor changes such as these, the dominant pedagogical orientation at Tech during the late fifties and early sixties was extremely traditional and rigid. Many faculty members seemed to believe that simply by forcing students through a series of demanding academic hurdles, a sort of academic variant on boot camp, graduates would be produced who could deal with the "real world." In curricular terms, Georgia Tech throughout the sixties continued to be somewhat insular, perhaps most accurately described by its student nickname, "The North Avenue Trade School."

A useful benchmark for understanding how far Georgia Tech had come in undergraduate curriculum revision and the many issues that still remained to be addressed is provided by the report on Tech's educational program which was included in the 1963 self-study. Although the 1963 report was in general agreement with the 1954 study on educational aims and objectives at Tech, the 1963 report only noted two specific recommendations of the earlier study that had been implemented—the raising of entrance requirements to Tech and the institution of final examinations. The 1963 report presented eleven specific recommendations, many of which went significantly beyond those of 1954. Among the new recommendations was that women be admitted to all curricula on the same basis as men and that the cooperative program be extended beyond the seven schools in the Engineering College then involved. To increase curricular flexibility, required course hours for a degree should be reduced, at least eighteen hours of unrestricted electives should be allowed, and an undesignated bachelor's degree should be instituted. Simultaneously, steps should be taken to strengthen student academic quality, improve teaching, and provide special programs for particularly able students. The report concluded by suggesting that a permanent committee distinct from the present Curriculum Committee of the Academic Senate be established to conduct a continuing and more effective study of curricular problems. Although many of the recommendations of the 1963 report were eventually implemented at Tech, many of them—especially those dealing with curricular flexibility—continued to be hotly debated throughout the 1960s.[156]

The introduction of revised curricula in Physics and in Chemistry at Tech during the 1965–66 school year helped break the ice for much subsequent curricular revision in other schools and departments in the institution. The case of Physics is particularly instructive. Since World War II, Physics at Tech had developed a strong undergraduate program, as well as starting a graduate program of increasing strength. The weaknesses and need for change that remained in Physics at Tech were highlighted for School Director Vernon Crawford, however, when he asked three students at three different levels of the program what they had just been studying. They all replied, "the particle in a box," a basic problem in quantum mechanics. Crawford and others realized that the program needed to be streamlined to reduce inefficiency and overlap. A curriculum review committee under David Wyly's leadership eventually proposed scrapping the existing program and consolidating the required course hours from 221 to 198. Although the proposal initially met stiff resistance from some faculty members, ultimately the revision was accepted and became highly praised by faculty members for both tightening and strengthening their program. Throughout much of the sixties, while some other programs still required as many as 232 credit hours to graduate and offered little freedom for choice, the Physics program attracted many of the brightest students who wanted a rigorous but flexible and more broadly based education. A similar, though less drastic reduction in required course hours in Chemistry from 219 to 209 also was associated with strengthening its already strong program.[157]

Despite discussion of possible revision of undergraduate curricula at Tech and some efforts at such reorganization during the 1950s and early 1960s, relatively few substantive changes were instituted until the late 1960s. The dominant engineering schools were especially slow to attempt significant revision of their curricula at the undergraduate level. Jesse Mason's comment in the 1963-64 annual report typified the situation of the early sixties. He wrote: "Because of the pressure of other duties, it has not been possible to make much progress in overall curriculum revision."[158] Not until the coming of Arthur G. Hansen as dean of engineering in 1966 would major steps be undertaken to revise the engineering programs and institute a "core curriculum."

Research and Graduate Programs

Throughout the 1950s and 1960s, Georgia Tech's formal statements of institute goals stressed three main areas: undergraduate education, research, and graduate education. Undergraduate education clearly remained the dominant focus of concern, but as the sixties progressed, profound changes gradually began to take place in the closely related areas of research and graduate education. These changes were not simply quantitative improvements in the dollar volume of research or in the number of graduate programs and students, important as these were, but also included substantial structural and qualitative modifications. At the same time that the dollar value of all research during Harrison's presidency was approximately doubling every five years, for example, a struggle over control of research projects was developing, culminating in 1964 in a major policy change in which research efforts in the Engineering Experiment Station and in the academic departments were formally separated. Graduate education, so intimately associated with research, also experienced significant but less drastic changes as new programs were started, the number of graduate students approximately quadrupled, and substantially more faculty members held doctorates by the mid-1960s. Yet despite all the improvements during Harrison's presidency, when he left Tech in the late 1960s most of the graduate programs still were rated far behind those of the top schools nationally.

The cold war of the 1940s and 1950s and the advent of Sputnik in 1957 contributed to efforts to expand research and graduate programs in engineering and the physical sciences, nationally and at Tech. By 1961, President Harrison's major policy statement attempting to define the "quality" goals sought by Tech focused heavily on research, "the most discussed and least understood" concern of the Institute. He stressed the importance of research expansion and of seeking to achieve a unification of effort in the areas of teaching, research, and graduate study.[159] As part of this effort, at the beginning of the 1960–61 school year Dean of Faculties Paul Weber began working with the Engineering Experiment Station director to seek "to achieve a closer alliance between the academic goals of the institution and those primarily concerned with research activities."[160] Intense controversy continued over the provisions under which research was conducted at Tech, including the ways in which the academic departments could better participate "in the expenditure and utilization of funds for research from state sources and from overhead."[161] Effective July 1, 1963, a new position was created as associate dean of faculties and administrator of research, headed by Robert E. Stiemke who had formerly headed the experiment station, to address the "complexities of expanded research activities involving institutional funds, grants, and contracts."[162] The major watershed,

The Post-Sputnik Era

one which would set the patterns in research for years to come, came with President Harrison's memorandum of April 14, 1964, which declared that research which in general served academic purposes, graduate education, and thesis-related goals should in the future be conducted by the academic departments and that nonacademic, contract research should be conducted primarily by the Engineering Experiment Station.[163] This decision to separate academic and contract research was predictably greeted with enthusiasm by many faculty members while being disapproved by many in the station.

Despite continuing tensions over the nature and control of research at Tech, institute research, especially at the Engineering Experiment Station, showed substantial growth throughout Harrison's presidency. Whereas expenditures for all budgeted research totaled $2,150,000 for the 1956–57 year, the figure rose to $4,100,000 by 1961–62, and to $8,298,800 by 1966–67.[164] For the station alone, expansion in expenditures went from $1,972,600 in 1956–57, to $3,855,000 in 1961–62, to $6,064,000 in 1966–67.[165] The Experiment Station consolidated many of its programs in new buildings. Looking at the achievements of the station as of November 1969, a report noted that during fiscal year 1968–69 the various divisions of the station held 1,200 contracts with industry, especially in Georgia, about half of which were extended contracts with the companies concerned. The report also noted that twenty-nine companies with annual sales of $25 million could be considered as spinoffs of Georgia Tech and that eighteen of those, including Scientific Atlanta, Inc., were started by EES personnel. The professional staff of the station then consisted of 207 full-time employees, 65 of whom were shared with other departments, and 62 graduate assistants. Approximately 60 of the full-time staff members were taking graduate courses on a part-time basis, and an estimated 25 of the full-time employees taught formal courses at Tech on an occasional basis. As of the end of May 1969, 104 undergraduates were also employed by the station.[166] Academic research, which in most departments had only begun to be separated from that of the station in 1964, also showed a significant though less substantial rise.

Concern with Georgia Tech's role in the growth of the economy of Georgia and the Southeast was also expressed in the previously mentioned Little report, *Georgia Tech: Impetus to Economic Growth* (1963). The report stressed that for Georgia Tech to be able to develop fully its graduate and research programs in order to aid the long-term development of the state and region, substantial sources of support beyond those from the state legislature must be sought. Toward that end, the report recommended establishing a permanent office of institutional planning and undertaking a nationwide fund-raising campaign. Other recommendations of the report focused on the Engineering Experiment Station and on the idea of establishing a model industrial park. The report argued that as the academic departments at Tech increasingly strengthened their independent research efforts "the EES will be freer to develop its contract research services for government and industry as well as its assistance to industrial development." Because of the present lack of demand within the region for the contract research services offered by the EES, however, clients from outside the region must be actively solicited. The report also noted the difficulties in administration of the Industrial Development Division of the EES, which operated as a semi-autonomous agency, physically apart from Tech or the EES, but recommended against separation of the division. The most far-reaching proposal of the Little report, one which has to date not been achieved despite much discussion, was that Tech help establish a "model industrial park" on "a site of approximately 500 acres suitable for research, pilot plant, or manufacturing operations that are oriented toward science and technology."[167]

If research activity at Tech was expanding and changing substantially during the 1960s, so too was graduate education. As Harrison's president's report for 1962 noted: "The graduate program is so closely linked to efforts of academic research that they may be considered mutually essential."[168] From a relatively small base of just over 300 students at the beginning of Harrison's presidency, graduate student enrollment expanded rapidly during the early 1960s to more than 1,300 by 1966–67. Looking back after ten years as president, Harrison observed: "In 1967 we awarded 56 Ph.D. Degrees and 312 Master's Degrees, while just five years ago we awarded only 13 doctorate degrees and 172 Master's Degrees. Tech has now awarded 65 percent of all its doctorate degrees during the past five years."[169] By 1965–66, doctorates were offered in most areas of engineering, the physical sciences, and mathematics. In that year, the major areas of graduate enrollment (including both master's and doctoral candidates) were electrical engineering (133), chemical engineering (110), industrial engineering (106), chemistry (100), mechanical engineering (95), industrial management (85), aerospace engineering (74), and physics (69).[170] Much impetus for the expansion of graduate education came as a result of increasing support from public and private donors, including a $680,000 three-year grant in 1961 from the Ford Foundation to improve graduate education in engineering at Tech.[171] Also significant were improvements in the numbers of faculty members with better credentials and research interests. In 1965, 224 (53 percent) of the faculty held doctorates, as compared to only 159 (38 percent) two years earlier.[172]

Despite some substantial improvements, there remained significant problems with the development of graduate education at Georgia Tech. The cost of graduate education was substantially more than for undergraduate education with a similar number of students. Faculty members who themselves often did little research work or who felt that the Institute's commitment should be to undergraduate teaching sometimes resisted what they saw as a diversion of funds from the primary goals of Georgia Tech. The state of Georgia remained reluctant to commit the amounts of money necessary to provide first-rate graduate education at Georgia Tech when funding for primary, secondary, and undergraduate education within the state lagged far behind the national average. And by the end of the decade of the sixties, federal funding for research and graduate education also was reduced.

The slow rate of change in graduate education was suggested by the fact that not until 1961 was Georgia Tech invited to become a member of the Council of Graduate Schools in the United States.[173] Georgia Tech also received only moderately good ratings in two reports by the American Council on Education—Allan Cartter's *An Assessment of Quality in Graduate Education*, the research for which was done in 1964, and Kenneth D. Roose and Charles Anderson's *A Rating of Graduate Programs*, done in 1969 using essentially Cartter's techniques. Georgia Tech was rated in four areas of engineering: chemical, electrical, mechanical, and civil; and in three basic sciences: chemistry, mathematics, and physics. Between the research of 1964 and that of 1969, Georgia Tech improved its ratings by one category in chemical, electrical, and mechanical engineering, and in physics, and remained in the same categories in chemistry and in civil engineering. In mathematics, however, Georgia Tech was not even ranked in the upper three categories in either report.

In the 1969 report, the "quality of graduate faculty" was ranked, using a scale of one to five with the top categories (the only ones reported) being distinguished or strong, good, and adequate-plus. Tech's faculties were rated adequate-plus in chemical engineering, physics, and chemistry; good in civil, electrical, and mechanical engineering; and unranked in mathematics. When schools were rated according to effectiveness of doctoral programs, with the top categories again being distinguished, good, and adequate-plus, Tech doctoral programs, with the exception again of unranked mathematics, were all indicated as adequate-plus. By contrast, Tech's most-mentioned rivals, Massachusetts Institute of Technology, California Institute of Technology, and Stanford University, each received a distinguished rating in all seven areas, both for quality of faculty and for doctoral programs. Clearly Tech had to undergo much improvement before its pretensions in graduate education could match its performance.[174]

Harrison's Departure

The administrative reorganization of 1965 had left many questions unanswered. Some powerful administrators such as Mason were removed or shifted to new positions, but a fully effective new administrative team was not put into place. The removal of Mason "left some scars that lasted,"[175] and powerful traditionalist elements of the Tech faculty dubious about substantial curricular reform, the growing emphasis on research and publication, and the efforts to expand graduate education significantly. At the same time, many of the most dynamic and ambitious faculty members advocated the expansion of research and graduate education and chafed at what they saw as inadequate steps in that direction under the Harrison administration. By the mid-1960s, pressures for faster expansion of research and graduate education were building nationally, as well as at the state level under the aggressive leadership of George L. Simpson, Jr., the new chancellor of the University System of Georgia. President Harrison faced an exceedingly difficult challenge in trying to satisfy the demands for expansion of research and graduate education without alienating powerful traditionalist forces whose cooperation was also necessary for the continuing success of Georgia Tech.

The effort to put together an effective new administrative team had mixed success. The number two administrative post as vice president for academic affairs was filled when Arthur Trabant, formerly the dean of engineering at the State University of New York in Buffalo, assumed that position on July 1, 1966. Also promptly hired as new dean of engineering at Tech was Arthur G. Hansen, most recently the chairman of the mechanical engineering department at the University of Michigan, who soon began energetic efforts to revise the engineering curriculum. While new administrators were being found, others were being lost. The departure of Mario Goglia as dean of the Graduate Division in July 1966 to become vice chancellor for research in the Georgia University System, removed one of the most committed internal advocates for graduate education at Tech. Ralph Hefner, dean of the General College since its inception in 1948, died on June 30, 1967, the day of his retirement, leaving another position to be filled. Harrison appointed Karl Murphy as acting dean of the Graduate Division and Sam Webb as acting dean of the General College. When Wyatt Whitley retired as director of the Engineering Experiment Station, Harrison attempted yet another reorganization to bring the station and the academic departments closer together. He renamed the Graduate Division the Division of Graduate Studies and Research, selecting Webb as dean and giving Maurice Long the double title of associate dean for research and director of the Engineering Experiment Station. Vernon Crawford moved from being director of the School of Physics, where he had recently presided over substantial curricular revision and strengthening of the program, to the position of dean of the General College. By the late spring of 1968, after more than two years of new arrivals, departures, and reshuffling of personnel, Harrison's administrative organization again appeared complete.[176]

Just two days before the new appointments were to be formally announced, however, the kingpin of the new administrative team was removed. Trabant announced that he was resigning as vice president for academic affairs, effective September 1, in order to assume the presidency of the University of Delaware. Trabant was bright and energetic, but he had stepped into an exceedingly difficult position as Weber's successor. Weber had run a tight ship, and as a result the pressures for change had been quietly building up over the years. With Weber's departure from the number two position, demands for change proliferated from all sides, and pleasing everyone proved impossible for Trabant. When he was offered a more prestigious, more powerful, and better-paid position as president of a major university, he therefore accepted it. Harrison was "visibly shaken" by Trabant's decision to leave, a decision that constituted only the latest of a series of problems he faced.[177] Increasingly, criticisms were being voiced internally and externally at Tech's failure to achieve national distinction in research and to secure fully satisfactory funding for its programs, an ongoing problem that was becoming worse as a result of federal cutbacks in research funding by 1968.

External pressure for change at Georgia Tech came especially from George L. Simpson, Jr., who became chancellor of Georgia's University System on July 15, 1965. Simpson's background had predisposed him toward a concern for research and graduate education. After receiving his bachelor's (1941), and his master's (1944) and doctorate (1951) in sociology, all from the University of North Carolina at Chapel Hill, he had served as the first director of North Carolina's Research Triangle, a cooperative effort of three universities, industry, and government to stimulate scientific and technological creativity. Simpson then moved on to a top position in the National Aeronautics and Space Administration. Simpson served the Georgia University System after 1965 as a "strong" chancellor who sought to get a system that had previously been allowed to drift moving again. He sought to focus on "certain areas of strength" at the University of Georgia and at Georgia Tech. When the new governor of Georgia, Lester Maddox, initially balked at the $10 million in "quality improvement" funds included in the 1967 budget, Simpson worked day and night for three weeks to get the funds restored. He also began to institute a "core curriculum" for the system, so that students could freely transfer credit throughout all units of Georgia's colleges and universities. By 1968, Simpson was presiding over a rapidly expanding state educational system with almost 70,000 students in fifteen senior colleges and universities, eight junior colleges, and a medical college, with three new junior colleges in preparation. Demanding of himself and of others, Simpson perhaps best expressed his philosophy shortly before he became chancellor when, as he dedicated the new Physics Building at Tech, he spoke of the "hard, uncompromising nature of science," seeing the building as "the place in which dedicated, often abstracted, people pursue a lonely, hard profession."[178]

Simpson may have given the Georgia University System a necessary shake-up, but his hard-driving approach also made many enemies. In attempting to provide stronger central direction for the University System, Simpson set up new systemwide administrative procedures. He also sought to exercise direct personal influence over important units of the system, including their major personnel decisions. To those whom he viewed as his reliable supporters, Simpson could be loyal and affable; to those whom he viewed as enemies or as unreliable, his hostility could be intense. Both institutional and personal factors thus sometimes contributed to tensions between the chancellor's office and the presidents of different institutions. Although Simpson initially came to Harrison for advice because of Harrison's strong political base in Atlanta, relations between the two men soon became cool at best. Both men clashed repeatedly over matters of institutional and personal prerogative.[179]

The story of Harrison's unexpected resignation as president of Georgia Tech in early July 1968 may be impossible to reconstruct in full, but the overall outlines can be suggested, based on written and interview sources. On July 2, Harrison wrote a five-page, single-spaced letter to Simpson regarding the search for a successor to Trabant. The letter apparently amplified an earlier Harrison letter of May 30 that had met criticism from Simpson and provided a response to Simpson's "Interim Procedure for Filling Major Faculty and Administrative Positions." Harrison defended at length the broadly based search process being conducted at Tech. He concluded: "I would appreciate your endorsement of this letter in order that I can proceed with instructions to the committee and begin searching for a replacement."[180]

Simpson's response evidently was not favorable. As one standard account succinctly notes: "Dr. Edwin D. Harrison handed in his resignation to Chancellor George L. Simpson, Jr., on the morning of July 3, 1968."[181] The resignation was to be effective at the end of the following school year, on June 30, 1969, or earlier if a successor were named. After presenting the resignation, Harrison left to spend the Fourth of July holiday with family at Daytona Beach, Florida, with the intention of announcing the decision to faculty, alumni, and friends following the holiday. The decision, however, was leaked to the press and on July 4 the combined holiday edition of the *Atlanta Journal and Constitution* reported Harrison's resignation as front-page news. The headline announced: "Tech President Resigns in Row with Regents"; and a subheading indicated: "Policies Reported as Issues." The newspaper reported "a high state Capitol source who declined to be named" as saying that there had been "a conflict over University System administration policies": "They've demanded certain things he (Harrison) doesn't feel like he can go through with. Evidently he's not being given the freedom he thinks he should have. Apparently there are programs and policies being pushed that he feels are not in the best interest of the school." Harrison's own statement, presented through a Georgia Tech spokesman, was simply: "I have long held a view that no college president should serve more than 10 years in the position. Because of Dr. Arthur Trabant's leaving to become the president of the University of Delaware, I feel this would be the most appropriate time to make a change in order that a new president can select his own vice president of academic affairs. This way the transition can be made as smoothly as possible."[182]

Harrison's resignation created much discussion in Atlanta. The standard denials were issued that the decision was anything but voluntary. Nevertheless, a variety of other factors were suggested to account for the resignation. Most were variants on the statement attributed to an unnamed regent that the board felt "Harrison was not moving Tech rapidly enough toward excellence on a national level" and that there seemed to be a mutual feeling on the part of Harrison and the board that "maybe it was time for a new man." A state senator, H. McKinley Conway, secretary of the University System Committee, called for a legislative investigation of the circumstances behind the resignation, but this action was not pursued.[183] On July 9, Harrison spoke for two hours to an alumni group about the events, breaking the silence he had maintained since confirming the story of his resignation. He also issued a memorandum to the faculty, staff, and students at Tech, noting: "I regret very much that you learned of my decision to retire from Georgia Tech through the news media rather than by a campus announcement as I had planned. . . . Unfortunately there are rumors, vicious in nature, circulating in great numbers. I urge you neither to believe them nor to pass them along. My decision was correctly quoted in the only press release or statement I have made. . . . I ask for your cooperation, understanding and effort in carrying forward our existing programs and especially the Master Plan for Graduate Study, the numerous service activities which we are undertaking and the progress in the academic and research areas."[184]

The next year would be a difficult one for President Harrison, unable as an outgoing figure to exercise full authority or to plan effectively for the institution he continued to serve. On January 17, 1969, J. P. Stevens and Company announced that as soon as Harrison completed his duties at Tech, he would serve as one of their executive vice presidents.[185] On February 12, 1969, in a move that surprised many people as much as his resignation, Harrison announced that the Board of Regents, at his request, had approved a four-month leave of absence for him beginning on March 1. Harrison needed that time, he said, "to concentrate on clearing up my affairs as President so that an orderly transition can be made to my successor."[186] During that time, Crawford, dean of the General College, served as acting president. In the 1969 president's report, Harrison obliquely alluded to the tensions of his final year by calling for cooperative rather than factionalized efforts to solve Tech's pressing problems. He emphasized that the Institute's goal of providing a first-class education for all its students "can be truly achieved only when factions at all levels with selfish interests have the courage, intelligence, and understanding to subjugate their personal, individual and collective ambitions for the good of the institution. . . . All higher educational complexes, even Georgia Tech, are vulnerable to bias and distortion of facts and views. . . . Team effort has accounted for past successes. Only a similar sustained effort can keep the boot-strap operation of the past on a course of steady progress in the future."[187]

The heartfelt admiration and respect that alumni, faculty members, and students held for President Ed Harrison was conveyed at a special testimonial dinner on January 17, 1969, attended by over 650 people from throughout the city, state, and nation.[188] Perhaps even more moving was "Wonderful Ed's Day," the farewell celebration planned by students for April 9, 1969. The warm, sunny day—variously described as "the finest, the most loving day in Tech's history, happy and sad, far more than just a party," and "the largest and most memorable demonstration of the sixties at Tech"—expressed the genuine affection students felt for Ed Harrison. Banners proclaimed "Thanks for the EDucation" and "Well Done, Dr. Harrison," balloons flew, a folk-rock group played, and Atlanta Mayor Ivan Allen spoke of his regard for Ed Harrison, proclaiming April 9 "Wonderful Ed's Day" in Atlanta, in honor of "the many contributions of Dr. Harrison to the growth of Tech and of the City." A high point of the celebration came when Tech students unveiled and presented to Harrison a five-foot tall T—a part of the four Tech signs around the top of the administration building that had mysteriously disappeared the preceding week—so that he would have what every Tech man needed, his own glowing yellow T for a conversation piece. The celebration ended and Harrison rode off in the rumble seat of the Tech Reck. In July, Harrison would move on to spend seven more productive years with J. P. Stevens and Company, until his final retirement in 1976.[189]

What was the overall balance sheet on Edwin Harrison's eleven-year presidency? In many ways, the period was one of expansion and positive changes for Tech. Major strides were made in improving the quality of the student body and faculty. Racial integration was achieved peacefully and without court order for the first time in any public institution of higher education in the Deep South. Alumni relations and fund raising were professionalized so that Tech became second to none in this area among public institutions in the country. Research and graduate education experienced significant improvements, though still falling far short of the highest levels of achievement nationally. With the aid of urban renewal, the campus experienced its greatest expansion and started its most sustained building effort. Perhaps most important and controversial, efforts were made to chart a new future for the institution and to reorganize its administrative structure so that it could more effectively handle the many challenges that it faced.

These rapid changes at Tech left many unresolved issues. While Harrison helped to accelerate efforts to transform the institution, he was unable to develop a fully effective new structure, administrative team, and policies himself. His successors until at least 1972 would similarly experience years of turmoil and transition at the administrative level. Perhaps the most balanced assessment of Harrison's efforts and accomplishments was the one he presented in 1968: "In retrospect, in evaluating the last eleven years, I am sure that there are some who would have attempted to move faster in some areas, others would have moved slower in the same areas, but in terms of academic caliber, overall faculty endorsement, increase in caliber of students, superior business operations, faculty-student-community relations, alumni relations, and national and international reputation, Tech stands proudly with the best."[190]

Chapter Nine

Years of Turmoil and Transition

Overleaf: Georgia Tech students became involved in community service through participation in the Techwood Tutorial Project involving youngsters from the Techwood and Clark Howell housing projects and O'Keefe High School. (Courtesy of the Georgia Tech Archives.)

The era between the end of Edwin D. Harrison's eleven-year presidency of Georgia Tech and the appointment of Joseph M. Pettit to that office was marked by rapid turnover in the Institute's top leadership. There was considerable uncertainty about future directions for the school on North Avenue, an unsettling situation paralleled on the national scene by upheavals in engineering education and American university life in general. And yet during this era, major initiatives, some of which had been launched under Harrison, began to bring into focus the outline of Tech as it would appear at its centennial.

Between 1969 and 1972, the land that had been added to the campus on the north and west during Harrison's tenure began to blossom with new buildings. There was a major revision of the undergraduate curriculum and continued effort to expand graduate education. Expectations were raised for research in the academic units, while the Engineering Experiment Station underwent another stormy reevaluation of its mission and administrative relationship to the Institute. And, for the first time in its history, Georgia Tech fired a head football coach. Tech's forward movement during those years, despite heated and sometimes highly publicized controversy, is a credit both to the three men who briefly served as chief executive officer and to what one of the three liked to call the Tech "community."

Vernon Crawford and Educational Reform

On July 1, 1968, just a few days before President Harrison's resignation, Vernon D. Crawford had become dean of the General College.

When, in March 1969, Harrison announced that he would take a leave of absence until his resignation became effective, Chancellor George L. Simpson named Crawford as acting president.

The man who became the fourth acting president in Georgia Tech's history had been a member of the Tech faculty for almost twenty years. A native of Nova Scotia, Crawford had received his undergraduate training in Canada and his doctorate in physics from the University of Virginia before coming to Tech in 1949 as associate professor of physics. Young Professor Crawford was struck, he later recalled, by the "no-nonsense" attitude of Tech's students, whom he enjoyed teaching.[1] In addition to his successes as a physics instructor, Crawford quickly established himself as part of the forward-looking, research-oriented wing of the faculty, both in the School of Physics and in the Engineering Experiment Station, where he held a research appointment and served during the 1950s as head of the physics branch. Crawford became a member of the Research Club and the Sigma Xi Club, which was the focal point of campus interest in research and graduate education. As director of the School of Physics beginning in 1964, Crawford promoted a thorough revision of the undergraduate physics curriculum, a development which not only attracted some of Tech's brightest students to that school in the 1960s, but also set the pattern for a more general revision of undergraduate curricula in the 1970s.[2]

Crawford's commitment to teaching was clearly evident in his brief tenure as acting president. In his inaugural address before the Faculty Senate, Crawford defined the Institute's mission: "My view of the primary aim of Georgia Tech, simply stated, is this: to provide a first class education for our students."[3] The acting president added weight to those words by encouraging the ferment of curricular innovation that was then developing across the campus. He supported the efforts of Dean Arthur G. Hansen and others in rethinking the engineering core curriculum and lent his support to expansion of undergraduate instruction in the humanities and social sciences. Finally, during Crawford's tenure, the School of Industrial Management achieved the status of a college, with School Director Sherman Dallas named as dean. At the end of the decade, industrial management was the most popular major on the campus, enrolling one-and-one-half times as many students as the largest engineering school.⁴

Throughout the late 1960s the Engineering College grappled with a major revision of the undergraduate curriculum, particularly the foundation or core courses of study. As was often the case before in Tech's history, a combination of local and national forces triggered the movement for change. This latest round of curriculum reform at Tech coincided with yet another national study of engineering education, this one conducted by the American Society for Engineering Education. Launched in 1963, the study entitled "Goals for Engineering Education" produced by 1965 a preliminary report that generated considerable debate among engineering educators.⁵

The portion of the study dealing with graduate education was directed by Joseph M. Pettit, then dean of engineering at Stanford University, but the findings that initially stirred the greatest interest on the Georgia Tech campus concerned undergraduate curricula. The preliminary report called for a reduction in the number of hours required for graduation, greater flexibility in the selection of engineering courses, an increase of coursework in the humanities and social sciences, and a lengthening of the basic professional degree to a five-year program.⁶

In one of his last acts as dean, Jesse Mason had appointed a faculty committee to review the preliminary "Goals" report. That committee's report, presented to the engineering faculty in 1966, contained echoes of the old shop culture–school culture debate. With the backing of the majority of the engineering faculty, the committee dismissed most of the "Goals" recommendations and concluded: "The education process must develop ingenuity—the ability to supply an answer when there is none available from science and mathematics. This requires a state of mind, involving intuition (developed by an understanding of the art of engineering), inspiration, and courage. It is seldom the subject of a formal course; instead it can be learned by exposure to the solution of real engineering problems and by the influence of teachers who had had real engineering experience."⁷

Yet, less than four years later, many of the "Goals" recommendations were implemented at Tech, with the strong backing of a new engineering dean and many of his faculty. Why the change? In the first place, the basic direction of modern engineering education—toward a firmer foundation in mathematics and science—was already well established, and the "Goals" report merely reaffirmed that trend. And in American higher education generally the end of the 1960s witnessed strong pressures for reduction of required courses and greater flexibility in curricula. By the end of the decade, the national decline in engineering enrollments pushed schools of engineering into lowering course-hour requirements to levels comparable to those in the physical sciences.[8]

All three of these national trends were visible at Georgia Tech. Mason's successor as dean of engineering, Arthur G. Hansen, though an engineer by profession, had taken his doctorate in applied mathematics and was supportive of the "Goals" study. Many Tech students expressed interest (politely stated, of course) in more flexibility in the engineering curricula, following the precedent set by the revision of the course of study in physics. Finally, by 1970 Georgia Tech was feeling the impact of the national decline in engineering enrollment.[9]

The new dean was strongly in favor of curricular reform. In 1967, Hansen appointed his own committee to consider changes in the engineering curriculum, specifically to define a "core curriculum" common to all engineering majors. Hansen selected as chairman Dale C. Ray, professor of electrical engineering, who, like himself, had joined the Tech faculty from the University of Michigan in 1966.[10] The committee surveyed engineering programs at other institutions and reviewed the final report of the "Goals" committee (published in January 1968) before suggesting a core curriculum for Georgia Tech engineering students. The Tech committee's recommendations, like the final "Goals" report, did not advocate a five-year bachelor's degree program—such programs had proven to be unpopular in the few engineering schools that had adopted them. The Tech committee did recommend a reduction in the total number of hours required for graduation from approximately 220 to 180–90, which more nearly matched the requirements at leading engineering schools at the time. The committee made specific recommendations for basic courses in science, mathematics, engineering, and humanities and social sciences, to provide a core of 101 quarter hours, a slight overall reduction from existing practice.[11]

The increased flexibility of the proposed new core extended to the humanities and social sciences, where required sequences in English and modern languages gave way to a choice of electives. The new core curriculum encouraged, but did not mandate, the study of technology as a historical-cultural subject and of the interaction between science and society. A joint committee of engineering and liberal arts professors proposed in 1969 an initiative to increase course offerings and faculty "in the area of technology and its impact on society."[12]

Expressions of interest in courses on science, technology, and society were of two kinds. Some among the engineering faculty viewed the lack of such emphasis in traditional liberal arts curricula as a serious oversight leading to a lack of appreciation for the contribution of scientists and engineers to human advancement. In addition, some students and faculty, influenced by the prevalent attitude of questioning the benign nature of science, called for study of the interplay between science and society without presupposing a positive connection. The call to make the study of science and technology a major enterprise in the humanities and social sciences component of engineering education paralleled the demands for Afro-American studies on American college campuses, including Tech's. Indeed, the beginning of course offerings in Afro-American literature and history and the recruitment of Tech's first black instructor, William Peace (social sciences), coincided with the introduction of courses on science, technology, and society and the creation of an endowed chair in that field. In both cases group pride was at work, a sense that an important segment of society had been left out of the telling of civilization's advance and that new courses and new instructional approaches were needed to correct the oversight.[13]

Although the Core Curriculum Committee circulated its proposed recommendations in the spring of 1968 and made a "final" report that fall, debate over the matter dragged on for two more years. At issue, as in the earlier discussions, were the questions of whether reduced course hours and a more flexible curriculum amounted to a dangerous watering down of Tech's demanding course of study. Specific points at issue included disagreement over whether traditional courses in engineering drawing should still be required (they were being phased out elsewhere) and whether instruction in classical mechanics should still be offered through the department of physics or transferred to the Engineering College's School of Engineering Science and Mechanics. To be sure, these and other disputes were in part struggles over academic turf, but they also reflected the old debate over practical versus theoretical education. There was also an echo of the old idea that what distinguished Tech's engineering program was the fact that it "overloaded" the students and thus better prepared them for the rigors of the working world.[14]

The proponents of reform in the core curriculum included not only many of the younger faculty and most of the engineering school directors but also Vernon Crawford (as acting president and then as vice president for academic affairs) and Arthur Hansen (first as dean of engineering and then as president). Hansen, having encouraged the process of undergraduate curricular reform, lobbied with the faculty and even with students for its acceptance. On the day of his appointment as president, Hansen told a group of students that the engineering curriculum needed to be more flexible: "I will propose a cutdown and opening up of the curriculum," Hansen said. "If you do not have freedom to explore, you will not learn, grow, and will not be a well educated person."[15] By 1970–71 the proposed changes had been adopted by the engineering schools. Along with parallel changes in the structure and organization of specialized engineering coursework at the beginning of the 1970s, this revision was, as of 1985, the last basic change in the undergraduate engineering curriculum.

Arthur Hansen Takes the Helm

Despite his active presence on campus as engineering dean, Hansen's appointment as president of Georgia Tech came as a surprise. Chancellor George Simpson had encouraged the selection of a nationally prominent engineer from outside the Institute to succeed Harrison. It was widely believed that the position would go to Raymond L. Bisplinghoff, then dean of engineering at MIT and formerly a senior official of NASA.[16] Immediately following Bisplinghoff's withdrawal from consideration, Chancellor Simpson recommended

Hansen to the Board of Regents, and on May 28, 1969, he was named as the seventh president of Georgia Tech.

Hansen, aged forty-four, brought to the presidency a youthful vigor that caused one member of the Tech faculty to label him as the "John Kennedy of Georgia Tech." Perhaps a more useful comparison was between Hansen and Kennedy's science advisor, Jerome B. Wiesner. As provost of MIT during the turbulent era of the late 1960s and early 1970s, Wiesner mediated student protest while at the same time leading his institution in new intellectual directions. Wiesner's student-oriented style of administration, coupled with his relatively liberal political stance, made him a highly visible champion of social causes within the context of a technological university.[17]

The affable, pipe-smoking Hansen was readily accessible to students (more so than to faculty, some complained) and shared with many of the student leaders a concern about contemporary social problems. Hansen had helped establish a committee of the American Society for Engineering Education to promote engineering education in historically black colleges. He had served as a visiting professor at Tuskegee Institute, during which time he observed the Selma-Montgomery civil rights march of 1965.[18] A political liberal by some standards, Hansen was certainly no flaming radical. With regard to the universities' role in solving the social problems that loomed so large at the end of the 1960s, Hansen, like Wiesner, can perhaps best be described as a cautious optimist.

Similarities between Wiesner and Hansen along these lines would not necessarily have been apparent to the Georgia Tech community at the time of his arrival. Hansen, a native of Wisconsin, had earned his bachelor's and master's degrees from Purdue (in electrical engineering and mathematics, respectively) before taking his doctorate in applied mathematics from Case Western Reserve University. At the time he became president of Georgia Tech, Hansen's career had been divided equally between engineering research and academia. Between 1948 and 1958 he had worked as a research scientist at NASA's Lewis Flight Propulsion Laboratory in Cleveland. Hansen had then briefly headed the Nucleonics Section of the Cornell Aeronautics Laboratory in Buffalo before joining the engineering faculty of the University of Michigan in 1959. During his last years at Ann Arbor he had served as chairman of Mechanical Engineering, and it was from that post that he moved to Atlanta in 1966 as dean of engineering.[19]

President Hansen quickly put his own stamp on the administrative plan that had been drawn in the 1965 reorganization. Vernon Crawford was named vice president for academic affairs, replacing Arthur Trabant, who had resigned to become president of the University of Delaware. The office of vice president controller was divided, with long-time fiscal officer Jamie R. Anthony assuming the new position of vice president for institutional services but relinquishing the role of chief financial officer to his associate, Ewell I. Barnes, who was named controller. (In 1970 Barnes's title was changed to vice president for business and finance.) The Office of Vice President for Programs was abolished, as was, with the retirement of Paul Weber, the Office of Vice President for Planning. With characteristic understatement, Weber concluded his final annual report as vice president by noting: "It is with a feeling of some pride that I view the advancements which have been made during the past 30 years."[20]

The administrative changes extended to the deans' level. Following Hansen's appointment to the presidency, Walter O. Carlson, professor of mechanical engineering, served as acting dean of engineering until the appointment in 1970 of Thomas E. Stelson of Carnegie-Mellon University. Similarly, following Crawford's appointment as acting president, William Eberhardt, professor of chemistry, served as acting dean of the General College until the selection of Henry C. Valk of the University of Nebraska, also in 1970. When Sherman Dallas stepped down as dean of industrial management in 1971 and was replaced the following year by Ferdinand K. Levy of Rice University, all three of the academic deanships were filled by men recently recruited for the positions from outside the faculty.[21] More than ever before in its history, Tech was being led by men who were new to the Institute. Coupled with other decisions to draw both leaders and ideas about the future of the Institute from the outside (recall the flurry of external studies in the mid-1960s), these new appointments help to delineate the late 1960s and early 1970s as a time when institutional leadership consciously, sometimes even enthusiastically, distanced itself from the image and the substance of what Tech had been before. The thirty years of service to which Paul Weber could point with pride had been witnesses to a great shift. The Georgia Tech to which Weber had come as a young professor in 1927 would have been recognizable to its founders. Despite some underlying continuities, the institution from which he retired in 1969 probably would not have been.

Campus and Community

The part of Tech's transformation most immediately visible to a casual visitor in 1969 was the unprecedented campus expansion and building boom that had begun under Edwin Harrison. By the time Hansen assumed the presidency, major buildings either recently completed or under construction included new homes for the Schools of Chemistry, Physics, and Civil Engineering, new buildings for the Engineering Experiment Station, and major expansions of the library and computer center, along with new dormitories and the student center.

Much of the new construction was on land west of Hemphill Street only recently acquired through the federal Urban Renewal Program. Between 1964 and 1971, the campus had increased in size from 153 to 255 acres, with almost all of the increase coming in the west campus area. In 1968 Tech began a second phase of land acquisition to the west and north under the Neighborhood Development Program. Federal programs such as this one seemed to provide Tech with the means of fulfilling the Perkins and Will Plan of 1965 that projected a four-hundred-acre campus bounded by North Avenue, Marietta Street, Northside Drive, Tenth Street and Interstate 75-85—a far cry from the four acres originally donated by the Peters Land Company in the 1880s. Before that goal could be fully realized, changes in federal urban renewal programs and reduction of building funds would slow expansion and bring new construction to a standstill. During Hansen's brief presidency, however, Georgia Tech pressed forward with the purchase of land to the north and west of the campus.[22]

The land within Tech's planned area of development was not standing vacant but was a heavily populated residential and commercial district. President Hansen, in his first official statement on the subject of campus expansion, likened conditions in the area to those in the Techwood neighborhood before 1933 when President M. L. Brittain encouraged federal authorities to build the first major federal housing project there. Like Techwood on the southern border of the campus, the land to the north and west was heavily built up with low-income residences. Unlike Techwood, however, the area into which Tech now hoped to expand included more well-defined communities. Although 80 percent of the homes had been declared substandard, many residents owned their own homes. This was especially true in the Home Park community, only a portion of which was within the projected growth area. Many residents worked or had worked at the adjacent Atlantic Steel Company mill or in other industrial jobs nearby. Particularly in the area more to the north of the campus, networks of extended families, churches, and schools tied the predominantly white community together. Among those with long-standing family ties in the neighborhood was Georgia's governor, Lester Maddox. Not only had Maddox been raised in the area, his Pickrick Restaurant was in the path of Tech's planned expansion and became in 1966 the Georgia Tech Placement Center.[23]

Tech's highly publicized expansion plans, linked as they were to urban renewal programs, had the potential for triggering both community and campus protests. Although no one seriously anticipated student reactions like those at Columbia University, where campus expansion into a nearby low-income neighborhood touched off protests including student occupation of campus buildings, Tech administrators were mindful that a sizable and influential group of students was concerned about the Institute's relationship with the poor neighborhoods, and they took quick steps to address those concerns.[24]

Throughout the 1960s several student-initiated projects had given Tech students opportunity for translating concern into community service. For example, since 1962 the Techwood Tutorial Program, initiated by the Episcopal student organization, had paired Tech students with youngsters from the Techwood and Clark Howell housing projects for counseling and academic tutoring. Similarly, the High School Tutoring Program had matched Tech students with teenagers from nearby O'Keefe High School.[25] In the fall of 1968 Numan V. Bartley, professor of history, worked with students to establish a series of courses that channeled students into community service projects, including tutoring of adults for high school equivalency exams in the nearby Bedford-Pines neighborhood, which, unlike Techwood Homes at the time, was predominantly black.[26]

The assassination of Martin Luther King, Jr., in April 1968 triggered several expressions of social concern on the campus, including the "Open Letter" initiated by campus leaders and signed by over five hundred students. Delivered to President Harrison on April 25, the same day that students were occupying the Lowe Library at Columbia, the letter requested that the administration expand its community service efforts. The letter included a ringing declaration that "Tech now has a moral obligation to look around its city and to work beyond Hemphill and North Avenue. As an educational institution, it must direct itself to a society of which the ghetto is a part."[27]

The community service initiatives announced by President Hansen were, to be sure, responsive to student concerns, but other forces were at work as well. When Tech began the second phase of its urban renewal expansion both public attitudes and federal laws had changed since the first phase was launched. The 1968 Neighborhood Development Program mandated that local governments and the developers of urban renewal land (Tech, in this case) allow greater participation by low-income citizens from the affected neighborhoods and pay more attention to the needs of the urban poor in the process of redeveloping the land. Locally, urban renewal programs for the Buttermilk Bottoms and Bedford-Pine areas (black neighborhoods within a mile of Tech) had in 1965 and 1966 generated strong community opposition to the closing of a neighborhood school (on the present site of the Atlanta Civic Center) and to the relocation of people from the neighborhood.[28] Thus, the Institute's legal and political imperatives converged with the idealistic concerns of some of the students. The result was a rather ambitious effort to harness student activism and add to it a measure of administrative support for community service activities in the urban renewal expansion zone.

Even in the first phase of Tech's urban renewal expansion, senior administrators had sought to defuse neighborhood protest by meeting personally with homeowners whose land was being purchased.[29] President Hansen continued this practice and also took steps immediately after his inauguration to launch a program of community service. Hansen pledged institutional support for existing student-initiated projects and a broadening of Tech's involvement in the urban renewal area through relocation counseling and other services.[30]

In the spring of 1969, before Hansen took office, staff members from the dean of students' office and the YMCA had organized a Community Service Coordinating Staff to facilitate campus involvement in the renewal area. Assistant Dean of Students Miller Templeton was soon joined in this effort by Donald Nelson, assistant director of the YMCA. Nelson had come to Tech in 1968 from a Y post in Providence, Rhode Island, where he had coordinated community service activities for local universities.[31]

In August 1969 Nelson joined the dean of students' staff, where he assumed overall leadership of the community service program. Working with the Campus Planning Office and the president, Nelson, Templeton, and an energetic group of students (including Y leader Tom Saylor, *Technique* staffer Bruce Cook, and student government officer Wally Bloom) developed an umbrella organization, the Community Service Task Force, that coordinated Tech's community involvement and served as the institutional agency with direct responsibility for carrying out the mandate for community service in the renewal area.[32]

With supervision from the Office of the Dean of Students, but with considerable student initiative, the Task Force secured funding through the federal Work-Study Program and the federally supported Economic Opportunity Atlanta (EOA) with which to support a variety of student-staffed service programs in the renewal area. These included a community center on Third Street that provided job and relocation counseling, child care, and medical assistance (with medical staff provided by EOA).[33]

Simultaneously, other community service programs got underway in 1969 and 1970. The Student Government Association sponsored construction of a playground in a nearby urban renewal area (Vine City), and former Student Body President Sam Williams, working with Mayor Ivan Allen and EOA executive Dan Sweat, helped organize an Atlanta Urban Corps, through which area college students took federally funded summer jobs doing community service work in the city.[34]

At their peak in 1970–71, Tech's community service programs were both highly visible and generally successful in easing tensions between the Institute and residents of the urban renewal area. Acquisition of land in the second phase of Tech's urban renewal expansion was accomplished without the neighborhood opposition that had occurred in Buttermilk Bottoms or, for that matter, would occur a decade later when Tech attempted to expand its holdings between Eighth and Tenth streets. Laudable as these efforts were, however, they involved a relatively small number of students. Coordinator of Community Programs Donald Nelson estimated that one thousand students were involved to some extent during 1970–71, but this figure included the most casual participants. A much smaller group (perhaps in the range of one hundred) made serious commitments of time and energy.[35] Furthermore, most of the projects quickly faded away in the early 1970s, leaving little residue in the surrounding neighborhoods.

Why the rapid decline of community service? One must acknowledge first of all the shifts in student interests and priorities. At Tech, as on college campuses elsewhere, the humanitarian zeal of the 1960s ran afoul of the job shortage of the 1970s. Indicative of this transformation were the topics of discussion at President Hansen's public conversations with students, the "Issues and Answers Forum." At the first of these, held in 1969, students pressed Hansen for clarification of Tech's role in the neighboring communities. By the summer of 1970 worried students were asking the president about the prospects of relief from the decline in the engineering job market.[36] Administrative changes played a role as well. With the departure of Hansen in 1971, the community service program lost a strong advocate at the top. Other members of his administration who were involved in campus planning and land acquisition had been much less committed to the outreach concept.[37] Furthermore, when the Student Center opened in 1971, Nelson joined its staff, and his involvement in the community service program decreased. Cutbacks in federal funds for community development programs such as EOA and the phaseout of the urban renewal programs removed the financial base for community service and changed the terms under which Tech would acquire property in the 1970s.[38] Finally, the community service spirit fell victim to a changed campus attitude toward the surrounding area in the early 1970s. At the end of the 1960s the population of Techwood and Clark Howell homes rapidly shifted from largely white to predominantly black, and even before that racial shift occurred, vandalism and assaults against students became more commonplace. The integration and rapid re-segregation of O'Keefe High School brought more black neighborhood youths onto the campus than before. For most students the "community" meant the area just beyond the dormitories to the east and south of the campus—the direction one walked to the Varsity and other nearby commercial establishments. The increased sense of danger on that side of the campus contributed to a widespread feeling of being under siege. In 1972 a Tech security official was quoted as saying to the Student Council, "From the Techwood Housing area to O'Keefe is becoming a corridor of crime." A year later the same official raised the possibility that crime and vandalism could be halted by fencing the campus.[39]

Tech's short-lived foray into community service was many things to many people. The administration's quick embrace of student-initiated programs demonstrated the concerns of an institution involved in a politically sensitive expansion project and one anxious to channel the student idealism that on other campuses had contributed to confrontation. Given the genuine concern of President Hansen and others for the families who were being displaced in the urban renewal area, it would be wrong to label the administration's actions as merely cooptation of youthful idealism, but there was a happy convergence of institutional self-interest and student activism. And from the perspective of the students who gave their most prized possession—time—to such activities as tutoring in Techwood and O'Keefe, building a playground in Vine City, or staffing a counseling center in the urban renewal area, Tech's brief venture into community service was tangible proof that the student activism of the 1960s did come to Tech, but in a particularly constructive fashion.

Student Life in the Protest Era

Another manifestation of activism on American college campuses in the late 1960s was opposition to the war in Vietnam. Here again, the Tech response was different from the highly publicized reactions on leading college campuses elsewhere. At the height of the war even the nation's most prestigious technological institutions were caught up in the wave of protest. Two weeks before Hansen was inaugurated as president of Georgia Tech, students at MIT picketed and blocked access to the Draper Laboratory, protesting its production of guidance systems for the Poseidon missile.[40]

On the Tech campus reactions to the war and the associated military buildup were quite different. Although the *Technique* editorialized again involvement of the United States in Vietnam and some student activists called for withdrawal of American forces, the Student Council soundly defeated a bill endorsing the Vietnam Moratorium in the fall of 1969. A poll of three thousand Tech students taken in the preceding spring revealed a plurality in favor of increased bombing of North Vietnam.[41] Unlike MIT, Stanford, Wisconsin, and other institutions where military research became a focal point of antiwar activities, there was virtually no public protest at Tech against the military electronics research conducted in the Engineering Experiment Station.

The American invasion of Cambodia in April 1970 touched off a new wave of antiwar demonstrations on college campuses. One of them, at Kent State University, resulted in the killing of four student protestors by Ohio National Guardsmen, an event which, in turn, triggered such a storm of protest that some 450 colleges were forced to suspend classes, some of them for the remainder of the spring term.[42]

On college campuses in Georgia the reaction was relatively restrained. At Emory University in Atlanta, however, some students boycotted classes and held demonstrations, and the faculty voted to downgrade Air Force ROTC from the status of an academic department to extracurricular activity. At the University of Georgia in Athens, several hundred students marched on the home of the president demanding that he close the university, and three students were arrested in connection with minor damage to a university building.[43]

Although no such demonstrations occurred on the Tech campus, the Institute was ordered closed on May 8 and 9, along with all other units of the University System.[44] Lack of protest demonstrations on the Tech campus did not mean there was no student concern over what had happened at Kent State. On Friday, May 8, four hundred people from the Tech community filled Bertha Square for a student-organized memorial service. Religious leaders and representatives of the faculty and student body addressed the gathering, along with President Hansen. As Hansen later recalled, given the emotional current then running on American college campuses that week, no one knew exactly what to expect, but when the memorial service was ended the students went quietly on their way.[45]

As with the community-oriented student activism and mild anti-war sentiment at the end of the 1960s, the fortunes of several student organizations at Georgia Tech followed national trends, but on a different scale and for different reasons. Fraternities had for decades attracted a large percentage of students and dominated campus organizations, but membership in the Greek letter organizations dropped from 37 percent of all male students in 1968 to 29 percent in 1970, and then declined even further to 22 percent in 1975 before making a recovery.[46] The decline had little to do with antifraternity sentiment in the Age of Aquarius (although there was more individualism, and some increased resistance to authoritarianism was observed, whether imposed by administrators or fellow students). Rather, the principal causes were the further relaxation of in loco parentis rules, the loosened restrictions on student use of automobiles, the opening of new dormitories, and the increased importance of nonfraternity organizations in campus affairs (including the Inter-dormitory Council), all of which reduced the advantages of fraternity membership.[47]

A similar decline occurred in ROTC participation. As noted above in chapter 8, the immediate source of this decline was the ending of compulsory ROTC training in 1965. While the buildup of the United States' military involvement in Vietnam no doubt discouraged some students from enrolling in ROTC, these decisions were for the most part based on personal career goals, since anti-ROTC peer pressure was minimal on the Tech campus. Enrollment in Air Force ROTC declined from 1,247 in 1964 to 524 in 1968 and 185 in 1972. The number of cadets actually commissioned declined also, but not as precipitously as the size of the cadet corps.[48]

While the decline in fraternity and ROTC membership at Georgia

Tech paralleled similar declines nationwide, and while political and social activism played a more important role on the Tech campus than one might suppose, neither should obscure the fact that the majority of Tech students held decidedly conservative views. In 1968 a survey of 1,605 students and faculty, employing a "liberal" to "conservative" scale of +12 to −12 in measuring of social and political attitudes, faculty members measured +0.87, freshmen −3.3, and upperclassmen −1.95.[49] The conservatism of Tech students may have derived as much from their southern origins as from their technological bent. During the presidential primary season in 1968 over 40 percent of Tech's students participated in a national presidential preference poll. Among Tech students, Richard Nixon received 39.2 percent while liberal Democrats Eugene McCarthy and Robert Kennedy received a total of 28.6 percent. Nationwide the results were reversed, with Nixon receiving 18 percent to McCarthy and Kennedy's 47 percent. The Tech results, however, more nearly resembled the statewide results among college students in Georgia.[50]

The idea that Tech students' social and political views were shaped by regional culture as well as by professional orientation seems to contradict the long-standing fact of geographical diversity among Tech's student body. In 1969–70, for example, 41 percent of Tech's students came from states other than Georgia (only Idaho was not represented that year), and another 5 percent came from 68 foreign countries. Of the students from other states, however, 47 percent came from the five states contiguous to Georgia, and a full 60 percent came from nine southern states.[51] At least with regard to its student body, Tech remained a decidedly southern school.

The profile of Tech's students at the end of the 1960s also resembled that of the earliest group in that a disproportionate number of the Georgia students came from the state's major cities. Forty-five percent came from Fulton and DeKalb counties (Atlanta and its suburbs), and 66 percent came from four metropolitan Atlanta counties plus the counties containing Macon, Savannah, Columbus, and Augusta. Furthermore, despite the admission of women in 1952 and blacks in 1961, Tech remained overwhelmingly a white male preserve. In 1969–70 only 2.7 percent of the students were women, and slightly under one percent were black.[52]

Despite the small number of women and blacks on the campus,

organizational changes were taking place at the end of the decade that presaged a dramatic increase in the enrollment and impact of both groups in the 1970s. In 1968 women were freely admitted to the industrial management program, making women at last eligible to enter all degree programs. In 1969 the first women's dorm opened (Fulmer Hall), and Judith E. Priddy was named to the newly created post of assistant dean of students for women.[53]

In 1968 the Georgia Tech Afro-American Association (GTAAA) was formally established, with Haywood Soloman as its first president. The following February, with GTAAA leadership, Tech for the first time observed Negro History Week. Also in 1969 Georgia Tech signed its first black athlete to a grant-in-aid. Eddie McAshan, an all-state performer in football and basketball from Jacksonville, Florida, became Georgia Tech's first black athlete to take part in intercollegiate competition.[54]

With the exception of the decline in ROTC and fraternity membership, the basic continuity in the composition of the student body was reflected to a considerable extent in the flavor of organized extracurricular activities. For example, intramural sports, long an important feature of campus life, still involved over one thousand students in organized competition. At the end of the 1960s women's athletics, which in the 1970s would develop into varsity programs, existed only as intramural activities.[55]

Campus religious organizations played an important role in the lives of many students, perhaps reaching a peak in their membership in the late 1960s. During the past decade several church-related organizations had constructed or purchased buildings on the campus. Groups such as the Wesley Foundation (Methodist), Newman Club (Catholic), Baptist Student Union, Presbyterian Student Center, and Episcopal student organization not only provided religious instruction and a churchlike environment, but also offered recreational, educational, and service programs for interested students. The role of the Episcopal student organization in establishing community service programs has already been noted. In addition, the Wesley Foundation organized the "Free University," which, beginning in 1968, provided a forum for faculty and student discussion of social issues not ordinarily addressed in the classroom.[56]

In the mid and late 1960s student government came to play a

much more important role in campus affairs than had previously been the case. In part, this increased stature was due to the Student Council's assertion of control over allocation of student activity fees beginning in 1966 and to a changing balance of responsibilities for campus affairs between the dean of students and the YMCA. The Student Council, however, also benefited during these years from exceptionally capable leadership. Among the outstanding student leaders of those years were three successive student body presidents. Carey Brown (1966–67) first mobilized student support for a Student Athletic Complex to house intramural and recreational sports activities. The committee of students, staff, and alumni that he called together laid plans for what would eventually become the Fuller Callaway III Student Athletic Complex. Sam Williams (1967–68) was the first nonfraternity man to be student body president. Working through the Student Government and with city officials, Williams played a major role in Tech's community service efforts. John Hayes (1968–69) presided over the Student Council during the year when responsibility for many student activities was shifting from the YMCA to the new Student Center, and he played a constructive role in that difficult transition, to which we now turn.[57]

From the YMCA to the Student Center

The late 1960s witnessed a greater centralization of responsibility for campus activities under the dean of students and his staff and a lesser role for the various independent organizations that had previously provided much of the leadership for student affairs. This shift was dramatically illustrated by two interrelated events: the long-awaited completion of the Student Center and the severance of a seventy-year-old tie between the Institute and the Georgia Tech YMCA.

As early as 1939 students and faculty members had discussed the need for a student center. For years, Management Professor Fred Wenn and Dean of Students George C. Griffin had pushed for such a facility.[58] The YMCA's North Avenue Building, constructed in 1911, had long since been inadequate to accommodate all student activities, but the construction of a modern facility for recreation, dining, and student gatherings did not necessarily threaten the Y's influential position in the organization and implementation of student activities. Conceivably, the YMCA could have become the programmatic arm of the Student Center.

By the 1960s some members of the Tech community were questioning the appropriateness of such close ties between a state institution and the Young Men's Christian Association, regardless of the Y's nonsectarian stance. At that time student activity fees were still being allocated on a per capita basis to support the YMCA, and Tech held title to the YMCA building on North Avenue and to 192 acres of land on the Chattahoochee River near Roswell that was used primarily for Y functions.

Neither the movement to build a Student Center nor the potential for "church and state" conflict seriously threatened the YMCA's dominant position so long as Charlie Commander remained Y secretary and George Griffin was dean of students. Only months before Commander's death in 1967, when planning for the new Student Center was getting underway, President Harrison urged closer cooperation between the YMCA and the dean of students (who was to have administrative responsibility for the center), but Harrison wrote the chairman of the Y Board, "I see no reason why the YMCA should not continue to sponsor" the programs that it then managed.[59]

But after Commander's death in 1967 and Griffin's retirement in 1964, personal ties no longer reinforced the institutional linkage between Tech and the Y. Carlton Parker, who succeeded Commander, was an experienced YMCA executive but lacked Commander's personal rapport with Tech administrators. Griffin's successor, James E. Dull, believed that many of the functions long carried out by the YMCA should logically be under his administrative direction as dean of students.[60]

In 1968 Tech broke ground for the new Student Center and hired as director of the facility Timothy F. Mitchell, formerly director of the University Union at Eastern Illinois University. It became increasingly clear that the new Student Center was intended to be much more than a building or, as its promoters put it, "the living room of the Georgia Tech campus." It was also designed to assume many of the programmatic functions of the YMCA, including freshman orientation, recreational programs, lecture series, student-faculty relations, and community service.[61]

While the Student Center was still under construction, Mitchell began assembling a professional staff. Simultaneously, the Center's network of student committees was expanded, coordinated by a Student Center Governing Board. In May 1968 Fred Krefetz was named as the first president of the Student Center. The Student Center thus had in place a programmatic structure closely paralleling that of the YMCA.[62]

Perhaps inevitably, the shift in the coordination of many student activities from the Y to the Student Center became a matter of personal conflict, both within the YMCA staff and board of directors and between the Y and the central administration. (The Tech Y, although affiliated with the national YMCA, was governed by a local board of directors made up of faculty, students, and civic leaders. By 1969 its student members were assuming a more active role in the policy decisions.) As a temporary solution to the jurisdictional dispute, Acting President Crawford instructed the Tech YMCA staff to report to the dean of students beginning July 1, 1969, "in the interest of harmonious working conditions in the interim."[63]

The disputes over personnel and program jurisdiction were compounded by the effect of the Y's increasing financial insecurity. When in 1966 the Student Council won the right to allocate student activity fees, Student Council members began almost immediately to question the Y's entitlement to student funding. Furthermore, collections for the YMCA-sponsored World Student Fund were declining, and the Y board was from time to time forced into short-term borrowing to keep the World Student Fund afloat.[64]

During the summer of 1969 a committee of the Y board worked to establish a plan for reorganizing the YMCA in light of present conditions. A draft of that committee's recommendations called for the YMCA to concentrate on international programs (turning community service and leadership development over to the dean of students); to acknowledge that "control over any assets rests in the hands of the Institute, not the YMCA"; to forego any claim to student activity fees; and to report administratively to the dean of students. In October the report, supported by most of the student members, was defeated by the whole board. The board instead sent to

President Hansen a proposal that the YMCA receive state funding from Tech sufficient to pay staff salaries, that the Y executive report directly to the president, and that the YMCA board and the president "determine as rapidly as possible the origin and ownership of the . . . assets of the YMCA."[65]

President Hansen's decision in the matter made official the separation that many had anticipated. He directed that "the YMCA should become an autonomous organization with non-state funds being employed for the support of the staff and [that] the use of the YMCA facilities and buildings would continue as in the past until all matters relating to property and resources are settled."[66] The separation became effective on July 1, 1970. At the same time, allocations of student activity funds for the YMCA ceased. The following month, the new Student Center opened its doors.

As is often the case in legal separations, there was a property settlement to be made. YMCA officials were of the opinion that the organization could survive only by selling its interest in one or both of the properties, yet both ethical and legal questions obscured the issue of ownership. The Roswell property had been purchased with Y funds, and John D. Rockefeller had provided the funds for the North Avenue Building; however, both had been deeded to the University System and, by law, such a transfer was irrevocable.[67] For over two years lawyers for the YMCA and the Board of Regents discussed the matter of title. The attorney general of Georgia was asked for a ruling on Tech's right to enter into a lease arrangement with the YMCA. (The YMCA board had proposed to sell the Roswell land for the benefit of the Y and lease the North Avenue property from the Institute for a nominal sum.) The attorney general ruled that Tech should enter into no such agreement, for it involved a potential violation of church and state relations.[68] Finally, in August 1972, an agreement was reached whereby the Tech YMCA retained title to the Roswell property (it was subsequently sold) and the Institute retained the North Avenue property. Initially, Tech planned to level the 1911 Rockefeller Building, but, happily, it was refurbished in 1979, and renamed the L. W. ("Chip") Robert Faculty/Alumni House.[69]

After 1970 the Georgia Tech YMCA continued to function, albeit on a much reduced scale. Its principal program activity was administration of the World Student Fund scholarship program. In 1969–70 the questions of the YMCA's role in student affairs unfortunately became tangled with personal differences. In the heat of the moment that fact probably obscured the inevitability of change in the Y's historic role on the campus. For better or worse, the end of the Y's central place in campus life was representative of a new era in Tech's institutional history in which formal bureaucratic structures replaced a relaxed, informal network held together by long-standing relationships of friendship and trust.

The Organization of Research

The transition from informal arrangements to highly structured bureaucracy in the late 1960s and early 1970s was nowhere more evident than in the area of academic research. To be sure, the Georgia Tech Engineering Experiment Station had long been organized more or less along the lines of a not-for-profit research facility in which research and development was the "product" and modern management techniques were employed to maximize its output. But research on the academic side was another matter. While faculty groups such as the Research Club and Sigma Xi had long fostered research, and the central administration had with increasing urgency proclaimed its importance to the Institute, research in the academic units depended very much on the particular set of individuals involved and the professional imperatives of the disciplines that they represented.

At the end of the 1960s some schools had flourishing research groups and high expectations for scholarly performance, while in other units scholarly research, whether funded by external sources or not, played a minor role. Aerospace Engineering and Chemistry are representative of the schools that by 1970 had well-established research traditions. Although Aerospace conducted some work related to the space program, much of the research effort there was in the school's initial area of expertise under Montgomery Knight, rotary-winged aircraft. These efforts culminated in the 1970s with national recognition for the school's rotary-winged aircraft research. Unlike Aerospace, Chemistry did not have a cooperating arrangement with the Engineering Experiment Station in research. Pursuing funds through private foundations and federal agencies (particularly the National Institutes of Health and the National Science Foundation), the School of Chemistry developed strong research programs, especially in organic chemistry and much later in biochemistry. Research in the school was closely tied to a flourishing graduate program that by 1971 produced the highest number of doctorates (fourteen) of any unit in the Institute.[70]

The intellectual strength of a research university is, of course, to be found in the laboratories and studies of scientists and scholars. But at the end of the 1960s two organizational changes were taking place that would, along with other new developments in the 1970s, alter the character and velocity of research activity on the campus.

One was the organization at Tech in the 1960s of interdisciplinary research centers. The interdisciplinary team approach to research was increasingly popular in the 1960s and was advocated, in particular, on the Tech campus by Vice President Trabant. The first of these units, established in 1963, was the Water Resources Center, directed by Carl E. Kindsvater, professor of civil engineering. Supported by federal and some state funds, the Water Resources Center was in the 1960s the principal research facility at Georgia Tech that addressed problems of water pollution and other environmental issues. Renamed the Environmental Resources Center in 1970, it continued to play a leading role in environmental matters, increasingly focused on nuclear and health physics.[71]

A second interdisciplinary research unit, the Bioengineering Center, came into being in 1969.[72] Led initially by E. J. Scheibner, research professor of physics and head of the Physical Sciences Division of the EES, the Bioengineering Center tended to focus its efforts on development of prototype medical instrumentation and prosthetic devices.[73]

In their first few years of operation the interdisciplinary research centers had relatively little direct impact on the organization and conduct of research in the academic units. However in the 1970s and 1980s the interdisciplinary centers would be used as vehicles for coordination of research activities that Tech considered central to its mission.[74]

A second development at the end of the decade had a more immediate effect on academic research. When Hansen moved from the engineering dean's post to the presidency he picked as his successor Thomas E. Stelson, who had spent his entire academic career at Carnegie-Mellon University as a student, professor of civil engineering, and chairman of the civil engineering department. But he had also been extensively involved in engineering consulting and had worked with the Pennsylvania state government in developing transportation policies.[75]

Stelson arrived at Tech with a determination to upgrade research among the engineering faculty. He pressed the various engineering schools to increase their pursuit of "mission-oriented" research contracts, as well as more basic research of the sort supported by the National Science Foundation. The result was an immediate sustained increase in the level of research funding. However, not all of the faculty agreed with Stelson's approach and its wider application beyond the Engineering College. In the course of the institutional self-study conducted in 1972–73, the committee reviewing graduate programs reported: "There is a substantial belief among a part of the faculty that the Institute is pursuing the available dollar rather than projects which are actually desired and that the faculty is being subjected to pressure simply to bring in money."[76] The debate of which that report is a part did not begin with the coming of Dean Stelson (one hears echoes of the school culture–shop culture dispute of a century ago), nor did it end in 1973.

At the end of the 1960s much of the research and development activity at Tech (as measured in dollar value) was still conducted in or through the Engineering Experiment Station. Once again, the recurring conflict between the station and the "academic side" of the Institute erupted into a heated and public confrontation.

Underlying the conflict were old antagonisms over organizational and budgetary prerogatives, but new pressures brought matters to a point of confrontation. Even before the resignation of President Harrison, the chancellor and the Board of Regents were expressing a "growing concern" about the station's mission and relation to the Institute. Both from the chancellor's office and from other sources came encouragement to make the station more self-supporting from research and development contracts *and* to integrate the station more closely into academic programs, particularly at the graduate level—all this while continuing to provide technical assistance to Georgia industries.[77]

By 1970 both the station and Georgia Tech itself were suffering from the overall cutback in federal funds for military research and the space program. In addition, both had other problems that focused attention on the relationship between the station and Tech.

On the academic side, the impact of federal research cuts was compounded by the decline in federal support for graduate education in science and technology. This cutback, along with the ending of draft deferments for graduate students, led to an actual decline in graduate enrollment in 1969–70. The post-Sputnik boom in federal aid had passed, and simultaneously the growth in state funding for the Institute began to taper off. Furthermore, the long-recognized need to upgrade Tech's graduate programs had been given new impetus by the publication in 1966 and 1970 of reports evaluating graduate programs in American universities. Despite the dangers of oversimplifying the results of such reports, there are always pressures to reduce them to a set of rankings, on the order of football polls. When viewed in this light, Georgia Tech's graduate programs did not fare particularly well in the 1966 Cartter report, nor was there substantial improvement in the 1970 Roose-Anderson report.[78]

Similarly, the station faced problems that triggered a reconsideration of its basic operating procedures and relation to the Institute. Under the terms of its charter in 1919 and in its early years of operation, the station's mission had resembled that of the Agricultural Experiment Stations financed by the United States Department of Agriculture and operated by the nation's land grant colleges. That is, the EES, operating largely with state funds, conducted development and testing work for Georgia industry and provided technical assistance to firms in the state. This aspect of the station's work continued and expanded during the 1950s and 1960s through the efforts of the Industrial Development Division of the station and its field offices throughout the state. However, since World War II, the station had shifted more and more of its attention to electronics research and development, under contract to the federal government. Thus, the station increasingly resembled general not-for-profit research organizations such as Battelle Memorial Institute, Stanford Research

Institute, and the Illinois Institute of Technology Research Institute.[79]

With its base of state support and with the flush times for space and military research in the early 1960s, the Georgia Tech EES had been less aggressively "client-oriented" than had been some of the free-standing research institutes, which had elevated the cultivation of research and development contracts to the status of an art form. Thus, the cutback in federal funding, along with reductions in state funding in 1971, left the station in a seriously weakened position.

In the fall of 1970, President Hansen began to explore a bold and controversial solution to the problems of both the Institute and the station: the complete integration of the EES into Tech's academic units. Acknowledging the major legal and administrative difficulties involved in such a step, Hansen argued that if they could be overcome, the administrative absorption of the station would be highly beneficial. With closer ties to the educational side of the Institute, the station would be less vulnerable to questioning of its state support. On the other hand, the move would instantly improve Tech's standing with regard to research funding (the station's research budget would be included in the Institute's for evaluation purposes), graduate students would have more options for financial aid and for thesis projects in applied areas of research, and greater administrative efficiency would be achieved. Another consideration, not always stated in just this bald a fashion, was that absorption of the station by the Institute would give the Institute control over the reserve fund (said to exceed one million dollars) held by GTRI.[80]

On March 8, 1971, Vice President Crawford, to whom the station director reported, announced that Dean of Engineering Stelson was to take charge of the reorganization of the station. Although Stelson's publicly stated assignment was to recommend a plan for reorganization, the administration's basic intent was clear: closer integration of the station and the Institute.

Response from the station was equally clear. The director, Maurice Long, viewed the move as contrary to the EES charter and a usurpation of its administrative autonomy. Long had been named director in July 1969. A Tech graduate (both bachelor's and doctorate), he was a veteran of the station's electronics division who had been with the organization since 1946. Unlike most of his predecessors as head of the station, Long had not held faculty rank in one of the academic units.[81]

Long pointed out the legislatively conferred independence of the EES and contended that Tech officials lacked the authority to merge the two. Long requested a meeting with the Board of Regents to discuss the matter. Station personnel and business executives with close ties to the station protested to influential members of the legislature and to Governor Jimmy Carter. Not surprisingly, the in-house controversy found its way into the local press.[82] The conflict remained very much unresolved when Hansen announced on April 27 that he was resigning, effective July 1, to become president of his alma mater, Purdue University.[83]

The selection of James E. Boyd as acting president was strongly influenced by his unequaled qualifications for resolving smoothly the conflict over the station. Boyd was highly regarded both by the academic faculty (he had been a member of the physics faculty from 1935 to 1961) and by the EES staff. He had been a leading figure in the development of the station's radar-related research after World War II and had served as director between 1957 and 1961, moving from there to the presidency of West Georgia College and then on to the chancellor's office where he held a senior administrative position. When selected to serve as acting president, Boyd was still a member of the GTRI Board of Directors.[84]

With Boyd in charge, planning for the literal absorption of the station into the Institute did not go forward, but the basic objectives of closer control and more aggressive solicitation of contracts by Hansen remained in place. Dean Stelson was named assistant vice president for academic affairs on a temporary basis, retaining the title of engineering dean as well. Working with Vice President Crawford, Stelson was to continue as the administration's principal point of contact with the station.[85]

Discussions about future relations with the station continued during the spring and summer. In July some members of the University System Committee of the State Senate met on the campus with administrative officials to hear both sides of the argument. By that time the proposal to integrate the station and the Institute completely was moribund.[86]

Although the merger did not take place, the financial crisis of the station forced a shift in orientation in 1971–72 that would substantially alter the character of the EES. Compounding the impact of the decline in federal funds, in July 1971 the station lost almost half of its state funding. There were large-scale layoffs of research personnel, and the station was reorganized to make it more financially independent through concentration on solicitation of revenue-generating contracts. The shift can be seen in Director Long's annual report of 1972–73. Long began by defining the station as "a client-oriented research center supported primarily by Federal and industrial grants." He went on to note that "there are some persons within EES who found it hard to realize that the glorious days of the 1960s for sponsored research are gone. Increased synergism is helping some of these persons to learn to respond and grow with a radically changed environment for financial support."[87] Electronics work remained the bread and butter of the station throughout the crisis period, but the relative decline in funding for those activities meant that the station would have to look elsewhere for contracts. In the early 1970s that shift in funding led them more in the direction of environmentally related research, including the development of alternative energy sources. Later, the revival of military and industrial electronics funding would lead to the resurgence of these activities in the station.

Crisis in Athletics

Boyd's skills as a peacemaker would be called upon once more in his brief tenure as acting president, this time in an area far removed from the familiar terrain of the Experiment Station. As president, Boyd chaired the Board of Directors of the Georgia Tech Athletic Association. At the end of the 1960s Tech's intercollegiate athletic program had taken a turn for the worse, both financially and on the playing field.[88] Athletic Director and former Head Football Coach Bobby Dodd had warned for years of impending disaster. In his annual report of 1969, Dodd said, "We regard the future of the Georgia Tech Athletic Association with concern, even pessimism."[89]

Even allowing for some overstatement (the Athletic Association was at that point seeking permission to solicit funds directly from private sources), Dodd had evidence to support his gloomy predictions. The coming of professional football to Atlanta eroded attendance at Tech games, as did the Yellow Jackets' less than outstanding record in the 1960s. (Dodd's successor as head coach, Leon H. "Bud" Carson, had only one winning season in five years.)[90] These reductions in football revenue came at a time when the Athletic Association, which received no state funds, had incurred additional obligation for expansion of Grant Field. In 1970 the Faculty Senate, alarmed about the financial picture, asked for and received a detailed presentation regarding the Athletic Association. Once again, talk of deemphasizing athletics was in the air.[91]

This unhappy situation faced Boyd when he assumed the presidency in 1971. The financial difficulty of the entire athletic program was compounded by the increasing chorus of demands for the ouster of Coach Carson. No head football coach had ever been fired at Georgia Tech. In the history of Tech football only three men had held the job, and each in his own way had become legendary: John Heisman, William A. Alexander, and Bobby Dodd. Under the best of circumstances Carson would have faced difficulty in following the legendary "Grey Fox." These were far from the best of circumstances.

Carson's cumulative record of 27–27 after five seasons was enough to start the grumbling among alumni and fans. No matter that Coach Dodd had warned for years that rising academic standards and Tech's limited curriculum would make it more difficult to field competitive teams than in the glory days of the 1950s and 1960s. A more important point of contention (or so it was claimed) was Carson's personal style of coaching, which contrasted sharply with that of his predecessor. As stated discreetly in the *Alumni* magazine, "The difference seemed to be in a hard-nosed go-for-broke-and-win approach as opposed to the comparatively relaxed, conservative approach to football that had been typical of Dodd."[92] In private many alumni were more explicit, accusing Carson of mistreating and humiliating players, of exhibiting "unsportsmanlike conduct" during games, and a host of other wrongdoings.[93]

Alumni opposition to Carson reached a crescendo at the end of the 1971 season, in which the Yellow Jackets had a 6–6 record, including a humiliating Peach Bowl loss to the University of Mississippi. Atlanta sportswriters picked up the scent of trouble and began the public speculation about Carson's impending ouster. The press reports hastened, but did not fundamentally alter, the decision-making process. At a specially called meeting on January 8, 1972, the Athletic Association's Board of Directors considered the need for a coaching change. Charges against Carson had been presented to the board, most extensively in a forty-two-page document drawn up by an alumnus. However, several participants in the board meeting confirm Boyd's statement made that day that "the Board did not honor any such charges nor undertake to give credence to those charges, nor to conduct a trial based thereon."[94] The board voted not to renew Carson's contract, but agreed not to accept the resignation of Athletic Director Bobby Dodd, which had been tendered at the meeting.[95] Carson, who had been a successful and innovative defensive coach, went on to an outstanding career in professional football. On January 21, Boyd announced the appointment of Bill Fulcher as head coach. Fulcher, who had come to Tech as a walk-on player in 1952, had lettered on the 1953, 1954, and 1955 teams and had played briefly with the Washington Redskins. His career had included high school coaching jobs in Georgia, assistant coaching posts at Tech, and one year as head coach at the University of Tampa.[96]

The controversy over Bud Carson and his dismissal momentarily shifted attention away from the chronic problems of Tech's athletic program, but not for long. Even before the coaching change was made, President-elect Joseph M. Pettit wrote to a Tech alumnus: "For myself, as a newcomer, I feel a need for thorough evaluation of the whole athletic program, including but not limited to football, assessing its strength and potential for the future."[97]

The Financial Picture: Better But Not Good

The painful controversies that Georgia Tech endured between 1969 and 1972 and the rapid turnover in top leadership (four presidents in three years) no doubt took their toll on the Institute. Energies that might otherwise have gone to charting the long-term course were too often diverted in meeting immediate crises. Rapid changes in the top administration inevitably raised questions on and off the campus about Tech's future direction.

Nevertheless, the Institute came through those difficult years with much to be proud of. Tech had dealt constructively with its immediate neighbors in the midst of a major expansion program, it had modernized its undergraduate programs and set itself on a course of improvement in graduate education, and it had begun to resolve the long-standing controversy between the Institute and the EES, while at the same time expanding the role of research on the "academic side" of Georgia Tech. In the first part of this brief era, Tech's financial situation also looked bright. But, in retrospect, at the end of the 1960s Georgia Tech missed a rare opportunity to achieve the adequate level of state funding that had eluded it since the founding.

In the 1960s, for one of the few times in its history, the state of Georgia had both the economic resources and the political will to increase substantially its financial support of higher education. Governor Carl Sanders, working closely with the Board of Regents and Chancellor Simpson, began the surge of support for the University System that raised support to competitive levels for the first time in history. Lester Maddox, elected as Sanders's successor by special act of the legislature in 1967, initially disagreed with the regents over the increased level of University System funding for 1967–68 that was proposed by the outgoing governor. However, the disagreement was resolved in favor of the University System by the General Assembly under the leadership of George L. Smith. From that point on, Governor Maddox strongly supported the new level of funding. Maddox, who had grown up in the shadow of Georgia Tech and dreamed of going there, resolved to help make possible for a new generation the college education that he had missed. During his term, funding for the University System increased by one-third.[98]

Tech felt an immediate financial boost in 1967 and 1968, including $1 million in quality improvement funds divided among four schools, Chemistry, Physics, Aerospace Engineering, and Civil Engineering. In relative terms, however, Tech was losing ground. Between 1966 and 1971 the Institute's fractional share of the overall state appropriation for higher education dropped by one-third. The largest single beneficiary of the budgetary increase was the University of Georgia. Between 1966 and 1969, Tech's state support dropped from one-half to one-third the size of the University of Georgia, and its funding per student from equal to 38 percent less. The massive infusion of new funds into the University at Athens was entirely justified. As Simpson has noted, the state appropriations to the university were well below the amount called for under the Board of Regents' per capita formula. Tech could make no such claim at the time, although the formula itself gave greater weight to graduate than undergraduate students (and Georgia Tech's students were overwhelmingly in the latter category) and did not take into account the higher costs of scientific and technological education.[99]

Several factors contributed to the relative decline in support. Georgia was also building junior colleges all across the state and expanding its four-year colleges. Chancellor Simpson had as a top priority the elevation of both the University of Georgia and Georgia Tech into the top rank of American graduate and research institutions. Given the chance to put major new funding behind that intention, his first move was toward the university in order to bring it up to levels authorized by the University System's funding formula. By 1970 the growth spurt in funding for higher education was over, and enrollment at Tech had begun to decline (most sharply in fields related to the aerospace industry), making additional funding harder to justify. Budgetary cuts in 1970–71 brought a warning from Vice President Crawford that any additional reductions would force a choice between "whether to sacrifice some of the hard-won quality in the Institute's leading schools or to stifle the development of some of the emerging programs."[100]

Georgia Tech's new president, installed in 1972, thus arrived at a moment of missed opportunity. Unfortunately, the health of the economy and the financial well-being of public higher education in Georgia would get even worse. But the recurring shocks to the American economy in the 1970s would present opportunities as well as problems for an institution approaching its one hundredth birthday.

Chapter Ten

Toward the Second Century

Overleaf: The CALMA Chips 220 integrated circuit design system represents an important part of the very large scale integration systems research being carried on at the Microelectronics Research Center. (Courtesy of the Georgia Tech Office of Research Communications.)

On October 5, 1971, Chancellor Simpson announced the appointment of Joseph M. Pettit, dean of engineering at Stanford University, as Georgia Tech's eighth president. Paul Weber, who had served under all but the first three of Tech's presidents, responded by noting that while all the men who had led the Institute in the past had their particular areas of strength, "this man tops them all in experience and eminence in engineering education before coming to Tech."[1] Weber was not given to hyperbole, nor had he overstated the facts in this instance. At the time of his selection Pettit was president-elect of the American Society for Engineering Education, a member of the National Academy of Engineering (the only member at Tech or in Georgia), and the dean of one of the nation's most distinguished engineering schools.

What made Pettit particularly attractive to those involved in the selection process, including the chancellor, the Board of Regents and Governor Carter, was his record of accomplishment in precisely those areas wherein Georgia Tech needed strengthening—graduate education and research. In an interview at Stanford on the day his appointment was announced Pettit called Georgia Tech a "first class undergraduate school." Noting that graduate work was relatively new at Tech, he added: "strengthening these programs provides a very challenging opportunity to use what I've learned here and do it there."[2]

Pettit's sense of what a technological university should be derived from his lengthy career in engineering and engineering education.

Over that career loomed the shadow of his mentor and colleague, Frederick E. Terman. A brief sketch of Pettit's professional life and the way in which it was influenced by Terman's vision may help explain the course that he would chart for Georgia Tech.

Pettit was born in Rochester, Minnesota, in 1916, but spent much of his youth in Portland, Oregon. A boyhood interest in radios nudged him toward a career in engineering rather than medicine (his father had been a surgeon). Pettit graduated from the University of California at Berkeley in 1938 and then moved on to Stanford to pursue graduate studies in electrical engineering under Terman, who was already recognized as a leading figure in the field. Upon completion of his doctorate in 1942, Pettit joined his graduate advisor at the Radio Research Laboratory at Harvard University. Terman had been selected to head the nation's wartime research in radar countermeasures, and he chose his young Stanford protégé as one of his lieutenants. After the war Terman returned to Stanford as dean of engineering. Pettit and the research group that he had directed at Harvard worked briefly at the Airborne Instruments Laboratory in New York. But in 1947 Pettit returned to Stanford as an associate professor of electrical engineering and spent the next twenty-four years on the Palo Alto campus as professor and dean.[3]

During that era Stanford emerged as a premier research university in science and engineering and as a vital element in the government-university-industry network that by the 1960s was being called Silicon Valley. Several factors contributed to the growth of this western hub of high technology. The concentration of military research made the San Francisco Bay area a magnet for budding electronics firms after the war. Two crucial events in Palo Alto itself were the establishment in 1946 of the Stanford Research Institute (located just off campus, and tied administratively to the university) and the formation of Stanford Industrial Park (situated on university-owned land, it provided space for many of the new high-technology firms).[4]

Terman himself was a galvanizing force. Even before World War II he had encouraged his students (notably William Hewlett and David Packard) to launch their own electronics firms. After the war, when the armed services shifted much of their research and development activities out of government labs and into universities, Terman helped ensure that Stanford attracted a major share of the contracts. The commercialization of the knowledge thus created provided further stimulus for new firms (Varian Associates, for example, founded by a group that included two of Terman's students). By the end of the 1960s both Stanford University and large firms in the area, particularly Fairchild Semiconductor Corporation, had spun off so many new companies and were operating in such close cooperation with one another that observers began to speak of a "critical mass" of technological expertise, capable of triggering still more growth.[5]

The metaphor that Terman used to describe what was happening came not from physics but from history. Likening the mix of technological expertise and entrepreneurship to the communities of scholars who banded together in medieval European towns to form the first universities, Terman spoke of a "modern community of technological scholars," centered in "universities which have strong programs in engineering and science, surrounded by companies emphasizing research and development, under conditions where there is continual interaction among all of the components."[6]

The modern community of technological scholars that Terman helped build became national and even international in orientation. Particularly in the early years, however, its rationale and objectives were distinctly local and regional. Terman encouraged his students to begin their own firms on a shoestring (Hewlett and Packard began building audio-oscillators in Packard's garage) so that they would not have to leave the area to find engineering jobs. At its founding the Stanford Research Institute was heavily committed to regional economic development; in fact, it was referred to as the "Research Center of the West."[7] Terman's vision and Henry Grady's dream were cut from the same cloth.

This was the environment in which Pettit came into his own. As coauthor of a major book with Terman, as a junior colleague, and as his mentor's successor as dean, Pettit elaborated on the Terman model. He supervised graduate students (four of whom founded their own firms), presided over the continued improvement of Stanford engineering, initiated the Stanford Instructional Television Network, and strengthened ties between the Engineering School and industry.[8] In the process he gained a reputation as one of the leading figures in American engineering education. However, between the heady days of Silicon Valley's beginnings and the area's "discovery" in the 1970s as a center of America's high-technology growth industries, Terman's community of technical scholars became the object of sharp, even violent, opposition from students and faculty who objected to the university's involvement in military research and development.

Opposition first focused in 1969 on defense work in the Stanford Research Institute. Radicals demanded that the university either sever its ties with the Institute or convert it to "socially useful" research. In May of 1969 militants shifted their attention to on-campus classified research, seizing the Applied Electronics Laboratory (which was under Dean Pettit's jurisdiction) and holding it for a week. Subsequently, the university trustees cut Stanford's ties with the Research Institute (its corporate name was changed to SRI International), and the university faculty voted to phase out classified research on campus.[9] In the aftermath of the Cambodian crisis in 1970, protest turned to violence as campus buildings were stoned and set fire. In the fall of 1971, while Pettit was under consideration for the presidency of Georgia Tech, a faculty-student study charged that reliance on Pentagon funding was "skewing" academic research and called for closer screening of research contracts.[10]

Dean Pettit responded that only the Department of Defense provided substantial support for engineering research. He told the Faculty Senate, "We have gone ahead, seeking research support where it existed, and where the arrangements were fully compatible with the free conduct of the work." The charge that accepting Department of Defense contracts implicated Stanford in weapons development "simply isn't true," Pettit asserted. But the time he made that latter statement, he had accepted the presidency of Georgia Tech.[11] A technological and scientific institute in the South, where the height of antiwar sentiment was a peaceful memorial service following the Cambodia and Kent State crises, must have had considerable appeal. In fact, Pettit later acknowledged of those troubled times, "Georgia Tech was my kind of place."[12]

Pettit arrived in Atlanta to assume his duties as president in March 1972 and was officially installed in ceremonies on May 9. In his inaugural address, Pettit outlined his sense of where Georgia

Toward the Second Century

Tech stood and what it ought to be striving for. To the Tech community, his ideas were at once familiar and challenging:

> Within the diversified university system Georgia Tech has the possibility of optimizing its role as a technological university, attracting students who have aptitude for abstract and quantitative thinking and who are motivated toward careers in engineering, science, or modern management.... We can conduct students through programs leading to the higher levels of master's and doctor's degrees. We can contribute to knowledge in our own fields. Our disciplines are rapidly evolving; research is active and abundant. Our professors need research involvement to keep our teaching programs modern. Both professors and the students themselves in their advanced degree programs can contribute new knowledge generated from research, which can be one of the major contributions to the University System....
>
> [As for future curricular developments,] I think we should only expand our field of study to add disciplines which emerge from . . . our current areas of strength. Along with this "horizontal" expansion, we can expand "vertically" to add more students in master's and doctor's programs.... At the same time, along with our highest level programs, we also provide a category of more practically-oriented technology programs not elsewhere available in the state. This we have at our Southern Tech campus. Our four-year technology programs exemplify a growing sector on the national educational scene....
>
> Assuming that we can continue to justify the unique function of Georgia Tech in the University System, namely a primarily technological institution of high degree, realistically, this means first the recruiting and retaining of increasingly better faculty, because from this much will flow. Internally, we need to raise our standards for appointment, promotion, and tenure.... To bring the best faculty to our Georgia students, we have to compete nationally with good colleges elsewhere. To fulfill our local and regional functions, therefore, we must be a national institution.[13]

Following his recital of aspirations for the Institute itself, Pettit turned to the theme of regional development through technology that had so strongly shaped the history of the institution which he now headed: "If we are successful in this course of action, potential benefits to the city and state lie ahead. [There is] a high correlation between the presence of excellent high level educational opportunities in engineering and science . . . and the presence of a prosperous high technology industry.... A growing high technology industry would mean increased employment opportunities."[14]

The goals that Pettit set for Georgia Tech grew out of his own experiences as an engineer, educator, and academic administrator. They also coincided with the plans and aspirations that were by 1972 the official policy of Georgia Tech, although not universally accepted within the Tech community. The strengthening of graduate programs and research followed the example of Stanford and other leading universities. Doctoral programs were already in place in most of Tech's academic units, and graduate work was being given a higher priority, although some believed that such a shift meant trouble for Tech's undergraduate programs.

The sharp focus on technological and scientific degree programs seemed to Pettit consistent with the formula for excellence that Terman and President Wallace Sterling had employed at Stanford, that of establishing "steeples of excellence." As Terman put it in a line that Pettit enjoyed repeating years later, "You can't be good in everything, so you should pick a few things."[15] Tech's singular focus on technological and scientific degree programs dated to its founding, and it had been maintained in recent years, with the full support of Chancellor Simpson, to a greater degree than almost any institution of higher learning in America. However, the increasing importance of management, architecture, the natural sciences and mathematics, and (to a lesser degree) the humanities and social sciences on the campus had lessened the extent to which Georgia Tech was an engineering college, pure and simple.[16]

The upgrading of faculty quality was Pettit's top priority in 1972.[17] Nationally, the soft job market for doctorates in engineering, as well as in the sciences and humanities, aided Tech's faculty recruitment, as did the relative improvement of faculty salaries in the late 1960s and the growing recognition of Atlanta as an attractive place to live and work. Locally, Georgia Tech students had for several years asked that systematic evaluation of teaching be part of the tenure review (an innovation that Pettit had championed at Stanford), while a combination of administrative prodding and academic peer pressure was beginning to result in increased rates of scholarly publication and external funding.[18]

Finally, the translation of scientific and technological knowledge into regional economic uplift was an objective equally at home in the Silicon Valley of Terman and Pettit and the New South of Henry Grady and his spiritual heirs. For reasons that we shall explore later, in the early 1970s there was relatively little local interest in promoting technology-based industrial development: certainly much less than would be shown in succeeding years.

In the first years of the Pettit administration progress toward all the goals that Tech and its new president had set for themselves was threatened by a series of problems, to which we now turn.

Challenges of the Early 1970s

President Pettit's agenda for progress at Georgia Tech rested, in part, on a set of projections formed in the 1960s about the future course of higher education in America, particularly its science and engineering component. By the time Pettit arrived in Atlanta, however, the trend lines from which those projections had been extrapolated had taken an unexpected turn.

The "Goals of Engineering Education" study, conducted between 1963 and 1968, had projected a steady increase in the number of college students entering engineering study and a higher percentage of those students going on for advanced work at the master's and doctoral levels.[19] As director of the section of the study dealing with graduate education, Pettit lauded those trends and championed advanced training for engineers. At professional meetings and through engineering journals, he argued that a fifth year of study (whether called a master's degree or not) be required for the "basic" professional degree. Pettit further proposed that doctoral programs should be expanded and viewed as preparatory for industrial employment as well as for college teaching. Brushing aside the argument that graduate work was of little use for professional engineers, Pettit contended that "advanced-degree engineers function more fully as members of a technical profession than do engineers possessing only the bachelors degree."[20]

Pettit's views about advanced education for engineers did not prevail, either within the professional societies (most of whose members held only bachelor's degrees) or in the marketplace. Opposition to raising professional entry to the master's level carried the day, and, at the end of the 1960s, the decade-long rise in graduate enrollments turned to decline, in engineering and science as well as in other fields.[21]

Simultaneously, the highly publicized job shortages in technical fields precipitated by cutbacks in the space and military research programs triggered a nationwide decline in undergraduate engineering enrollments. As noted above in chapter 9, Georgia Tech had first experienced an overall enrollment drop in 1970–71. Between then and 1973–74, the student body declined by 7 percent with most of the decline coming in engineering. In the hardest hit school, Aerospace Engineering, enrollment dropped from 1,100 to 250 between 1970 and 1973.[22]

In his first annual report to the Board of Regents, President Pettit took note of the declining enrollment, but attempted to put it into national and historical perspective: "Our particular fields of study are currently less popular . . . [but] the tides of popularity change from decade to decade . . . and there is no question but that our technological society will soon bring a return of interest in the fields of study which Georgia Tech offers."[23]

In addition to the temporary problem of declining enrollments, Georgia Tech in the 1970s faced a more persistent problem in the erosion of state financial support. Two years before Pettit came to Tech, Georgia ranked fourteenth among the fifty states in per capita support for higher education, a distinction achieved through the surge of spending in the late 1960s. A decade later, however, the state had dropped to thirty-third. The main culprit was a stagnant national economy, plagued by spiraling inflation together with recurring recessions. This national decline seriously weakened the economy of the Southeast, which in the previous two decades had begun to reverse centuries-old patterns of impoverishment.

In Georgia, where the state constitution forbade governmental deficit spending, public funding for higher education was extremely sensitive to short-term economic fluctuations and generally incapable of keeping up with the inflationary spiral. Furthermore, higher education in Georgia fared less well than it had in the 1960s in competing for scarce state dollars. A particular quirk in the formula for allocating funds within the University System further reduced

Tech's state support. Budgetary allocations for the various colleges were reduced by the amount of income that each anticipated for the coming year, including "indirect income" or "overhead" produced by research grants and contracts. A faculty committee studying Tech's financial affairs for the institutional self-study in 1973 said of the practice: "This is eminently unfair and serves as a deterrent to the Institute's quest for outside funding."[24]

The effects of this financial erosion were not felt all at once. In fact, during the period of declining enrollments (1970–74) Tech actually maintained its fractional share of state funds for higher education and experienced an increase in support per student. As the decade wore on, however, the cumulative effect of slowly rising state aid (in 1975 there was an actual decline), along with skyrocketing inflation, created serious strains. In the midst of the major recession of 1974–76, Vice President Crawford, who had served Tech for twenty-six years, reported to the regents: "Many people who have been at Tech for a lengthy period . . . consider the 1975–76 academic year to have been the most difficult year in their experience."[25]

Funds for equipment and capital improvements were slashed, leaving the Institute without resources to modernize its laboratory facilities, much less to construct new buildings, and in two out of five years statewide salary freezes affected University System faculty and staff along with other state employees. Faced with declining revenues, Chancellor Simpson opted to concentrate available funds in salaries rather than equipment and capital improvements. While this may have made faculty and staff members grumble somewhat less than they otherwise would have, it worked a particular hardship on institutions such as Georgia Tech where scientific laboratory equipment was in constant need of updating.[26]

One victim of the financial squeeze in the 1970s (and of changing federal priorities as well) was the further expansion of the campus and the addition of new buildings. The Perkins and Will plan of 1965 had projected a 400-acre campus by 1985. In 1971, total campus size was 255 acres, but the boom in land acquisition had ended. In the next seven years Tech purchased only small parcels within the Perkins and Will area, using endowment and other internal funds for almost all of it.[27]

Only two major buildings were constructed during the 1970s. In

1973 the campaign for a student athletic complex, launched in 1968 by Student Body President Carey Brown, finally paid off. The Board of Regents allocated $2.5 million toward its construction, and the Callaway Foundation contributed a like amount. When completed in 1977, the facility was named the Fuller Callaway III Student Athletic Center, in memory of a Tech graduate of 1952 who had died in 1971. Managed by the Physical Education and Recreation Department, the center provided modern facilities for both individual recreation and for many of the popular intramural athletic programs.[28]

At the beginning of the decade the top academic priority for construction had been a "Systems Science" Building to house the College of Management and the School of Industrial and Systems Engineering. Second on the list was a new Architecture Building. Both the College of Management and the School of Architecture were seriously overcrowded at the time. In 1974, President Pettit reversed the order of priority, and the Board of Regents allocated funds for preliminary work on the Architecture Building. For months prior, architecture students, their parents, and alumni had lobbied regents and legislators for construction of the new building. (Architecture labs were at that time crowded into several buildings scattered around the campus.) On two occasions architecture students had even staged sit-in demonstrations in the labs to express their concerns. Of greater weight in the decision was the fact that in a 1971 review of the school, architecture was threatened with the loss of its accreditation because of, among other things, inadequate space.[29]

In addition to problems of enrollment and funding, Pettit was faced immediately with the unresolved controversy over Tech's relationship with the Engineering Experiment Station. Under Acting President Boyd's leadership the public furor had subsided, but the basic structural problems remained. Furthermore, personal animosities had reached such a point that there was some sentiment in the station for a complete break with the Institute.

Even before his arrival on campus, Pettit indicated that the organization of research and the "optimum mode of operation" for the station were uppermost in his mind. Having recently witnessed the separation of Stanford University and Stanford Research Institute, he was determined that Georgia Tech's EES should remain directly on the campus and work in harmony with the Institute.[30]

President Pettit continued the temporary administrative arrangement initiated by Boyd, whereby Dean Stelson doubled as an assistant vice president to coordinate research activities. As such, Stelson oversaw the painful reduction in EES staff and the internal reorganization in March 1972 that oriented the station toward more aggressive pursuit of contract work. The reorientation produced quick financial results, and the value of contract research increased sharply throughout the 1970s. Although electronics work continued to be the mainstay, the station responded in the 1970s to increased federal and state support for environmentally related research and development, including biomass conversion and solar energy. At the end of the 1970s and beyond, Georgia Tech was a major beneficiary of increased spending for research and development by the Department of Defense, whose funding supported not only Tech's traditionally strong military electronics work, but also research efforts in the EES and the academic units ranging from Electrical Engineering to Mathematics and Psychology. In the mid-1980s, Department of Defense funds accounted for over one-half of the total external research funding in the Institute.[31]

In 1975 Maurice Long retired as director of EES. After an interim period in which Stelson presided over the station, Donald J. Grace was named director in 1976. Grace came to Tech directly from the University of Hawaii where he had headed the Center for Engineering Research; however, he had spent most of his career at Stanford University. After taking his doctorate there in electrical engineering in 1962, he held joint appointments on the faculty of electrical engineering and the staff of the Systems and Techniques Laboratory. He subsequently directed that lab and served as associate dean under Pettit before going to Hawaii in 1969.[32]

The confrontation between the station and the Institute's central administration proved to be something of a standoff. Hansen's plan for the wholesale integration of EES functions into the academic units died quietly. At the same time, the station's much-heralded legislative autonomy proved to be a moot point. The station *was* administratively accountable to the president of the Institute. The need to clarify that line of reporting contributed to a significant administrative realignment in 1974.

In February of that year, President Pettit announced the creation of a new administrative position, vice president/research, and the appointment of Stelson to the post.[33] The creation of a research vice presidency had been discussed as early as the Van Leer administration (see above, chapter 7), and in the intervening years Tech's presidents had employed a variety of administrative devices to stimulate research activity on the campus. In recent years, as we have noted, Acting President Boyd and President Pettit had assigned Stelson to a research coordinating role as temporary assistant to the academic vice president. In addition, Stelson was at that point being courted for the presidency of another technological university, a circumstance that affected at least the timing, if not the fact, of his promotion to such a strategic post at Georgia Tech.[34]

In the new administrative arrangement, the EES and the Office of Interdisciplinary Programs reported directly to Stelson, and he controlled the financial side of research administration, including the allocation of state research funds and indirect revenues from research contracts, in academic units as well as in the EES. From this financial vantage point Stelson moved aggressively to promote more contract research in academic units campuswide, as he had already begun to do in the Engineering College. His carrot-and-stick approach involved allocating state funds in proportion to indirect revenues brought in.

The pressure on professors to become more research-oriented was part of an overall effort to upgrade the quality of the faculty. President Pettit pressed for more thorough evaluation of candidates for reappointment and tenure, as well as greater care in the initial appointment of faculty members. He insisted on reviewing the files in all such cases himself. In addition to the directive to fill faculty positions with research-oriented professors, in the early 1970s department heads were discouraged from hiring faculty members whose highest degrees were from Georgia Tech, which was common practice before that time.[35]

Tech's effort to raise faculty standards did not, of course, begin with the arrival of Pettit. The year before he came, for example, three endowed chairs were filled with well-known scholars from other universities, but there was a notable shift in faculty review procedures. The 1973 self-study acknowledged that "faculty tenure is in a state of disarray," with no clear understanding of who held tenure. Changes instituted on the campus by Pettit and in the University System as a whole had by 1975 systematized appointment and tenure procedures.[36] The results, when measured in the most accessible terms, were impressive. By 1975, 77 percent of the faculty held doctorates, as compared to 51 percent ten years earlier. Research funding in the academic units more than tripled between 1971 and 1976.[37] Qualitative assessment of these changes would prove to be more difficult.

The administration's effort to raise faculty standards and to emphasize heavily external research funding met with mixed reaction. Although many welcomed efforts to enhance academic quality, the managerial style employed to achieve it was less well received. Furthermore, the very change in the faculty brought about by the new policies was itself a source of tension. Many of the new professors brought with them expectations for institutional support that could not be met in the early 1970s. All this was happening within the unsettling context of declining engineering enrollments nationwide and of a topsy-turvey economy in which faculty salaries were caught in an inflationary squeeze.

Never at Georgia Tech had there been a strong tradition of faculty governance, but in the 1970s faculty frustrations were focused rather sharply on the upper administration. In the 1973 self-study no fewer than four faculty committees made a point of criticizing administrative practices, particularly for developing new policies without significant faculty involvement.[38] A faculty evaluation of top administrators conducted by the campus chapter of the American Association of University Professors was equally critical. Forty-one percent of the faculty participated in issuing "grades" for administrators that, had they belonged to students, would have left almost all of them on academic probation.[39]

Academic Vice President Crawford acknowledged the strained campus relations in his annual report of 1976: "As real as our needs for additional fiscal resources are, they may rank second in importance to the intangible but no less real need for a sense of community within the Institute." This long-term member of the Tech community pledged that a primary goal of his would be "to work toward the restoration of the once prevalent belief that we are all seeking a common good, an academically excellent Georgia Tech, and that we can pursue it with complete confidence in the motives and integrity of one another."[40]

Two innovations in the 1980s may be viewed as efforts to improve the flow of information between faculty and administration. One, instituted by President Pettit, is the ongoing survey and evaluation of administration and management known as the Georgia Tech Organizational Leadership Development Project (GOLD), conducted by the Higher Education Management Institute (HEMI) of the American Council of Education. The other innovation, initiated by the faculty with strong encouragement from the president, was a restructuring of the Academic Senate and General Faculty into a representative system of faculty governance. Both projects were undertaken with high expectations. At this writing it is too soon to know what their full impact will be.

New Initiatives, New Faces

Despite its various difficulties in the early 1970s, Georgia Tech moved ahead with new academic initiatives, all related to the Institute's traditional areas of strength. At the same time, the groundwork was being laid for some decided breaks with tradition in Tech's athletic program in the years after the Bobby Dodd era.

Changes in the academic program included subtractions as well as additions. The sharp reduction of required courses in engineering graphics in 1973 marked the end of an era. Among the thousands of students who had struggled through drawing courses had been a president of the United States and a United States senator.[41] With encouragement from Thomas Stelson, dean at that time, Tech followed the national trend in deemphasizing drawing courses. The objection raised to the change by the head of the graphics department, a member of the faculty for thirty-three years, contained an echo from the days of Isaac Hopkins and Nat Harris. Such courses were still needed by Tech graduates, he argued, because of the underdeveloped state of industry in the Southeast, where the engineer still needed to be a "jack of all trades."[42] Another victim of curricular moderniziation in 1973 was the degree in general management. The change was part of a larger initiative to align Industrial Management more closely with the science- and mathematics-based curricula in engineering.[43]

The Architecture School underwent the most sweeping curricular change of any unit during the early 1970s. The architecture profession, unlike engineering, had agreed to make the master's the first professional degree. With prompting from the same 1971 accreditation report that had stressed the need for more laboratory and studio space, the architecture faculty proposed a "4 + 2" curriculum to bring Tech into compliance with the profession's national standards. Under this curriculum, which was approved in 1973, students received an undesignated bachelor's degree at the end of four years and then completed two years of graduate work before receiving the degree master of architecture.[44] In 1975, the School of Architecture, historically situated within the College of Engineering, became the Institute's fourth college. With the retirement of Paul M. Heffernan, long-time director of the school and designer of a number of campus buildings, William L. Fash of the University of Illinois was named dean of architecture.[45]

Even with the removal of Architecture, the Engineering College remained Tech's largest. In 1974 William M. Sangster succeeded Stelson as engineering dean. In 1967 Sangster had come to Tech as director of civil engineering from the University of Missouri at Columbia. In the same year that he was named dean, Sangster was honored with the presidency of the American Society of Civil Engineers. Sangster became the first Tech professor named to the presidency of one of the founding engineering societies in the 1970s, the second being Stothe P. Kezios, director of mechanical engineering, who was president of the American Society of Mechanical Engineers in 1977.[46]

These new administrative faces on the "hill" were matched by new athletic leadership on the "flats." But no matter how striking the rapid turnover in coaches and athletic directors during the 1970s, a transformation of the financing, administration, and orientation of Georgia Tech's athletic program that began in those years was of more lasting significance.

The financial troubles to which Dodd had pointed for years were very real. Information available to Pettit when he assumed the presidency indicated that if current trends continued the Athletic Association would face financial ruin within five years.[47] In 1973 Pettit convened a panel of athletic directors from the Universities of Miami, Delaware, and North Carolina to review Tech's program and recommend changes that would put it on a sound financial footing. (The visiting athletic director from Chapel Hill was Homer Rice, who became Tech's director seven years later.) The panel proposed direct solicitation from alumni (which Dodd had long requested) and priority seating at football games for major contributors. They further recommended that an athletic fee be levied on all students. The panel also strongly recommended that Tech rejoin a conference so as to share in pooled revenues from bowl and television appearances. The opportunity to keep all of Tech's bowl and television earnings had been a strong incentive when the Yellow Jackets had left the Southeastern Conference during the Dodd heyday, but the football shoe was now on the other foot.[48]

Direct solicitations through the Alexander-Tharpe Fund began in 1974, as did the use of priority seating as an incentive for giving. Both initially triggered complaints from alumni and friction with the Alumni Association's annual fund-raising efforts.[49]

In 1975 Tech joined the Metropolitan Collegiate Athletic Conference, consisting largely of former members of the Missouri Valley Conference with strong basketball traditions. The newly formed Metro Conference held championship competition in basketball but not in other sports, including football. The conference included none of Tech's traditional regional or intersectional rivals, and conference membership did not alleviate Tech's financial problems; however, no further change in the Yellow Jackets' conference status would come about until after some important personnel changes had been made.

Immediately following the 1973 football season Head Coach Bill Fulcher resigned, after only two years in the job. His decision was, by all accounts, unforced. With the urging of Bobby Dodd the Athletic Association Board quickly named Tech alumnus Franklin C. "Pepper" Rodgers as Fulcher's successor.[50] Rodgers, an Atlanta native, had first viewed Tech football games as a boy scout usher at Grant Field. After a varsity career at Tech in the 1950s, Rodgers enjoyed a successful coaching career, including head coaching jobs at the University of Kansas and UCLA. In 1974, he brought his flashy personality and successful wishbone offense to Atlanta in what promised to be a long stay at his alma mater. Neither the wishbone nor the personality had the desired effect.

After six seasons Rodgers's teams posted a record of 34–31–2 (including a 4–6–1 mark in 1979). That record, along with what some considered to be an excessively flamboyant style, cost Rodgers his job. A month after the 1979 season had ended the Athletic Association Board announced that "in the best interest of Georgia Tech, with full respect to Coach Pepper Rodgers, a change should be made in the position of head football coach." Although the manner and timing of Rodgers's dismissal took most within the Tech community by surprise, it was less a matter of contention than the firing of Bud Carson had been in 1972. It did, however, result in a lawsuit filed by Rodgers against the Athletic Association for breach of contract with regard to certain "fringe benefits" associated with the head coaching job. The case, which might have led to a landmark decision regarding the status of football coaches, was resolved after lengthy litigation through an out of court settlement.[51]

In 1976, Bobby Dodd reached what was for University System employees the age of mandatory retirement. The Athletic Association had no comparable rule and Dodd was not eager to retire, but he agreed to step down, after forty-six years at Tech. The naming of his replacement came as a surprise. Although the current assistant athletic director was Dodd's personal choice and had seemingly been groomed for the job, the board selected Douglas Weaver, then athletic director at Southern Illinois and former assistant coach to Pepper Rodgers at Kansas and UCLA.[52]

During his four-year stay as athletic director (he left to become athletic director at his alma mater, Michigan State, in 1980), Weaver presided over a change that would have sweeping implications for the future of Tech's athletic program. Tech expressed interest in rejoining the SEC, but was rebuffed because the SEC did not wish to expand beyond its ten member size. The ACC, which had recently become a seven-member conference with the withdrawal of the University of South Carolina, was more interested. Not only was Tech academically compatible with most of the ACC schools but, as one conference athletic director pointed out, admission of Georgia Tech would give the conference entrance to television markets from Washington, D.C., to Atlanta.[53]

In 1978 Georgia Tech withdrew from the Metro Conference and joined the ACC. The sports editor of the student newspaper expressed the feelings of a good many alumni and students just before the decision was made when he urged that Tech not join the ACC. He thought that the Yellow Jackets could not hope to compete in basketball against the ACC's perennial national contenders, while in football, "Georgia Tech would probably finish in the top two or three every year. . . . Beating Virginia or Wake Forest isn't the same as beating Tennessee or Auburn. Clemson isn't even a thrill since they have good teams once in a blue moon."[54]

The editorial illustrates the perils of journalistic forecasting (Clemson promptly won a national championship in football; Tech did not soon reach the top of the ACC standing in football but quickly established itself as a legitimate contender in basketball under Coach Bobby Cremins). More important, the editorial also suggests, at least by implication, the change in orientation called for in the decision to join the Atlantic Coast Conference. The ACC was not only a strong basketball conference, but it also had a history of strong competition in "minor" intercollegiate sports. Georgia Tech's decision to join the ACC signaled a shift away from the Institute's long-standing athletic concentration on football and a commitment to improve sports programs across the board.

Growing Pains: Student Life in Tech's Tenth Decade

In 1973, at a low point in Tech's enrollment, the various vice presidents and deans, along with the registrar, predicted that enrollment would hold steady in the next few years at 8,200 to 8,600 students.[55] Their projection may even have been wishful thinking (enrollment that year had dropped to around 8,000), but in fact, Georgia Tech, like other professional schools across the country, was on the verge of a boom. In 1974 enrollments began to grow, and by 1982 the number of students had jumped to 11,393, an increase of 42 percent over the low point of 1973.[56]

In some respects, the student profile remained remarkably constant during the rapid rise in enrollment. Between 1972 and 1982 the ratio of undergraduate to graduate students held constant at about five to one. Approximately 60 percent of the students were from Georgia, and the fraction of those who came from metropolitan Atlanta and the state's other largest cities increased slightly (to around 77 percent in 1976). The dramatic shift in the student body during those years came in the number of women and black students. Between 1972 and 1976 the number of women doubled, and by 1980 it had doubled again. In 1982, 2,421 women were enrolled, approximately 20 percent of the total. The number of black students also increased dramatically from fewer than 100 in 1972 to 700 in 1982.[57]

The increase in black and women students in the 1970s was, again, in line with the national trend. The increase, however, also reflected a shift within Tech from *accepting* women and minority students to actively recruiting them. Associate Dean of Engineering William Schutz led an aggressive recruiting effort to attract both women and black students. Schutz also served as coordinator of the Institute's "three-two" program, in which after five years the student received a degree from a liberal arts college and an engineering degree from Georgia Tech. Although it dated back to 1954, the program was drastically expanded in the late 1960s and early 1970s to include a number of historically black and women's colleges. In 1968 and 1969 first Morehouse College and then the other undergraduate institutions of the Atlanta University Center established three-two programs with Georgia Tech. In 1974 the first students from the Atlanta University Center completed dual degree programs.[58]

In the 1970s the number of campus organizations open to women multiplied. In 1969 and 1970 ROTC programs first began recruiting women. In 1973 the campus's second sorority was founded (Alpha Gamma Delta), and the Tech student section of the Society of Women Engineers was reactivated with Helen E. Grenga of the metallurgy faculty serving as faculty advisor. The following year the Student Center Activities Committee announced that it would no longer charter organizations which discriminated against women. Change came more slowly in athletics. Women's basketball began as an intramural and club sport in the 1970s. By 1975 the team received token support from the Athletic Association and the Student Government and was coached by Jim Culpepper, intramural director. In 1981 women's basketball became a funded intercollegiate sport, and that year Bernadette McGlade, a former All-American athlete at the University of North Carolina, was hired as coach.[59]

By the late 1970s women students were much more integrated into campus life than in the previous twenty years of coeducation. By 1982, 57 percent of the women students were majoring in engineering, as compared to 34 percent in 1972. (Typically, 70 percent of all men students are engineering majors at Tech.) In 1977 women students won or shared the top two awards at Honors Day, and in 1978, Amy Wepking became the first woman to be elected student body president.[60] Tech remained predominantly a men's institution, but less decisively and militantly so.

While women were generally accepted into the mainstream as they increased in numbers, the same was not altogether true for black students. To be sure, at the personal level racial integration of the student body and most of its organizations proceeded during the 1970s (Hamilton Barksdale was elected SGA vice president in 1978), but divisions continued. The fraternity-sorority system remained almost all white until the establishment of black fraternities and sororities in 1978. The Georgia Tech Afro-American Association, established in 1968, remained a focal point of black student life, along with the National Society of Black Engineers, founded in the mid-1970s.[61]

In 1975 and again in 1979 the GTAAA presented grievances concerning campus conditions for blacks to the administration. The discussions in 1979, led by Francine McCauley and Merlin Todd, focused on a student request for establishment of an office of minority affairs. Prior to that time, Professor Dorothy Cowser Yancy of the Department of Social Sciences had served as unofficial faculty advisor for black students. Although President Pettit initially expressed reservations about the need for an arrangement of the size originally demanded, the Office of Minority Educational Development was established in 1980 with Thomas Parker of the Counseling Center serving as interim director.[62]

Except for presentation of grievances by black students, there was little evidence of student protest on the Tech campus during the

1970s. In this regard Tech in the 1970s more closely resembled the national norm than it had in the tumultuous 1960s. A small number of students continued to channel their social concerns into community services coordinated by the Student Center staff and religious organizations. During the decade student interests in environmental issues and alternative energy could be detected in various activities, including award-winning solar energy projects entered in the 1977 Student Competition for Relevant Engineering at Washington State University and demonstrations of various alternative energy systems at Tech's first "Sun Day" in 1979.[63]

Tech students did reveal some emotion and much of their anatomy when the "streaking" craze hit the campus in 1974. The first reported incident occurred on a February evening when two students clad only in ski masks and scarves dashed through a crowded chemistry class. Two weeks later Tech students claimed a record for the largest number of streakers. On two separate evenings a bare multitude of six hundred paraded around the campus ("milling" more accurately describes their pace than "streaking"). President Pettit issued the obligatory stern warning—"the Institute cannot and does not condone this behavior"—but the streaking craze was allowed to fade away without administrative intervention.[64]

On a more prosaic note, traditionally strong campus organizations held their own or gained ground in the 1970s. ROTC continued its recovery, fraternity-sorority membership stabilized at just over 20 percent of the student body, and the intramural athletic program continued to attract a substantial percentage of the students. In fact, a survey conducted by the University of Pittsburgh in 1977 rated Georgia Tech's intramural program among the nation's top 5 percent in the level of student participation.[65]

In the late 1970s and early 1980s the student government and other campus organizations mobilized students politically around campus issues. Not since the gubernatorial campaign of 1942 had Tech students been so directly involved in state politics on matters of interest to the Institute. In 1980 the Student Government Association launched a lobbying campaign in support of funding for a new dormitory. (The rapid expansion in enrollment had strained the housing system to the breaking point.) Although neither President Pettit nor the chancellor believed the dormitory should have top priority, the student lobbying effort was so effective with regents, legislators, and the governor, that Tech received funding for the dorm *and* the Institute's top academic building priority, the long-delayed Management/Industrial and Systems Engineering Building.[66]

Two other student projects, though lacking the immediate success of the dorm campaign, demonstrated student interest and skill in public advocacy. In 1981–82 the Student Government Association sponsored a study of the quality of undergraduate education at Georgia Tech. The report, entitled *A Question of Priorities: The Status of Georgia Tech Academics,* concluded that "the quality of a Georgia Tech education has slipped in the past decade and continues to decline." The report, which placed the blame on inadequate state financial support to the Institute, was used by students lobbying for increased appropriations and by other members of the Tech community wishing to make the same point.[67] In 1983–84 the SGA produced a "high-tech" exhibit that demonstrated Georgia Tech's contributions to the state through research and education. The exhibit was prominently displayed in the state capitol office complex and, like the academic priorities report, was used as part of a lobbying campaign to overcome what the students perceived as a lack of public support. These expressions of student concern about the quality of their education differed from student statements a decade before. In the 1980s version the source of the problems was located outside the Institute, in the funding priorities of the state, whereas in the late 1960s the focus of student concern was on how the Institute could reform itself. Both the students and the times had changed.

Academic Life in the Tenth Decade

Crowded classrooms and inadequate laboratories were, as the SGA survey noted, a fact of life in the early 1980s. Between 1974 and 1982 the ratio of students to instructional faculty rose from 15.8:1 (which was considered too high for a graduate and research-oriented university) to 21.6:1. The concentration of enrollment growth in a few areas (particularly electrical and mechanical engineering and computer science) sent class sizes in the most popular majors zooming upward at a time when the national shortage of qualified faculty in these fields made recruitment difficult. Increased student demand, plus greater faculty involvement in sponsored research (labeled "peddle or perish" by one student editorialist) meant that more and more of the teaching was done by graduate assistants. The faculty committee evaluating educational programs for the 1983 institutional self-study concurred with the SGA report of the previous year: "Every measure of quality which this committee has investigated clearly demonstrates that the instructional program has deteriorated in the past ten years."[68]

More than one explanation was offered on the campus for this state of affairs. The SGA report was one eloquent statement of the view that Georgia Tech was not getting its fair share of state resources. In a 1981 letter to the regents, President Pettit made the same point when he again called attention to the budgetary procedure that seemed to penalize Tech for attracting sponsored research: "We cannot help but feel that . . . this internally generated support has resulted in a decrease in the state appropriation which we would otherwise be entitled to." Compounding this problem was the fact that in 1982 and 1983, for the second time in less than a decade, a major recession reduced the amount of state funds from which Tech hoped to take a reasonable share.[69]

The 1983 self-study acknowledged that "there are those who contend that the resources available are not adequate to provide the quality of education which has been available to our students in the past," but added, "a second contention is that a dynamic institution such as Tech will never have adequate resources and the issue is one of resource management." Some members of the faculty believed that the undergraduate enrollment should never have been allowed to grow so rapidly. Others pointed out that while enrollment was increasing by over 30 percent (1976–81) the size of the instructional faculty remained almost constant, but administrative personnel increased by 38 percent. The self-study labeled this trend "disquieting." The campus community was painfully aware that in 1980, 1981, and 1983 unanticipated internal budgetary shortfalls ranging from $600,000 to over $1 million caused further financial distress. When enough time has passed to render objective historical judgment on the two contentions noted in the self-study, both may prove to have some merit.[70]

By the mid-1980s some relief was in sight. Relatively more state funds were being channeled into laboratory equipment (reversing a decade-long trend in University System budgeting), and, as in the days of Lyman Hall, private firms were easing the burden with contributions of advanced equipment, ranging from microcomputers to the makings of a major teaching and research facility in Computer Aided Design/Computer Aided Manufacturing. In the wake of the microcomputer revolution of the 1980s, computers were increasingly integrated into the instructional program in areas ranging from engineering, physics, computer science, and mathematics (all of which had pioneered in the instructional use of computers) to the humanities and social sciences. Undergraduate enrollment leveled off and then declined somewhat by 1983, due in large measure to the establishment of enrollment ceilings in the most popular major fields. Admissions officers and others interested in curbing the growth also looked forward to the end of the 1980s when the post–"baby boom" generation would have reached college age, thereby reducing the pool of potential students in the 18–21 age bracket. The experiences of the preceding decade, however, should make the historian, as well as the admissions officer, wary of predictions.[71]

Since the arrival of Pettit as president and even before then, Tech's long-range goal had been to hold undergraduate enrollments steady or let them decline slightly, while substantially increasing the number of graduate students, particularly at the doctoral level. Neither term of that ratio behaved as expected. Although the number of graduate students at the master's level grew by two-thirds between 1969 and 1981, the number of doctoral students remained constant, and the number of doctorates awarded declined by 10 percent before turning upward slightly. The fact that these figures were consistent with national trends in science and engineering did not lessen their impact. In 1982 Demetrius Paris, director of the School of Electrical Engineering, was commissioned to review the status of graduate studies and to recommend steps for improving the situation. In his report Paris noted that since 1973 the fivefold increase in sponsored research in the academic units had not been matched by a corresponding increase in graduate degrees awarded: "Emphasis must be placed on achieving substantial growth in high quality student centered research, on effecting better linkages between graduate students and research funds, and on creating an amiable environment for faculty and graduate students." In line with his assessment, and similar views expressed elsewhere on the campus, administrative leaders were by the mid-1980s developing plans for improving graduate education, several of which would be recognized by anyone familiar with the Institute's recent history. They included an administrative reorganization to link graduate education and research more closely, and increased use of EES projects for graduate student employment and thesis research.[72]

The Paris report raised an important question about the qualitative measurement of research, a question also raised in many quarters on the campus. The faculty committee that evaluated research for the 1983 self-study expressed frustration at the lack of agreement on criteria for evaluating research and the scarcity of information on faculty research other than dollar value of sponsored projects. President Pettit raised the same concern in 1983 when he noted his research vice president's "responsibility to foster research, not dollars as such. How should we measure it? How much progress have we made in the past decade?"[73] While the questions Pettit raised have as yet no definitive answer, this much is clear: Georgia Tech had, by its centennial year, come a long way from the time when almost all "research" was conducted in the EES and was concentrated in a handful of applied areas. By the mid-1980s Tech faculty were engaged in activities ranging from the most basic scientific research to development and commercialization of new technologies, from interdisciplinary work in electronics and biotechnology to scholarly publication in the humanities and social sciences. In scope and quality, those efforts defied measurement on any single scale.

The hoped-for growth in graduate education would come, if at all, in existing areas of strength, for Tech launched only a few graduate programs in its tenth decade. New doctoral programs were authorized in applied biology and architecture (the latter making Tech one of only a handful of institutions offering a doctorate in that field). A master's program in technology and science policy was established in the School of Social Sciences, and several interdisciplinary master's degrees were initiated. But in 1982 the School of Health Systems was merged back into Industrial and Systems Engineering, and in 1983 one of the Institute's youngest schools, Nuclear Engineering, became part of the oldest, Mechanical.[74]

Tech's historical involvement in nontraditional and off-campus instruction took some new turns during this era. The programs in continuing education and industrial education still provided noncredit short courses on scores of subjects within the Institute's areas of expertise. Industrial education, which had long provided training courses for Georgia textile firms and other old-line industries in the state, branched out into overseas job training programs. In 1978 the Center for Media Based Instruction was established to coordinate credit courses (mostly at the graduate level) offered off-campus through live microwave transmission and videotape. One of Tech's oldest off-campus educational ventures, the cooperative program, was flourishing in the 1980s. In 1982–83, 2,483 undergraduates were enrolled in the cooperative plan, double the number and almost double the percentage of students ten years earlier. In 1983 the cooperative program was broadened to include graduate students.[75]

Several campus units were renamed during that era. The College of Industrial Management dropped "Industrial" from its name, and the General College became the College of Sciences and Liberal Studies. Another long-anticipated name change occurred in October 1984 when after fifty years the Engineering Experiment Station changed its name to the Georgia Tech Research Institute. The existing contracting agency of that name became the Georgia Tech Research Corporation.

The decade-long drought of new buildings ended in the early 1980s. A major addition to the Architecture Building was completed in 1981, as was the Arthur B. Edge Intercollegiate Athletic Center, which housed athletic administration and at last provided first-class training facilities for Tech's varsity athletes. The year 1983 saw the completion of a multibuilding facility housing the College of Management and the School of Industrial and Systems Engineering. The hard-won dormitory complex was also completed that year, as was the first phase of a large research facility to house the Advanced Technology Development Center.[76]

There were important changes in top-level administrative personnel during the tenth decade, although they reflected individual transitions rather than a sweeping change of direction. The most noteworthy change came in 1979 with the announcement that Vernon Crawford, Tech's academic vice president and a former acting president of the Institute, was to serve as acting chancellor of the University System of Georgia, succeeding George Simpson. In 1980 Crawford was named chancellor in his own right and served with distinction in that post until his retirement in 1985. Crawford was succeeded as academic vice president by Henry C. Bourne, an MIT graduate who had held faculty positions in electrical engineering at Berkeley and Rice, and had then served as deputy head of the Engineering Directorate of the National Science Foundation before coming to Tech.[77]

In 1977, Gene M. Nordby succeeded the retiring Ewell Barnes as vice president for business and finance. Nordby left after only three years and was succeeded in 1980 by Richard Fuller. Joe Guthridge, vice president for Institute relations and development and a key figure in Tech's growth during the 1960s, died in 1978, his death following by only a few days that of Dean of Graduate Studies Sam Webb. Guthridge was succeeded by Warren Heemann, who had held a similar post at the College of William and Mary. Also in 1978, Charles E. Gearing succeeded Ferdinand K. Levy as dean of the College of Management, a post that Gearing held for three years. In 1981, Les A. Karlovitz, director of the School of Mathematics, became dean of the College of Sciences and Liberal Studies, succeeding Henry Valk, who returned to full-time teaching in the School of Physics.[78]

In April 1980, Homer C. Rice became director of athletics and assistant to the president, joining Tech graduate Bill Curry who had just been named head football coach to succeed Pepper Rodgers. Rice launched an ambitious five-year plan to strengthen Tech's athletic program, the outlines of which can be seen in the review that Rice helped to conduct in 1973. It included expanding the program's financial base and investing in facilities and scholarships to upgrade Tech's overall program, beginning with those sports that would particularly enhance Tech's standing in the ACC.[79]

One other transition in this era is particularly worthy of note. In 1980, the Southern Technical Institute in Marietta became independent of Georgia Tech. Southern Tech was established as a two-year affiliate of Georgia Tech in 1947 and in 1971 was raised to the level of a four-year institution, awarding degrees in engineering technology. Even under the best of circumstances, many of Southern Tech's faculty, students, and local supporters perceived their institution to be a neglected stepchild of Georgia Tech. In the late 1970s the move to separate gained enough support that Chancellor Simpson appointed a committee to consider a division. Simpson left office before the matter was resolved, and it fell to Crawford to make the final decision. In retrospect, Southern Tech and its supporters wanted the separation more than Georgia Tech opposed it. Steven Cheshier of Purdue University was named as Southern Tech's first president, and the Marietta school has flourished under his leadership. Like its parent institution, Southern Tech defined for itself a specialized role in fulfilling the dream of southern economic development.[80]

Variations on a Theme by Henry Grady

In the 1970s and 1980s Georgia and the nation experienced a series of economic shocks almost as severe as those that had wracked the country in the era of Georgia Tech's founding. This time, however, the problems were not those of an emerging industrial nation and an agricultural South. The crises of the late twentieth century were those of a mature industrial economy threatened by the escalating price and uncertain availability of essential raw materials (crude oil being only the most obvious) and by apparent loss of global mastery in industrial technology and productivity. In the South, the economic trauma of the mid-1970s threatened to undo the gains made since World War II in overcoming the region's historic status as "the nation's number one economic problem."[81]

By the late 1970s many Americans feared that the problems ran deeper than the recessions which had periodically slowed the nation's phenomenal economic growth since 1945. Experts in various fields and of differing political persuasions began to speak of longterm, even permanent decline in the nation's economic system and of a parallel decline in America's standard of living.[82]

As always in a crisis, the nation did not lack for proposed remedies, two of which had particular bearing on Georgia Tech's history at the end of its first century. First, many policy makers thought instinctively of the crash programs in research and development that had produced the nuclear weapons and sophisticated electronics of World War II and had sent an American to the moon in 1969. A similar focusing of expertise and resources, it was argued, could resolve the energy crisis and restore America's industrial supremacy. As with the earlier crash programs, such efforts would harness the resources of universities, private industry, and the federal government.

A second and related approach captured considerable attention at the end of the 1970s and in the early 1980s. Some analysts, taking note of the role of government in Japan's economic miracle, called for a national industrial policy to bring about a revitalization or "reindustrialization" of the American economy. Under such a policy, the federal government would stimulate the growth of certain industries, and firms within those industries would be encouraged to cooperate in the development of new technologies. In one version of the proposal federal support would flow to the *universities* under a new "high technology Morrill Act," which would do for science- and technology-based industry what the original land-grant legislation had done for agriculture in the nineteenth century.[83]

For a time, the writing of articles and books on industrial policy itself became a flourishing minor industry,[84] but all the words printed and spoken did not translate into a national policy. The whole idea was antithetical to the economic policies of the Reagan administration, and although versions of industrial policy had some considerable support among corporate leaders, it seemed to smack of a more centralized and planned economy (whether controlled by government or by large corporations) and was thus politically unacceptable to many Americans. (In fact, though billed as a new departure, the proposed industrial policies of the 1970s resembled in broad outlines Herbert Hoover's "corporatist" policies of the 1920s and early 1930s, and the call for a new Morrill Act was older still.)[85] Furthermore, the easing of the recession of 1980–83 lessened the demand for sweeping governmental intervention. By the mid-1980s, the only place where one could discern a federal "industrial policy"

438   Engineering the New South

was in the Department of Defense's concentration of research and development funds on certain technologies and industries thought to be of national security interest.

While plans for a *national* industrial policy sputtered and failed to get off the ground, many of the *states* proceeded with programs of their own to promote high technology industrial growth. ("High technology industry" has no agreed upon definition. As used here it refers both to research-intensive industries that produce new sophisticated products—microelectronics and biotechnology, for example—and the application of technological innovations to existing industries—textiles being the leading example in the Southeast.) State leaders were enamored of the highly publicized success of California's Silicon Valley, Massachusetts' Route 128, and North Carolina's Research Triangle (only the last of which was state-sponsored). A study conducted in 1983 by the Congressional Office of Technology Assessment identified 153 state-supported programs ranging from traditional efforts to secure industrial plant location and provide job-specific manpower training to state support for high technology research and development and for venture capital formation. The authors of the study concluded that "state and local leaders are attracted to [high technology development] because they believe it promises new jobs, clean industry, and rapid growth."[86]

In the last decade of its first century, Georgia Tech would find itself very much involved in both these approaches to economic recovery and reform: crash programs in energy and industrial research and development, and state-level "industrial policy." The Institute and its leaders were not strangers to either. Many of the men who led Georgia Tech in the 1970s and 1980s had come of age professionally in the massive defense-related research and development projects of World War II and the Korean War. And, for better or worse, Georgia had had its own industrial policies of sorts for two centuries. One hundred years before Georgia Tech was founded the legislature offered a bounty of cash and land to anyone who would produce iron from Georgia ore. Fifty years later the state had constructed and operated a railroad to open northwestern Georgia to commercial agriculture.[87] Georgia Tech itself was chartered in the 1880s as part of a strategy to harness public and private resources in support of economic growth. And one hundred years after Nat Harris first introduced legislation to establish a school of technology, Governor George Busbee stood before a gathering of would-be high technology developers in an Atlanta hotel ballroom named for Henry W. Grady and said:

> As we plan ways to escape the current economic contraction, I'm convinced that our state needs to concentrate on building a base of high technology employment. The state cannot accomplish all that is needed because it does not have the resources nor does it have all the expertise that is needed. Instead, I want to propose that the public sector in Georgia forge an alliance with business to focus our best resources on finding and implementing solutions to our economic growth problems.[88]

The governor's strategy, in which Georgia Tech was to play a leading role, may well be called variations on a theme by Henry Grady.

In 1975–77 and 1983 Georgia Tech led efforts to secure major new research facilities for the state, one federally mandated and the other established by a consortium of electronics firms. In the end, neither bid was successful, but both drew attention to continuing research and development activities at Tech, which strove for the fulfillment of Grady's dream.

In the aftermath of the oil embargo and escalation of world oil prices, Congress in 1974 authorized the establishment of a Solar Energy Research Institute (SERI) to lead the nation's search for solar alternatives to fossil fuel.[89] By the time that legislation was passed, researchers from Georgia Tech's Colleges of Engineering and Architecture and from the EES had developed considerable expertise in high temperature materials, conversion of solar energy to electrical power, and demonstration-scale application of various solar technologies. Tech's first solar research, high temperature materials tests, conducted in 1971 at a giant solar furnace in France, had a military application unrelated to alternative energy, but after 1973 Tech pioneered in solar thermal conversion and other aspects of solar energy. At the federally financed "new town" of Shenandoah, Georgia, Tech engineers designed what was described as the "largest solar system in the world for heating and cooling a building."[90] In 1975,

Tech began construction of a 325-kw solar test facility, which when completed helped establish Georgia Tech as a leader in university-based solar research.

When in 1975 the state government decided to bid for location of SERI in Georgia, Vice President Stelson was asked to coordinate the effort.[91] The Georgia proposal, submitted to the Energy Research and Development Administration (ERDA) in July 1976, included a privately donated site at Shenandoah, a state-financed research facility at Georgia Tech and leased office space in Atlanta (both to be used until permanent quarters were constructed at Shenandoah), and establishment of a Solar Consortium (SOLCON) consisting of Georgia Tech and five industrial, engineering, and architectural firms that would operate SERI. The Georgia plan called for a management team including Stelson as director and key subordinates from Tech and two other members of the consortium, Westinghouse Electric and the firm that managed the Air Forces' Arnold Engineering Development Center.[92]

Among the twenty research organizations submitting SERI proposals were Battelle Memorial Institute (with the state of Arizona), SRI International (with New Mexico), and Midwest Research Institute (with Colorado). Despite the heavy competition, Stelson predicted that Georgia had "at least a 20 percent chance" of securing the facility.[93] Final selection was delayed until early in 1977, after inauguration of a new president. Local opinion was divided as to whether Jimmy Carter's presence in the White House would help or hurt Tech's chances. When it was announced in March 1977 that SERI would be located in Golden, Colorado, and operated by Midwestern Research Institute, many in Georgia, including the governor and the state's senior senator, believed that the SOLCON proposal had been disadvantaged by the new administration's desire to avoid the appearance of home state favoritism. That suggestion was strongly denied by the president.[94] Nonpolitical factors (not the least of which was the law of averages) could certainly explain the loss. Georgia Tech's solar research was heavily concentrated in the demonstration and commercialization phase, and although the government's specifications for SERI were not clearly defined, ERDA's plans seemed to favor a broadly based approach ranging from basic research to commercialization and even economic and policy assessments.

Despite losing in the SERI competition, Tech's solar and renewable energy research program continued to flourish. In August 1979, President Carter focused attention on the work at Tech by participating, along with his secretary of energy, in a day-long solar energy conference on the campus. Soon thereafter he appointed Vice President Stelson to be assistant secretary of energy with responsibility for renewable energy programs, a post which Stelson held for one year. (President Carter returned to the campus the following February to receive an honorary doctorate and deliver a major foreign policy address. He thus became the fourth sitting president to visit the Tech campus.) Also in 1979, Georgia Tech researchers worked with Senator Herman Talmadge, chairman of the Senate agriculture committee, in drafting legislation that promoted research in biomass conversion from wood fiber. By the end of the decade Georgia Tech researchers were introducing solar and biomass conversion technologies to a variety of traditional industries in Georgia, with a little help from Washington.[95] Sunshine and trees, both of which Georgia had in abundance, were to be enlisted in the cause of economic development.

At the same time, an increasing share of Georgia Tech's renewable energy work was taking place in third world countries. Activities ranged from design of test facilities in Kuwait similar to the power tower on the Atlanta campus, to introduction in sub-Saharan Africa of a simple, low-cost spiral solar concentrator, called the "curly cooker," that had been invented by a Georgia Tech student, Rich Steenblick. Overseas diversification and continuing (though diminished) congressional support for solar research enabled Tech's program to continue in the 1980s when public interest in finding alternatives to fossil fuel had waned, at least for the moment.[96]

In 1983, Georgia Tech initiated another attempt to secure a major research facility for the Atlanta area, this one in the microelectronics field. In 1982, William C. Morris, chairman of Control Data Corporation, proposed a joint venture research facility that would pool talent and money from leading American electronics firms in order to meet the challenge of Japanese efforts in advanced electronics. Morris's initiative led to the creation of the Microelectronics and Computer Technology Corporation (MCC), which tapped the resources of twelve leading electronics firms.[97] MCC proposed to establish a $50 million per year research facility near a university with strong programs in microelectronics and computer technology. Georgia Tech officials considered the Institute to be a viable contender. President Pettit was himself widely regarded as an important figure in the development of Silicon Valley in the 1950s and 1960s, and Georgia Tech had, within the past year, begun to coordinate its research in areas of interest to MCC through a Microelectronics Research Center.

A bidding process ensued, similar to that for the location of SERI. Georgia Tech's officials learned of the site selection only ten days before preliminary screening, but President Pettit and Governor Joe Frank Harris flew to Chicago and made a presentation to the selection committee on March 18. Pettit began his remarks with a reflection on Terman's concept of a "modern community of scholars," which, he said, "we regard as our model for Atlanta."[98] Based on the presentations made in Chicago by Pettit and Harris, Atlanta was included among the four cities to be given further consideration. In the succeeding weeks the governor's office and Georgia Tech officials prepared a formal proposal that included an offer of building space for MCC on the Tech campus and, more important, the creation of a $30 million Georgia Research Consortium to support a "center of excellence" in microelectronics and computer technology. Half of the funding for the consortium was to come from state appropriation and half from the private sector.[99]

On May 17, MCC President Bobby R. Inman announced that the research facility would be located in Austin, Texas, and would work in cooperation with the University of Texas and Texas A&M University. Backers of the Austin proposal "had money in hand," whereas the Georgia Research Consortium was contingent on legislative appropriation and private fund raising. Furthermore, Georgia Tech could not match the combined engineering and computer expertise already in place and to be hired at the University of Texas and Texas A&M; and finally, according to one published account, Atlanta ranked fourth among the competing cities in "quality of life."

The whirlwind effort to lure MCC to Atlanta, though unsuccessful, paid major dividends for the Institute. More than any single event, it focused the attention of policy makers on the possibility of replicating Terman's modern technological community of scholars in Atlanta. We now turn to the question of how that might come to be, and why it has not already happened.

The efforts of Georgia Tech and the state of Georgia to attract research facilities being established for "crash programs" (SERI and MCC) publicized Tech's expertise in solar energy and electronics, even though neither facility was placed in Georgia. The state government's participation in those efforts may well have been less of a new departure than just another version of the old strategy of luring industry to the state. The outlines of a more far-reaching strategy to promote economic growth in Georgia through high technology may be seen in the formation in the 1980s of the Advanced Technology Development Center and the Microelectronics Research Center, and in the less glamorous but no less significant efforts to bring new technologies to existing industries.

In 1963, studies conducted for the governor's office (by Spindletop Research Center) and the Georgia Tech Alumni Association (by Arthur D. Little, Inc.) recommended that a state-supported research park be established in association with Georgia Tech and private industry. Neither recommendation was followed, leading to the conclusion in a 1982 study that "the quest for high technology industrial development in the state of Georgia is a story with numerous episodes and no resolutions."[100] What made the lack of a center of high technology such as Silicon Valley or Boston's Route 128 so galling to some civic boosters was that neighboring North Carolina seemed to have put itself on the high technology map with the Research Triangle Institute and Research Triangle Park. Established in 1956 under the leadership of Governor Luther Hodges, the Research Triangle was formed to pool the scientific and technological expertise of Duke University, the University of North Carolina, and North Carolina State University, and private industry to promote economic development in the state. By the late 1970s Research Triangle Park was home to an impressive array of chemical and electronics research facilities and federal laboratories.[101]

One of the principal architects of the Research Triangle, George Simpson, had been chancellor of the University System of Georgia since 1965. Since World War II, Georgia Tech researchers had been engaged, albeit on a relatively modest scale, in electronics research that, in the Palo Alto and Boston areas, had translated into industrial growth. And since 1972 one of the leading figures in the rise of Silicon Valley had been the president of Georgia Tech. Why then did Georgia and Atlanta lag behind?

The answer is quite similar to the explanation of why the Worcester-style school of technology founded in the 1880s by Porter, Harris, Higgins, and the rest did not in itself transform Atlanta into a booming manufacturing center. Atlanta in the 1880s lacked the mature manufacturing culture—the extensive network of machinists and other skilled personnel—that the city of Worcester had. The business leadership of Atlanta was more interested in commerce and finance than in industry, and as Grady so often said, the city and region lacked the investment capital needed for large-scale industrialization.

So also was the case in the 1960s. Whether one referred to a "critical mass" of technological expertise or a "community of technological scholars," Atlanta did not have the accumulation of talent and resources needed to touch off a chain reaction of high technology firms. As one close observer of the situation noted, "Atlanta's problem is that the rest of the world regards it as a one-company High Tech town.... The standard question is, 'after Scientific Atlanta, what is there?'" As we have seen in discussion of the formation of Scientific Atlanta as a spinoff of sorts from the EES (chapter 7), Georgia Tech itself had reservations about the easy interchange between its own research faculty and private industry.[102]

In the 1960s the business and financial leadership of Atlanta for the most part was too caught up in the city's real estate boom and related ventures to concern itself with science- and technology-based development. The city's traditional role as regional transportation and distribution hub was only beginning to be redefined in a high technology information-based economy. Within the closely knit civic leadership only a handful of men, many of them Tech graduates, spoke out in favor of the sort of development which was at that moment turning scrub pineland between Raleigh, Durham, and Chapel Hill into the Research Triangle.[103]

The lack of capital that hampered high technology entrepreneurial growth cannot be blamed altogether on the disinclination of local financial institutions to invest. Generally speaking, banks have played a minor role in financing high technology development.

Banks, accustomed or even required to secure commercial loans with company assets, are not well-equipped to finance the electronics whiz whose stock in trade is an idea for a new product and whose "physical plant" is his dining room table. Financing for this new breed of entrepreneurs has largely come through "venture capital," loaned in return for equity ownership (a slice of the company) or extended as unsecured debt. Until the 1980s the availability of venture capital was severely limited except in a handful of areas, including the existing centers of high technology development on the East and West coasts.[104]

One exception to the general disinterest in high technology development was the creation in 1971 of Technology Park by a group of Georgia Tech alumni. They anticipated that the park in suburban Gwinnett County would become a magnet for high technology firms in the same manner as Stanford Industrial Park, although unlike its Palo Alto model, Technology Park was located over a dozen miles from the Tech campus. Technology Park weathered the recession and real estate collapse of the mid-1970s and was by 1982 home to some forty companies employing 2,500 people. By that time the northern suburban rim of Atlanta was rapidly becoming the focal point of technology-based firms in the area.[105]

By the mid-1980s all three conditions needed for growth had begun to materialize: the clustering of technical expertise, the support of business and educational leaders, and the availability of venture capital. The late 1970s and early 1980s saw a substantial influx of electronics and avionics firms into the Atlanta area, including the facilities of Bell Laboratories, Rockwell International, and Northern Telecom. In addition, several start-up firms with Tech connections made a name for themselves in electronics and computer fields, among them Hayes Microcomputing and Management Science America. The handful of long-time advocates of high technology development in Atlanta (including the founders of Scientific Atlanta and Technology Park) were joined by a group of energetic young Tech graduates who were established with successful high technology firms. Working through the Committee of Twenty of the Tech Alumni Association, they interjected a strong appeal for new high technology initiatives into the councils of the city's business and financial leadership. And finally, changes in federal tax laws in 1978 and 1981 facilitated venture capital formation, and more of that capital began finding its way to Atlanta.[106]

Georgia Tech's efforts in support of entrepreneurial high technology development were concentrated in the Advanced Technology Development Center (ATDC). In 1979, Governor Busbee commissioned researchers at the EES to conduct yet another study of how scientific and technological resources could be employed to promote economic development. The researchers also brought into the discussion young Tech alumni from the Committee of Twenty who helped to formulate recommendations and sell them to the Atlanta business community. Like the Georgia legislators who had journeyed to Worcester and Boston a century before, the research team visited the national centers of high technology growth, including, of course, Silicon Valley and the Research Triangle. They then issued a report calling for the establishment at Georgia Tech of an Advanced Technology Development Service (later changed to "Center") to "create a community of advanced technology companies in Georgia."[107] The idea (similar to one then being developed by Rensselaer Polytechnic Institute and the state of New York) was to nurture infant high technology enterprises by providing "incubator space," access to Tech research facilities, business management assistance, and introduction to sources of venture capital. In addition, the ATDC would assist state and local governments in recruitment of new high technology firms. The proposal was, in a sense, a high technology version of the EES's old Industrial Development Division.[108]

Governor Busbee, a strong advocate of government-industry cooperation, took a personal interest in the project, as did President Pettit. Busbee helped secure legislative support, and Pettit activated another important constituency: "I have made extensive contacts," he reported to the chancellor, "with entrepreneurs and venture capital persons in California who have played major roles in making Silicon Valley a successful high-technology reality."[109]

The ATDC began operation in late 1980 in temporary facilities in the O'Keefe School. Construction began that same year on a $5 million building capable of housing up to forty start-up firms.[110] By April 1984, ATDC had "graduated" six companies, and thirty more were in the program. Most of the companies focused on one or a few products in computer software or peripherals (areas in which Atlanta was becoming a leading center), but others ran the gamut from biotechnology to millimeter wave technology, to computer applications for the textile industry.[111]

Equally important as the ATDC's incubator function was its role in introducing potential investors to would-be entrepreneurs through venture capital conferences. The ATDC itself became home to a venture capital fund specializing in start-up investment in southeastern high technology firms. Although it is impossible to measure precisely, the ATDC contributed substantially to a shift in local business attitudes toward high technology development.

If Milton P. Higgins could return to Georgia Tech for its centennial, he would no doubt want to have a look at the ATDC. The commercialization of high technology is separated more by time than by philosophy from the commercial shop that Higgins founded. But if he returned for a visit, the old shop superintendent might have a word of caution for the ATDC's capable director, Jerry Birchfield (who at times sounded for all the world like a latter-day Henry Grady): the public and political forces that brought both the ATDC and Tech itself into being create such high expectations that anything short of an economic miracle could be viewed as failure.

If the ATDC represented Georgia Tech's most ambitious effort in the field of entrepreneurial commercialization of high technology, the Microelectronics Research Center, proposed by President Pettit in 1980 and established the following year, represented a major commitment to focus basic research efforts on the campus so as to achieve major advances in an area of great importance. By the 1970s Georgia Tech had established strong research capabilities in such areas as digital signal processing, semiconductor materials research, and computer science and computer engineering. Much of that expertise was related to Tech's long-standing research effort in military electronics. By 1980 there was growing interest in bringing these and other related research activities together in a concentrated effort in microelectronics, particularly in the development of the newest generation of integrated circuits known as VLSI (for Very Large Scale Integration). The movement to focus campuswide research in this "hot" area under a single research leader stemmed in part from the interdisciplinary nature of the work. Real advances were to be made by linking the work of strong but previously unconnected research groups.[112] In addition, an old and familiar argument was heard. One senior member of the EES staff, noting the establishment of the North Carolina Microelectronics Center with strong support from the state, said: "Why should we let North Carolina be the dominant factor in the buildup of this technology in the Southeast? What we need is some comparable financial and political support."[113] Officials have been quick to point out the dissimilarities between microelectronics research in the two states, but nevertheless the level of state support for such an effort in North Carolina was viewed with some envy on the Atlanta campus.

As with the ATDC, President Pettit took direct interest in the coordination of microelectronics research. In November 1981 he announced the formation of the Microelectronics Research Center and the appointment of John W. Hooper as director. A Regents' Professor of Electrical Engineering and a former vice chancellor of the University System, Hooper was highly regarded on the campus as a researcher and administrator. The MCR began operation with advanced equipment donated by industry, and with funds generated from within the Institute and from contract research. A hoped-for multimillion-dollar infusion of state funding had not materialized by the end of 1984.

Hooper was quick to acknowledge that while a great many universities were establishing microelectronics centers, the finite pool of funds for such costly operations would limit the number of "survivors" to a handful, perhaps a half dozen.[114] Given the high stakes, the centers that flourished would be the ones which were not content with small incremental gains but succeeded in making major advances in microelectronics. Georgia Tech naturally hoped to be among the latter group.[115]

At the end of Georgia Tech's first hundred years, advances in such esoteric fields as microelectronics and biotechnology held promise for enhancing the quality of life in Georgia through science and technology. Yet, that century of experience which we have now reviewed also suggests some grounds for caution in projecting what the impact of high technology will be.

Georgia Tech's founders were motivated, in part, by a concern for the social and political consequences of a large body of unemployed and underemployed people in the state. One hundred years later, experts warn that high technology will continue to account for only a small percentage of total employment in the United States.[116] While these emerging industries certainly hold great promise for engineers and skilled technicians, structural unemployment threatens to create in the last years of the twentieth century a large segment of society that, if employable at all, will have hope only of the most poorly paying jobs. The goal of the "New South Creed" to broaden employment opportunities through new technology remains elusive. The experience of the founders might lead one to ask whether the current enthusiasm for high technology might turn to cynicism and loss of public support if economic miracles are not forthcoming.

One promising approach to broadening the pool of potential beneficiaries of the high technology revolution is to preserve jobs in the older "smokestack" industries by application of the most up-to-date technologies. Efforts to "retrofit" older industries with recent technological innovations are ongoing at Georgia Tech and range from application of computer technology in the textile industry to development of renewable energy systems for poultry producers and processors. These efforts, though less visible to the public than the glamorous research, development, and commercialization activities described above, may prove in the long run to be of at least equal importance.

The technological marvels of the age of semiconductors and recombinant DNA would no doubt amaze Tech's founding fathers. They might also marvel at the school's recent efforts to move beyond engineering a New South toward the application of science and engineering on a national and international scale. But the modern day aspiration for improving the way people live, as well as the pitfalls and dilemmas of engineering a better world, would be to them altogether familiar.

Tech Between Two Centuries

N. E. Harris, Henry Grady, and the other founders of Georgia Tech achieved their first victory with the legislative chartering of the George School of Technology in 1885. As the centennial of that event approached, the Georgia Tech community plunged into a crowded schedule of events which looked back on the Institute's first century, celebrated its one hundredth birthday, and reflected on the second century of a major technological university.

Centennial festivities began in the fall of 1984. In October, Sandra Day O'Connor, associate justice of the Supreme Court, spoke to a near-capacity audience at Alexander Memorial Coliseum, launching a lecture series that would bring a variety of distinguished speakers to the campus during the following year and a half. In November an elaborate exhibition of ancient Chinese technology opened under Tech's sponsorship at Atlanta's High Museum of Art. Dignitaries, including China's ambassador to the United States, Zhang Wenjing, and Georgia's governor, Joe Frank Harris, were on hand for opening ceremonies of *China: 7,000 Years of Discovery*.

As the centennial year of 1985 began, student exhibits and special entertainment enlivened the campus. In March, Georgia Tech formally launched its Centennial Campaign to raise $100 million for endowment and long-range development. Not since the Greater Georgia Tech campaigns of the 1920s had any such private fundraising effort been attempted. Among the many centennial events still to come as this book went to press were a convocation in October 1985 marking the actual anniversary of the Institute's chartering and a symposium in the spring of 1986 that would conclude the centennial celebration with reflections on the role of a technological university in the twenty-first century.

The centennial year was also a time for taking stock of the Institute's mission and academic programs. Georgia Tech's long range plan called for strengthening academic programs already in place rather than creating new ones. It also envisioned maintaining Tech's enrollment at about 11,000 students, but changing the mixture by increasing the number of graduate students to about 3,000. In the fall quarter of 1984, 8,730 undergraduates and 2,228 graduate students were enrolled.[117]

The engineering disciplines still accounted for the lion's share of degrees awarded, both at the undergraduate and graduate levels. In 1983–84, Georgia Tech ranked fourth among American universities in the number of bachelors degrees awarded in engineering with 1,315.[118] Further changes in the structure of engineering education came in 1985 when a new school of materials engineering was established, bringing together Tech's well-established instructional and research programs in that field from ceramics and metallurgy. Tech continued to graduate a relatively small number of doctoral students in engineering, but enrollments and degrees awarded at the doctoral level were increasing in the centennial year.[119]

Georgia Tech remained committed to increasing the quality as well as the size of its graduate programs. Although qualitative assessment was problematic at best and comparative evaluation even less reliable, Georgia Tech inevitably kept track of the national "rankings" of graduate programs, much as it and other universities followed the sports polls. A 1982 study of doctoral programs in America, which resembled the Cartter and Roose-Anderson reports of the 1960s and 1970s, evaluated eight of Georgia Tech's doctoral programs. The report categorized most of Tech's programs as strong, and some approaching excellence, but none in the first rank nationally in their respective fields.[120] For Georgia Tech, taking the next qualitative step in graduate education loomed as one of the principal tasks for the opening years of the second century.

Georgia Tech's increasing emphasis on graduate education and its selective admissions policies for undergraduates added new weight to a long-standing appeal in the state for creation of another engineering college that would concentrate on applied undergraduate training. Ironically, the discussion of a new engineering college echoed the shop culture–school culture debate of the 1880s, with proponents of a new school sounding for all the world like Georgia's converts to the Worcester system in the 1880s. This time Georgia Tech was cast in the role of Boston Tech. Institute officials, including President Pettit and Dean of Engineering William Sangster, agreed that a second public engineering school of the type mentioned might be of value to the state, but with a certain reservation. Sangster was quoted as saying, "We're not opposed to a second engineering school. We're opposed to a second underfunded engineering school. We'd like to see Georgia Tech fully funded before we start another one."[121]

Late in 1984 Mercer University announced plans to open an engineering school on its campus in Macon. However, Mercer's decision to establish a private engineering school did not curb the appeals of college officials and community leaders from around the state to establish a new engineering school in their area. Understandably, Southern Tech's president, Stephen Cheshier, argued that his institution was already prepared to fill such a role.[122]

The pursuit of academic excellence at Georgia Tech was matched by efforts to strengthen the athletic program. At the time of the centennial the Georgia Tech Athletic Association was making progress toward providing full support for a broad range of men's and women's varsity teams. Handsome new facilities were completed in 1985 for tennis and track, the latter named for longtime dean of students and track coach George C. Griffin. In football, Coach Bill Curry's team posted a winning record in 1984, including a 35–18 victory over arch-rival Georgia. The 1984–85 basketball season marked the arrival of Georgia Tech as a national contender. On the way to a record 27–8 season, the Yellow Jackets three times defeated perennial powerhouse North Carolina, captured the Atlantic Coast Conference championship (Tech's first in any sport since joining the ACC), and advanced to the NCAA regional finals before narrowly losing to defending champion Georgetown. The Yellow Jackets' stunning success in basketball was followed by conference championships in baseball and golf, making the spring of 1985 one of the most memorable athletic seasons in Tech's history.

In 1985, as had been the case since the beginning, the heart and soul of Georgia Tech was the community of students and faculty who shared the enterprise of learning, teaching, and research. The student body remained a diverse and highly qualified group. Every state in the union and eighty-five foreign nations were represented. Fifty-eight percent came from Georgia and three-fourths were from Georgia and the surrounding states.[123] The freshman class of 1984–85 included ninety-four National Merit and twenty-four National Achievement scholars, giving Georgia Tech the highest percentage of freshmen in both categories among public universities in the United States.[124]

In 1984, 608 academic faculty members and 777 research faculty practiced their professions at Georgia Tech and the Georgia Tech Research Institute. In the classroom, the hard-nosed traditions of John Saylor Coon and Lyman Hall were alive and well. Said one senior professor of electrical engineering, "We expect a lot of our undergraduates. We work them very hard. . . ."[125]

Research underway at Georgia Tech at the end of its first century included work in a rich variety of fields as well as in the highly visible "peaks of excellence" in electronics and other areas of science and engineering. Faculty research ranged from efforts by a team of chemists to produce new anticancer drugs from readily available natural sources to the development by an engineering group of a widely used integrated computer software system (called GTSTRUDL) that tremendously enhanced the design productivity of practicing engineers, to the historical and policy-related scholarship of the "founding father" of the history of technology in America.

As noted earlier, the Microelectronics Research Center (MRC) became in the 1980s an important focal point of Tech's multidisciplinary research in the electronics field. In 1985, Governor Joe Frank Harris proposed and the General Assembly approved a $15 million appropriation for the MRC, contingent upon the Institute's raising an additional $15 million from nonstate sources. The appropriation was larger than any single state award made to the Institute, but the requirement for matching funds was identical to the arrangement under which early presidents like Lyman Hall and K. G. Matheson had labored to expand Georgia Tech's facilities.

Both the research and instructional activities of the Institute continued to be well supported by the Price Gilbert Memorial Library. In 1984, Miriam Drake, a nationally recognized pioneer in the library application of computer technology, succeeded the retiring E. Graham Roberts as director.

From the earliest days Georgia Tech and its advocates had used an industrial metaphor to express its contributions to the state of Georgia and to the larger society: the "product" most often mentioned was the body of alumni and former students who had left the North Avenue campus to assume positions of leadership. The scope of their contributions was illustrated in the careers of the four men who received Tech's first Alumni Exceptional Achievement Awards in March 1985: Ivan Allen, Jr., former mayor of Atlanta; John Portman, world-renowned architect; C. J. "Pete" Silas, president and chief operating officer of Phillips Petroleum Company; and John Young, astronaut and chief of the NASA astronaut office. At the end of Tech's first century alumni were to be found in a broad range of endeavors, including public service (a former president of the United States and Georgia's senior United States senator among them), the professions, and military service. Not surprisingly, the largest concentration was to be found in business corporations, particularly in firms involving science and technology. In 1985 almost four thousand of Tech's fifty-one thousand known alumni were senior officers of business firms.[126] At the same time, 42 percent of Tech's graduates were working in Georgia, and 65 percent in Georgia plus surrounding states, suggesting that the Institute, through its alumni, was still engaged in engineering a new South. But former students were also to be found in every state of the union and in many foreign countries.[127] Among the alumni, as well as within the campus community, Georgia Tech's original focus on the state and region had expanded to a global scale.

In an address to the faculty in 1984, President Pettit spoke of the Tech community at the time of the centennial as the "New Founders" of Georgia Tech. Certainly, the challenges of Tech's second century called for men and women prepared to make their own history, as had Harris, Grady, and all the others who first envisioned the school and invested themselves in the struggle to make it a reality in the face of great adversity.

Notes

Chapter One

1. John Hubbel Weiss, *The Making of Technological Man: The Social Origins of French Engineering Education* (Cambridge: MIT Press, 1982), pp. 6–25, 89–90.
2. Anthony F. C. Wallace, *The Social Context of Innovation* (Princeton: Princeton University Press, 1982), p. 101.
3. Weiss, *The Making of Technological Man*, pp. 4–5, 110.
4. Ibid., p. 5.
5. Ibid., p. 236.
6. Charles Alpheus Bennett, *History of Manual and Industrial Education up to 1870* (Peoria, Ill.: Manual Arts Press, 1926), pp. 76–156.
7. Winton U. Solberg, *The University of Illinois, 1867–1894* (Urbana: University of Illinois Press, 1968), pp. 1–9.
8. Ibid., pp. 12–29.
9. Ibid., pp. 47, 51.
10. Kenneth Coleman, gen. ed., *A History of Georgia* (Athens: University of Georgia Press, 1977), p. 244; Solberg, *The University of Illinois*, pp. 54–57, 60.
11. Robert Preston Brooks, *The University of Georgia Under Sixteen Administrations, 1785–1955* (Athens: University of Georgia Press, 1956), pp. 53–54, 93.
12. Coleman, *A History of Georgia*, p. 243.
13. Louis R. Harlan, *Booker T. Washington: The Making of a Black Leader, 1856–1901* (New York: Oxford University Press, 1975), p. 64.
14. Ibid., pp. 58–64, 141.
15. Bruce Sinclair, *Philadelphia's Philosopher Mechanics: A History of the Franklin Institute, 1824–1865* (Baltimore: Johns Hopkins University Press, 1974).

16. Ibid., pp. 298–99; Bruce Sinclair, *A Centennial History of the American Society of Mechanical Engineers, 1880–1980* (Toronto: University of Toronto Press, 1980).
17. Monte A. Calvert, *The Mechanical Engineer in America, 1830–1910* (Baltimore: Johns Hopkins University Press, 1967), pp. 11, 62.
18. Wallace, *The Social Context of Innovation*; Calvert, *The Mechanical Engineer in America*, pp. 70, 281.
19. Calvert, *The Mechanical Engineer in America*, pp. 56–57.
20. William Frederick Durand, *Robert Henry Thurston: A Biography* (New York: American Society of Mechanical Engineers, 1929).
21. Robert H. Thurston, "On the Necessity of a Mechanical Laboratory: Its Province and Its Methods," *Journal of the Franklin Institute* 100 (1875): 1409–18.
22. Charles A. Bennett, *History of Manual and Industrial Education, 1870 to 1917* (Peoria, Ill.: Manual Arts Press, 1937), pp. 310–12.
23. R. H. Thurston, "Instruction in Mechanical Engineering," *Scientific American Supplement* 17 (1884): 6904–5.
24. R. H. Thurston, "Technical Training Considered as a Part of a Complete and Generous Education," *Scientific American Supplement* 24 (1887): 9614–16.
25. R. H. Thurston, "Technical Education in the United States: Its Social, Industrial and Economic Relations to Our Progress," *Transactions of the American Society of Mechanical Engineers* 14 (1893): 855–1013.
26. Paul M. Gaston, *The New South Creed: A Study in Southern Mythmaking* (New York: Vintage Books, 1973), pp. 17–34.
27. Walter G. Cooper, *Official History of Fulton County* (Atlanta: Walter W. Brown Publishing Co., 1934), pp. 282, 839–40.
28. Ibid., pp. 830–37; "Henry Grady and South Rise Together," *Atlanta Constitution*, 7 March 1983.
29. Jack Blicksilver, "The International Cotton Exposition of 1881 and Its Impact upon the Economic Development of Georgia," *Atlanta Economic Review* 7 (June 1957): 12.
30. *Dictionary of American Biography*, Allen Johnson et al., eds., 27 vols. (New York: Scribner's, 1928–), 1:406–7; Daniel Nelson, *Managers and Workers: Origins of the New Factory System in the United States, 1880–1920* (Madison: University of Wisconsin Press, 1975), p. 13.
31. Cooper, *Official History of Fulton County*, pp. 301–4.
32. "The Exposition Opening and the New Era Dawning upon the South," *Atlanta Constitution*, 6 October 1881.
33. "New England and the New South," *Atlanta Constitution*, 2 November 1881.

34. "The Industries," *Atlanta Constitution*, 4 November 1881.
35. Ibid.
36. "The Exposition as a Teacher," *Atlanta Constitution*, 16 November 1881.
37. "Atlanta's Own Citizens: Their Personal and Public Affairs," *Atlanta Constitution*, 3 March 1882.
38. "The Big Industry," *Atlanta Constitution*, 4 March 1882; "Southern Spindles," *Atlanta Constitution*, 6 September 1882.
39. "How We Grow," *Atlanta Constitution*, 4 February 1883.
40. "Busy Atlanta," *Atlanta Constitution*, 22 March 1883.
41. "A City of Small Industries," *Atlanta Constitution*, 19 September 1886.
42. "Atlanta and Her Industries" *Atlanta Constitution*, 21 November 1886.
43. "Atlanta's Growth," *Atlanta Constitution*, 21 November 1886.
44. See obituaries of Hanson in the *New York Times*, 16 December 1910; *Atlanta Constitution*, 16 December 1910; and *Atlanta Journal*, 15 December 1910. Also see Kenneth Coleman and Charles Stephen Gurr, eds., *Dictionary of Georgia Biography*, 2 vols. (Athens: University of Georgia Press, 1983), 1:389–90.
45. For a reprint of the Edwards editorial, see James E. Brittain and Robert C. McMath, Jr., *A Documentary History of Georgia Tech's Beginnings* (Atlanta: Georgia Institute of Technology, 1977), pp. 1–3.
46. Nathaniel E. Harris, *Autobiography: The Story of an Old Man's Life with Reminiscences of Seventy-Five Years* (Macon, Ga.: J. W. Burke, 1925); Marion L. Brittain, *The Story of Georgia Tech* (Chapel Hill: University of North Carolina Press, 1948), pp. 3–4. Also see the *Dictionary of Georgia Biography*, 1:405–6.
47. "Practical Education," *Atlanta Constitution*, 23 May 1882.
48. "The Legislature," *Atlanta Constitution*, 25 November 1882; Brittain, *The Story of Georgia Tech*, p. 8.
49. "The Legislature," *Atlanta Constitution*, 9 December 1882.
50. "Schools for Georgia Boys," *Atlanta Constitution*, 14 December 1882.
51. "Cost of a School of Technology," *Northeast Home Journal*, 13 July 1883; "The Free Institute—What Is Said About It by Visiting Committee from Georgia," *Worcester Daily Spy*, 9 August 1883; clippings located in scrapbook in the Archives of the Worcester Polytechnic Institute.
52. Harris stated later in his *Autobiography* that he had written the report.
53. The Report of the Legislative Committee is reprinted in Brittain and McMath, *A Documentary History*, pp. 4–5.

54. Ibid., p. 6.
55. Ibid., pp. 7–8.
56. Ibid., pp. 9–10.
57. "Technical Training in Georgia," *Atlanta Constitution*, 27 June 1883.
58. "Technical Education Again," *Atlanta Constitution*, 13 July 1883.
59. "The Legislature," *Atlanta Constitution*, 25 July 1883; Brittain, *The Story of Georgia Tech*, p. 9.
60. "Practical Education," *Atlanta Constitution*, 5 August 1883; "The Legislature," *Atlanta Constitution*, 15 September 1883.
61. Harris, *Autobiography*, p. 209.
62. *Dictionary of American Biography*, 9:210–11; *National Cyclopaedia of American Biography*, 76 vols. (New York: James T. White and Co., 1898–), 1:520–21; *Dictionary of Georgia Biography*, 1:476–78; obituary in *Atlanta Constitution*, 4 February 1914.
63. Isaac Stiles Hopkins, "Industrial Education," in *Sources and Reprints* (Atlanta: Emory University Publications, 1952), pp. 1–4, 14.
64. Ibid., pp. 8–10, 14–15.
65. Harris, *Autobiography*, p. 211.
66. "The Technological School," *Atlanta Constitution*, 28 July 1885.
67. "Mind and Hand," *Atlanta Constitution*, 29 July 1885.
68. Ibid.
69. "The Technological School," *Atlanta Constitution*, 29 July 1885.
70. "Technology OK," *Atlanta Constitution*, 30 July 1885; "What the Bill Is," *Atlanta Constitution*, 30 July 1885; "A Good Thing for Georgia," *Atlanta Constitution*, 30 July 1885; Harris, *Autobiography*, p. 214.
71. "The Legislature," *Atlanta Constitution*, 8–9 October 1885.
72. "The Legislature," *Atlanta Constitution*, 13 October 1885; Harris, *Autobiography*, p. 214.
73. A reprint of the enabling legislation appears in Brittain and McMath, *A Documentary History*, pp. 11–14.
74. "The Technological School Commission," *Atlanta Constitution*, 23 March 1886.
75. *Dictionary of Georgia Biography*, 1:505–6; *National Cyclopaedia of American Biography*, 2:443; Cooper, *Official History of Fulton County*, pp. 846–48; obituary in *Atlanta Constitution*, 13 January 1915.
76. *National Cyclopaedia of American Biography*, 33:73; Brittain, *The Story of Georgia Tech*, pp. 13–14.
77. Brittain, *The Story of Georgia Tech*, pp. 14–15.
78. Ibid., p. 15; obituary in *Atlanta Constitution*, 13 February 1920.
79. Minutes of the Board of Trustees, 5 April 1886, Georgia Tech Archives, hereafter cited as GTA.

459 Notes to Pages 27–33

80. "Atlanta and the Technological School," *Atlanta Constitution*, 9 September 1886.
81. "The Technological School," *Atlanta Constitution*, 19 September 1886.
82. "Technological Talk," *Atlanta Constitution*, 27 September 1886.
83. "The Tactics of the Macon Ring," *Atlanta Constitution*, 17 June 1886; Judson C. Ward, "Augustus Octavus Bacon and Joseph E. Brown: An Exchange of Letters," *Atlanta Historical Journal* 26 (1982–33): 64–67.
84. "We Are Satisfied with It," *Atlanta Constitution*, 12 September 1886.
85. "The Technological School," *Atlanta Constitution*, 19 September 1886.
86. P. H. Mell to the editor, *Atlanta Constitution*, 27 September 1886.
87. "The Technical School," *Atlanta Constitution*, 26 September 1886.
88. Edward Atkinson to Samuel Inman, 28 September 1886, reprinted in *Atlanta Constitution*, 1 October 1886; "The Technological School," *Atlanta Constitution*, 1 October 1886.
89. Minutes of the Board of Trustees, 1 October 1886, GTA.
90. "Teaching the Hand," *Atlanta Constitution*, 2 October 1886.
91. Ibid.
92. "Technological School," *Atlanta Constitution*, 14 October 1885.
93. "Teaching the Hand," *Atlanta Constitution*, 2 October 1886.
94. Ibid.
95. Ibid.
96. Minutes of the Board of Trustees, 2 October 1886, GTA; "Atlanta and the Technological School," *Atlanta Constitution*, 3 October 1886.
97. Minutes of the Board of Trustees, 19 October 1886, GTA.
98. "Twenty-One Ballots," *Atlanta Constitution*, 20 October 1886.
99. There remains a slight discrepancy in the documentary evidence concerning the final ballot with the official minutes of the Commission indicating that Hodgson voted for Atlanta rather than Heard. All other evidence however indicates that it was in fact Heard who cast the deciding ballot for Atlanta.
100. Minutes of the Board of Trustees, 20 October 1886, GTA; "Atlanta Gets It—School of Technology Located at Last," *Atlanta Journal*, 20 October 1886.
101. "Atlanta Selected," *Atlanta Constitution*, 21 October 1886.
102. "Hanging Fire," *Atlanta Constitution*, 26 January 1887; Minutes of the Board of Trustees, 24–25 January 1887, GTA.
103. Minutes of the Board of Trustees, 26 January 1887, GTA.
104. "The Site Selected," *Atlanta Constitution*, 27 January 1887.

460   Notes to Pages 33–41

105. "North Avenue," *Atlanta Constitution,* 27 June 1883.
106. "Peters Park—Model Town Projected," *Atlanta Constitution,* 30 March 1884.
107. "Atlanta Selected," *Atlanta Constitution,* 21 October 1886; Cooper, *Official History of Fulton County,* pp. 319–20.
108. "Peters Park—A Magnificent Suburb," *Atlanta Constitution,* 30 March 1884.
109. "The Peters Park Purchase," *Atlanta Constitution,* 30 March 1884.
110. For biographical information on Grant and Peters, see Cooper, *Official History of Fulton County,* pp. 858–61; also see Helen K. Lyon, "Richard Peters—Atlanta Pioneer," *Atlanta Historical Bulletin* 10 (1957): 21–39.
111. "The Peters Park Purchase," *Atlanta Constitution,* 30 March 1884.
112. Cooper, *Official History of Fulton County,* pp. 314–19.

Chapter Two

1. Minutes of the Board of Trustees, 8 December 1886, Georgia Tech Archives, hereafter cited as GTA.
2. "Higgins Laboratories," *Journal of the Worcester Polytechnic Institute* 44 (1941): 2; "The Elevator Business," *Journal of the Worcester Polytechnic Institute* 41 (1938): 14–15; J. M. Perry, "Sketch of the Life and Work of Milton Prince Higgins, 1842–1918," *Bulletin of the Business Historical Society* 18 (1941): 33–54; M. P. Higgins, "WPI: The Washburn Shops," pamphlet dated October 1904, Worcester Polytechnic Institute Archives, Worcester, Mass., hereafter cited as WPI Archives.
3. Minutes of the Board of Trustees, 24 January 1887, GTA.
4. Clipping dated 26 February 1887, WPI Archives.
5. Ibid.
6. Minutes of the Board of Trustees, 8 April 1887, GTA.
7. Clipping from *Worcester Home Journal,* 30 April 1887, scrapbook, WPI Archives.
8. Minutes of the Board of Trustees, 4 July 1887, GTA. The entry states that there was no quorum due to the absence of Porter and Inman. The invitation to Thurston to speak at the Worcester Commencement was mentioned in a clipping from the *Worcester Home Journal* of 30 April 1887, WPI Archives.
9. R. H. Thurston, "Technical Training Considered as a Part of a Com-

plete and Generous Education," *Scientific American Supplement* 24 (1887): 9614–16.
10. "Training the Hand," *Atlanta Constitution*, 4 September 1887.
11. Minutes of the Board of Trustees, 3 November 1887, GTA.
12. Board of Trustees Meeting Records, 12 and 23 November 1887, WPI Archives.
13. Clipping from the *Worcester Telegram*, 20 November 1887, scrapbook, WPI Archives.
14. Board of Trustees Meeting Records, 20 April 1887, 7 November 1891, 19 June 1895, 18 January 1896, 18 April 1896, WPI Archives.
15. Minutes of the Board of Trustees, 15–16 March 1887, GTA.
16. Ibid., 5 May 1887 and 2 June 1887, GTA.
17. Ibid., 1 September 1887, GTA.
18. "Training the Hand," *Atlanta Constitution*, 4 September 1887.
19. Minutes of the Board of Trustees, 1 October 1887, 1 December 1886, 1 March 1887, and 5 April 1887, GTA.
20. "Technology," *Atlanta Constitution*, 24 December 1887.
21. Minutes of the Board of Trustees, 3 November 1887, GTA.
22. Copy of Minutes of the University of Georgia Board Meeting of 21 December 1887, in Minutes of the Board of Trustees, GTA.
23. Minutes of the Board of Trustees, 1 December 1887, GTA.
24. "Technology," *Atlanta Constitution*, 24 December 1887.
25. "Atlanta and the University Fund," *Atlanta Constitution*, 17 July 1887.
26. "The University and the School," *Atlanta Constitution*, 1 January 1888.
27. "The University and the School," *Atlanta Constitution*, 12 February 1888. Chancellor Mell died 26 January 1888. See the *National Cyclopaedia of American Biography* 9:181–82.
28. Minutes of the Board of Trustees, 1 March 1888, GTA.
29. Robert Preston Brooks, *The University of Georgia Under Sixteen Administrations, 1785–1955* (Athens: University of Georgia Press, 1956), pp. 78–93.
30. Minutes of the Board of Trustees, 5 April 1888 and 3 May 1888, GTA.
31. On Hopkins, see Kenneth Coleman and Charles Stephen Gurr, eds., *Dictionary of Georgia Biography*, 2 vols. (Athens: University of Georgia Press, 1983), 1:476–78; *Dictionary of American Biography*, Allen Johnson et al., eds., 27 vols. (New York: Scribner's, 1928–), 9:210–11; *National Cyclopaedia of American Biography*, 76 vols. (New York: James T. White and Co., 1898–), 1:520–21.
32. "The Technological School," *Atlanta Constitution*, 2 June 1888.

33. Minutes of the Board of Trustees, 7 June 1888, GTA.
34. On Hall, see *Dictionary of Georgia Biography*, 1:384–85; *National Cyclopaedia of American Biography*, 29:265–66.
35. Minutes of the Board of Trustees, 5 July 1888, GTA.
36. Ibid., 1 March 1888, GTA.
37. Ibid., 5 July 1888, GTA.
38. Monte A. Calvert, *The Mechanical Engineer in America, 1830–1910* (Baltimore: Johns Hopkins University Press, 1967), p. 50.
39. Minutes of the Board of Trustees, 2 August 1888, GTA.
40. Obituary of Emerson in *Atlanta Constitution*, 14 November 1924.
41. D. S. Tarbell, Ann T. Tarbell, and R. M. Joyce, "The Students of Ira Remsen and Roger Adams," *ISIS* 71 (1980): 620–25.
42. W. H. Emerson, "The Solubility of Stearic Acid in Ethyl Alcohol at Zero," *Journal of American Chemical Society* 29 (1907): 1750–56.
43. "Hand and Brain: The Technological School Ready for Scholars," *Atlanta Constitution*, 5 September 1888.
44. James E. Brittain and Robert C. McMath, Jr., *A Documentary History of Georgia Tech's Beginnings* (Atlanta: Georgia Institute of Technology, 1977), pp. 25–27; prospectus, 1888, GTA.
45. "The Technological School," *Atlanta Constitution*, 5 October 1888; "The Formal Opening," *Atlanta Constitution*, 6 October 1888. The ceremonial starting of a steam engine by a young girl was not without precedent and evidently was viewed as demonstrating that even great power could be controlled with little physical effort. In April 1881, George Pullman's eleven-year-old daughter had been given the task of starting the famous Corliss steam engine that had provided motive power for machinery exhibited at the Philadelphia Exhibition of 1876. Pullman had purchased the engine and installed it at his factory in Illinois. See Dian O. Belanger, "The Corliss at Pullman," *Technology and Culture* 25 (1984): 86.
46. "Professor Higgins' Address," *Atlanta Constitution*, 7 October 1888.
47. "The Formal Opening," *Atlanta Constitution*, 6 October 1888.
48. W. H. Emerson, "The First President—Dr. I. S. Hopkins," probably 1913, uncataloged, GTA.
49. Faculty Minutes, 5 October 1888, GTA.
50. Minutes of the Board of Trustees, 5 December 1888, 3 January 1889, 2 May 1889, and Faculty Minutes, 14 June 1889, GTA. The faculty drafted a letter in Shepherd's behalf.
51. Minutes of the Board of Trustees, 2 May 1889, GTA.
52. Obituary in *Transactions of the American Society of Mechanical Engineers* 63 (1941): 52–53. Articles by Coon appeared in *Transactions of*

the *American Society of Mechanical Engineers* 3 (1882): 290–99 and 9 (1887): 476–83.
53. Marion L. Brittain, *The Story of Georgia Tech* (Chapel Hill, University of North Carolina Press, 1948), p. 14.
54. Early volumes of the *Transactions of the American Society of Mechanical Engineers* containing Porter's bookplate are now in the Georgia Tech Library.
55. Obituary in *Transactions of the American Society of Mechanical Engineers* 63 (1941): 52–53.
56. W. H. Emerson, "Dr. Coon," *Georgia Tech Alumnus* 1 (May 1923): 64–66; "A Last Fling with the Steam Gauge," *Georgia Tech Alumnus* 1 (May 1923): 62, GTA.
57. Minutes of the Board of Trustees, 2 October 1890, GTA.
58. Ibid., 1 January 1891, GTA.
59. Walter G. Cooper, *Official History of Fulton County* (Atlanta: Walter W. Brown, 1934), pp. 314–15, 319–20.
60. Brittain and McMath, *A Documentary History*, pp. 16–17, 20.
61. Georgia School of Technology Catalog, 1888–89, GTA; also annual catalogs of the Worcester Polytechnic Institute, 1888–94, WPI Archives.
62. M. P. Higgins Letterbook, 27 March 1889 to 17 June 1889, GTA.
63. Ibid., and Shop Correspondence, 30 August 1889 to 6 February 1890, GTA.
64. M. P. Higgins Letterbook, 27 March 1889 to 17 June 1889, 17 June 1889 to August 1889, GTA.
65. S. M. Inman to W. F. Cole, 11 May 1889, copy in M. P. Higgins Letterbook, GTA.
66. Obituary of Cole in *Journal of Worcester Polytechnic Institute* 46 (1943): 15, WPI Archives.
67. W. F. Cole to F. M. Higer Company, October 22, 1889; W. F. Cole to Thomson-Houston Company, 6 April 1890; W. F. Cole to Davis Water Wheel Company, 8 July 1890, Shop Correspondence, GTA.
68. W. F. Cole to O. S. Porter, 2 July 1980, Shop Correspondence, GTA.
69. Minutes of the Board of Trustees, 1 May 1890, and W. F. Cole to Atlanta National Bank, 30 August 1890; D. Parkhurst to O. S. Porter, 5 September 1890, Shop Correspondence, GTA.
70. G. E. Cassidy to Pratt Furnace, 6 December 1890; G. E. Cassidy to Lynchburg Coal Company, December 1890, Shop Correspondence, GTA.
71. "A Disastrous Fire," *Atlanta Journal*, 21 April 1892.
72. "The Tech Fire," *Atlanta Constitution*, 22 April 1892.

73. Minutes of the Board of Trustees, 29 April 1892, 21 June 1892, GTA.
74. Minutes of Executive Committee (filed in Minutes of the Board of Trustees), 21 December 1892, GTA.
75. Cooper, *Official History of Fulton County*, p. 315.
76. A. Jessop to Board of Trustees, 15 August 1893, Shop Correspondence, GTA.
77. Minutes of the Board of Trustees, 3 January 1896, GTA.
78. Georgia School of Technology Catalog, 1896–97, GTA.
79. Ibid.
80. Georgia School of Technology Prospectus, 1888, and Catalog, 1888–89, GTA.
81. Ibid.
82. Ibid.
83. Georgia School of Technology Catalog, 1889–90, GTA.
84. Minutes of the Board of Trustees, 7 January 1891, GTA; Georgia School of Technology Catalog, 1890–91, GTA; James E. Brittain and Robert C. McMath, Jr., "Engineers and the New South Creed: The Formation and Early Development of Georgia Tech," *Technology and Culture* 18 (April 1977): 189.
85. Correspondence of Lyman Hall, 19 January 1899, vol. 2, GTA.
86. Georgia School of Technology Catalog, 1889–90, 1893–94, 1898–99, GTA; also see Brittain, *The Story of Georgia Tech*, p. 27.
87. "Football," *Atlanta Constitution*, 29 October 1892; Georgia School of Technology Catalog, 1889–90, 1890–91, GTA.
88. "A Great Sport—How the Modern Game of Football Is Played," *Atlanta Constitution*, 15 October 1893.
89. "The Techs Won," *Atlanta Constitution*, 5 November 1893.
90. Georgia School of Technology Catalog, 1889–95, GTA.
91. Based on data from Georgia School of Technology Catalog, 1893–1900, GTA.
92. Based on data from Georgia School of Technology Catalog, 1893–96, GTA.
93. Brittain, *The Story of Georgia Tech*, pp. 24–25.
94. *National Cyclopaedia of American Biography*, 28:210.
95. Georgia School of Technology Catalog, 1883–99, GTA; biographical item in the Georgia Tech *Whistle*, 5 December 1983.
96. Georgia School of Technology Catalog, 1893–99, GTA.
97. Faculty Minutes, 21 May 1895, 23 May 1895, GTA.
98. Minutes of the Board of Trustees, 25 June 1895, GTA.
99. Ibid., 26 June 1895, GTA.

100. "Are All to Resign?," *Atlanta Constitution*, 3 January 1896.
101. Minutes of the Board of Trustees, 3 January 1896, GTA.
102. "Lyman Hall Named," *Atlanta Constitution*, 4 January 1896.
103. Minutes of the Board of Trustees, 24 June 1896, GTA.
104. *Dictionary of American Biography*, 9:210–11.
105. *National Cyclopaedia of American Biography*, 1:520–21; *Dictionary of Georgia Biography*, 1:476–78.
106. Obituaries of Hopkins, *Atlanta Constitution*, 4 February 1914, and *Atlanta Journal*, 3 February 1914.
107. Transcript of Hopkins's talk "Pioneer Work for Technological School in Georgia," vertical files, GTA.

Chapter Three

1. See review in *Science* 224 (18 May 1984): 717.
2. Lyman Hall to J. A. Finger, 4 August 1898; Hall to D. J. Lucas, 9 August 1898, Correspondence of Lyman Hall, Georgia Tech Archives, hereafter cited as GTA.
3. For a perceptive discussion of the socializing function of military drill and discipline, see William H. McNeill, *The Pursuit of Power: Technology, Armed Force and Society Since A.D. 1000* (Chicago: University of Chicago Press, 1982), pp. 131–32.
4. Minutes of the Board of Trustees, 7 November, 30 December 1896, GTA.
5. Faculty Minutes, 8 January 1897, GTA; Lyman Hall to George Winship, 16 August 1898, Correspondence of Lyman Hall, GTA.
6. Minutes of the Board of Trustees, 7 November 1896, GTA.
7. "$25,000 for the Tech," *Atlanta Constitution*, 25 November 1896.
8. "Some Features of the Legislature's Work," *Atlanta Constitution*, 25 November 1896.
9. "Mr. Knowles' Good Work," *Atlanta Constitution*, 26 November 1896.
10. "Tech's Bill Is Up," *Atlanta Constitution*, 2 December 1896.
11. "For the School of Technology," *Atlanta Constitution*, 3 December 1896.
12. "One Was Left, the Other Taken," *Atlanta Constitution*, 10 December 1896.
13. Minutes of the Board of Trustees, 30 December 1896, GTA.
14. Ibid., 23 June 1897, GTA.
15. Ibid., 1 September 1897, GTA.

16. Georgia School of Technology Catalog, 1897–98, GTA.
17. Lyman Hall to Mrs. R. N. Jones, 30 August 1898, and Hall to J. H. Williams, 16 October 1898, Correspondence of Lyman Hall, GTA.
18. Lyman Hall to N. E. Harris, 10 October 1898, Correspondence of Lyman Hall, GTA.
19. Lyman Hall to Governor Atkinson, 22 October 1898, Correspondence of Lyman Hall, GTA.
20. Faculty Minutes, 19 March 1897, GTA.
21. Georgia School of Technology Catalog, 1897–98, pp. 72–75, GTA.
22. Lyman Hall to B. Skalowski, 20 October 1898, Correspondence of Lyman Hall, GTA.
23. Lyman Hall to N. E. Harris, 19 January 1899, Correspondence of Lyman Hall, GTA.
24. Lyman Hall to N. E. Harris, 1 October 1899, Correspondence of Lyman Hall, GTA.
25. Minutes of the Board of Trustees, 30 December 1896, 23 June 1897, GTA.
26. Robert Belfield, "The Niagara System: The Evolution of an Electrical Power Complex at Niagara Falls, 1883–1896," *Proceedings of the Institute of Electrical and Electronics Engineers* 64 (September 1976): 1344–50.
27. Robert Rosenberg, "The Origins of EE Education: A Matter of Degree," *IEEE Spectrum* 21 (July 1984): 60–68.
28. From an item with biographical data on Tech faculty, filed in the Correspondence of Lyman Hall, November 1898, GTA; also see an obituary of Quick in the *Atlanta Constitution*, 5 September 1899.
29. Georgia School of Technology Catalog, 1897–98, GTA.
30. Faculty Minutes, 30 September 1899, GTA; obituary in the *Atlanta Constitution*, 5 September 1899; Lyman Hall to George Winship, 7 September 1899, Correspondence of Lyman Hall, GTA; Minutes of the Board of Trustees, 20 June 1901, GTA.
31. See a biographical sketch on Ford in "Electrical Engineers of the Times," *Electrical World and Engineer* 46 (1905): 518; Minutes of the Board of Trustees, 1 October 1902, GTA.
32. Minutes of the Board of Trustees, 22 June 1898, GTA.
33. Based on data from Georgia School of Technology Catalog, 1910–11, GTA.
34. See the *Textile History Review* 4 (1963): 150; *Georgia Historical and Industrial* (Atlanta: Georgia Department of Agriculture, 1901), p. 337.
35. Minutes of the Board of Trustees, 3 November 1897; Faculty Minutes, 5

November 1897, 10 December 1897, GTA; Lyman Hall to G. R. Glenn, 16 August 1898, Correspondence of Lyman Hall, GTA.
36. Faculty Minutes, 10 December 1897; Minutes of the Board of Trustees, 13 January 1898; Lyman Hall to C. P. Brooks, 31 January 1898, Correspondence of Lyman Hall, all in GTA.
37. See "Aaron French," *Dictionary of American Biography*, Allen Johnson et al., eds., 27 vols. (New York: Scribner's, 1928–), 7:23–24; Lyman Hall to William Stearns, 8 February 1898; Hall to A. French, February 1898, Correspondence of Lyman Hall, GTA.
38. Lyman Hall to John D. Rockefeller, 15 February 1898, Correspondence of Lyman Hall, GTA.
39. Copy of Hall's circular filed with letter to N. E. Harris, 9 February 1898; also a list of mills contacted, 4 June 1898; Lyman Hall to Clarence Knowles, 7 March 1898, all in Correspondence of Lyman Hall, GTA.
40. Lyman Hall to Clark Howell, 7 March 1898, Correspondence of Lyman Hall, GTA. Hall's letter stimulated an editorial entitled "We Must Have Textile School," *Atlanta Constitution*, 10 March 1898.
41. Lyman Hall to A. French, 28 February 1898, Correspondence of Lyman Hall, GTA.
42. Lyman Hall to N. E. Harris, 11 March 1898; Hall to A. French, 23 March 1898, both in Correspondence of Lyman Hall, GTA.
43. Lyman Hall to C. P. Brooks, 9 March 1898, Correspondence of Lyman Hall, GTA.
44. Lyman Hall to N. E. Harris, 25 March 1898, 10 October 1898; Hall to O. S. Porter, 2 May 1898, Correspondence of Lyman Hall; Georgia School of Technology Catalog, 1899–1900, pp. 101, 124, all in GTA.
45. Lyman Hall to the Governor, 25 June 1898, Correspondence of Lyman Hall, GTA.
46. Lyman Hall to A. French, 5 July 1898, 14 July 1898; Hall to H. G. Kittridge, 16 July 1898; Hall to Clark Howell, 16 July 1898, Correspondence of Lyman Hall, all in GTA; editorial "Atlanta Ought to Have It," *Atlanta Constitution*, 17 July 1898.
47. "President Lyman Hall," *Atlanta Constitution*, 7 August 1898.
48. Lyman Hall, information for state legislature, 19 November 1898, Correspondence of Lyman Hall, GTA.
49. J. A. Stewart, "Cotton Trade Schools in the South," *Scientific American* 82 (2 June 1900): 342.
50. "Georgia School of Technology," *Scientific American Supplement* 52 (1901): 21439–42.

51. Lyman Hall to N. E. Harris, 28 March 1899, 1 April 1899; Hall to A. French, 10 May 1899, all in Correspondence of Lyman Hall, GTA.
52. Lyman Hall to N. E. Harris, 23 May 1899, Correspondence of Lyman Hall, GTA.
53. Lyman Hall to N. E. Harris, 5 June 1899, Correspondence of Lyman Hall, GTA; Robert Preston Brooks, *The University of Georgia Under Sixteen Administrations, 1785–1955* (Athens: University of Georgia Press, 1956), p. 111; Kenneth Coleman, gen. ed., *A History of Georgia* (Athens: University of Georgia Press, 1977), pp. 327–28.
54. Lyman Hall to A. French, 8 October 1899, Correspondence of Lyman Hall; analysis of data from Georgia School of Technology Catalog, 1901–5, all in GTA.
55. "Tech Dorms Open This Monday," *Atlanta Constitution*, 27 September 1899; editorial, *Atlanta Constitution*, 31 October 1899.
56. Lyman Hall to A. French, 10 May 1899, 23 September 1899; Hall to N. E. Harris, 6 October 1899, 1 November 1899; Hall to W. B. Miles, 15 November 1899, all in Correspondence of Lyman Hall, GTA; Minutes of the Board of Trustees, 11 January 1900, all in GTA.
57. Minutes of the Board of Trustees, 3 October 1900, GTA; "The Tech Appropriation," *Atlanta Constitution*, 9 November 1900.
58. Lyman Hall to S. M. Inman, 4 October 1900; Hall to James Swann, 24 October 1900, both in Correspondence of Lyman Hall, GTA; obituary of James Swann and editorial "Death of James Swann," *Atlanta Constitution*, 2 May 1903.
59. "The School of Technology," *Atlanta Constitution*, 3 December 1900; also see "The Scene at Tech," *Atlanta Constitution*, 28 November 1900.
60. "Money for Tech Was Made Good," *Atlanta Constitution*, 14 December 1900; "Tech Will Be Given $87,000 to Expend for Improvement," *Atlanta Constitution*, 15 December 1900. The newspaper's arithmetic evidently was confused although some confusion was understandable in view of the various overlapping conditional contributions and appropriations. See also "The Tech Wins Out," *Atlanta Constitution*, 16 December 1900; letter to the editor, "Georgia's Greatest Educational Enterprise," *Atlanta Constitution*, 17 December 1900.
61. Lyman Hall to Fulton County Commission, 2 January 1901; Hall to A. French, 18 February 1901, 1 March 1901; Hall to James Swann, 25 January 1901, 24 April 1901; Hall to W. B. Miles, 19 August 1901, Correspondence of Lyman Hall, GTA; Georgia School of Technology Catalog, 1900–1901, GTA; "H. H. Miles Awarded Dormitory Contract," *Atlanta Constitution*, 11 April 1901. An additional gift of $2000 from Alfred Austell and $1500 from James Swann was announced in April 1901 to

enable completion of the Swann Dormitory according to the architect's specifications. See "Big Gift for Tech from Alfred Austell," *Atlanta Constitution*, 12 April 1901.

62. John W. Servos, "The Industrial Relations of Science: Chemistry at MIT, 1900–1939," *ISIS* 71 (December 1980): 531–49.
63. Minutes of the Board of Trustees, 2 January 1901, 30 April 1901, GTA; Georgia School of Technology Catalog, 1900–1901, GTA.
64. Georgia School of Technology Catalog, 1905–6, GTA; *Journal of the American Chemical Society* 26 (1904): 96; Robert B. Wallace, *Dress Her in White and Gold: A Biography of Georgia Tech and the Men Who Led Her*, rev. ed. (Atlanta: Georgia Tech Foundation, 1969), p. 112.
65. *Georgia Tech*, November 1900, January 1901, December 1901, and May 1902, GTA; Georgia School of Technology Catalog, 1895–6, GTA; Faculty Minutes, 16 November 1901, GTA. Lyman Hall wrote in 1898 that the Tech faculty did not care to join an oratorical association since "our courses here are exclusively scientific and we have but little time to devote to oratory." The statement is from Lyman Hall to J. R. Stratton, 27 October 1898, Correspondence of Lyman Hall, GTA.
66. *Georgia Tech*, December 1901, GTA; Faculty Minutes, 16 November 1901, GTA; Georgia School of Technology Catalog, 1898–99, 1909–10, GTA; Marion L. Brittain, *The Story of Georgia Tech* (Chapel Hill University of North Carolina Press, 1948), p. 36; for biographical information on Floyd Furlow, see *National Cyclopaedia of American Biography*, 76 vols. (New York: James T. White and Co., 1898–), 20:240–41, and *Dictionary of American Biography*, 7:75.
67. C. H. Kicklighter, "Future of the Technological School," *Georgia Tech*, December 1900, GTA; "A Trip to Birmingham," *Georgia Tech*, April 1902; Georgia School of Technology Catalog, 1909–10, GTA.
68. *Georgia Tech*, January 1901, March 1901, November 1901, and January 1902, GTA; Faculty Minutes, 3 January 1902, GTA.
69. Wallace, *White and Gold*, pp. 48–60, 467–68. On Heisman, see Kenneth Coleman and Charles Stephen Gurr, eds., *Dictionary of Georgia Biography* (Athens: University of Georgia Press, 1983), 1:433–34.
70. Brittain, *The Story of Georgia Tech*, p. 45; Minutes of the Board of Trustees, 25 June 1900, GTA.
71. Data with letter from Lyman Hall to Clarence Knowles, 8 November 1898, Correspondence of Lyman Hall, GTA; Georgia School of Technology Catalog, 1898–99, GTA; James E. Brittain and Robert C. McMath, Jr., "Engineers and the New South Creed: The Formation and Early Development of Georgia Tech," *Technology and Culture* 18 (April 1977): 195; Lyman Hall to Clarence Knowles, 24 November 1898, Cor-

respondence of Lyman Hall, GTA; Georgia School of Technology Catalog, 1905–6, GTA.
72. Lyman Hall to N. E. Harris, 10 June 1898; Hall to W. J. Holmes, 12 July 1898, Correspondence of Lyman Hall, GTA; data comparing Tech with twelve other schools collected by faculty committee chaired by W. H. Emerson, in Faculty Minutes, 21 May 1904, GTA.
73. Georgia School of Technology Catalog, 1898–99, GTA; Brittain and McMath, "Engineers and the New South Creed," p. 196.
74. From a list of graduates of Clemson College, S.C., and occupations represented, 1896–1901, Clemson University Archives, Clemson, S.C.; also see Brittain and McMath, "Engineers and the New South Creed," p. 196.
75. Brittain and McMath, "Engineers and the New South Creed," p. 197.
76. From Georgia School of Technology Catalog, 1905–6, GTA.
77. Brittain and McMath, "Engineers and the New South Creed," p. 193.
78. H. L. Smith, first presidential address on "United Effort the Herald of Success," 28 June 1899, vertical files (Alumni Association), GTA.
79. Lyman Hall to A. French, 14 October 1901, Correspondence of Lyman Hall, GTA.
80. Brittain, *The Story of Georgia Tech*, pp. 36–37; "Technological Fund Needs $1000," *Atlanta Constitution*, 17 June 1902; "The Tech's Good Fortune," *Atlanta Constitution*, 20 June 1902; "Tech Ends Year with $20,000 to Her Credit," *Atlanta Constitution*, 20 June 1902; "New Department Created at Tech," *Atlanta Constitution*, 20 June 1902; Minutes of the Board of Trustees, 19 June 1902, GTA.
81. Minutes of the Board of Trustees, 7 January 1903, 1 October 1902, 6 January 1904, 7 October 1903, and 6 April 1904, GTA.
82. "Georgia Tech Receives $5000 as Gift from William R. Hearst and "The School of Technology," *Atlanta Constitution*, 19 June 1903.
83. Transcript of Samuel Spencer's talk entitled "Industrial Education," in booklet, *Georgia School of Technology 1904*, unclassified box of Hall materials, GTA. The booklet also contains Hall's remarks at the commencement exercises.
84. Minutes of the Board of Trustees, 5 April 1905, 23 August 1905, GTA; Lyman Hall to George F. Peabody, 18 February 1905, 15 March 1905, unclassified box of Hall materials, GTA; Faculty Minutes, 21 August 1905, GTA; "Hall's Memory to Be Honored," *Atlanta Constitution*, 11 November 1905; "New Laboratory Was Dedicated," *Atlanta Constitution*, 26 November 1905. The Atlanta newspapers reported in August 1905 that Hall's health had slowly been failing for the past twelve months. His death was attributed to the accumulated stress of overwork

that had caused "nervous prostration." See "Captain Hall Grows No Better," *Atlanta Journal*, 11 August 1905; "Captain Hall Is Slowly Sinking," *Atlanta Journal*, 13 August 1905; "Lyman Hall, President of Tech, Passes Away—His Useful Career Ends," *Atlanta Journal*, 17 August 1905; "Hall Succumbs to Prostration," *Atlanta Constitution*, 18 August 1905.
85. J. S. Akers to K. G. Matheson, 30 October 1905, unclassified box of Hall materials, GTA.

Chapter Four

1. "Kenneth G. Matheson," *Who's Who*, vol. 1, p. 788, copy in presidential files, uncatalogued, Georgia Tech Archives, hereafter cited as GTA; *National Cyclopaedia of American Biography*, 76 vols. (New York: James T. White and Co., 1946), 23:23; *Blue Print* 1908. Matheson also did graduate work at the University of Chicago and Columbia. He received honorary degrees from Washington and Lee, the University of Georgia, and the University of Pennsylvania. *Georgia Tech Alumnus*, January 1932, pp. 51–52.
2. K. G. Matheson to William G. Perry, 20 December 1900; Lyman Hall to William G. Perry, 21 December 1900, vertical files (William Gilmer Perry), GTA; William Gilmer Perry, Tribute to Lyman Hall, 21 August 1905, presidential files, uncatalogued, GTA; "Memories of Georgia Tech, 1904–1913," presidential files (J. B. Crenshaw), GTA.
3. William Gilmer Perry, J. B. Crenshaw, and J. B. Edwards, Tribute to Kenneth G. Matheson, 29 November 1931, presidential files, uncatalogued, GTA.
4. *Annual Report* of the Georgia Institute of Technology for the years 1905–6, pp. 3–9, 11, 55–56.
5. M. L. Brittain, *Outline of the Laws, Appropriations, Gifts and History of the Georgia School of Technology, 1885–1923* (Atlanta: n.p., 1923), p. 36; *Annual Announcements of the Georgia School of Technology*, 1906, p. 94; *Bulletin of the Georgia School of Technology*, 1919–20, p. 30. For a full description of Tech's expansion in land and buildings, see Warren Drury, "The Architectural Development of Georgia Tech," unpublished M.Arch. thesis, Georgia Institute of Technology, 1984; N. E. Harris, N. P. Pratt, and J. S. Akers, Tribute to K. G. Matheson on his resignation, filed with Minutes of the Board of Trustees, 5 October 1921, and *Bulletin*, April 1922, pp. 33–34.
6. K. G. Matheson's correspondence with R. B. Ridley, 26 December

1906; D. C. Peacock, 25 July 1906; George Foster Peabody, 16 August 1906; L. G. Myers, 1 October 1906; Edwin C. Peters, 13 June, 6 November 1906; J. Carol Payne and George W. Parrott, 30 November 1906; form letter, 21 December 1906, all in presidential files, uncatalogued, GTA. See also E. C. Peters to Athletic Association, October 1909, vertical files (Athletic Association Contracts), GTA; J. B. Crenshaw, "History of Grant Field," vertical files (Buildings and Grounds), GTA; M. L. Brittain, *The Story of Georgia Tech* (Chapel Hill: University of North Carolina Press, 1948), p. 47.

7. *Annual Report,* 1912–13, pp. 20–22; ibid., 1913–14, p. 63; ibid., 1914–15, p. 17; *Technique,* 17 January 1912; *Annual Announcements,* 1911–12, p. 26; ibid., 1912–13, p. 33; J. B. Crenshaw, "History of Grant Field," vertical files (Buildings and Grounds), GTA.

8. For a full account of the details concerning the acquisition of Grant Field, see J. B. Crenshaw, "History of Grant Field," vertical files (Buildings and Grounds, Grant Field), GTA, and, by the same author, "The Georgia Tech Athletic Association, 1922–1923," *Georgia Tech Alumnus,* March 1923, pp. 19–23. For Matheson's efforts and the board's response, see Minutes of the Executive Committee of the Board of Trustees, 24 April, 18 September 1919; 25 May, 13 July 1921; 16 January 1922; and Minutes of the Board of Trustees, 7 January 1920; 4 October 1921; 5 January 1922.

9. The board was not interested in disposing of the Texas lands because it was hoped they might produce oil. Brittain, *The Story of Georgia Tech,* pp. 100–108; Robert B. Wallace, *Dress Her in White and Gold: A Biography of Georgia Tech and the Men Who Led Her,* rev. ed. (Atlanta: Georgia Tech Foundation, 1969), pp. 65–67.

10. *Annual Announcements,* 1900–1901, p. 96; Annual Reports of the Librarian, 1901–2, 1904–5, 1905–6, vertical files (Reports of Librarian), GTA; Laura Hammond, "History of Georgia Tech Library Opening," clipping, no date, vertical files (Georgia Tech Library), GTA; Jas. Bartram to K. G. Matheson, 16 March 1906, copy in vertical files (Library Book Shower), GTA.

11. *Annual Announcements,* 1909–10, pp. 10–11, 98; *Technique,* 17 November 1911; Martha C. Trnavsky, R.N., "A History of Health Care at Tech," vertical files (Health Services–History), GTA. Tech students raised the last portion of the money necessary to open the hospital.

12. W. H. Glenn to Walter Nash, 22 June 1910, vertical files (W. H. Glenn), GTA; Faculty Minutes, 30 August 1910; *Annual Announcements,* 1911–12, pp. 34, 112; ibid., 1920–21, p. 34; Minutes of the Executive Committee of the Board of Trustees, 2 February 1920; *Annual Report,*

1910–11, p. 20; ibid., 1911–12, p. 46; ibid., 1919–20, pp. 58–59; ibid., 1920–21, pp. 53–54; Wallace, *White and Gold*, pp. 65, 412.
13. *Annual Report*, 1912–13, p. 20.
14. *Bulletin*, July 1916, p. 24; *Blue Print*, 1916; "Tech Newsletter," 12 March, 1 June 1912, vertical files (World Student Fund), GTA; *Annual Report*, 1909–10, pp. 11, 14–15; ibid., 1911–12, p. 46; Faculty Minutes, 10 March 1911; clipping, no date, vertical files (Buildings), GTA.
15. Ultimately, Mr. Grant's contributions to Grant Field facilities totaled $50,000. J. B. Crenshaw, "The Georgia Tech Athletic Association, 1922–23," *Georgia Tech Alumnus*, March 1923, pp. 19–23. See also Wallace, *White and Gold*, p. 69; J. B. Crenshaw, "History of Grant Field," vertical files (Buildings and Grounds), GTA; John W. Grant, to J. S. Akers, 17 January 1920, vertical files (Georgia Tech History), GTA; *Annual Announcements*, 1912–13, p. 33; ibid., 1913–14, p. 168; Minutes of the Executive Committee of the Board of Trustees, 24 April, 18 September 1919; *Annual Report*, 1915–16, p. 14.
16. *Technique*, 17 January 1912; *Annual Report*, 1911–12, p. 49. Drury states that Phinehas V. Stephens provided the initial design for the power plant. As finally executed, it represented the work of Francis P. Smith, head of Tech's Department of Architecture. "Architectural Development of Georgia Tech," pp. 106–7.
17. *Annual Report*, 1912–13, pp. 22–23; ibid., 1913–14, pp. 63–65; ibid., 1914–15; pp. 14–15; *Annual Announcements*, 1914–15, p. 29; Phinehas V. Stephens, "General Outline Greater Georgia Tech Movement," 26 February 1921, pp. 2–4, Matheson Family Papers, GTA.
18. *Annual Report*, 1914–15, p. 17; ibid., 1915–16, pp. 17–18; *Annual Announcements*, 1914–15, p. 29; ibid., 1916–17, p. 29. More extravagant predictions of what the power laboratory could mean to Georgia and its people are contained in fund-raising brochures issued in 1914 and 1918. See *Georgia's Greater Tech*, brochure [1914], vertical files (History), GTA, and pamphlet, 1918, in Matheson Family Papers, GTA.
19. *Annual Report*, 1905–6, p. 11.
20. Faculty Minutes, 31 March 1909, 30 October 1913, 10 October 1914; *Annual Announcements*, 1906, pp. 101–2; ibid., 1911–12, p. 46; J. E. Brittain and R. C. McMath, "Engineers and the New South Creed: The Formation and Early Development of Georgia Tech," *Technology and Culture* 18 (April 1977): 189.
21. Faculty Minutes, 12 November 1908, 28 October, 11 November, 23 December 1909, 28 January, 24 February 1910.
22. *Annual Report*, 1911–12, pp. 7–8; ibid., 1915–16, p. 16; Faculty Minutes, 6 January, 1 December 1910, 30 October, 7 November 1913, 5

March, 16 April, 9 October 1914, 22, 30 September 1915, 19 November 1920; Brittain, *Outline of Laws, Appropriations, Gifts,* p. 31; *Annual Announcements,* 1913–14, pp. 182–89; Society for the Promotion of Engineering Education, *Report of the Investigation of Engineering Education, 1923–29* (University of Pittsburgh, 1930), 1:446–48.
23. Faculty Minutes, 28 September 1906; *Annual Announcements,* 1917–18, p. 19; *Technique,* 8 October 1920; Minutes of the Board of Trustees, 4 October 1921; Brittain, *The Story of Georgia Tech,* pp. 73, 83. Annual enrollment figures from 1888 through April 1922 appear in the *Bulletin* of the Georgia School of Technology, April 1922, p. 35. While they do not agree exactly with those given above for the years after World War I, they are generally similar.
24. Faculty Minutes, 12 June 1906, 4 March 1908, 25 November 1910, 12 January 1911, 15 May 1912; Wallace, *White and Gold,* p. 396.
25. K. G. Matheson to the Carnegie Foundation, 13, 14 December 1906, presidential files, uncatalogued, GTA; *Technique,* 31 January, 20 March 1912; Faculty Minutes, 7 March 1912.
26. *Annual Report,* 1905–6, pp. 8, 55–56.
27. Ibid., 1911–12, pp. 10, 21, 44; ibid., 1909–10, pp. 7–10, 14, 16–17; ibid., 1913–14, pp. 54–58.
28. *Annual Report,* 1917–18, pp. 16–18, 19.
29. "Memories of Georgia Tech, 1904–1913," presidential files (J. B. Crenshaw), GTA; "Statutes," 21 July 1944, presidential files (W. C. Perry), GTA.
30. 21 July 1944, presidential files (W. G. Perry), GTA; Faculty Minutes (styled variously Council Minutes, Reports of the committee to the council, or Steering Committee Minutes but in all cases filed with Faculty Minutes), 5 December 1919, 9, 23, 30 January, 24 February, 5 March 1920, 1, 7 April 1921. Tech's governance accorded with that found in the great majority of American engineering schools. See Charles Riborg Mann, "A Study of Engineering Education," Bulletin no. 11, p. 29, in *Carnegie Foundation for the Advancement of Teaching,* Bulletin nos. 9–11 (New York, 1916).
31. Faculty Minutes, 12 October, 1 December 1911, 17 October 1912, 26 February 1914, 13 February, 19 December 1918.
32. Faculty Minutes, 28 October 1909, 17 February, 27 October 1910; Horage Sturges to Joseph Pettit, 8 March 1979, vertical files (Southern Association of Colleges and Secondary Schools), GTA. This folder contains a copy of *A Short History of the Southern Association of Colleges and Secondary Schools* by Guy Snavely.
33. Faculty Minutes, 1 February 1912, 8 May, 18 October 1913, 13 November 1914, 8 June 1917; Gilbert Boggs to Charles Holmes Herty, 1907,

Notes to Pages 118–22

Herty Papers, Special Collections, Robert W. Woodruff Memorial Library, Emory University.
34. *Technique*, 28 February 1912; Faculty Minutes, 19, 20 October 1916; *Annual Announcements*, 1915–16, pp. 38–39. See chapter 2 for references to Coon and Emerson.
35. Faculty Minutes, 11 March, 25 April, 19 May, 16 August, 4 November 1921. The master of science degree was approved by the Board of Trustees in June 1921. Minutes of the Board of Trustees, June 11, 1921. A graduate program at Tech was first considered in 1911 but the idea was quickly rejected "under existing conditions." Faculty Minutes, 16 November 1911.
36. "History of Modern Languages," no date, vertical files (Modern Languages), GTA; "History 1888–1938," vertical files (J. B. Crenshaw), GTA; Faculty Minutes, 25 November 1910, 12 January 1911. The English department also taught economic theory, general history, and physical geography, according to the *Annual Announcements*, 1907–8, p. 38. Matheson advised his faculty in 1910 that in the Board of Trustees and among friends of the school there was much discussion about liberalizing the course of study at Tech. Many southern schools had come to the conclusion that it would be wise to do so. "The Worcester Polytechnic Institute," Tech's original model, "had practically done this although there was no distinct acknowledgment of the fact," Matheson told his colleagues. Faculty Minutes, 25 November 1910.
37. *Annual Announcements*, 1905–6, p. 69; Faculty Minutes, 27 February 1908.
38. Faculty Minutes, 27 February 1908; *Annual Announcements*, 1907–8, p. 79; ibid., 1908–9, p. 75.
39. Paul Weber, copy of manuscript, "History of Chemical Engineering at Georgia Tech," School of Social Sciences file; *Annual Announcements*, 1907–8, p. 27; vertical files (Bulletins), GTA.
40. *Annual Announcements*, 1907–8, p. 97; ibid., 1909–10, p. 100; *Bulletin*, Night Class Number [1908]; *Annual Report*, 1911–12, pp. 44–45, 47; ibid., 1915–16, p. 13; ibid., 1919–20, pp. 50, 54; Engineering Evening School, Minutes of the Night School Committee, 1923–42, with insert by R. S. Howell, director of the Engineering Extension Division, "Engineering Evening School, 1908–58."
41. Faculty Minutes, 14 January, 8 May, 10 June 1909.
42. Kapp's remarks appeared in the *Technique*, 3 December 1920. See also *Technique*, 24 January 1912, 14 January, 8 April 1921; Faculty Minutes, 10 June 1909, 11 January, 9 May 1912, 29 November, 19 December 1918, 8 January 1919; *Annual Announcements*, 1912–13, pp. 20, 70–71; ibid., 1913–14, p. 18; *Annual Report*, 1912–13, p. 19; ibid., 1915–

16, p. 14; *Bulletin,* 1919–20, pp. 82–83; Minutes of the Executive Committee, Board of Trustees, 30 July 1920; Minutes of the Board of Trustees, 13 October 1920, 9 March 1922. For a full discussion of the cooperative movement in American engineering education through 1925, see Society for the Promotion of Engineering Education, *Bulletin* no. 12, *Report of the Investigation of Engineering Education,* 1923–29, vol. 1 (Pittsburgh: University of Pittsburgh, 1930), and David F. Noble, *America by Design: Science, Technology and the Rise of Corporate Capitalism* (New York: Alfred A. Knopf, 1977), especially chap. 8, pp. 184–202.
43. Society for the Promotion of Engineering Education, *Bulletin* no. 11, *Report of the Investigation of Engineering Education,* 1923–29, pp. 538, 548–49.
44. *Technique,* 31 January 1912.
45. Richard Teach, History of IMMS, unpublished manuscript, no date, copy in Tech Project File, School of Social Sciences, pp. 1–2; Faculty Minutes, 5 October 1911; *Technique,* 21 February, 10 April 1912.
46. Teach, History of IMMS, pp. 2–3; Faculty Minutes, 7 March 1912; *Annual Announcements,* 1912–13, pp. 8, 203–4; *Annual Report,* 1911–12, p. 49.
47. Faculty Minutes, 16, 20 September, 6 November 1913; Teach, History of IMMS, pp. 3–4; *Annual Announcements,* 1913–14, pp. 158–61; *Bulletin,* July 1916, p. 22. Initial funding for the School of Commerce came entirely from a group of "guarantors," many of whom were Tech alumni and prominent bankers, lawyers, and certified public accountants. The school expected to assume the obligation "at an early date." *Blue Print,* 1922.
48. *Annual Report,* 1913–14, pp. 59, 61–62; ibid., 1914–15, p. 10; ibid., 1915–16, p. 13; ibid., 1916–17, p. 12; Teach, History of IMMS, pp. 5–7; *Annual Announcements,* 1916–17, pp. 80–81; *Technique,* 23 October 1917; *Bulletin,* 1918–19, p. 4. According to the *Technique,* 27 April 1979, Ms. Wise began teaching in 1920. Teach and M. L. Brittain disagree about the time spent by the Evening School in its various rented quarters.
49. Faculty Minutes, 13 April, 12 October 1916, 15 February, 1 November 1917; Minutes of the Executive Committee of the Board of Trustees, 2 November 1917; *Annual Announcements,* 1917–18, pp. 125–26.
50. *Annual Report,* 1920–21, p. 50; Wallace, *White and Gold,* p. 71.
51. *Annual Report,* 1914–15, pp. 12–13; ibid., 1917–18, pp. 18–19; ibid., 1918–19, pp. 15–16; ibid., 1919–20, p. 56; ibid., 1921–22; *Annual Announcements,* 1920–21, p. 51; *Technique,* 14 January 1921.
52. *Annual Report,* 1919–20, pp. 59–60.

53. "Technical Training," brochure, vertical files (Georgia Tech History), GTA; vertical files (William Howard Taft), GTA; vertical files (Commencement, 1917), GTA; *Technique,* 27 May 1921; Faculty Minutes, 9 January, 21 April, 15, 29 May, 7 November 1913, 19 February, 16 April 1914, 15 October 1915.
54. "Memories of Tech, 1904–13," presidential files (J. B. Crenshaw), GTA; Faculty Minutes, 4 May 1911.
55. Faculty Minutes, 24 April 1912, 20 March 1913, 2 December 1915, 24 March 1916.
56. *Annual Report,* 1919–20, pp. 61–62.
57. W. A. Emerson, "Description of Early Days at Tech," *Blue Print,* 1916; Faculty Minutes, 9 November 1916, 6 January, 29 April, 13 November 1913, 11 February 1916, 16 December 1921.
58. Clipping, *Technique,* 28 October 1915, vertical files (World Student Fund), GTA; *Blue Print,* 1908.
59. For example, as part of a regional program conducted on southern campuses in 1912, about ninety-five Tech students began an exhaustive project under the direction of Professor George B. Franklin to study "Negro Life in the South." *Technique,* 28 February 1912, 28 October 1915; *Annual Announcements,* 1906–7, p. 121.
60. Faculty Minutes, 27 September 1915, 7 March 1921, 8 February 1922; *Technique,* 2 October, 6 November 1917, 30 April 1918, 8 October 1920; vertical files (World Student Fund), GTA.
61. *Georgia Tech,* scattered issues from November 1900–June 1904; vertical files (Textile Engineering School), GTA; *Yellow Jacket,* October 1910–December 1911; *Annual Announcements,* 1908–9, pp. 100–101; *Blue Print,* 1908, 1912. The *Georgia Tech,* begun in 1894, was preceded by a publication called the *Technologian.* First issued in the spring of 1891, it did not last a year. The *Yellow Jacket* lasted from 1908 to 1955, with time out for bad behavior. Wallace, *White and Gold,* pp. 20, 350–51.
62. *Technique,* 6 March 1912; *Annual Announcements,* 1911–12, p. 156. Walter Read (Doc) Boyd states that E. A. Turner, secretary of the YMCA, started the *Technique.* "Some Firsts at Georgia Tech . . . 1908 to . . . 1913," vertical files (Walter Boyd), GTA. But J. B. Crenshaw, writing in the *Yellow Jacket,* May 1913, claims founding honors for Professor Albert Blohm of the English department.
63. Faculty Minutes, 20 March 1913; *Annual Announcements,* 1911–12, p. 156.
64. *Technique,* 21 January, 11 February, 18 March, 15, 22 April 1921; Minutes of the Executive Committee of the Board of Trustees, 12 November 1921. The *Technique,* noting that the *Tornado* had joined the

478 Notes to Pages 130–34

Yellow Jacket as a "deceased member," promised that Tech would have an approved "comic paper" of its own by the next academic year. It did. The *Yellow Jacket* was revived as a humor magazine. *Technique*, 22 April 1921.

65. *Technique*, 5 March 1918, 8 April, 20 May 1921; Faculty Minutes, 8 June 1914; *Annual Report*, 1913–14, p. 62; ibid., 1916–17, p. 11; ibid., 1917–18, p. 20.
66. Vertical files (Honor Society; Phi Kappa Phi), GTA; *Technique*, 20 March 1912.
67. Faculty Minutes, 3 November 1910; *Technique*, 21 November 1911; *Annual Announcements*, 1911–12, pp. 159–60.
68. *Technique*, 8 December 1911, 21 February 1912, 9 October 1917; Faculty Minutes, 17 October 1912; *Blue Print*, 1913; "Some Firsts at Georgia Tech," p. 15, vertical files (Walter Boyd), GTA; vertical files (Glee Club 1911), GTA. Cobb was a well-known drama coach in Atlanta. The Drama Club was renamed the Marionettes a few years after its founding.
69. *Technique*, 7 February, 6 March, 13 March 1912; Faculty Minutes, 19 December 1912.
70. *Technique*, 7 May 1918, 25 February 1921.
71. *Technique*, 4 December 1917, 19 February 1918; Faculty Minutes, 6 February 1922; *Atlanta Constitution*, 8 May 1949; Wallace, *White and Gold*, 103–6.
72. Faculty Minutes, 11 March 1915; *Blue Print*, 1910, 1916, 1917, and 1921, p. 208; Minutes of the Executive Committee of the Board of Trustees, 19 April 1921.
73. Faculty Minutes, 18 October 1919, 16 December 1921; *Technique*, 25 February 1921, 11 December 1917, 3 December 1920; *Blue Print*, 1922.
74. *Technique*, 6 March 1912; *Blue Print*, 1922; Faculty Minutes, 16 October 1913, 14 January, 19, 26 May 1921, 27 April, 4 May 1922. An official history of Alpha Epsilon Pi suggests that existing chapters of Phi Epsilon Pi and Tau Epsilon Phi, Jewish fraternities already established on the Tech campus, may have felt threatened by the effort to establish a chapter of Alpha Epsilon Pi. Allegedly they complained to the faculty that there was "no room for the new group." George S. Toll, *Alpha Epsilon Pi: The First Sixty-Five Years, 1913–1978* (Fulton, Mo: Ovid Bell Press, Inc., 1978), pp. 469–73. After years as a "social club," a chapter of the fraternity was finally recognized in 1946.
75. Faculty Minutes, 9 May 1912, 8 April 1915; *Technique*, 5 June 1912; *Blue Print*, 1913, p. 98.
76. *Technique*, 17 December 1920.

77. Faculty Minutes, 19 May 1922; Wallace, *White and Gold*, p. 391.
78. *Technique*, 27 May 1921; *Annual Announcements*, 1920–21, p. 100. Wallace provides a good description of this historic "first." *White and Gold*, p. 153–5.
79. J. B. Crenshaw, "The Georgia Tech Athletic Association, 1922–23," *Georgia Tech Alumnus*, March 1923, pp. 19–23; Athletic Association History, no date, vertical files (Buildings and Grounds—Grant Field), GTA; Faculty Minutes, 20 March 1913, 19, 26 February 1914, 3 May 1917; *Annual Announcements*, 1911–12; Wallace, *White and Gold*, p. 124.
80. Faculty Minutes, 29 June, 7 July 1914, 23, 25 September, 2, 7 December 1915. The incident involved an SIAA challenge of a Tech player's eligibility. *Blue Print*, 1916. Tech joined another conference, the Southern Intercollegiate Conference, in 1922. *Technique*, 4 March 1921; vertical files (Southern Intercollegiate Conference), GTA. For a history of the Southern Intercollegiate Athletic Association, see Nathan W. Daugherty, *Educators and Athletes: The Southeastern Conference, 1894–1972* (Knoxville: University of Tennessee Press, 1976), pp. 20–30.
81. Minutes of Executive Committee of the Board of Trustees, 17 September 1917; Minutes of the Board of Trustees, 27 October 1917.
82. Faculty Minutes, 2 November 1917, 29 November 1918.
83. Faculty Minutes, 13 January 1919; *Annual Report*, 1918–19, p. 15; ibid., 1919–20, p. 57.
84. *Technique*, 4 March 1921; W. T. Alexander, "Athletics at Tech," *Georgia Tech Alumnus*, March 1923, p. 13; Wallace, *White and Gold*, pp. 52–54; vertical files (Basketball 1906), GTA; *Blue Print*, 1910, 1913; *Technique*, 24 November 1911, 10 January 1912, 12 February 1918; Faculty Minutes, 5 December 1919.
85. Georgia Tech Track Team Records, 1907–13, vertical files (Track Team), GTA; correspondence, 25 February, 23 October, 26 November 1919, vertical files (Golf), GTA; vertical files (Robert T. Jones), GTA; *Technique*, 14 January 1921; Faculty Minutes, 18 September 1920, 21 January 1921.
86. Vertical files (Football, misc.), GTA; Wallace, *White and Gold*, p. 468; W. N. Randle, football article, *Blue Print*, 1908; *Technique*, 7 November 1911.
87. Vertical files (Athletic Association Contracts, 1903–19), GTA.
88. Vertical files (John W. Heisman), GTA. For other profiles of Heisman, see Wallace, *White and Gold*, pp. 55–60; Al Thomy, *The Ramblin' Wreck: A Story of Georgia Tech Football* (Huntsville, Ala.: Strode Publishers, [1973]), pp. 33–38; John T. Brady, *The Heisman: A Symbol of Excellence*, ed. John A. Walsh (New York: Atheneum, 1984), chap. 1;

480   Notes to Pages 139–42

and L. F. Woodruff, *A History of Southern Football, 1890–1928*, 3 vols. (Atlanta, Ga.: Walter W. Brown Publishing Co., 1928), 1:142–43.
89. Wallace, *White and Gold*, p. 468.
90. Quoted in *Technique*, 30 October 1917.
91. Ibid., 30 October, 6 November 1917.
92. *Technique*, 6 November 1918. The *Philadelphia Ledger* was also highly complimentary about Tech's "splendid record." Noting that Tech's team was composed of eleven men under military age, three who had been rejected, and five who planned to enlist when the season ended, the *Ledger* thought Tech was not only doing its bit but playing good football besides. Quoted in *Technique*, 20 November 1917.
93. Quoted in *Technique*, 4 December 1917. The game with Auburn was filmed from two cameras atop the wooden stands and one on the sidelines. Besides the *Sun*, the New York *Globe, Evening Mail*, and *Telegram* all awarded the national football championship to Georgia Tech. But W. R. Hearst's *Journal* voted for Pittsburgh, undefeated in three seasons.
94. *Technique*, 15 October, 22 September, 8 October 1920; clipping, *Georgian*, 11 June 1912, vertical files (Commencement 1912), GTA; *Blue Print*, 1916; Minutes of the Executive Committee of the Board of Trustees, 12 April 1920; Minutes of the Board of Trustees, 8 June 1920.
95. Wallace, *White and Gold*, p. 469; *Technique*, 12, 19 November, 17 December 1920; vertical files (Football 1920), GTA.
96. *Technique*, 12 November, 17 December 1920, 11 February, 18 March 1921.
97. Excerpts from an unidentified biography of Leonard Wood, no date, vertical files (General Leonard Wood), GTA; Thomy, *The Ramblin' Wreck*; Wallace, *White and Gold*, pp. 467–68; K. G. Matheson to J. B. Crenshaw, 20 November 1923; vertical files (Football, 1923), GTA.
98. Exactly who those enemies were is not clear, but among some of the individuals supporting the charges against Tech were an Atlanta attorney, Marion Smith, a son of Hoke Smith, and Eugene Talmadge, then a student at the University of Georgia. Vertical files (Red Box), GTA. Georgia was also under investigation in 1907–8 because of charges that her team was loaded with "ringers." Correspondence between W. D. Hooper, athletic director at the university, and his brother-in-law, Charles H. Herty at the University of North Carolina, November and December 1907, in Herty Papers, Special Collections, Robert W. Woodruff Memorial Library, Emory University.
99. Faculty Minutes, 25 May, 22 September 1911; *Technique*, 24 November, 1 December 1911.

100. Faculty Minutes, 18, 26 May 1916; Memo, no date, presidential files (J. B. Crenshaw), GTA.
101. *Atlanta Journal*, 18 May 1919, vertical files (Football, 1919), GTA; J. B. Crenshaw to the Board of Trustees, 27 May 1919, vertical files (Athletic Association Annual Report), GTA; J. B. Crenshaw to S. V. Sanford, 19 May 1919, S. V. Sanford to J. B. Crenshaw, 22 May 1919; Faculty Minutes, 23 May 1919; "Memories of Tech," presidential files (J. B. Crenshaw), GTA; Minutes of the Board of Trustees, 14, 19 June 1919.
102. For early efforts to resume relations see Minutes of the Board of Trustees, 13 October 1920. For faculty objections see Faculty Minutes, 15, 20 October 1920, 1, 4, 5, 10 November 1921. Additional material appears in vertical files (Football, 1921), GTA; and student reaction occurs in the *Technique*, 15, 22 October 1920, 14 January 1921. For the resumption of relations see vertical files (Southern Conference), GTA. For J. B. Crenshaw's private opinion of the alumni, businessmen, journalists, and politicians who wanted to restore relations with Georgia, see J. B. Crenshaw to Henry W. Grady, 10 November 1921, vertical files (Football, 1921), GTA.
103. Noble, *America by Design*, pp. 224–26. For a full discussion of American colleges during the First World War, see Parke R. Kolbe, *The Colleges in Wartime and After: A Contemporary Account of the Effect of the War upon Higher Education in America* (New York: Appleton, 1919), and Arthur Dean, *Our Schools in Wartime and After* (Boston: Ginn, 1918).
104. Stephens first brought Georgia Tech to the Aero Club's attention in 1915, when he presented a slide show at the First Pan American Aeronautical Exposition in New York. "General Outline Greater Georgia Tech Movement," 26 February 1921, p. 3, Matheson Family Papers, GTA. Faculty Minutes, 19 October 1916; Minutes of the Board of Trustees, 6 March, 4 April 1917.
105. Faculty Minutes, 16, 28, 29 May 1917; Minutes of the Board of Trustees, 29 May, 8 June 1917; contract, 1 July 1917, vertical files (Military Aeronautics, School of), GTA. See also Kolbe, *The Colleges in Wartime and After*, pp. 41–43, and Dean, *Our Schools in Wartime and After*, p. 98. The seven other schools were the University of California, the University of Illinois, the University of Texas, Ohio State, Cornell, Princeton, and MIT.
106. Minutes of the Executive Committee of the Board of Trustees, 8 May, 3 August 1917; *Blue Print*, 1918; *Technique*, 2 October 1917. Aware that the University of Virginia, Tulane, and North Carolina A&M hoped to lure the aviation school away from Tech by offering better facilities,

Matheson appealed to the Public Safety Committee of the Chamber of Commerce to pay for the alterations. They responded handsomely and the evicted freshmen moved to rented quarters in the Old Washington Seminary Building. Faculty Minutes, 30 September 1917.

107. *Technique,* 2, 30 October 1917, 15 January, 17 May 1918; *Annual Announcements,* 1917–18, pp. 184–86; Minutes of the Executive Committee of the Board of Trustees, 26 December 1917, 8, 18 January 1918; Reorganization of Aeronautics School, 12 January 1918, vertical files (Military Aeronautics, School of), GTA.

108. *Annual Announcements,* 1915–16, pp. 96–97, 189; ibid., 1917–18, p. 191; Minutes of the Board of Trustees, 18 January, 14 May, 10 June 1918; Faculty Minutes, 28 November 1917, 16 January, 7 February, 21, 26 August 1918; Minutes of the Executive Committee of the Board of Trustees, 4 May 1918. See also Kolbe, *The Colleges in Wartime and After,* pp. 62–65.

109. Faculty Minutes, 1 May, 13, 30 August 1917; *Technique,* 2, 20, 27 October, 4 December 1917.

110. "History of the Georgia Institute of Technology Army ROTC," typescript, March 1969, pp. 1–3, vertical files (Major John H. Matthews), GTA.

111. Minutes of the Board of Trustees, 8 June, 16 August 1917; *Annual Announcements,* 1917–18, p. 190; *Technique,* 2 October 1917, 15 January 1918.

112. *Annual Announcements,* 1917–18, p. 190; Minutes of the Board of Trustees, 18 January 1918; *Technique,* 12, 19 February, 12 March, 9 April 1918; Faculty Minutes, 13 February, 7 March 1918.

113. *Blue Print,* 1919; *Bulletin,* 1918–19, pp. 178–80; Minutes of the Executive Committee of the Board of Trustees, 12, 14 September 1918; Faculty Minutes, 24 September–15 November 1918; William G. Perry, "War Activities of the Georgia School of Technology," *Proceedings* of the Georgia Historical Association, 1919, pp. 43–47; *Bulletin,* Register of Graduates, extra, April 1920. For a full discussion of the forces that gave rise to the SATC, see Noble, *America by Design,* pp. 207–23, and Kolbe, *The Colleges in Wartime and After,* pp. 70–75.

114. *Blue Print,* 1919; Faculty Minutes, 12 December 1918. For a friendlier appraisal of the SATC, see Kolbe, *The Colleges in Wartime and After,* pp. 76–81.

115. Faculty Minutes, 19 December 1918, 9 January, 14 February 1919; Minutes of the Board of Trustees, 8 January 1919; *Annual Bulletin* of Georgia School of Technology, 1918–19, p. 151; *The Barrage,* Yearbook of ROTC at Georgia Institute of Technology, 1922–23, p. 26.

116. K. G. Matheson to A. H. Purdue, 2 May 1907, presidential files, uncatalogued, GTA. As explained earlier, Tech abandoned its Department of Mining in 1908.
117. Tech began receiving Smith-Hughes funds to train vocational teachers in the fall of 1917. Minutes of the Executive Committee of the Board of Trustees, 2 November 1917; Faculty Minutes, 3 January 1919; Minutes of the Board of Trustees, 8 January 1919. In 1920 Congress passed the Industrial Rehabilitation Act, another federal-state matching program, directed in Georgia by M. L. Brittain, state superintendent of public schools. Brittain arranged for Tech to accept industrially disabled Georgians in the existing federally supported Disabled Veteran's Program begun at Tech in 1919. Minutes of the Board of Trustees, 3 February, 29 March 1921.
118. Faculty Minutes, 4 May, 12 October 1916; Minutes of the Executive Committee of the Board of Trustees, 27 October 1917, 8 January 1918; Minutes of the Board of Trustees, 18 January, 15 October 1918; *Technique*, 19 February 1918; Donald J. Kevles, "Federal Legislation for Engineering Experiment Stations: The Episode of World War I," *Technology and Culture* 12 (April 1971): 182–89. Stephens did not give up. In the spring of 1922 he was still working to have a bill on the same subject introduced in Congress. P. V. Stephens to K. G. Matheson, 22 March 1922, and P. V. Stephens to N. P. Pratt, 18 March 1922, Matheson Family Papers, GTA.
119. Minutes of the Executive Committee of the Board of Trustees, 28 October, 26 November 1919; Minutes of the Board of Trustees, 8 October 1919; Faculty Minutes, 15 October 1918, 2 April 1919.
120. Minutes of the Board of Trustees, 7 January, 8 June 1920; Minutes of the Executive Committee of the Board of Trustees, 20 February 1920, 3 December 1921, 1 February 1922.
121. Minutes of the Board of Trustees, 5 April 1922.
122. *Annual Report*, 1918–19, pp. 13, 19.
123. *Annual Report*, 1918–19, pp. 20–21; Faculty Minutes, 8, 9 May, 19 September 1919; Minutes of the Executive Committee of the Board of Trustees, 27 June, 2 August 1919, 12 April 1920.
124. Minutes of the Executive Committee of the Board of Trustees, 12 April, 9 July 1920; Minutes of the Board of Trustees, 14 August, 13 October 1920; Stephens, "Greater Georgia Tech Movement," p. 16. For an explanation of the competition for legislative appropriations by the several branches of the University System, see Thomas G. Dyer, *The University of Georgia: A Bicentennial History, 1785–1985* (Athens: University of Georgia Press, 1985), pp. 167–70, 175.

125. Minutes of the Board of Trustees, 14 August, 13 October 1920; Minutes of the Executive Committee of the Board of Trustees, 21 December 1920; Faculty Minutes, 12 November 1920. After a moving plea by the president, the City of Atlanta also came through, doubling its annual appropriation to the school which, with the amount it gave the Night School, amounted to $44,000. *Technique*, 8 October 1920, 21 January 1921.
126. Minutes of the Executive Committee of the Board of Trustees, 10 March, 11 August 1921; Minutes of the Board of Trustees, 17 August 1921; Faculty Minutes, 2 June, 16 August 1921. The legislature did vote an amount large enough to repay the Rotary loan contracted during the 1920–21 session. Matheson tried to talk the Rotarians into canceling the loan, but they refused. Minutes of the Board of Trustees, 17 August 1921, 5 April 1922.
127. Faculty Minutes, 20 October 1914; Minutes of the Board of Trustees, 4 October 1916, 29 May, 14, 16 August 1917, 15 October 1918, 2 April 1919; Minutes of the Executive Committee of the Board of Trustees, 3 August, 2 November, 26 December 1917, 24 April, 4 August, 28 October, 26 November 1919; *Blue Print*, 1915; *Technique*, 12, 19 February 1918. For a self-serving account of these events, see Phinehas V. Stephens, "General Outline of the Greater Georgia Tech Movement," 26 February 1921, and brochure, "Greater Georgia Tech," 26 January 1918, both in Matheson Family Papers, GTA.
128. Minutes of the Board of Trustees, 7 January 1920; Minutes of the Executive Committee of the Board of Trustees, 2 February, 27 April, 9 June, 7 October 1920; Stephens, "Greater Georgia Tech Movement," p. 5.
129. Stephens, "Greater Georgia Tech Movement," pp. 5, 6; vertical files (Alumni Association: Financial Records, Constitution and By Laws, Charter), GTA; Wallace, *White and Gold*, pp. 178–80; Minutes of the Board of Trustees, 13 October 1920; *Blue Print*, 1921, p. 269; ibid., 1922, p. 316; *Annual Report*, 1919–20, p. 58.
130. Minutes of the Executive Committee of the Board of Trustees, 27 April, 9 June, 7 October 1920; Faculty Minutes, 5 October, 5 November 1920; *Technique*, 29 October, 19, 26 November 1920; Stephens, "Greater Georgia Tech Movement," pp. 6, 7.
131. Minutes of the Executive Committee of the Board of Trustees, 21 December 1920; Minutes of the Greater Georgia Tech Campaign Committee, 28 December 1920; Minutes of the Board of Trustees, 5 January 1921. A breakdown of what Tech planned to do with the five million dollars appears in the *Technique*, 11 February and 18 March 1921. The

1914 Greater Tech Campaign sought $500,000; by 1919–20 the goal had climbed to one million. The five million dollar figure, scaled down from the ten million proposed by Phinehas V. Stephens, was unveiled at a December 1920 meeting in Matheson's office. Stephens, "Greater Georgia Tech Movement," 26 February 1921, pp. 2–3, 4–5, 8; *Annual Report*, 1919–20, p. 58.

132. *Technique*, 18, 25 March, 15, 22 April 1921; Faculty Minutes, 18 March, 1, 21, 22 April 1921; Minutes of the Board of Trustees, 12 April 1921. See Drury, "Architectural Development of Georgia Tech," for a full discussion and illustration of the architectural plans for a Greater Tech.

133. K. G. Matheson to Chas. A. Greene Optical Company, 4 June 1921, vertical files (Georgia Tech Campaign), GTA; Minutes of the Board of Trustees, 11 June, 10 November 1921; Minutes of the Executive Committee of the Board of Trustees, 13 July, 11 August, 21 September, 10, 26 October, 11, 12 November, 17 December 1921, 13 March, 24 August 1922; Kenneth G. Matheson to Ivy Lee, 16, 25 March 1922, Percy Brooks to Ivy Lee, 20 March 1922, P. V. Stephens to N. P. Pratt, 18 March 1922, P. V. Stephens to K. G. Matheson, 22 March 1922, all in Matheson Family Papers, GTA.

134. Willis J. Milner, "Campaign Facts," *Georgia Tech Alumnus*, March 1923, p. 9; *Annual Report*, 1921–22; Minutes of the Board of Trustees, 5 April 1922; Minutes of the Executive Committee of the Board of Trustees, 29 May, 14 June, 3 August, 13 December 1922; *Technique*, 24 January 1930; *Blue Print*, 1922, p. 317.

135. *Atlanta Constitution*, 9 October 1921; Minutes of the Executive Committee of the Board of Trustees, 21, 22 September 1921; Minutes of the Board of Trustees, 5 October 1921; Faculty Minutes, 30 September, 7 October 1921.

136. *Atlanta Constitution*, 9 October 1921.

137. Ibid.

138. Ibid. Matheson's reasons for leaving Tech, as expressed in his private correspondence, did not differ from those in his public statement, but they were more emphatic. To the president of Alabama Polytechnic Institute he wrote, "Had I been accorded even partial support by indifferent and antagonistic legislatures, I would have concluded my life work here." Matheson to Dr. Spright Dowell, 31 October 1921. To W. P. Fleming of Macon he wrote on 15 October 1921, "I did not care to court the untimely end of Lyman Hall and therefore decided to resign on time." Both letters appear in the Matheson Family Papers, GTA.

Chapter Five

1. *Annual Report* of the Georgia School of Technology for the year ending 31 May 1923. Brittain's political and personal contacts throughout the state were mentioned by others as well and were his main assets as president throughout his tenure at Tech. See interview with W. Harry Vaughan, 15 February 1984; interview with Ellis Arnall, 27 February 1984. On Watson, see Marion L. Brittain, *The Story of Georgia Tech* (Chapel Hill: University of North Carolina Press, 1948), pp. 275–80.
2. Robert B. Wallace, Jr., *Dress Her in White and Gold: A Biography of Georgia Tech and the Men Who Led Her*, rev. ed. (Atlanta: Georgia Tech Foundation, 1969), pp. 142–45; *Annual Report*, 1923; *Technique*, 6 October 1922, 22 February 1924, 26 September 1924, 10 October 1924, 19 December 1924, 9 January 1925, 20 February 1925, 22 January 1926, 12 February 1926, 9 April 1926, 21 May 1926, 17 September 1926, 16 November 1927, 17 February 1928, 19 December 1924.
3. *President's Report*, 1930–31, pp. 9–10; *Technique*, 17 February 1928, 4 May 1928.
4. *President's Report*, 1927, pp. 7, 8; *Annual Report*, 1925, pp. 10–11, 17–18; *Technique*, 25 September 1925, 22 January 1926, 17 September 1926, 28 September 1928.
5. *Annual Report*, 1923, 1924, 1927; *President's Report*, 1927, pp. 7, 15, and 1931–32; *Technique*, 22 January 1926.
6. The earliest discussion of a ceramics engineering department was in 1907. See chapter 4, n. 41. *Annual Report*, 1923, 1924; *Technique*, 7 November 1924, 25 September 1925; *Bulletin of Georgia School of Technology* 21 (15 November 1924): 16–18; interview with Vaughan; Wallace, *White and Gold*, p. 143.
7. *President's Report*, 1927, p. 13.
8. In 1928, Henry was elected chairman of the Southern Board of Governors of the American Mining Congress, indicating his stature in the field. *Technique*, 30 March 1928. On the dedication, see *Technique*, 7, 14 November 1924.
9. *Technique*, 26 September 1924, 17 October 1924, 24 April 1925, 12 February 1926; *Annual Report*, 1925, p. 16; *Technique*, 19 February 1926. Ceramic engineering courses also became part of the co-op program in 1926. *Technique*, 12 March 1926.
10. *Technique*, 21 May 1926, 27 January 1928, 21 October 1927, 7 October 1927, 14 October 1927. An attempt was made to secure support for an aeronautical engineering department as early as 1915, and Tech did get a ground school during World War I.
11. *Technique*, 2 December 1926, 7 March 1930; *Bulletin of the Georgia*

School of Technology 27 (April 1930); Wallace, White and Gold, p. 146; Richard P. Hallion, Legacy of Flight: The Guggenheim Contribution to American Aviation (Seattle: University of Washington Press, 1977), pp. 62–65.
12. President's Report, 1938–39, pp. 6–7, and 1930–31, p. 3; Macon Telegraph, 13 April 1930; Technique, 14 March 1930.
13. Clipping, vertical files (Brittain), Georgia Tech Archives, hereafter cited as GTA; interview with Ida Brittain Patterson (President Brittain's daughter), 3 June 1983; Brittain, The Story of Georgia Tech, p. 154; Kirkland is quoted in Wallace, White and Gold, p. 147.
14. Brittain, The Story of Georgia Tech, pp. 94–96; Technique, 26 February 1926, 21 May 1926; President's Report, 1927, pp. 9, 15; Wallace, White and Gold, p. 141.
15. Technique, 17 September 1926; Macon Telegraph, 13 April 1930; John H. Matthews, History of the Georgia Institute of Technology Army ROTC, March 1969, p. 13, in vertical files (ROTC), GTA; President's Report, 1927; Brittain, The Story of Georgia Tech, p. 128.
16. Technique, 26 February 1926; President's Report, 1927, p. 13; Technique, 25 September 1925.
17. Annual Report, 1924, p. 25, and 1925, p. 15; Technique, 7 March 1924, 13 November 1925, 21 May 1926, 17 September 1926; Atlanta Constitution, 9 October 1938. For the letter specifying the conditions of the resumption of athletic competition and Student Council approval see Faculty Minutes, 28 February 1924, p. 162, and 5 March 1924, p. 164.
18. Quoted in Wallace, White and Gold, pp. 92–93.
19. On 1928 team and Rose Bowl game, see vertical files (Sports-Football, 1929), GTA; Brittain, The Story of Georgia Tech, pp. 149–51.
20. Technique, 22 February 1929, 21 September 1928; Wallace, White and Gold, pp. 94–95.
21. Vertical files (Brittain), GTA; M. L. Brittain Diary, 1928.
22. Interview with Ida Brittain Patterson; Wallace, White and Gold, pp. 155–56; Technique, 18 January 1924, 17 October 1924, 28 November 1924, 16 January 1925. See chapter 4 for the beginnings of an interest in radio on the Tech campus.
23. Faculty Minutes, 18 September 1922, pp. 9–10; Technique, 24 November 1922, 15 January 1926, 10 March 1926, 26 September 1924, 27 September 1929, 9 April 1926, 6 February 1925; Wallace, White and Gold, pp. 131, 391–92.
24. See, for example, Atlanta Journal, 17 June 1923; Technique, 5 March 1926; Tech Alumnus editorial, reprinted in Technique, 12 February 1926.
25. Technique, 23 April 1926, 7 May 1926.

488   Notes to Pages 176–81

26. Wallace, *White and Gold*, pp. 163–65. A bill had been introduced in the legislature as early as 1921 and again in 1922 to substitute a Board of Regents for the separate boards of Trustees but no action was taken on the proposal. Apparently the time was not yet right for this type of reorganization. *Journal* of the House of Representatives of Georgia, 15 July 1921, pp. 490–91, and 28 June 1922, p. 238. For other discussions of reorganization see Thomas G. Dyer, *The University of Georgia: A Bicentennial History* (Athens: University of Georgia Press, 1985).

27. *Technique*, 15 January 1932; Wallace, *White and Gold*, p. 171. A Tech man was not appointed until W. Elliott Dunwoody was given a seat on the Board at the end of 1932, replacing a member who had resigned. The underrepresentation of Tech alumni on the Board of Regents is referred to by a number of individuals as hurting Tech—see, for example, interview with Ida Brittain Patterson; interview with Ellis Arnall.

28. Wallace, *White and Gold*, pp. 167–71.

29. H. P. Hammond, "Report on Engineering Education in the University System of Georgia," February 1942, p. 81; Brittain to all Tech faculty, vertical files (Brittain), GTA; Faculty Minutes, 14 April 1932, p. 229; *President's Report*, 1933–34, p. 3, and 1930–31, p. 6; *Technique*, 24 January 1930.

30. Brittain, *The Story of Georgia Tech*, pp. 201–3; Wallace, *White and Gold*, pp. 172–73; *Annual Report from the Regents of the University System of Georgia to His Excellency Hon. Eugene Talmadge*, 1933, p. 11.

31. *Technique*, 19, 28 April 1933; interview with Ivan Allen, Jr., 17 November 1983 (Allen was president of the Student Council at this time).

32. Brittain, *The Story of Georgia Tech*, p. 204; *Technique*, 1 December 1933; *President's Report*, 1931–32, p. 6; Brittain to Chancellor Philip Weltner, 8 November 1934, Regents files, GTA.

33. *Technique*, 1 December 1933.

34. Wallace, *White and Gold*, p. 174.

35. *Technique*, 23 February 1934, 2 March 1934; Wallace, *White and Gold*, p. 196; copy of interview with Paul Weber (conducted by Jack Markwalter and Ben Mathis), 24 April 1981; *Technique*, 25 September 1936.

36. *President's Report*, 1931–32, pp. 5, 6, 11; 1930–31, p. 10, 11; 1934–35, pp. 2, 15; and 1938–39, p. 7. See also "Outline of Needs," 10 August 1938, vertical files (Brittain), GTA; Hallion, *Legacy of Flight*, p. 224.

37. Wallace, *White and Gold*, p. 96; *Technique*, 13 January 1932, 13 January 1933, and also 19 January 1934; Edward Peters to Brittain, 8 December 1932, presidential files, uncatalogued, GTA. According to Harold Friedman, professor of chemistry from 1929 to 1942, the loss of the Com-

merce School severely hurt the football program. Interview with Harold Friedman, 19 April 1984.
38. *Technique*, 10 February 1933, 17 March 1933, 16 March 1934, 23 March 1934, 6 April 1934, 11 October 1935; Wallace, *White and Gold*, p. 107; Faculty Minutes (Student Council Minutes), 25 April 1933, 10 January 1933, p. 275, and 20 March 1934, p. 68; *Technique*, 10 January 1936, 15 January 1937.
39. Wallace, *White and Gold*, pp. 187–90.
40. *President's Report*, 1933–34, p. 8.
41. *Technique*, 23 February 1934, 9 March 1934, 18 October 1935; *Annual Report from the Regents*, 1940, p. 103; *Technique*, 9 October 1936, 3 October 1930; *President's Report*, 1931–32, p. 7, and 1933–34, p. 5; *Technique*, 1 April 1938; Co-Op Department, "Annual Report," 1937–38, vertical files (Co-Op Division), GTA; George Griffin to Brittain, 4 March 1938, vertical files (Personnel Department), GTA; Wallace, *White and Gold*, p. 135.
42. *Atlanta Journal*, 30 September 1934; John Lear, "Special Report on Conditions of Techwood Slums," 1933, quoted in Howard W. Pollard, "The Effect of Techwood Homes on Urban Development in the United States," (M.A. thesis, Georgia Institute of Technology, 1968), pp. 6–7.
43. "Outline of Needs of the Georgia School of Technology," Brittain to Chancellor and Board of Regents, 10 August 1938, vertical files (Brittain), GTA; Brittain, *The Story of Georgia Tech*, p. 222; *Atlanta Journal*, 15 September 1935; *Technique*, 27 September 1935, and 22, 28 November 1935.
44. "Report on Housing, 1934," vertical files (Advisory Committee), GTA; *Annual Report from the Regents*, 1935, p. 54.
45. Pollard, "The Effect of Techwood Homes," p. 22; Faye Hamby Goolrick, "Who Wants Techwood?" *Atlanta Weekly*, 15 March 1981, p. 13; Brittain, *The Story of Georgia Tech*, p. 224. Earlier, Brittain had been one of Roosevelt's supporters, having become a member of the Roosevelt Business and Professional League organized at Tech during the 1932 campaign. *Technique*, 21 October 1932.
46. *Annual Report from the Regents*, 1935, p. 55; *Technique*, 26 September 1941.
47. Interview with W. Harry Vaughan; Faculty Minutes, 15 March 1934, p. 65; interview with Harold Friedman.
48. Interview with Vaughan.
49. Interview with Vaughan; interview with Vaughan by Martha Ann Steger, in "History, Contributions to Georgia, Organization, and Enabling Legislation, Engineering Experiment Station," 23 July 1971, p. 5.

50. Interview with Vaughan, 15 February 1984.
51. Vertical files (Fiftieth Anniversary), GTA; Faculty Minutes, "Program of Fiftieth Anniversary," 7–8 October 1938, p. 118; *Annual Report from the Regents*, 1938, p. 104.
52. Vertical files (Fiftieth Anniversary), GTA; Faculty Minutes, "Program of Fiftieth Anniversary," p. 118; *Atlanta Constitution*, 6 October 1938; *New York Times*, 25 October 1938.
53. See sources cited in notes 51 and 52 above.
54. Interview with Vaughan; see also interview with Paul Weber; interview with Harold Friedman.
55. *Technique*, 2 March 1928, 27 August 1929, 10 October 1924, 12 February 1926, 22 January 1926, 2 October 1925, 2 March 1928, 11 November 1927, 23 September 1927, 19 March 1926.
56. Brittain, *The Story of Georgia Tech*, p. 123; interview with Ida Brittain Patterson; clipping, vertical files (Brittain), GTA; *President's Report*, 1938–39, pp. 5–6; for student opinion on training in English, see *Technique*, 19 April 1929.
57. *Annual Report from the Regents*, 1937, pp. 46–47; *Technique*, 23 February 1934; Edward J. Noble, chairman, Civil Aeronautics Authority to Brittain, 14 January 1939, vertical files (Aeronautical Engineering), GTA; *Technique*, 16 February 1940.
58. *Annual Reports*, 1922; *Technique*, 22 February 1929; *Report of the Investigation of Engineering Education, 1923–1929* (Society for the Promotion of Engineering Education, 1930, vol. 1, pp. 140, 549, 554; 1934, vol. 2, pp. 1247–48.
59. Harry P. Hammond, "Engineering Education in Georgia," 1932, pp. 32–34; Michael Bezilla, *Engineering Education at Penn State* (University Park: Pennsylvania State University Press, 1981), pp. 127–28, 134.
60. Harry P. Hammond, "Report on Engineering Education in the University System of Georgia," February 1942, p. 21; Hammond, 1932, pp. 29–31.
61. Hammond, "Engineering Education in Georgia," pp. 14–17, 30, 52–53, 63.
62. Hammond, "Report on Engineering Education," pp. 2, 8, 10, 41; Hammond, "Engineering Education in Georgia," p. 3.
63. "Outline of the Needs of the Georgia School of Technology," Brittain to Chancellor and Board of Regents, 10 August 1938, vertical files (Brittain), GTA; Brittain to Chancellor S. V. Sanford, 22 February 1937, 12 April 1937, presidential files, uncatalogued, GTA; Brittain to Committee on Finance and Education, Board of Regents, 24 March 1932, presidential files, uncatalogued, GTA; interview with Vaughan; S. V. Sanford

491 Notes to Pages 193–99

to Brittain, 9 September 1938, Regents files, GTA; interview with Arnall; *Technique,* 2 April 1937, 15 October 1937.
64. *Atlanta Constitution,* 20 January 1935, 20 October 1935; *Atlanta Journal,* 22 January 1935, 5 February 1935.
65. *Atlanta Journal,* 27 May 1941; Brittain, *The Story of Georgia Tech,* pp. 282–83; interview with Ida Brittain Patterson; Wallace, *White and Gold,* p. 205.
66. *Atlanta Journal,* 27 May 1941; *Atlanta Constitution,* 29–31 May 1941; *Technique,* 13 October 1922; L. R. Siebert, secretary of Board of Regents, to Brittain, 25 June 1941, Regents files, GTA: Brittain to Siebert, 26 June 1941; Brittain to Chancellor Sanford, 25 November 1941, Regents files, GTA; Wallace, *White and Gold,* p. 207.
67. *Atlanta Journal,* 25 December 1941; *Atlanta Constitution,* 15 October 1941; *Atlanta Journal,* 21 November 1941; interview with Arnall.
68. *Atlanta Journal,* 5 December 1941.
69. Ibid. and 15 October 1941; *Annual Report from the Regents,* 1941, p. xii; *Atlanta Constitution,* 2 November 1941; clipping, 3 November 1941, vertical files (University System Accreditation), GTA.
70. Interview with Herman Talmadge, 18 January 1984; William Anderson, *The Wild Man from Sugar Creek: The Political Career of Eugene Talmadge* (Baton Rouge: Louisiana State University Press, 1975), p. 198, 201–2; interview with Arnall.
71. *Technique,* 24 October 1941; *Atlanta Journal,* 26 October 1941, 2 November 1941; Faculty Minutes, 22 October 1941, p. 445; 27 October 1941, p. 447; 5 November 1941, p. 457; *Atlanta Constitution,* 5 November 1941; *Technique,* 7 November 1941. Jimmy Carter, a student at Tech at this time, noted that he first became interested in state politics due to the Talmadge dispute. Interview with Hon. Jimmy Carter, 20 March 1984.
72. *Atlanta Journal,* 19 October 1941, 1 September 1942; Brittain to Fernando Payne, 6 November 1941, Regents files (1941–42), GTA; Payne to Brittain, 18 November 1941, Regents files (1941–42), GTA; Brittain to O. C. Carmichael, 24 October 1941, vertical files (Brittain), GTA; Brittain to W. Elliott Dunwoody, Jr., 14 August 1942, Regents files (1941–42), GTA.
73. *Atlanta Constitution,* 16 October 1941; Faculty Minutes, 11 December 1941, p. 464; Brittain, *The Story of Georgia Tech,* pp. 298–99; *Atlanta Constitution,* 31 May 1942; *Atlanta Journal,* 12 July 1942.
74. Interview with Arnall; interview with Herman Talmadge; Anderson, *The Wild Man from Sugar Creek,* pp. 211, 200–201; *Atlanta Journal,* 23 August 1942.

75. Interview with Arnall; Brittain, *The Story of Georgia Tech*, pp. 300, 302; *Report from the Regents*, 1942–43, pp. 9, 11; Wallace, *White and Gold*, pp. 210–11; S. V. Sanford to M. C. Huntley, 24 November 1942, Regents files (1941–42), GTA.
76. Wallace, *White and Gold*, pp. 210–11; interview with Arnall; *Report from the Regents*, 1942–43, pp. 9, 11.
77. *Report from the Regents*, 1942–43, pp. 9, 11; Wallace, *White and Gold*, pp. 211–12.
78. *President's Report*, 1941–42, pp. 6–8, 13.
79. Harold Friedman noted that when he arrived at Tech in 1929, he found the school impoverished, although the quality of scholarship was high. When he left in 1942, Tech was slightly better off but still a financially poor school. Interview with Friedman.

Chapter Six

1. See Carroll Pursell, "Science Agencies in World War II: The OSRD and Its Challengers," and Harvey M. Sapolsky, "Academic Science and the Military: The Years Since the Second World War," in Nathan Reingold, ed., *The Sciences in the American Context: New Perspectives* (Washington, D.C.: Smithsonian Institution Press, 1979); John Ziman, *The Force of Knowledge: The Scientific Dimension of Society* (Cambridge: Cambridge University Press, 1976).
2. *Atlanta Constitution*, 19 May 1939; *Atlanta Journal*, 4 June 1940.
3. *Technique*, 5 October 1939.
4. Calvin B. T. Lee, *The Campus Scene: 1900–1970* (New York: David McKay Co., 1970), p. 73.
5. *Technique*, 21 March 1941.
6. *Atlanta Journal*, 29 May 1941; *Atlanta Constitution*, 30 May 1941; Robert B. Wallace, Jr., *Dress Her in White and Gold: A Biography of Georgia Tech and the Men Who Led Her*, rev. ed. (Atlanta: Georgia Tech Foundation, 1969), pp. 207–9; Marion L. Brittain, *The Story of Georgia Tech* (Chapel Hill: University of North Carolina Press, 1948), pp. 281–87; *Technique*, 24, 31 October 1941, 12 December 1941.
7. *Atlanta Constitution*, 22 June 1941.
8. *Technique*, 6 March 1942.
9. Frank Knox to M. L. Brittain, 11, 14 April 1942, presidential files (Navy, World War II), uncatalogued, Georgia Tech Archives, hereafter cited as GTA.
10. Fred W. Ajax to M. L. Brittain, 25 June 1942, presidential files (Navy, World War II), uncatalogued, GTA; *Technique*, 26 September 1941.

Notes to Pages 207–11

11. M. L. Brittain to S. V. Sanford, 14 June 1942, Regents files (1941–42), GTA; *Annual Report of the President of the Georgia School of Technology*, 1941–42, pp. 5–6.
12. Fred W. Ajax to M. L. Brittain, 25 June 1942; *Annual Report*, 1941–42, pp. 6–12; interview with Edward A. Moulthrop, 17 November 1983.
13. *Annual Report*, 1941–42, p. 2, and 1943–44, p. 3; "Enrollment, Fall Quarter, 1943," Regents files (Statistics), GTA.
14. Bulletin no. 33, 21 September 1942; bulletin no. 40, 4 December 1942, "Higher Education and National Defense," American Council on Education, presidential files (World War II), uncatalogued, GTA; William P. Layton, Headquarters, Army Fourth Service Command, to College Presidents, 26 December 1942; memo ("Highly Confidential"), Navy College Training Program, undated, presidential files (Navy, World War II), uncatalogued, GTA; Col. Herman Beukema, Director, ASTD, to M. L. Brittain, 27 February 1943, presidential files (Miscellaneous), uncatalogued, GTA.
15. *Technique*, 12 February 1943; *Atlanta Constitution Magazine*, 21 March 1943.
16. *Atlanta Constitution*, 7 March 1943; *Technique*, 5, 19 March 1943; W. A. Alexander to M. L. Brittain, 24 April 1943, presidential files (Military, World War II), uncatalogued, GTA; *Atlanta Journal*, 6 April 1943.
17. Brig. Gen. Joe N. Dalton to M. L. Brittain, 28 April 1943; Brittain to Dalton, 3 May 1943; Col. S. W. Harrelson to Brittain, 25 March 1943, presidential files (Military, World War II), uncatalogued, GTA; Brittain to S. V. Sanford, 22 April 1943, Regents files (1942–43), GTA; *Atlanta Journal*, 27 June 1943; *Atlanta Journal Magazine*, 19 September 1943.
18. A. H. Armstrong and W. A. Alexander to M. L. Brittain, 18 March 1941; Brittain to Alexander, 25 March 1941; "Report of the Department of Physical Training, 1941," vertical files (Physical Training), GTA; Alexander to S. V. Sanford, 14 May 1942, Regents files (1941–42), GTA; interview with R. L. "Bobby" Dodd, 5 July 1983.
19. *Annual Report*, 1943–44, p. 6; S. V. Sanford to M. L. Brittain, 4 January 1944, Regents files (1943–44), GTA.
20. L. R. Siebert to M. L. Brittain, 28 December 1943, Regents files (1943–44), GTA.
21. *Annual Report*, 1943–44, p. 6; Gen. F. E. Uhl to M. L. Brittain, 15 March 1944; War Department News Release, 18 February 1944, presidential files (Military, World War II), uncatalogued, GTA; interview with Jamie R. Anthony, 8 February 1984.
22. *Atlanta Journal*, 19 December 1943; Capt. J. V. Babcock to M. L. Brittain, 27 March 1944, presidential files (Navy, World War II), uncatalogued, GTA.

23. *Technique*, 16 April 1943; *Annual Report*, 1943–44, p. 7.
24. Brittain, *The Story of Georgia Tech*, pp. 305–6; *Annual Report*, 1943–44, p. 14, and 1944–45, pp. 69–70; *Atlanta Journal*, December 19, 1943.
25. *Technique*, 9 November 1939; *Atlanta Constitution*, 17 April 1942; *Technique*, 12 March 1943.
26. "Report on Faculty, 1939–40," Regents files (Statistics), GTA; interview with Phil C. Narmore, 27 September 1983; interview with Homer S. Weber, 3 March 1984.
27. Memorandum, W. Harry Vaughan to Faculty, 7 May 1940, vertical files (EES to 1957), GTA.
28. *Annual Report of the State Engineering Experiment Station*, 1940–41, pp. 1–7; interview with W. Harry Vaughan, 15 February 1984; Paul Weber, "History of Chemical Engineering at Georgia Tech," unpublished manuscript, unpaginated, Paul Weber Papers, GTA.
29. *Technique*, 26 September 1941; *Annual Report*, 1941–42, pp. 12–13.
30. L. R. Siebert to H. E. Dennison, 23 October 1942, Regents files (1942–43), GTA.
31. *Annual Report*, 1943–44, p. 15; *Annual Report, EES*, 1943–44, pp. 1–3.
32. *Annual Report, EES*, 1943–44, p. 8.
33. *Annual Report, EES*, 1943–44, pp. 2–3, 17–18.
34. *Annual Report, EES*, 1944–45, pp. 1–2, 10; "List of All A and B Projects performed by the Engineering Experiment Station," 1 July 1965, GTA.
35. Pursell, "Science Agencies in World War II," pp. 359–60.
36. Ibid., p. 364.
37. Brittain, *The Story of Georgia Tech*, pp. 281–97; M. L. Brittain to S. V. Sanford, 28 May 1943, Regents files (1942–43), GTA.
38. Georgia Tech Alumni Association to Marion Smith, 4 August 1943, Regents files (1942–43), GTA.
39. Ibid.; Vaughn interview; Henrietta M. Larson, Evelyn H. Knowlton, and Charles S. Popple, *New Horizons: History of the Standard Oil Company (New Jersey), 1927–1950* (New York: Harper and Row, 1971), pp. 152, 446–47, 492.
40. Minutes of the Meeting of the Board of Regents, 8 September 1943; L. R. Siebert to Cherry L. Emerson, 9 September 1943, Regents files (1942–43), GTA.
41. "Physical Development Program," M. L. Brittain to S. V. Sanford, 16 June 1942, presidential files (Future Plans), GTA.
42. Ibid.; see also M. L. Brittain to S. V. Sanford, 21 January 1942, Regents files (1941–42), GTA.
43. *Technique*, 12 October 1948; L. R. Siebert to Frank M. Spratlin, 14 July 1944, Regents files (1943–44), GTA; Wallace, *White and Gold*, pp. 158–59.

495   Notes to Pages 220–27

44. *Annual Report*, 1943–44; Harold Bush-Brown to M. L. Brittain, 9 December 1943, 29 February 1944; "School Development Program, 15 November 1943–15 July 1944," presidential files (Future Plans), GTA.
45. Reports, Post-War Planning Committees I, II, and III, verticle files (Post-War Planning Committees), GTA.
46. S. V. Sanford to M. L. Brittain, 13 January 1944; Brittain to Sanford, 14 January 1944, Regents files (1943–44), GTA.
47. *Atlanta Constitution*, 14 September 1943; telephone interview with Mae Evelyn Dodd, 9 February 1984.
48. *Atlanta Constitution*, 16 February 1944; *Annual Report*, 1943–44, p. 18.
49. *Atlanta Journal*, 4 May 1944; interview with Ella Wall Van Leer, 31 August 1983.
50. "Biographical Data Concerning Col. Blake Ragsdale Van Leer," vertical files (Blake Van Leer), GTA; Ella Wall Van Leer interview; *Atlanta Constitution*, 16 February 1944.
51. Ibid.
52. *Atlanta Journal*, 4 May 1944; Blake Van Leer to L. R. Siebert, 1 May 1944, Regents files (1942–43), GTA.
53. *Atlanta Constitution*, 4 May 1944.
54. Interview with Glenn Rainey, 27 June 1983; interview with Leslie F. Zsuffa, 2 April 1984; Phil C. Narmore interview; interview with Mario Goglia, 10 February 1984; interviews with Jamie R. Anthony, 22 March 1983, 8 February 1984; interview with Elizabeth Koenig Armsby, 6 September 1983; Homer S. Weber interview; Ella Wall Van Leer interview; Bobby Dodd interview; *Atlanta Constitution*, 5 July 1944.
55. *Statues of Georgia School of Technology*, Atlanta, 1891; Blake Van Leer to S. V. Sanford, 13 June 1945, Regents files (1944–45), GTA.
56. Blake Van Leer to Ralph Hefner, 8 July 1944, presidential files (Statutes), GTA.
57. William Gilmer Perry to R. A. Hefner, 21 July 1944; "A Short History of the Government of Georgia Tech: Report of the Dean of General Subjects and Personal Comment," presidential files (Statutes), GTA.
58. *Annual Report*, 1944–45, p. 2; Blake Van Leer to S. V. Sanford, 28 February 1945, presidential files (Statutes), GTA.
59. *Annual Report*, 1944–45, p. 81; *Technique*, 17 March 1945, 14 July 1945; Minutes of the Meeting of the Board of Regents, 14 March 1945, Regents files (1944–45), GTA.
60. *Annual Report*, 1944–45, pp. 16, 20; "Georgia School of Technology Advanced Planning Report, December 1944," presidential files (Future Plans), pp. 10, 111, GTA.
61. R. S. King to Blake Van Leer, 27 July 1944; W. V. Skiles to Van Leer, 29 July 1944; Lloyd W. Chapin to Van Leer, 29 July 1944; D. P. Savant to

Van Leer, 31 July 1944; J. L. Daniel to Van Leer, 31 July 1944; R. S. Howell to Van Leer, 3 August 1944, all in presidential files (Future Plans), GTA; Harold Bush-Brown to Van Leer, 15 July 1944; "Progress Report #3," presidential files (Development Plans), GTA.

62. *Annual Report, 1944–45*, pp. 4–5; "1944 Development Plan," presidential files (Campus Planning), GTA; *Atlanta Journal*, 22 October 1944.
63. Zsuffa interview; *Atlanta Journal*, 16 September 1945; Minutes of the Meeting of the Board of Regents, 11 July 1945, Regents files (1945–46), GTA; *Technique*, 8 September 1945; Glenn Rainey interview; Phil C. Narmore interview.
64. Clipping, "Vet Rehabilitation Center Awarded at Tech," undated, vertical files (Veterans Affairs), GTA; *Annual Report, 1944–45*, p. 14; Joseph E. Moore to Dr. Ira D. Scott, 16 July 1948, presidential files (Veterans Guidance Center), GTA; *Atlanta Constitution*, 12 October 1945.
65. *Technique*, 17 March 1945; Minutes of the Meeting of the Board of Regents, 14 March 1945, Regents files (1945–46), GTA.
66. Blake Van Leer to Frances Perkins, 15 January 1945; Perkins to Van Leer, 27 December 1944; Henry S. Heald to Blake Van Leer, 2 April 1945; Van Leer to Heald, 5 April 1945; "Safety Engineering at Georgia Tech," undated report, presidential files (Safety Engineering), GTA; *Technique*, 7 July 1945.
67. *Annual Report, 1944–45*, pp. 7–9, 17; Marion Smith to Blake Van Leer, 21 September 1945; Van Leer to Smith, 20 September 1945, Regents files (1945–46), GTA.
68. Minutes of the Meeting of the Board of Regents, 14 August 1945, Regents files (1945–46), GTA; Richard D. Teach, IMMS, unpublished manuscript, p. 19; *Digest of the Annual Report of the President of the Georgia School of Technology, 1945–46*, p. 16; *Bulletin of the Georgia School of Technology, 1945–46*, pp. 209–10; interview with Tommy Plaxico, 21 June 1984.
69. *Annual Report, 1944–45*, p. 9.
70. *Atlanta Journal*, 6 September 1945.
71. L. R. Siebert to Blake Van Leer, 29 September 1945; Van Leer to Siebert, 11 April 1946; Siebert to Van Leer, 10 April 1946, Regents files (1945–46), GTA; *Technique*, 15 December 1945; *Digest of Annual Report, 1945–46*, p. 12.
72. *Annual Report, 1944–45*, p. 104–6; Lt. Gen. A. A. Vandergrift to Blake Van Leer, 15 January 1945, presidential files (Navy, World War II), uncatalogued, GTA; Gen. George C. Marshall to Van Leer, 2 April 1945; Van Leer to Marshall, 7 April 1945, presidential files (ROTC 1945–46), uncatalogued, GTA; Hon. Carl Vinson to Van Leer, 10 March 1945; Van

Leer to Vinson, 19 March 1945, presidential files (Navy, World War II), uncatalogued, GTA.
73. L. W. Robert to L. R. Siebert, 24 March 1944, Regents files (1941–42), GTA; Edwin Camp, *Alexander of Georgia Tech* (Atlanta: Georgia Institute of Technology, 1950), pp. 41–43; Bobby Dodd interview.
74. Camp, *Alexander*, pp. 44–45; *Technique*, 9 November 1944; Bobby Dodd interview.
75. *Technique*, 7 December 1946; *Atlanta Journal*, 5 January 1947; *Atlanta Constitution*, 18 December 1946; *Atlanta Journal*, 29 December 1946; *Atlanta Journal*, 11 January 1948; Digest of *Annual Report*, 1947–48, pp. 20–21.
76. *Atlanta Journal*, 3 November 1948; Wallace, *White and Gold*, pp. 289–90; Bobby Dodd interview.

Chapter Seven

1. W. L. Hughes, "A Brief History of the Technical Institute Movement in America" (American Society for Engineering Education, 1947), presidential files (Technical Institutes), Georgia Tech Archives, hereafter cited as GTA; L. R. Siebert to Blake Van Leer, 8 May 1945, Regents files (1944–45), GTA.
2. Committee on Technical Institutes to Blake Van Leer, 7 August 1945; Donnell W. Dutton, R. S. Howell, and R. I. Sarbacher to Van Leer, 3 December 1945; L. R. Siebert to Technical Institute Committee, 8 December 1945; and Van Leer to Regents Committee on NATTC, 3 December 1945; presidential files (Technical Institutes), GTA; interview with Leslie F. Zsuffa, 21 April 1984.
3. Minutes of the Meeting of the Board of Regents, 9 January 1945, Regents files (1945–46), GTA; L. R. Siebert to Van Leer, 24 May 1946, and Van Leer to Sandy Beaver, 23 April 1947, presidential files (Technical Institutes), GTA.
4. C. W. Beese, "Technical Institutes," paper delivered at the meeting of the Association of Land Grant Colleges and Universities, 17 December 1946; L. V. Johnson to Blake Van Leer, 5 February 1947, presidential files (Technical Institutes), GTA.
5. A. D. Kenney to Blake Van Leer, 7 June 1947; Kenney to Marion Smith, 7 June 1947; Mayor W. B. Haley, Albany, Georgia, to Smith, 5 June 1947; Frank Neely to Chancellor Raymond Paty, 7 July 1947; and L. R. Siebert to Van Leer, 8 October 1947, presidential files (Technical Institutes), GTA; Zsuffa interview.

6. R. W. Mayer to Blake Van Leer, 30 April 1947; Van Leer to Mayer, 31 May 1947; Van Leer to Raymond Paty, 31 May 1947, 16 July 1947; Van Leer to Administrative Council, 22 December 1947; and Jamie R. Anthony to Van Leer, 17 September 1947, presidential files (Technical Institutes), GTA; *Atlanta Constitution*, 1 February 1948; *Technique*, 4 October 1947.
7. Blake Van Leer to R. I. Sarbacher, 6 October 1947; L. V. Johnson to Van Leer, 3 October 1947; and Sarbacher to Van Leer, 29 September 1947, presidential files (Technical Institutes), GTA.
8. *Digest of the Annual Report of the President of the Georgia Institute of Technology,* 1947–48, pp. 11–12; memorandum, Blake Van Leer to L. V. Johnson, 15 July 1948, presidential files (STI, 1948–49), GTA; Zsuffa interview; L. V. Johnson to Van Leer, 8 March 1948, presidential files (Technical Institutes), GTA.
9. C. L. Emerson to Blake Van Leer, 17 December 1948; H. P. Hammond to Van Leer, 23 April 1949; and L. R. Siebert to Van Leer, 12 May 1949, presidential files (STI, 1948–49), GTA.
10. C. L. Emerson to Blake Van Leer, 7 December 1948, presidential files (STI, 1948–49), GTA.
11. *Technique*, 12 August 1944; Calvin B. T. Lee, *The Campus Scene, 1900–1970* (New York: David McKay Co., 1970), p. 77.
12. *Atlanta Journal Magazine*, 21 October 1941; *Atlanta Journal*, 12 July 1946; C. L. Emerson to L. R. Siebert, 11 July 1946, Regents files (1945–46), GTA.
13. Brochure, "Geogia Tech," p. 10, vertical files (Georgia Tech Campus), GTA.
14. *Technique*, 26 September 1948; *Atlanta Constitution*, 14 August 1946; *Atlanta Journal*, 13 August 1946.
15. *Technique*, 11 October 1947; *Yellow Jacket* 50, no. 2 (1947): 12, 28.
16. Interview with Dr. Homer S. Weber, 7 March 1984; Blake Van Leer to Regents, 12 June 1946, presidential files (Development Plans no. 2), GTA.
17. *Technique*, 19 April 1947, 14 April 1948.
18. Faculty Bulletin, vol. 3, p. 13, 24 January 1948, vertical files (Faculty Bulletins), GTA; *Digest of Annual Report*, 1947–48, p. 11.
19. Blake Van Leer to Raymond Paty, 12 July 1948, presidential files (Reorganization, 1948), GTA.
20. *Technique*, 15 December 1945, 13 August 1948; Blake Van Leer to Raymond Paty, 12 July 1948, presidential files (Reorganization, 1948), GTA; *Digest of Annual Report*, 1948–49, pp. 13–17.
21. Blake Van Leer to Cherry L. Emerson, 16 August 1948, presidential

files (Vice President, 1948–50), GTA; Administrative Memorandum no. 1, presidential files (Reorganization, 1948), GTA.

22. Blake Van Leer to Raymond Paty, 12 July 1948, presidential files (Reorganization 1948), GTA; *Atlanta Constitution*, 10 April 1946; interview with Jamie R. Anthony, 8 February 1984; *Technique*, 9 July 1948, p. 3.
23. *Technique*, 13 August 1948; *Digest of Annual Report*, 1948–49, p. 9.
24. *Technique*, 9 July 1948; *Digest of Annual Report*, 1947–48, p. 17.
25. "Legislative Visitation Report," 5 April 1945, Regents files (1944–45), GTA.
26. *Digest of Annual Report*, 1945–46, p. 35; Blake Van Leer to L. R. Siebert, 1 March 1946; Regents resolution, 14 February 1946; Van Leer to J. D. Robinson, Jr., Trust Company Bank, 20 March 1946; L. R. Siebert to Van Leer, 16 March 1946; and L. R. Siebert to Cherry L. Emerson, 27 March 1946, Regents files (1947), GTA; *Atlanta Constitution*, 2 September 1946; Anthony interview; "Permanent Buildings Constructed Since September 1, 1941," presidential files (Development Plans no. 2), GTA.
27. Blake Van Leer to Harold Bush-Brown, 9 March 1945, 18 December 1945, presidential files (Development Plan, 1944), GTA; L. R. Siebert to Van Leer, 18 November 1945, presidential files (Development Plans, 1945–47), GTA; *Digest of Annual Report*, 1947–48, pp. 3–4.
28. *Digest of Annual Report*, 1945–46, p. 6; *Atlanta Journal*, 10 September 1947; *Digest of Annual Report*, 1943–44, p. 10; Zsuffa interview.
29. Blake Van Leer to Acting Governor M. E. Thompson, 1 November 1948; C. L. Emerson to Roy B. Wilhoit, Trust Company Bank, 26 September 1949; L. R. Siebert to Van Leer, 10 January 1950; and Board of Regents Minutes, 16 December 1949, presidential files (Research Building), GTA.
30. Fuller E. Callaway, Jr., to Cherry L. Emerson, 28 January 1948; program of groundbreaking ceremony and text of Van Leer talk, 22 May 1948; L. R. Siebert to Blake Van Leer, 8 October 1948; Frank Neely to Van Leer, 8 September 1948; Van Leer to Neely, 1 September 1948; and L. R. Siebert to Cherry L. Emerson, 4 March 1948, presidential files (President's House), GTA; interview with Fuller E. Callaway, Jr., 15 September 1983.
31. *Digest of Annual Report*, 1948–49, pp. 4–7; "Georgia Institute of Technology General Education Board Grants"; and Dorothy Crosland to Dr. Gilbert Mann, General Education Board, 6 April 1943, Crosland files (General Education Board), GTA; Cherry L. Emerson to R. J. Thiesen, Alumni Association, 12 September 1946; Emerson to Crosland, 20

November 1946; Blake Van Leer to Crosland, 15 October 1946; and memorandum, "A Method of Facilitating the Purchase of Back Periodicals for Tech's Library," Paul Weber (1946?), vertical files (Dorothy Crosland), GTA.

32. "Report on Georgia Tech," 5 April 1945, Crosland files (Correspondence), GTA; Hollis Edens to Dorothy Crosland, 10 September 1948; Crosland to Blake Van Leer, 13 September 1948; and Crosland to Hollis Edens, 14 October 1948, Crosland files (General Education Board), GTA.

33. Groundbreaking address, "Judge Stirling Price Gilbert," vertical files (Dorothy Crosland), GTA; Dorothy Crosland to Judge Price Gilbert, 26 November 1947, 6 December 1947, Crosland files (Presidential House File), GTA.

34. Dorothy Crosland to Julian P. Boyd, 28 February 1939, Crosland files (Julian P. Boyd), GTA; Blake Van Leer to Harmon Caldwell, 1 March 1949, Crosland files (Caldwell), GTA; *Atlanta Journal*, 21 February 1951; and Dorothy Crosland, "The Price Gilbert Library," speech given to Library Building Institute, St. Paul, Minnesota, 20 June 1954, vertical files (Dorothy Crosland), GTA; *Digest of Annual Report*, 1953–54, pp. 25–26, 28, 53–54; Crosland to John E. Burchard, 16 August 1954, Crosland files (Correspondence), GTA.

35. Hughes Spalding to Blake Van Leer, 17, 24, 27 April 1950; and Van Leer to Spalding, 21, 26, April 1950, presidential files (Development Plans, 1949–55), GTA; Harold Bush-Brown, "Notes on the Architecture Building," vertical files (Architecture Building), GTA; *Digest of Annual Report*, 1951–52, p. 3.

36. Blake Van Leer to Cherry L. Emerson, 5 November 1951, Emerson files (Building), GTA. Bush-Brown, Gailey, and Heffernan had changed some of the details of the master plan, reducing the number of fraternity houses, without consulting or informing Van Leer.

37. *Digest of Annual Report*, 1951–52, pp. 4–5, and 1952–53, p. 5; Blake Van Leer to Harmon Caldwell, 24 November 1953; Cherry L. Emerson to Van Leer, 6 November 1953; and Van Leer to Emerson, 7 December 1953, presidential files (Development Plans, 1951–54), GTA.

38. Edwin Camp, *Alexander of Georgia Tech* (Atlanta: Georgia Institute of Technology, 1950), pp. 47–50; *Atlanta Constitution*, 26 April 1950; *Technique*, 29 April 1950.

39. *Atlanta Journal*, 24 April 1955; *Atlanta Constitution*, 24 April 1955; Anthony interview; *Digest of Annual Report*, 1954–55, p. 5; Robert B. Wallace, Jr., *Dress Her in White and Gold: A Biography of Georgia*

Tech and the Men Who Led Her, rev. ed. (Atlanta: Georgia Tech Foundation, 1969), pp. 267–68.
40. *Atlanta Journal*, 14 April 1954; Blake Van Leer to Ben R. Gordon, 17 March 1954, Emerson files (Rich Computer Center), GTA; *Digest of Annual Report*, 1953–54, pp. 7–8; and 1954–55, p. 28.
41. *Digest of Annual Report*, 1944–45, pp. 21–22; Blake Van Leer to S. V. Sanford, 6, 11, 26, 30 July 1945, Regents files (1944–45), GTA; interview with Elizabeth Koenig-Armsby, 6 September 1983.
42. Blake Van Leer to W. Wilson Noyes, 26 March 1945, Regents files (1944–45), GTA.
43. Minutes of the Meeting of the Board of Regents, 24 September 1945; and Blake Van Leer to L. R. Siebert, 27 October 1945, Regents files (1945–46), GTA. Wallace, *White and Gold*, pp. 185–86; Zsuffa interview; *Digest of Annual Report*, 1945–46, p. 5, 1951–52, p. 6, and 1948–49, pp. 8–9; *Technique*, 3 March 1948; interview with Senator Herman Talmadge, 18 January 1984.
44. *Technique*, 24 January 1950; *Digest of Annual Report*, 1951–52, p. 6, 1952–53, p. 16, and 1953–54, p. 15.
45. Blake Van Leer to Committee on Southern Technical Institute, 10 March 1951; Van Leer to Hughes Spalding, 27 March 1951; and Van Leer to STI students, 26 March 1951, presidential files (STI, 1950–51), GTA.
46. L. V. Johnson, "Statement on the Southern Technical Institute, 1951"; Roy V. Harris to L. V. Johnson, 28 March 1951; Blake Van Leer to Jim Cherry, 17 April 1951; Cherry to Van Leer, 20 April 1951; and handwritten memo, undated, "STI Agreement," presidential files (STI, 1950–51), GTA.
47. L. V. Johnson to Roy N. Emmet, 30 March 1951; and night letter, H. P. Hammond to Blake Van Leer and L. V. Johnson, 4 April 1951; presidential files (STI, 1950–51), GTA; *Technique*, 6 April 1951.
48. Zsuffa interview; L. R. Siebert to Blake Van Leer, 7 May 1951; Minutes of the Meeting of the Board of Regents, 11 April 1951; Van Leer to Harmon Caldwell, 9 April 1951; and L. R. Siebert to Van Leer, 12 April 1951, presidential files (STI, 1950–51), GTA.
49. Telegram, Blake Van Leer to Commanding General, Scott Air Force Base, Illinois, 13 April 1951; telegram, Commanding General, Scott Air Force Base, to Van Leer, 12 April 1951; Col. Harold L. Neely, USAF, to Van Leer, 25 April 1951; and L. V. Johnson to Hon. Prince H. Preston, 28 May 1951, presidential files (STI, 1950–51), GTA; Van Leer to Headquarters, Air Force Air Material Command, 8 December 1951, presi-

dential files (STI, 1951–52, GTA; *Digest of Annual Report,* 1953–54, p. 23, and 1954–55, pp. 31–32.
50. *Digest of Annual Report,* 1954–55, p. 3.
51. *Atlanta Journal,* 30 November 1947, 7 April 1949.
52. R. A. Hefner to Sigma Xi members, 7 January 1946, 8 February 1946; W. M. Spicer to Blake Van Leer, 29 April 1946; and Van Leer to George A. Baitsell, 14 June 1946, Sigma Xi files, GTA; *Technique,* 8 June 1946; interview with Waldemar T. Ziegler, 12 July 1983; interview with W. H. Eberhardt, 1 September 1983.
53. W. T. Ziegler to P. K. Calaway, 14 April 1947; Lane Mitchell to Monie A. Ferst, 12 October 1949; Ziegler to George A. Baitsell, 18 November 1950; Ziegler to Sigma Xi Executive Committee, 14 March 1951; and Blake Van Leer to Sigma Xi Executive Committee, 15 July 1952, Sigma Xi files, GTA; Ziegler interview; Eberhardt interview; *Technique,* 2 June 1953; *Digest of Annual Report,* 1952–53, p. 4.
54. Blake Van Leer to Sigma Xi headquarters, 15 July 1952, Sigma Xi files, GTA; *Digest of Annual Report,* 1949–50, p. 13, and 1950–51, p. 12; Ziegler interview; interview with Vernon Crawford, 15 July 1983; interview with Mario J. Goglia, 2 February 1984; M. A. Honnell to Gerald A. Rosselot, 23 January 1947, Emerson files (EES), GTA.
55. L. R. Siebert to Blake Van Leer, 13 July 1945; and Van Leer to S. V. Sanford, 6 July 1945, Regents files (1945–46), GTA.
56. Handwritten memo, "GTRI," 21 September 1945; Cherry L. Emerson to R. B. Wilby, 23 November 1945; and Fuller E. Callaway, Jr., to Emerson, 17 January 1946, Emerson files (EES), GTA; interview with Fuller E. Callaway, Jr., 15 September 1983; Fuller E. Callaway, Jr., to Harry L. Baker, Jr., 19 January 1946; M. A. Ferst to Cherry L. Emerson, 6 February 1946; Callaway to Emerson, 6 February 1946; memo, "GTRI," G. A. Rosselot, 21 February 1946; Emerson to Blake Van Leer, 9 January 1946; Frank A. Hooper, Jr., to Emerson, 1 February 1946; Frank Neely to Emerson, 31 January 1946; and Emerson to Raymond Jones, 19 February 1946, Emerson files (GTRI), GTA.
57. Harry L. Baker, Jr., to Fuller E. Callaway, Jr., G. A. Rosselot, and Cherry L. Emerson, 15 March 1946, Emerson files (GTRI), GTA.
58. *Digest of Annual Report,* 1945–46, p. 14; L. R. Siebert to Blake Van Leer, 8 March 1946, Regents files (1945–46), GTA; booklet, "The Georgia School of Technology of Atlanta Presents the Country's Largest and Most Complete A. C. Network Calculator Circuit," vertical files (EES to 1957), GTA; H. P. Peters, "Georgia Tech A. C. Network Calculator," *Research Engineer,* January 1948, p. 3.

Notes to Pages 261–64

59. *Annual Report of the Engineering Experiment Station,* 1947–48, p. 18; interview with James A. Boyd, 20 February 1984, "List of All A & B Projects," EES, 1946–47, GTA.
60. *Technique,* 17 April 1848, p. 3; news release, L. F. Zsuffa, 9 March 1948, Emerson files (EES), GTA; T. H. Evans to Blake Van Leer, 27 April 1948; and Evans to Cherry L. Emerson, 11 October 1948, Emerson files (Research), GTA; Evans to Van Leer, 29 January 1949; and G. A. Rosselot to EES Advisory Committee, 4 February 1949, Emerson files (EES no. 2), GTA.
61. *Digest of Annual Report,* 1949–50, p. 16; *EES Annual Report,* 1949–50, pp. 1–2; Cherry L. Emerson to Blake Van Leer, 18 February 1949; Van Leer to Emerson, 21 February 1949; and Robert W. July to Van Leer, 8 April 1949, Emerson files (Fund: Additional Research), GTA.
62. Blake Van Leer to Cherry L. Emerson, 24 July 1950, Emerson files (Fund: Additional Research), GTA; Sandy Beaver to Van Leer, 12 October 1950; and Van Leer to Beaver, 19 October 1950, Regents files (1950), GTA; Van Leer to L. M. K. Boelter, 6 December 1949, presidential files (EES, 1948–49), GTA.
63. *Digest of Annual Report,* 1950–51, p. 14.
64. G. A. Rosselot to Blake Van Leer, 7 April 1950, presidential files (EES, 1948–54), GTA; *Digest of Annual Report,* 1951–52, pp. 13–14. For information on the nature of the work undertaken by Redgrave in this capacity, see his extensive correspondence and copies of his reports in the Emerson files (Capt. D. C. Redgrave), GTA.
65. G. A. Rosselot to Blake Van Leer, 7 April 1950; and Cherry L. Emerson to Rosselot, 19 June 1950, presidential files (EES, 1948–54), GTA; Emerson to Rosselot, 20 April 1951, Emerson files (Budget, Research, 1951–52), GTA; Anthony interview; Goglia interview; Koenig-Armsby interview; Boyd interview.
66. *Moody's Industrial Manual,* vol. 2 (New York: Moody's Industrial Service, 1983), p. 5938; Anthony interview; Boyd interview; Goglia interview; J. S. Hollis to Blake Van Leer, 12 April 1955; Maurice Long to Van Leer, 10 November 1953; W. W. Wright to Van Leer, 26 January 1954; and J. E. Boyd to Van Leer, 21 August 1953, Emerson files (Outside Activities, Research Personnel), GTA.
67. *Digest of Annual Report,* 1951–52, p. 13; James A. Blissit to Blake Van Leer, 11 September 1952, Regents files (1952), GTA.
68. Blake Van Leer to Cherry L. Emerson, Harry L. Baker, Jr., and Jamie R. Anthony, 12 September 1952, Emerson files (EES no. 2), GTA; Van Leer to Harmon Caldwell, 30 October 1952; and memo, Van Leer to Emer-

son and Rosselot, 27 October 1952, Emerson files (Blissit Report), GTA; James A. Blissit to Van Leer, 7 November 1952, presidential files (EES, 1948–54), GTA.
69. Harmon Caldwell to Cherry L. Emerson, 13 November 1952; and notice to all EES Personnel, 24 November 1952, presidential files (EES, 1948–54), GTA; Blake Van Leer to Caldwell, 21 November 1952, Regents files (1953–54), GTA; Emerson to Ben H. Weil, 10 December 1952, Emerson files (Future Research), GTA; *Technique*, 29 January 1954.
70. Anthony interview; G. A. Rosselot to Paul Weber, 13 March 1955, Weber Papers. As further evidence of the apparent friendly relationship that continued between Van Leer and Rosselot, see their correspondence in Rosselot's personnel file which continues after his leaving Georgia Tech (out-of-service files [G. A. Rosselot], GTA).
71. Herschel Cudd to Blake Van Leer, 20 January 1953; and Cherry L. Emerson to Van Leer, 22 January 1953, presidential files (EES, 1948–54), GTA.
72. James A. Blissit to Jamie R. Anthony, 16 January 1953; and Minutes of the Meeting of the Board of Regents, 11 February 1953, 13 March 1953, presidential files (EES, 1948–54), GTA; Cherry L. Emerson to Fuller E. Callaway, Jr., 7 February 1953; and "Memorandum of Understanding Between GIT and GTRI," Emerson files (Blissit Report), GTA.
73. Herschel Cudd to Blake Van Leer, 9 December 1952; Harmon Caldwell to Cherry L. Emerson, 13 November 1952; and Van Leer to Cudd, 7 January 1953, presidential files (EES, 1948–54), GTA; *Annual Report, 1952–53*, p. 13.
74. Herschel Cudd to Paul Weber, Chair, Rules and Regulations Committee, 21 January 1953, 6 February 1953; Cudd to Cherry L. Emerson, 19 May 1953; and Emerson to Blake Van Leer, 25 May 1953, Emerson files (H. H. Cudd), GTA.
75. Blake Van Leer to Harmon Caldwell, 23 December 1954, presidential files (Reorganization, 1954–55), GTA; "Statutes, Part II," 1 April 1952, vertical files (Statutes), GTA; Herschel Cudd to F. W. Cox, W. N. Cox, Jr., H. E. Dennison, D. W. Dutton, Cherry L. Emerson, R. L. Sweigert, Blake Van Leer, and Paul Weber, 5 January 1953, Emerson files (H. H. Cudd), GTA.
76. "The Aims and Objectives of the Georgia Institute of Technology" (p. 41), vertical files (Educational Objectives and Methods Committee), GTA.
77. Eberhardt interview; Cherry L. Emerson to Sen. Richard B. Russell, 1 September 1951; and memo, "Statement in Regards to Proposed Ap-

plication to Grants to the NSF," Cherry L. Emerson, 1952?, Emerson files (NSF), GTA; Ziegler interview; Crawford interview; Goglia interview.
78. *Digest of Annual Report*, 1953–54, p. 21; Anthony interview; Blake Van Leer to Fuller E. Callaway, Jr., 16 March 1954; and Callaway to Van Leer, 11 March 1954, presidential files (EES, 1955–56), GTA.
79. Cherry L. Emerson to Herschel Cudd, 13 November 1953; Cudd to Blake Van Leer, 30 November 1953; and Van Leer to Cudd, 7 December 1953, Emerson files (H. H. Cudd), GTA; *Digest of Annual Report*, 1953–54, p. 21; *Technique*, 29 January 1954; Boyd interview.
80. Cherry L. Emerson to Blake Van Leer, 17 December 1953, 11 February 1954, Emerson files (EES no. 2), GTA; *Technique*, 2 February 1954; *Digest of Annual Report*, 1953–54, pp. 3, 8–9, 21.
81. *Digest of Annual Report*, 1954–55, pp. 8–9, 24–26.
82. Ibid., 1955–56, pp. 37–41, and 1953–54, p. 3.
83. Henry K. Stanford to Blake Van Leer, 10 April 1952, vertical files (Women at Tech), GTA; Blake Van Leer to L. R. Siebert, 9 June 1945, Regents files (1944–45), GTA; "Unique," 1 April 1946; interview with Ella Wall Van Leer and Samuel Van Leer, 31 August 1983.
84. *Faculty Bulletin*, vol. 2, no. 26 (31 May 1947), vertical files (Faculty Bulletins), GTA; *Atlanta Journal*, 8 May 1947; *Technique*, 17 May 1947; Blake Van Leer to H. A. Dickert et al., 23 May 1947, presidential files (Co-education), GTA.
85. Hamilton Lokey to H. A. Dickert, 13 June 1947; Dickert to Blake Van Leer, 14 June 1947; and L. R. Siebert to Van Leer, 7 July 1947, presidential files (Co-education), GTA.
86. Marie K. Hudson to Blake Van Leer, 10 March 1948, presidential files (Technical Institutes), GTA; *Atlanta Journal*, 7 November 1948; Van Leer to Gen. Sandy Beaver, 8 November 1948; J. R. Anthony to Van Leer, 2 November 1948; and Beaver to Van Leer, 20 October 1948, Regents files (1948), GTA; L. R. Siebert to Miss Anne Bonds, 10 November 1948, presidential files (Co-education), GTA; John Hope Franklin, *From Slavery to Freedom: A History of American Negroes* (New York: Knopf, 1961), pp. 541–42; *Atlanta Journal*, 22 November 1948.
87. Handwritten memo, "This Is the Accurate Story of the Co-education of Georgia Tech," Dorothy Crosland, undated, vertical files (Co-education), GTA; Blake Van Leer to Cherry L. Emerson, 15 November 1952, Emerson files (Co-ed Women), GTA; Van Leer to Harmon Caldwell, 28 December 1948, Regents files (1948), GTA.
88. Rutherford L. Ellis to Mrs. J. Henly Crosland, 22 April 1952, vertical

files (Co-education), GTA; *Technique,* 26 February 1953; L. R. Siebert to Blake Van Leer, 6 March 1952, vertical files (Co-education), GTA: Minutes of the Meeting of the Board of Regents, 12 March 1952, vertical files (Women), GTA; *Technique,* 7 March 1952.

89. Minutes of the Meeting of the Board of Regents, 12 March 1952, vertical files (Women), GTA; Blake Van Leer to Harmon Caldwell, 6 March 1952; and Amber W. Anderson to Van Leer, 6 April 1952, presidential files (Co-education), GTA.

90. *Technique,* 11 April 1952; *Atlanta Journal,* 9 April 1952; Minutes of the Meeting of the Board of Regents, presidential files (Co-education), GTA; Henry King Stanford to Blake Van Leer, 10 April 1953; and Van Leer to W. L. Carmichael, 11 April 1952, vertical files (Women), GTA.

91. Amber W. Anderson to Rutherford L. Ellis, 23 April 1953; and Blake Van Leer to Colonel A. D. Amoroso, 16 April 1952, presidential files (Co-education), GTA; *Technique,* 22 August 1952; Ella Wall Van Leer interview; *Technique,* 25 November 1952.

92. *Digest of Annual Report,* 1952–53, p. 24; *Technique,* 22 May 1953, 23 February 1952, 22 November 1955; *Atlanta Constitution,* 21 April 1954, 16 October 1953, 4 October 1954; Ella Wall Van Leer interview; *Digest of Annual Report,* 1955–56, p. 34.

93. *Technique,* 28 September 1946.

94. *Atlanta Constitution,* 14 August 1946; *Technique,* 21 January 1949, 4 March 1949, 7, 10 March 1950, 19 February 1952; Gordon Albury, Jr., "On the Hill," *Georgia Tech Alumnus,* February 1956, p. 18.

95. *Technique,* 5 October 1951, 31 January 1948, 13 December 1949, 9 October 1953.

96. *Technique,* 5 January 1946, 9 May 1952, 27 September 1947, 14 February 1948.

97. Lee, *The Campus Scene,* pp. 88–92; for a good narrative discussion of attitudes in the 1950s, see Eric F. Goldman, *The Crucial Decade and After: America, 1945–1960* (New York: Vintage, 1960). *Technique,* 14 March 1950, 14 April 1950.

98. *Technique,* 23 November 1946, 18, 21 April 1950; Zsuffa interview; *Yellow Jacket,* November 1953; *Technique,* 24 November 1953, 8 December 1953, 3 June 1955; Minutes of the Academic Senate Meeting, 31 May 1955; Faculty Minutes, 1952–53; *Digest of Annual Report,* 1954–55, p. 17.

99. Wallace, *White and Gold,* pp. 404–7; interview with George C. Griffin, 7 July 1983; *Technique,* 2 October 1951; George C. Griffin to Blake Van Leer, 7 April 1952; and Van Leer to Griffin, 9 April 1952, presidential

files (Development Plans), GTA; *Technique,* 10 April 1953, 21 May 1954, 19 November 1954.
100. Blake Van Leer to Cherry L. Emerson, 15 December 1948, Emerson files (Fraternities, Housing), GTA; *Technique,* 5 October 1948, 12, 23 October 1951; *Digest of Annual Report,* 1951–52, p. 4.
101. Blake Van Leer to G. Everitt Millican, Hamilton Lokey, M. R. Smith, and Hoke Smith, 5 May 1954; John Pershing to G. C. Griffin, 12 January 1955; and memo, Pershing to Georgia Tech Fraternities, 12 October 1955, presidential files (Fraternity Matters, 1948–58), GTA; *Technique,* 19 December 1954; Crawford interview.
102. *Technique,* 24 August 1951, 7 December 1951.
103. *Atlanta Journal,* 22 May 1968; *Atlanta Constitution,* 5 April 1953.
104. *Technique,* 2 November 1951; "WSF: A History," World Student Fund, Georgia Tech YMCA.
105. *Technique,* 3 December 1954, 8 December 1953, 5, 12, 19 November 1954, 14 January 1955, 8 April 1955.
106. Minutes of the Advisory Committee of the Administrative Council, 18 February 1953, Faculty Minutes, 1952–53; L. R. Siebert to Calvin Jackson, 11 February 1953; Siebert to Robert Cheeseboro, 9 March 1953; Blake Van Leer to Siebert, 19 February 1953; Siebert to Van Leer, 23 February 1953; and Van Leer to Siebert, 25 February 1953, Regents files (1953), GTA.
107. Wallace, *White and Gold,* p. 270; *Technique,* 6 December 1955; interview with Robert L. "Bobby" Dodd, 5 July 1983.
108. *Technique,* 6 December 1955; Blake Van Leer to Harmon Caldwell, 5 January 1956; and George C. Griffin to Van Leer, 4 January 1956, presidential files (Regents, Student Demonstrations), GTA.
109. L. R. Siebert to Blake Van Leer, 14 December 1955, presidential files (Regents, Student Demonstrations), GTA; Wallace, *White and Gold,* pp. 272–73; *Technique,* 6 December 1955.
110. Dodd interview; Blake Van Leer to Harmon Caldwell, 5 January 1956; George C. Griffin to Van Leer, 4 January 1956; and Ben Fortson to Van Leer, 7 December 1955, presidential files (Regents, Student Demonstrations), GTA; Zsuffa interview; *Technique,* 6 December 1955, 10 January 1956.
111. Wallace, *White and Gold,* p. 273; Ella Wall Van Leer interview; Koenig-Armsby interview.
112. *Technique,* 5 December 1950, 4 December 1951.
113. *Atlanta Journal,* 23 July 1951, 24 May 1951.
114. Sandy Beaver to Regents, 3 October 1951; Beaver to Regents, 10 Oc-

tober 1951; and Bob Arnold to Blake Van Leer, 5 October 1951, presidential files (Football De-emphasis), GTA; *Atlanta Constitution*, 4 October 1951.

115. *Atlanta Constitution*, 4 October 1951; *Technique*, 9 October 1951, p. 4; L. R. Siebert to Blake Van Leer, 4 February 1952; and Minutes of the Meeting of the Board of Regents, 14 November 1951, presidential files (Football De-emphasis), GTA; *Atlanta Journal*, 5 October 1951.

116. *Technique*, 16 January 1953; Dodd interview; clipping, Ed Danforth editorial, *Atlanta Journal*, January 1954?, presidential files (Football De-emphasis), GTA; *Atlanta Constitution*, 21 December 1955.

117. *Technique*, 13 November 1951; Roy McArthur to Bobby Dodd, 30 April 1951, presidential files (Athletic Association, 1953–57), GTA; *Technique*, 11 January 1955, 4 February 1955.

118. *Technique*, 15 September 1955.

119. "Aims and Objectives," vertical files (Educational Objectives and Methods Committee), GTA; American Society for Engineering Education, *Report on Evaluation of Engineering Education* (ASSE, 1955), pp. 1–3, 35–36.

120. "Aims and Objectives," vertical files (Educational Objectives and Methods Committee), GTA.

121. Samuel J. Mantel, "Critique of the Aims and Objectives of GIT from the Social Sciences Department," vertical files (Curriculum), GTA; H. P. Hammond, "Report of the Committee on Engineering Education After the War," *Journal of Engineering Education* 34, no. 5 (January 1944): 589–614.

122. *Report on Evaluation of Engineering Education*, 1955, p. 2; *Digest of Annual Report*, 1955–56, p. 14.

123. *Technique*, 2 October 1951, 29 January 1954; *Digest of Annual Report*, 1953–54, p. 32.

124. *Report on Evaluation of Engineering Education*, 1955, p. 3; *Digest of Annual Report*, 1954–55, pp. 47–48.

125. *Digest of Annual Report*, 1953–54, pp. 34–37, and 1955–56, p. 5.

126. Blake Van Leer to L. R. Siebert, 21 March 1946; Phil C. Narmore, Cherry L. Emerson, and Ralph Hefner to Van Leer, 19 March 1946; Siebert to Heads of Units, University System, 4 June 1946; Emerson to Siebert, 13 June 1946; and Van Leer to Marion Smith et al., 12 June 1946, Regents files (1945–46), GTA.

127. Blake Van Leer to Marion Smith et al., 12 June 1946, Regents files (1945–46), GTA; Van Leer to Raymond Paty, 13 February 1948, Regents files (1948), GTA; Sandy Beaver to Regents, 10 March 1951; and Van Leer to Harmon Caldwell, 22 March 1951, Regents files (1951), GTA;

Van Leer to Caldwell, 20 April 1949, Regents files (1949), GTA; Faculty Bulletin, vol. 3, no. 12 (17 January 1948), vertical files (Faculty Bulletins), GTA; Eberhardt interview; L. R. Siebert to Van Leer, 24 June 1951, Eberhardt Papers, GTA.

128. Harmon Caldwell to Blake Van Leer, 28 April 1954; and memo, Lloyd Chapin to Van Leer, 7 May 1954; Regents files (1953–54), GTA; L. R. Siebert to Van Leer, 18 August 1952; Van Leer to Caldwell, 26 August 1952; and memo, Chapin to Van Leer, 22 August 1952, Regents files (1952), GTA; *Atlanta Journal,* 9 June 1953; *Atlanta Constitution,* 9 June 1953.

129. *Atlanta Journal,* 16 March 1954; Harmon Caldwell to Blake Van Leer, 8 March 1949, Regents files (1949), GTA; interview with George F. Wheeler, 11 June 1984; Minutes of the Special Meeting of the General Faculty, 16 March 1954, Faculty Minutes, 1952–55; *Atlanta Journal,* 16 March 1954.

130. Telegram, Ralph E. Himstead to Blake Van Leer, 15 March 1954; Van Leer to Himstead, 17 March 1954; and Harmon Caldwell to Van Leer, 24 March 1954, presidential files (Sedition and Subversive Activities), GTA; *Atlanta Journal,* 16 March 1954; *Digest of Annual Report,* 1953–54, p. 14.

131. *Digest of Annual Report,* 1949–50, p. 13, and 1950–51, p. 13; *Technique,* 2 October 1951.

132. *Digest of Annual Report,* 1952–53, pp. 19, 21; Maj. Gen. K. L. Hastings to Blake Van Leer, 23 September 1953, Zsuffa Papers; Zsuffa interview.

133. Wallace, *White and Gold,* pp. 147–52; *Technique,* 28 April 1954, p. 1.

134. *Technique,* 23 February 1951, 2 July 1953; Cherry L. Emerson to Blake Van Leer, 21 May 1951; and Van Leer to Emerson, 24 May 1951, presidential files (Development Plans, 1949–51), GTA; Van Leer to Harmon Caldwell, 24 May 1954, presidential files (Development Plans, 1951–54), GTA.

135. Blake Van Leer to Harmon Caldwell (confidential), 15 September 1954; Caldwell to Van Leer, 22 September 1954, presidential files (Reorganization, 1954–55), GTA.

136. Sandy Beaver to Blake Van Leer, 10 February 1950, presidential files (STI, 1949–50), GTA; Koenig-Armsby interview; G. A. Rosselot to Paul Weber, 13 March 1955, Weber Papers, GTA.

137. Blake Van Leer to Harmon Caldwell, 27 September 1954, presidential files (Reorganization, 1954–55), GTA.

138. *Report on Evaluation of Engineering Education,* pp. 3–4; news release, 9 March 1955, presidential files (Reorganization, 1954–55), GTA.

139. Phil C. Narmore to Ralph E. Himstead, 21 May 1954; and George F.

Wheeler to Blake Van Leer, 16 June 1948, out-of-service files (George F. Wheeler), GTA; Wheeler interview.
140. Wheeler interview; interview with Glenn W. Rainey, 27 June 1983.
141. Wheeler interview; Phil C. Narmore to Ralph E. Himstead, 21 May 1954; J. H. Howey, R. A. Hefner, and L. W. Chapin to Blake Van Leer and Regents of the University System, 31 May 1954; Van Leer to Harmon Caldwell, 31 May 1954; and Caldwell to Van Leer, 11 June 1954, out-of-service files (George F. Wheeler), GTA.
142. See Executive Dean Reports, 1951–55, vertical files (Executive Dean Reports), GTA; Narmore interview; interview with anonymous source; G. A. Rosselot to Paul W. Weber, 13 March 1955, Weber Papers.
143. Blake Van Leer to Harmon Caldwell, 23 December 1954; memorandum of meeting, 3 February 1955; and Van Leer to Caldwell, 17 February 1955, presidential files (Reorganization, 1954–55), GTA; Goglia interview.
144. Minutes of the Meeting of the Board of Regents, 9 March 1955; Harmon Caldwell to Blake Van Leer, 11 March 1955; and news release, 9 March 1955, presidential files (Reorganization, 1954–55), GTA; *Technique*, 11 March 1955; Minutes of the Special Meeting of the General Faculty, 10 March 1955, Faculty Minutes, 1952–55.
145. G. A. Rosselot to Paul W. Weber, 13 March 1955, Weber Papers, GTA; Blake Van Leer to Administrative Council, 6 June 1955, presidential files (Reorganization, 1954–55), GTA; *Technique*, 9 August 1955.
146. *Digest of Annual Report*, 1955–56, pp. 3–4; Koenig-Armsby interview; *Atlanta Constitution*, 24 January 1945; *Technique*, 24 January 1945; *Digest of Annual Report*, 1955–56, pp. 9–10.
147. Ella Wall Van Leer and Samuel Van Leer interview; Koenig-Armsby interview; memorandum, Clyde Robbins to Lawrence Foster, 2 August 1984; *Technique*, 27 January 1956; "Blake R. Van Leer's Georgia Tech," *The Georgia Tech Alumnus*, February 1956, pp. 5–17; Stephen G. Hardy, "Statistical Breakdown of Funding: Georgia Tech and the University of Georgia"; *Technique*, 27 January 1956; *Atlanta Constitution*, 24 January 1956.
148. *Technique*, 27 January 1956; Talmadge interview.

Chapter Eight

1. Interview with Paul Weber, 24 April 1981, conducted by the academic honorary Omicron Delta Kappa, copy in the Georgia Tech Archives hereafter cited as GTA. Interviews by Tech historians with Edwin D.

Harrison, 26 October 1983; Mario J. Goglia, 10 February 1984; Vernon D. Crawford, 15 July 1983; Glenn Rainey, 27 June 1983; Jamie R. Anthony, Sr., 22 March 1983; and Waldemar T. Ziegler, 12 July 1983. The most convenient summary of Weber's career is found in Robert B. Wallace, Jr., *Dress Her in White and Gold: A Biography of Georgia Tech and the Men Who Led Her,* rev. ed. (Atlanta: Georgia Tech Foundation, 1969), pp. 291–309. Wallace's book, though largely a collection of documents linked by narrative, provides an assessment of people and events he knew well during the 1950s and 1960s. The account often is remarkably candid for the work of a college publications director.
2. Wallace, *White and Gold,* pp. 294–95.
3. A letter from Harmon Caldwell to L. W. Robert, Jr., 19 April 1957, was sent by Robert to Weber with an additional note encouraging Weber to pursue the presidency vigorously. Weber responded to L. W. Robert, Jr., 29 April 1957: "I still prefer to go back to a position which does not involve so much outside work and entertaining activities. However, if the Regents can not find someone they and the alumni and the faculty can agree on for a new president, I shall be glad to carry on as best I know how. With the knowledge that the faculty and persons like you would favor this, the task would not be so difficult." Presidential files (President, Selection of), GTA.
4. Harrison interview, 9 November 1983.
5. On the search process, see Frederick G. Storey, "As I See It," *Georgia Tech Alumnus,* July 1956, p. 4. For discussion about the delay, see *Technique,* 27 September 1956, 12 April 1957, and 19 April 1957. On the problems posed by impending integration, see William M. Spicer, "History of the School of Chemistry, 1955–73," p. 5, ms. in GTA; and Wallace, *White and Gold,* p. 308.
6. The most detailed summary of Georgia Tech's development under Weber's presidency is found in *Annual Report of the President, Georgia Institute of Technology,* 1955–56 and 1956–57. A shortened version of the *Annual Report,* containing only the president's report and statistical data but omitting other administrative reports, was published as *The President's Report.*
7. Wallace, *White and Gold,* pp. 304–5.
8. *Atlanta Journal and Constitution,* 7 July 1957; Wallace, *White and Gold,* pp. 310–11; Harrison interview, 26 October 1983.
9. Wallace, *White and Gold,* p. 308.
10. Harrison interview, 26 October 1983.
11. Ibid.; Robert B. Wallace, Jr., "North Avenue Enigma," *Atlanta Magazine,* October 1963, pp. 65–66, 106, 108; *President's Report,* 1966, p. 4;

Edwin D. Harrison to George L. Simpson, Jr., 2 July 1968, vertical files (Annual Reports—Misc.), GTA.
12. *President's Report*, 1958, p. 8.
13. Ibid., p. 9.
14. Ibid.
15. Ibid., pp. 10–11.
16. Ibid., p. 15.
17. Ibid., pp. 15–19; Wallace, *White and Gold*, p. 318.
18. For general overviews, see Benjamin Muse, *Ten Years of Prelude: The Story of Integration Since the Supreme Court's 1954 Decision* (New York: Viking, 1964), and Reed Sarratt, *The Ordeal of Desegregation: The First Decade* (New York: Harper and Row, 1966).
19. Numan V. Bartley, *The Rise of Massive Resistance: Race and Politics in the South During the 1950s* (Baton Rouge: Louisiana State University Press, 1969).
20. *Technique*, 16 January 1959.
21. *Technique*, 30 January 1959, discusses methods of avoiding integration.
22. Ronald H. Bayor, "A City Too Busy to Hate: Atlanta's Business Community and Civil Rights," in Harold Sharlin, ed., *Business and Its Environment* (Westport, Conn.: Greenwood, 1983).
23. *Technique*, 5 December 1958.
24. Ibid., 23, 30 January 1959.
25. Wallace, *White and Gold*, pp. 333–34.
26. James E. Dull to Edwin D. Harrison, 16 January 1961, copy in possession of James E. Dull; interview with James E. Dull, 21 July 1983.
27. Wallace, *White and Gold*, pp. 334–40, provides a transcript of most of the meeting; also see *Technique*, 20 January 1961.
28. Wallace, *White and Gold*, pp. 335–36.
29. James E. Dull to Edwin D. Harrison, 27 March 1961, copy in possession of James E. Dull.
30. Wallace, *White and Gold*, pp. 341–42. A letter from nine of the ten black students who were rejected, requesting an explanation for their rejection, was reported in the *Atlanta Constitution*, 21 June 1961. The original letter is in the presidential files (January Confusion), GTA.
31. *Technique*, 12 May 1961.
32. Letters to Harrison, presidential files (January Confusion), GTA; file of letters and clippings in possession of Edwin D. Harrison.
33. *Technique*, 26 May 1961.
34. Fred W. Ajax, "Information for News Media," copy in possession of James E. Dull.

35. *Technique,* 6 October 1961.
36. Ibid.
37. Ibid., 9 November 1963. Apparently the concert was actually held in the spring of 1963. Ibid., 31 January 1964.
38. Ibid., 31 January 1964.
39. *Annual Report,* 1966–67, p. 12.
40. *Technique,* 26 April 1963, 30 April 1965, 30 June 1965, 16 May 1969.
41. Ibid., 9 February 1968.
42. Ibid., 31 May 1968, 1 November 1968, 14 November 1969.
43. Ibid., 11 October 1968.
44. Ibid., 14 February 1969.
45. *Annual Report,* 1961–62, p. 97.
46. Keck Engineering Associates, *Formula for Growth: Georgia Institute of Technology* (1962); Perkins & Will Partnership, *Comprehensive Campus Development Plan* (1965); Booz, Allen & Hamilton, Inc., *Top Organization Plan: Georgia Institute of Technology, Atlanta, Georgia* (1965); Arthur D. Little, Inc., *Georgia Tech: Impetus to Economic Growth* (1963). Wallace, *White and Gold,* pp. 389–401, discusses the four studies and their impact.
47. *Annual Report,* 1961–62, p. 97. Joe Guthridge made the statement.
48. *An Institutional Self-Study of the Georgia Institute of Technology* (May 1963), 1:1.
49. Ibid., 1:1–2.
50. Ibid., "The Purpose of the Institution," 1:18–68.
51. For the complete text of the address, see vertical files (75th Anniversary), GTA. The core of the address is printed in *President's Report,* 1961, pp. 7–16, and in Wallace, *White and Gold,* pp. 327–33.
52. *Self-Study,* 1963, 1:56–57.
53. Ibid., 1:57–58.
54. M. R. Carstens to M. J. Goglia, 14 November 1961, presidential files (75th Anniversary), GTA.
55. Goglia interview, 15 February 1984.
56. Untitled, unpaginated manuscript prepared by a member of the 75th Anniversary Committee, vertical files (75th Anniversary), GTA. Material in this section that is not cited is either from this manuscript or from Wallace, *White and Gold,* pp. 380–88.
57. 75th Anniversary manuscript; interview with Paul G. Mayer, 6 June 1983; *Technique,* 26 October, 9 November, 30 November, and 12 December 1962, 18 January 1963.
58. Letters in presidential files (75th Anniversary—Earl Warren Incident), GTA.

59. *Technique*, 1, 8, and 15 February 1963; *North Side News*, 31 January 1963, presidential files (75th Anniversary—Earl Warren Incident), GTA.
60. Letters in presidential files (75th Anniversary—Earl Warren Incident), GTA.
61. *Technique*, 15 February 1963. For the full text of the speech, see vertical files (75th Anniversary), GTA.
62. 75th Anniversary manuscript; program for the symposium, vertical files (75th Anniversary), GTA; Wallace, *White and Gold*, pp. 381–82.
63. 75th Anniversary manuscript.
64. Wallace, *White and Gold*, p. 383. For the issue, see vertical files (75th Anniversary), GTA.
65. Robert B. Wallace, Jr., *Dress Her in White and Gold: A Biography of Georgia Tech and of the Men Who Led Her*, 1st ed. (Atlanta: Georgia Tech Foundation, 1963). This edition of *White and Gold* includes pictures and a chronology which were omitted from the enlarged 1969 edition. All citations in this chapter are to the revised edition.
66. Edwin D. Harrison to John F. Kennedy, 3 January 1963, presidential files (75th Anniversary—Convocation), GTA.
67. Edwin D. Harrison to Kenneth O'Donnell, 22 May 1963; Kenneth O'Donnell to Edwin D. Harrison, 28 May 1963; and Edwin D. Harrison to Kenneth O'Donnell, 1 June 1963, presidential files (75th Anniversary—Convocation), GTA.
68. *Technique*, 31 May 1963.
69. See the news article, "Fuqua Says He Persuaded Kennedy to Cancel Talk," and the editorial by Eugene Patterson, "Could Dallas Have Happened Here?" in *Atlanta Constitution*, 25 November 1966.
70. Kenneth F. O'Donnell to Edwin D. Harrison, 13 August 1963, presidential files (75th Anniversary—Convocation), GTA; *Technique*, 4 September 1963.
71. *Atlanta Journal*, 7 October 1963; *Technique*, 11 October 1963. The program for the convocation is in vertical files (75th Anniversary), GTA.
72. Wallace, *White and Gold*, p. 386.
73. Robert B. Wallace, Jr., to Edwin D. Harrison, 12 August 1964, vertical files (75th Anniversary), GTA.
74. Wallace, *White and Gold*, p. 303.
75. Crawford interview, 15 July 1983.
76. *Atlanta Journal and Constitution*, 14 November 1965.
77. For a discussion of the role of the Dean of Engineering in the admin-

istrative chain of command at Georgia Tech during the late fifties and early sixties, see *Technique,* 20 February 1959.
78. Among the most useful of the interviews that discussed Mason's role are those with Edwin D. Harrison, 26 October 1983, 3 November 1983; Mario J. Goglia, 10, 15 February 1984; Samuel C. Barnett, 6 July 1983; Arnold Ducoffe, 12 September 1983; Janice Gosdin-Sangster, 9 September 1983; Vernon D. Crawford, 15 July 1983; Glenn Rainey, 27 June 1983; James D. Young, 24 June 1983; William H. Eberhardt, 1 September 1983; and Rudy Yobs, 16 July 1984.
79. *Technique,* 8 May 1959.
80. Harrison interview, 26 October 1983.
81. Faculty Senate Minutes, 5 October 1965; Booze, Allen & Hamilton, *Top Organization Plan,* p. ii.
82. *President's Report,* 1966, p. 4.
83. Booze, Allen & Hamilton, *Top Organization Plan,* p. 17.
84. Ibid., p. 9.
85. Harrison interview; 26 October 1983; Goglia interviews; correspondence in Georgia Institute of Technology, Central Administrative Records (Reorganization—1965), hereafter cited as CAR.
86. Ibid.
87. Faculty Senate Minutes, 5 October 1965.
88. Edwin D. Harrison, "Notes for Faculty Meeting," CAR (Reorganization—1965).
89. Faculty Senate Minutes, 5 October 1965.
90. Correspondence in CAR (Reorganization—1965); Harrison interview, 26 October 1983.
91. Correspondence in CAR (Reorganization—1965).
92. Ibid.
93. Clyde D. Robbins to Lawrence Foster, 21 August 1984; Wallace, *White and Gold,* p. 408. Wallace's figures for the expansion of campus size are incomplete.
94. Robbins to Foster, 21 August 1984. For the architectural history of Georgia Tech prior to Harrison's presidency, see Warren E. Drury III, "The Architectural Development of Georgia Tech" (M.S. thesis, School of Architecture, Georgia Institute of Technology, 1984). On the expansion of the Van Leer era, also see chapter 7.
95. Clarence N. Stone, *Economic Growth and Neighborhood Discontent: System Bias in the Urban Renewal Program of Atlanta* (Chapel Hill: University of North Carolina Press, 1976), chapters 4, 5, and 6.
96. *Self-Study,* 1963, p. 1.

97. Keck Engineering Associates, *Formula for Growth*; Wallace, *White and Gold*, pp. 390–91; interview with Clyde D. Robbins, 26 August 1983.
98. For a convenient summary of the plan, see Lee Robinson, "Georgia Tech: Dateline 1985," *Georgia Tech Engineer*, April 1965, pp. 16–27. Also see Lee Robinson, "Engineer Interview: Mr. Clyde Robbins, Campus Planner," *Georgia Tech Engineer*, April 1965, pp. 12–15. *A Bold Future* is available in vertical files (Georgia Tech Campus), GTA.
99. Perkins & Will, *Comprehensive Campus Development Plan*, p. 13.
100. Ibid., pp. 5–6.
101. Wallace, *White and Gold*, pp. 391–92; Robbins interview, 26 August 1983.
102. Ibid.
103. Ibid.
104. Compilation of information on campus buildings by Warren E. Drury III, copy in GTA.
105. See *President's Reports* and *Annual Reports* for 1961 through 1970, and Wallace, *White and Gold*, pp. 402–8.
106. Ibid., p. 406.
107. For introductions to student academic unrest during the sixties, see David Riesman and Verne A. Stadtman, eds., *Academic Transformations: Seventeen Institutions Under Pressure* (New York: McGraw-Hill, 1973), and Mitchell Cohen and Dennis Hale, eds., *The New Student Left* (Boston: Beacon, 1967).
108. Interview with Miller Templeton and Edwin Kohler, 23 June 1983; *Technique*, 26 September 1958, 22 October 1965.
109. *Technique*, 30 May 1958; interviews with Carlton Parker, 23 June 1983; William Landiss, 22 June 1983; Glenn Rainey, 27 June 1983; James E. Dull, 21 July 1983; James D. Young, 24 June 1983; and Miller Templeton and Edwin Kohler, 23 June 1983.
110. *Technique*, 5 April 1963.
111. Ibid., 4 October 1961.
112. Ibid., 14 May 1965.
113. Ibid., 4 and 11 November 1960.
114. Ibid., 4 and 11 March, 29 April 1960.
115. Ibid., 21 October 1960.
116. Ibid., 4 November 1960.
117. Ibid., 24 October 1958.
118. Ibid., 23 September, 2 December 1960.
119. Ibid., 5 October 1962.
120. Ibid., 29 July 1960.
121. Ibid., 14 May 1965.

122. Ibid.
123. Ibid., 30 April 1965.
124. Ibid., 12 July 1957.
125. Ibid., 6 September 1956.
126. The removal of Guinn Leverett—the outstanding *Technique* editor for 1963–64, who had not personally approved the entire issue—was a less severe sanction than that taken in the case of the 1953 April Fool's issue of the *Technique*, entitled *Feel and Scream*, which resulted in the firing of the entire staff. *Technique*, 27 February 1959.
127. Interview with George C. Griffin, 7 July 1983; George C. Griffin, *Griffin—You Are a Great Disappointment to Me: The Tales of Georgia Tech's Dean Emeritus George C. Griffin* (Atlanta: Georgia Tech National Alumni Association, 1971); Wallace, *White and Gold*, pp. 132–38.
128. *Technique*, 10 December 1965, 28 January 1966.
129. Ibid., 5 March 1965.
130. *Annual Report*, 1968–69, p. 5.
131. *Technique*, 26 April 1968; *New York Times*, 30 September 1968; Wallace, *White and Gold*, pp. 359–70. Another letter with wide support from student leadership appeared in May 1969 and called for substantial curriculum revision. *Technique*, 9 May 1969.
132. Terry Connolly and Alan L. Porter, *The Recruitment and Retention of Women as Undergraduate Engineers* (Atlanta: School of Industrial and Systems Engineering, Georgia Institute of Technology, 1979); Helen E. Grenga, "Women in Engineering at Georgia Tech," *Georgia Professional Engineering Magazine*, September–October 1983, pp. 7–8, 14; Bruce Toth, "Tech Since 1964: A World of Difference," *Exponent*, October 1974, pp. 10–15 (*Exponent* was a short-lived magazine supplement to *Technique*); *Technique*, 1 March 1968. For the effort to attract women, see the pamphlet printed in the early 1970s, *Women in Engineering at Georgia Tech*, copy in possession of Helen Grenga. Despite the small percentage of women engineers at Tech, throughout the sixties more women were studying at Georgia Tech than at any other technical school in the country. *Annual Report*, 1967–68, p. 152.
133. *Technique*, 30 May 1958. *Technique* issues of 7 November 1958 and 29 January 1965 provide a description of the house.
134. *Exponent*, October 1974, p. 11.
135. Grenga, "Women in Engineering," p. 7; interview with Helen E. Grenga, 9 June 1983. Humor often could be vicious, as in the article entitled "Dog Run over by ATO's; Later Found to be Coed," *Technique*, 22 November 1968.

135. Wallace, *White and Gold*, p. 354.
137. *Technique*, 9 January 1959, 22 January 1960.
138. Lynn Jones, ed., *The Freshman Girl's Handbook, 1966–1967: Georgia Institute of Technology*, in vertical files (Co-education), GTA, provides an historical overview of the changes. The pace of change was even slower for women instructors than for women students. The first female instructor at Tech, Dr. Mary K. Cabell in Math, did not join the faculty until the fall of 1960. *Technique*, 14 October 1960; *Atlanta Journal and Constitution*, 30 October 1960.
139. *Technique*, 1 March 1968.
140. Ibid., 2 September 1957.
141. *Sports Illustrated*, 19 September 1960, pp. 62–63; *Technique*, 12 December 1958; Robert B. Wallace, Jr., "The Tall Grey Fox," *Georgia Tech Alumnus*, September 1960, pp. 6–11; interview with Robert L. Dodd by Steve Branscombe, in *Exponent*, April 1976, pp. 11–12; interview with Robert L. Dodd, 5 July 1983.
142. Dodd interview, 5 July 1983.
143. *Technique*, 12 December 1958.
144. Dodd interview, 5 July 1983.
145. Such efforts became public under Dodd's successor, Bud Carson. *Atlanta Journal*, 16 December 1968.
146. *Atlanta Constitution*, 25 November 1961.
147. *Technique*, 26 January 1962.
148. Ibid., 16 August 1963, 31 January 1964; *President's Report*, 1964, pp. 15–16; Dodd interview, 5 July 1983; Harrison interview, 3 November 1983; Wallace, *White and Gold*, pp. 283–84.
149. *Technique*, 8 October 1965.
150. Ibid., 13 January 1967.
151. *Atlanta Constitution*, 7 February 1967; Wallace, *White and Gold*, pp. 285–90.
152. On the revitalization of Tech's basketball program, see Wallace, *White and Gold*, p. 283. On "drownproofing," see Fred R. Lanoue, *Drownproofing: A New Technique for Water Safety* (Englewood Cliffs, N.J.: Prentice-Hall, 1963). For minor sports, see "Report of the Athletic Director," in *Annual Reports*.
153. *Technique*, 31 January 1958, says that approximately three thousand students per year, over half the enrollment, participated in intramurals. *Exponent*, October 1974, p. 21, indicated that intramural participation was approximately 40 percent each year.
154. Committee on Educational Objectives and Methods, *The Aims and Objectives of the Georgia Institute of Technology* (September 1954), pp. 12–42.

155. *Technique*, 6 December 1957, 4 December 1959.
156. "Educational Program," *Self-Study*, 1963, 4:1–17.
157. *President's Report*, 1966, pp. 11–12; Crawford interview, 15 July 1983; David Wyly, "History of Georgia Tech Physics Department, 1888–1967," manuscript in possession of School of Physics, p. 28.
158. *Annual Report*, 1963–64, p. 36.
159. *President's Report*, 1961, pp. 8–9.
160. Ibid., 1961, p. 25.
161. Ibid., 1962, pp. 20–21.
162. *Annual Report*, 1962–63, pp. 14–15.
163. *President's Report*, 1964, p. 6.
164. *Annual Report*, 1966–67, p. 2.
165. Ibid., 1956–57, p. 86, 1961–62, p. 59, and 1966–67, p. 62.
166. "Industrial and Educational Involvement of the Georgia Tech Engineering Experiment Station," 25 November 1969, pp. 5, 7–8, 9.
167. Arthur D. Little Report, *Georgia Tech: Impetus to Economic Growth*; "Georgia Tech: Impetus to Economic Growth—A Summary of the Arthur D. Little Report," *Georgia Tech Alumnus*, December 1963, pp. 7–11; Wallace, *White and Gold*, pp. 393–95.
168. *Annual Report*, 1961–62, p. 2.
169. Ibid., 1966–67, p. 2.
170. Ibid., 1965–66, p. 30.
171. *President's Report*, 1961, p. 20.
172. Ibid., 1965, p. 8.
173. *Annual Report*, 1961–62, p. 55.
174. Allan M. Cartter, *An Assessment of Quality in Graduate Education* (Washington, D.C.: American Council on Education, 1966); Kenneth D. Roose and Charles J. Andersen, *A Rating of Graduate Programs* (Washington, D.C.: American Council on Education, 1970); *Atlanta Journal*, 1 August 1974.
175. Wallace, *White and Gold*, p. 400.
176. Ibid., pp. 400–401.
177. Ibid., p. 401.
178. Margaret Shannon, "Chancellor of Georgia's University System," *Atlanta Journal and Constitution Magazine*, 10 March 1968, pp. 8–9, 58, 59. 61.
179. The disagreements between Harrison and Simpson are common knowledge and have been discussed in virtually every interview we have conducted which deals with the mid to late 1960s.
180. Edwin D. Harrison to George L. Simpson, Jr., 2 July 1968, vertical files (Annual Reports—Misc.), GTA.
181. Wallace, *White and Gold*, p. 432. *Atlanta Journal and Constitution*, 4

July 1968, indicates that Simpson was the source of the information on the time of Harrison's resignation. A student assessment of the reasons for the resignation, *Technique*, 28 February 1969, links it to the Board of Regents' July 2 decision to place the Urban Life Center at Georgia State rather than at Georgia Tech. Interviews have not corroborated the importance of this action for Harrison's resignation, however.
182. *Atlanta Journal and Constitution*, 4 July 1968.
183. *Atlanta Journal*, 9 July 1968.
184. E. D. Harrison to all faculty, staff, and students, 9 July 1968, vertical files (Edwin D. Harrison), GTA; reported in *Atlanta Constitution*, 10 July 1968.
185. *Atlanta Journal*, 17 January 1969; Harrison interview, 8 November 1983.
186. E. D. Harrison to members of the faculty and staff, 12 February 1969, vertical files (Edwin D. Harrison), GTA.
187. *President's Report*, 1969, p. 4.
188. Wallace, *White and Gold*, p. 440.
189. *Atlanta Constitution*, 9 April 1969; Wallace, *White and Gold*, pp. 440–43; Harrison interview, 8 November 1983.
190. *President's Report*, 1968, p. 12.

Chapter Nine

1. Interview with Vernon D. Crawford, 15 July 1983.
2. David Wyly, "History of the Georgia Tech Physics Department, 1888–1967," manuscript in possession of School of Physics, p. 28. Professor Wyly chaired the faculty committee that planned the revision of the physics curriculum.
3. Faculty Senate Minutes, 11 March 1969.
4. *Annual Report of the President*, 1969–70, p. 517.
5. "Reactions to the Preliminary Report of the ASEE Goals Study," *Engineering Education* 57 (February 1967): 437–44.
6. "Final Report: Goals of Engineering Education," *Engineering Education* 58 (January 1968): 15–22.
7. "Report to the Engineering College, Georgia Institute of Technology, on *Goals of Engineering Education—The Preliminary Report*, by the Goals Committee Report Committee of the Engineering College," 9 December 1966, in the Dean of Engineering File, Central Administrative Records, hereinafter cited as CAR.

8. Interview with Dale C. Ray, 29 June 1983.
9. "A Statement of Academic Concern," reprinted in *Annual Report, 1969–70*, pp. 5–6.
10. Interview with Arthur G. Hansen, 19 August 1983; Ray interview, 29 June 1983. Hansen and Ray had known each other slightly at Michigan, having served together on a Ph.D. examining committee.
11. "Final Report: Goals of Engineering Education," pp. 387–94; *Technique*, 12 April 1968; memorandum, Dale C. Ray to Walter O. Carlson, 26 July 1968, in possession of Professor Ray.
12. *Annual Report, 1968–69*, p. 7.
13. Robert B. Wallace, Jr., *Dress Her in White and Gold: A Biography of Georgia Tech and the Men Who Led Her*, rev. ed. (Atlanta: Georgia Tech Foundation, 1969), p. 368; *Annual Report, 1969–70*, p. v.
14. Ray interview.
15. *Technique*, 2 June 1969; Hansen interview; interview with Walter O. Carlson, 20 July 1983.
16. *Technique*, 28 May 1969; interviews with present and former members of Georgia Tech faculty; interview with George L. Simpson, Jr., 5 March 1984. In 1962 Simpson and Bisplinghoff toured Georgia's state universities on behalf of NASA and at the request of President Kennedy.
17. "A Visit with Dr. Wiesner," *Change* 4 (1972): 19–20.
18. Biographical sketch of Arthur G. Hansen, vertical files (Arthur G. Hansen), Georgia Tech Archives, hereafter cited as GTA; Hansen interview; interview with Donald R. Nelson, 25 September 1983.
19. Hansen biographical sketch.
20. Memorandum, Arthur G. Hansen to Members of the Georgia Tech Faculty, 31 July 1969, CAR (Administrative Memoranda); "Report of Vice President for Planning," in *Annual Report, 1968–69*, p. 133.
21. "Report of Vice President for Academic Affairs, in *Annual Report, 1970–71*, pp. 70–71; *Georgia Institute of Technology Self-Study*, 1973, 2:19.
22. Dan Green, "Tech's Building Boom," *The Georgia Tech Engineer*, May 1969, *President's Report, 1970–71*, p. 107.
23. Interview with Lester G. Maddox, 25 October 1983; "Proposed Campus Expansion Plan," Georgia Institute of Technology, Campus Planning Office, no date.
24. Wallace, *White and Gold*, pp. 359–70. As an advisor to top campus administrators until his untimely death in 1970, Robert Wallace was a participant in decision making as well as a chronicler of Tech's history. In retrospect, his detailed account of Tech's response to student concerns about community problems in the late 1960s overstates the level

of student activism, but it reflects accurately the attention that Tech administrators, for a variety of reasons, were giving to such matters.
25. Arthur G. Hansen, "Presidential Memorandum Number 1," 12 November 1969, vertical files (Arthur G. Hansen), GTA; interview with William Landiss, 22 June 1983.
26. Interview with Numan V. Bartley, 24 May 1983; Nelson interview.
27. *Technique*, 30 April, 24 May, 15 November 1968; Bartley interview.
28. Clarence N. Stone, *Economic Growth and Neighborhood Discontent: System Bias in the Urban Renewal Program of Atlanta* (Chapel Hill: University of North Carolina Press, 1976), chapters 7 and 8.
29. Jamie Anthony, who had fiscal responsibility for Tech's real estate acquisitions throughout the period, recalls making numerous visits to homes in the urban renewal area, accompanied by Paul Weber and other Tech officials. Interview with Jamie Anthony, 7 February 1984.
30. Hansen, "Presidential Memorandum Number 1."
31. "Report of the Dean of Students," in *Annual Report*, 1968–69, pp. 178–79; Nelson interview.
32. *Technique*, 31 October 1969.
33. *Atlanta Journal*, 8 April 1970; *EOA News*, 29 April 1970; *Technique*, 23 July 1971.
34. *Technique*, 7 February, 18 July, 12 December 1969.
35. "Report of the Dean of Students," in *Annual Report*, 1970–71, p. 155.
36. *Technique*, 17 October 1969, 21 August 1970.
37. Interview with Clyde Robbins, 26 August 1983.
38. "Report of the Dean of Students," in *Annual Report*, 1971–72, pp. 66–67.
39. *Technique*, 12 November 1971, 21 January 1972, 2 March, 25 May 1973.
40. Benson Snyder, "Change Despite Turmoil at MIT," in David Reisman and Verne A. Stadtman, eds., *Academic Transformation: Seventeen Institutions Under Pressure* (New York: McGraw-Hill, 1973), p. 155.
41. *Technique*, 9 February 1968, 17 May 1968, 17 October 1969.
42. Milton Viorst, *Fire in the Streets: America in the 1960s* (New York: Simon and Schuster, 1979), p. 539.
43. *Atlanta Constitution*, 7 May 1970; Thomas G. Dyer, *The University of Georgia: A Bicentennial History* (Athens: University of Georgia Press, 1985), pp. 349–51.
44. Arthur G. Hansen, Memorandum to Administrative Personnel, 7 May 1970, CAR (Administrative Memoranda). The order to close the colleges was given in the name of the Board of Regents, but according to

newspaper accounts, both Chancellor Simpson and Governor Maddox participated in the decision.
45. *Technique*, 15 May 1970; Hansen interview.
46. Fraternity/Sorority Scholastic Reports, Fall Quarters, 1968–75, in possession of the Dean of Students.
47. Interview with Edward Kohler and Miller Templeton, 23 June 1983; interview with Rush Smith, 24 May 1983.
48. AFROTC statistics provided by Col. Robert W. Bush, June 1984.
49. *Technique*, 17 January 1969.
50. Ibid., 17 May 1968. The survey had been conducted in April, when the McCarthy-Kennedy battle for primary votes was still taking shape. Southern regional director for the national straw vote was Sam Williams, who had just completed his term as student body president at Tech.
51. *Annual Report*, 1969–70, pp. 517–25.
52. Ibid., pp. 527–53.
53. *Technique*, 9 February 1968; *Annual Report*, 1968–69, p. 168; ibid., 1969–70, p. 174–75.
54. *Technique*, 1 November 1968, 14 February, 10 October 1969.
55. Interview with Tommy Plaxico, 21 June 1984.
56. Landiss interview; Nelson interview.
57. *Technique*, 2 March 1968, 22 November 1968, 7, 21 February 1969.
58. Ben L. Moon, "Anatomy of a Dream," *Georgia Tech Alumnus Magazine*, November–December 1970, p. 5.
59. W. T. Ziegler to E. D. Harrison, 12 January 1967; Harrison to Ziegler, 11 April 1967, both in CAR (YMCA).
60. Harrison to Ziegler, 11 April 1967, CAR (YMCA).
61. *Annual Report*, 1968–69, 170–71; Moon, "Anatomy of a Dream," p. 5.
62. *Technique*, 16 May 1969.
63. Vernon Crawford to Carlton Parker et al., 13 June 1969, CAR (YMCA). Crawford had himself been a member of the YMCA Board of Trustees.
64. YMCA Board of Trustees, *Minutes*, 9 October 1969, CAR (YMCA).
65. "Proposal for Reorganization of the Georgia Tech YMCA" (presented to YMCA Board), 9 October 1969; "A Proposal for Reorganization of the Georgia Tech YMCA" (approved by the YMCA Board for transmittal to Arthur G. Hansen), 12 October 1969, both in CAR (YMCA).
66. A. G. Hansen to Board of Trustees of Georgia Tech YMCA, 29 December 1969, CAR (YMCA); interview with Carlton Parker, 23 June 1983.
67. Robert Coleman to Henry G. Neal, 16 February 1972, CAR (YMCA).

68. W. T. Ziegler to A. G. Hansen, 25 September 1970; J. Robert Coleman to Henry G. Neal, 16 February 1972; both in CAR (YMCA).
69. *Annual Report,* 1979–80, p. 49.
70. *Annual Report,* 1969–70, p. 82; interview with Arnold Ducoffe, 12 September 1983; interview with William E. Eberhardt, 1 September 1983.
71. "Report of the Director, Water Resources Center," in *Annual Report,* 1968–69, pp. 117–18; ibid., 1969–70, p. 87; interview with Paul G. Mayer, 12 May 1983.
72. "Report of the Director, Bioengineering Center," in *Annual Report,* 1969–70, pp. 97–103; interview with Walter Bloom, 13 September 1983. Dr. Bloom, who had come to Tech in 1967 from Emory Medical School and the staff of Piedmont Hospital in Atlanta, also played a key role in establishing the Bioengineering Center. The Health Systems Center was also established in 1969, but with the primary objective of organizing a new academic unit in that field.
73. *Annual Report,* 1969–70, pp. 180–81.
74. See chapter 10, especially the discussion of the Microelectronics Research Center.
75. *American Men and Women of Science: Physical and Biological Science,* 15th ed., vol. 6 (New York: R. R. Bowker Co., 1982), p. 979; interview with Thomas E. Stelson, 2 August 1983.
76. *Self-Study,* 1973, 2:419.
77. George L. Simpson, Jr., to Edwin Harrison, 27 March 1968; H. F. Robinson to Arthur G. Hansen, 25 March 1970, both in CAR (Engineering Experiment Station).
78. Allan M. Cartter, *An Assessment of Quality in Graduate Education* (Washington, D.C.: American Council on Education, 1966); Kenneth D. Roose and Charles J. Andersen, *A Rating of Graduate Programs* (Washington, D.C.: American Council on Education, 1970).
79. Harold Vagtborg, *Research and American Industrial Development* (New York: Pergamon Press, 1976), chapters 6 and 7. I am grateful to Professor Stothe P. Kezios for bringing to my attention Vagtborg's pioneering contributions to the development of technological research institutes.
80. Arthur G. Hansen to Vernon Crawford, 1 September 1970; Hansen to Deans, Directors, and Division Chiefs, 14 April 1971, both in CAR (Engineering Experiment Station); *Atlanta Constitution,* 1 April 1971.
81. *American Men and Women of Science,* 4:822.
82. "Report of the Director, Engineering Experiment Station," in *Annual Report,* 1970–71, pp. 83–85; *Atlanta Constitution,* 1 April 1971;

Technique, 23 April 1971; Clayton Brown, Jr., to Arthur G. Hansen, 6 April 1971, CAR (Engineering Experiment Station); interview with Hon. Jimmy Carter, 30 March 1984.
83. Faculty Senate Minutes, 27 April 1971.
84. Technique, 30 April 1971; interview with James E. Boyd, 20 February 1984.
85. Memorandum, James E. Boyd to Vice Presidents, Deans, Directors, and Department Heads, 15 July 1971, CAR (Engineering Experiment Station). Stelson's term was to coincide with Boyd's term as acting president.
86. Technique, 6 August 1971. The committee assigned to formulate a reorganization plan was disbanded in July without making a final report. Thomas E. Stelson to Albert B. Sheppard, 22 July 1971, CAR (Engineering Experiment Station).
87. "Report of the Director, Engineering Experiment Station," in *Annual Report*, 1972–73, p. 54.
88. "Athletics" was still virtually synonymous with "football," even though Tech fielded competitive teams in nine other sports.
89. "Report of the Athletic Director," in *Annual Report*, 1968–69, p. 186–87; ibid., 1969–70, p. 181.
90. Coach Dodd did not share the view of some that Tech's departure from the Southeastern Conference had contributed to the drop in attendance.
91. Faculty Senate Minutes, 3 February 1970; Technique, 12 May 1970; telephone interview with W. T. Ziegler, 14 April 1984.
92. "The End of an Era," *Georgia Tech Alumnus Magazine*, Winter 1972, p. 24.
93. File of letters and memoranda in possession of James E. Boyd.
94. Statement to the press of Dr. James E. Boyd, 8 January 1972, in possession of Dr. Boyd; interview with James E. Boyd, 8 March 1984; interview with Waldemar T. Ziegler, 12 July 1983; Technique, 14 January 1972 (editorial by Rush Smith). As editor of Technique, Smith was a voting member of the Athletic Board.
95. Boyd press statement, 8 January 1972.
96. Technique, 28 January 1972; *Georgia Tech Alumnus Magazine*, Winter 1972, pp. 27–28.
97. Joseph M. Pettit to James P. Poole, 22 December 1971, copy in possession of James E. Boyd.
98. See chapter 8. Maddox interview; Simpson interview.
99. University System of Georgia, Board of Regents, *Annual Report*, 1967–72.

100. Simpson interview; "Report of the Academic Vice President," *Annual Report,* 1970–71, p. 4.

Chapter Ten

1. *Technique,* 8 October 1971; Ben Moon, "Dr. Joseph M. Pettit. . . ." *Georgia Tech Alumnus Magazine* 50 (Fall 1971): 7.
2. Interview with George L. Simpson, 5 March 1984; interview with Hon. Jimmy Carter, 30 March 1984; interview with J. M. Pettit, 18 July 1983; press release, Stanford University News Service, 5 October 1971, Stanford University Archives.
3. Pettit interview, 18 July 1983; biographical sketch, J. M. Pettit, President's Office.
4. *National Cyclopaedia of American Biography,* 76 vols. (New York: James T. White and Co., 1946), 6:546; John Walsh, "Stanford's Search for Solutions," in David Reisman and Verne A. Stadtman, eds., *Academic Transformation: Seventeen Institutions Under Pressure* (New York: McGraw-Hill, 1973), pp. 305–7; Pettit biographical sketch.
5. Gene Bylinsky, "California's Great Breeding Ground for Industry," *Fortune,* June 1974, pp. 130–31.
6. Frederick E. Terman, "The Newly Emerging Community of Technical Scholars," reprinted in Carroll W. Pursell, Jr., ed., *Readings in Technology and American Life* (New York: Oxford University Press, 1969), pp. 431–32.
7. Bylinsky, "California's Great Breeding Ground for Industry," p. 131; Harold Vagtborg, *Research and American Industrial Development* (New York: Pergamon Press, 1976), p. 238.
8. Pettit interview, 18 July 1983.
9. John Walsh, "Stanford's Search for Solutions," pp. 312–13; Immanuel Wallerstein and Paul Starr, eds., *The University Crisis Reader,* 2 vols. (New York: Random House, 1969), 1:228–29.
10. Walsh, "Stanford's Search for Solutions," pp. 313–20; Stanton A. Glantz, "Stanford and the Pentagon," *Change,* September 1972, pp. 17–19.
11. Press releases, Stanford University News Service, 27 May 1970 and 6 December 1972, Stanford University Archives.
12. *Atlanta Journal and Constitution,* 24 June 1984, p. 20-E.
13. Inaugural Address, President Joseph Mayo Pettit, Georgia Institute of Technology, 9 May 1972, manuscript in possession of Dr. Pettit.
14. Pettit inaugural address.

15. Pettit interview, 18 July 1983; Walsh, "Sanford's Search for Solutions," p. 306; Gene Griessman, "Joseph M. Pettit Fosters Continuity and Leadership," *Georgia Tech Alumni Magazine* 58 (Winter 1983): 11.
16. Upon his arrival President Pettit discouraged plans that were then well advanced for further curricular expansion in the liberal arts, telling one faculty forum that "we should capitalize on our uniqueness." *Technique*, 5 May 1972.
17. Pettit interview, 18 July 1983.
18. Interview with Thomas E. Stelson, 2 August 1983; press release, Stanford University News Service, 13 November 1968, Stanford University Archives; *Annual Reports*, 1969–73.
19. "Final Report: Goals of Engineering Education," *Engineering Education* 58 (January 1968): 380–81.
20. Joseph M. Pettit, "The Changing Status of Graduate Engineering Education," *Engineering Education* 58 (January 1967): 363–68; "Final Report: Goals of Engineering Education," p. 406; interview with J. M. Pettit, 31 August 1983.
21. Pettit interview, 31 August 1983.
22. University System of Georgia, Board of Regents, *Annual Reports*, 1970–73; interview with Arnold Ducoffe, 12 September 1983. Enrollment is measured here in full-time equivalents.
23. *Annual Report*, 1971–72, p. v.
24. *Georgia Institute of Technology Self-Study*, 1973, 2:82.
25. "Report of the Vice President for Academic Affairs," in *Annual Report*, 1975–76, p. 1; Board of Regents, *Annual Reports*, 1970–76.
26. Simpson interview; George L. Simpson to Hon. Paul C. Broun and Hon. Joe Frank Harris (cc. Hon. George D. Busbee), in RG 1–1–5, Governor's Correspondence File, "Regents," box 63, Georgia Department of Archives and History.
27. Interview with Clyde Robbins, 26 August 1983; *Annual Report*, 1970–71, p. 107.
28. *Technique*, 11 May, 17 August 1973.
29. *Annual Report*, 1973–74, p. 30; *Technique*, 16 November 1973; Associated Student Chapters, American Institute of Architecture, to J. M. Pettit et al., 6 November 1973, in the Architecture file, Central Administrative Records, hereafter cited as CAR.
30. Memorandum, Vernon D. Crawford to Thomas E. Stelson, 15 November 1971 (report of telephone conversation, Crawford and J. M. Pettit, 11 November 1971), in CAR (Policy); interview with J. M. Pettit, 14 September 1983.
31. *Annual Reports*, 1971–72, p. 203; 1976–77, p. 80.
32. *Georgia Tech Alumni Magazine* 53 (November 1976): 23–24; *Ameri-*

can *Men and Women of Science*, 15th ed., 7 vols. (New York: R. R. Bowker, Co., 1982), 3:251.
33. Memorandum, J. M. Pettit to Georgia Tech Faculty, 14 February 1974, CAR (Vice President, Research).
34. Pettit interview, 14 September 1983; interview with Thomas E. Stelson, 10 August 1983.
35. Memorandum from Vernon D. Crawford to Academic Deans, 23 July 1974, CAR (Academic Vice President).
36. *Self-Study*, 1973, 2:42, 46, 114, 258–59, 443.
37. "Report of the Vice President for Academic Affairs," in *Annual Report*, 1974–75, p. v.
38. *Self-Study*, 1973, 2:42, 46, 114, 258–59, 443.
39. Faculty Senate, *Minutes*, 9 November 1976; *Technique*, 28 May 1976, p. 5.
40. "Report of the Academic Vice President," *Annual Report*, 1975–76, p. 5.
41. Carter interview; *Exponent*, April 1976, pp. 15–16.
42. *Technique*, 23 April 1971; report of R. K. Jacobs, Head of Engineering Graphics, in *Annual Report*, 1972–73, p. 16.
43. Faculty Senate, *Minutes*, 22 April 1973.
44. "Meeting the Challenge of Academic Excellence," *Georgia Tech Alumni Magazine* 58 (Winter 1983): 15; *Technique*, 21 January 1972; memorandum, Thomas E. Stelson to J. M. Pettit, 18 January 1974, CAR (Architecture).
45. *Annual Report*, 1975–76, p. 3.
46. *Annual Report*, 1974–75, p. 2; *American Men and Women of Science*, 6:415.
47. Interview with J. M. Pettit, 29 September 1983. As was always the case, no state funds could be used to support the intercollegiate athletic program.
48. Interview with Homer Rice, 20 June 1984; Pettit interview, 29 September 1983; *Annual Report*, 1973–74, p. 256.
49. "Report of the Executive Secretary, Alumni Association," in *Annual Report*, 1973–74, p. 300–301.
50. *Technique*, 18 January 1974.
51. *Technique*, 11 January, 11 April 1980; Pettit interview, 29 September 1983.
52. *Technique*, 9 April 1976.
53. Rice interview.
54. *Technique*, 2 December 1977.
55. *Self-Study*, 1973, 2:161.

56. John Dunn, "Growing Pains," *Georgia Tech Alumni Magazine* 58 (Winter 1983): 20; Patrick J. Sheridan, "Engineering and Engineering Technology Enrollments," *Engineering Education* 70 (October 1970): 58; William J. Jannan, "The Enrollment Crunch: A National Survey," *Engineering Education* 71 (April 1981): 705–8.
57. *Annual Reports, 1972–82.*
58. Paula L. Loring, "Women Engineers: Progress and Challenge," *Engineering Education* 70 (January 1980): 337–39; Helen E. Grenga, "Women in Engineering at Georgia Tech," *Georgia Professional Engineering Magazine,* September–October 1983, pp. 7–8; *1973 Self-Study,* 2:367; "Report of the Dean of Engineering," in *Annual Report, 1971–72,* pp. 88–89; "Report of the Academic Vice President," in *Annual Report, 1973–74,* p. 4.
59. AFROTC information provided by Col. Robert Bush; *Technique,* 10 July 1970, 10 October 1975; "Report of the Dean of Students," in *Annual Report, 1972–73,* p. 187; *1973–74,* p. 381; Grenga, "Women in Engineering," p. 14; *Exponent,* February 1975, pp. 18–23; *Georgia Tech Alumnus Magazine* 58 (Fall 1982): 9–13.
60. Dunn, "Growing Pains," p. 20; Grenga, "Women in Engineering," p. 5.
61. *Blue Print,* 1977, 1978.
62. *Georgia Institute of Technology Self-Study,* 1983, 2:452; conversations with participating faculty members.
63. *Technique,* 1 July 1977, 11 May 1979.
64. *Technique,* 22 February, 8 March 1974.
65. "Fall Quarter Fraternity/Sorority Scholarship Reports," 1975–84, in possession of the Dean of Students; *Georgia Tech Alumni Magazine* 54 (October 1977): 13.
66. Interview with Vernon D. Crawford, 30 January 1984. Cf. correspondence to and from Governor George D. Busbee in RG 1–1–5, box 81. Receipts of funds for the dormitory was a mixed blessing. Tech's authorization for two major buildings virtually depleted the entire University System's building fund that year, a circumstance that may well have cost Tech additional support for construction in future years.
67. Academic Priorities Committee, Student Government Association, *A Question of Priorities: The Status of Georgia Tech Academics,* 1982.
68. *Self-Study,* 1983, 2:56, 72; *Technique,* 19 May 1978.
69. Statement of J. M. Pettit, in *Annual Report, 1980–81,* unpaginated.
70. *Self-Study,* 1983, 2:35, 101–2; *Annual Report, 1980–81,* p. 27.
71. *Annual Reports,* 1980–83.
72. Demetrius Paris, *Graduate Study and Research: A Prospectus for Improved Quality,* Georgia Institute of Technology, 1982.

73. *Self-Study,* 1983, 2:559–601; memorandum, J. M. Pettit to Thomas E. Stelson, 8 March 1982, CAR (Vice President, Research).
74. *Annual Report,* 1978–83.
75. *Self-Study,* 1983, 2:441–42.
76. Ibid., 2:442. This list of new buildings does not include several smaller administrative and service buildings or the O'Keefe School, purchased in 1979 and used for various research purposes.
77. *Technique,* 23 May 1980; *American Men and Women of Science,* 4:295.
78. *Annual Reports.*
79. *Annual Report,* 1979–80, p. 54; Pettit interview, 29 September 1983; Rice interview.
80. Crawford interview; interview with Walter O. Carlson, 20 July 1983; *Annual Report,* 1970–71, p. 32; Faculty Senate Minutes, 22 August 1978, 6 November 1979; *Technique,* 2 November 1979, 1 July 1980.
81. The phrase was Franklin D. Roosevelt's (1938), but the poverty of which he spoke was chronic in the region.
82. One such study, which apparently influenced President Jimmy Carter's thinking on the subject, was Christopher Lasch, *The Culture of Narcissism: American Life in an Age of Diminishing Expectations* (New York: W. W. Norton, 1979).
83. "Debate Grows over Adoption of National Industrial Policy," *New York Times,* 19 June 1983; James Botkin, Dan Dimancescu, and Ray Stata, *Global Stakes: The Future of High Technology in America* (Cambridge, Mass.: Belinger Publishing Co., 1982), pp. 154–55.
84. "The Reindustrialization of America," *Business Week* (special issue), 30 June 1980; Barry Bluestone and Bennett Harrison, *The Deindustrialization of America* (New York: Basic Books, 1982).
85. Joan Hoff Wilson, *Herbert Hoover, Forgotten Progressive* (Boston: Little, Brown and Co., 1975), chapter 4. See chapter 4 in this book for earlier attempts to expand the land grant concept to industrial research.
86. "Technology, Innovation, and Regional Economic Development: Encouraging High-Technology Development—Background Paper no. 2" (Washington, D.C.: U.S. Congress, Office of Technology Assessment, OTA-BP-STI-25, February 1984), p. 13; *Technology, Innovation, and Regional Economic Development* (Washington, D.C.: U.S. Congress, Office of Technology Assessment, OTA-STI-238, July 1984), p. 5. I am indebted to my colleague J. David Roessner, a member of the OTA advisory panel on Technology and Regional Economic Development, for this information.
87. Kenneth Coleman, gen. ed., *A History of Georgia* (Athens: University

of Georgia Press, 1977), p. 157. For information on Georgia's iron subsidy, I am indebted to Steven G. Hardy, a chemical engineering graduate of Georgia Tech (1984) and a dedicated student of eighteenth-century history.

88. "Remarks of Governor George Busbee, Advanced Technology Strategy Conference, Peachtree Plaza Hotel, Henry Grady Room," 5 October 1982, in CAR (ATDC).
89. Dennis R. Costello, "The National Solar Energy Research Institute: Function, Organization, and the First Six Months," unpublished report in possession of J. David Roessner.
90. Martha Ann Stegar, "Solar Energy Research Shines at Georgia Tech," *Georgia Tech Alumni Magazine* 59 (Spring 1984): 22–26.
91. Interview with George D. Busbee, 1 November 1983; interview with Thomas E. Stelson, 2 August 1983; memorandum to Potential SERI Site Sponsors from Thomas E. Stelson, 30 July 1975, RG-1-1-5, Governor's Executive Correspondence, box 36, pp. 4327–38.
92. "Proposal to ERDA for Establishment of SERI in Georgia, Submitted by the State of Georgia for the Solar Consortium," 15 July 1976; George L. Simpson to Hon. George Busbee, RG-1-1-5, box 63, pp. 4344–29. Until one month before the final submission date Tech had also been part of a National Solar Energy Research Consortium, organized by the president of George Washington University and consisting of twelve universities. Tech withdrew from that group after it decided to recommend a Miami site for SERI over Tech's Shenandoah proposal. Memorandum, T. E. Stelson to J. M. Pettit, 24 February 1976; "Synopsis of Organizational Meeting," NSERC, 4 June 1976; Pettit to Lloyd H. Elliot, 18 June 1976; all in CAR (Solar Energy).
93. ERDA Press Release, 21 July 1976; Special Memorandum to Georgia Tech Faculty, 8 July 1976, both in CAR (Solar Energy).
94. *Atlanta Journal*, 25 March 1977; Busbee interview; interview with Hon. Herman Talmadge, 18 January 1984; interview with Hon. Jimmy Carter, 30 March 1984. President Carter reaffirmed in that interview that the decision was made without interference from him.
95. Engineering Experiment Station, *Annual Report*, 1982–83, pp. 22–27; *Technique*, 21 September 1979; Stelson interview, 2 August 1983; Talmadge interview; interview with Jerry Birchfield, 24 May 1984. Senator Talmadge credits Birchfield, then an EES engineer, with playing a major role in drafting the Renewable Energy Act of 1979.
96. Stegar, "Solar Energy Research," pp. 24–26; Stelson interview, 2 August 1983.
97. "MCC Moves out of the Idea Stage," *Science* 220 (17 June 1983): 1256–

532   Notes to Pages 441–46

97. The twelve companies were Advanced Micro Devices, Allied, Control Data, Digital Equipment, Harris, Honeywell, Mostek, Motorola, National Semiconductor, NCR, RCA, and Sperry.
98. Presentation of J. M. Pettit to Microelectronics and Computer Technology Corporation, 18 March 1983, CAR (MCC); confidential administrative correspondence.
99. *Atlanta Business Chronicle*, 30 May 1983; "MCC Moves Out of the Idea Stage," p. 1257.
100. Mary Bosch, "High Technology Development: Its Origin, Success, and Place in Atlanta," Georgia Power Company, 1982, p. 20, CAR (ATDC).
101. Ibid., pp. 4–6.
102. Neil Shister, "The High Tech Revolution," *Atlanta* (August 1982), p. 57.
103. Ibid., pp. 56–57; Bosch, "High Technology Development," pp. 22–24. Chancellor Simpson did recall attempting to interest community and academic leaders in developing a private research park adjacent to the Tech campus in the late 1960s, but to no avail.
104. *Technology and Growth: State Initiatives in Technological Innovation* (Washington, D.C.: National Governor's Association, 1983), pp. 87–88.
105. Pettit interview, 28 July 1983; Shister, "The High Tech Revolution," pp. 58–59. For a decade after its founding, a controlling interest in Technology Park was held by the Georgia Tech Foundation.
106. *Technology and Growth*, p. 88; Birchfield interview.
107. "Final Report, State Science, Engineering, and Technology Program," prepared for the Office of the Governor, February 1980, p. 84, copy in possession of Professor Fred Tarpley.
108. "Final Report, STTEP," pp. 75–78; *Technology and Growth*, pp. 73–74; John Walsh, "RPI Takes the High Road," *Science* 212 (29 May 1981): 1005–8.
109. Interview with Rudy Yobs, 16 July 1984; Birchfield interview; Busbee interview; Pettit interview, 28 July 1983; J. M. Pettit to Vernon Crawford, 6 May 1982, CAR (ATDC).
110. Construction of the ATDC building touched off an outcry within the Home Park community. Campus relations with the adjacent community were less harmonious than had been the case during the urban renewal expansion of the 1960s. The administration seemed more anxious (in the words of the Vice President for Planning) to "plant the flag" at the northernmost boundary of the urban renewal zone, while some community leaders were better organized to resist. Letters of protest flooded the office of the Governor, as well as local officials, and

Notes to Pages 446–52

neighborhood residents launched a "Redirect High Tech" campaign. However, the construction of the new facility moved ahead, and it was opened in 1984. Interview with Clyde Robbins, 28 August 1983; *Home Park Newsletter*, 8 March 1980; "Letters re Home Park," in RG 1–1–5, Governor's Executive Correspondence, box 80.

111. "Directory of ATDC Member Companies," April 1974.
112. Interview with John W. Hooper, 11 April 1984; Demetrius Paris to J. M. Pettit, 28 August 1980; Jack Spurlock, "A Synopsis of Microelectronics Programs at the Georgia Institute of Technology," May 1980, both in CAR (Microelectronics).
113. G. R. Harrison to J. C. Wiltse et al., 8 August 1980, copy in CAR (Microelectronics).
114. Hooper interview.
115. Stelson interview, 2 August 1983; Amitai Etzioni, "The Two-Track Society," *National Forum: The Phi Kappa Phi Journal* 64 (Summer 1984): 3–5; Eva C. Galambos, "A 'High-Tech' or a Service Economy Future," ibid., pp. 38–39.
116. *Technology, Innovation and Regional Economic Development*, pp. 4–5.
117. Vice President's Long Range Planning Documents, CAR (Long Range Planning), 1984–85.
118. Tech followed Pennsylvania State University, the University of Illinois at Urbana, and Texas A&M University. Comparative data provided by W. Denny Freeston, associate dean of engineering.
119. Sue Palmer, ed., *1984–85 Fact Book Georgia Tech* (Atlanta, 1985), p. 31. While doctorates awarded in the engineering fields outnumbered those in the sciences by two to one, the largest single doctoral program, in terms of graduates, was in chemistry.
120. Lyle V. Jones, et al., eds., *An Assessment of Research-Doctorate Programs in the United States: Engineering* (Washington, 1982), pp. 36, 37, 44, 54, 55, 62, 74, 75, 82, 94, 95, 102; Lyle V. Jones, et al., eds., *An Assessment of Research-Doctorate Programs in the United States: Mathematics and Physical Sciences* (Washington, 1982), pp. 40, 41, 52, 62, 63, 68, 100, 101, 122–23, 134. The authors of the reports cautioned against using their findings as a basis for ranking programs, and critics have pointed to numerous methodological difficulties. Nevertheless, the reports' overall assessment of Georgia Tech's programs seems generally correct.
121. *Atlanta Journal and Constitution*, 27 January 1985.
122. Ibid.
123. Palmer, ed., *1984–85 Fact Book*, pp. 28, 29. These figures represent a continuation of long-standing patterns, as does the fact that 61 percent

of in-state students were residents of five metropolitan Atlanta counties.
124. Information provided by William Lee, director of financial aid.
125. John Dunn, "The Making of a Hell of an Engineer," *Georgia Tech Alumni*, Fall 1984, p. 36.
126. "Senior officer" is defined here as chairman of the board, chief executive officer, president, and executive vice president. Information supplied by Paul Brown, Georgia Tech Alumni Association.
127. Palmer, ed., *1984–85 Fact Book*, p. 58.

Bibliographical Note

Engineering the New South is based primarily upon manuscript and printed records and reports, presidential correspondence, institutional and student publications, newspaper clippings and tape-recorded interviews. M. L. Brittain's *The Story of Georgia Tech* (Chapel Hill: University of North Carolina Press, 1948), and Robert Wallace, Jr.'s *Dress Her in White and Gold: A Biography of Georgia Tech and the Men Who Led Her*, rev. ed. (Atlanta: Georgia Tech Foundation, 1969), are also valuable sources. Brittain was president of Tech from 1922 to 1945. Wallace, a 1949 graduate of the Institute, edited the *Georgia Tech Alumnus* for almost twenty years and served as director of information services and publications until his death in 1971. Consequently both books are in many ways memoirs as well as history.

Most of the research material for *Engineering the New South* is located in the Georgia Tech Archives. However, collections at Clemson, Emory, and Worcester Polytechnic Institute also provided useful information, especially for the early history of Georgia Tech. The Georgia Department of Archives and History and the Stanford University Archives supplied material concerning Tech's current president, Joseph M. Pettit, and Mrs. J. O. Pearson of Wheeling, West Virginia, contributed papers and correspondence relating to the presidency of her father, K. G. Matheson. James E. Boyd, acting president of Georgia Tech in 1971–72, also made correspondence in his possession available.

The Georgia Tech Archives contains sizable quantities of published and unpublished materials as well as an extensive vertical file. Among the most valuable unpublished records consulted were Faculty Minutes and Minutes of the Board of Trustees, shop correspondence and shop ledgers, and what the authors have cited as "presidential files." Uncatalogued but arranged by subject, the presidential files contain correspondence, departmental records, and reports. There is little pertaining to the years before the presidency of M. L. Brittain (1922–45). However ten letter books containing copies of the Lyman Hall correspondence, 1898–1905, provide valuable insights into the administration of Tech's second president.

Another valuable body of unpublished and uncatalogued material is the regents file, consisting of correspondence between the Board of Regents and Georgia Tech presidents. It is particularly useful for the administrations of M. L. Brittain and Blake Van Leer. For the recent period, however, the most important materials can be found in the Central Administrative Records, currently under the control of the president's office. This collection consists of administrative correspondence and other records pertaining to various divisions and departments of the Institute.

Additional unpublished materials in the Georgia Tech Archives that contributed to this volume include a brief diary kept by M. L. Brittain in 1928 and short histories of the schools of industrial management and chemical engineering by R. M. Teach and Paul Weber, respectively. (A history of the Tech physics department by David Wyly in possession of the School of Physics was also consulted.) The Dorothy Crosland and Cherry Emerson papers were equally helpful. Mrs. Crosland served as director of the Tech library for many years. Her papers are especially useful for the library building campaign and the integration of women at Georgia Tech. Vice President Emerson's correspondence sheds much light on the Engineering Experiment Station, campus expansion, and the growth of research at the Institute. A box of material pertaining to the scientific research honorary society, Sigma Xi, also supplied information about research activity during the Van Leer presidency. Finally, out-of-service personnel records, undergraduate theses, and a recently completed master's thesis, "The Architectural Development of Georgia Tech" by Warren Drury, contributed to this history.

Published materials consulted for this volume range from official reports to a student humor magazine. The *Annual Report* of the Georgia School of Technology, which included the *President's Report* until 1945, constitutes the single most important printed source used by the authors. For the years after World War II, a *Digest of the Annual Report of the President*, later called the *President's Report* or the *Annual Report of the President*, serves the same purpose. Also valuable are the *Annual Reports of the Board of Regents of the University System of Georgia* and the several official publications of Georgia Tech. These include the *Annual Announcements, Annual Catalogs,* and various *Bulletins* published intermittently throughout the school's history. The *Annual Report of the State Engineering Experiment Station* is useful for tracing the station's growth and development after 1940, and two collections of state statutes by Hal G. Newell and M. L. Brittain trace the legislative and financial history of Georgia Tech from its creation in 1885 through the Matheson presidency in 1922.

The archives also contains materials designed to promote Georgia Tech's image with the public. Two examples include *Engineering Evening School, 1908–58*, by R. S. Howell and *Research Engineer*, which chronicles the growth of the Experiment Station. More objective assessments of the Institute can be found in self-studies, internal and external reports relating to the economic and institutional growth of Georgia Tech, status reports, and proposals for the school's academic development. Among these, the following were especially useful: H. P. Hammond, *Report on Engineering Education in the University System of Georgia* (Athens: University of Georgia, 1932), and a follow-up study by the same author produced in 1942; *Self Studies of the Georgia Institute of Technology* for 1963, 1973, and 1983; four external studies of Georgia Tech, including Keck Engineering Associates, *Formula for Growth, Georgia Institute of Technology*; Arthur D. Little, Inc., *Georgia Tech: Impetus to Economic Growth* (1963); Perkins and Will Partnership, *Comprehensive Campus Development Plan* (1965); Booz, Allen and Hamilton, *Top Organization Plan: Georgia Institute of Technology, Atlanta, Georgia* (1965); Academic Priorities Committee, Student Government Association, *A Question of Priorities: The Status of Georgia Tech Academics* (Georgia Institute of Technology, 1982); and Demetrius Paris, *Graduate Study and Research: A Prospectus for Improved Quality* (Georgia Institute of Technology, 1982). Finally, an indispensable source for any historical assessment of American engineering education is a two-volume work produced by the Society for the Promotion of Engineering Education entitled *Report of the Investigation of Engineering Education, 1923–29* (University of Pittsburgh, 1930). Georgia Tech is included in many of the comparative studies that compose the *Report*.

Student publications also constitute essential source material for the writing of educational history. The Georgia Tech Archives contains only scattered copies of the *Georgia Tech*, a "serious" publication begun in the 1890s and reborn somewhat later as the *Yellow Jacket*. Published until the 1950s, the *Yellow Jacket* became Tech's humor magazine around 1921. Tech's first annual, the *Blue Print*, made its appearance in 1908 and the *Georgia Tech Alumnus*, later the *Georgia Tech Alumni Magazine*, began publishing in 1923. But the most important publication, for students as well as historians, is the school newspaper, the *Technique*, first produced in 1911. Its coverage of sports, extracurricular activities, and student opinion contributed immensely to the authors' understanding of everyday life at Tech. So did the columns of Atlanta's two newspapers, the *Constitution* and the *Journal*.

One major source for *Engineering the New South*, the vertical file, defies easy description or categorization. Arranged alphabetically by subject, it consists of newspaper clippings, pamphlets, photographs, faculty publications, memoirs of former students and professors, correspondence, and much more. It yielded vast amounts of information as the notes make clear.

Oral interviews with more than sixty individuals provided invaluable material to complement the written and printed sources for this history. A list of those persons who contributed their time and memories is appended below.

Ivan Allen, Jr., 17 November 1983
Jamie R. Anthony, 22 March 1983; 8 February 1984
Elizabeth Koenig Armsby, 6 September 1983
Hon. Ellis Arnall, 27 February 1984
Samuel C. Barnett, 6 July 1983
Numan V. Bartley, 24 May 1983
Jerry Birchfield, 24 May 1984
Walter Bloom, 13 September 1983
Henry C. Bourne, 9 August 1983
James E. Boyd, 20 February 1984; 8 March 1984
George P. Burdell, 1 April 1983
Hon. George D. Busbee, 1 November 1983
Beatrice Caine, 30 May 1983
Fuller E. Callaway, Jr., 15 September 1983
Walter D. Carlson, 20 July 1983
William L. Carmichael, 4 May 1983
Hon. Jimmy Carter, 30 March 1984
Vernon D. Crawford, 15 July 1983; 30 January 1984
Mae Evelyn Dodd (by telephone), 9 February 1984
Robert L. "Bobby" Dodd, 5 July 1983
Arnold Ducoffe, 12 September 1983
James E. Dull, 21 July 1983
William H. Eberhardt, 1 September 1983
Harold Friedman, 19 April 1984
Edward A. Gaston, 2 February 1984
Mario J. Goglia, 10 February 1984; 15 February 1984
Helen Grenga, 9 June 1983
George C. Griffin, 7 July 1983
Arthur G. Hansen, 19 August 1983
Julian Harris, 8 August 1984
Edwin D. Harrison, 26 October 1983; 3 November 1983; 8 November 1983
John W. Hooper, 11 April 1984
Stothe P. Kezios, 30 May 1984

Edward Kohler, 23 June 1983
William Landiss, 22 June 1983
Edward Loveland, 17 May 1983
Hon. Lester G. Maddox, 25 October 1983
Paul G. Mayer, 12 May 1983
Edward A. Moulthrop, 17 November 1983
Phil C. Narmore, 27 September 1983
Donald R. Nelson, 25 September 1983
Carlton Parker, 23 June 1983
Ida Brittain Patterson, 3 June 1983
Mary M. Pearson, 19 October 1983
Joseph Mayo Pettit, 18 July 1983; 28 July 1983; 31 August 1983; 14 September 1983; 29 September 1983; 11 April 1984
Tommy Plaxico, 21 June 1984
Glenn W. Rainey, 27 June 1983; 24 August 1983
Dale C. Ray, 29 June 1983
Homer C. Rice, 20 June 1984
Clyde D. Robbins, 26 August 1983; 28 August 1983; 4 October 1983
Hon. Carl Sanders, 20 October 1983
Janice Gosdin Sangster, 9 September 1983
George L. Simpson, 5 March 1984
Rush Smith, 24 May 1983
Thomas E. Stelson, 2 August 1983; 10 August 1983
Hon. Herman E. Talmadge, 18 January 1984
Fred A. Tarpley, Jr., 16 May 1983
Miller Templeton, 23 June 1983
Sandra W. Thornton, 7 June 1983
Ella Wall Van Leer, 31 August 1983
Samuel Wall Van Leer, 31 August 1983
W. Harry Vaughan, 15 February 1984
Homer S. Weber, 7 March 1984
Paul Weber, transcript of ODK interview, 8 May 1981; videotaped interview, 20 December 1978
George F. Wheeler, 11 June 1984
Ward Winer, 19 July 1983
Rudy Yobs, 16 July 1984
James D. Young, 24 June 1983
Waldemar T. Ziegler, 12 July 1983
Leslie F. Zsuffa, 21 April 1984

Index

Accreditation, 196–200, 205
Aderhold, O. C., 284
Administration, 49, 50, 66–67, 72, 103
Administrative reorganization: under Matheson, 115–17; 1944 statutes, 224–26; 1948 statutes, 245–46; cf 1955, 292–99; of 1965, 330–36; faculty reaction to, 333, 334–35; long-range significance of, 335–36, 362–64; under Hansen, 380–81
Admissions requirements, 48, 84, 310–11
Advanced Technology Development Center, 434, 443, 446–47
Aero Club of America, 144–45
Aerospace Engineering, School of, 168–70, 180, 190, 200, 205, 214–15, 241, 308, 395, 404, 416, 486 (n. 10)
"Affirmation Vietnam," 347
Afro-American studies, 377
Agnes Scott College, 26, 343
Agriculture and the Mechanic Arts, Georgia State College of, 7
Ajax, Fred W., 206–7, 279–80, 317
Alden, George I., 40–42
Aldrich, Professor, 50
Alexander, W. A., 140, 141, 147, 172, 181, 208–9, 232, 292, 402
Alexander Memorial Coliseum, 251–52, 308, 354
Alexander-Tharpe Fund, 424
Allen, Ivan, Jr., 327, 337, 368, 384, 453
Alumni Association. *See* Georgia Tech Alumni Association

Alumni Exceptional Achievement Award, 453
Alumni Roll Call, 253
American Association for the Advancement of Science, 118
American Association of University Professors, 290, 291, 296, 421
American Chemical Society, 47, 93, 118
American Council on Education, 208, 268
American Engineering Council, 223
American Expeditionary Force, 147
American Institute of Electrical Engineers, 80
American Society for Engineering Education, 231, 253, 286, 288, 295, 375, 379
American Society of Mechanical Engineers, 8, 40, 51, 118, 223, 227
American Telephone and Telegraph, 256
American Viscose Corporation, 269
Americus, Ga., 45
Amoskeag Manufacturing Company, 40
Anaconda Copper Company, 51
Anderson, Charles, 361
Anderson, W. D., 176
Anniversary celebrations, 187–89, 320, 323–29, 450
Anthony, Jamie R., 246, 297, 309, 334, 339, 380, 522 (n. 29); named vice president and controller, 332
Anzio, 210
Architecture, College of, 120, 171, 190, 207, 219, 250, 251, 414, 439; curriculum, 423; Ph.D. program in, 433

Arkwright, Preston, Sr., 187
Armour Research Foundation, 260
Armstrong, Samuel C., 7
Army Specialized Training program. See Military training
Arnall, Ellis, 196, 198–99, 217
Arnold, H. H., 206
Arnold, Howard, 314
Arnold, Robert A., 282, 285
Arthur B. Edge Intercollegiate Athletic Center, 434
Arthur D. Little, Inc., 443
Associated Industries of Georgia, 240, 255
Association of American Universities, 189, 196–97
Association of Land-Grant Colleges and Universities, 151, 240, 261
Association of Southern Colleges and Preparatory Schools, 114. See also Southern Association of Colleges and Secondary Schools
Athens, Ga., 17, 27, 28, 29, 30, 31, 32, 80
Athletic Association. See Georgia Tech Athletic Association
Athletics, intercollegiate, 171–73, 180–81, 354; baseball, 96, 137; "professionalism" decried, 136–37; track, 138; boxing, 138; golf, 138; swimming, 138; tennis, 138; origins of Tech-Georgia rivalry, 141; Tech-Georgia relations strained, 142–44; integration of, 318; for women, 390. See also Basketball, Football
Athletics, intramural, 351, 354, 390
Atkinson, Edward, 13, 16, 29, 30
Atlanta, Ga., 13, 14, 15, 17, 26, 27, 28, 29, 30, 31, 32, 33, 34, 35, 40, 43, 49, 53, 57, 62, 63, 73, 74, 80, 85, 87, 93, 95, 98, 112, 126, 209, 246–47, 313; as source of Tech students, 389; high technology in, 444–45
Atlanta Athletic Club, 138
Atlanta Baseball Association, 138
Atlanta Basketball League, 137
Atlanta Bridge and Axle Company, 35, 52, 56

Atlanta Chamber of Commerce, 110, 126
Atlanta City Council, 27, 86, 121, 154
Atlanta Constitution, 158
Atlanta Cotton Factory, 54
Atlanta Cotton Mill, 35
Atlanta Georgian, 133
Atlanta Housing Authority, 339
Atlanta Manufacturers Association, 15, 33, 52
Atlanta Paper Company, 54
Atlanta Radio Club, 134
Atlanta University, 7
Atlanta University Center, 427
Atlanta Veterans Hospital, 294
Atlantic Coast Conference, 425–26; basketball championship (1985), 452
Atlantic Steel Corp., 241
Auburn University, 28, 60, 61, 99, 137, 138, 139, 140
Augusta, Ga., 14, 21, 81, 389

Babcock, J. V., 211
Bacon, Augustus O., 27–28
Bacon, Raymond, 156
Baker, Harry, Jr., 259–60
Baldwin, George, 118
Bankhead-Jones Act, 253
Baptist Student Union, 390
Barksdale, Hamilton, 428
Barnes, Ewell I., 264, 380, 435
Barnes, Roy, 280
Barnesville, Ga., 15
Barron, David I. "Red," 194–96, 205
Bartley, Numan V., 382–83
Basketball, 353, 354; in the Matheson era, 137; success in the early 1950s, 285–86; women's, 427–28; 1985 season, 452
Battelle Memorial Institute, 260, 398, 440
Beard, Roane, 329
Beaver, Sandy, 262, 271, 284, 290
Bedford-Pines community, 383
Beese, C. W., 240
Bell Aircraft Corp., 242
Bender, Thomas, 71
Bendix Corporation, 265

Bibb County, Ga., 74
Bibb Manufacturing Company, 15
Bioengineering Center, 396
Biology, School of, 189, 433
Biotechnology, 448
Birchfield, Jerry, 447
Birmingham, Ala., 95
Bisplinghoff, Raymond L., 378
Black, Homer V., 93, 101
Black and Hilliard Company, 75
Blacks, 195, 368, 512 (n. 30); industrial college for, 7; and the Gaines decision on equal educational opportunity, 272; and first rumblings of integration in the 1950s, 280–81; and Sugar Bowl incident of 1956, 281–84; first admitted to Georgia Tech, 312–19; proportion in student body, 318, 389, 427; first instructor at Tech, 377
Blaik, Earl, 284
Blake, Morgan, 139
Blissit, James, 264
Bloom, Wally, 384
Bloom, Walter (Dr.), 524 (n. 72)
Board of Regents (1932–), 176–79, 193–96, 198–200, 307, 333, 488 (nn. 26, 27); discontinue Department of Industrial Education, 125; and funding, 253; and Southern Tech shortfall, 255–56; and selection of Edwin Harrison, 309; and racial integration, 313; and Engineering Experiment Station, 397
Board of Trustees (1885–1932), 24, 25, 26, 27, 29, 32, 33, 35, 39, 40, 42, 43, 44, 46, 48, 50, 54, 56, 57, 63, 64, 65, 72, 73, 74, 75, 77, 79, 80, 82, 83, 93, 94, 102, 109, 111, 112, 114, 118, 119, 129, 132, 136, 145, 150, 152, 153, 154, 155, 157, 158, 167, 170, 176–77
Boggs, Gilbert H., 93, 118, 130, 213
Boggs, William E., 44, 87
Bonds, Anne, 272
Booz, Allen and Hamilton study: goals and recommendations of, 331–32; implementation by Harrison, 332–33
Boston Manufacturers Mutual Insurance Company, 13

Bourbon Democrats, 12, 15, 27
Bourne, Henry C., 425
Bowl games. *See* Football
Boyd, James E., 400–403; and postwar electronics research, 260–61; becomes director of EES Physics Division, 262; becomes assistant director for scientific affairs at EES, 269; and athletics, 401–3; and Engineering Experiment Station, 418
Boyd and Baxter Foundry Company, 35
Boynton, John, 10
Bradley Building, 278
Bradley Foundation, 278
Branch, T. P., 80
Brisbine Park, 137
Brittain, Marion L., 51, 63, 336, 382; chosen for presidency, 163, 486 (n. 1); early career of, 163–64; and funding, 166, 175, 180, 192, 200; Ceramic Engineering, School of, 166–67; Guggenheim Award, 168–70, 180, 192, 200; and Navy ROTC, 171, 197; and curriculum, 171, 189; and athletics, 171–73; and the University System, 175–76, 178–79; and Techwood Homes, 184–85; Experiment Station, 186; and Eugene Talmadge, 194, 198; and retirement, 194, 217–18, 221–22, 233; and accreditation, 197–99; administrative style of, 204; World War II, 206, 209, 211, 214; named President Emeritus, 221; death of, 293; and Franklin Roosevelt, 489 (n. 45)
Brittain Dining Hall, 209
Brooklyn Navy Yard, 263
Brooks, C. P., 82, 85
Brown, Carey, 391, 418
Brown, Joseph E., 13, 16
Brown, Julius, 16, 222; bequest to Georgia Tech, 109
Brownell, Florence H., 222
Brown University, 5, 9
Brown v. Board of Education, Topeka, Kansas, 280
Bruce and Morgan Company, 42, 75
Bryan, William Jennings, 126

544 Index

Bryant, Paul "Bear," 352
Buildings. See Physical plant
Bunger, Harold, 186, 213, 214
Burdell, George P., 346
Burge, Flippen, 184, 247
Burrowes, Robert M., 147
Busbee, George D., 439, 446
Bush-Brown, Gailey, and Heffernan, 251
Bush-Brown, Harold, 165, 207, 218–19, 227

Cabell, Mary K., 518 (n. 138)
Caldwell, Harmon W., 195, 266, 309
California Institute of Technology, 238, 287, 362
Calaway, Paul K., 246, 257
Callaway, Fuller E., Jr., 248, 259
Callaway Apartments, 247
Callaway Foundation, 418
Callaway Institute, Inc., 260
Calumet and Hecla Mining Company, 51
Calvert, Monte A., 8, 9
Camp, Walter, 139
Campus expansion, 100, 312, 373, 381–86; under Matheson, 108–9; under Brittain, 173, 336; during World War II, 218–20; postwar, 227, 246–48; under Harrison, 336–41; during Van Leer's tenure, 336–37; and urban renewal programs, 337; and Sputnik I, 337; alumni support for, 337; 1965 Perkins and Will proposal, 338–39
Campus planning, 319, 381, 417
Campus safety, 386
Capital City Club, 135, 297
Carlisle Indians, 139, 140
Carlson, Walter O., 380
Carmichael, O. C., 198
Carmichael, W. L., 273–74
Carnegie, Andrew, 72, 110
Carnegie Foundation, 152, 158, 164, 249
Carnegie Steel Company, 63
Carson, Leon H. "Bud," 402–3; succeeds Dodd as coach, 354
Carter, Jimmy, 400, 409; and solar energy research facility, 440; visits Tech campus, 441, 491 (n. 71)
Cartter, Allan, 361

Cassidy, G. E., 54, 55, 56, 57
Castleberry, Clint, 232
Centennial Campaign, 450
Center for Media Based Instruction, 434
Central of Georgia Railroad, 15, 166–67
Centre College, 141
Ceramic Engineering, School of, 166–67, 486 (nn. 6, 9)
Chapin, Lloyd W., 245, 290, 295–96, 297
Chatham County, Ga., 62
Chemical Engineering, School of, 72, 92, 93, 177, 213–14, 306
Chemistry, School of, 47, 102, 120–21, 177, 213–14, 356–57, 395–96, 404; and criticism of EES contract research, 258, 268
Cherry, Jim, 255
Cheshier, Steven, 436, 452
China: 7,000 Years of Discovery, 450
Citadel, 107
Civil Engineering, School of, 71, 77, 80, 81, 88, 292, 308, 381, 396, 404; and creation of hydraulics laboratory, 256–57; offers first doctorate, 288–89
Civilian Conservation Corps, 209
Clay, Lucius D., 324
Clay, R. A., 147
Clemson University, 96, 98, 99, 138
Cobb, Carolyn, 131
Cobb County, Ga., 96
Cocking, Walter, 195–96
Coeducation, 300, 356, 517 (n. 132); first woman graduate, 124; World War II, 212; and 1952 change in policy, 270–75; student attitudes toward, 271, 273; first women admitted, 274; mixed reaction of males to, 348–50; limited enrollment of women, 348, 350; proportion of women in student body, 389, 427; women admitted to Industrial Management, 390; housing for women, 390; and engineering programs, 428; and first female instructor, 518 (n. 138)
Cole, W. F., 54, 55
Colquitt, Senator, 46
Columbia University, 79, 116, 127, 382–83
Columbus, Ga., 14, 17, 30, 84, 389

Comer, H. F., 128
Commander, Robert C. "Charlie," 276, 280, 343, 344, 392
Commerce, School of, 177–79, 271; organization of, 123–24; day school, 124; evening division, 124; admits women, 124. *See also* Management, College of
Committee of Twenty, 445–46
Community relations, 246–47; under Matheson, 126–28; and commencement services, 126–27, 532 (n. 110); student efforts to improve, 347–48; Home Park, 382
Community service, 382–85
Community Service Task Force, 384
Comprehensive Campus Development Plan (1965), 338
Computer Aided Design/Computer Aided Manufacturing, 432
Computer Center. *See* Rich Computer Center
Consolidated Street Railway Company, 63
Continuing education, 434
Conway, H. McKinley, 366
Cook, Bruce, 384
Coon, John S., 26, 50, 51, 52, 58, 59, 79, 95, 111, 118, 119, 123, 129–30, 131
Cooper Union, 17
Cooperative education, 189, 356, 434, 486 (n. 9); introduced at Tech, 122; World War II, 220; with Norfolk Naval Shipyard, 288; fiftieth anniversary of, 324
Corliss engine, 462 (n. 45)
Cornell University, 51, 52, 79, 97, 98, 127, 208
Cotton States Exposition, 26
Council of Graduate Schools, 361
Covington, Ga., 27
Cox, W. N., Jr., 230
Crawford, George G., 63, 127
Crawford, James M., 243
Crawford, Vernon D., 356–57, 378, 421, 436; named dean of General College, 363; as acting president, 367; biographical sketch of, 374; named vice president, 380; and YMCA, 393; and reorganization of Engineering Experiment Station, 399–400; and financial problems of the Institute, 405, 417; named chancellor, 435
Cremins, Bobby, 426, 452
Crenshaw, J. B., 115, 116, 119, 136, 137, 138, 143, 144
Crisler, Fritz, 284
Crosland, Dorothy, 249, 250, 272–73
Crystal Palace, 131, 133, 137
Cudd, Herschel H., 264, 266–69
Culpepper, Jim, 428
Cumberland College, 138
Curriculum, 53, 58, 59, 60, 79, 98, 171, 189–91, 310, 373, 415, 452; revision in Matheson era, 119–26; World War II, 207–10; World War II trimester calendar, 207, 230; ASTP and Navy V-12, 208; and postwar planning, 220–21; changes under Van Leer, 228–31; hotel management program, 230; for athletes, 232; evaluation of (1950s), 286–89; improvement of basic sciences, 287–88; adoption of "three-two" program, 288; accreditation of engineering programs, 299–300; and rising academic standards, 351–55; revision of undergraduate program, 354–57; and "core curriculum," 357; engineering core, 374–78
Curry, Bill, 435, 452

Dallas, Sherman, 375, 380
DallaValle, J. M., 290
Dalton, Ga., 63
Daniel, J. L., 213, 246
Daniels, Earl M., 334
Daniels, Josephus, 126
Dartmouth College, 40
Dasher, Ben, 334
Davidson College, 139
Davis, James C., 295
Davis Water Wheel Company, 55
Dean, Norris, 207
DeKalb County, Ga., 62, 97, 255
De Leon, Edwin, 12
Dennison, H. F., 214, 246
Department of Defense, 419, 438; and EES research, 268

Dickert, Herman A., 271
Division of Emergency Training, 211
Dodd, R. L. "Bobby," 232–33, 238, 281–86, 292, 350–54, 424; becomes head football coach, 232; becomes athletic director, 251; resignation as coach, 353–54; predicts troubles for athletic program, 401–2; retirement of, 425
Dormitories. *See* Housing
Dorsey, Hugh, 156
Downing, Walter T., 92
Drake, Miriam, 453
Drama Tech, 276
Dress Her in White and Gold, 324, 326
Drexel Institute, 107, 154, 157, 158
Duke University, 443
Dull, James E.: and racial integration, 315
Dunlop, Edgar, 273
Dunwoody, Elliott, Jr., 198
Du Pont Company, 292

Eberhardt, William, 257
Ecole Centrale, 4
Ecole Polytechnique, 4, 46
Economic development, 223–24, 320, 359–60, 413–15, 436–49; World War II, 213–14
Edens, A. Hollis, 249
Edson, William A., 292
Education, industrial, 6, 13, 22, 23, 28, 102; for Georgia women, 7
Edwards, Harry S., 15–16
Edwards, J. B., 80, 134
Eisenhower, Dwight D., 228
Eldred, C. P., 134
Electrical Engineering, School of, 65, 66, 71, 77, 78, 80, 88, 90, 92, 101, 292, 419
Electronics research, 239, 260–61, 270, 401, 441–43, 447–48, 453; World War II, 216
Ellis, Rutherford, 227, 272–73
Elsas, Jacob, 33
Elsas, Oscar, 54, 85
Emerson, Cherry L., 127, 229, 242, 294; becomes temporary vice president, 217–18; becomes dean of engineering, 226; as dean of engineering, 245; becomes vice president, 245; and building program, 250–51; comments on GTRI, 259; applies for salary supplement grants, 261; and friction with Gerald Rosselot, 262–65; management of EES, 269; on President Van Leer, 289; retirement of, 293, 297; and building construction, 500 (n. 36)
Emerson, Ralph W., 5
Emerson, William H., 47, 50, 60, 92, 93, 117, 118, 128, 134
Emory University, 21, 22, 44, 45, 67, 343, 387
Empire Chemical Company, 27
Empty Stocking Fund, 133
Engineering, College of, 246, 321, 439
Engineering Chemistry. *See* Chemical Engineering, School of
Engineering drawing: reduction of required courses in, 378
Engineering education (national trends), 190–91, 231, 238–39, 286–89, 295, 299–300, 354–55, 358–59
Engineering Experiment Station (EES), 112, 186–87, 335, 338, 340, 381, 395; and State Agricultural College, 150, 151; faculty advisory council, 261, 267; World War II, 204, 212–17; budget, 214–15, 260–62, 299; postwar growth, 246; plant expansion, 248; wartime growth, 258–59; and management of funds, 259–60; and faculty relations, 266–70, 358–59; administrative reorganization, 262–70; adoption of new research personnel titles, 267; and expansion of research in the 1950s, 270; growth in the 1960s, 359; commercial spinoffs, 359; personnel, 359; Industrial Development Division, 360; relation to Georgia Tech, 397–401, 418–20; mission of, 398–99; financial crisis, 401; expansion of, 419; and graduate education, 433; name change to Georgia Tech Research Institute, 434

Engineering extension: World War II, 211–12
Engineering graphics, 422
Engineering Science and Management War Training, 211
Engineering Science and Mechanics, School of, 125, 378
Engineers' Council for Professional Development, 231, 239, 241, 288
English, Department of, 45, 119, 123, 124
English, J. W., 91
Enrollment, 62, 96, 114–15, 177, 180, 198; World War II, 204, 207–8; postwar, 244, 246, 253–54; national decline in engineering, 254, 376; decline in (1970–74), 416; increase (1974–), 426; undergraduate to graduate ratio, 432
Environmental Resources Center, 396
Episcopal student organization, 390
Evans, Thomas H., 229, 261
E. Van Winkle Company, 35
Experimental Engineering, Department of, 101
Exposition Cotton Mill, 14, 35, 52, 54

Faculty, 50, 64, 95, 452; efforts to form club, 115; salaries, 115–16, 153, 170, 175, 177, 192, 289–91, 307; recruitment of, 116, 170, 197–98; World War II, 212–13, 220, 226; qualifications (1950s), 288; terms and conditions of employment, 289–91; promotion and tenure in 1950s, 290; sabbatical policy for, 290; first Regents' Professors appointed, 290–91; and loyalty oath issue, 291; quality of, 311; perception of Georgia Tech, 322–23; teaching loads, 355, 430; improved qualifications, 361, 414, 421; research activities of, 420; unhappiness with upper administration (1970s), 421; and first female instructor, 518 (n. 138)
Faculty Senate, 402, 422

Fairchild Semiconductor Corporation, 411
Fambrough, W. M., 123
Fash, William L., 423
Federal Communications Commission (FCC), 219
Federal programs, 182–85, 193–94, 200, 203, 204–5, 209, 211, 220, 238, 241, 242–43, 253, 255, 268, 269; Smith-Hughes Act, 125, 149; during World War I, 149–50; Newlands Bill, 150, 151; Smith-Howard Bill, 150, 151; Morrill Acts of 1862 and 1890, 151, 152; Neighborhood Development Program, 381–83; Urban Renewal, 381–83
Ferst, Monie, 257
Field, Floyd, 194–95, 245
Finances, 307, 404–5; Greater Georgia Tech Campaigns of 1906, 109. 154; of 1914, 112, 154–55; of 1918, 155; of 1921, 135, 152, 155–58; lack of funds, 165–66, 175, 177, 180, 191–92, 492 (n. 79); and the University System of Georgia, 238; postwar building construction, 247–52; postwar funding, 252–56; budget growth under Van Leer, 299–300; cutback in federal funds, 398; in the University System, 404–5; problems of in the 1970s, 416–17, 431–32
Flowers, R. B., 134
Floyd County, Ga., 62, 96
Football, 60, 61, 95, 96, 171–73, 181, 373; under Heisman, 138–40; W. A. Alexander named coach, 140; W. A. Alexander's record through 1922, 140–41; during World War II, 210, 231–33; and the 1956 Sugar Bowl game, 281–83; success in the early 1950s, 283–85; deemphasis movement in 1951, 284–85; in the 1960s, 350–54; scholarships, 353. See also Georgia Tech Athletic Association
Ford, Albert H., 79–80
Ford Foundation, 361
Formula for Growth, 320, 337

Fort McPherson, 61, 137, 147
Frank H. Neely Nuclear Research Center, 340
Franklin Institute, 8
Fraternities: honorary, 174–75, 181, 278; Anak, 130, 134; Koseme, 130, 131; Phi Kappa Phi, 130; Scabbard and Blade, 133; Omicron Delta Kappa, 278, 341
Fraternities and sororities, social: Alpha Epsilon Pi, 133, 174; first sorority formed, 274; administrative support of in the postwar era, 278–79; dominant role of, 343; decline in membership, 388; increase in membership (1970s), 429
"Free University," 390
Freeman, Y. Frank, 182
Freeman Traveling Scholarship, 223
French, Aaron, 72, 82, 84, 85, 87–90, 100
Fulcher, Bill, 403, 424
Fuller, Richard, 435
Fuller Callaway III Student Athletic Complex, 391, 418
Fulton Bag and Cotton Mill, 14, 33, 54, 63, 85
Fulton County, Ga., 62, 73, 92, 96, 109, 111, 112, 125–26
Fuqua, J. B., 327
Furlow, Floyd C., 94, 101
Furman University, 139

Gate City Guard, 63, 72
Gearing, Charles E., 435
General College, 321, 335. *See also* Sciences and Liberal Studies, College of
General Education Board, 100–101, 154, 157, 249, 253, 261–62; and graduate fellowships, 231
General Electric Company, 79, 111, 127
Geophysical Sciences, School of, 125
Georgia Educational Association, 117
Georgia Federation of Women's Clubs, 110
Georgia Institute of Technology: name change, 238, 244–45, 299
Georgia Medical College, 22, 45
Georgia Military Academy, 45
Georgia Military and Agricultural College, 63
Georgia Military College, 107
Georgia Normal and Industrial School, 8
Georgian Terrace Hotel, 132
Georgia Power Company, 248, 260
Georgia Railroad, 34
Georgia Research Consortium, 442
Georgia Rotary Clubs, 153, 154, 157
Georgia State College for Women, 249
Georgia state government: 18, 21, 23, 24, 26, 28, 65, 72–74, 82, 85, 86, 89–92, 96, 101, 102, 167, 176, 193–200, 313, 361; approves tuition charges, 154; visitation committee, 247; postwar funding by, 252–56, 361; legislative investigation of Engineering Experiment Station, 400. *See also* Finances
Georgia Tech Afro-American Association, 318, 390, 428
Georgia Tech Alumni Association, 63, 100, 175, 320, 329, 443; and Greater Georgia Tech Campaign of 1921, 155, 158; and Annual Roll Call, 253; Committee of Twenty, 445–46
Georgia Tech Athletic Association, 95, 96, 109, 111, 131, 135, 136, 138, 165, 181, 243, 251–52, 282, 284, 452; during World War II, 209; and the firing of Bud Carson, 401–3; financial difficulties of, 423–24; and the firing of Pepper Rodgers, 425
Georgia Tech Foundation, 63, 181, 244, 309, 320; and faculty salary supplement, 308
Georgia Tech graduates, 98–100
Georgia Tech: Impetus for Economic Growth, 320
Georgia Tech Organizational Leadership Development Project (GOLD), 422
Georgia Tech Research Corporation, 434
Georgia Tech Research Institute (GTRI), 215, 252, 299; founded in 1945, 259; and EES financial arrangements, 263–70; name change, 434

Georgia Tech shops, 33, 49, 52–58, 64
GI Bill, 203, 220, 238, 242–43, 255, 341
Gilbert, Judge S. Price, 249–50
Gilbert, S. Price, Jr., 249
Gill, John, 318, 348
Glenn, William H., 63, 182
"Goals for Engineering Education," 375–76, 415
Goglia, Mario J., 290, 309, 321; proposed as vice president for academic affairs, 332; nomination as vice president for academic affairs withdrawn, 333; becomes vice chancellor, 363
Gordon, John B., 27, 32
Grace, Donald J., 419
Graduate education, 119, 192, 415–16, 433; during World War II, 215, 226, 228; industrial management, 230; first doctoral program, 231; enrollment in 1948, 254; postwar expansion of, 258; enrollment in mid-1950s, 288; expansion of in 1960s, 360–62; quality of, 361–62; reorganization in 1967, 363; and Harrison master plan, 367; evaluations of, 398, 451
Graduates: career patterns of, 416, 453
Grady, Henry, 7, 12, 13, 16, 26, 30–33, 43, 44, 46, 223, 411, 415, 439
Graning, Chick, 352
Grant, Hugh Inman, 111
Grant, John W., 111
Grant, Lemuel P., 32, 34, 35
Grant Field, 109, 111; seats expanded, 233, 402; stands double-decked, 340–41
Grant Park, 32
Graves, Frank P., 188
Great Depression, 175, 177, 180–83
Greene, Fred, 318
Greene County, Ga., 25, 26, 30
Greensboro, Ga., 26
Gregg, Robert, 182
Grier, Bob, 282–83
Griffin, George C., 184, 206, 245, 277–78; devotion and service to Georgia Tech, 346–47; retirement of, 347; advocates student center, 391; track facility named for, 452

Griffin, Marvin, 282–83, 300, 311
Grinter, L. E., 286
Grinter Report, 287–88, 354
Groseclose, Frank F., 229
Gruen, E. C., 124
GTSTRUDL, 453
Guthridge, Joe, 309, 319–20, 329, 334, 435; named vice president for development, 332

Hall, Lyman: election to mathematics chair, 45–46; elected faculty secretary, 50; captain of Gate City Guard, 63; informs trustees of Tech's needs, 64; proposed as Tech president, 65; selected as faculty chairman, 66; managerial approach, 67, 72; themes of his presidency, 71; proposes dormitory regulations, 76–77; interest in civil engineering, 80; campaign for textile engineering degree, 81–86; considered for chancellor of University of Georgia, 87–88; dormitory campaign, 89–92; collects data on student origins, 96–97; effort to expand campus, 100; announces gifts to Tech, 101; death of, 102; legacy of, 103
Hall County, Ga., 74
Hammond, Harry P., 190–91, 226, 241, 255
Hammond Report, 286
Hampton Institute, 7
Handy, W. C., 132
Hansen, Arthur G.: becomes dean of engineering, 357, 363; and curriculum reform, 374–76; named president, 379; biographical sketch of, 379–80; and students, 379, 385; and campus expansion, 381–86; and Kent State memorial service, 388; and YMCA, 394; resignation of, 400; and reorganization of Engineering Experiment Station, 399–400, 419
Hanson, John F., 15, 16, 27
Harris, David, 327
Harris, Joe Frank, 442
Harris, Nathaniel E., 115, 147, 167, 190; elected to state legislature, 16; chairs

Harris, Nathaniel E. (cont'd)
  technological school committee, 17;
  introduces legislation for
  technological school, 21, 23;
  appointed to technological school
  commission, 25; supports Macon as
  site for Tech, 27, 31–32; speech at
  opening ceremony, 49; role in
  selection of chancellor at University
  of Georgia, 87–88; reluctance to
  abolish subfreshman class, 114;
  decries low faculty salaries, 116; first
  Blue Print dedicated to, 129; meets
  with representatives of State
  Agricultural College, 151; and
  Brittain, 163; and funding, 165; and
  shop culture–school culture debate,
  190
Harris, Roy, 283, 285
Harrison, Edwin D., 300, 325, 374, 383;
  biographical sketch of, 308–9;
  leadership style of, 309–10;
  educational goals of, 310; and racial
  integration, 312–18; and self-study,
  321; and administrative
  reorganization, 329–36; and
  curricular reform, 354–55; and
  control of research, 358–59; and
  controversy over resignation, 362–68,
  520 (n. 181); resignation of, 365–67;
  "Wonderful Ed's Day," 368;
  assessment of his leadership, 368–69;
  and YMCA, 392
Hart, J. C., 30
Hartsfield, William, 313
Harvard University, 8, 29, 71, 116, 138,
  141
Hayes, John, 391
Hayes Microcomputing, 445
Health Systems, School of, 433–34
Heard, Columbus, 25, 26, 30–33, 42, 43
Hearst, William R., 101
Heemann, Warren, 435
Heffernan, Paul, 250, 423
Hefner, Ralph A., 225–26, 257, 296, 363
Heifner, F. P., 57
Heisman, John W., 96, 129, 137, 138–40,
  142, 147, 402

Henika, John, 293
Henry, A. V., 167, 486 (n. 8)
Herbert, Walter C., 276
Hermance, Radcliffe, 148
Herndon, Elizabeth, 274
Hewlett, William, 410
Hiawatha College, 26
Higgins, Milton P., 40–43, 47, 49, 53–
  55, 57, 82, 94, 447
High Museum of Art, 450
High School Tutoring Program, 382
"High technology Morrill Act," 437
Hightower, William Harrison, 248
Hightower Textile Building, 247–48
Hill, Banjamin H., 12
Hill, Walter B., 16, 88
Himstead, Ralph E., 291, 296
Hinman, Florence, 202
Hinman, Phillip, 248
Hinman Research Building: completed
  in 1951, 262
Hodges, Luther, 443
Hodgson, Edward R., 25, 27, 31–33, 43
Hodgson Oil Company, 27
Holt, Darwin, 352
Home Park community, 382, 532–33 (n.
  110)
Hooper, John W., 448
Hoover, Herbert, 437
Hopkins, Isaac S., 21–23, 39, 44, 45, 47,
  50, 64–67, 72, 79, 103
Hosmer, J. B., 214
Hotel Management, 230
Housing, 64–66, 71, 73–77, 89, 90, 92,
  101, 164–65, 183–84, 247, 308, 429,
  434; Knowles Dormitory, 108, 145;
  World War II, 209, 211; for veterans,
  242–43; expansion under Van Leer,
  300; dormitory construction in the
  1960s and 1970s, 340, 341; inadequate
  facilities for women, 349; first
  women's dormitory, 390
Houston, Frank I., 246
Howard, William S., 150
Howell, Clark, 83
Howell, Park, 61
Howell, R. S., 121
Howey, J. H., 296

551 Index

Hubbard, E. W., 146, 147
Hudson, Barbara, 272
Humanities, 377, 414
Hunnicut, C. W., 33
Hunt. Joel, 123
Hyder, John "Whack," 354

Ickes, Harold, 184
Illinois College, 6
Illinois Institute of Technology, 229, 260
Illinois Institute of Technology Research Institute, 260, 399
Industrial and Systems Engineering, School of: creation of, 229
Industrial Development Council, 187, 214–15, 259
Industrial Education, 434; Department of, 125, 149
Industrial League, 6
Industrial Management. *See* Management, College of
Industrial policy, 437–38
Inman, Bobby R., 442
Inman, Nellie, 48
Inman, Samuel M., 13, 25, 26, 29–33, 35, 41, 42, 45, 46, 52, 54, 65, 90, 92, 123
Institute of Paper Chemistry, 260
Integration, 280–83, 312–19
Intercollegiate Golf Association, 138
Intercollegiate Intelligence Agency, 144
Interdisciplinary Research Centers, 396
Inter-Dormitory Council, 388
Interfraternity Council, 316, 318, 343
International Cotton Exposition, 12–14, 16, 26, 34
Iowa State University, 54
Ivey, Mary Nell, 276

Jessop, Alfred, 57
Johns Hopkins University, 45, 47, 71, 93, 257
Johnson, Edgar H., 67
Johnson, Lawrence V., 255; becomes head of Southern Tech, 240–41
Joint Tech-Georgia Development Fund, 309
Jones, R. T. "Bobby," 138, 187

Jones, Raymond, 259
Jones and Laughlin Steel Company, 63
Journal of Engineering Education, 295
J. P. Stevens and Company, 367–68

Kapp, Cecil A., 122
Karlovitz, Les A., 435
Keck Engineering Associates: 1962 report shapes campus expansion plans, 337–38
Kell, Wayne S., 124
Kennedy, John F., 326–27
Kent State University, 387–88, 412
Kezios, Stothe P., 423
Kicklighter, Charles H., 95
Kimball, Hannibal I., 33, 34
Kimbrough, Frank, 232
Kindsvater, Carl E., 256, 291, 396
King, Martin Luther, Jr., 383
King, R. S., 211
Kirk, Richard, 147
Knight, Montgomery, 169, 186, 205, 214, 395
Knowles, Clarence, 73–75, 83
Knox, Frank, 206
Korean War, 251, 262
Krefetz, Fred, 393

Land, Emory S., 169
Land-grant acts, 6, 7, 44, 253
Lane, Charles, 46, 47, 64, 65, 107
Lanoue, Fred, 209, 354
Lawson General Hospital, 243
Lee, Ivy, 157
Leeds University, 249
Levy, Ferdinand K., 380, 435
Lewis, David S., 326
Library, 168, 189; creation of, 109–10; campaign for new building, 249–50. *See also* Price Gilbert Memorial Library
Lindbergh, Charles A., 168
Little, Arthur D., 156
Little, W. A., 21, 23
Little Report, 360, 443
Lockheed Aircraft, 256
Long, Maurice, 325, 363, 399–401, 419
Long, Ralph, Jr., 318

552 Index

Lowell Textile School, 82–83, 85
Lowndes, F. E., 260
Lucas, J. H., 51
Lucy Cobb Institute for Girls, 61
L. W. "Chip" Robert Faculty/Alumni House, 394
Lynch, R. S., 241

McArthur, Roy, 285
McAshan, Eddie, 318, 390
McCarthyism, 280
McCauley, Francine, 428
McCrary, J. B., 51, 63, 123
McDaniel, Henry D., 24–27, 48, 88
McDaniel, James E., 141, 292
McGill, Ralph, 223–24, 324
McGilvray, Angus, 42, 43
McGlade, Bernadette, 428
McKee, G. A., 147
MacLaurin, R. C., 150
McNamara, Robert S., 327–28
Macon, Ga., 15–17, 25, 27, 30–32, 46, 65, 88, 389
Maddox, Lester, 364, 386, 404, 523 (n. 44)
Madison, Ga., 63
Management, College of, 180, 351, 352, 414; grants first master's degree, 230; achieves college status, 374; curriculum of, 422–23; name change, 434. See also Commerce, School of
Management/Industrial and Systems Engineering Building, 430
Management Science America, 445
Manhattan Project, 203, 228
Mantel, Samuel J., Jr., 287
Marchmont, George, 182
Marionette, 276
Maryville College, 26
Mason, Jesse W., 214, 245, 292, 297, 323, 332, 336, 357, 362, 375; personal and administrative qualities, 330–31; relations with Harrison, 330, 331, 333, 334; refuses nomination as vice president for special projects, 333; removal as dean of engineering, 333, 334, 336; reaction to his removal as dean of engineering, 333, 334–35

Massachusetts Institute of Technology, 4, 8, 9, 17, 20, 29, 93, 97, 116, 127, 150, 222, 238, 260, 288, 362, 378
Materials Engineering, School of, 451
Mathematics, School of, 45, 80, 414, 419; becomes school, 288; offers computer science courses, 288
Matheson, Kenneth G., 102–3, 203, 219, 225, 253; education and employment before 1897, 107; and inadequate funding, 108, 152–54; relations with Lyman Hall, 107–8; academic reforms of, 113–14; attempts to rename Georgia School of Technology, 115; encourages professionalism, 117–19; and curricular innovation, 119–26; supports modern languages, 119–20; and mining engineering, 120, 149; and architecture degree, 120; and chemistry degree, 120–21; and night school, 121; service in World War I, 147; and the Engineering Experiment Station, 150–52; and the Greater Georgia Tech Campaign, 154–58; resignation of, 158–59
Mayer, Paul G., 324
Mayer, R. W., 240
Mechanical Engineering, School of, 45, 46, 50–52, 55, 59, 88, 200, 308
Mechanics, Department of. See Engineering Science and Mechanics, School of
Mell, P. H., 28, 44
Mercer University, 25, 26, 30, 45, 60, 451
Metcalfe, W. R., 277
Metropolitan Collegiate Athletic Conference, 424
Michel, Barbara Diane, 274
Microelectronics and Computer Technology Corporation, 441–43
Microelectronics Research Center, 442–43, 447–48, 453
Midwest Research Institute, 440
Miles, Harry H., 92
Miles, W. B., 35, 52, 56, 90
Military Science, Department of, 146–47

553 Index

Military training, 171, 355; Reserve Officers' Training Corps (ROTC), 132, 134–35, 137, 144; ROTC, creation of, 144, 147; ROTC, suspension of, 148; ROTC, reactivation after World War I, 148–49; School of Military Aeronautics, 145, 146, 147, 149; Student Army Training Corps and athletics, 138; Student Army Training Corps, creation of, 148; Student Army Training Corps, cancellation of, 148, 149; Supply Officers' Training School, 145, 146; in World War II, 203, 206–10, 212, 231; for women, 274, 427; compulsory ROTC abolished, 342, 347; decline in ROTC membership, 388; increase in ROTC enrollment, 429
Milledgeville, Ga., 27, 30–32, 63
Milner, W. J., 157, 158
Minor, Leo D., 46
Mission of Georgia Tech, 322
Missouri Military Academy, 107
Mitchell, Timothy F., 392–93
Mizell, Warner, 173
Model Cities Program, 348
"Modern community of technological scholars," 411–12
Modern Languages, Department of, 118–19
Montgomery, W. F., 80
Moore, J S., 63
Moore, Joseph E., 228–29, 298
Morehouse College, 427
Moreland Park Military Academy, 46
Morrill, Justin S., 6
Morrill Act, 253
Morris, William C., 441
Morton, A. B. "Froggy," 121
Murphy, Karl, 363
Murray, Arthur, 132
Muscogee County, Ga., 23

Narmore, Phil C., 213, 226, 242, 245, 293, 296, 297–98
Nashville Banner, 139
National Academy of Engineering, 409
National Advisory Committee on Aeronautics, 215, 261
National Aeronautics and Space Administration, 340, 364, 378, 453
National Association of State Mining Schools, 149
National Athletic Association, 137
National Cash Register Company, 252
National Collegiate Athletic Association, 284–85; basketball tournament (1985), 452
National Defense Act of 1916, 144
National Defense Research Committee, 216
National Institutes of Health, 396
National Park Service, 339
National Research Council, 150
National Safety Council, 230
National Science Foundation, 396; act passed in 1950, 268; and impact on research programs, 268
National Society of Black Engineers, 428
National Student Association, 276
National Tube Company, 111
National Youth Administration, 204
Navy V-12 program. *See* Military training
Neely, Frank, 182, 240, 248
Neighborhood Development Program, 381–83
Neill, J. L., 128
Nelson, Donald, 384–85
Nesbit, J. N. G., 121, 147
New Jersey: industrialization in, 11
New South, 128
New South Creed, 3, 7, 11, 12, 35, 47, 78, 81, 83, 86, 99, 223–24, 237, 449
New York Sun, 140
New York University, 229
Newman Club, 390
Newton County, 25, 26
Neyland, Robert, 285
Niagara Falls Power Plant, 78
Night school: creation of, 121
Nordby, Gene M., 435
North Carolina Microelectronics Center, 448
North Carolina State University, 99, 223, 443

554 *Index*

Norton Emery Wheel Company, 41
Notre Dame University, 141
Noyes, W. Wilson, 253
Nuclear Engineering, School of, 434
Nuclear reactor, 311, 340

O'Brien, Eugene, 227
O'Connor, Sandra Day, 450
Office of Interdisciplinary Programs, 420
Office of Scientific Research and Development (OSRD), 214, 216, 265
Oglethorpe University, 296
O'Keefe High School, 386, 446, 530 (n. 76)
"Open Letter" of 25 April 1968, 348, 383
Otis Elevator Company, 94
Outlook, 141
Oxford, Ga., 21

Packard, David, 410
Panama Canal, 81
Parker, Carlton, 392–94
Parker, Thomas, 428
Parrott, George W., 35
Patterson, Ed, 345
Paty, Raymond A., 240, 244
Peace, William, 319, 377
Peachtree and Marietta Street Railway, 33
Peck, Maryly Van Leer, 271, 274–75
Penfield, Ga., 25–27, 30–32, 45
Perkins, Frances, 229
Perkins and Will, 320, 338, 339
Perkins and Will plan, 381, 417
Perry, William Gilmer, 118, 225, 246
Pershing, John, 279, 345
Pestalozzi, John H., 4, 5
Peters, E. C., 111
Peters, Richard, 33–35
Peters Land Company, 109, 111
Peters Park, 32–34, 39, 42
Peters Park Development Company, 33–35, 42, 96
Petit and DeHaven Company, 43
Petroleum Industry War Council, 218
Pettit, Joseph M.: and "Goals for Engineering Education," 375; and athletics, 403; appointment as president, 409; biographical sketch of, 410; as engineering dean at Stanford, 411–12; inaugural address, 413; attitude toward graduate education, 414, 415; and Engineering Experiment Station, 418–19; and creation of Office of Minority Education Development, 428; and research quality, 433; and Microelectronics and Computer Technology Corporation, 442; and Advanced Technology Development Center, 446; and Microelectronics Research Center, 447–48; and second engineering college, 451; "New Founders" address, 453–54
Phillips, G. M. "Pup," 181–82
Physical Education and Recreation, Department of, 209–10, 230, 418; under William Jackson, 135; and "mass athletics," 135, 137
Physical plant, 52, 72, 103, 164–65, 177, 180, 182–83, 192, 311–12, 418, 434, 529 (n. 66); expansion under Matheson, 109–13; postwar expansion, 218–19, 227, 247–52, 299–300; expansion under Van Leer, 336–37; new construction during the 1960s, 340–41
Physics, School of, 66, 80, 356–57, 381, 404; curriculum revision, 374
Picha, Kenneth G., 335
Pittman, Marvin, 195–96
Placement, 184, 206–7; in the 1950s, 279–80, 382
Plunger Elevator Company, 55, 94
Pollard, William G., 324
Porter, Oliver S., 25, 26, 31–33, 41, 42, 46, 50–52, 54–56, 66
Porterdale, Ga., 54
Porterdale Mill, 26
Portman, John, 453
Power plant, 111–13
Pratt, N. P., 152, 154, 157
Pratt Furnace, 56
Presidential search (1956–57), 307
President's home, 248

555 Index

Price Gilbert Memorial Library, 249–50, 381, 453; graduate library completed, 340
Priddy, Judith E., 390
Princeton University, 26, 116, 138
Pringle, W. F., Jr., 81
Psychology, School of, 419; creation of, 228–29
Public relations, 240; origins of Tech News Bureau, 141; creation of program, 227–28
Pullman, George, 34, 462 (n. 45)
Pund, Peter, 173
Purdue University, 222, 260, 261, 400
Pursell, Carroll, 216

A Question of Priorities: The Status of Georgia Tech Academics, 430
Quick, Robert M., 66, 77, 79

Radio, 133, 173–74, 194, 219, 279; early facilities, 134–35; and "wireless dance," 135; during World War I, 146
Radioisotopes and Bioengineering Laboratory, 308
Radio Research Laboratory (Harvard University), 410
Ramblin' Reck Club, 345, 350
Randall, William N., 95, 135, 136
Ray, Dale C., 376
Redgrave, Dewitt C., 263, 503 (n. 64)
"Red Scare," 280, 291
Religious organizations, 390, 429; and community service, 382
Remington-Rand Corp., 252
Remsen, Ira, 47
Rensselaer Polytechnic Institute, 446
Research, 186–87, 192, 452–53; under Matheson, 118–19; during World War II, 203, 212–17; postwar expansion of, 256–70; department-based, 268–69, 358–59; in the 1960s, 357–60; separation of EES and academic departments, 358; student attitudes toward, 387; faculty, 395; electronics, 401, 447; environmental, 401; qualitative evaluation of, 433; solar energy, 439–41

Research Club, 186, 257, 374, 395
Research Engineer, 260
Research Triangle, 438, 443
Rice, David, 282–83
Rice, Grantland, 139
Rice, Homer, 424, 435
Rich Computer Center, 252, 282, 381
Rich Foundation, 252
Richmond County, Ga., 62, 96
Rich's Department Store, 240
Riegels, Roy, 172–73
Rivers, E. D., 187–88
Robert, L. W. "Chip," Jr., 130, 192–93, 511 (n. 3)
Robert and Company, 217, 218
Roberts, E. Graham, 453
Robbins, Clyde D.: appointed campus planner, 339; education and professional experience of, 339; land acquisition through urban renewal program, 339–40
Rockdale County, Ga., 63
Rockefeller, John D., 82, 83, 100, 111
Rockefeller Foundation, 152
Rodgers, Franklin C. "Pepper," 424–25, 435
Rogers, William B., 8
Roman, Frank "Wop," 132, 147, 157, 174
Rome, Ga., 17
Roosevelt, Franklin D., 184, 203–4
Rose Bowl Field, 173
Rosenberg, Robert, 78
Rose Polytechnic Institute, 9
Rosse, Kenneth D., 361
Rosselot, Gerald A., 213–15, 258, 298, 504 (n. 70); and conflict with faculty, 261; and friction with Cherry Emerson, 262–65; resignation from EES, 262–65
ROTC. *See* Military training
Rucker, J. W., 30, 89
Russell, Richard B., Jr., 176
Russell, Robert P., 217–18

Safety Engineering, Department of, 229–30
Sanders, Carl E., 326–27, 404

Sanford, S. V., 144, 184, 186, 194–95, 199, 210, 217, 220, 252
Sangster, William, 451; becomes engineering dean, 423
Sarbacher, Robert Irving, 226, 229, 241, 258
Savannah, Ga., 17, 389
Savannah Power and Electric Company, 118
Savant, D. P., 226, 292
Savini, David O., 339
Saylor, Tom, 384
Scattergood, Ezra F., 79
Scheibner, E. J., 396
Schneider, Herman, 122
School colors, 61
Schutz, William, 427
Schwab, Charles, 127
Science, industrial, 4
Science, technology, and society: courses in, 377
Sciences and Liberal Studies, College of, 246, 363; name change, 434
Scientific Associates. *See* Scientific Atlanta
Scientific Atlanta, 263, 359, 444–45
Sears, Zenas, 276
Segadlo's, 131, 132
Self-study and planning, 246–49, 319, 321, 354, 356; World War II, 217–21; mid-1950s, 286–88; Harrison proposes self-study, 337
Sewanee. *See* University of the South
Shenandoah, Ga., 439
Shepherd, R. B., 46, 50
Shop culture–school culture conflict, 9–11, 18, 41, 42, 48, 66, 78, 93, 190, 239, 300, 331, 336, 375, 397, 451
Siebert, L. R., 309
Sigma Xi, Society of, 186, 257–58, 395
Sigma Xi Club, 374
Silas, C. J. "Pete," 453
Silicon Valley, 410, 415, 438, 443
Simpson, George L., Jr., 374, 378, 397, 404–5, 409, 415, 417, 435, 443–44, 523 (n. 44), 532 (n. 103); and conflict with Harrison, 363–67; biographical sketch of, 364
Sisk, Glenn L., 246

Skiles, William Vernon, 186, 205, 207, 225–26, 245; building named for, 308
Sloss Iron and Steel Company, 63
Smith, D. M., 170, 292
Smith, Henry L., 63, 100
Smith, Hoke, 150
Smith, Marion, 227
Smith-Lever Act, 253
Smith Manufacturing Company, 63
Snow, Franklyn C., 229
Social Sciences, School of, 189–90, 246, 287, 377, 414
Society for the Promotion of Engineering Education, 47, 80, 118
Society of Women Engineers: Tech student chapter organized, 349
Solar Energy Research Institute, 439–41
Solomon, Haywood, 390
Soule, A. M., 150, 151
South Carolina Military Academy, 46, 47, 60
Southeastern Conference, 352–53
Southern Agricultural Works, 35, 57
Southern Association of Colleges and Secondary Schools, 117, 171, 189, 195–96, 198–99, 205
Southern Broadcasting Company, 219
Southern Intercollegiate Athletic Association, 135–36, 141, 142
Southern Intercollegiate Athletic Association Tournament, 137
Southern Medical College, 63
Southern Railroad Company, 102
Southern Technical Institute, 299, 452; formation, 238–42; 1951 budgetary crisis, 254–56; and admission of women, 272; campus of, 312; moves to Marietta, 340; separates from Georgia Tech, 435–36
Southern University, 22, 45
Soviet Union, 239
Space Science and Technology Center: construction begun, 340
Spain, F. O., 60
Spalding, Hughes, 179, 250
Sparta, Ga., 16
Speer, D. N., 35, 52, 56
Speer, Frank, 173
Spencer, Samuel, 102

557 Index

Spicer, W. M., 257, 268
Spindletop Research Center, 443
Spratlin, Frank M., 219, 227
Standard Oil Company (New Jersey), 217
Stanford Industrial Park, 410
Stanford Research Institute, 398, 410, 412, 418
Stanford University, 107, 362, 410–12
Statutes: adopted 1891, 224; adopted 1944–45, 224–26; amended 1953, 267
Steenblick, Rich, 441
Stelson, Thomas E., 370, 422; and "mission-oriented" research, 397, 420; and reorganization of Engineering Experiment Station, 399–400; and Engineering Experiment Station, 419; named vice president for research, 420; and solar energy research, 440
Stephens, Phinehas V., 134, 144, 145, 150, 151, 152, 155, 156, 157
Stevens, P. D., 184
Stevens Institute of Technology, 9, 10, 17
Stevenson, Paula, 349, 350
Stiemke, Robert E., 292, 358
Stratton, W. S., 156
Strayer Report, 255
Streaking, 429
Strickler, G. B., 44
Strite, Robert, 246
Strupper, Everett, 182
Stubbs, W. P., 134
Student activities, 60, 76, 77, 93, 94, 181; in the Progressive era, 128–35; Bull Dogs, 131; Glee Club, 131, 133, 157, 276; Drama Club, 131, 276; Cotillion Club, 131; Panhellenic Organization, 131; band, 132, 133, 157, 276; Kluck Kluck Klan, 132; Ku Klux Klan, 132; American Legion, 133; Student Activities Committee, 133; Georgia Tech Student Association, 133–34; during World War II, 231–33; postwar, 243–44; in the 1950s, 275–81, 341–42; in the Harrison era, 341–48; the 1960s and expanding student awareness, 342

Student Activities Night, 346
Student Center, 341, 343, 391–94; supported in 1950s, 278; construction of, 392–93
Student Center Governing Board, 393
Student Competition for Relevant Engineering, 429
Student-faculty relations: efforts to improve, 345
Student government, 174, 181, 194, 196–97, 276, 316; efforts to develop, 133–34; increasing role of, 342, 346; expanded role of, 390–91; and political lobbying, 429
Student Government Association: and community service, 384; and academic quality, 430
Student political attitudes, 347
Student protest, 178, 194, 196–98; over football seating, 243; over contract feeding, 275; and 1956 Sugar Bowl; on the national scene, 342; limited nature of at Tech, 342–43, 344–45; over architecture building, 418
Student publications, 60, 95, 243–44; Technique, 114, 115, 123, 131, 133, 137, 139, 140, 141, 142, 145, 146, 147, 154, 156, 165–67, 171, 174–75, 179–81, 183, 243, 314, 346, 387; creation of, 129–30; Georgia Tech, 129; Yellow Jacket, 129, 243–44, 277–78; Blue Print, 129, 132, 133, 148; Tornado, 130
Students: academic quality of, 452; attitude toward racial integration, 314; geographical origins of, 389, 427; political attitudes of, 389
Students, dean of, 184, 194–95, 206–7, 277, 279; and community service, 384–85; increased authority of, 391–93
Sullivan, Ed, 276
Swann, James, 90–92, 101
Swann, Janie Austell, 92
Sweat, Dan, 384
Sweigert, R. L., 258
Symposium on Engineering for Major Scientific Programs, 324, 325
Symposium on Utilization of Research Reactors, 324, 325

Talmadge, Eugene, 193–98, 205, 217
Talmadge, Herman, 291, 295, 300, 441
Taft, William Howard, 126
Tappan, Henry, 5
Teaching, evaluation of, 414
Tech Greek Week, 346
Tech High School, 115
Technique. See Student publications
Technological school: legislative committee on, 17–21
Technology Park, 445
Techwood Homes, 184–85, 209, 247, 382; shift to black population, 386
Techwood Tutorial Project, 347, 382
Templeton, Miller, 384
Tennessee Coal, Iron and Railroad Company, 63, 127
Tennessee Valley Authority, 213
Terman, Frederick E., 410–12
Texas A&M University, 260, 442
Textile Engineering, School of, 54, 72, 81–84, 86–88, 90, 92, 101
Textile industry, 449
Thompson, Melvin E., 248
Thomson Houston Electric Company, 55
Thoreau, Henry D., 5
"Three-two" program, 288, 427
Thurston, Robert H., 9–11, 41
Todd, Merlin, 428
Toolcraft and Design, School of (Emory University), 22
Topping, Dan, 233
Trabant, Arthur, 363, 364, 366, 380, 396
Tulane University, 139
Tunnel Hill, Ga., 47
Turner, E. A., 128
Turner, Jonathan, 6
Tuskegee Institute, 7, 379

United States Air Force, 256
United States Army Chemical Warfare Service, 261
United States Army Corps of Engineers, 81
United States Army Ordnance Department, 214
United States Army Quartermaster Corps, 292
United States Army Signal Corps, 145, 146, 215
United States Department of Education, 127
United States Forestry Service, 338
United States Military Academy, 45, 46, 72, 108, 140
United States Naval Academy, 9, 46, 47, 61, 141
United States Naval Air Station, Chamblee, Ga., 239–40, 340
United States Navy, 239
United States Navy Bureau of Ordnance, 260–61
United States Navy Bureau of Ships, 261
United States Navy Engineering Corps, 9
United States Steel Company, 63, 127
United States War Department, 144, 146, 148, 149, 208; and Committee on Education and Special Training, 148
University of Alabama, 135, 352
University of California, 222, 229
University of Cincinnati, 122
University of Colorado, 79
University of Florida, 95, 138, 223
University of Georgia, 113, 137, 138, 139, 141, 142, 143, 144, 149, 151, 152, 153, 154, 171–72, 175–78, 195, 314; Benjamin Hill speech to Alumni Association, 12; civil engineering at, 19, 21, 80; land-grant fund, 44; football games, 61; Lyman Hall considered as chancellor of, 87–88; Walter B. Hill elected chancellor of, 88; and list of accredited high schools, 113; plays Tech in Southern Intercollegiate Athletic Association tournament, 137; and first football game with Tech, 138; competition with Tech for funds, 149–53, 252–53; breakdown and restoration of athletic relations with Tech, 141–44; and Board of Trustees, 142, 152; and Prudential Committee, 151, 152; forced to withhold faculty salaries, 154; and commerce school, 178–79; and Walter Cocking, 195–96; antiwar protest at, 387

Index

University of Kansas, 260
University of Kentucky, 286
University of Michigan, 5, 379
University of North Carolina, 60, 139, 364, 443
University of Pennsylvania, 127, 139, 140
University of Pittsburgh, 140, 141, 281, 283
University of the South, 115, 136, 138, 288
University of Tennessee, 51, 107, 138
University of Texas, 442
University of Toledo, 308
University of Tübingen, 63
University of Virginia, 7, 60
University of Wisconsin, 79
University System Building Authority, 250–51
University System of Georgia, 175–78, 193–200, 210, 252, 364–65; World War II, 218; postwar planning, 220–21; funding, 238; building program, 250; closed after Kent State affair, 387; finances, 404–5; Tech's role in, 413
Urban Corps, 348
Urban renewal, 312, 381–83

Valk, Henry C., 380, 435
Vanderbilt University, 60, 135, 139, 141
Vandiver, Ernest, 313
Van Leer, Blake, 336; administrative style of, 204, 224; selection as president, 220–22; biographical sketch of, 222–23; adopts new statutes, 224–27; adopts plan for campus expansion, 227; creates office of public relations, 227–28; and changes wrought, 237–38; pushes for creation of Technical Institute, 238–42; on state support of Georgia Tech, 252–53; and funding problems, 252–56; and EES controversy, 264–70; and attitudes on coeducation, 270–75; and relationship with student body, 275–76, 286; health, 283, 293–94, 298–99; on faculty salaries and benefits, 289–91; on 1955 reorganization, 294; and tension with the Board of Regents,
 296–98; assessment of his presidency, 299–300; and relationship with G. Rosselot, 504 (n. 70)
Van Leer, Ella Wall, 223, 271, 274
Vaughan, W. Harry, 186–87, 213, 214
Very Large Scale Integration, 447–48
Veterans affairs, 203, 220, 228–29, 233; post–World War II, 242–44
Veterans Guidance Center, 228–29
Venture capital, 445
Vietnam War: student attitudes toward, 386–88
Vine City playground, 348
Vocational Education for National Defense, 211
Von Fellenberg, Philip, 5

Waddey, Frank, 172
Wake Forest University, 139
Walker, A. J., 246
Wallace, Anthony, 4, 9
Wallace, S. S., 124
Wallace, Robert B., Jr., 314, 324, 326, 329
Wamboldt, Wickes, 155, 156, 157
War Assets Administration, 241
Warren, Earl, 323–25
Washburn, Ichabod, 10, 40
Washburn shops, 40, 41, 53–55
Washington, Booker T., 7
Washington and Jefferson College, 223
Washington University, 20
Water Resources Center. *See* Environmental Resources Center
Watson, Tom, 164
Watters, J. M., 124
Wayland, Francis, 5
Weaver, Douglas, 425
Webb, Sam, 363, 435
Weber, Homer S., 213
Weber, Paul, 213–14, 245, 275, 297–99, 300, 309, 329, 358, 409, 552 (n. 29); as acting president, 305–8; career at Georgia Tech, 306; named vice president for planning, 332–33; named acting vice president for academic affairs, 333–34; retirement of, 380; on being president, 511 (n. 3)
Webster County, Ga., 23
Weems, T. R., 147

Weil, Ben H., 260
Weltner, Philip, 179, 186–87
Wenn, Fred, 391
Wepking, Amy, 428
Wesley Foundation, 390
West, E. E., 60–61
Western and Atlantic Railroad, 33, 35, 57
Western Electric Company, 79
West Georgia College, 400
Westinghouse Electric Company, 111, 127
WGST, 219, 222
Wheeler, George F., 295–96
Whitaker, A. D., Jr., 134
White, Henry C., 7, 30, 43, 44
Whitehead, Mrs. Joseph Brown, 110
Whitley, Wyatt, 363
Wickenden Report, 286
Wiesner, Jerome B., 379
Williams, Lawrence, 318
Williams, Sam, 384, 391, 523 (n. 50)
Williford, Jim, 243
Winship, George, 35, 52, 75, 79
Winship Machine Company, 35, 52, 85
Wise, Anna Teitelbaum, 124
Wohlford, J. G., 272
Women. *See* Coeducation
Women's Chamber of Commerce, 272
Wood, H. P., 111, 130, 134, 147
Wood, Leonard, 61, 126, 138, 141
Worcester, Mass., 18, 35, 41
Worcester Polytechnic Institute, 3, 9, 10, 17, 19, 20, 24, 25, 39–41, 43, 48, 53, 54
World Student Fund, 275, 280, 344, 393, 395
World War I, 116, 118, 124, 125, 129, 132, 144; impact on curriculum, 125, 146; effect on student activities, 132, 146; Department of Military Science created, 146–47; faculty in service, 147
World War II, 200, 203, 341; coming of war, 204–5; impact on campus, 204–12
WREK, 277
WTJY. *See* WREK
Wyly, David, 357

Yale University, 8, 116, 138
Yancy, Dorothy Cowser, 428
Yellow Jacket, 243; demise of, 277–78
YMCA, 60, 245, 275–76, 341; building erected and dedicated, 110–11; in the Progressive era, 128–29; and National War Work Council, 147; and World Student Fund, 280; and racial integration, 316; expanding influence of, 342; continued importance of, 343, 344; as unofficial student center, 343; and Callaway Gardens conferences, 344; and Annual Leadership Conference, 345; sponsors first women's freshman camp, 349–50; Gamma Psi organized, 350; and community service, 384–85; conflict over role on campus, 391–95; property settlement with Tech, 394; separation from Georgia Tech, 394–95
YMCA Building: becomes Faculty/Alumni House, 394
Young, John, 453
Young Americans for Freedom, 347

Zhang Wenjing, 450
Ziegler, Waldemar, 257–58
Zsuffa, Leslie A., 227–28, 240, 243, 253, 292